MARVEL マーベル MANGAVERSE

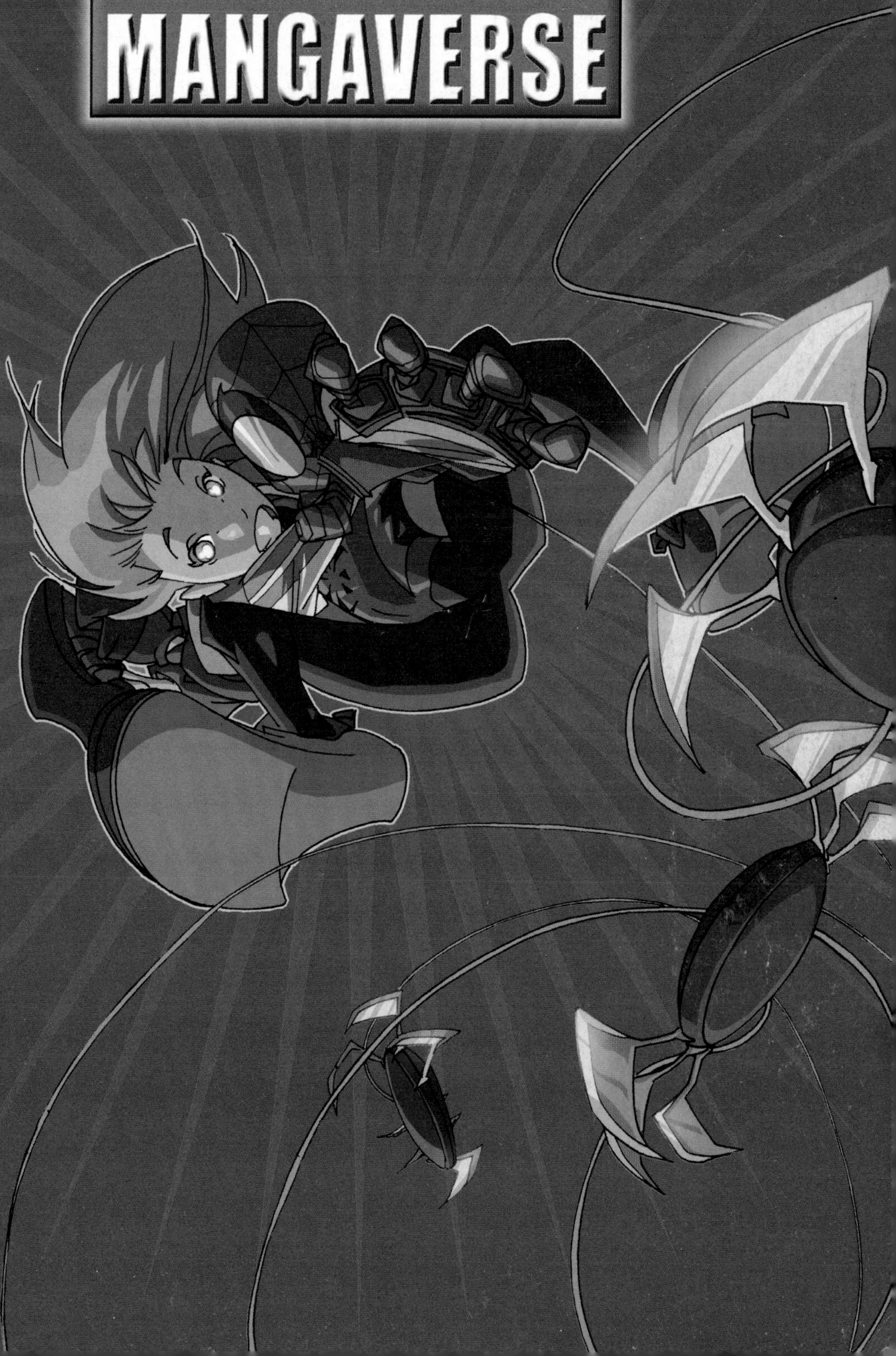

NEW DAWN
writer/artist BEN DUNN • colors GURU eFX • lettering BENN DUNN & GURU eFX

AVENGERS ASSEMBLE
art/story by UDON - writer KEN SIU-CHONG • art ALVIN LEE, ARNOLD TSANG, OMAR DOGAN, SHANE LAW • chief ERIK KO • letters COMICRAFT

FANTASTIC FOUR
writer ADAM WARREN • art by ARMADA - pencils KERON GRANT • inks ROB STULL • colors CHRIS WALKER • letters RICHARD STARKINGS & COMICRAFT

GHOST RIDERS
writer/artist CHUCK AUSTEN • concept BRIAN SMITH & CHUCK AUSTEN

THE PUNISHER
writer PETER DAVID • pencils/inks LEA HERNANDEZ • color art GURU eFX • background inks, pages 7-11 ROB ESPINOZA • letters COMICRAFT

SPIDER-MAN
writer/artist KAARE ANDREWS • colors DAVE McCAIG • assists RUSTY BEACH • letters RICHARD STARKINGS & COMICRAFT'S OSCAR GONGORA

X-MEN
writer C.B. CEBULSKI • pencils JEFF MATSUDA • art assist A.J. JOTHIKUMAR • inks ANDY OWENS • colors LIQUID • letters RS & COMICRAFT'S OSCAR GONGORA

ETERNITY TWILIGHT
writer/artist BEN DUNN • story assist KEVIN GUNSTONE • colors GURU eFX • lettering BENN DUNN & GURU eFX

MARVEL MANGAVERSE VOL. 1.   Contains material originally published in magazine form as MARVEL MANGAVERSE: NEW DAWN #1, MARVEL MANGAVERSE: AVENGERS ASSEMBLE! #1, MARVEL MANGAVERSE: FANTASTIC FOUR #1, MARVEL MANGAVERSE: GHOST RIDERS #1, MARVEL MANGAVERSE: PUNISHER #1, MARVEL MANGAVERSE: SPIDER-MAN #1, MARVEL MANGAVERSE: X-MEN #1 and MARVEL MANGAVERSE: ETERNITY TWILIGHT #1 . Second printing 2002. ISBN# 0-7851-0935-8. Published by MARVEL COMICS, a division of MARVEL ENTERTAINMENT GROUP, INC. OFFICE OF PUBLICATION: 10 East 40th Street, New York, NY 10016. Copyright © and 2002 Marvel Characters, Inc. All rights reserved. $24.95 per copy in the U.S. and $39.95 in Canada (GST #R127032852). Canadian Agreement #40668537. All characters featured in this issue and the distinctive names and likenesses thereof, and all related indicia are trademarks of Marvel Characters, Inc. No similarity between any of the names, characters, persons, and/or institutions in this magazine with those of any living or dead person or institution is intended, and any such similarity which may exist is purely coincidental. Printed in the U.S.A. STAN LEE, Chairman Emeritus. For information regarding advertising in Marvel Comics or on Marvel.com, please contact Russell Brown, Executive Vice President, Consumer Products, Promotions and Media Sales at 212-576-8561 or rbrown@marvel.com

10 9 8 7 6 5 4 3 2

MARVEL マーベル MANGAVERSE

editor BRIAN SMITH
consulting editor RALPH MACCHIO
editor in chief JOE QUESADA
president BILL JEMAS

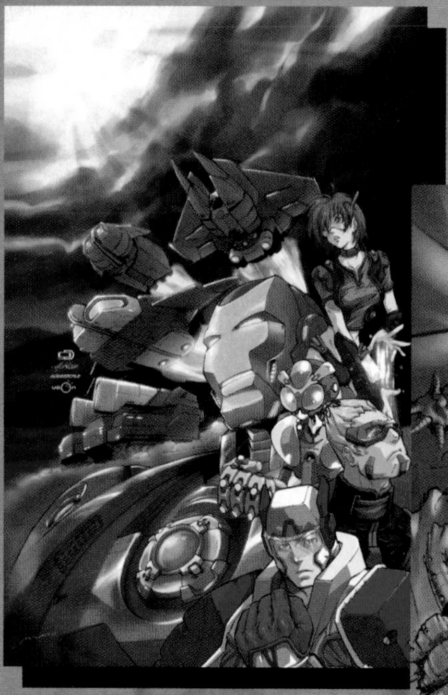

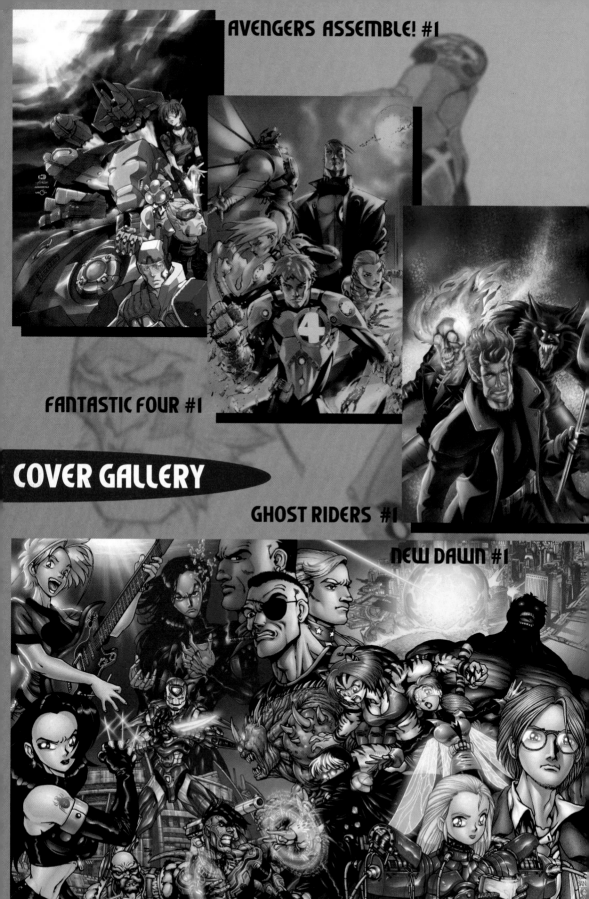

AVENGERS ASSEMBLE! #1

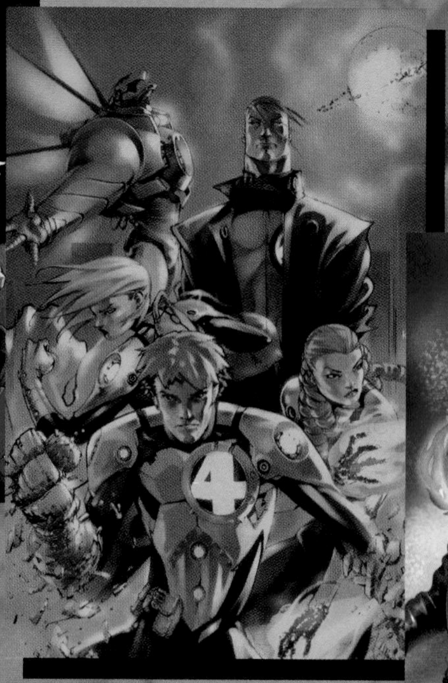

FANTASTIC FOUR #1

COVER GALLERY

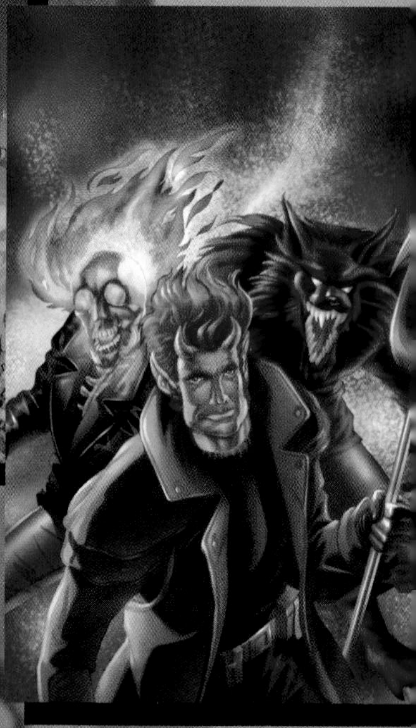

GHOST RIDERS #1

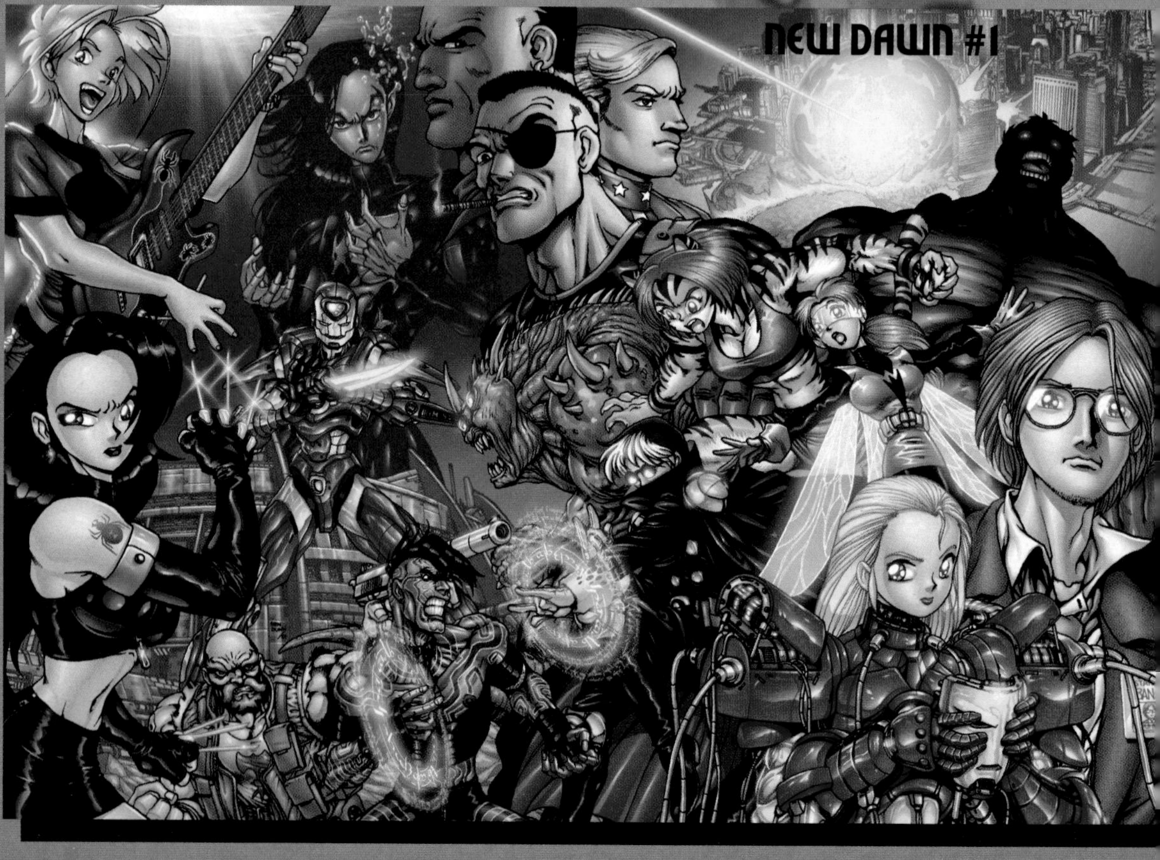

NEW DAWN #1

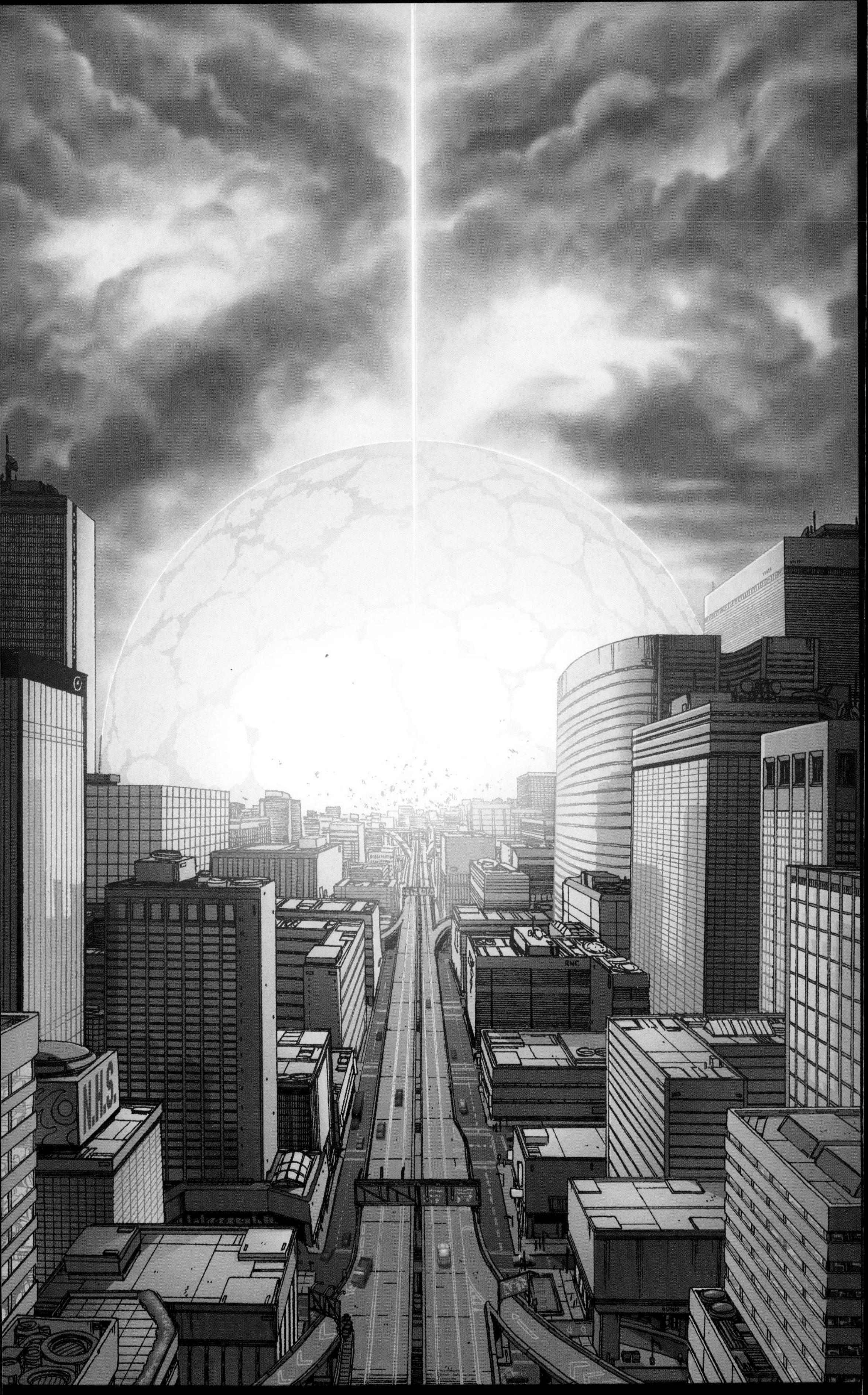
N.H.S.

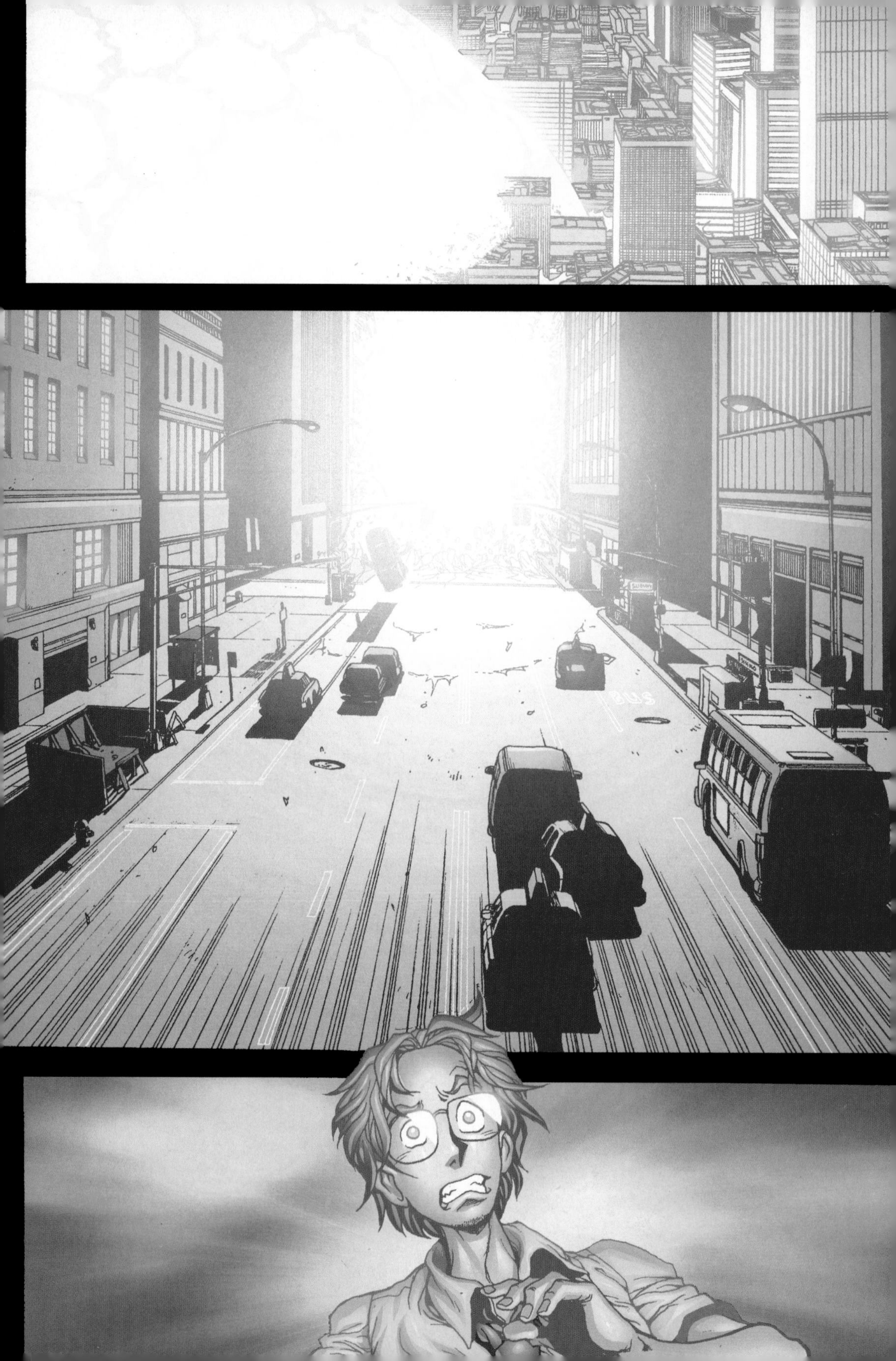
BUS

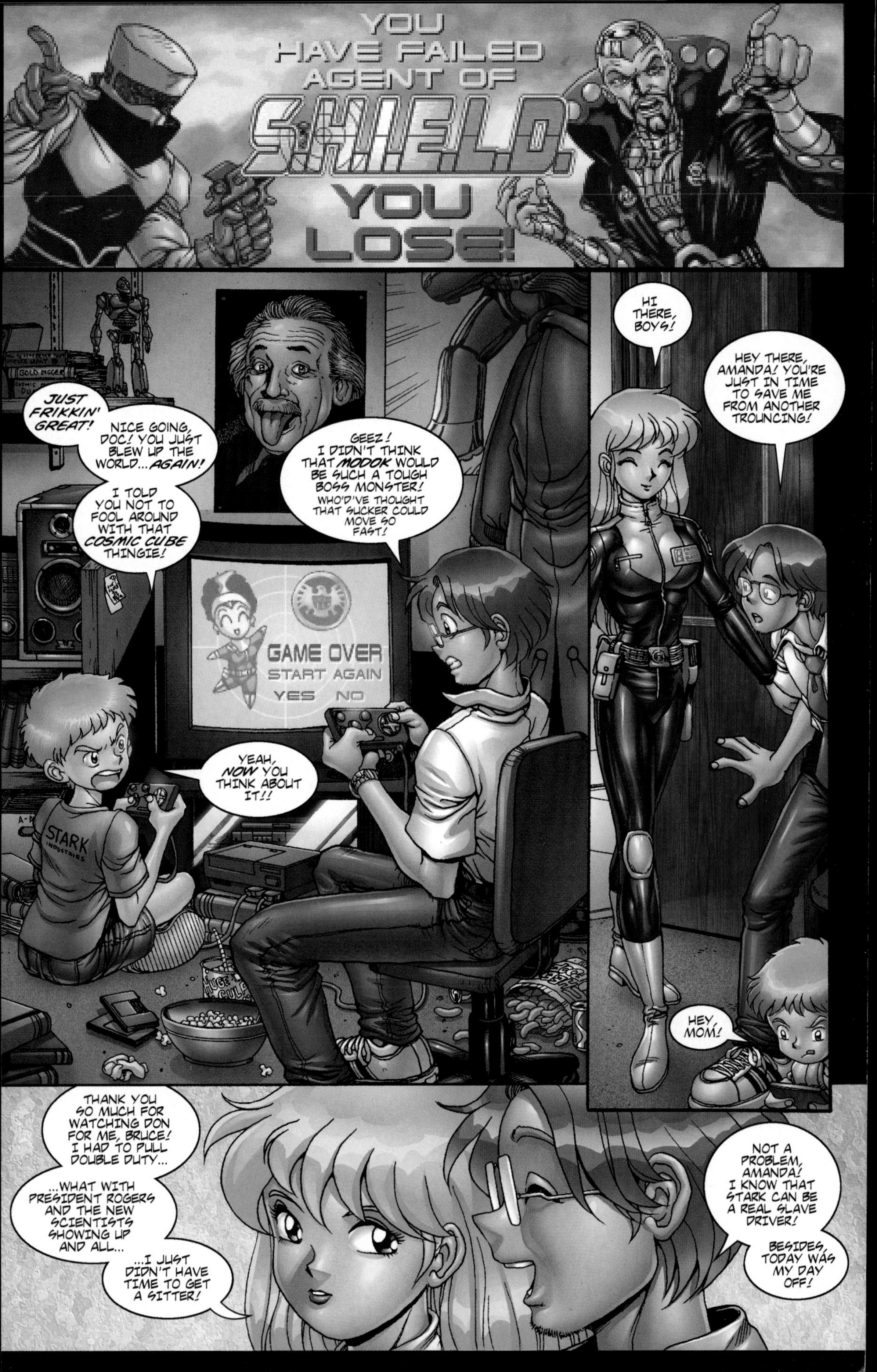
YOU HAVE FAILED AGENT OF S.H.I.E.L.D.
YOU LOSE!
GOLD DIGGER
JUST FRIKKIN' GREAT!
NICE GOING, DOC! YOU JUST BLEW UP THE WORLD... AGAIN!
I TOLD YOU NOT TO FOOL AROUND WITH THAT COSMIC CUBE THINGIE!
GEEZ! I DIDN'T THINK THAT MODOK WOULD BE SUCH A TOUGH BOSS MONSTER!
WHO'D'VE THOUGHT THAT SUCKER COULD MOVE SO FAST!
GAME OVER
START AGAIN
YES NO
YEAH, NOW YOU THINK ABOUT IT!!
STARK INDUSTRIES
HI THERE, BOYS!
HEY THERE, AMANDA! YOU'RE JUST IN TIME TO SAVE ME FROM ANOTHER TROUNCING!
HEY, MOM!
THANK YOU SO MUCH FOR WATCHING DON FOR ME, BRUCE! I HAD TO PULL DOUBLE DUTY...
...WHAT WITH PRESIDENT ROGERS AND THE NEW SCIENTISTS SHOWING UP AND ALL...
...I JUST DIDN'T HAVE TIME TO GET A SITTER!
NOT A PROBLEM, AMANDA! I KNOW THAT STARK CAN BE A REAL SLAVE DRIVER!
BESIDES, TODAY WAS MY DAY OFF!

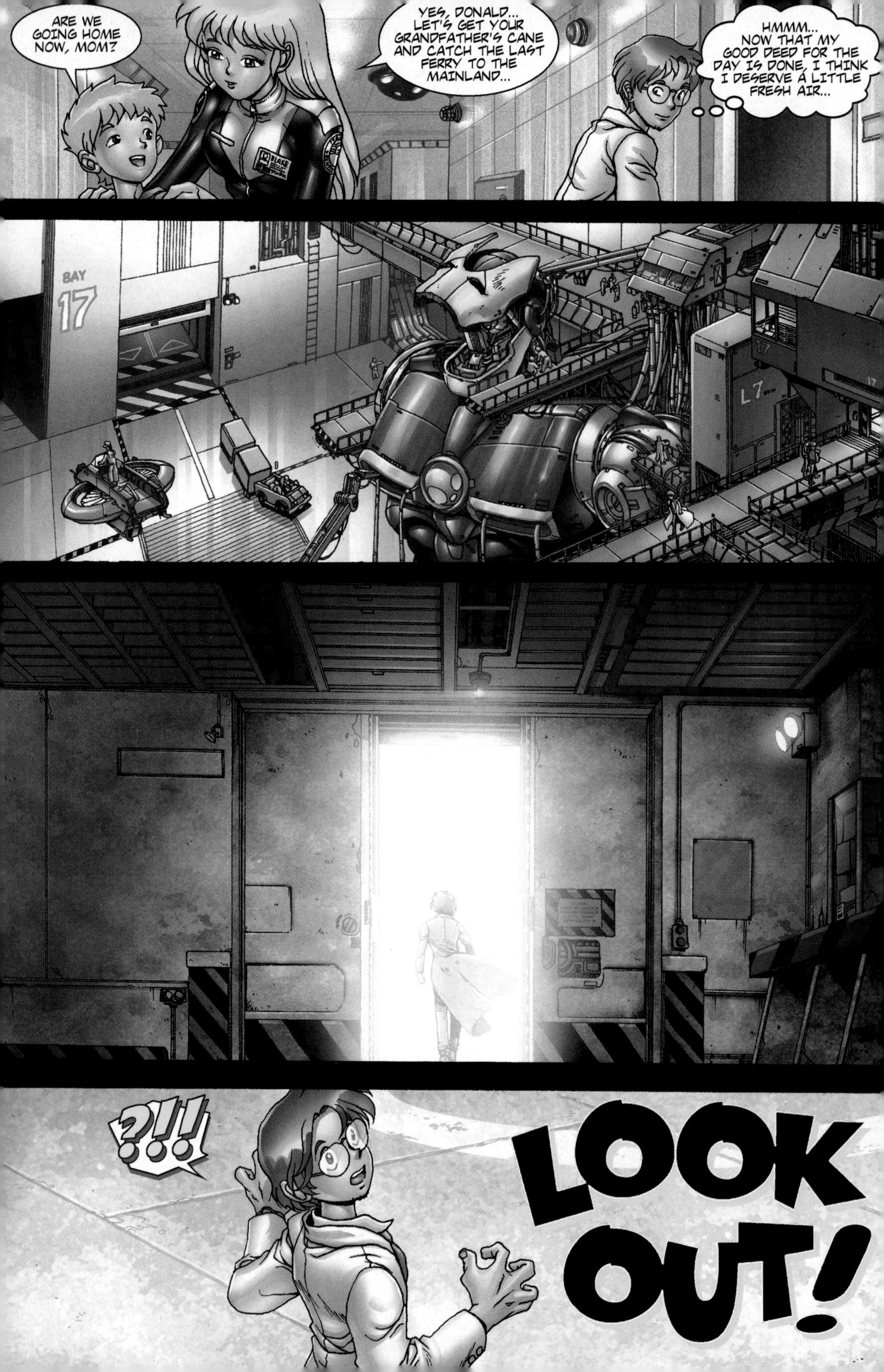
ARE WE GOING HOME NOW, MOM?
YES, DONALD... LET'S GET YOUR GRANDFATHER'S CANE AND CATCH THE LAST FERRY TO THE MAINLAND...
HMMM... NOW THAT MY GOOD DEED FOR THE DAY IS DONE, I THINK I DESERVE A LITTLE FRESH AIR...
BAY
17
L7
?!!
LOOK OUT!

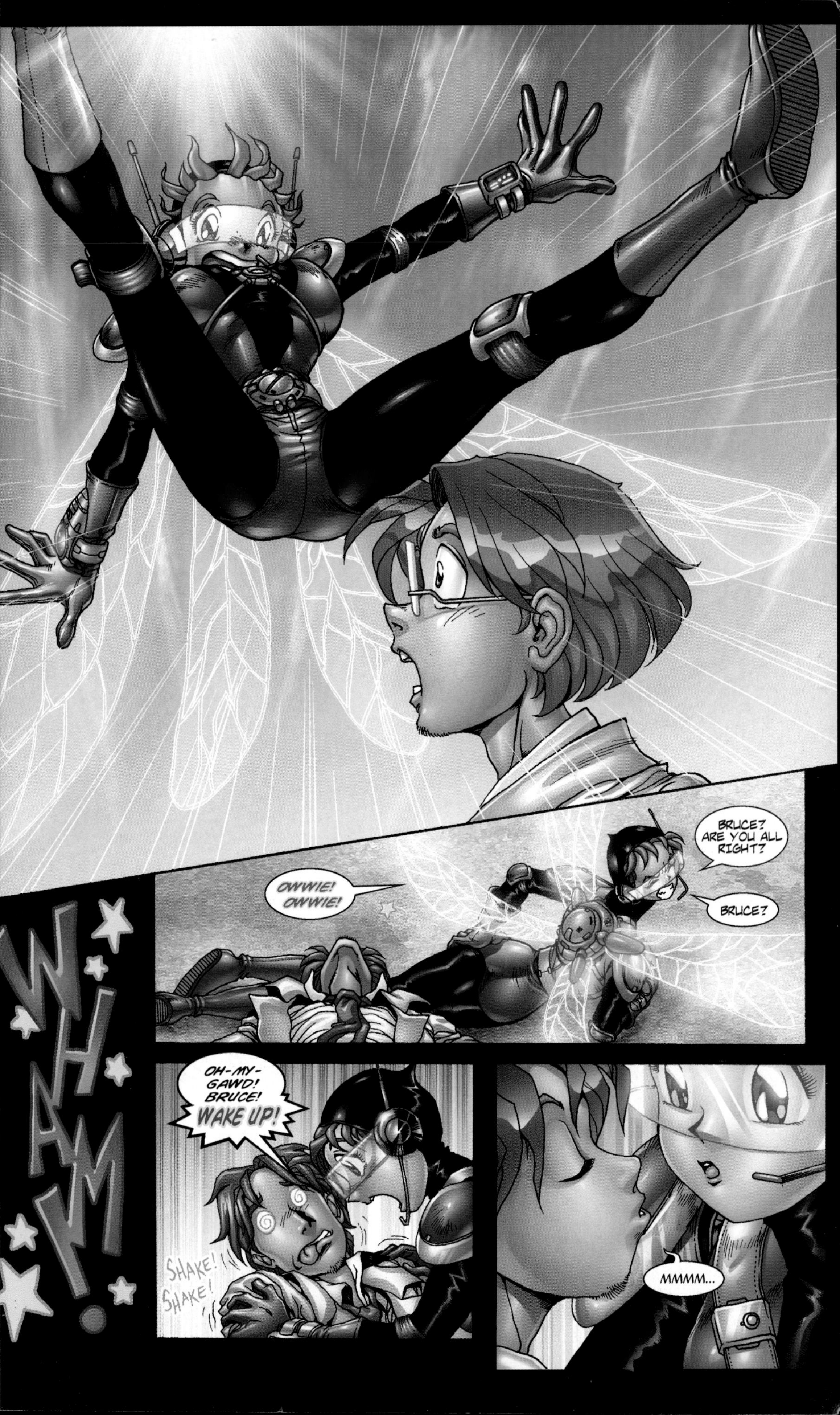

WHAM!
BRUCE? ARE YOU ALL RIGHT?
OWWIE! OWWIE!
BRUCE?
OH-MY-GAWD! BRUCE! WAKE UP!
SHAKE! SHAKE!
MMMM...

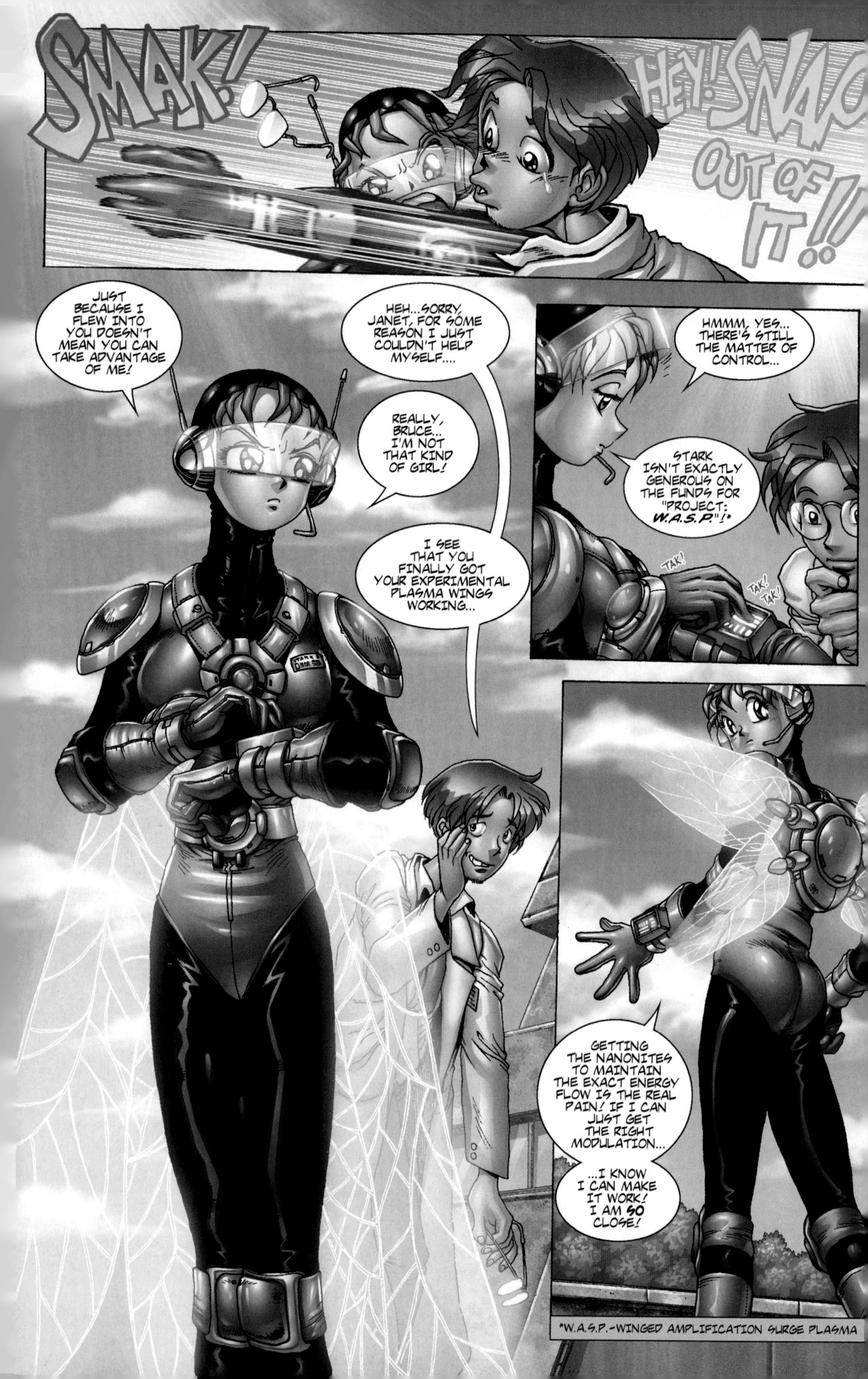
SMAK!
HEY! SNAP OUT OF IT!!
JUST BECAUSE I FLEW INTO YOU DOESN'T MEAN YOU CAN TAKE ADVANTAGE OF ME!
HEH...SORRY, JANET, FOR SOME REASON I JUST COULDN'T HELP MYSELF....
REALLY, BRUCE... I'M NOT THAT KIND OF GIRL!
I SEE THAT YOU FINALLY GOT YOUR EXPERIMENTAL PLASMA WINGS WORKING...
HMMM, YES... THERE'S STILL THE MATTER OF CONTROL...
STARK ISN'T EXACTLY GENEROUS ON THE FUNDS FOR "PROJECT: W.A.S.P."!*
TAK!
TAK! TAK!
GETTING THE NANONITES TO MAINTAIN THE EXACT ENERGY FLOW IS THE REAL PAIN! IF I CAN JUST GET THE RIGHT MODULATION...
...I KNOW I CAN MAKE IT WORK! I AM SO CLOSE!
*W.A.S.P.-WINGED AMPLIFICATION SURGE PLASMA

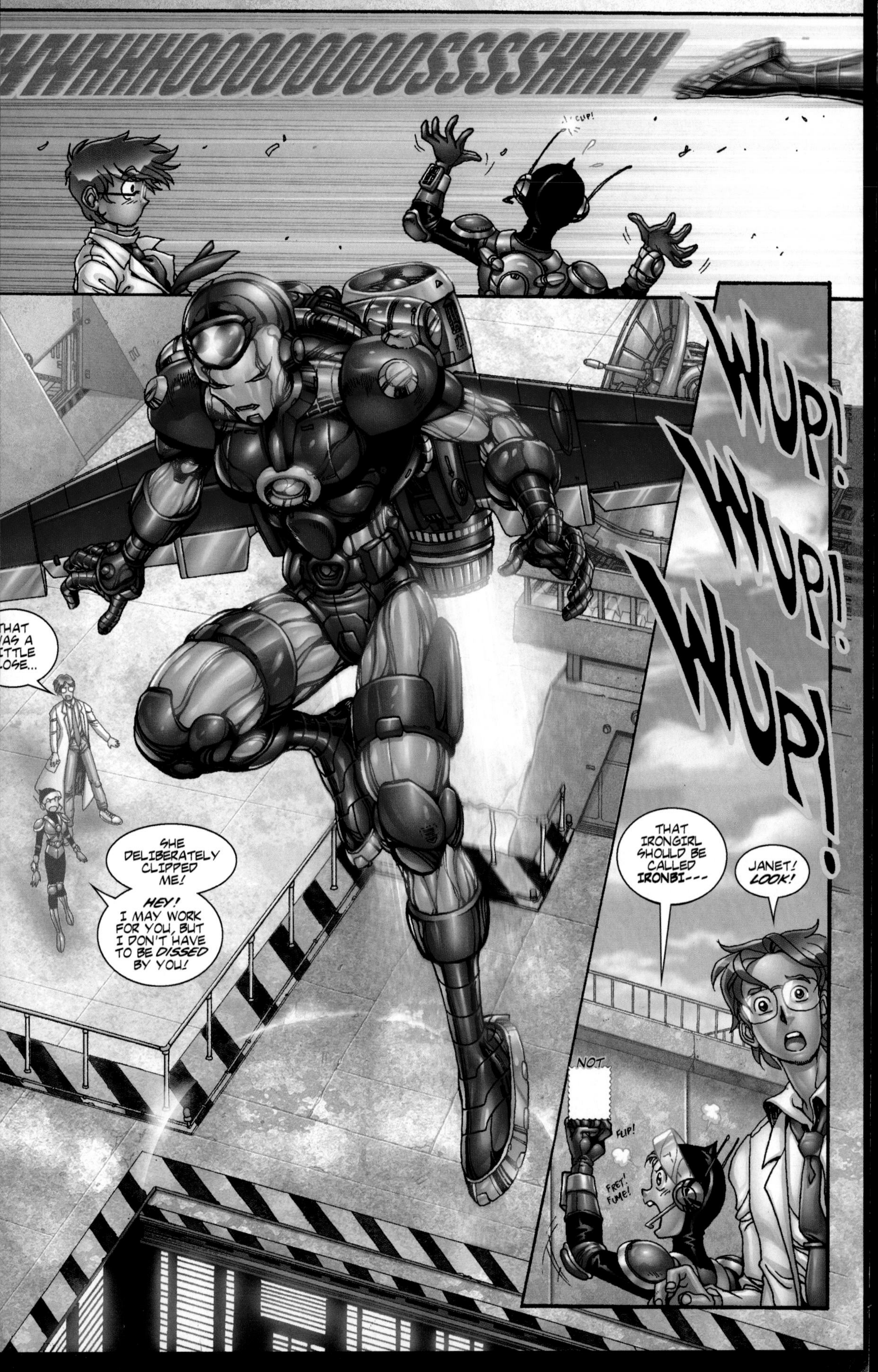
WHHHOOOOOOOOOSSSSSHHHH
CLIP!
WUP! WUP! WUP!
THAT AS A ITTLE LOSE...
SHE DELIBERATELY CLIPPED ME!
HEY! I MAY WORK FOR YOU, BUT I DON'T HAVE TO BE DISSED BY YOU!
THAT IRONGIRL SHOULD BE CALLED IRONBI---
JANET! LOOK!
NOT
FLIP!
FRET! FUME!

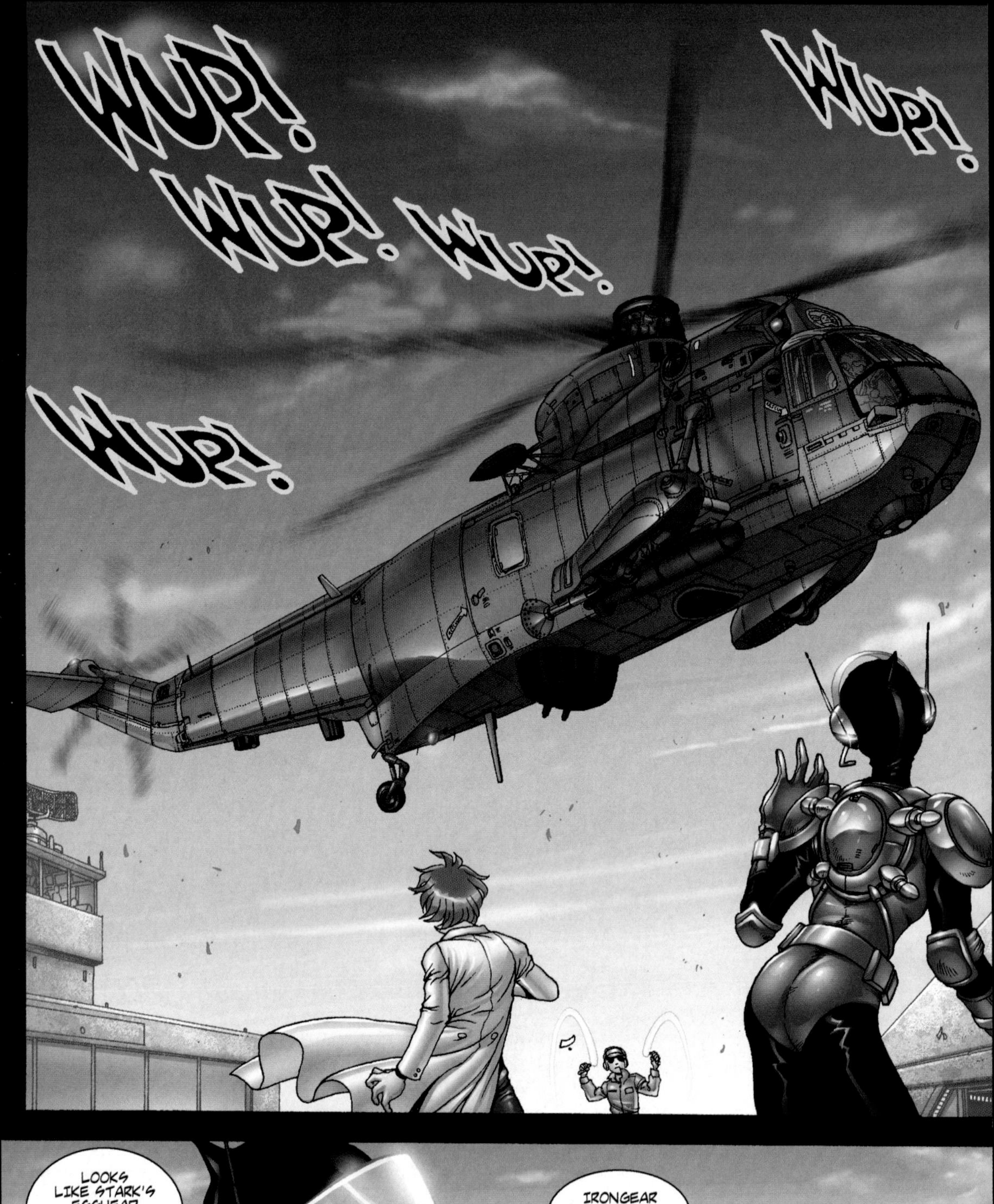
WUP!
WUP!
WUP!
WUP!
WUP!

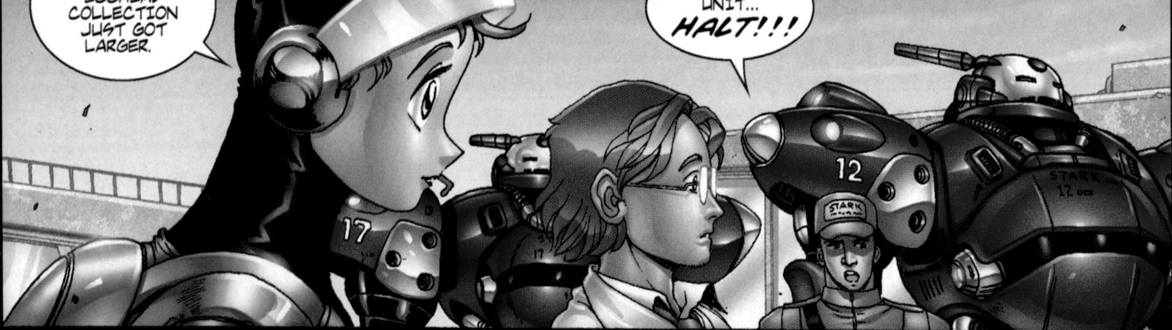
LOOKS LIKE STARK'S EGGHEAD COLLECTION JUST GOT LARGER.
IRONGEAR UNIT... HALT!!!

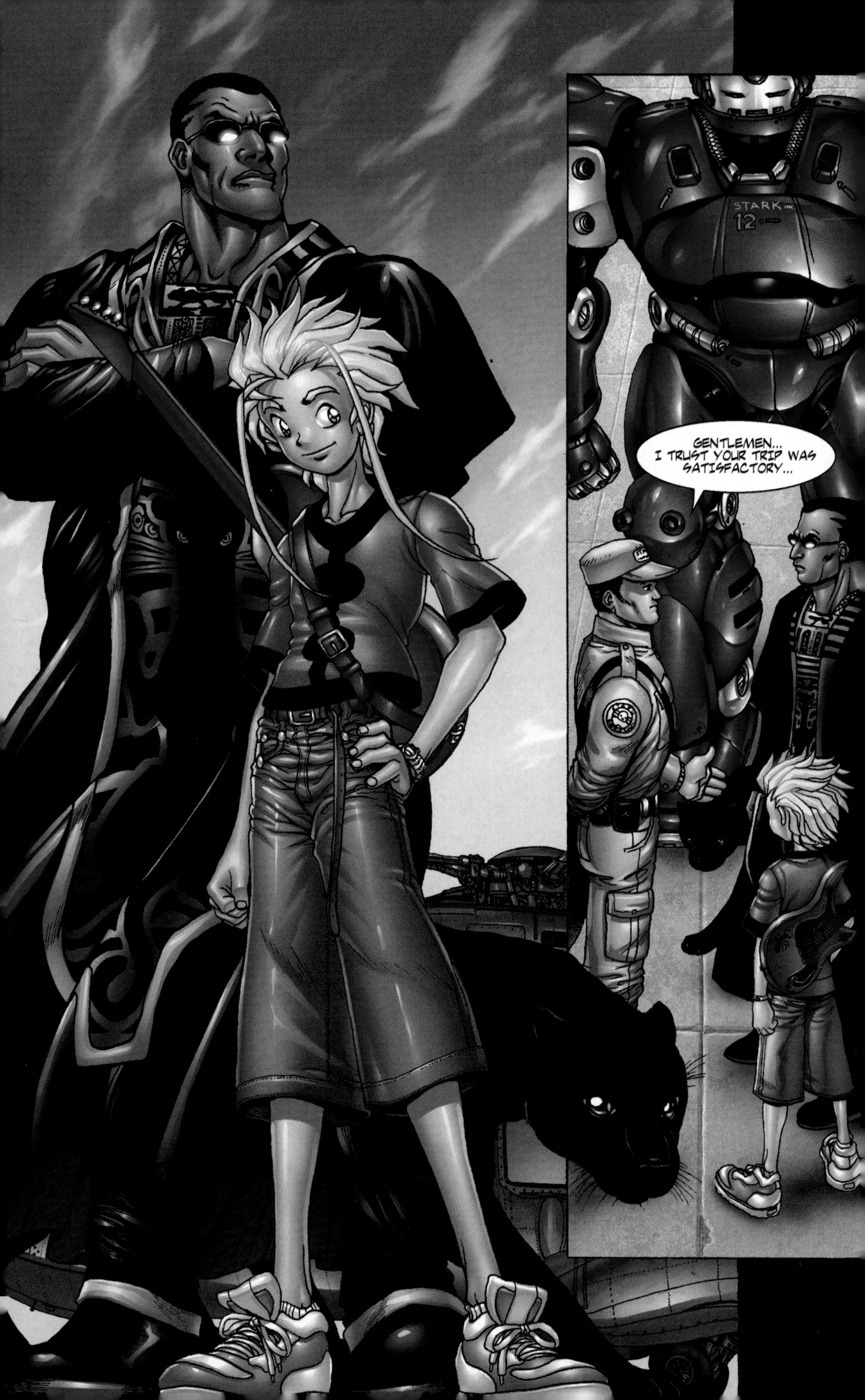
STARK INC
12
GENTLEMEN...
I TRUST YOUR TRIP WAS
SATISFACTORY...

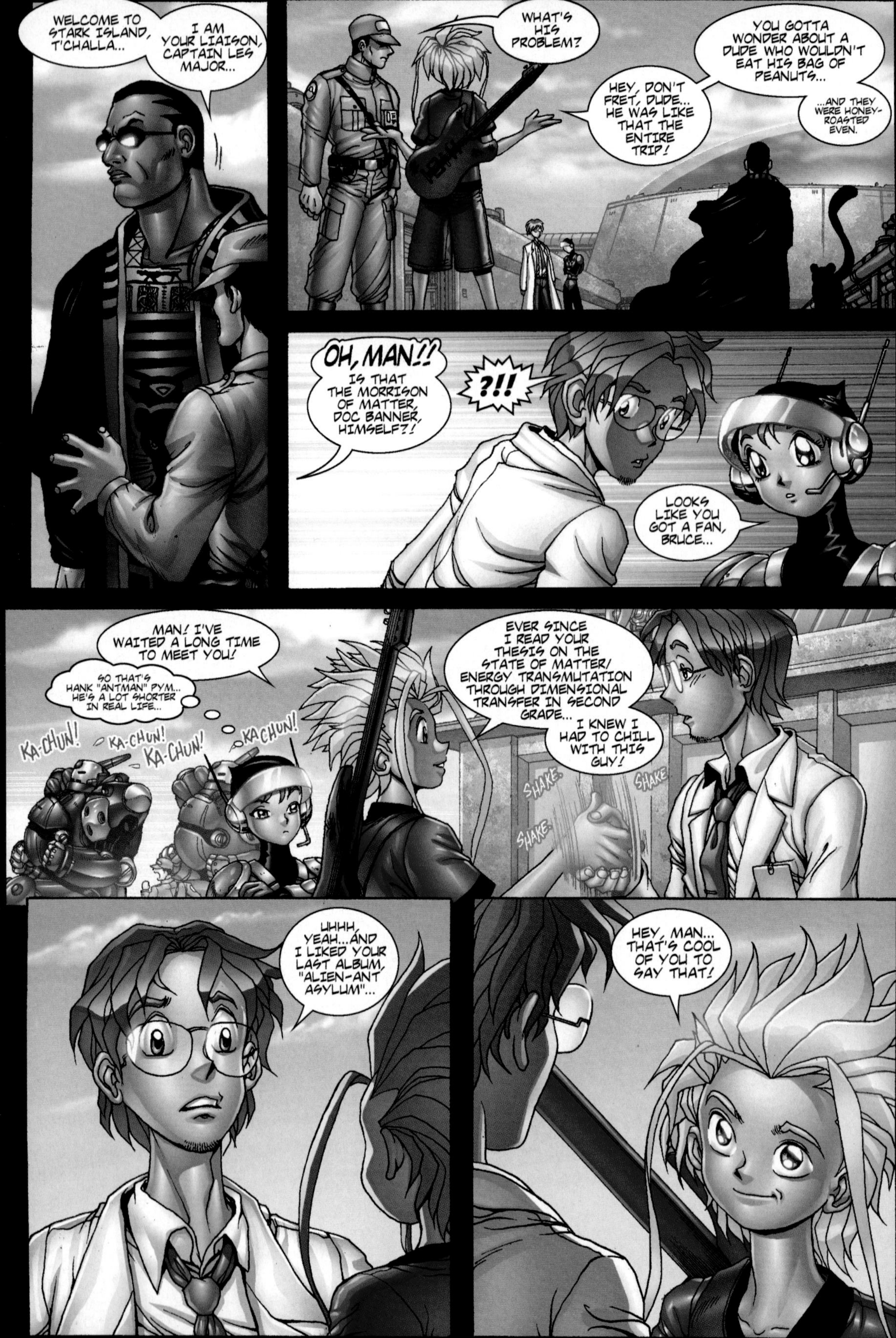
WELCOME TO STARK ISLAND, T'CHALLA...
I AM YOUR LIAISON, CAPTAIN LES MAJOR...
WHAT'S HIS PROBLEM?
HEY, DON'T FRET, DUDE... HE WAS LIKE THAT THE ENTIRE TRIP!
YOU GOTTA WONDER ABOUT A DUDE WHO WOULDN'T EAT HIS BAG OF PEANUTS...
...AND THEY WERE HONEY-ROASTED EVEN.
OH, MAN!! IS THAT THE MORRISON OF MATTER, DOC BANNER, HIMSELF?!
?!!
LOOKS LIKE YOU GOT A FAN, BRUCE...
MAN! I'VE WAITED A LONG TIME TO MEET YOU!
SO THAT'S HANK "ANTMAN" PYM... HE'S A LOT SHORTER IN REAL LIFE...
KA-CHUN! KA-CHUN! KA-CHUN! KA-CHUN!
EVER SINCE I READ YOUR THESIS ON THE STATE OF MATTER/ ENERGY TRANSMUTATION THROUGH DIMENSIONAL TRANSFER IN SECOND GRADE...
I KNEW I HAD TO CHILL WITH THIS GUY!
SHAKE. SHAKE. SHAKE.
UHHH, YEAH...AND I LIKED YOUR LAST ALBUM, "ALIEN-ANT ASYLUM"...
HEY, MAN... THAT'S COOL OF YOU TO SAY THAT!

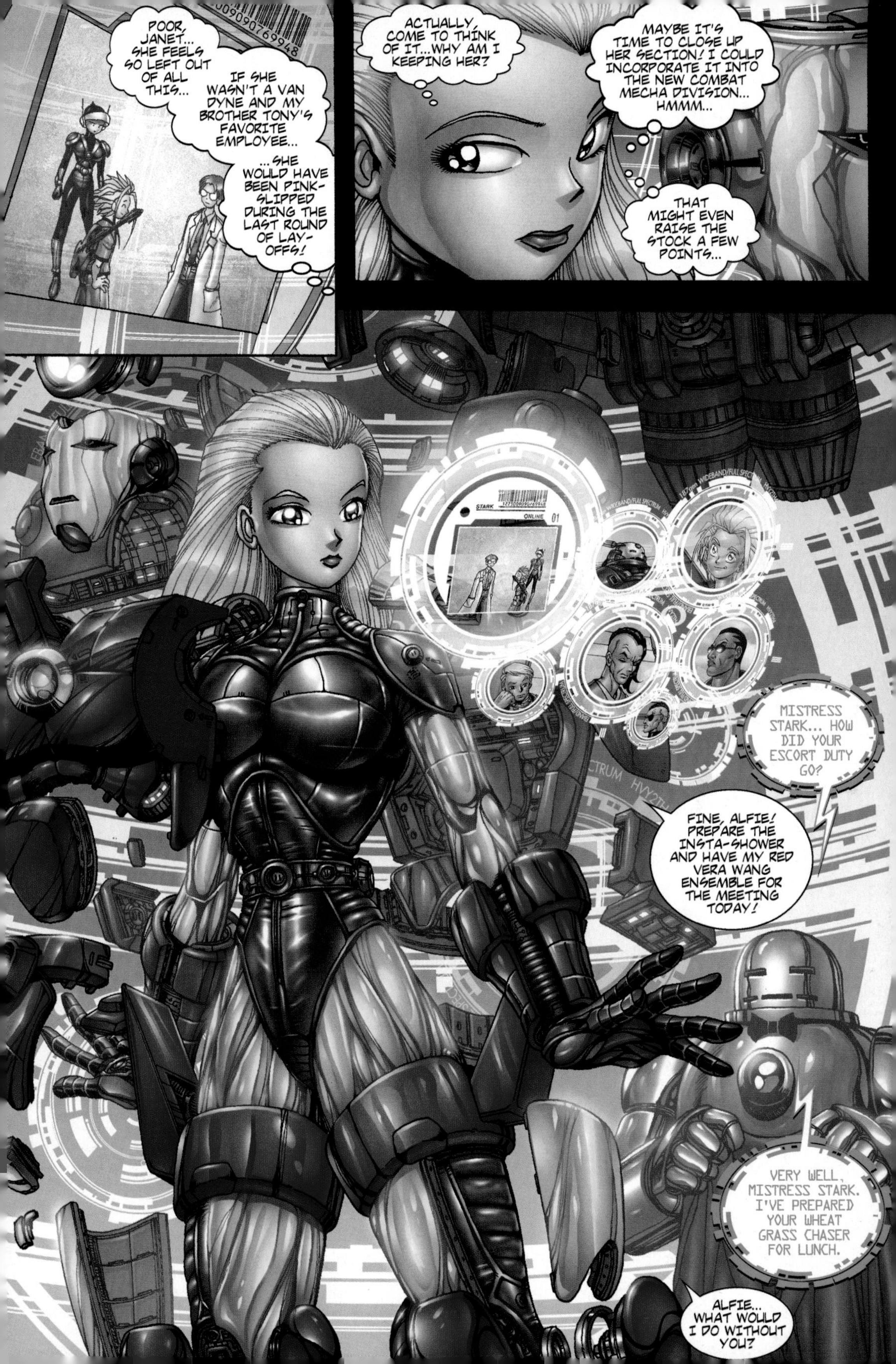
POOR, JANET... SHE FEELS SO LEFT OUT OF ALL THIS...
IF SHE WASN'T A VAN DYNE AND MY BROTHER TONY'S FAVORITE EMPLOYEE...
...SHE WOULD HAVE BEEN PINK-SLIPPED DURING THE LAST ROUND OF LAY-OFFS!
ACTUALLY, COME TO THINK OF IT...WHY AM I KEEPING HER?
MAYBE IT'S TIME TO CLOSE UP HER SECTION! I COULD INCORPORATE IT INTO THE NEW COMBAT MECHA DIVISION... HMMM...
THAT MIGHT EVEN RAISE THE STOCK A FEW POINTS...
MISTRESS STARK... HOW DID YOUR ESCORT DUTY GO?
FINE, ALFIE! PREPARE THE INSTA-SHOWER AND HAVE MY RED VERA WANG ENSEMBLE FOR THE MEETING TODAY!
VERY WELL, MISTRESS STARK. I'VE PREPARED YOUR WHEAT GRASS CHASER FOR LUNCH.
ALFIE... WHAT WOULD I DO WITHOUT YOU?

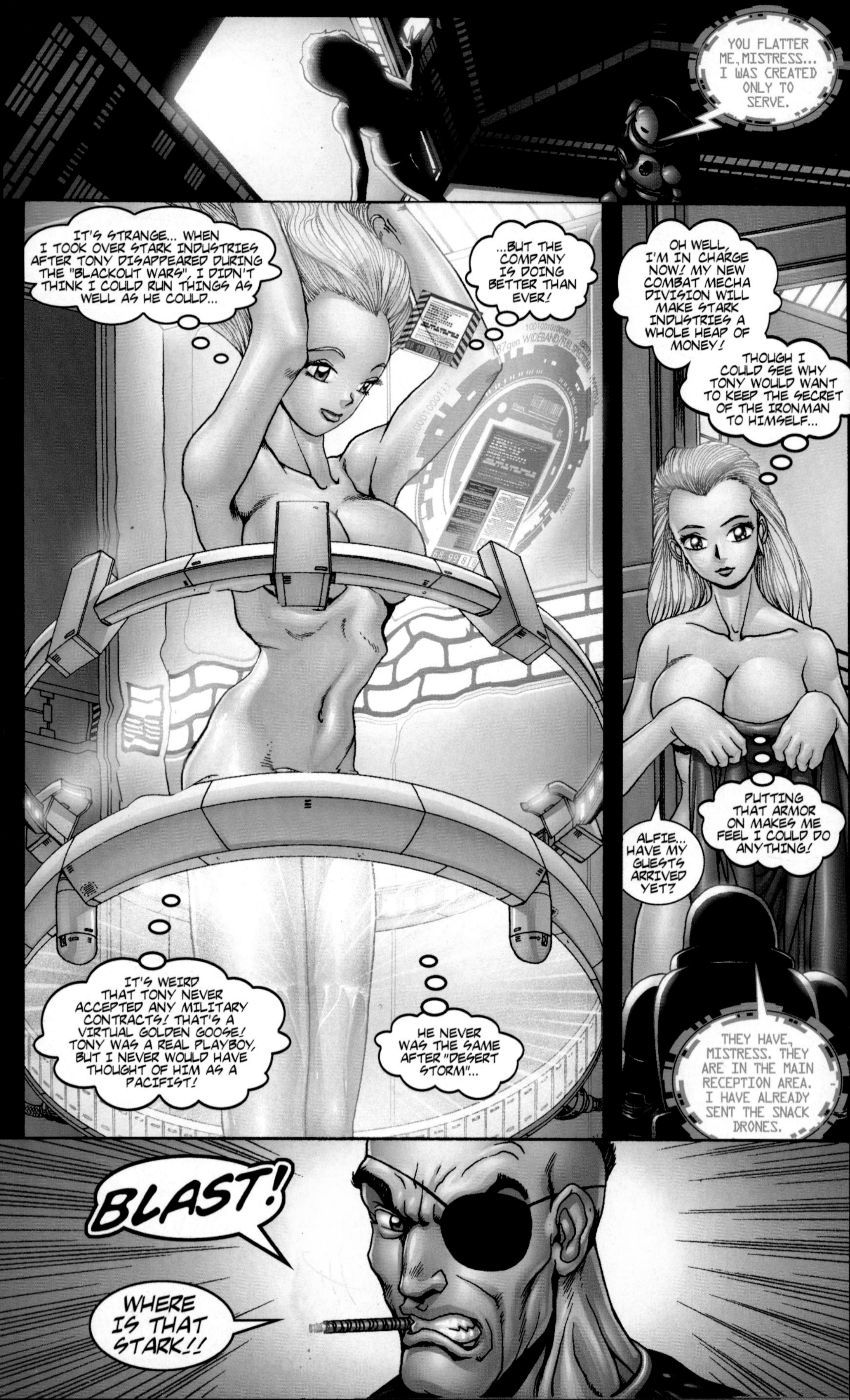

YOU FLATTER ME, MISTRESS... I WAS CREATED ONLY TO SERVE.
IT'S STRANGE... WHEN I TOOK OVER STARK INDUSTRIES AFTER TONY DISAPPEARED DURING THE "BLACKOUT WARS", I DIDN'T THINK I COULD RUN THINGS AS WELL AS HE COULD...
...BUT THE COMPANY IS DOING BETTER THAN EVER!
IT'S WEIRD THAT TONY NEVER ACCEPTED ANY MILITARY CONTRACTS! THAT'S A VIRTUAL GOLDEN GOOSE! TONY WAS A REAL PLAYBOY, BUT I NEVER WOULD HAVE THOUGHT OF HIM AS A PACIFIST!
HE NEVER WAS THE SAME AFTER "DESERT STORM"...
OH WELL, I'M IN CHARGE NOW! MY NEW COMBAT MECHA DIVISION WILL MAKE STARK INDUSTRIES A WHOLE HEAP OF MONEY!
THOUGH I COULD SEE WHY TONY WOULD WANT TO KEEP THE SECRET OF THE IRONMAN TO HIMSELF...
PUTTING THAT ARMOR ON MAKES ME FEEL I COULD DO ANYTHING!
ALFIE... HAVE MY GUESTS ARRIVED YET?
THEY HAVE, MISTRESS. THEY ARE IN THE MAIN RECEPTION AREA. I HAVE ALREADY SENT THE SNACK DRONES.
BLAST!
WHERE IS THAT STARK!!

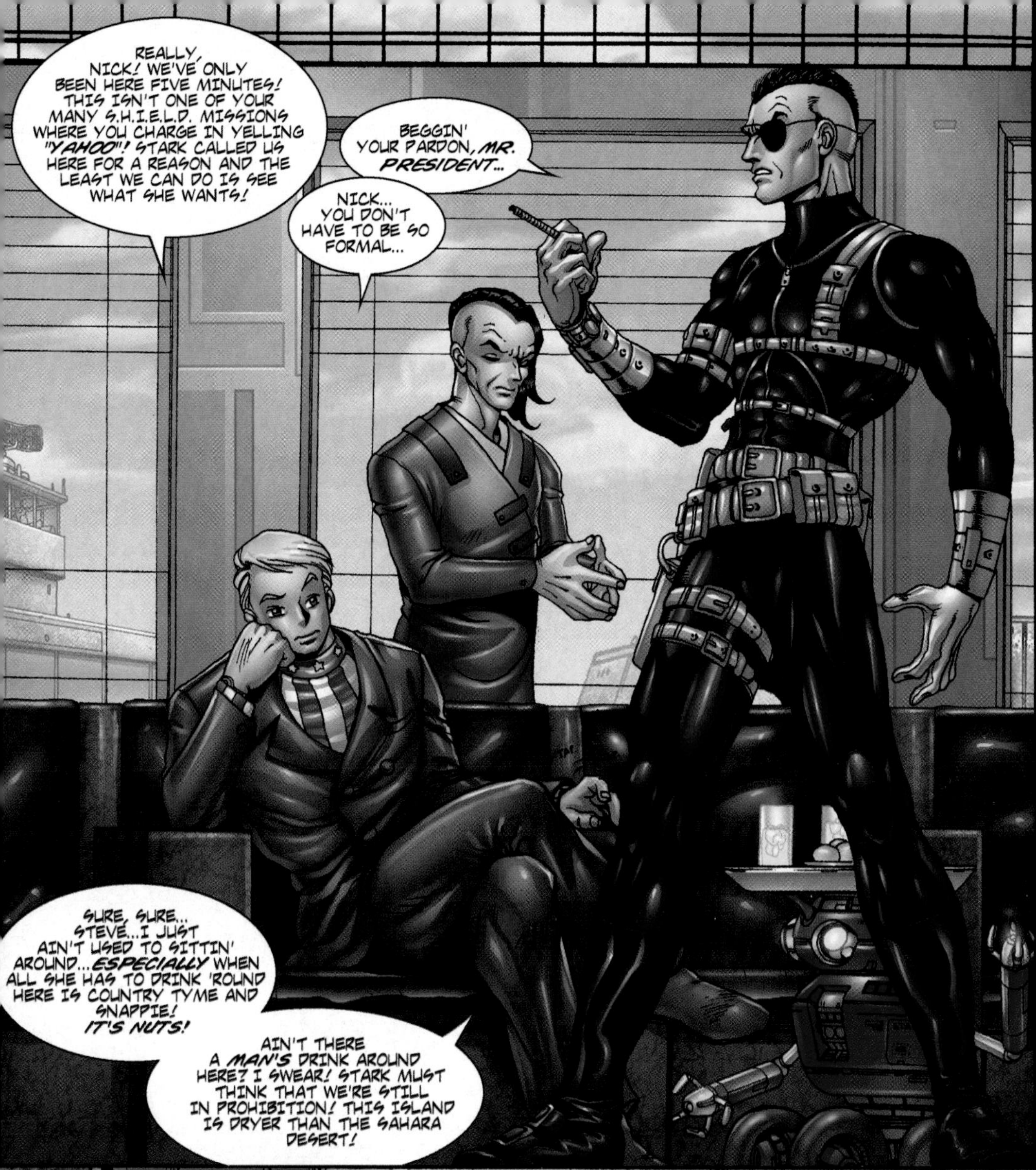
REALLY, NICK! WE'VE ONLY BEEN HERE FIVE MINUTES! THIS ISN'T ONE OF YOUR MANY S.H.I.E.L.D. MISSIONS WHERE YOU CHARGE IN YELLING "YAHOO"! STARK CALLED US HERE FOR A REASON AND THE LEAST WE CAN DO IS SEE WHAT SHE WANTS!
BEGGIN' YOUR PARDON, *MR. PRESIDENT*...
NICK... YOU DON'T HAVE TO BE SO FORMAL...
SURE, SURE... STEVE...I JUST AIN'T USED TO SITTIN' AROUND...*ESPECIALLY* WHEN ALL SHE HAS TO DRINK 'ROUND HERE IS COUNTRY TYME AND SNAPPIE! *IT'S NUTS!*
AIN'T THERE A *MAN'S* DRINK AROUND HERE? I SWEAR! STARK MUST THINK THAT WE'RE STILL IN PROHIBITION! THIS ISLAND IS DRYER THAN THE SAHARA DESERT!

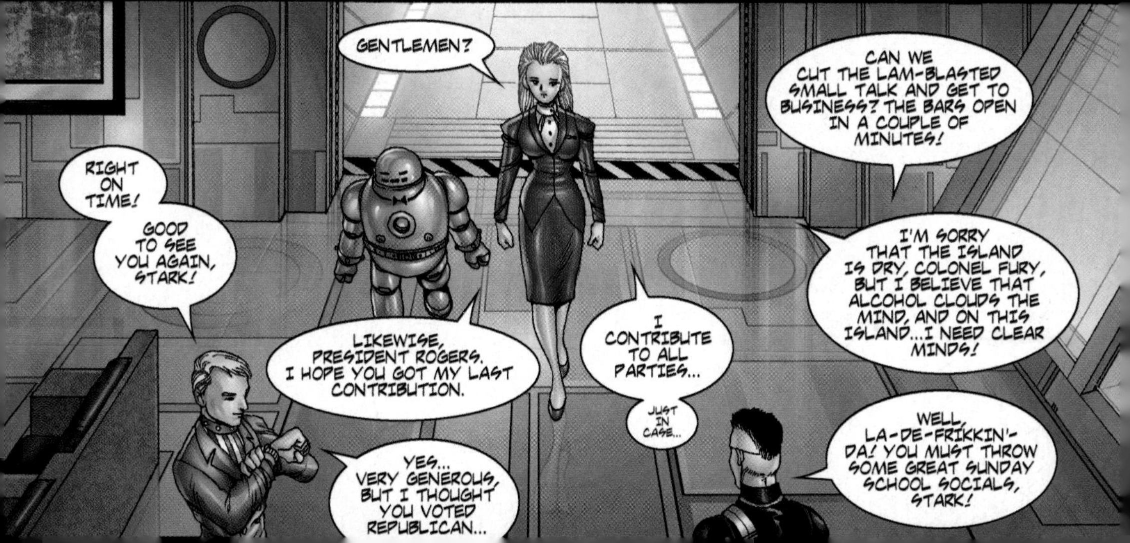
GENTLEMEN?
RIGHT ON TIME!
GOOD TO SEE YOU AGAIN, STARK!
CAN WE CUT THE LAM-BLASTED SMALL TALK AND GET TO BUSINESS? THE BARS OPEN IN A COUPLE OF MINUTES!
LIKEWISE, PRESIDENT ROGERS. I HOPE YOU GOT MY LAST CONTRIBUTION.
YES... VERY GENEROUS, BUT I THOUGHT YOU VOTED REPUBLICAN...
I CONTRIBUTE TO ALL PARTIES...
JUST IN CASE...
I'M SORRY THAT THE ISLAND IS DRY, COLONEL FURY, BUT I BELIEVE THAT ALCOHOL CLOUDS THE MIND, AND ON THIS ISLAND...I NEED CLEAR MINDS!
WELL, LA-DE-FRIKKIN'-DA! YOU MUST THROW SOME GREAT SUNDAY SCHOOL SOCIALS, STARK!

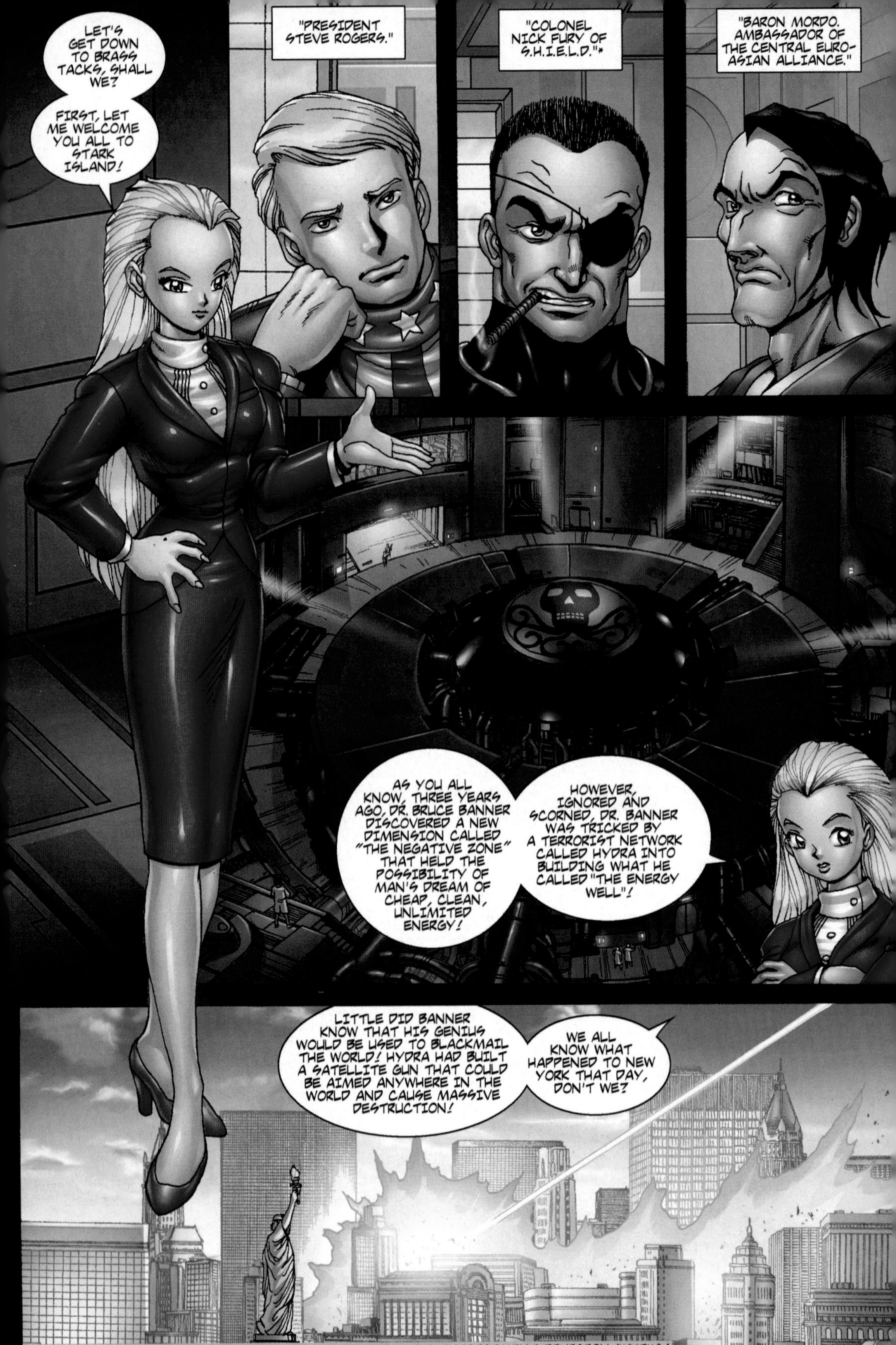
LET'S GET DOWN TO BRASS TACKS, SHALL WE?
FIRST, LET ME WELCOME YOU ALL TO STARK ISLAND!
"PRESIDENT STEVE ROGERS."
"COLONEL NICK FURY OF S.H.I.E.L.D."*
"BARON MORDO. AMBASSADOR OF THE CENTRAL EURO-ASIAN ALLIANCE."
AS YOU ALL KNOW, THREE YEARS AGO, DR. BRUCE BANNER DISCOVERED A NEW DIMENSION CALLED "THE NEGATIVE ZONE" THAT HELD THE POSSIBILITY OF MAN'S DREAM OF CHEAP, CLEAN, UNLIMITED ENERGY!
HOWEVER, IGNORED AND SCORNED, DR. BANNER WAS TRICKED BY A TERRORIST NETWORK CALLED HYDRA INTO BUILDING WHAT HE CALLED "THE ENERGY WELL"!
LITTLE DID BANNER KNOW THAT HIS GENIUS WOULD BE USED TO BLACKMAIL THE WORLD! HYDRA HAD BUILT A SATELLITE GUN THAT COULD BE AIMED ANYWHERE IN THE WORLD AND CAUSE MASSIVE DESTRUCTION!
WE ALL KNOW WHAT HAPPENED TO NEW YORK THAT DAY, DON'T WE?

*SUPREME HEADQUARTERS INTERNATIONAL ESPIONAGE LAW-ENFORCEMENT DIVISION (WHEW)!

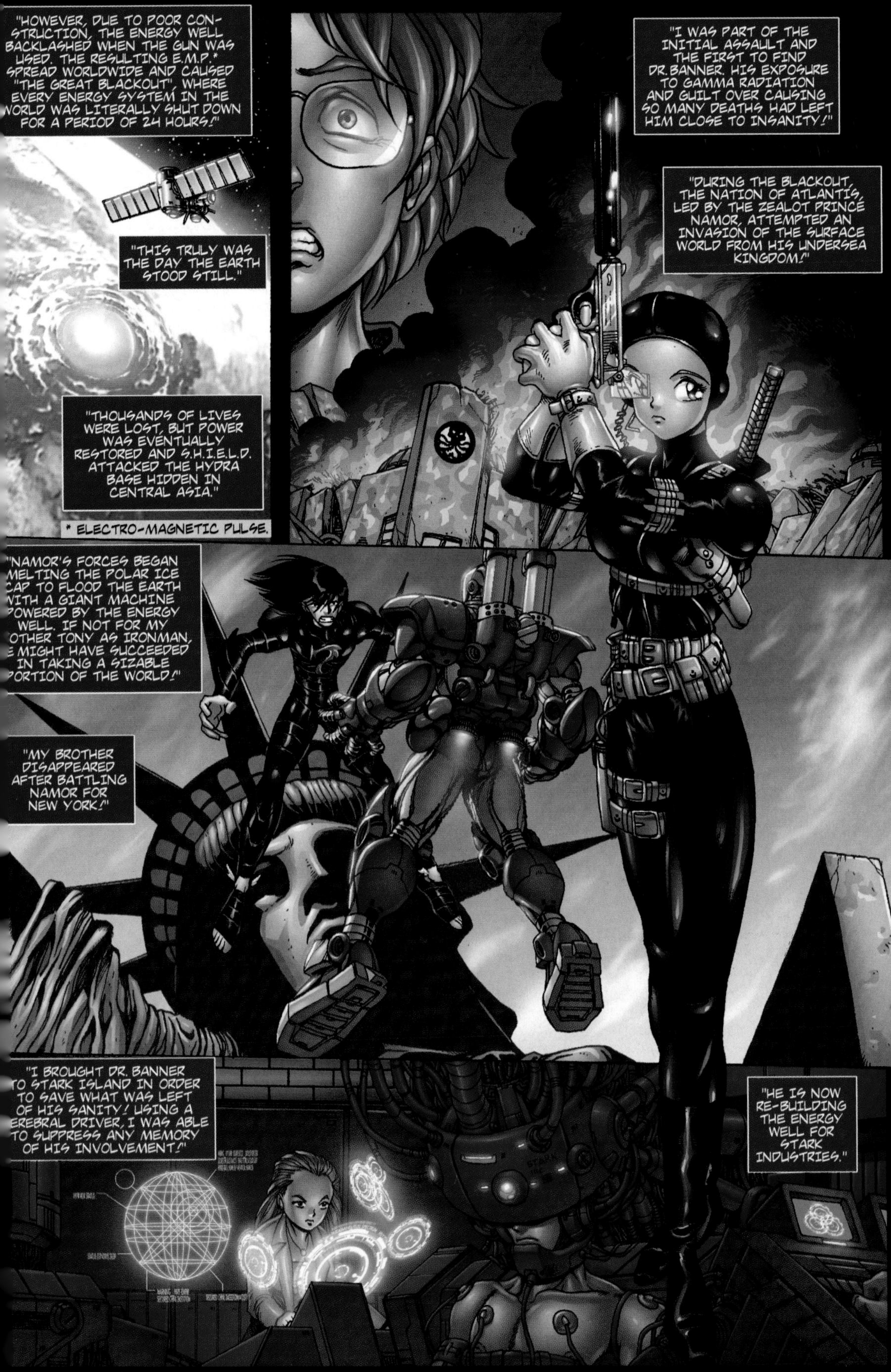
"HOWEVER, DUE TO POOR CONSTRUCTION, THE ENERGY WELL BACKLASHED WHEN THE GUN WAS USED. THE RESULTING E.M.P.* SPREAD WORLDWIDE AND CAUSED "THE GREAT BLACKOUT", WHERE EVERY ENERGY SYSTEM IN THE WORLD WAS LITERALLY SHUT DOWN FOR A PERIOD OF 24 HOURS!"
"THIS TRULY WAS THE DAY THE EARTH STOOD STILL."
"THOUSANDS OF LIVES WERE LOST, BUT POWER WAS EVENTUALLY RESTORED AND S.H.I.E.L.D. ATTACKED THE HYDRA BASE HIDDEN IN CENTRAL ASIA."
* ELECTRO-MAGNETIC PULSE.
"I WAS PART OF THE INITIAL ASSAULT AND THE FIRST TO FIND DR. BANNER. HIS EXPOSURE TO GAMMA RADIATION AND GUILT OVER CAUSING SO MANY DEATHS HAD LEFT HIM CLOSE TO INSANITY!"
"DURING THE BLACKOUT, THE NATION OF ATLANTIS, LED BY THE ZEALOT PRINCE NAMOR, ATTEMPTED AN INVASION OF THE SURFACE WORLD FROM HIS UNDERSEA KINGDOM!"
"NAMOR'S FORCES BEGAN MELTING THE POLAR ICE CAP TO FLOOD THE EARTH WITH A GIANT MACHINE POWERED BY THE ENERGY WELL. IF NOT FOR MY OTHER TONY AS IRONMAN, E MIGHT HAVE SUCCEEDED IN TAKING A SIZABLE PORTION OF THE WORLD!"
"MY BROTHER DISAPPEARED AFTER BATTLING NAMOR FOR NEW YORK!"
"I BROUGHT DR. BANNER TO STARK ISLAND IN ORDER TO SAVE WHAT WAS LEFT OF HIS SANITY! USING A EREBRAL DRIVER, I WAS ABLE TO SUPPRESS ANY MEMORY OF HIS INVOLVEMENT!"
"HE IS NOW RE-BUILDING THE ENERGY WELL FOR STARK INDUSTRIES."

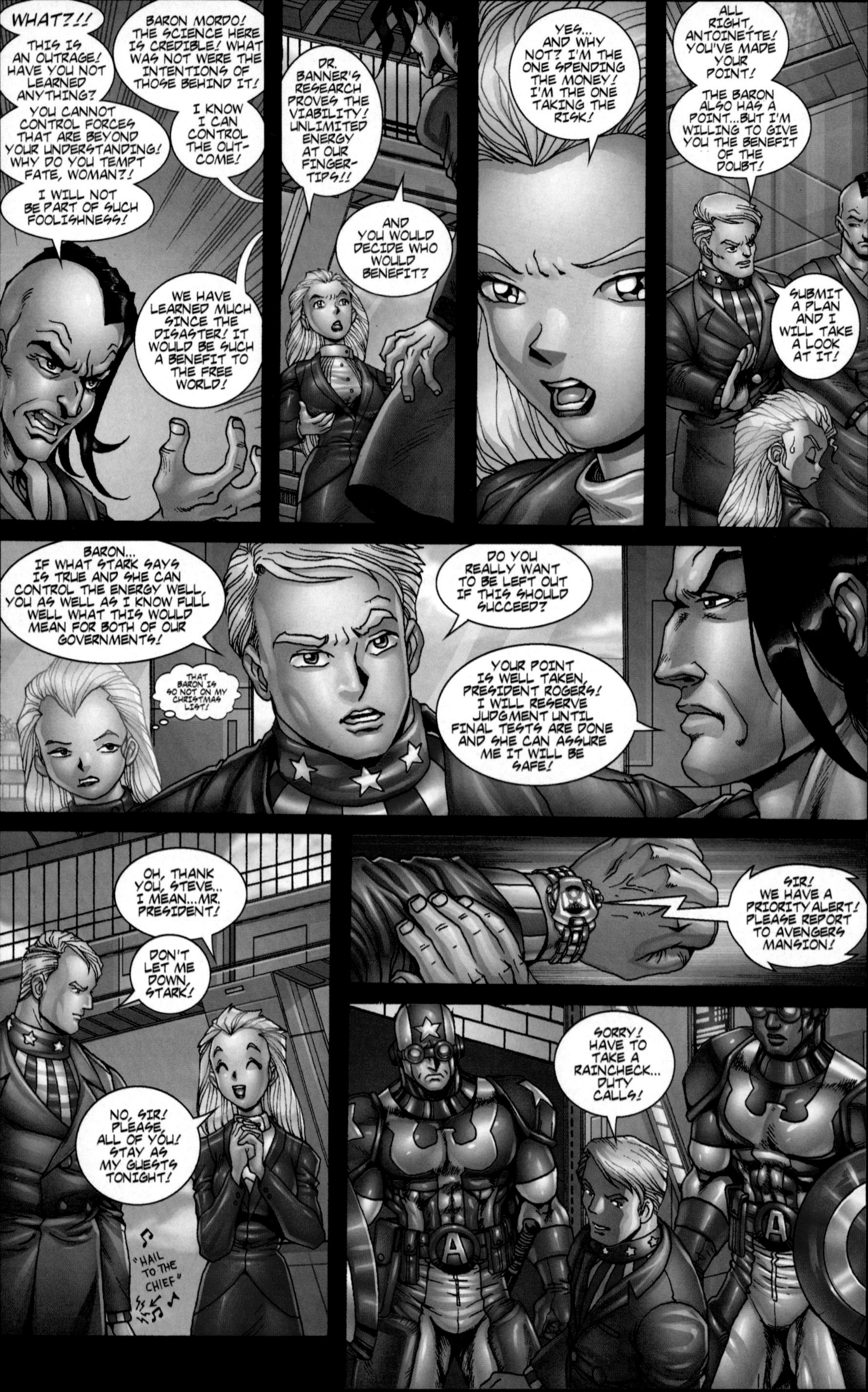
WHAT?!!
THIS IS AN OUTRAGE! HAVE YOU NOT LEARNED ANYTHING?
YOU CANNOT CONTROL FORCES THAT ARE BEYOND YOUR UNDERSTANDING! WHY DO YOU TEMPT FATE, WOMAN?!
I WILL NOT BE PART OF SUCH FOOLISHNESS!
BARON MORDO! THE SCIENCE HERE IS CREDIBLE! WHAT WAS NOT WERE THE INTENTIONS OF THOSE BEHIND IT!
I KNOW I CAN CONTROL THE OUT-COME!
WE HAVE LEARNED MUCH SINCE THE DISASTER! IT WOULD BE SUCH A BENEFIT TO THE FREE WORLD!
DR. BANNER'S RESEARCH PROVES THE VIABILITY! UNLIMITED ENERGY AT OUR FINGER-TIPS!!
AND YOU WOULD DECIDE WHO WOULD BENEFIT?
YES... AND WHY NOT? I'M THE ONE SPENDING THE MONEY! I'M THE ONE TAKING THE RISK!
ALL RIGHT, ANTOINETTE! YOU'VE MADE YOUR POINT!
THE BARON ALSO HAS A POINT...BUT I'M WILLING TO GIVE YOU THE BENEFIT OF THE DOUBT!
SUBMIT A PLAN AND I WILL TAKE A LOOK AT IT!
BARON... IF WHAT STARK SAYS IS TRUE AND SHE CAN CONTROL THE ENERGY WELL, YOU AS WELL AS I KNOW FULL WELL WHAT THIS WOULD MEAN FOR BOTH OF OUR GOVERNMENTS!
THAT BARON IS SO NOT ON MY CHRISTMAS LIST!
DO YOU REALLY WANT TO BE LEFT OUT IF THIS SHOULD SUCCEED?
YOUR POINT IS WELL TAKEN, PRESIDENT ROGERS! I WILL RESERVE JUDGMENT UNTIL FINAL TESTS ARE DONE AND SHE CAN ASSURE ME IT WILL BE SAFE!
OH, THANK YOU, STEVE... I MEAN...MR. PRESIDENT!
DON'T LET ME DOWN, STARK!
NO, SIR! PLEASE, ALL OF YOU! STAY AS MY GUESTS TONIGHT!
"HAIL TO THE CHIEF"
SIR! WE HAVE A PRIORITY ALERT! PLEASE REPORT TO AVENGERS MANSION!
SORRY! HAVE TO TAKE A RAINCHECK... DUTY CALLS!

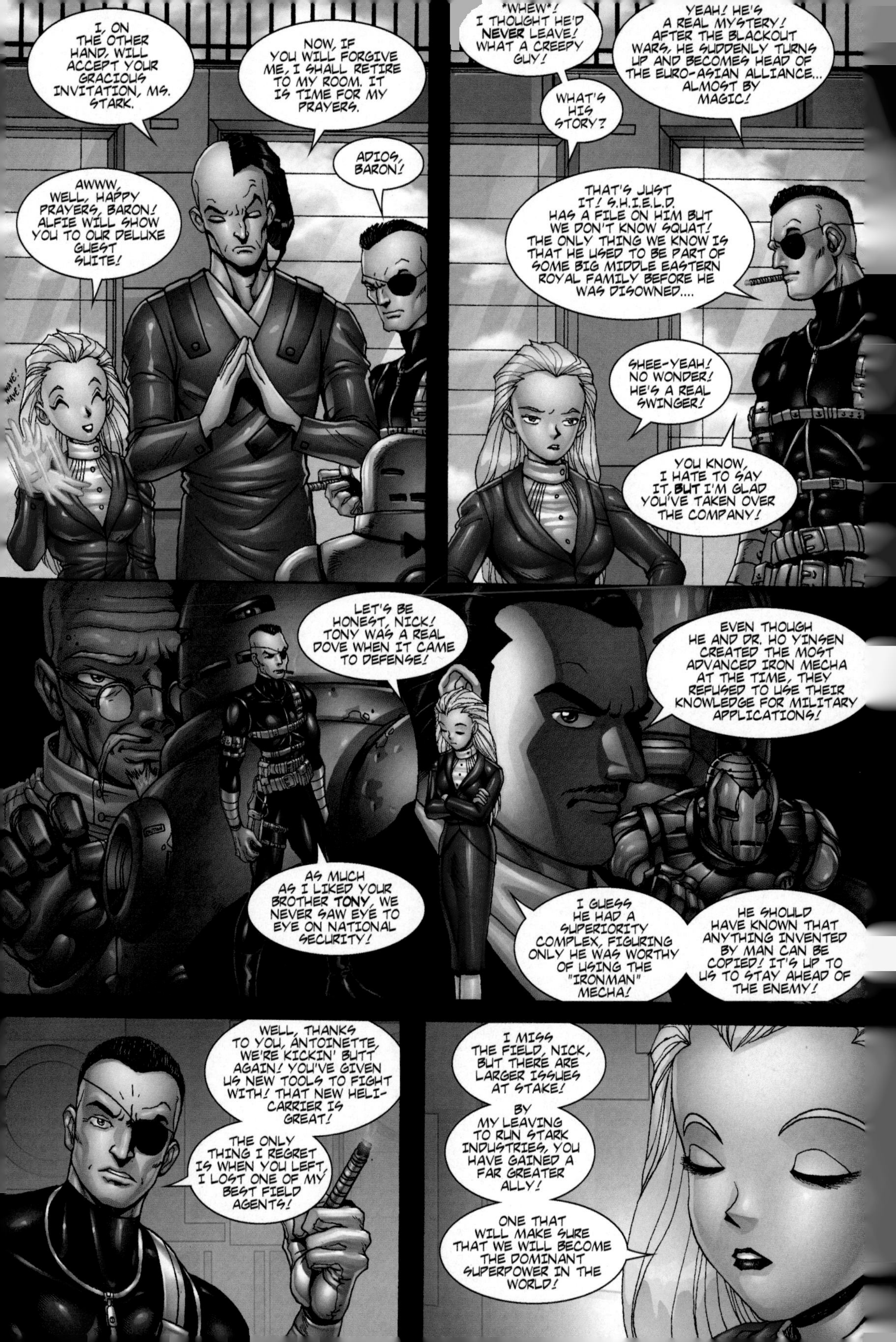
I, ON THE OTHER HAND, WILL ACCEPT YOUR GRACIOUS INVITATION, MS. STARK.
NOW, IF YOU WILL FORGIVE ME, I SHALL RETIRE TO MY ROOM. IT IS TIME FOR MY PRAYERS.
ADIOS, BARON!
AWWW, WELL, HAPPY PRAYERS, BARON! ALFIE WILL SHOW YOU TO OUR DELUXE GUEST SUITE!
WAVE! WAVE!
WHEW! I THOUGHT HE'D NEVER LEAVE! WHAT A CREEPY GUY!
WHAT'S HIS STORY?
YEAH! HE'S A REAL MYSTERY! AFTER THE BLACKOUT WARS, HE SUDDENLY TURNS UP AND BECOMES HEAD OF THE EURO-ASIAN ALLIANCE... ALMOST BY MAGIC!
THAT'S JUST IT! S.H.I.E.L.D. HAS A FILE ON HIM BUT WE DON'T KNOW SQUAT! THE ONLY THING WE KNOW IS THAT HE USED TO BE PART OF SOME BIG MIDDLE EASTERN ROYAL FAMILY BEFORE HE WAS DISOWNED....
SHEE-YEAH! NO WONDER! HE'S A REAL SWINGER!
YOU KNOW, I HATE TO SAY IT, BUT I'M GLAD YOU'VE TAKEN OVER THE COMPANY!
LET'S BE HONEST, NICK! TONY WAS A REAL DOVE WHEN IT CAME TO DEFENSE!
AS MUCH AS I LIKED YOUR BROTHER TONY, WE NEVER SAW EYE TO EYE ON NATIONAL SECURITY!
EVEN THOUGH HE AND DR. HO YINSEN CREATED THE MOST ADVANCED IRON MECHA AT THE TIME, THEY REFUSED TO USE THEIR KNOWLEDGE FOR MILITARY APPLICATIONS!
I GUESS HE HAD A SUPERIORITY COMPLEX, FIGURING ONLY HE WAS WORTHY OF USING THE "IRONMAN" MECHA!
HE SHOULD HAVE KNOWN THAT ANYTHING INVENTED BY MAN CAN BE COPIED! IT'S UP TO US TO STAY AHEAD OF THE ENEMY!
WELL, THANKS TO YOU, ANTOINETTE, WE'RE KICKIN' BUTT AGAIN! YOU'VE GIVEN US NEW TOOLS TO FIGHT WITH! THAT NEW HELI-CARRIER IS GREAT!
THE ONLY THING I REGRET IS WHEN YOU LEFT, I LOST ONE OF MY BEST FIELD AGENTS!
I MISS THE FIELD, NICK, BUT THERE ARE LARGER ISSUES AT STAKE!
BY MY LEAVING TO RUN STARK INDUSTRIES, YOU HAVE GAINED A FAR GREATER ALLY!
ONE THAT WILL MAKE SURE THAT WE WILL BECOME THE DOMINANT SUPERPOWER IN THE WORLD!

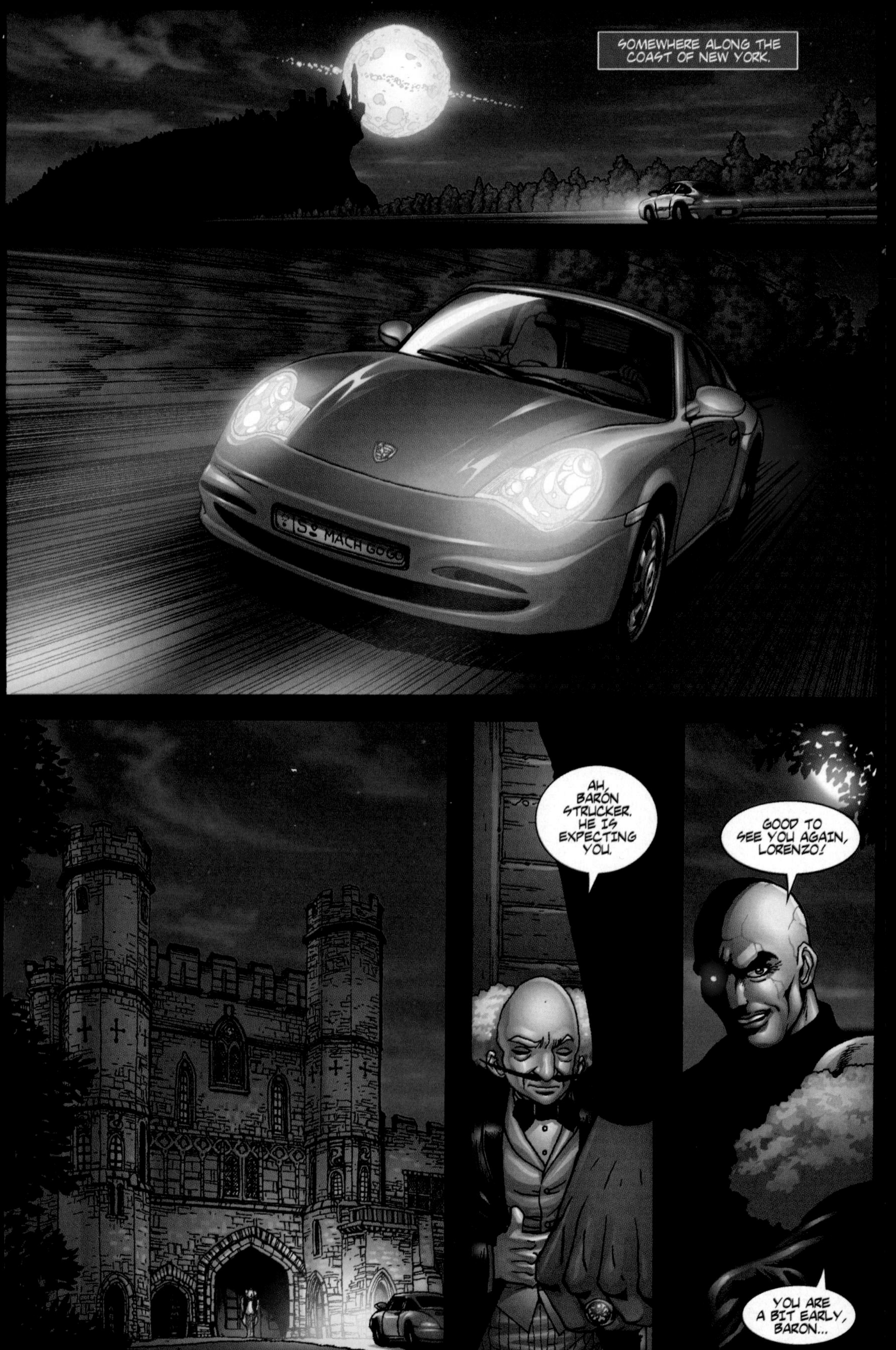
SOMEWHERE ALONG THE COAST OF NEW YORK.
S MACH GO GO
AH, BARÓN STRUCKER. HE IS EXPECTING YOU.
GOOD TO SEE YOU AGAIN, LORENZO!
YOU ARE A BIT EARLY, BARON...

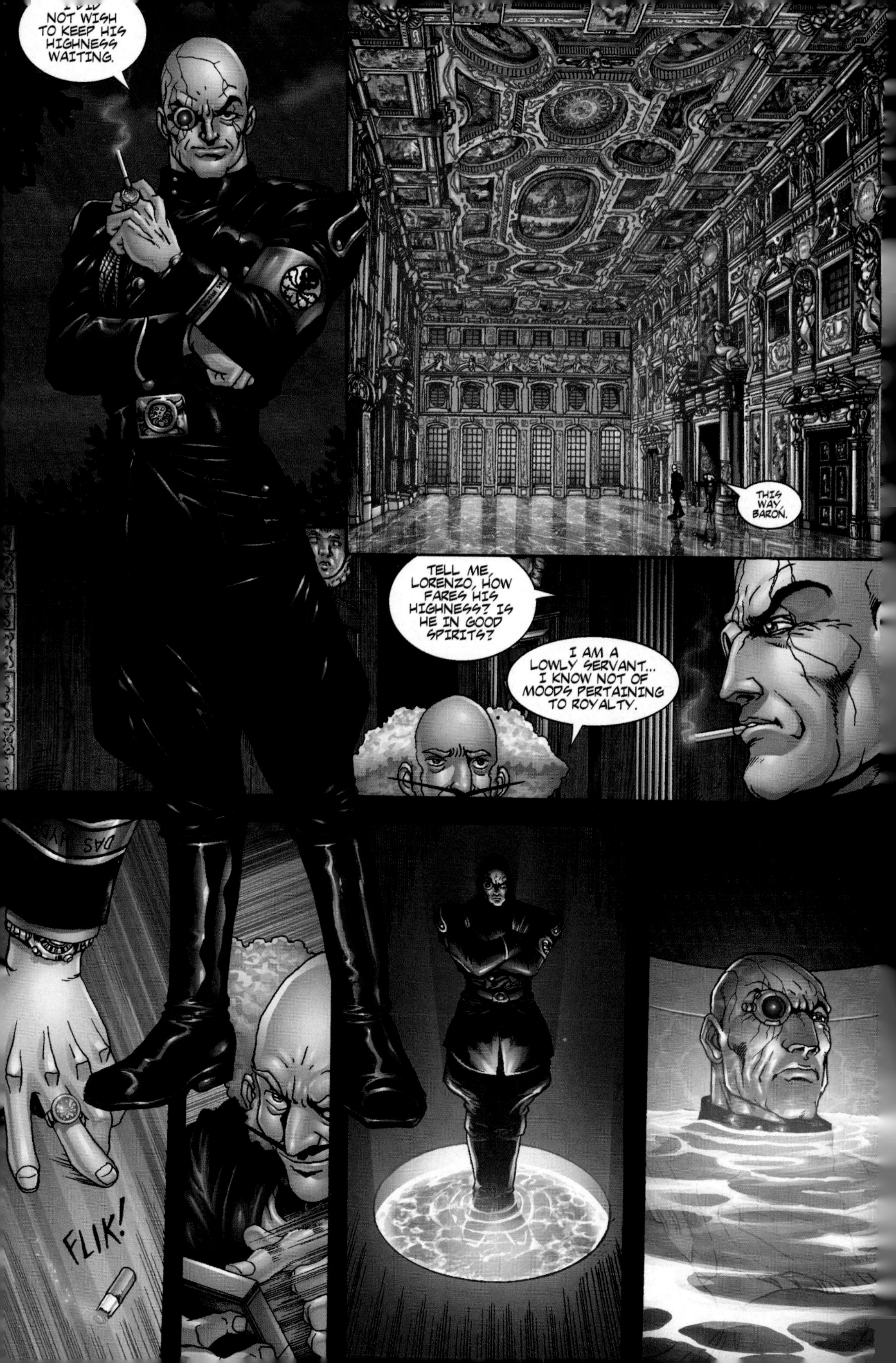
NOT WISH TO KEEP HIS HIGHNESS WAITING.
THIS WAY, BARON.
TELL ME, LORENZO, HOW FARES HIS HIGHNESS? IS HE IN GOOD SPIRITS?
I AM A LOWLY SERVANT... I KNOW NOT OF MOODS PERTAINING TO ROYALTY.
FLIK!

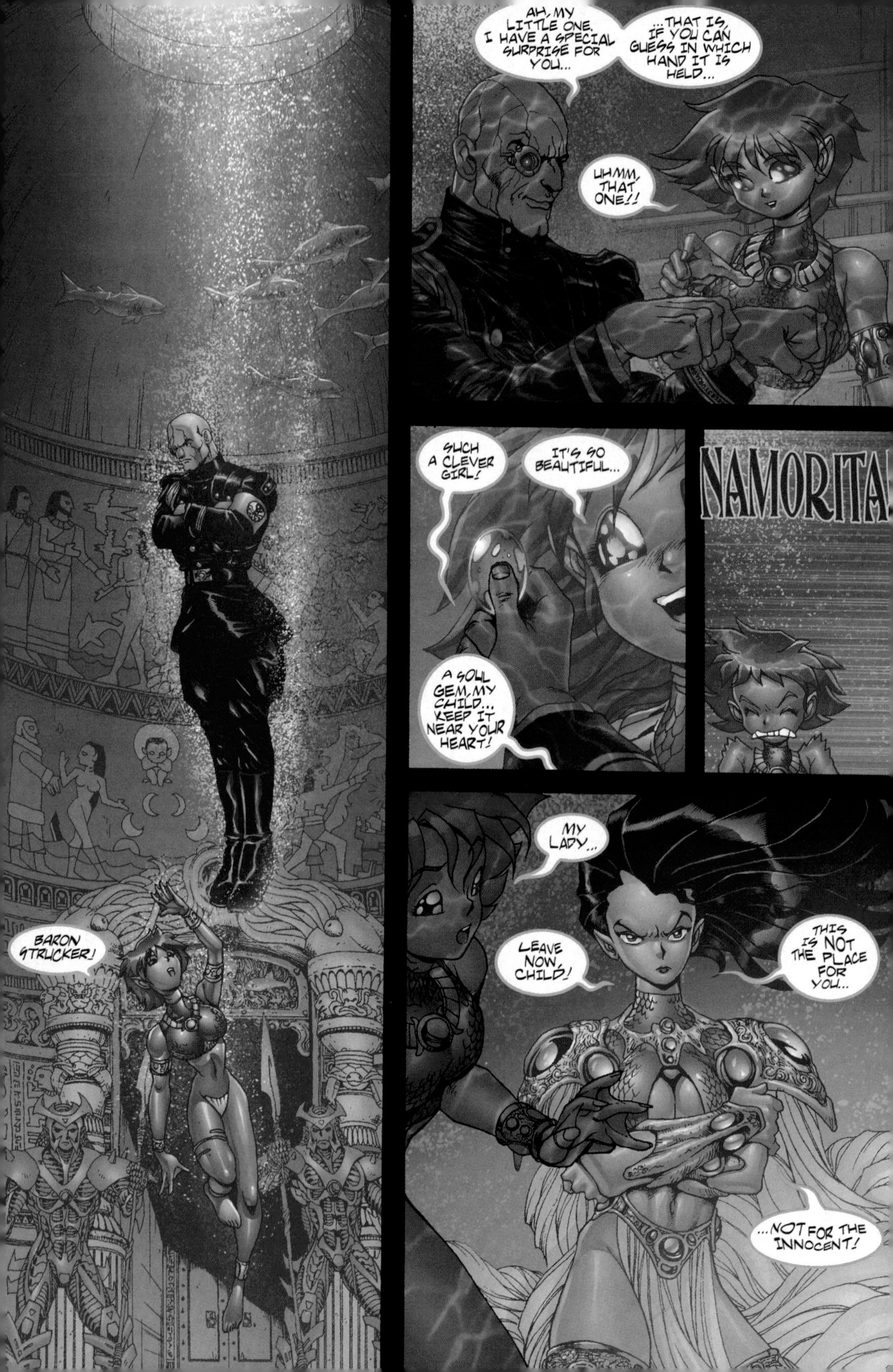
BARON STRUCKER!
AH, MY LITTLE ONE. I HAVE A SPECIAL SURPRISE FOR YOU...
...THAT IS, IF YOU CAN GUESS IN WHICH HAND IT IS HELD...
UHMM, THAT ONE!!
SUCH A CLEVER GIRL!
IT'S SO BEAUTIFUL...
A SOUL GEM, MY CHILD... KEEP IT NEAR YOUR HEART!
NAMORITA
MY LADY...
LEAVE NOW, CHILD!
THIS IS NOT THE PLACE FOR YOU...
...NOT FOR THE INNOCENT!

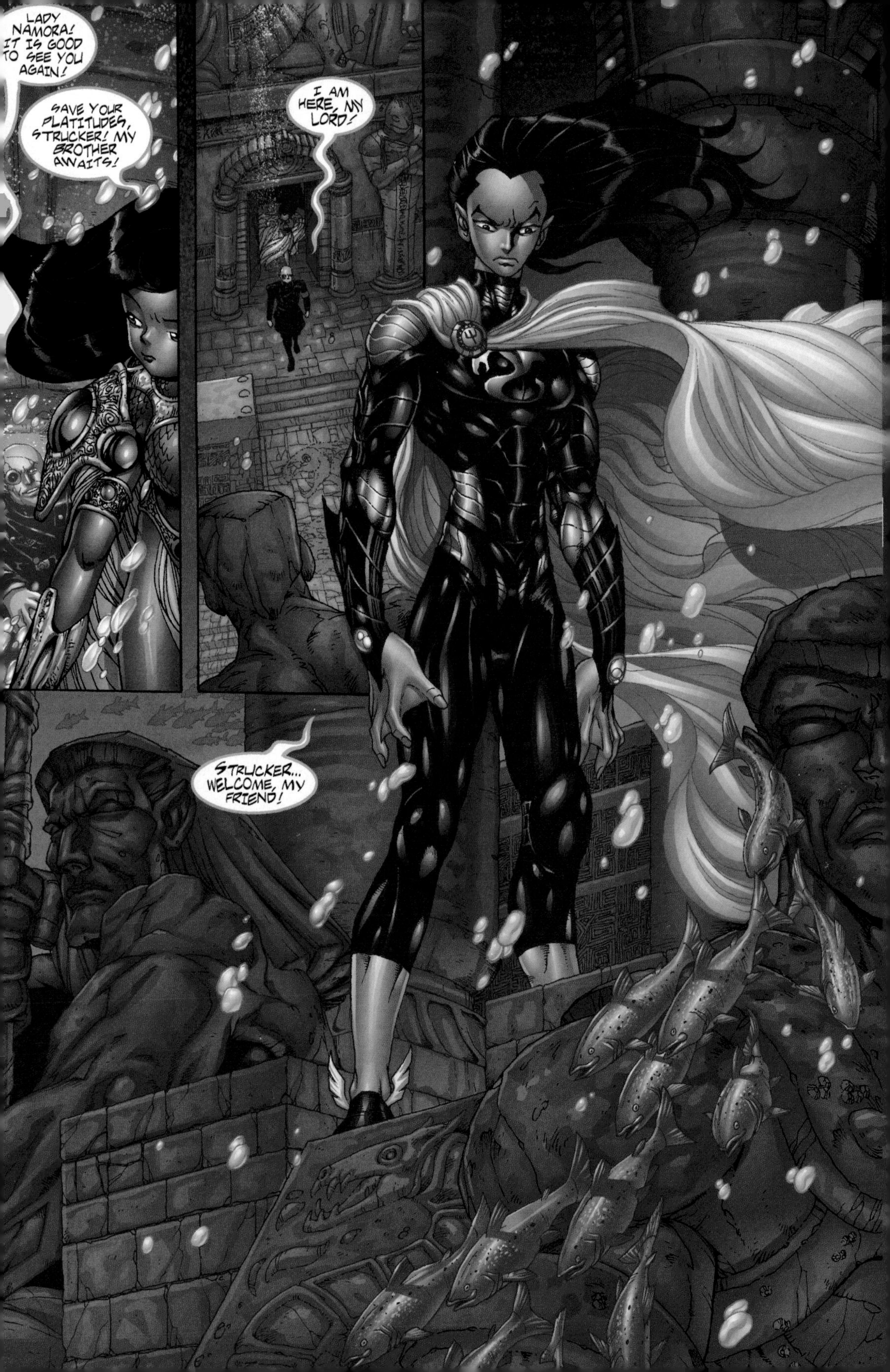
LADY NAMORA! IT IS GOOD TO SEE YOU AGAIN!
SAVE YOUR PLATITUDES, STRUCKER! MY BROTHER AWAITS!
I AM HERE, MY LORD!
STRUCKER... WELCOME, MY FRIEND!

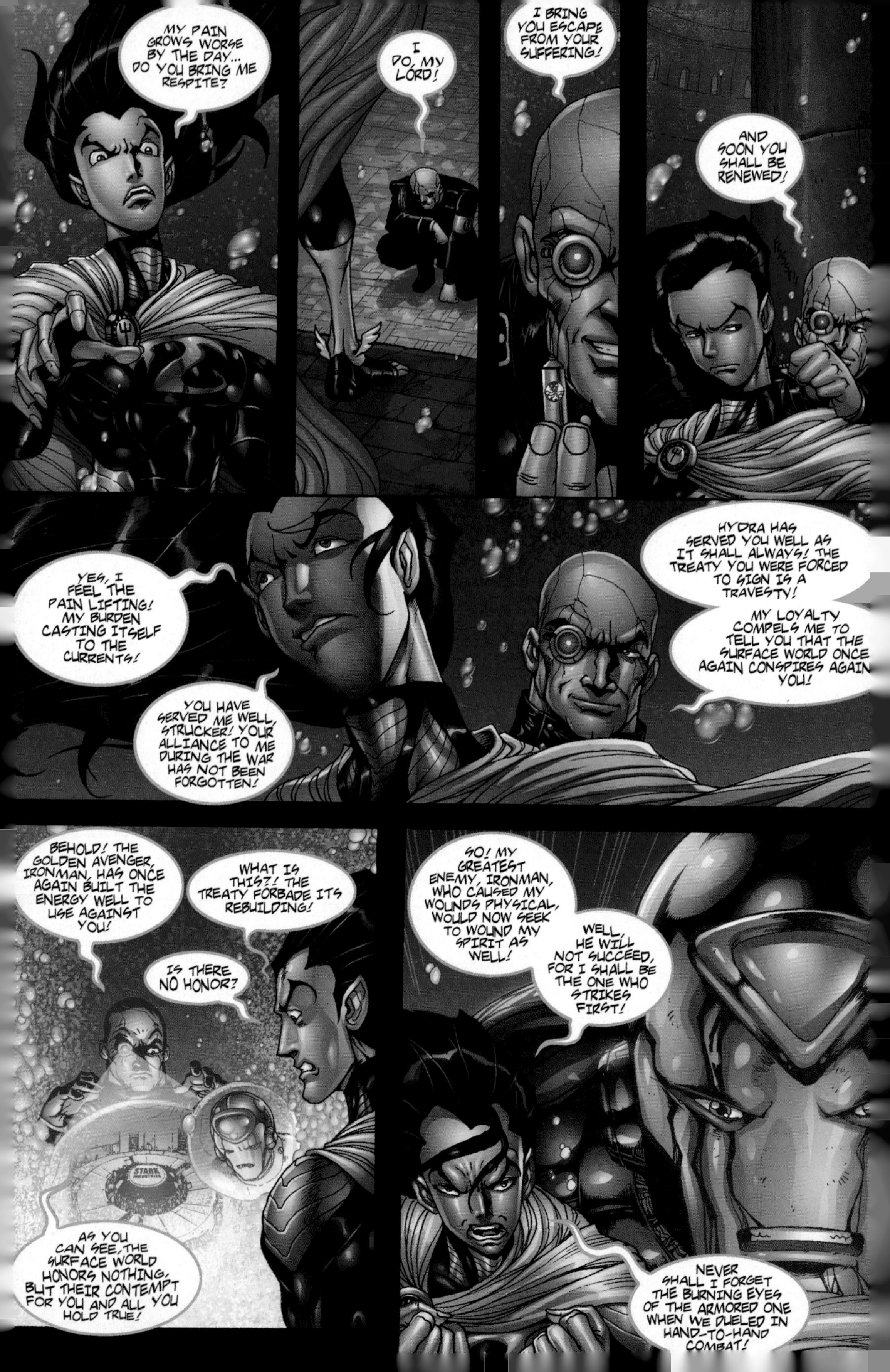
MY PAIN GROWS WORSE BY THE DAY... DO YOU BRING ME RESPITE?
I DO, MY LORD!
I BRING YOU ESCAPE FROM YOUR SUFFERING!
AND SOON YOU SHALL BE RENEWED!
YES, I FEEL THE PAIN LIFTING! MY BURDEN CASTING ITSELF TO THE CURRENTS!
YOU HAVE SERVED ME WELL, STRUCKER! YOUR ALLIANCE TO ME DURING THE WAR HAS NOT BEEN FORGOTTEN!
HYDRA HAS SERVED YOU WELL AS IT SHALL ALWAYS! THE TREATY YOU WERE FORCED TO SIGN IS A TRAVESTY!
MY LOYALTY COMPELS ME TO TELL YOU THAT THE SURFACE WORLD ONCE AGAIN CONSPIRES AGAIN YOU!
BEHOLD! THE GOLDEN AVENGER, IRONMAN, HAS ONCE AGAIN BUILT THE ENERGY WELL TO USE AGAINST YOU!
WHAT IS THIS?! THE TREATY FORBADE ITS REBUILDING!
IS THERE NO HONOR?
AS YOU CAN SEE, THE SURFACE WORLD HONORS NOTHING, BUT THEIR CONTEMPT FOR YOU AND ALL YOU HOLD TRUE!
SO! MY GREATEST ENEMY, IRONMAN, WHO CAUSED MY WOUNDS PHYSICAL, WOULD NOW SEEK TO WOUND MY SPIRIT AS WELL!
WELL, HE WILL NOT SUCCEED, FOR I SHALL BE THE ONE WHO STRIKES FIRST!
NEVER SHALL I FORGET THE BURNING EYES OF THE ARMORED ONE WHEN WE DUELED IN HAND-TO-HAND COMBAT!

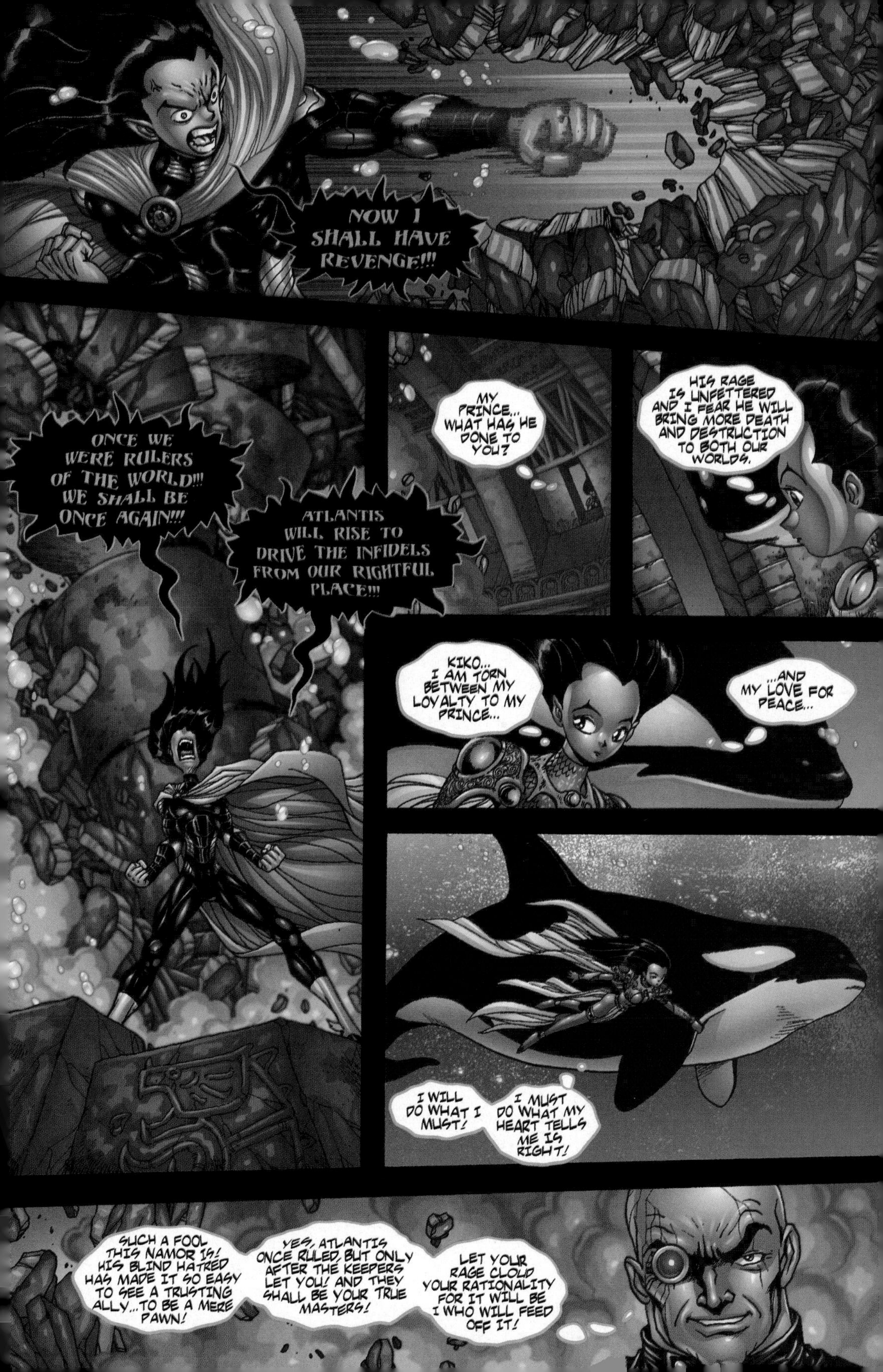
NOW I SHALL HAVE REVENGE!!!
ONCE WE WERE RULERS OF THE WORLD!!! WE SHALL BE ONCE AGAIN!!!
ATLANTIS WILL RISE TO DRIVE THE INFIDELS FROM OUR RIGHTFUL PLACE!!!
MY PRINCE... WHAT HAS HE DONE TO YOU?
HIS RAGE IS UNFETTERED AND I FEAR HE WILL BRING MORE DEATH AND DESTRUCTION TO BOTH OUR WORLDS.
KIKO... I AM TORN BETWEEN MY LOYALTY TO MY PRINCE...
...AND MY LOVE FOR PEACE...
I WILL DO WHAT I MUST!
I MUST DO WHAT MY HEART TELLS ME IS RIGHT!
SUCH A FOOL THIS NAMOR IS! HIS BLIND HATRED HAS MADE IT SO EASY TO SEE A TRUSTING ALLY...TO BE A MERE PAWN!
YES, ATLANTIS ONCE RULED, BUT ONLY AFTER THE KEEPERS LET YOU! AND THEY SHALL BE YOUR TRUE MASTERS!
LET YOUR RAGE CLOUD YOUR RATIONALITY FOR IT WILL BE I WHO WILL FEED OFF IT!

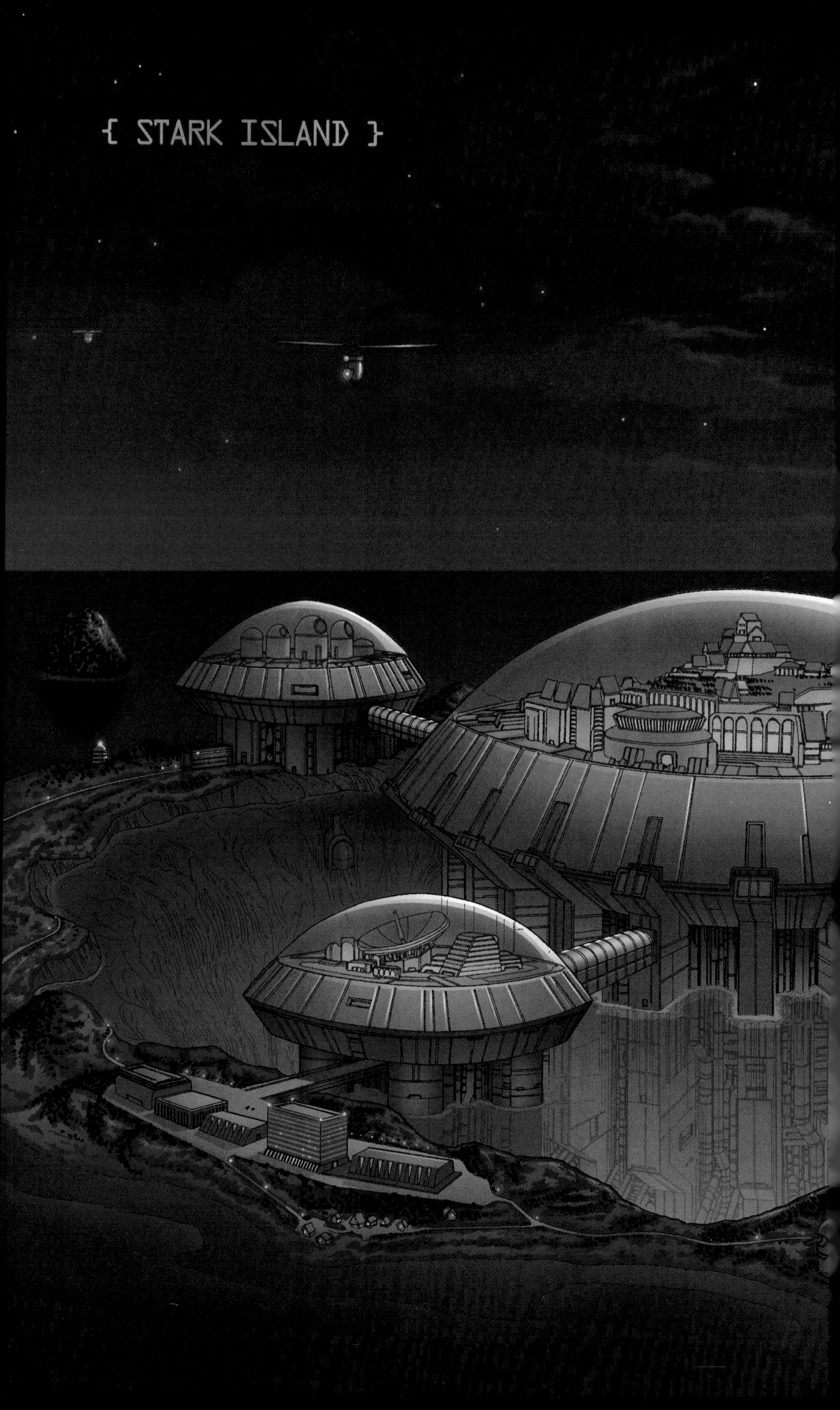
{ STARK ISLAND }

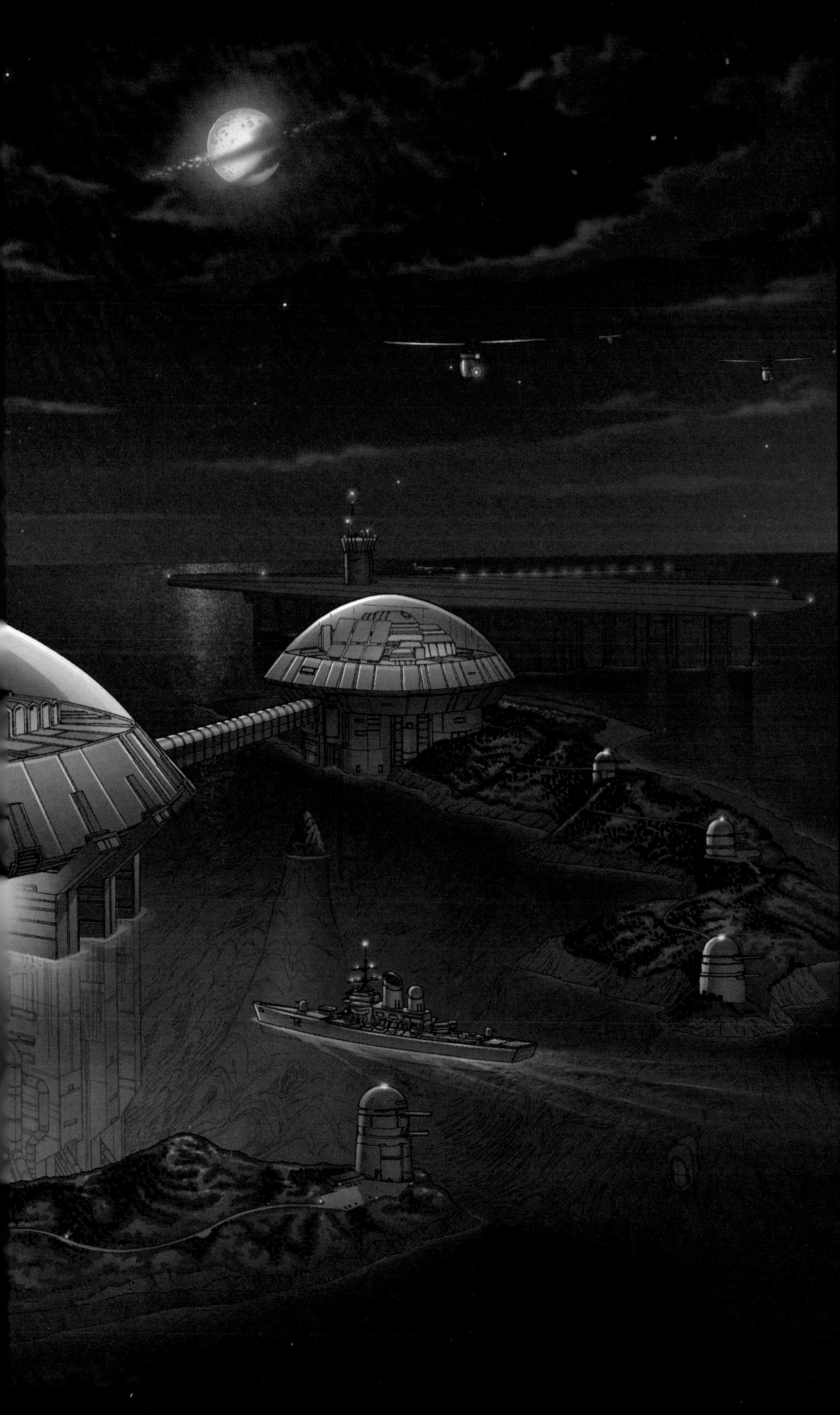

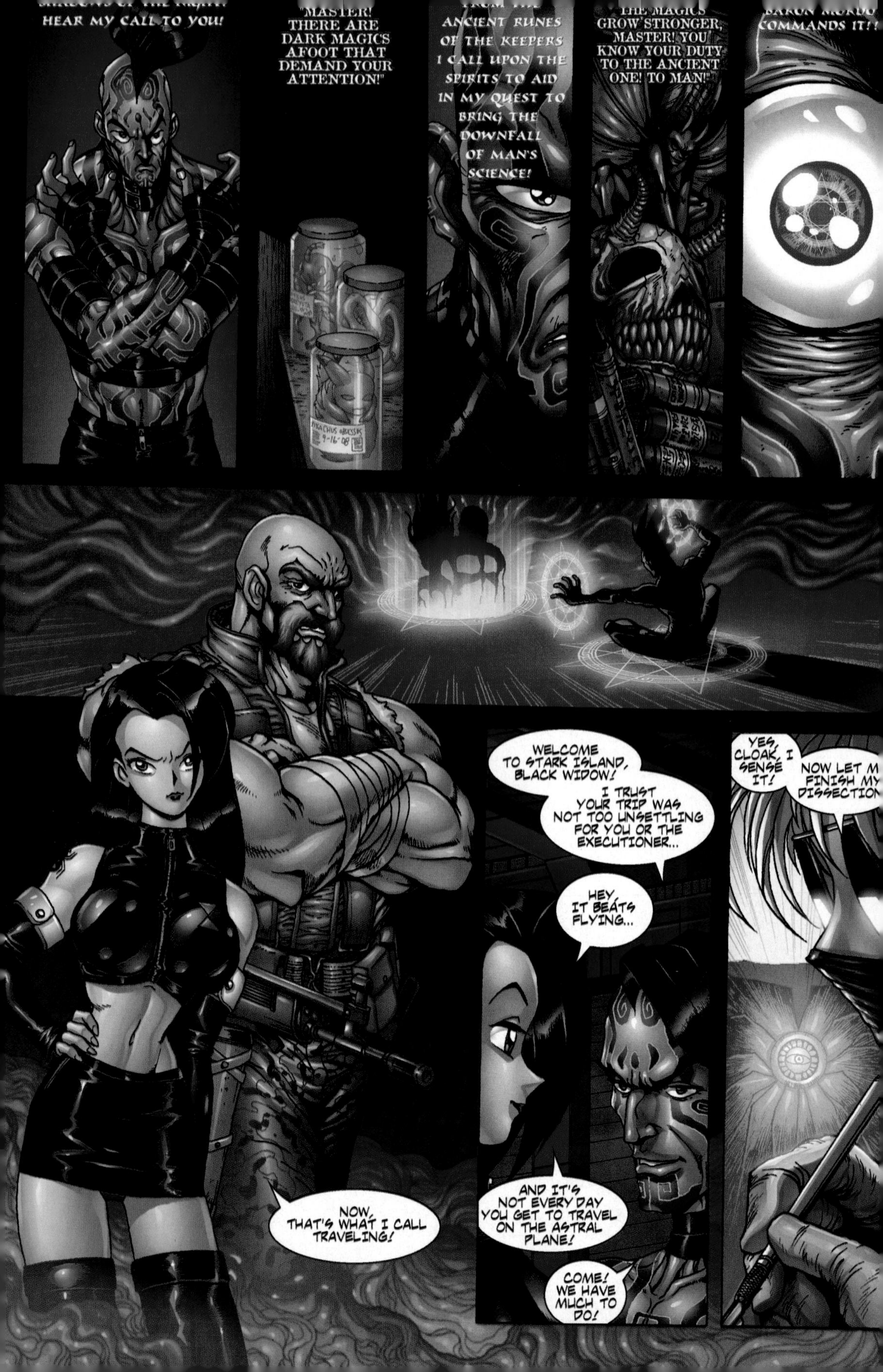
HEAR MY CALL TO YOU!
"MASTER! THERE ARE DARK MAGICS AFOOT THAT DEMAND YOUR ATTENTION!"
ANCIENT RUNES OF THE KEEPERS I CALL UPON THE SPIRITS TO AID IN MY QUEST TO BRING THE DOWNFALL OF MAN'S SCIENCE!
THE MAGICS GROW STRONGER, MASTER! YOU KNOW YOUR DUTY TO THE ANCIENT ONE! TO MAN!"
COMMANDS IT!!
PIKACHUS 9-16-08
NOW, THAT'S WHAT I CALL TRAVELING!
WELCOME TO STARK ISLAND, BLACK WIDOW!
I TRUST YOUR TRIP WAS NOT TOO UNSETTLING FOR YOU OR THE EXECUTIONER...
HEY, IT BEATS FLYING...
AND IT'S NOT EVERY DAY YOU GET TO TRAVEL ON THE ASTRAL PLANE!
COME! WE HAVE MUCH TO DO!
YES, CLOAK, I SENSE IT!
NOW LET M FINISH MY DISSECTION

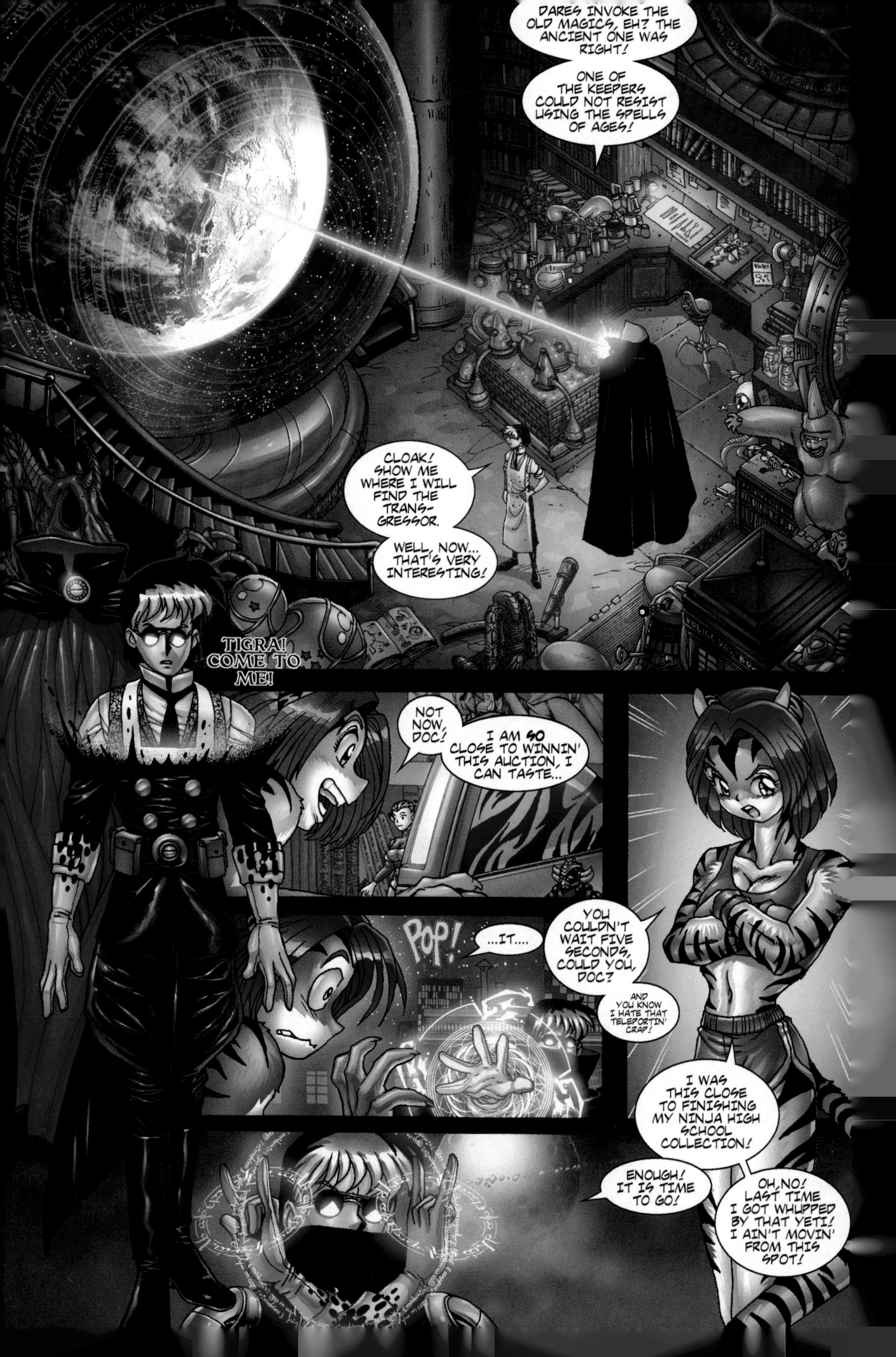

DARES INVOKE THE OLD MAGICS, EH? THE ANCIENT ONE WAS RIGHT!
ONE OF THE KEEPERS COULD NOT RESIST USING THE SPELLS OF AGES!
CLOAK! SHOW ME WHERE I WILL FIND THE TRANS-GRESSOR.
WELL, NOW... THAT'S VERY INTERESTING!
TIGRA! COME TO ME!
NOT NOW, DOC!
I AM SO CLOSE TO WINNIN' THIS AUCTION, I CAN TASTE...
POP!
...IT....
YOU COULDN'T WAIT FIVE SECONDS, COULD YOU, DOC?
AND YOU KNOW I HATE THAT TELEPORTIN' CRAP!
I WAS THIS CLOSE TO FINISHING MY NINJA HIGH SCHOOL COLLECTION!
ENOUGH! IT IS TIME TO GO!
OH, NO! LAST TIME I GOT WHUPPED BY THAT YETI! I AIN'T MOVIN' FROM THIS SPOT!

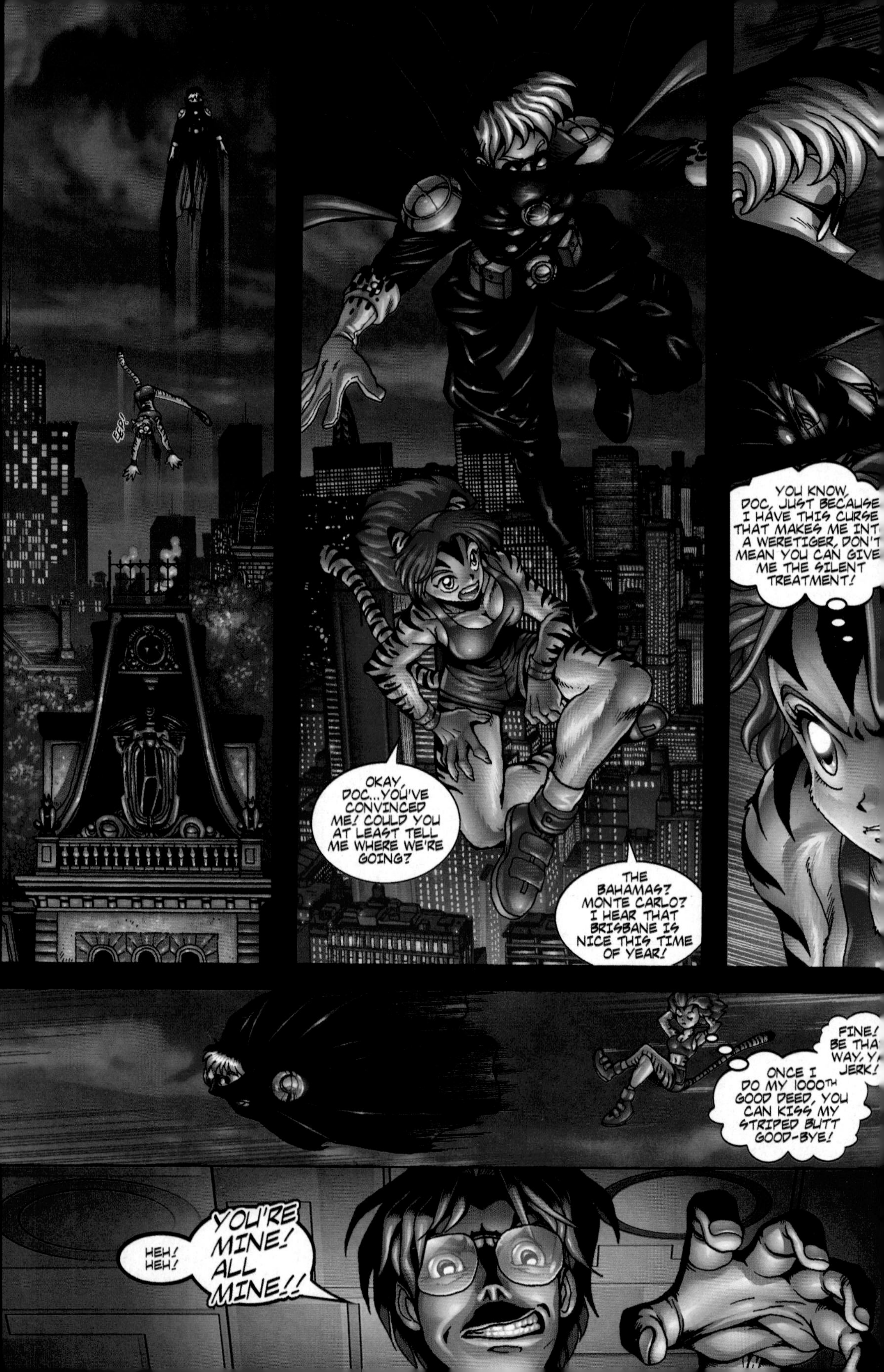
EEP!
OKAY, DOC...YOU'VE CONVINCED ME! COULD YOU AT LEAST TELL ME WHERE WE'RE GOING?
THE BAHAMAS? MONTE CARLO? I HEAR THAT BRISBANE IS NICE THIS TIME OF YEAR!
YOU KNOW, DOC, JUST BECAUSE I HAVE THIS CURSE THAT MAKES ME INT A WERETIGER, DON'T MEAN YOU CAN GIVE ME THE SILENT TREATMENT!
FINE! BE THA WAY, Y JERK!
ONCE I DO MY 1000TH GOOD DEED, YOU CAN KISS MY STRIPED BUTT GOOD-BYE!
HEH! HEH!
YOU'RE MINE! ALL MINE!!

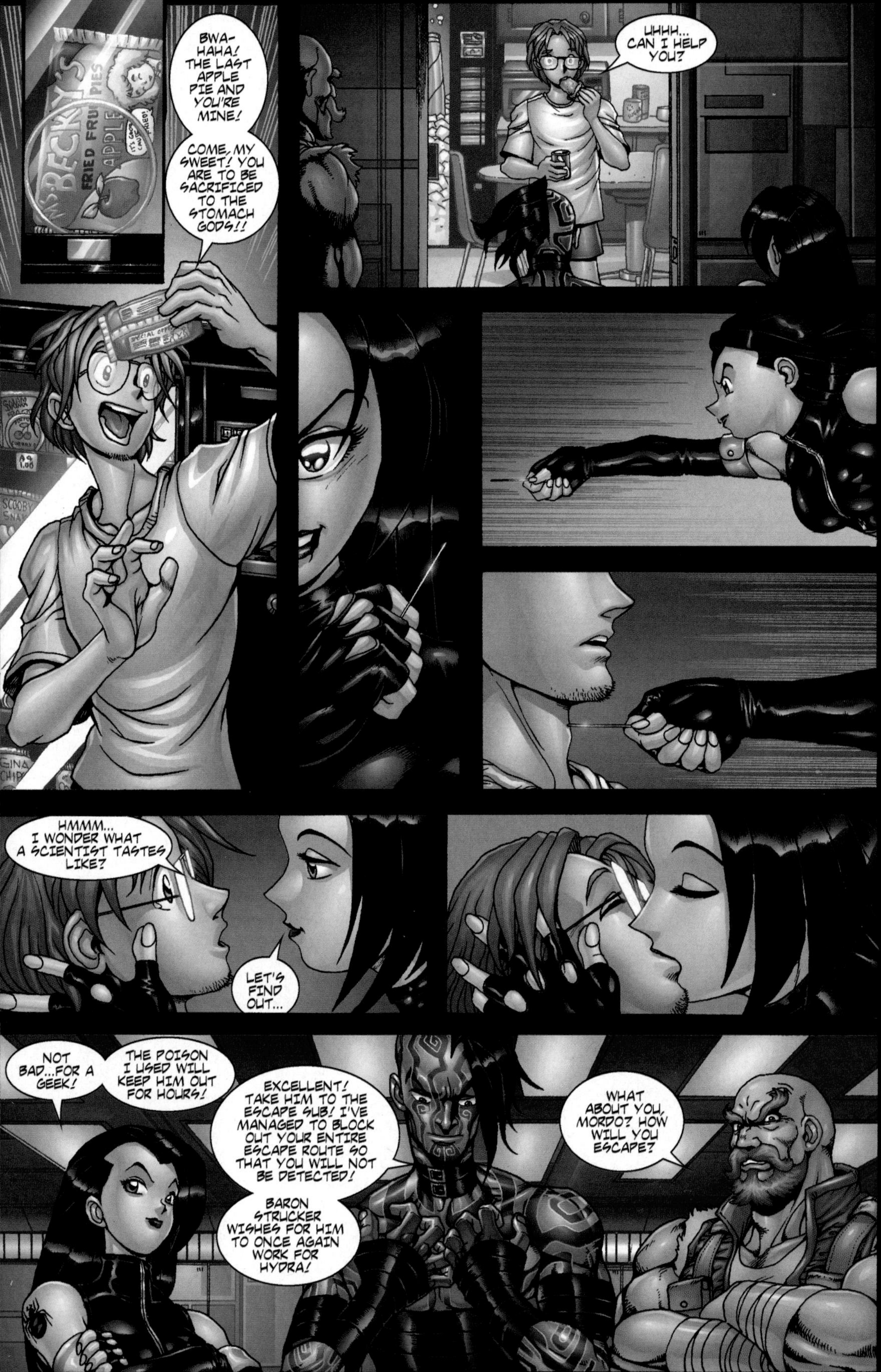
MS. BECKY'S
FRIED FRUIT PIES
APPLE
BWA-HAHA! THE LAST APPLE PIE AND YOU'RE MINE!
COME, MY SWEET! YOU ARE TO BE SACRIFICED TO THE STOMACH GODS!!
UHHH... CAN I HELP YOU?
HMMM... I WONDER WHAT A SCIENTIST TASTES LIKE?
LET'S FIND OUT...
NOT BAD...FOR A GEEK!
THE POISON I USED WILL KEEP HIM OUT FOR HOURS!
EXCELLENT! TAKE HIM TO THE ESCAPE SUB! I'VE MANAGED TO BLOCK OUT YOUR ENTIRE ESCAPE ROUTE SO THAT YOU WILL NOT BE DETECTED!
BARON STRUCKER WISHES FOR HIM TO ONCE AGAIN WORK FOR HYDRA!
WHAT ABOUT YOU, MORDO? HOW WILL YOU ESCAPE?

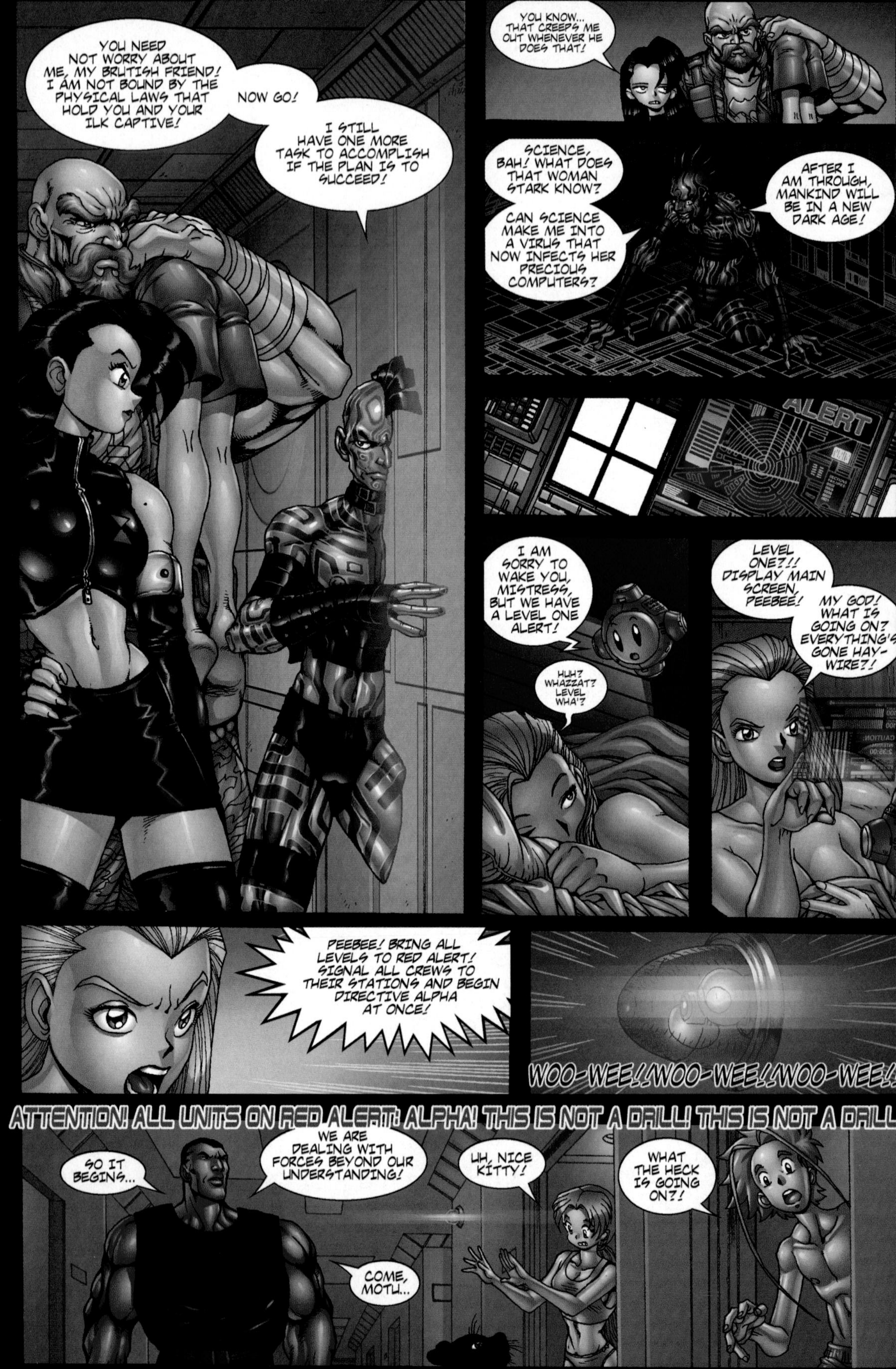
YOU NEED NOT WORRY ABOUT ME, MY BRUTISH FRIEND! I AM NOT BOUND BY THE PHYSICAL LAWS THAT HOLD YOU AND YOUR ILK CAPTIVE!
NOW GO!
I STILL HAVE ONE MORE TASK TO ACCOMPLISH IF THE PLAN IS TO SUCCEED!
YOU KNOW... THAT CREEPS ME OUT WHENEVER HE DOES THAT!
SCIENCE, BAH! WHAT DOES THAT WOMAN STARK KNOW?
CAN SCIENCE MAKE ME INTO A VIRUS THAT NOW INFECTS HER PRECIOUS COMPUTERS?
AFTER I AM THROUGH, MANKIND WILL BE IN A NEW DARK AGE!
ALERT
I AM SORRY TO WAKE YOU, MISTRESS, BUT WE HAVE A LEVEL ONE ALERT!
HUH? WHAZZAT? LEVEL WHA'?
LEVEL ONE?!! DISPLAY MAIN SCREEN, PEEBEE!
MY GOD! WHAT IS GOING ON? EVERYTHING'S GONE HAYWIRE?!
PEEBEE! BRING ALL LEVELS TO RED ALERT! SIGNAL ALL CREWS TO THEIR STATIONS AND BEGIN DIRECTIVE ALPHA AT ONCE!
WOO-WEE!! WOO-WEE!! WOO-WEE!!
ATTENTION! ALL UNITS ON RED ALERT: ALPHA! THIS IS NOT A DRILL! THIS IS NOT A DRILL!
SO IT BEGINS...
WE ARE DEALING WITH FORCES BEYOND OUR UNDERSTANDING!
COME, MOTU...
UH, NICE KITTY!
WHAT THE HECK IS GOING ON?!

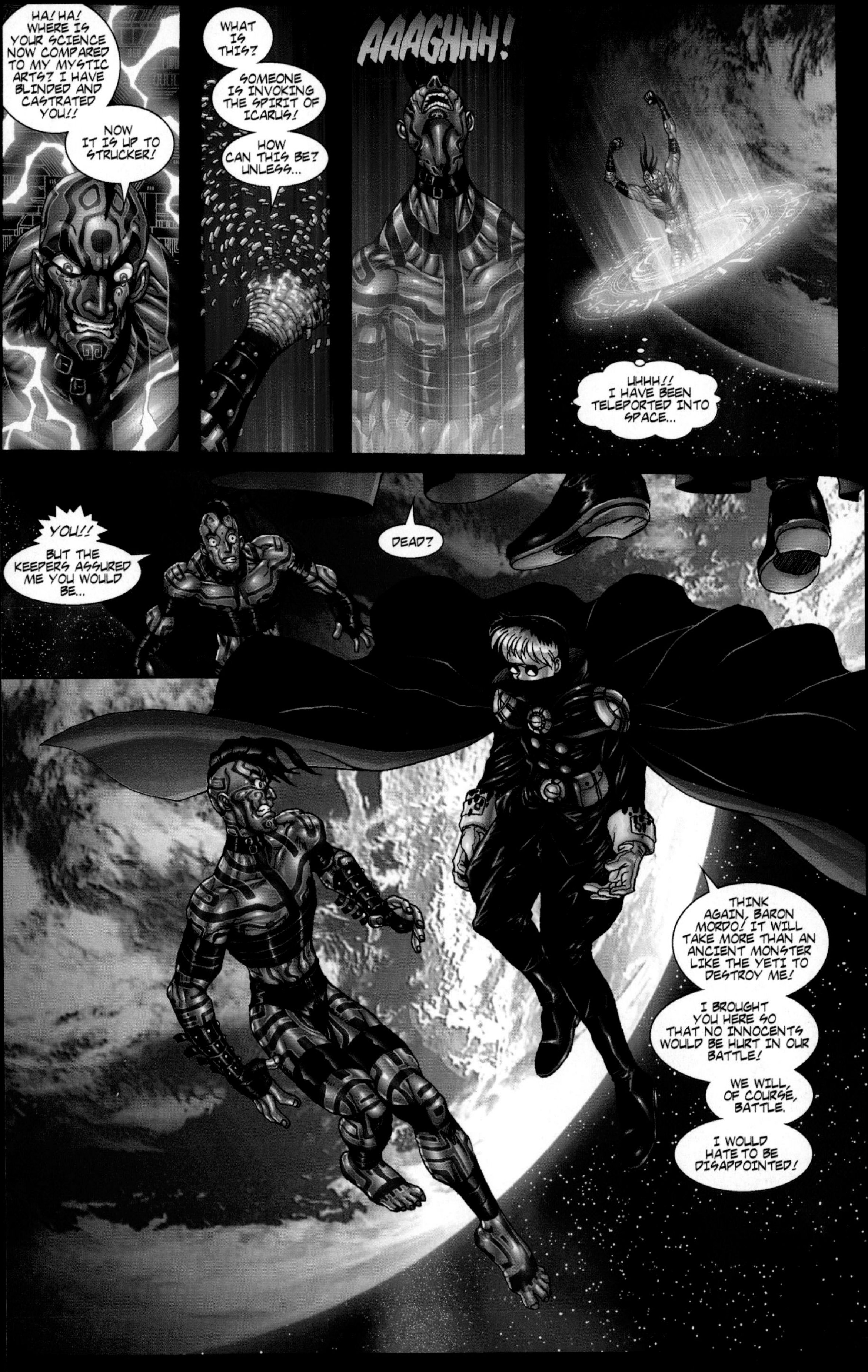
HA! HA! WHERE IS YOUR SCIENCE NOW COMPARED TO MY MYSTIC ARTS? I HAVE BLINDED AND CASTRATED YOU!!
NOW IT IS UP TO STRUCKER!
WHAT IS THIS?
SOMEONE IS INVOKING THE SPIRIT OF ICARUS!
HOW CAN THIS BE? UNLESS...
AAAGHHH!
UHHH!! I HAVE BEEN TELEPORTED INTO SPACE...
YOU!! BUT THE KEEPERS ASSURED ME YOU WOULD BE...
DEAD?
THINK AGAIN, BARON MORDO! IT WILL TAKE MORE THAN AN ANCIENT MONSTER LIKE THE YETI TO DESTROY ME!
I BROUGHT YOU HERE SO THAT NO INNOCENTS WOULD BE HURT IN OUR BATTLE!
WE WILL, OF COURSE, BATTLE.
I WOULD HATE TO BE DISAPPOINTED!

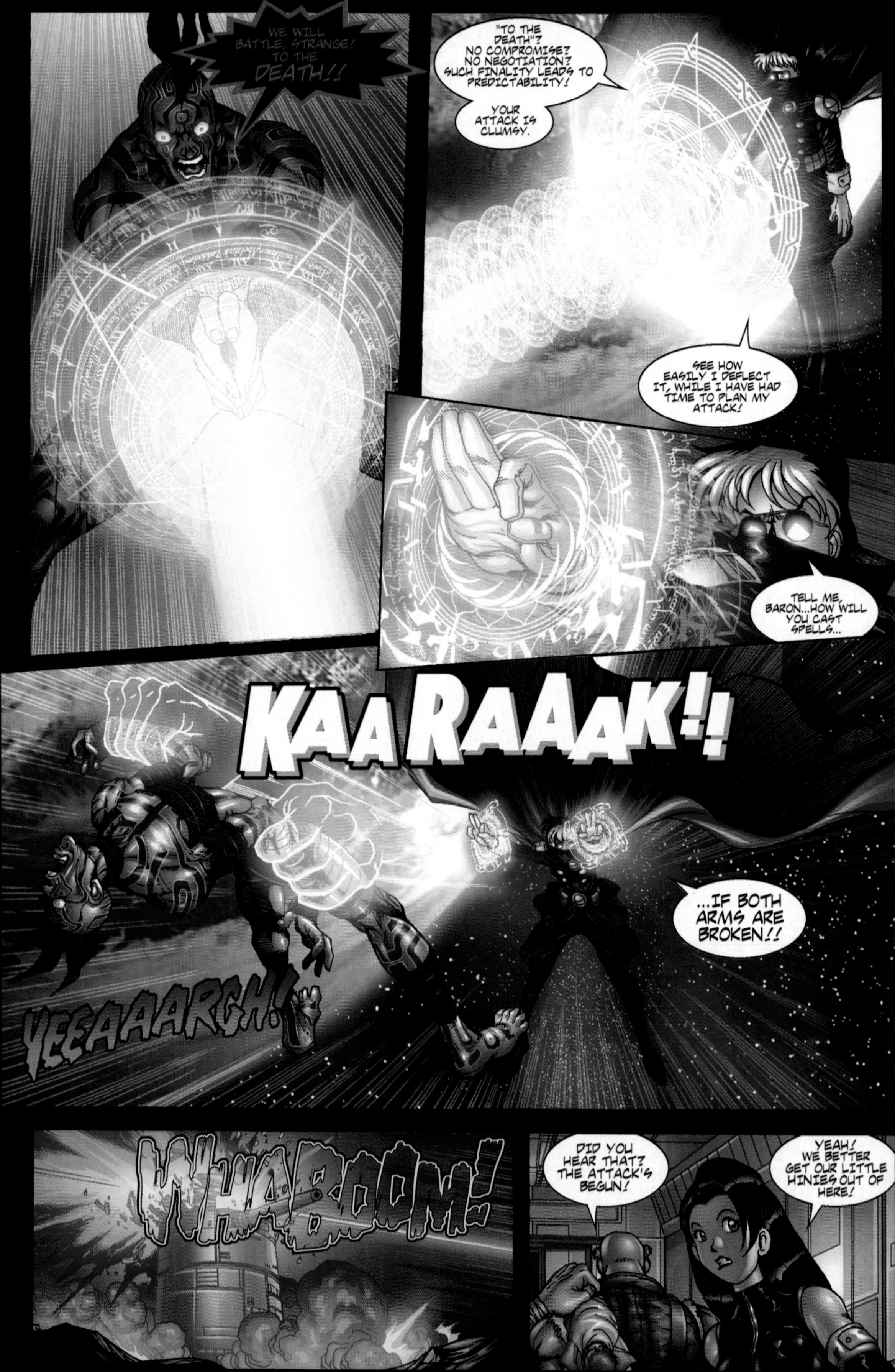
WE WILL BATTLE, STRANGE! TO THE DEATH!!
"TO THE DEATH"? NO COMPROMISE? NO NEGOTIATION? SUCH FINALITY LEADS TO PREDICTABILITY!
YOUR ATTACK IS CLUMSY.
SEE HOW EASILY I DEFLECT IT, WHILE I HAVE HAD TIME TO PLAN MY ATTACK!
TELL ME, BARON...HOW WILL YOU CAST SPELLS...
KAARAAAK!!
...IF BOTH ARMS ARE BROKEN!!
YEEAAARGH!
WHABOOM!
DID YOU HEAR THAT? THE ATTACK'S BEGUN!
YEAH! WE BETTER GET OUR LITTLE HINIES OUT OF HERE!

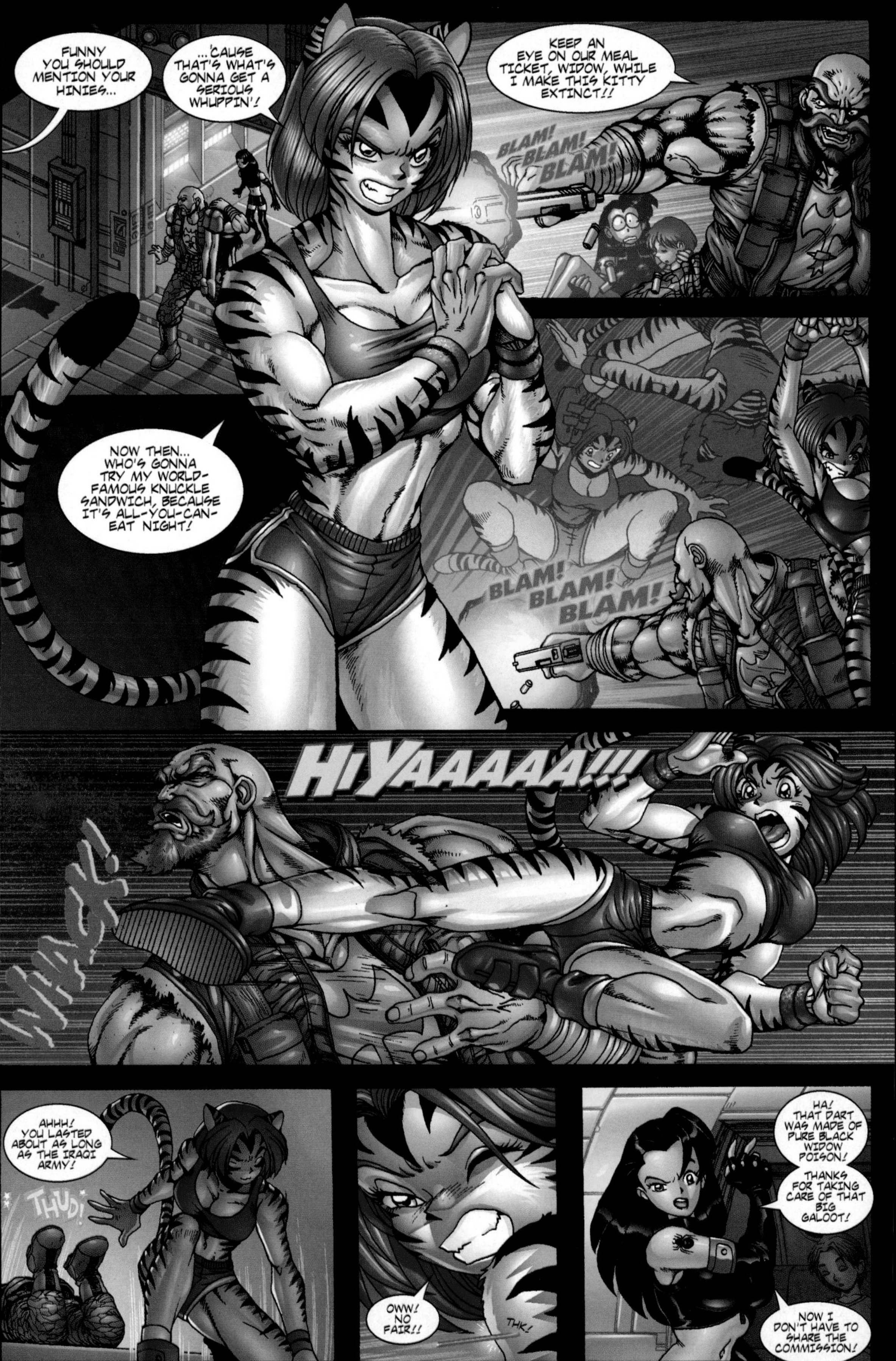
FUNNY YOU SHOULD MENTION YOUR HINIES...
...'CAUSE THAT'S WHAT'S GONNA GET A SERIOUS WHUPPIN'!
KEEP AN EYE ON OUR MEAL TICKET, WIDOW, WHILE I MAKE THIS KITTY EXTINCT!!
BLAM! BLAM! BLAM!
NOW THEN... WHO'S GONNA TRY MY WORLD-FAMOUS KNUCKLE SANDWICH, BECAUSE IT'S ALL-YOU-CAN-EAT NIGHT!
BLAM! BLAM! BLAM!
HIYAAAAAA!!!
WHACK!
AHHH! YOU LASTED ABOUT AS LONG AS THE IRAQI ARMY!
THUD!
OWW! NO FAIR!!
THK!
HA! THAT DART WAS MADE OF PURE BLACK WIDOW POISON!
THANKS FOR TAKING CARE OF THAT BIG GALOOT!
NOW I DON'T HAVE TO SHARE THE COMMISSION!

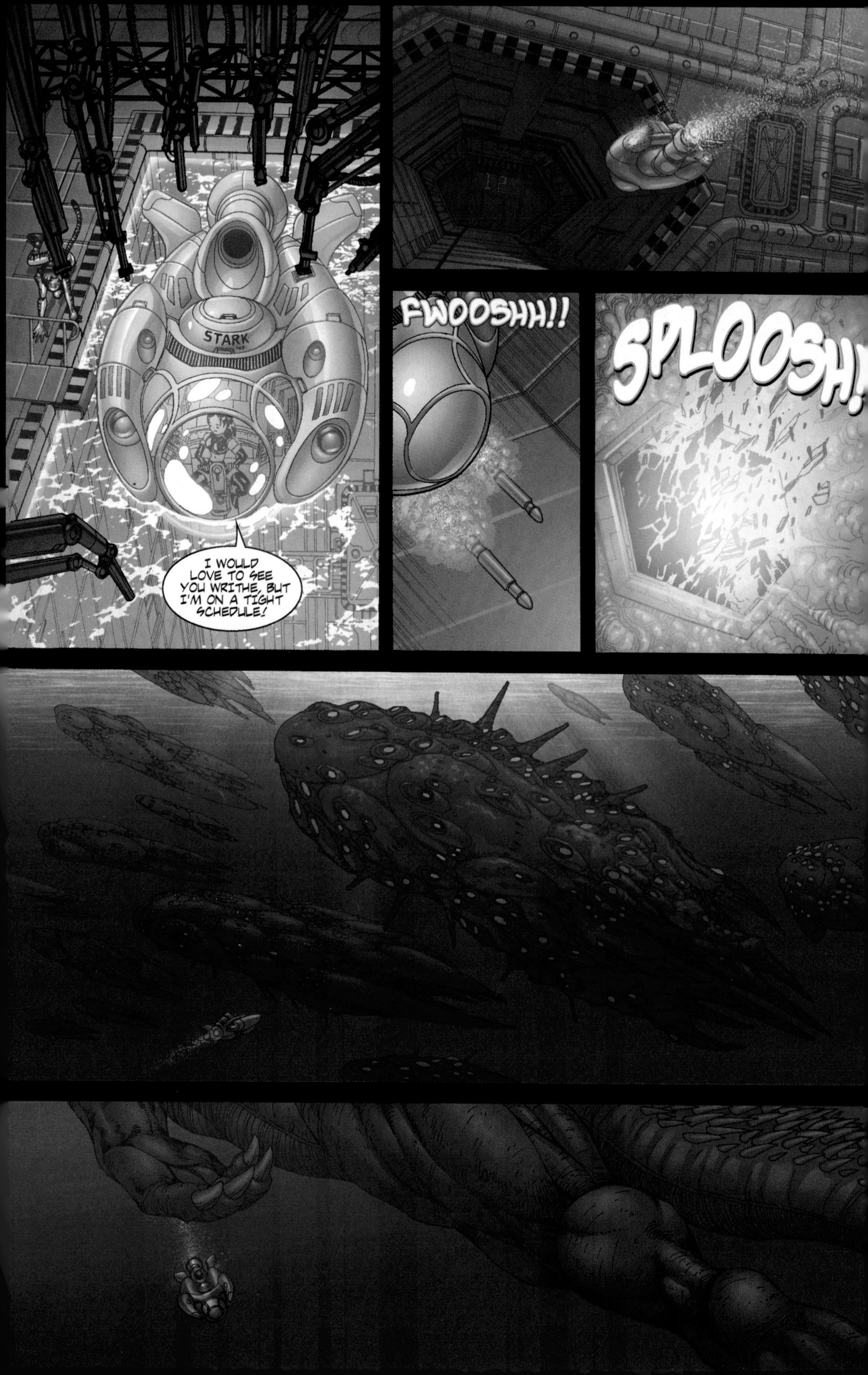
I WOULD LOVE TO SEE YOU WRITHE, BUT I'M ON A TIGHT SCHEDULE!
FWOOSHH!!
SPLOOSH!

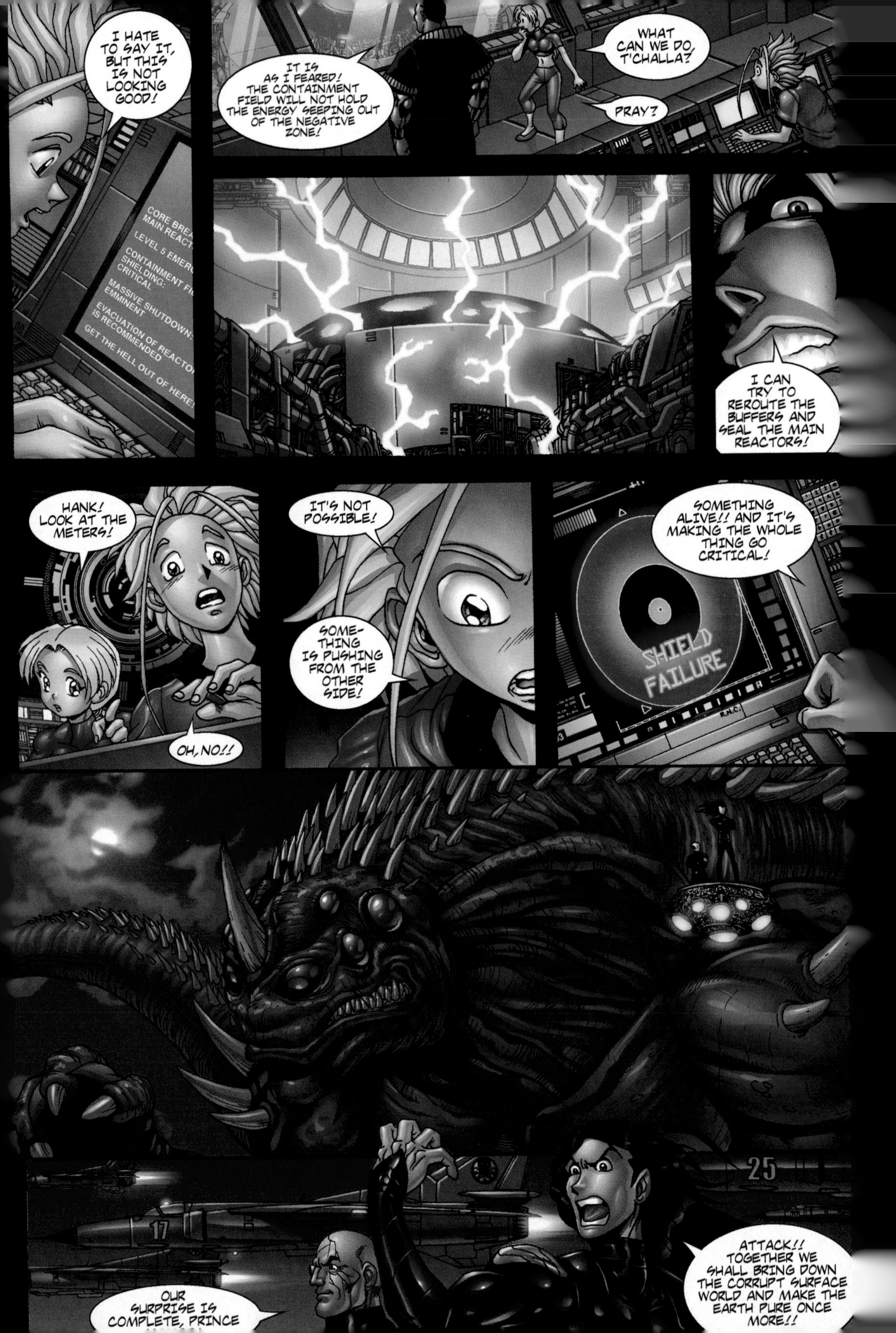
I HATE TO SAY IT, BUT THIS IS NOT LOOKING GOOD!
IT IS AS I FEARED! THE CONTAINMENT FIELD WILL NOT HOLD THE ENERGY SEEPING OUT OF THE NEGATIVE ZONE!
WHAT CAN WE DO, T'CHALLA?
PRAY?
SHIELDING: CRITICAL
MASSIVE SHUTDOWN: EMMINENT
EVACUATION OF REACTOR IS RECOMMENDED
GET THE HELL OUT OF HERE!
I CAN TRY TO REROUTE THE BUFFERS AND SEAL THE MAIN REACTORS!
HANK! LOOK AT THE METERS!
OH, NO!!
IT'S NOT POSSIBLE!
SOME-THING IS PUSHING FROM THE OTHER SIDE!
SOMETHING ALIVE!! AND IT'S MAKING THE WHOLE THING GO CRITICAL!
SHIELD FAILURE
R.M.C.
17
25
OUR SURPRISE IS COMPLETE, PRINCE
ATTACK!! TOGETHER WE SHALL BRING DOWN THE CORRUPT SURFACE WORLD AND MAKE THE EARTH PURE ONCE MORE!!

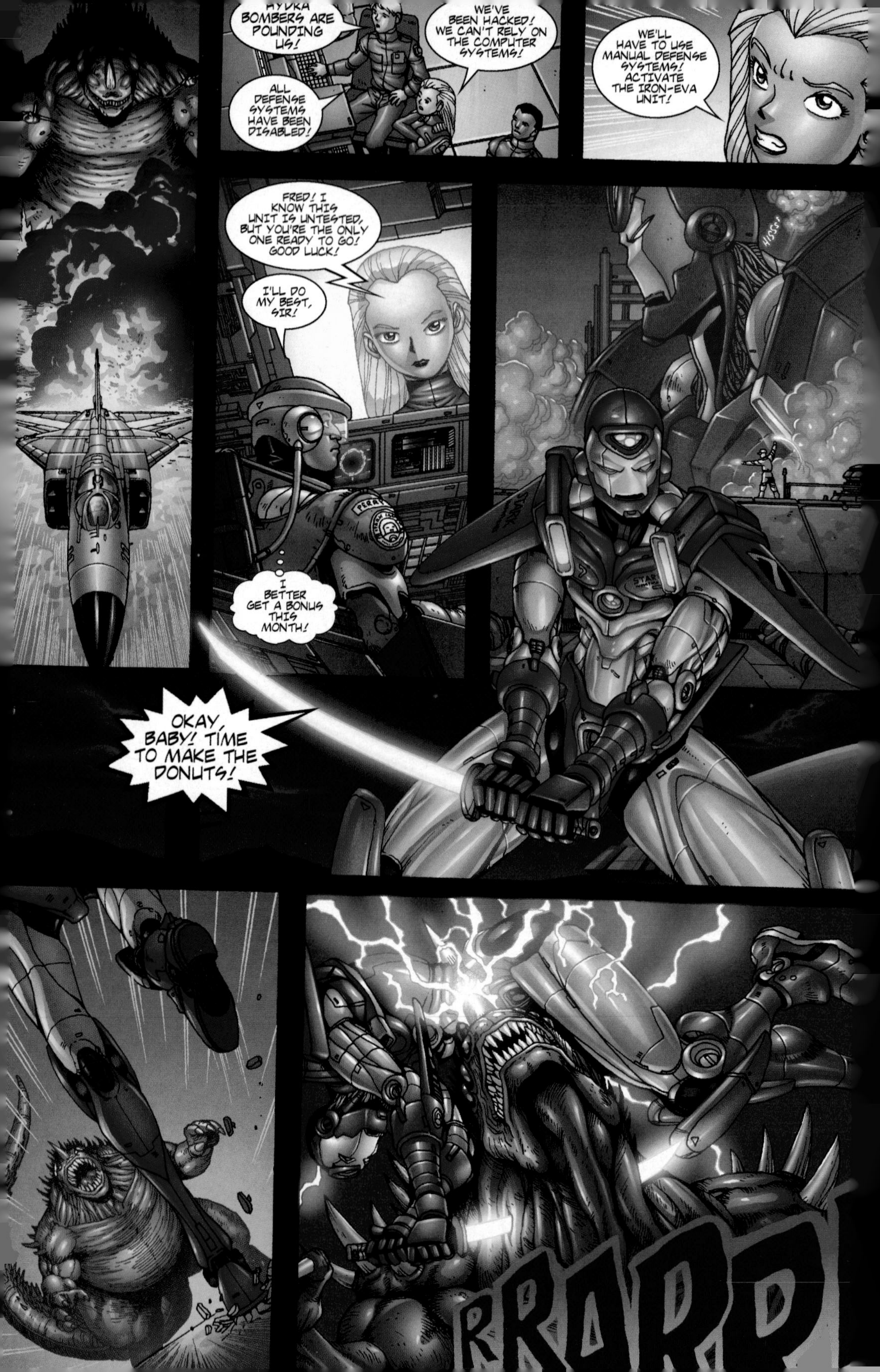
HYDRA BOMBERS ARE POUNDING US!
ALL DEFENSE SYSTEMS HAVE BEEN DISABLED!
WE'VE BEEN HACKED! WE CAN'T RELY ON THE COMPUTER SYSTEMS!
WE'LL HAVE TO USE MANUAL DEFENSE SYSTEMS! ACTIVATE THE IRON-EVA UNIT!
FRED! I KNOW THIS UNIT IS UNTESTED, BUT YOU'RE THE ONLY ONE READY TO GO! GOOD LUCK!
I'LL DO MY BEST, SIR!
I BETTER GET A BONUS THIS MONTH!
HISSS
OKAY, BABY! TIME TO MAKE THE DONUTS!
RRARR

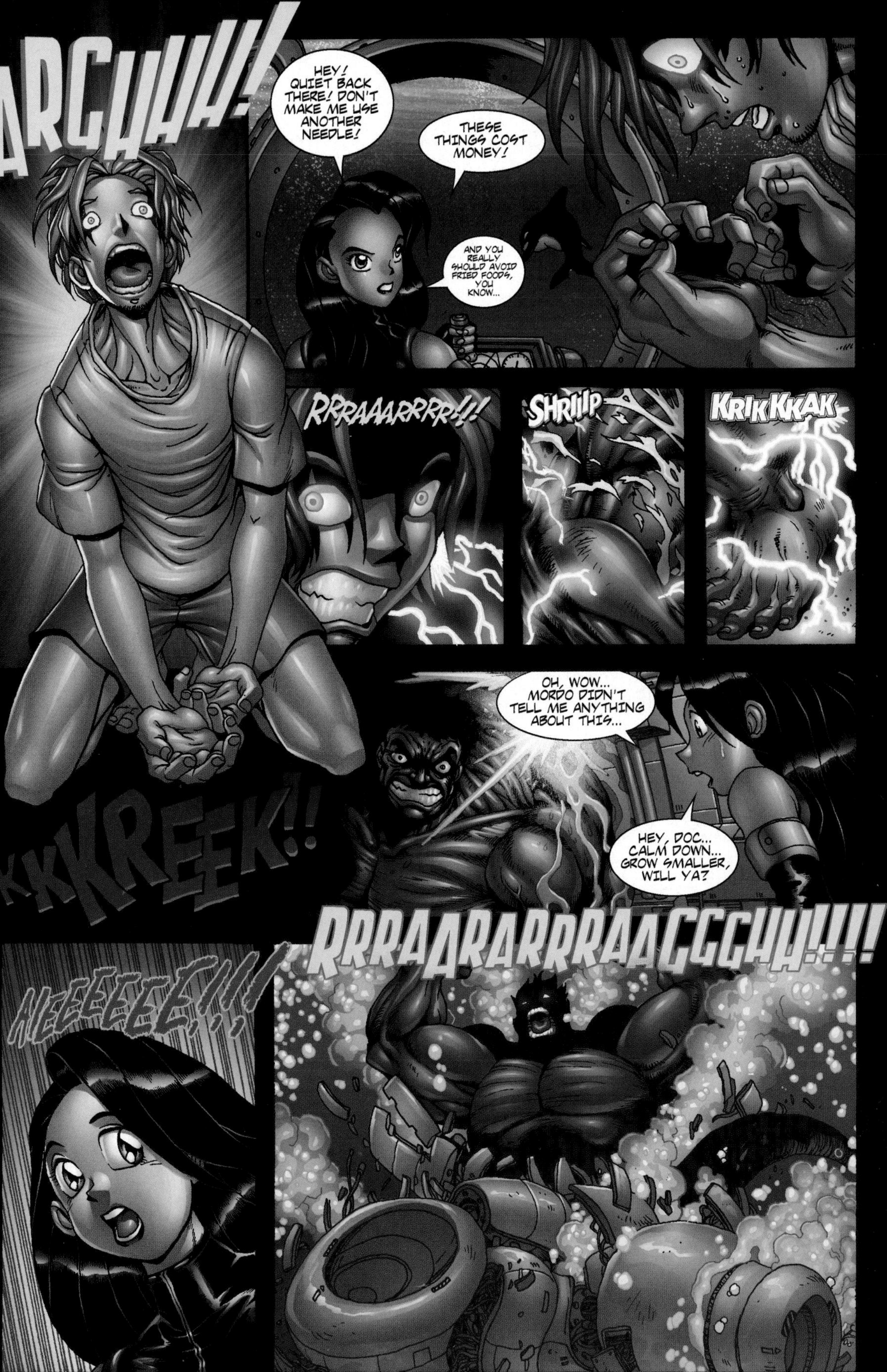

ARCHHH!
HEY! QUIET BACK THERE! DON'T MAKE ME USE ANOTHER NEEDLE!
THESE THINGS COST MONEY!
AND YOU REALLY SHOULD AVOID FRIED FOODS, YOU KNOW...
RRRAAARRRR!!!
SHRIIIP
KRIKKKAK
KKKREEK!!
OH, WOW... MORDO DIDN'T TELL ME ANYTHING ABOUT THIS...
HEY, DOC... CALM DOWN... GROW SMALLER, WILL YA?
AIEEEEEE!!!
RRRAARARRRAAGGGHH!!!!

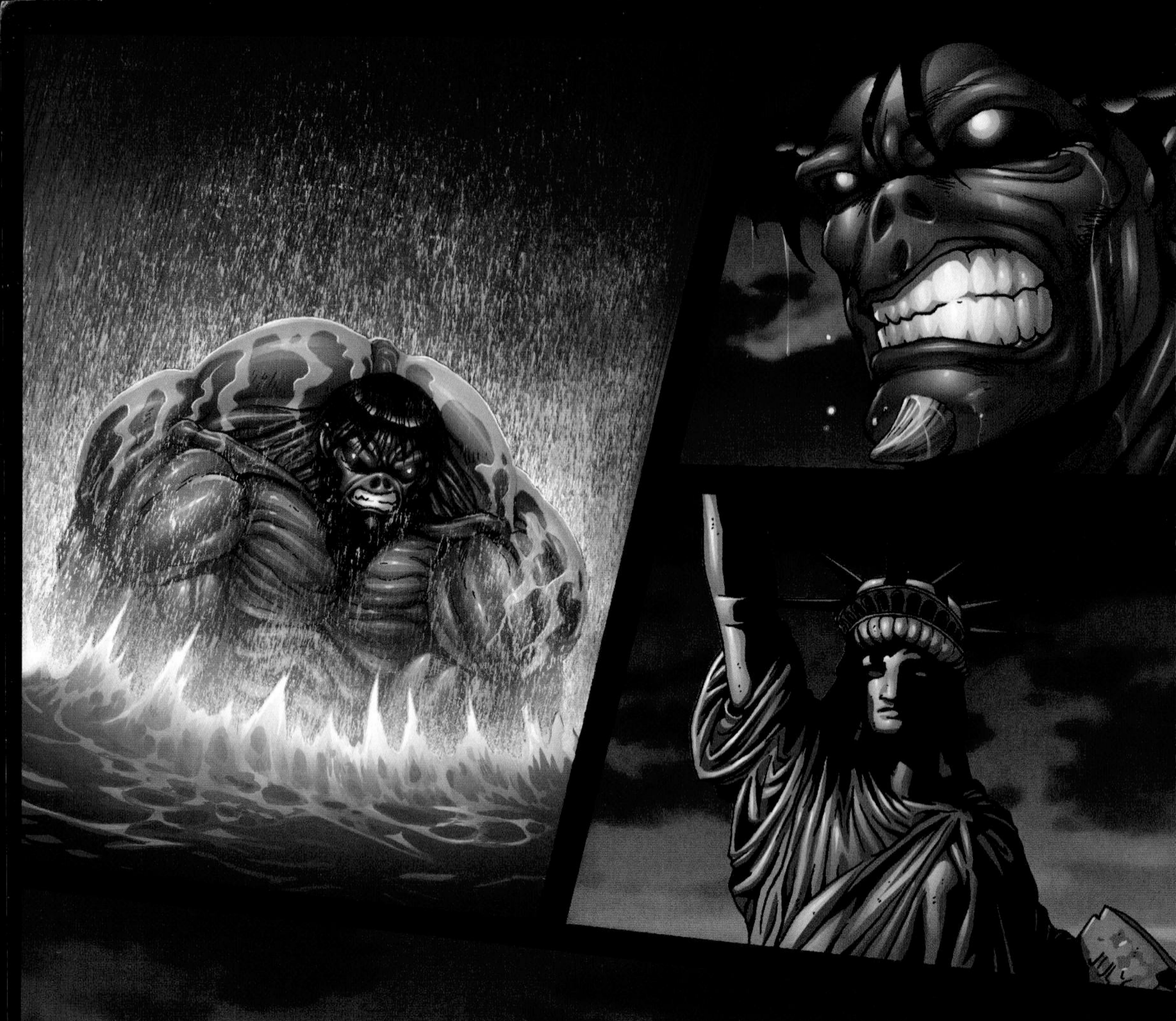

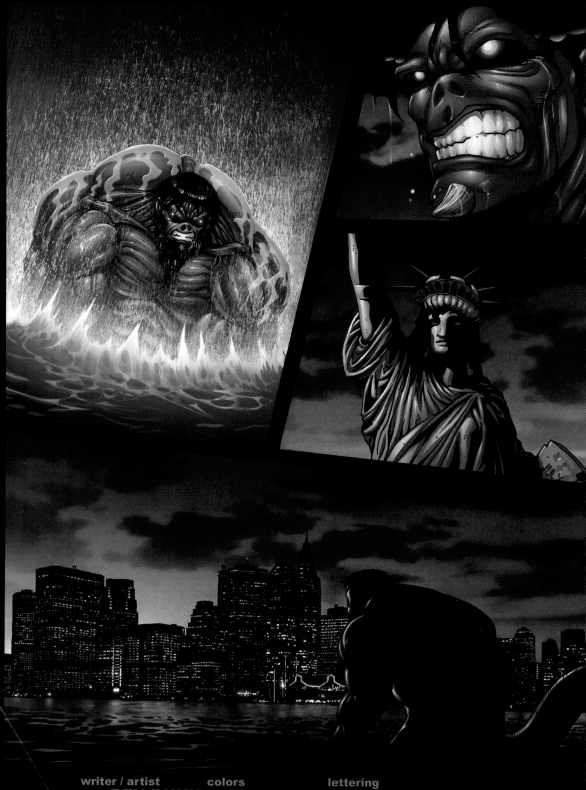

writer / artist
BEN DUNN

colors
GURU eFX

lettering
BEN DUNN / GURU eFX

editor
BRIAN SMITH

consulting editor
RALPH MACCHIO

editor-in-chief
JOE QUESADA

president
BILL JEMAS

special thanks to: ROD ESPINOSA / ROBBY BEVARD / DAVID HUTCHISON

dedicated to: JACK KIRBY

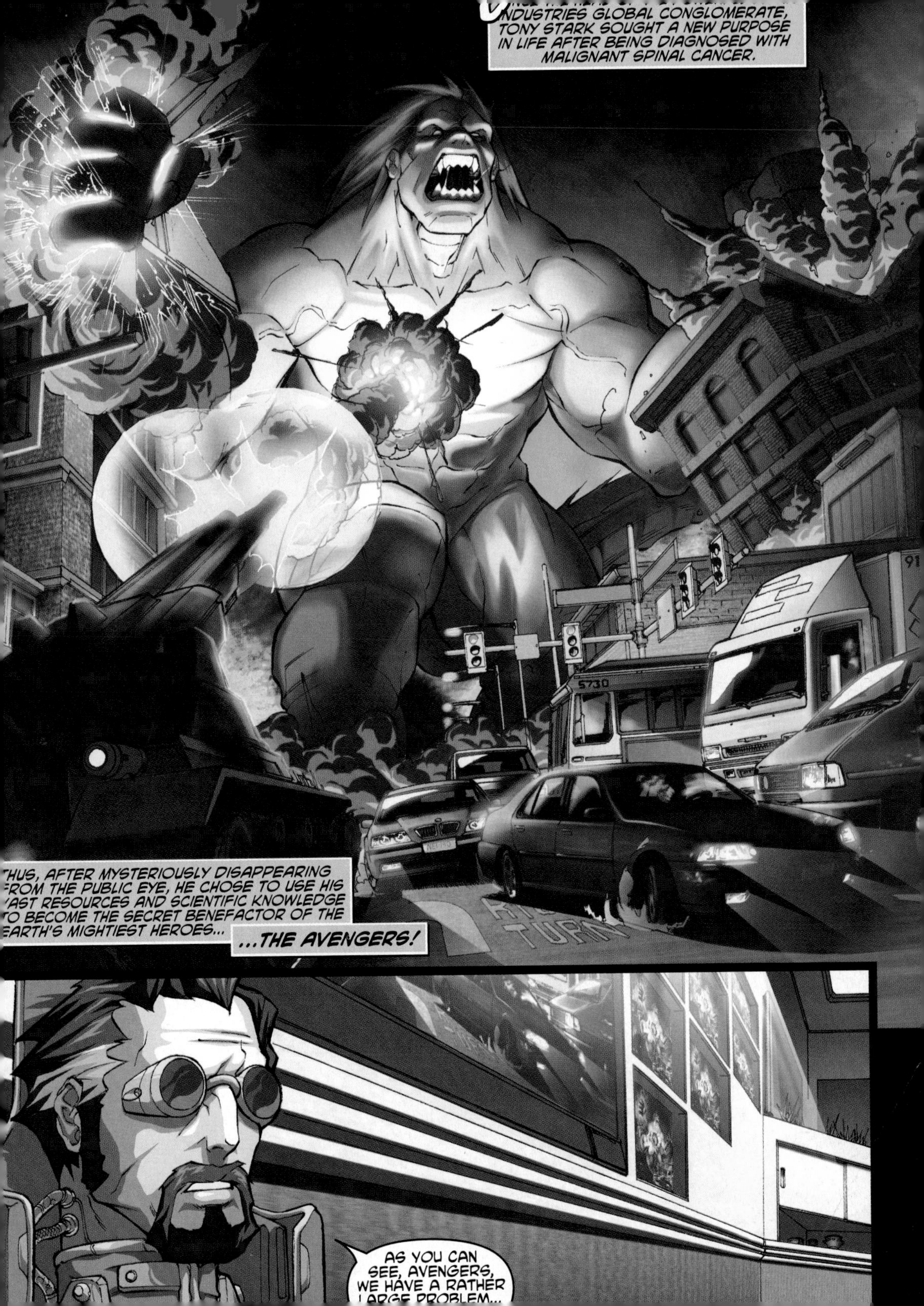
NDUSTRIES GLOBAL CONGLOMERATE, TONY STARK SOUGHT A NEW PURPOSE IN LIFE AFTER BEING DIAGNOSED WITH MALIGNANT SPINAL CANCER.
THUS, AFTER MYSTERIOUSLY DISAPPEARING FROM THE PUBLIC EYE, HE CHOSE TO USE HIS VAST RESOURCES AND SCIENTIFIC KNOWLEDGE TO BECOME THE SECRET BENEFACTOR OF THE EARTH'S MIGHTIEST HEROES...
...THE AVENGERS!
AS YOU CAN SEE, AVENGERS, WE HAVE A RATHER LARGE PROBLEM...

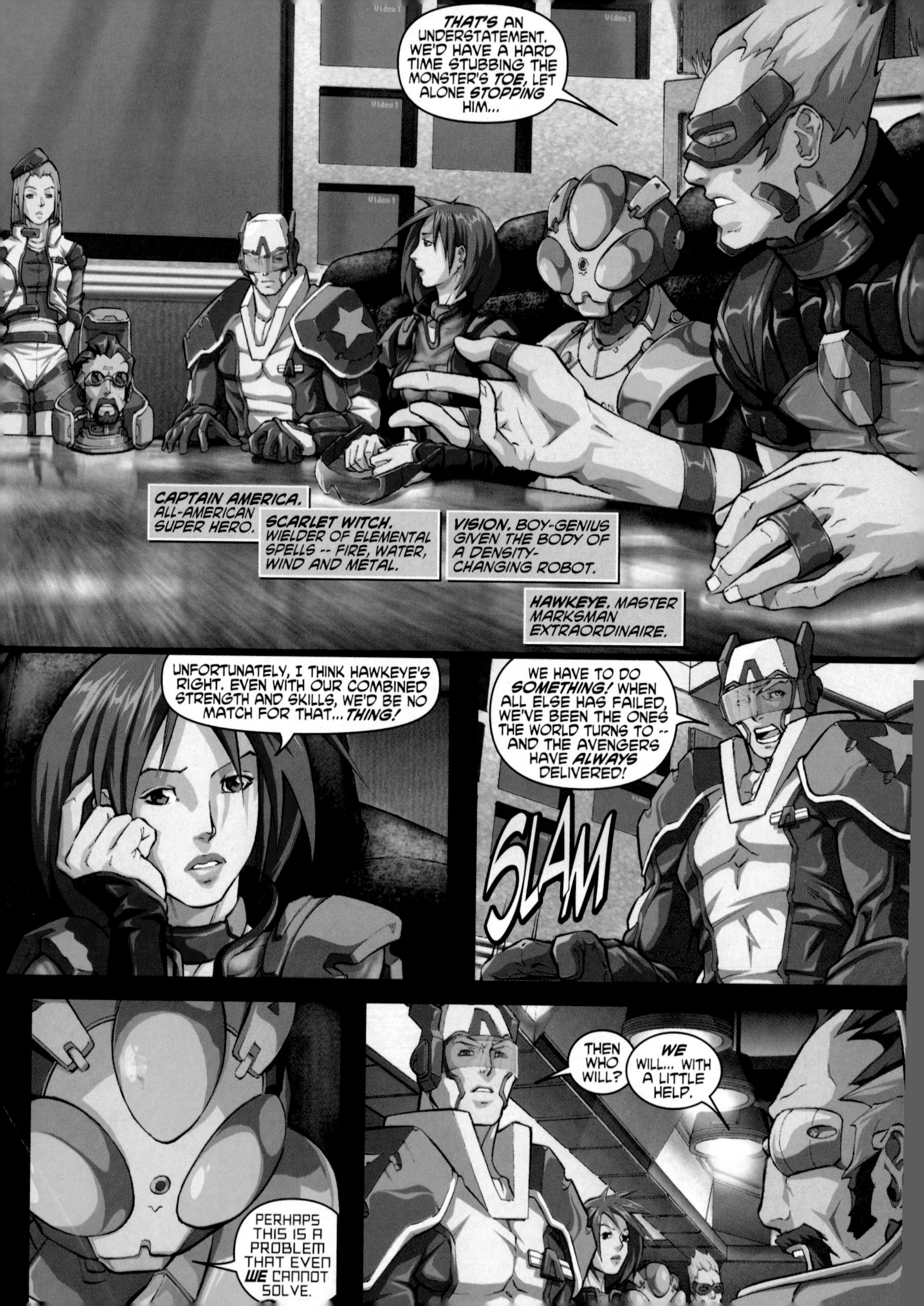

THAT'S AN UNDERSTATEMENT. WE'D HAVE A HARD TIME STUBBING THE MONSTER'S TOE, LET ALONE STOPPING HIM...
CAPTAIN AMERICA. ALL-AMERICAN SUPER HERO.
SCARLET WITCH. WIELDER OF ELEMENTAL SPELLS -- FIRE, WATER, WIND AND METAL.
VISION. BOY-GENIUS GIVEN THE BODY OF A DENSITY-CHANGING ROBOT.
HAWKEYE. MASTER MARKSMAN EXTRAORDINAIRE.
UNFORTUNATELY, I THINK HAWKEYE'S RIGHT. EVEN WITH OUR COMBINED STRENGTH AND SKILLS, WE'D BE NO MATCH FOR THAT...THING!
WE HAVE TO DO SOMETHING! WHEN ALL ELSE HAS FAILED, WE'VE BEEN THE ONES THE WORLD TURNS TO -- AND THE AVENGERS HAVE ALWAYS DELIVERED!
SLAM
PERHAPS THIS IS A PROBLEM THAT EVEN WE CANNOT SOLVE.
THEN WHO WILL?
WE WILL... WITH A LITTLE HELP.

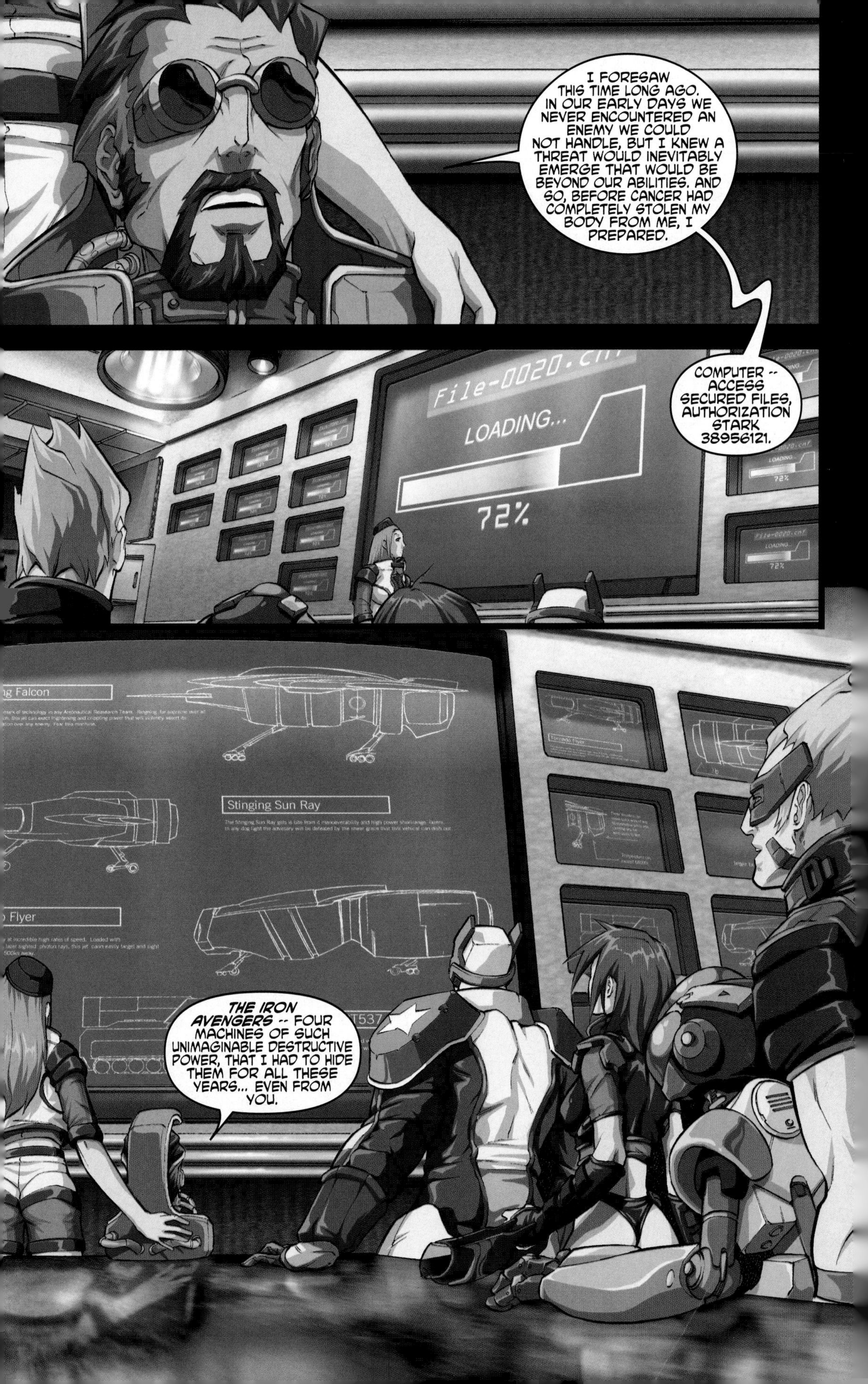
I FORESAW THIS TIME LONG AGO. IN OUR EARLY DAYS WE NEVER ENCOUNTERED AN ENEMY WE COULD NOT HANDLE, BUT I KNEW A THREAT WOULD INEVITABLY EMERGE THAT WOULD BE BEYOND OUR ABILITIES. AND SO, BEFORE CANCER HAD COMPLETELY STOLEN MY BODY FROM ME, I PREPARED.
COMPUTER -- ACCESS SECURED FILES, AUTHORIZATION STARK 38956121.
LOADING...
72%
Stinging Sun Ray
THE IRON AVENGERS -- FOUR MACHINES OF SUCH UNIMAGINABLE DESTRUCTIVE POWER, THAT I HAD TO HIDE THEM FOR ALL THESE YEARS... EVEN FROM YOU.

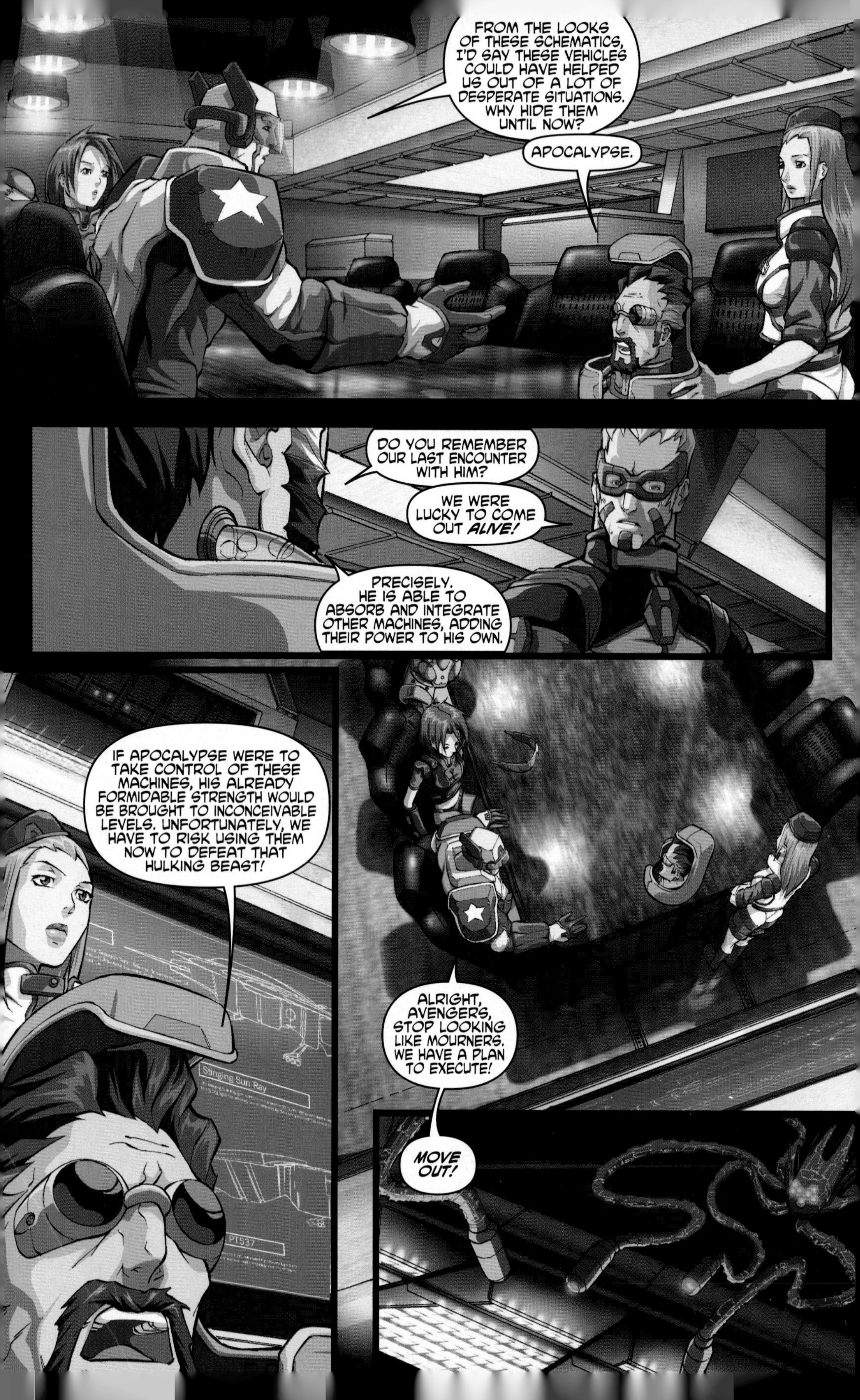
FROM THE LOOKS OF THESE SCHEMATICS, I'D SAY THESE VEHICLES COULD HAVE HELPED US OUT OF A LOT OF DESPERATE SITUATIONS. WHY HIDE THEM UNTIL NOW?
APOCALYPSE.
DO YOU REMEMBER OUR LAST ENCOUNTER WITH HIM?
WE WERE LUCKY TO COME OUT ALIVE!
PRECISELY. HE IS ABLE TO ABSORB AND INTEGRATE OTHER MACHINES, ADDING THEIR POWER TO HIS OWN.
IF APOCALYPSE WERE TO TAKE CONTROL OF THESE MACHINES, HIS ALREADY FORMIDABLE STRENGTH WOULD BE BROUGHT TO INCONCEIVABLE LEVELS. UNFORTUNATELY, WE HAVE TO RISK USING THEM NOW TO DEFEAT THAT HULKING BEAST!
Stinging Sun Ray
PT537
ALRIGHT, AVENGERS, STOP LOOKING LIKE MOURNERS. WE HAVE A PLAN TO EXECUTE!
MOVE OUT!

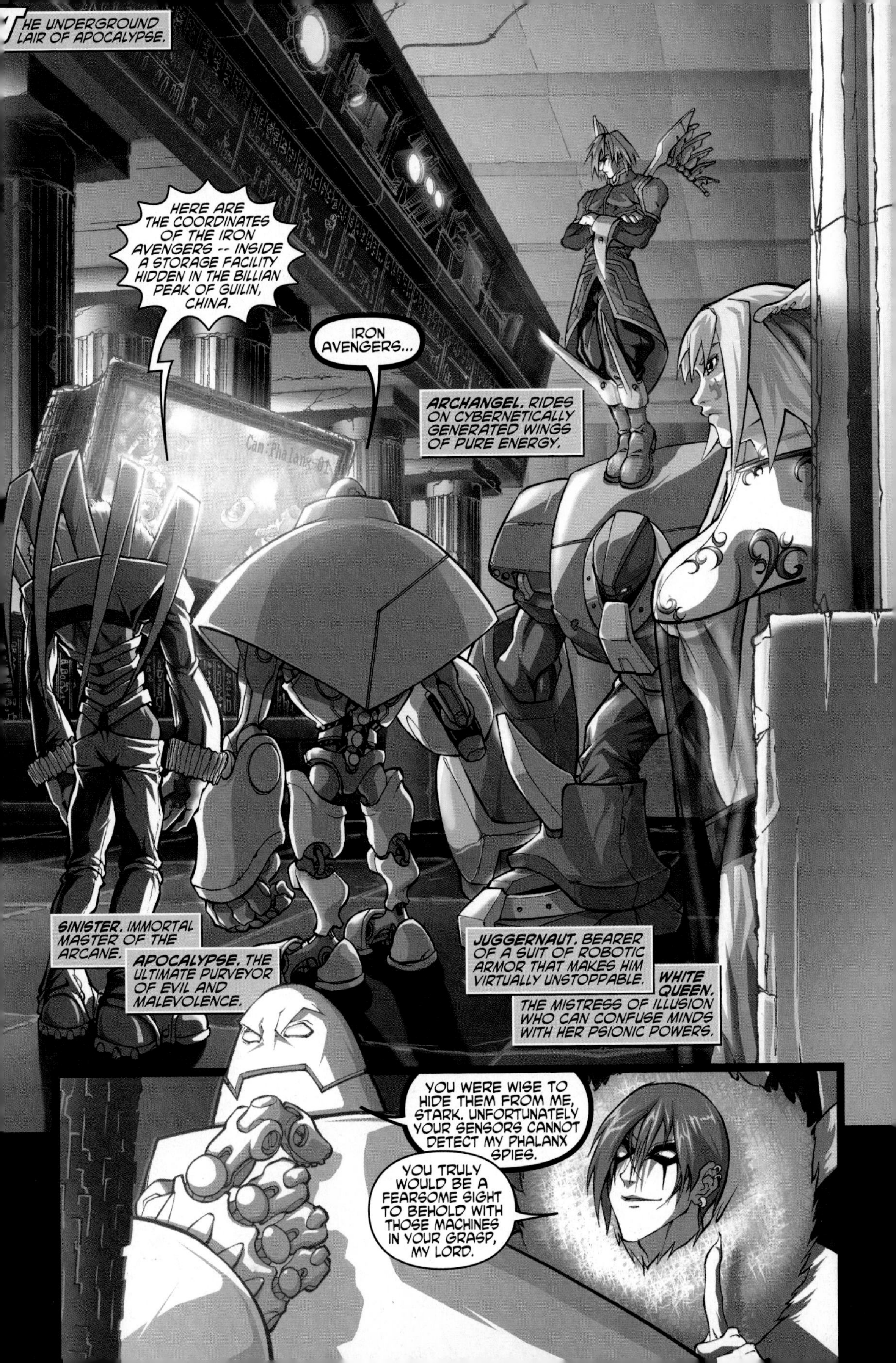
THE UNDERGROUND LAIR OF APOCALYPSE.
HERE ARE THE COORDINATES OF THE IRON AVENGERS -- INSIDE A STORAGE FACILITY HIDDEN IN THE BILLIAN PEAK OF GUILIN, CHINA.
IRON AVENGERS...
Cam:Phalanx-01
ARCHANGEL. RIDES ON CYBERNETICALLY GENERATED WINGS OF PURE ENERGY.
SINISTER. IMMORTAL MASTER OF THE ARCANE.
APOCALYPSE. THE ULTIMATE PURVEYOR OF EVIL AND MALEVOLENCE.
JUGGERNAUT. BEARER OF A SUIT OF ROBOTIC ARMOR THAT MAKES HIM VIRTUALLY UNSTOPPABLE.
WHITE QUEEN. THE MISTRESS OF ILLUSION WHO CAN CONFUSE MINDS WITH HER PSIONIC POWERS.
YOU WERE WISE TO HIDE THEM FROM ME, STARK. UNFORTUNATELY YOUR SENSORS CANNOT DETECT MY PHALANX SPIES.
YOU TRULY WOULD BE A FEARSOME SIGHT TO BEHOLD WITH THOSE MACHINES IN YOUR GRASP, MY LORD.

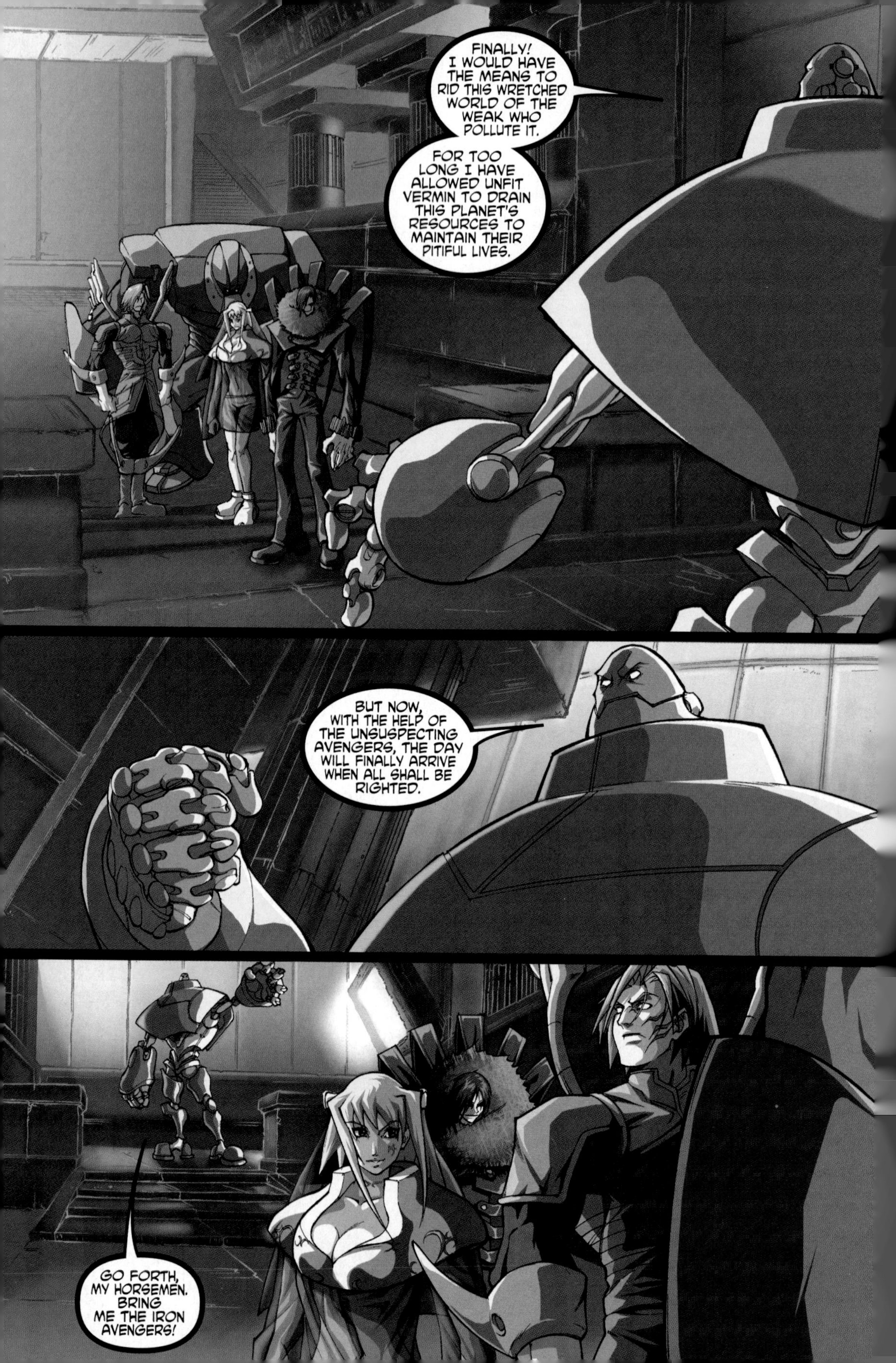
FINALLY! I WOULD HAVE THE MEANS TO RID THIS WRETCHED WORLD OF THE WEAK WHO POLLUTE IT.
FOR TOO LONG I HAVE ALLOWED UNFIT VERMIN TO DRAIN THIS PLANET'S RESOURCES TO MAINTAIN THEIR PITIFUL LIVES.
BUT NOW, WITH THE HELP OF THE UNSUSPECTING AVENGERS, THE DAY WILL FINALLY ARRIVE WHEN ALL SHALL BE RIGHTED.
GO FORTH, MY HORSEMEN. BRING ME THE IRON AVENGERS!

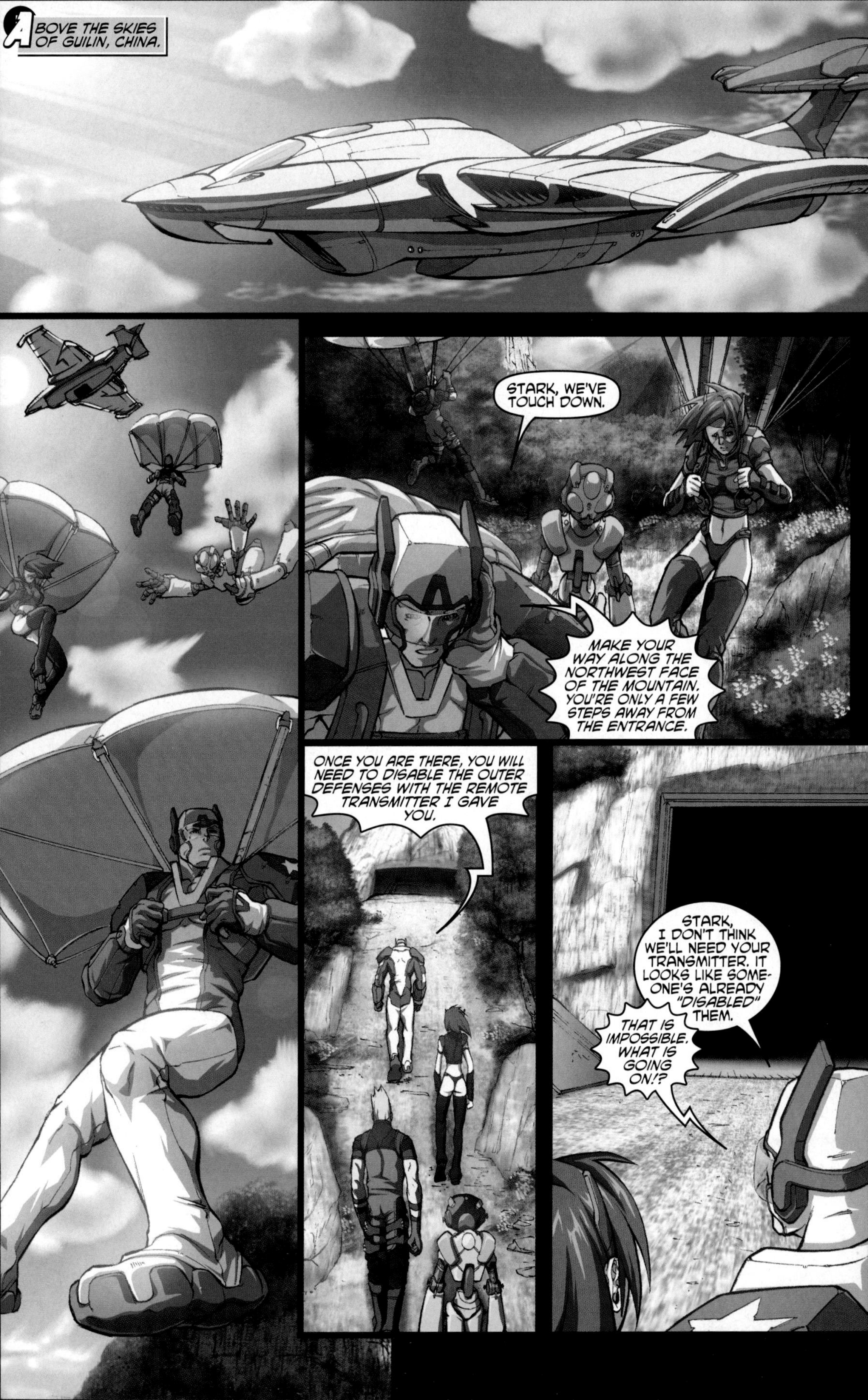
ABOVE THE SKIES OF GUILIN, CHINA.
STARK, WE'VE TOUCH DOWN.
MAKE YOUR WAY ALONG THE NORTHWEST FACE OF THE MOUNTAIN. YOU'RE ONLY A FEW STEPS AWAY FROM THE ENTRANCE.
ONCE YOU ARE THERE, YOU WILL NEED TO DISABLE THE OUTER DEFENSES WITH THE REMOTE TRANSMITTER I GAVE YOU.
STARK, I DON'T THINK WE'LL NEED YOUR TRANSMITTER. IT LOOKS LIKE SOME-ONE'S ALREADY "DISABLED" THEM.
THAT IS IMPOSSIBLE. WHAT IS GOING ON!?

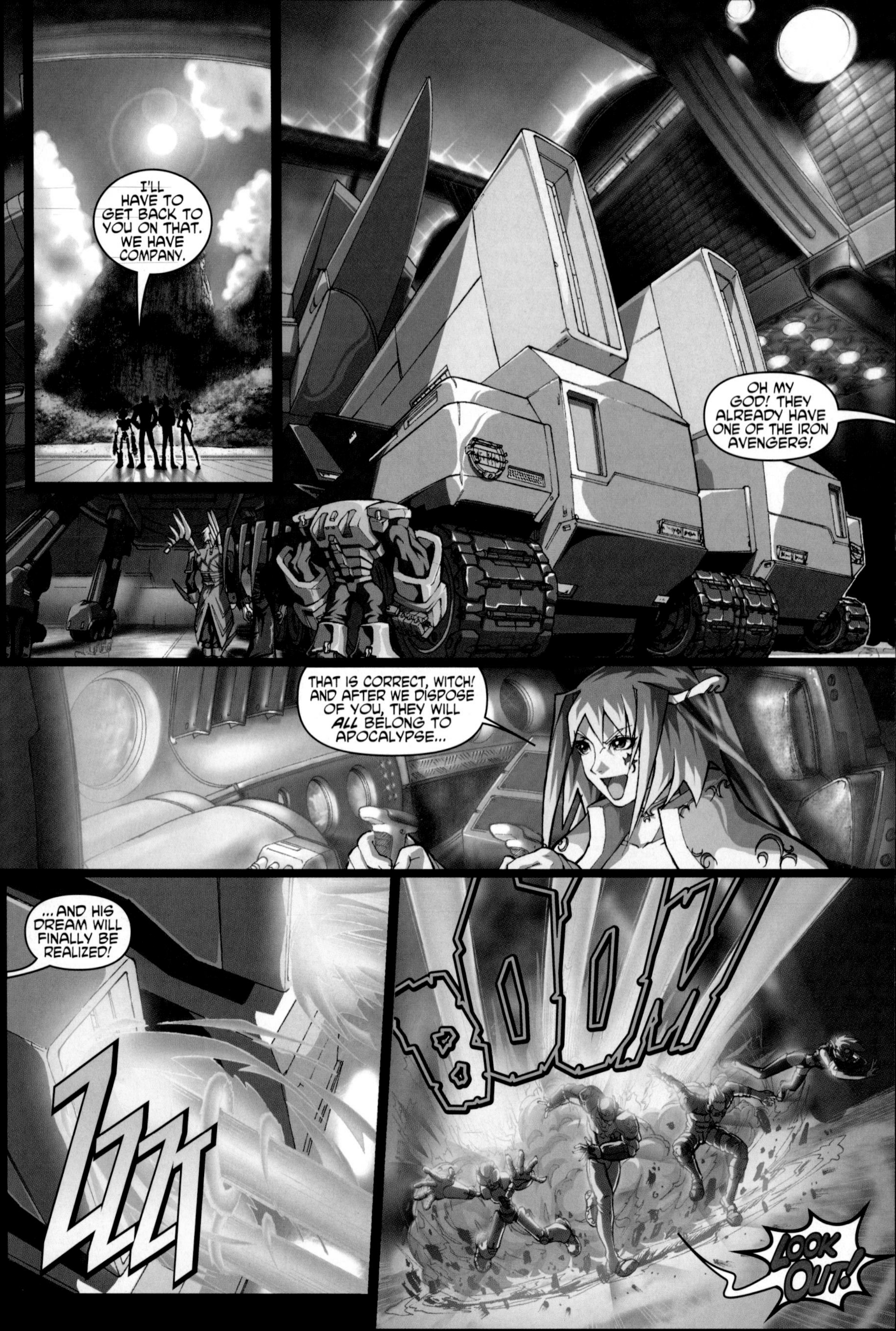
I'LL HAVE TO GET BACK TO YOU ON THAT. WE HAVE COMPANY.
OH MY GOD! THEY ALREADY HAVE ONE OF THE IRON AVENGERS!
THAT IS CORRECT, WITCH! AND AFTER WE DISPOSE OF YOU, THEY WILL ALL BELONG TO APOCALYPSE...
...AND HIS DREAM WILL FINALLY BE REALIZED!
ZZZZT
BOOM
LOOK OUT!

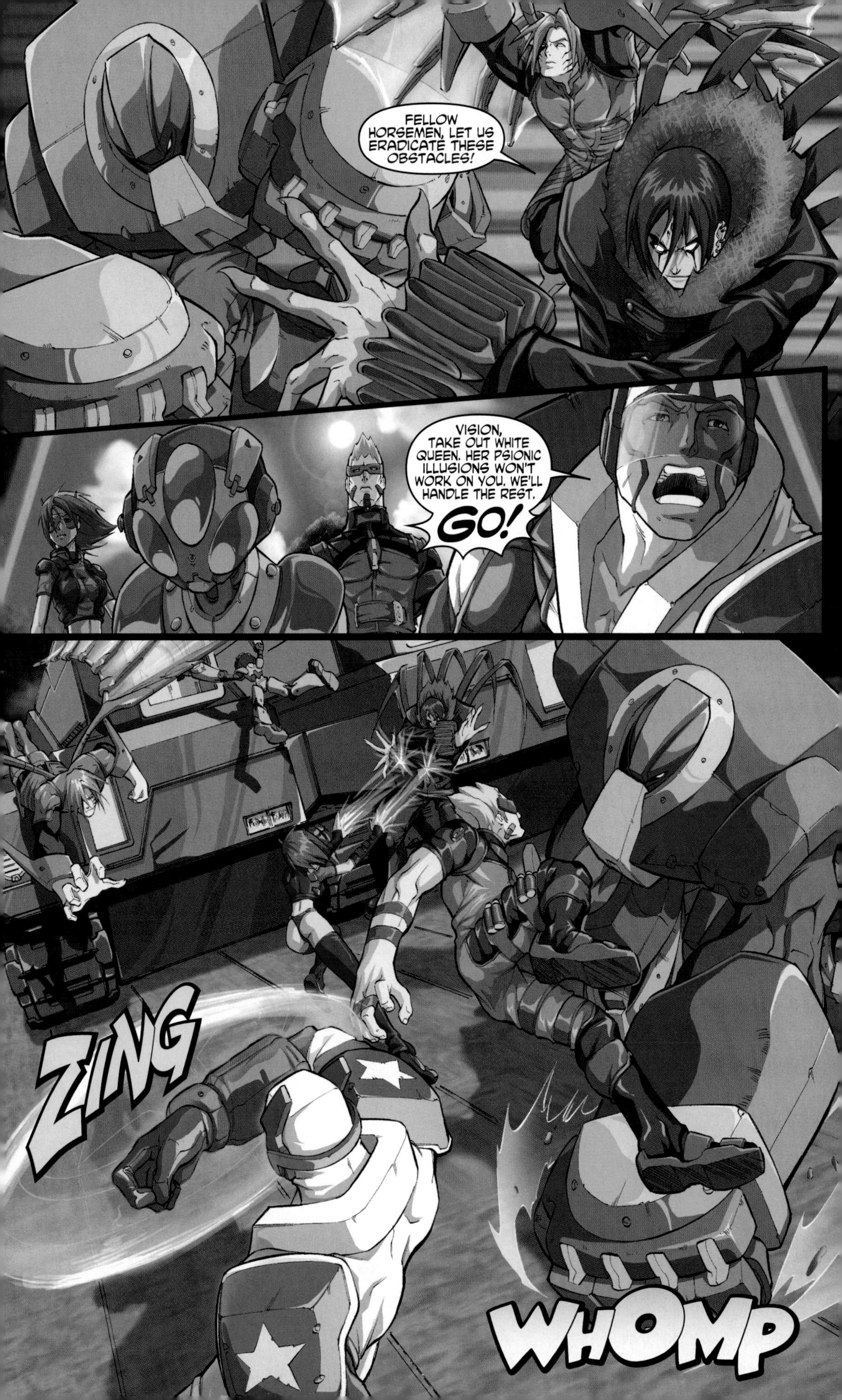

FELLOW HORSEMEN, LET US ERADICATE THESE OBSTACLES!
VISION, TAKE OUT WHITE QUEEN. HER PSIONIC ILLUSIONS WON'T WORK ON YOU. WE'LL HANDLE THE REST. GO!
ZING
WHOMP

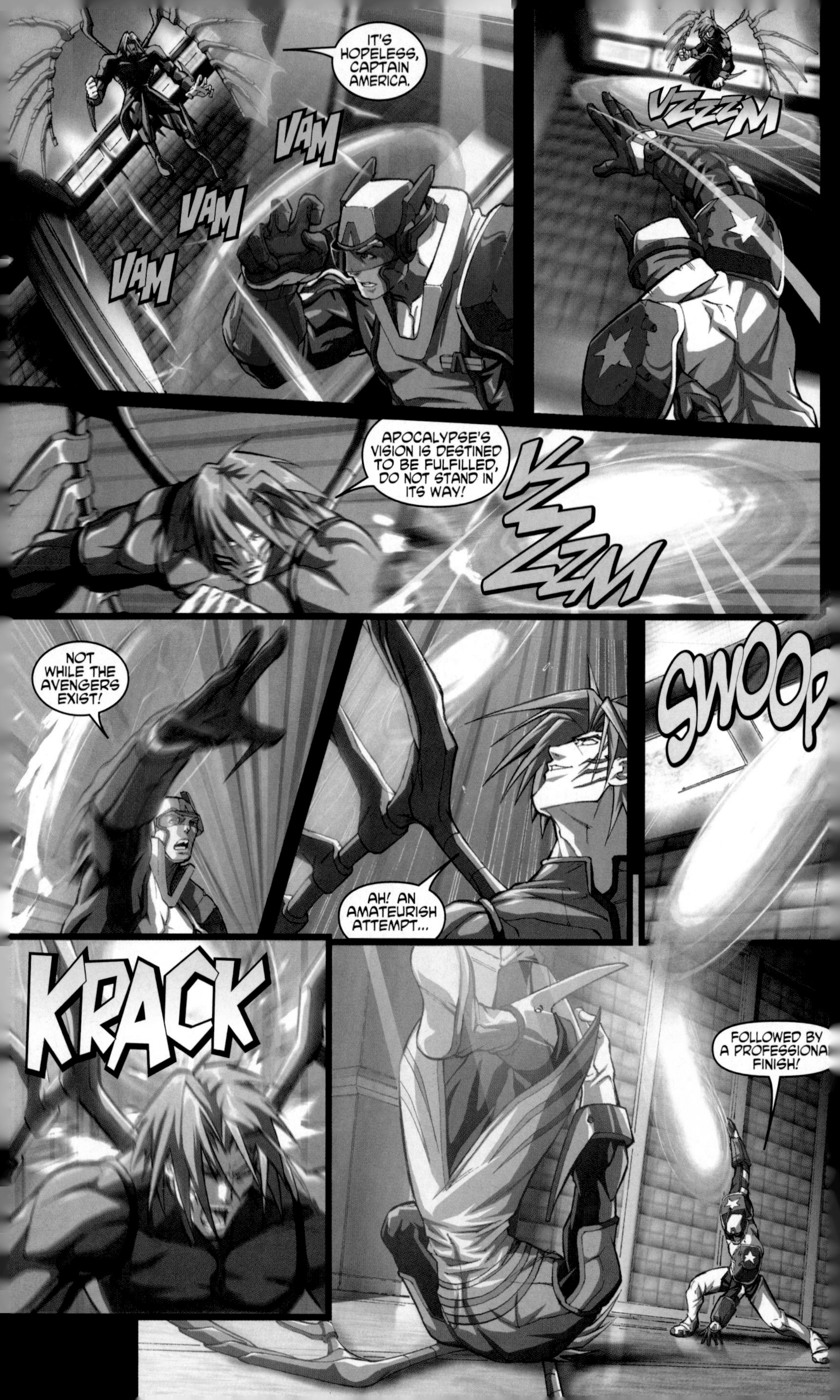
IT'S HOPELESS, CAPTAIN AMERICA.
VAM
VAM
VAM
VZZZM
APOCALYPSE'S VISION IS DESTINED TO BE FULFILLED, DO NOT STAND IN ITS WAY!
VSZZM
NOT WHILE THE AVENGERS EXIST!
AH! AN AMATEURISH ATTEMPT...
SWOOP
KRACK
FOLLOWED BY A PROFESSIONAL FINISH!

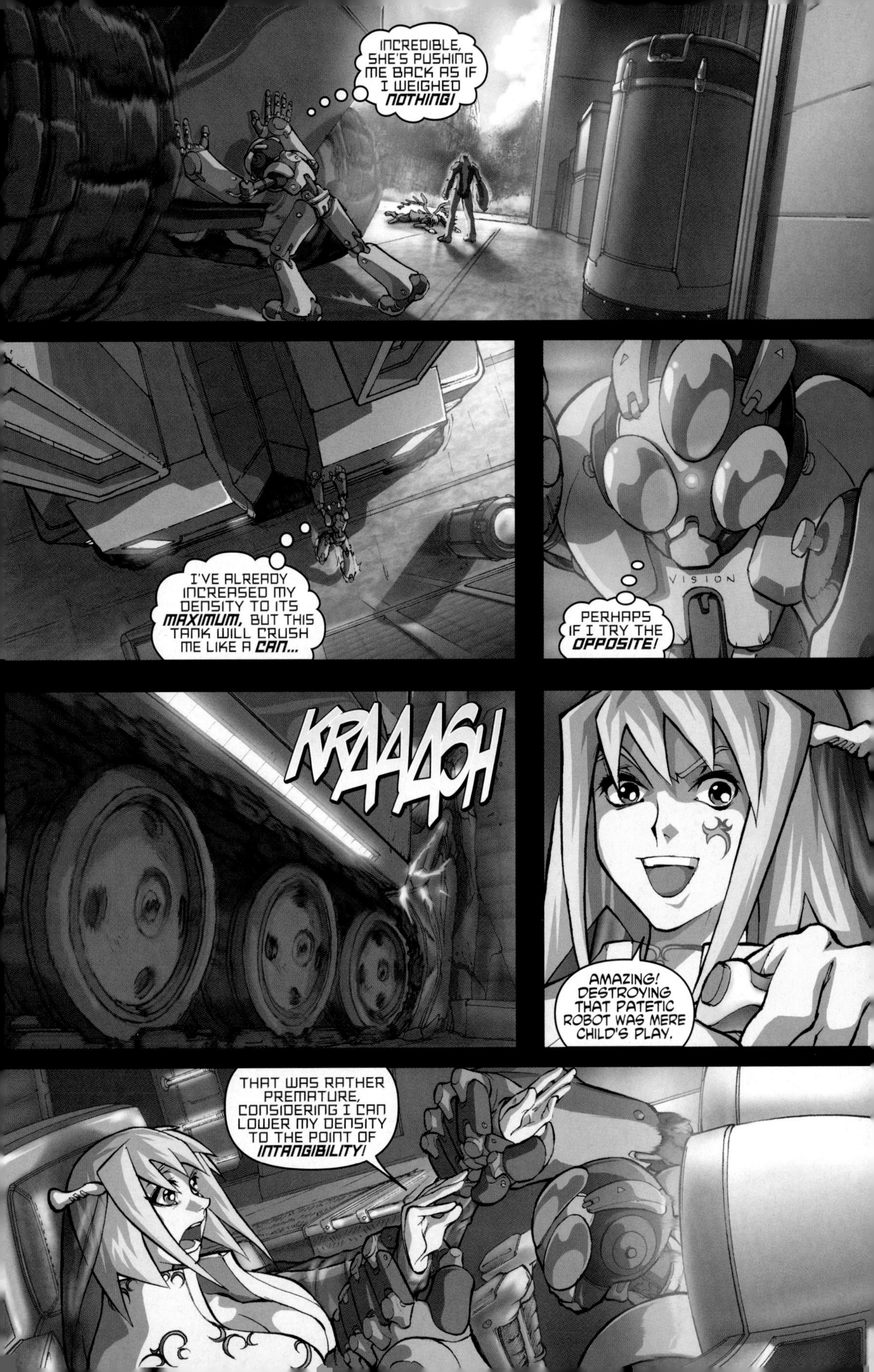

INCREDIBLE, SHE'S PUSHING ME BACK AS IF I WEIGHED *NOTHING!*
I'VE ALREADY INCREASED MY DENSITY TO ITS *MAXIMUM,* BUT THIS TANK WILL CRUSH ME LIKE A *CAN...*
VISION
PERHAPS IF I TRY THE *OPPOSITE!*
KRAAASH
AMAZING! DESTROYING THAT PATETIC ROBOT WAS MERE CHILD'S PLAY.
THAT WAS RATHER PREMATURE, CONSIDERING I CAN LOWER MY DENSITY TO THE POINT OF *INTANGIBILITY!*

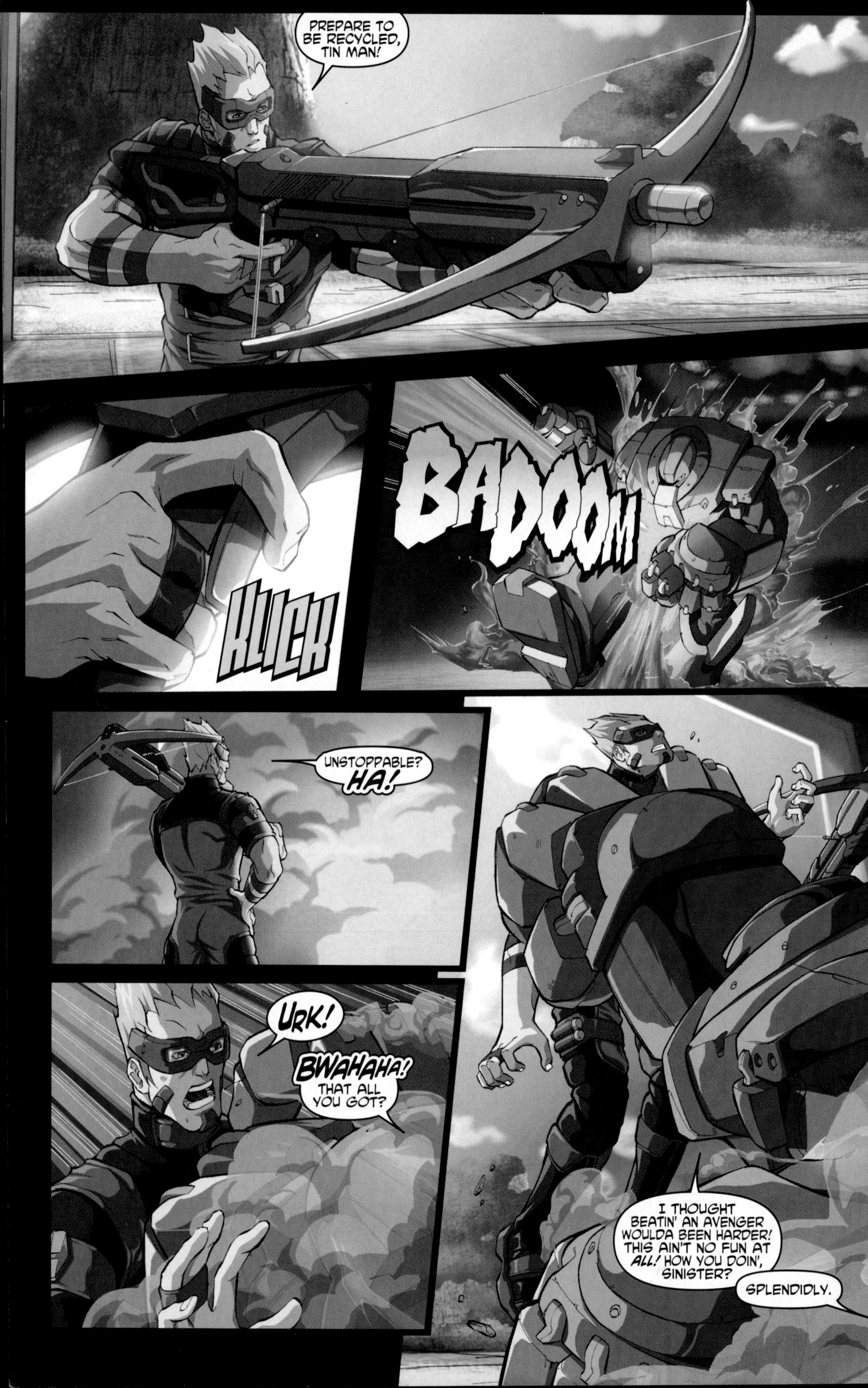
PREPARE TO BE RECYCLED, TIN MAN!
KLICK
BADOOM
UNSTOPPABLE? HA!
URK!
BWAHAHA! THAT ALL YOU GOT?
I THOUGHT BEATIN' AN AVENGER WOULDA BEEN HARDER! THIS AIN'T NO FUN AT ALL! HOW YOU DOIN', SINISTER?
SPLENDIDLY.

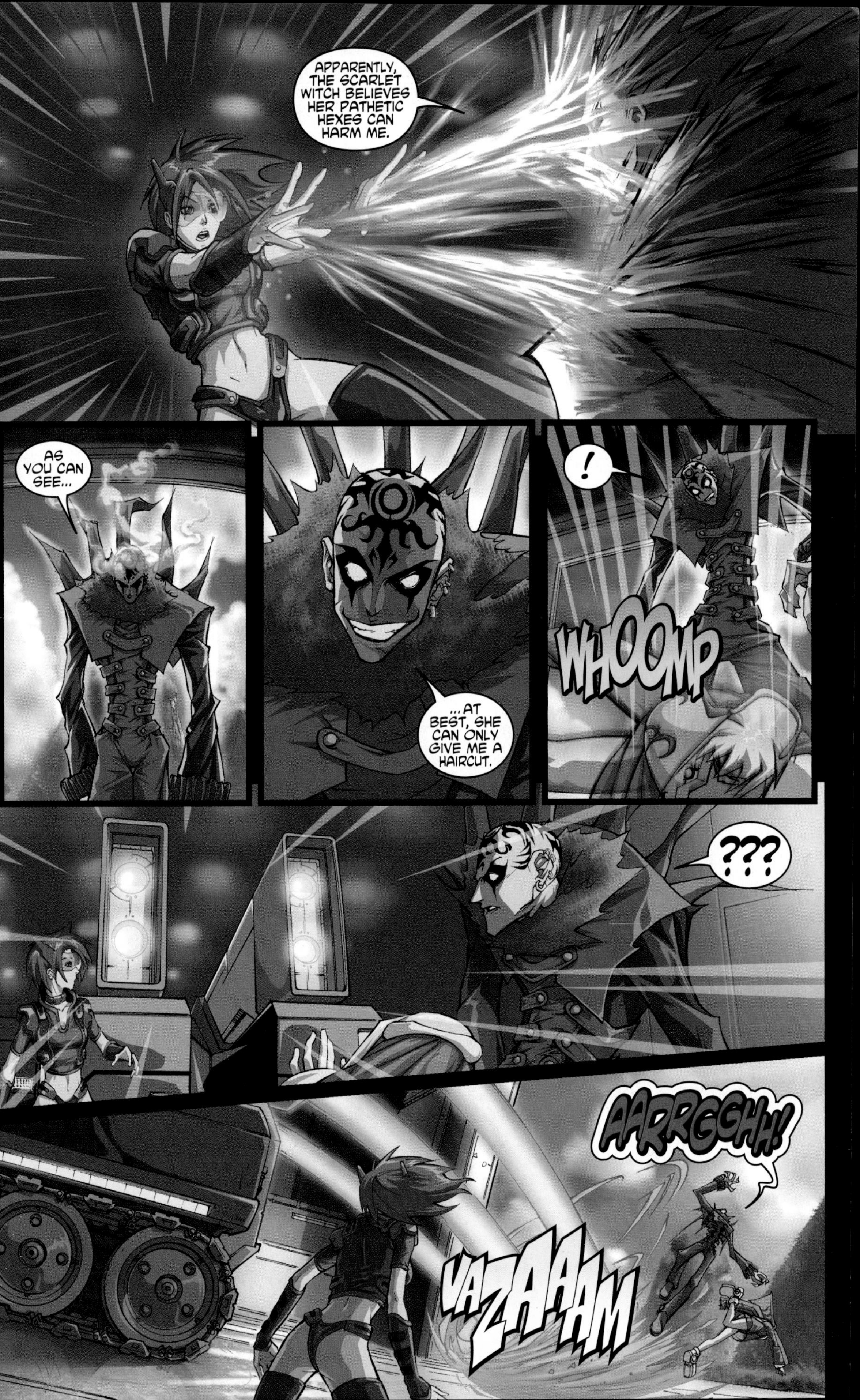
APPARENTLY, THE SCARLET WITCH BELIEVES HER PATHETIC HEXES CAN HARM ME.
AS YOU CAN SEE...
...AT BEST, SHE CAN ONLY GIVE ME A HAIRCUT.
!
WHOOMP
???
AARRGGHH!
VAZAAAAM

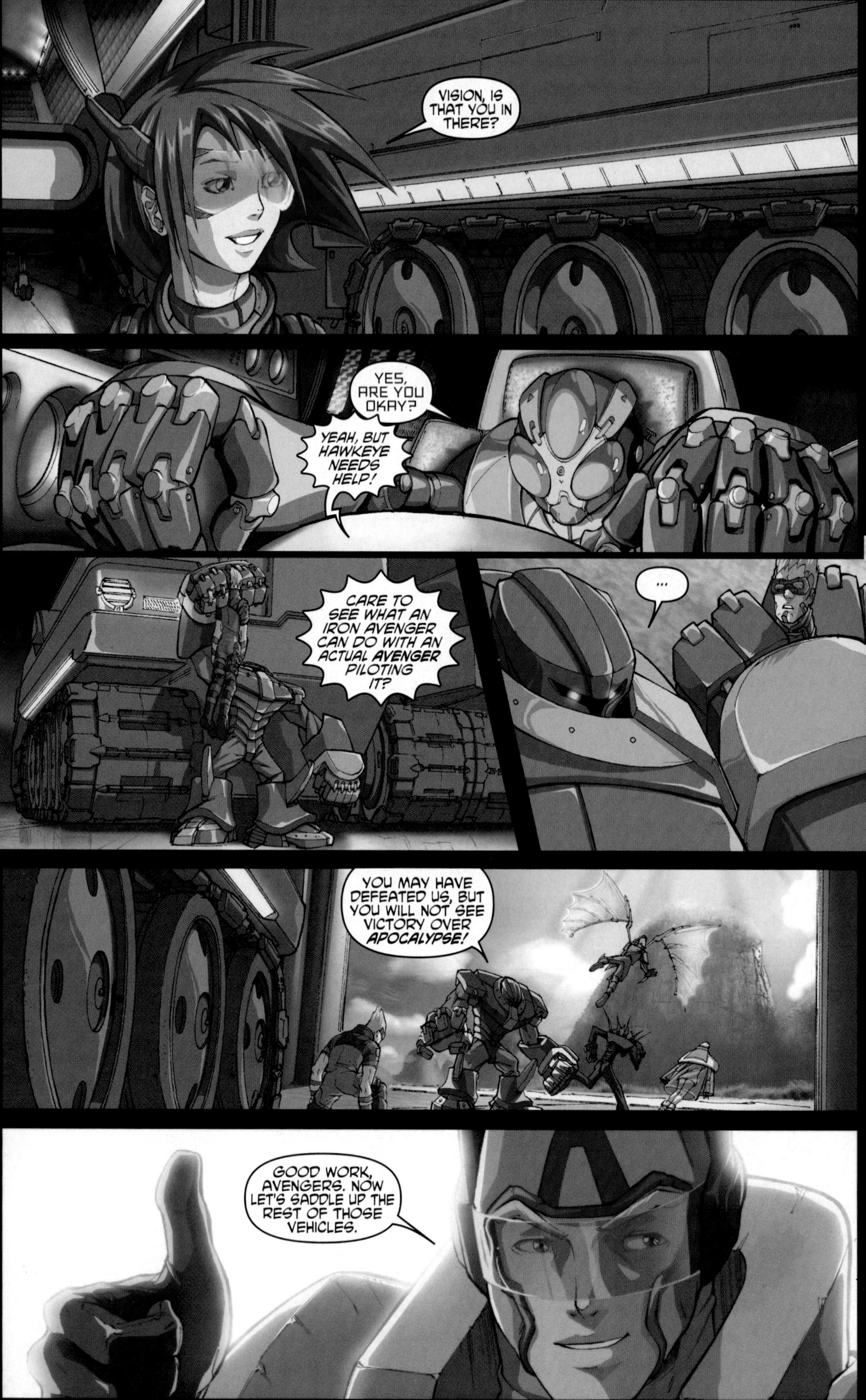
VISION, IS THAT YOU IN THERE?
YES, ARE YOU OKAY?
YEAH, BUT HAWKEYE NEEDS HELP!
CARE TO SEE WHAT AN IRON AVENGER CAN DO WITH AN ACTUAL AVENGER PILOTING IT?
...
YOU MAY HAVE DEFEATED US, BUT YOU WILL NOT SEE VICTORY OVER APOCALYPSE!
GOOD WORK, AVENGERS. NOW LET'S SADDLE UP THE REST OF THOSE VEHICLES.

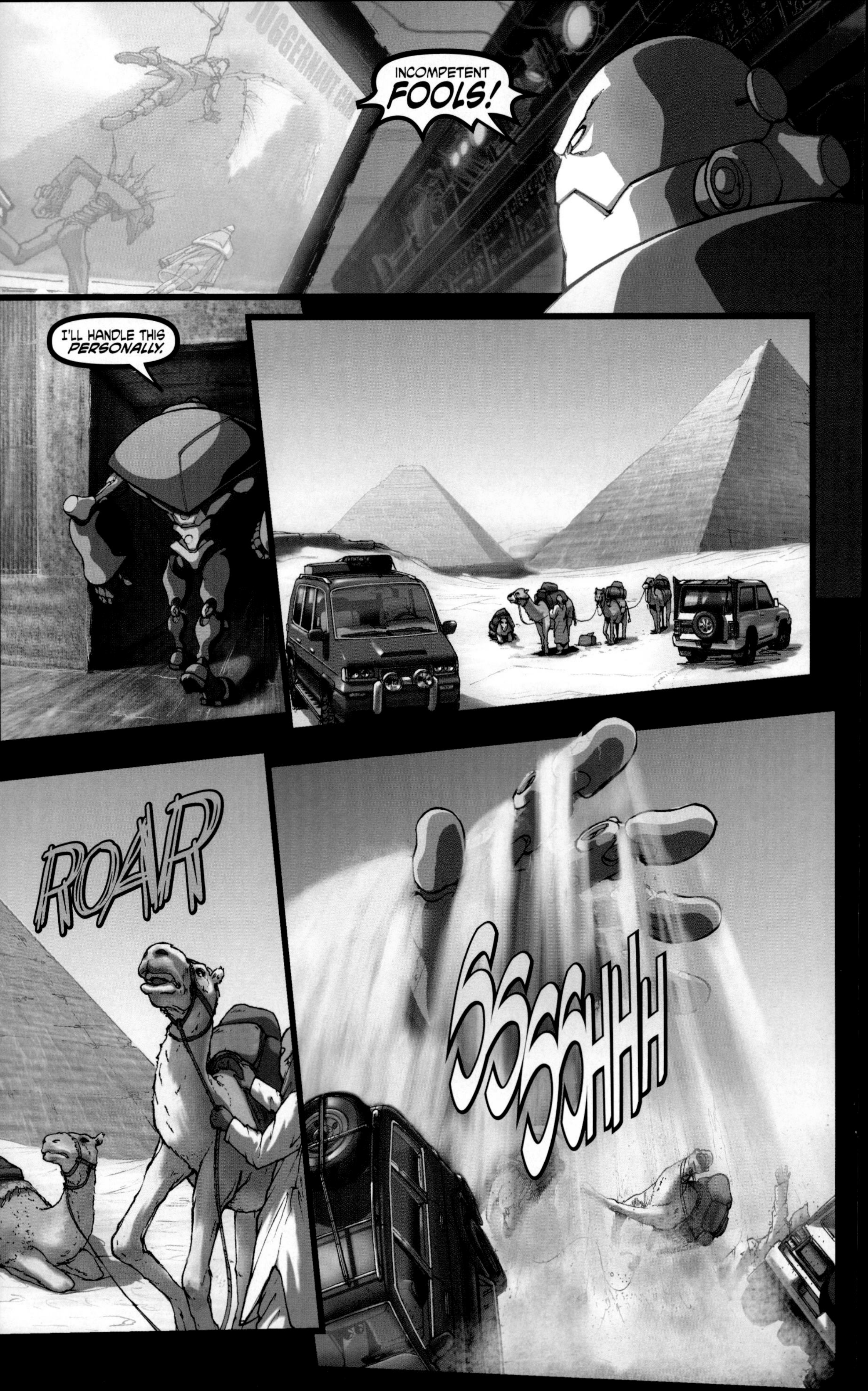
JUGGERNAUT
INCOMPETENT FOOLS!
I'LL HANDLE THIS PERSONALLY.
ROAR
SSSSHHH

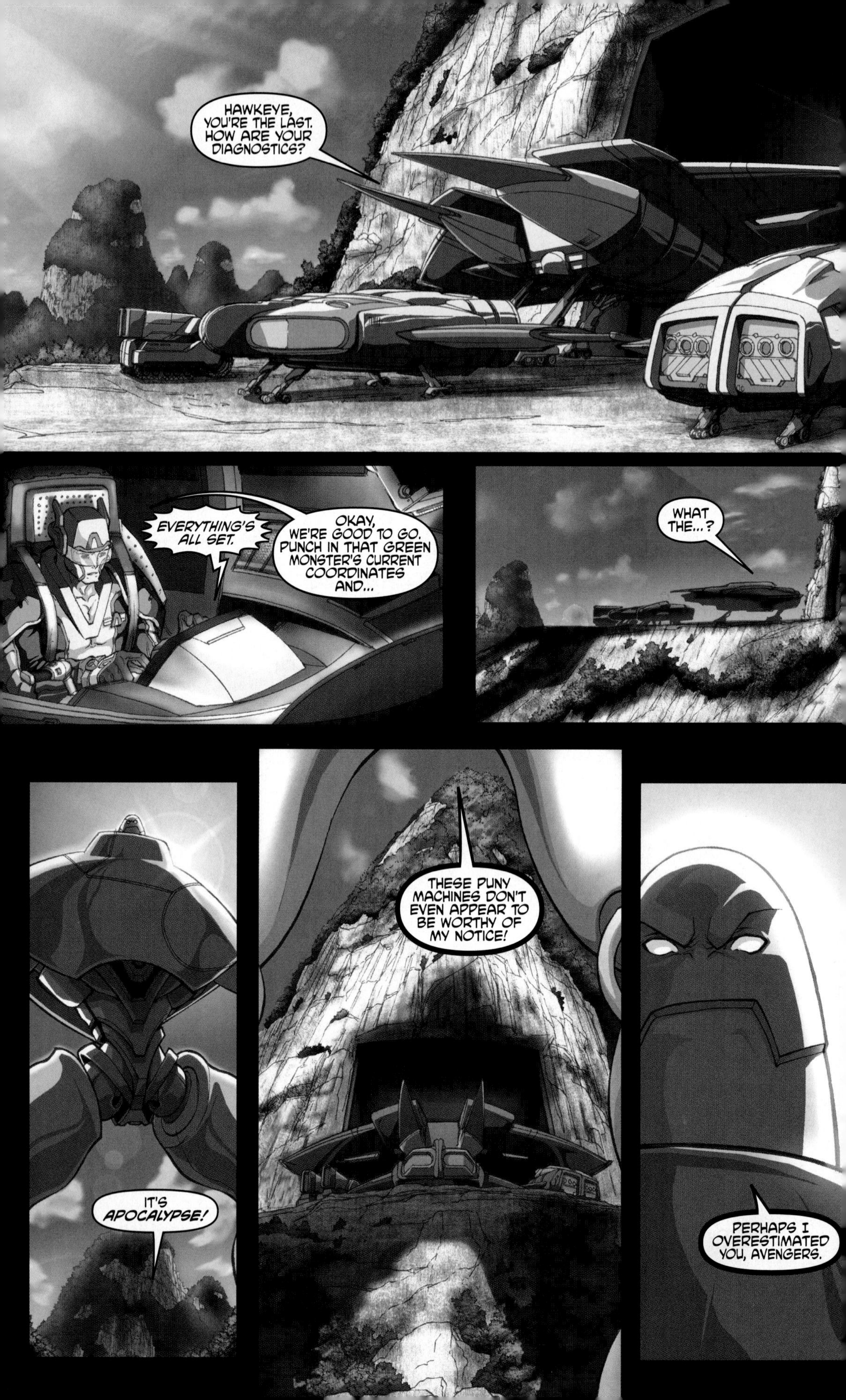
HAWKEYE, YOU'RE THE LAST. HOW ARE YOUR DIAGNOSTICS?
EVERYTHING'S ALL SET.
OKAY, WE'RE GOOD TO GO. PUNCH IN THAT GREEN MONSTER'S CURRENT COORDINATES AND...
WHAT THE...?
IT'S APOCALYPSE!
THESE PUNY MACHINES DON'T EVEN APPEAR TO BE WORTHY OF MY NOTICE!
PERHAPS I OVERESTIMATED YOU, AVENGERS.

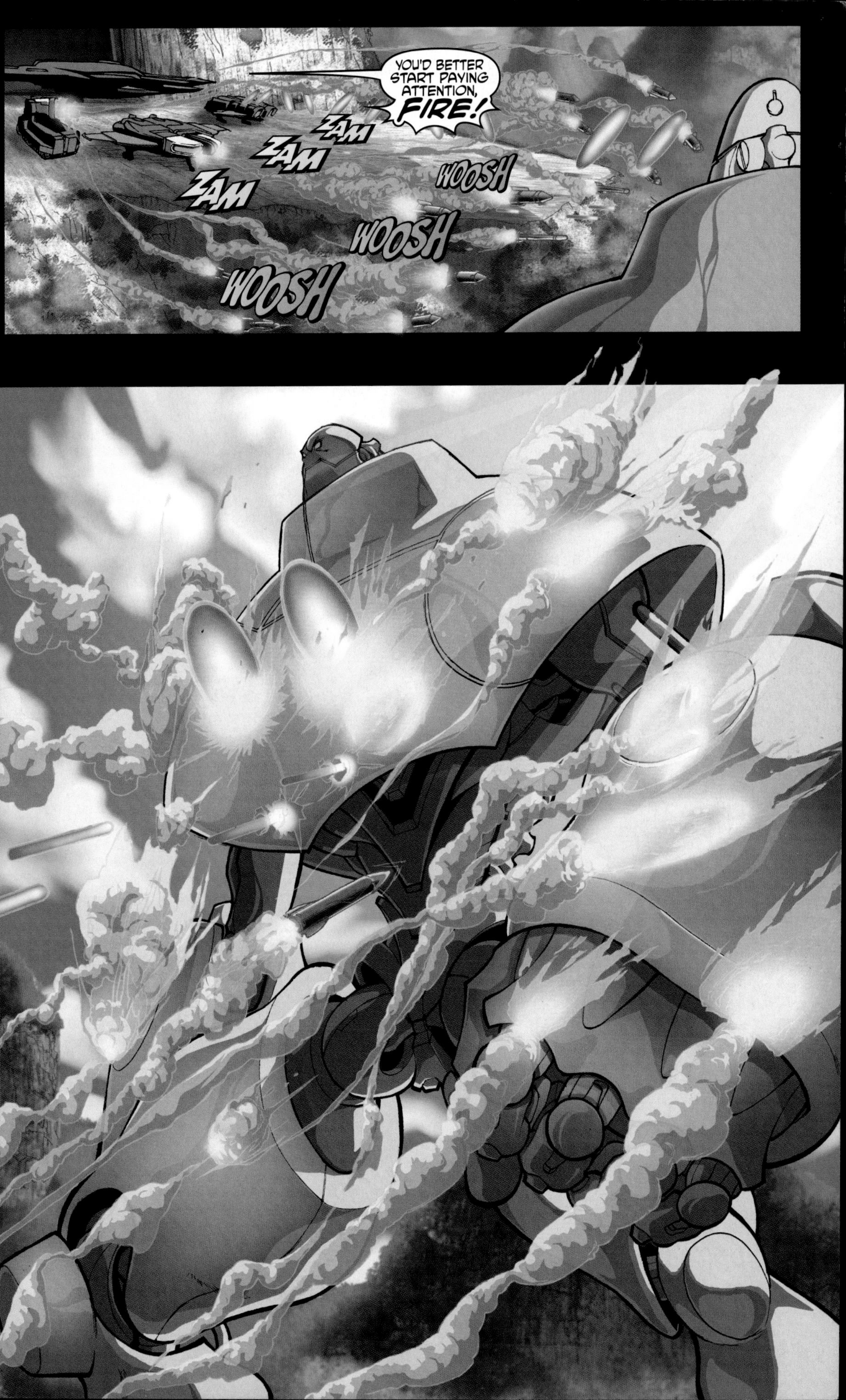
YOU'D BETTER START PAYING ATTENTION, FIRE!
ZAM
ZAM
ZAM
WOOSH
WOOSH
WOOSH

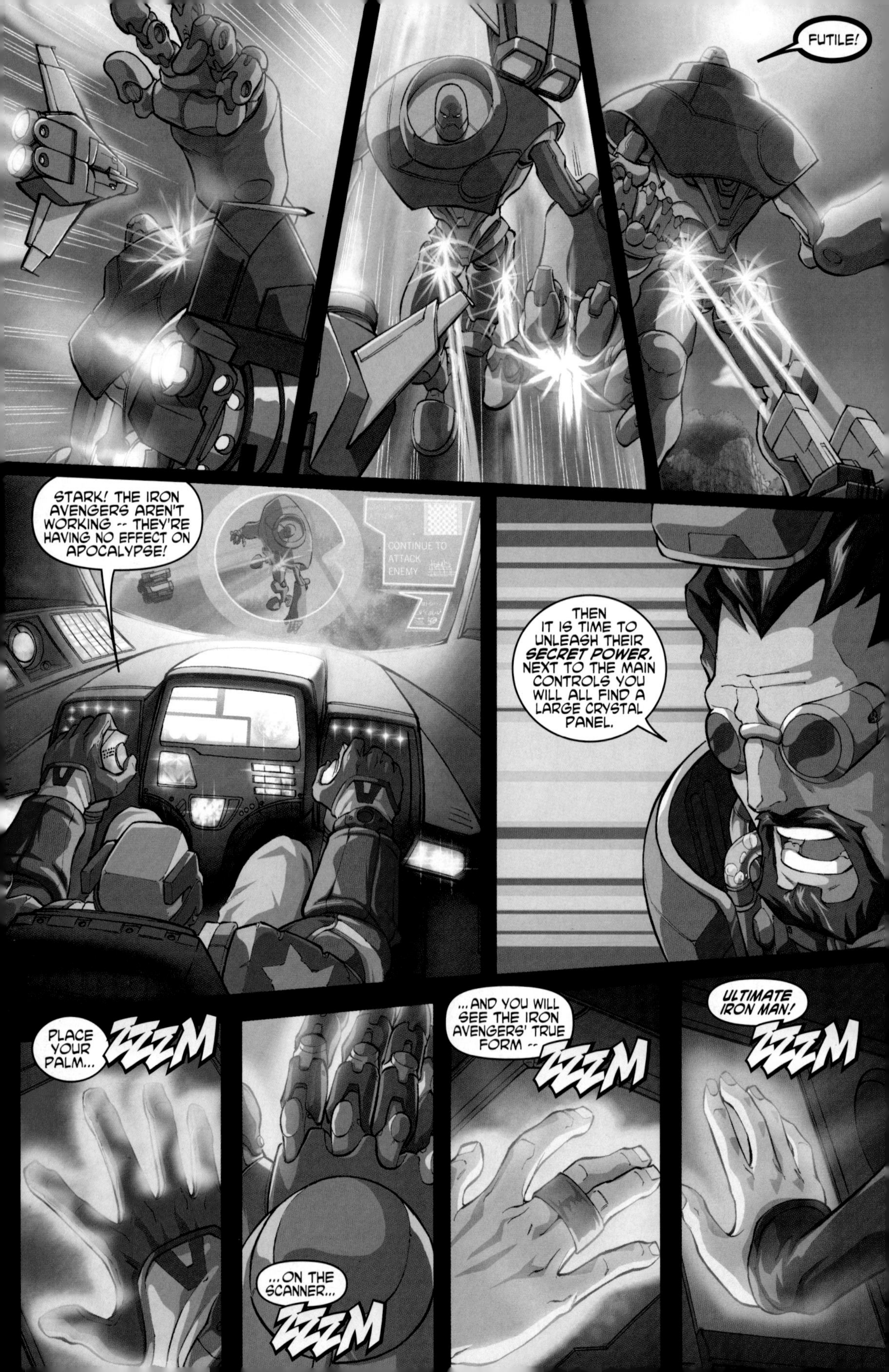
FUTILE!
STARK! THE IRON AVENGERS AREN'T WORKING -- THEY'RE HAVING NO EFFECT ON APOCALYPSE!
CONTINUE TO ATTACK ENEMY
THEN IT IS TIME TO UNLEASH THEIR SECRET POWER. NEXT TO THE MAIN CONTROLS YOU WILL ALL FIND A LARGE CRYSTAL PANEL.
PLACE YOUR PALM...
ZZZM
...ON THE SCANNER...
ZZZM
...AND YOU WILL SEE THE IRON AVENGERS' TRUE FORM --
ZZZM
ULTIMATE IRON MAN!
ZZZM

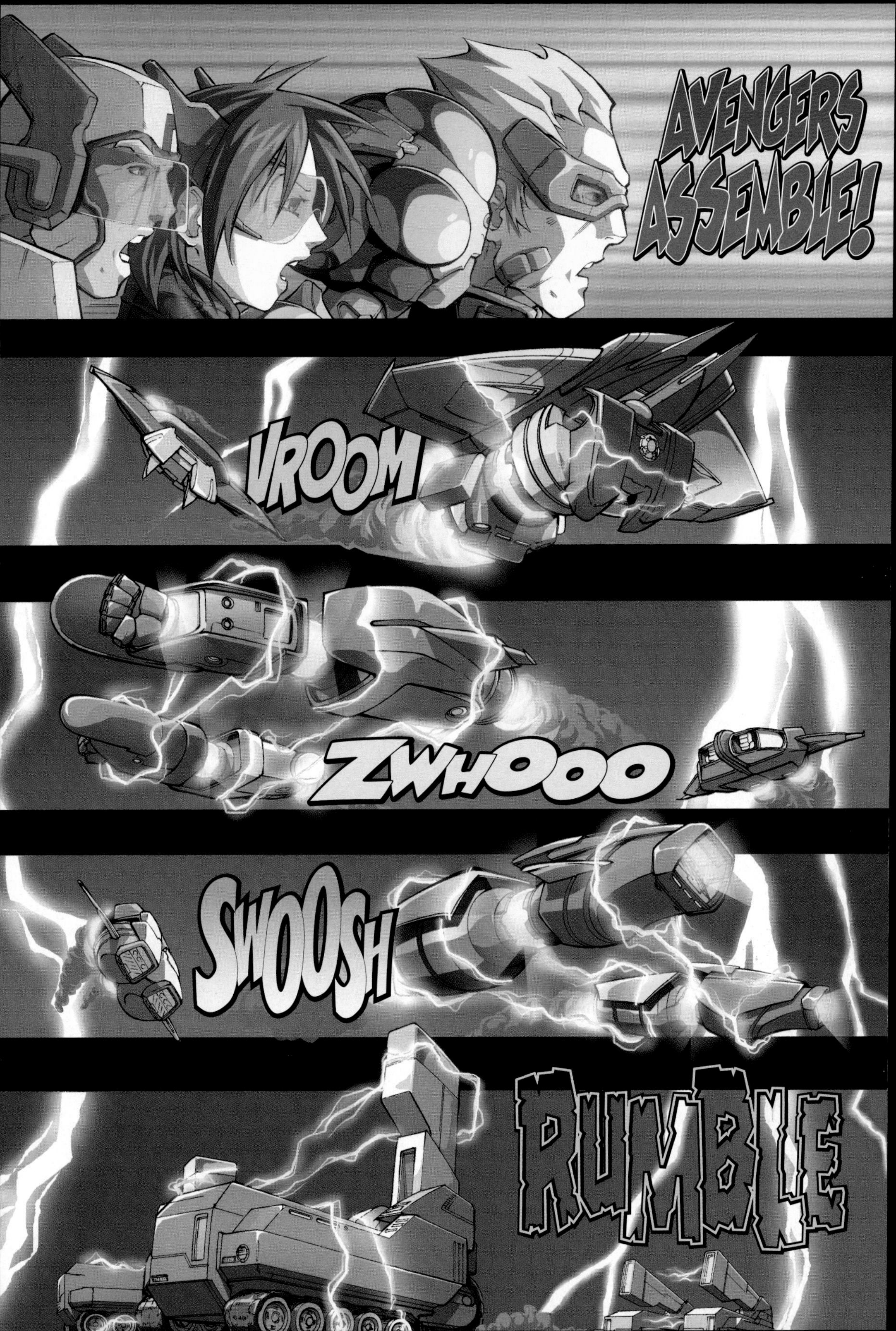
AVENGERS ASSEMBLE!
VROOM
ZWHOOO
SWOOSH
RUMBLE

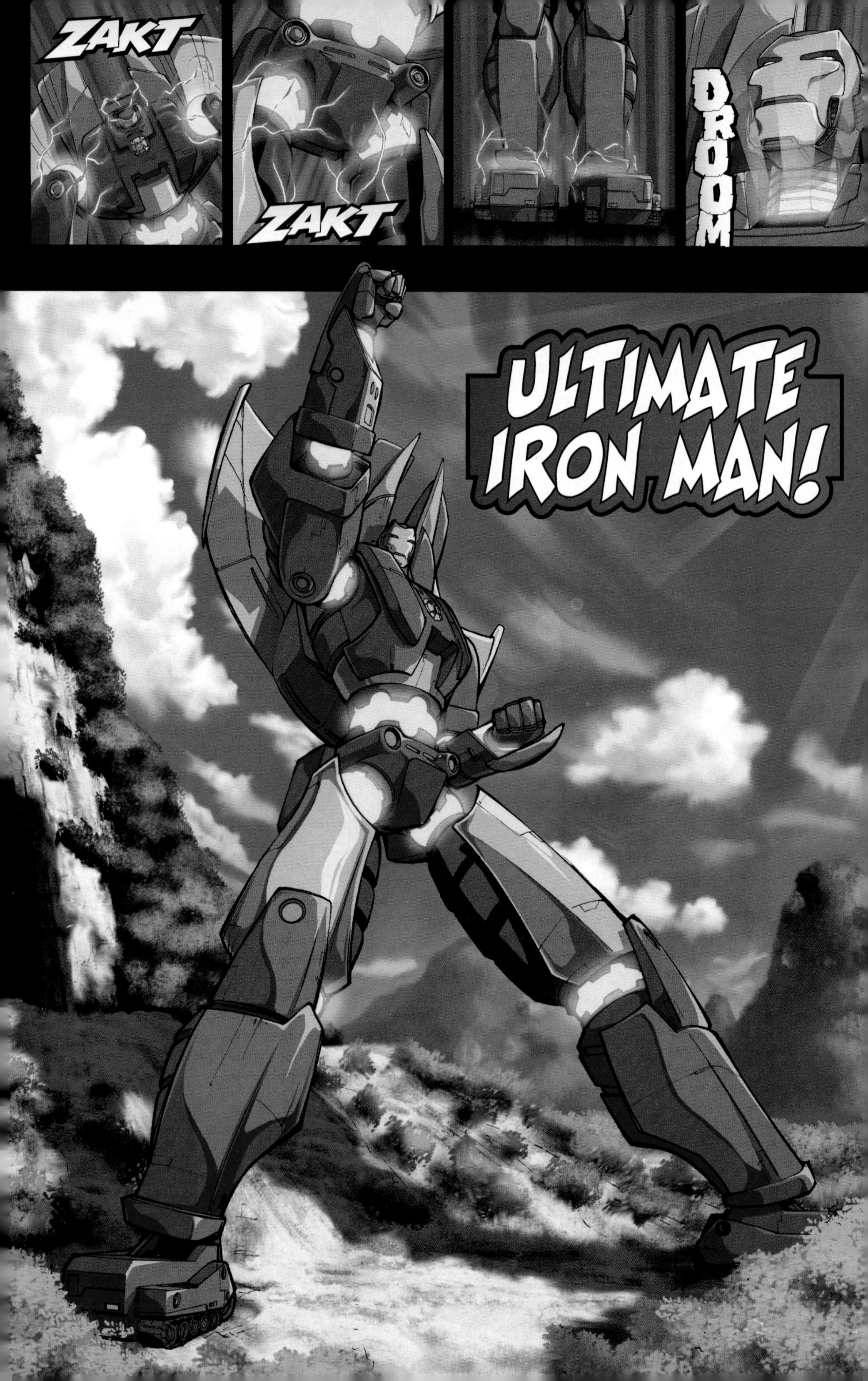
ZAKT
ZAKT
DROOM
ULTIMATE IRON MAN!

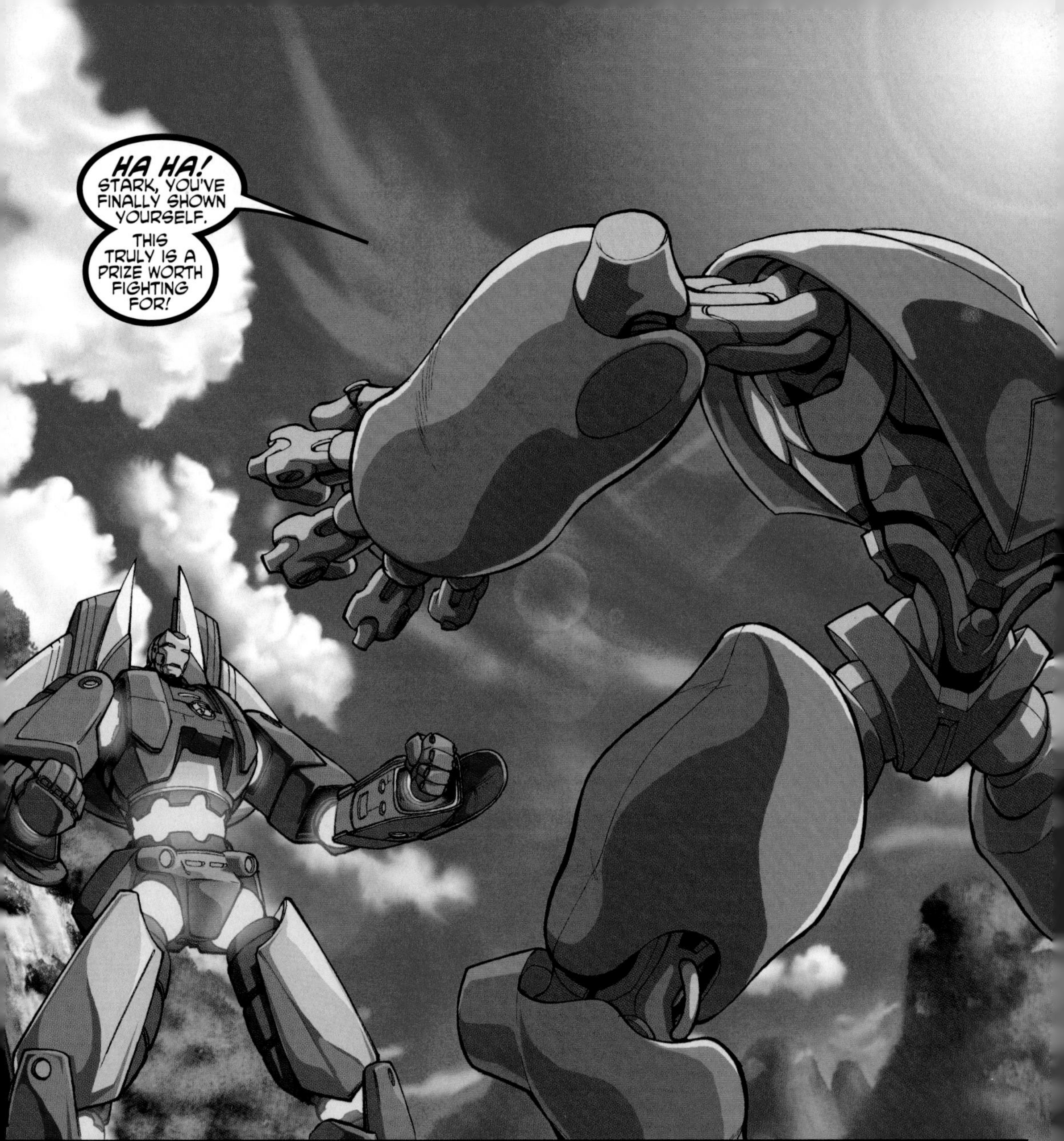
HA HA! STARK, YOU'VE FINALLY SHOWN YOURSELF.
THIS TRULY IS A PRIZE WORTH FIGHTING FOR!

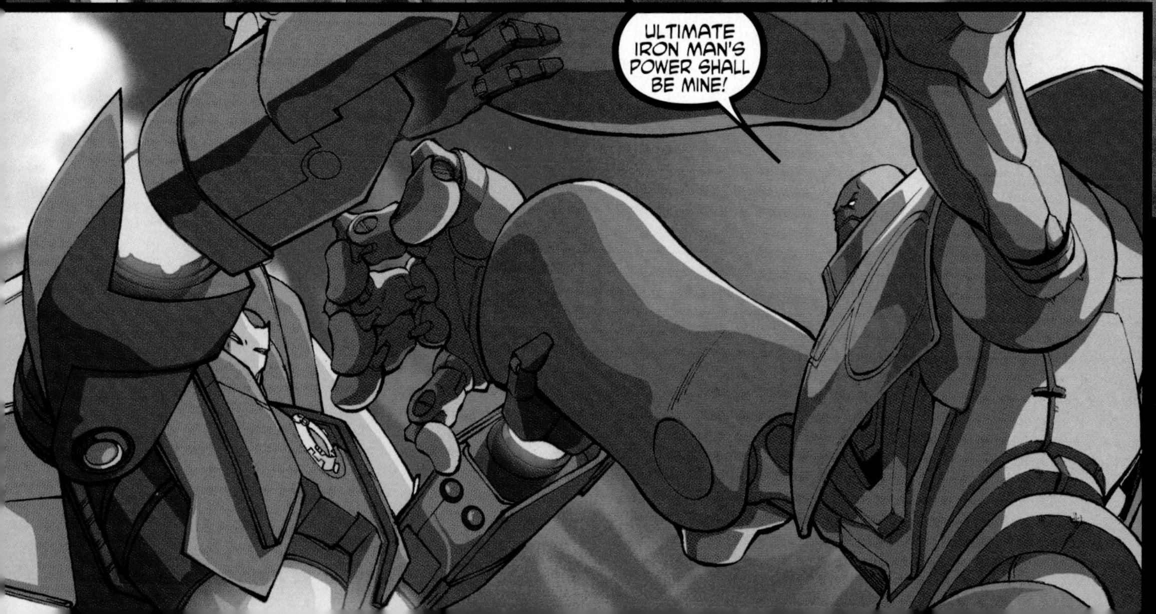
ULTIMATE IRON MAN'S POWER SHALL BE MINE!

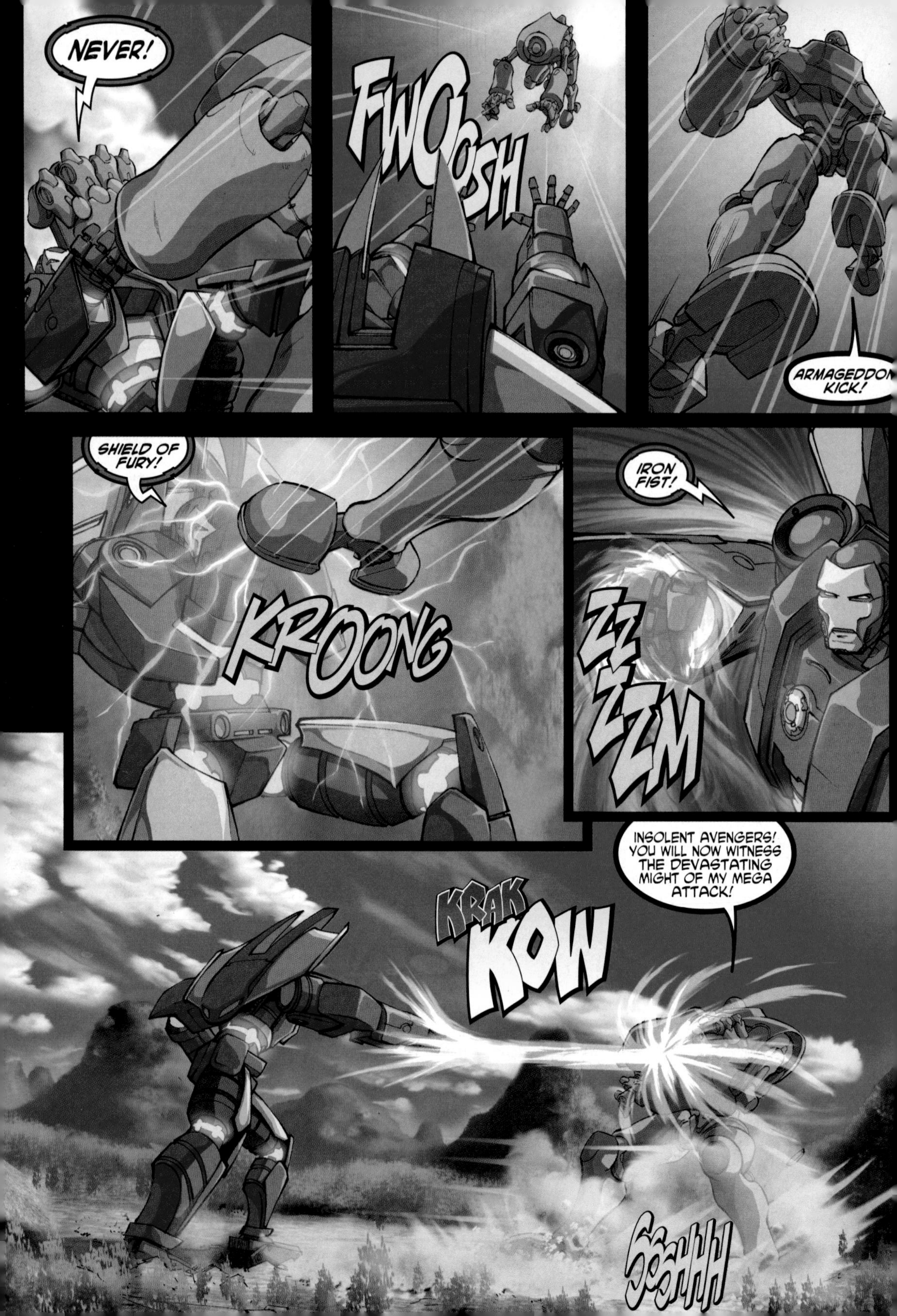

NEVER!
FWOOSH
ARMAGEDDON KICK!
SHIELD OF FURY!
KROONG
IRON FIST!
ZZZZZM
INSOLENT AVENGERS! YOU WILL NOW WITNESS THE DEVASTATING MIGHT OF MY MEGA ATTACK!
KRAK
KOW
SSSHHH

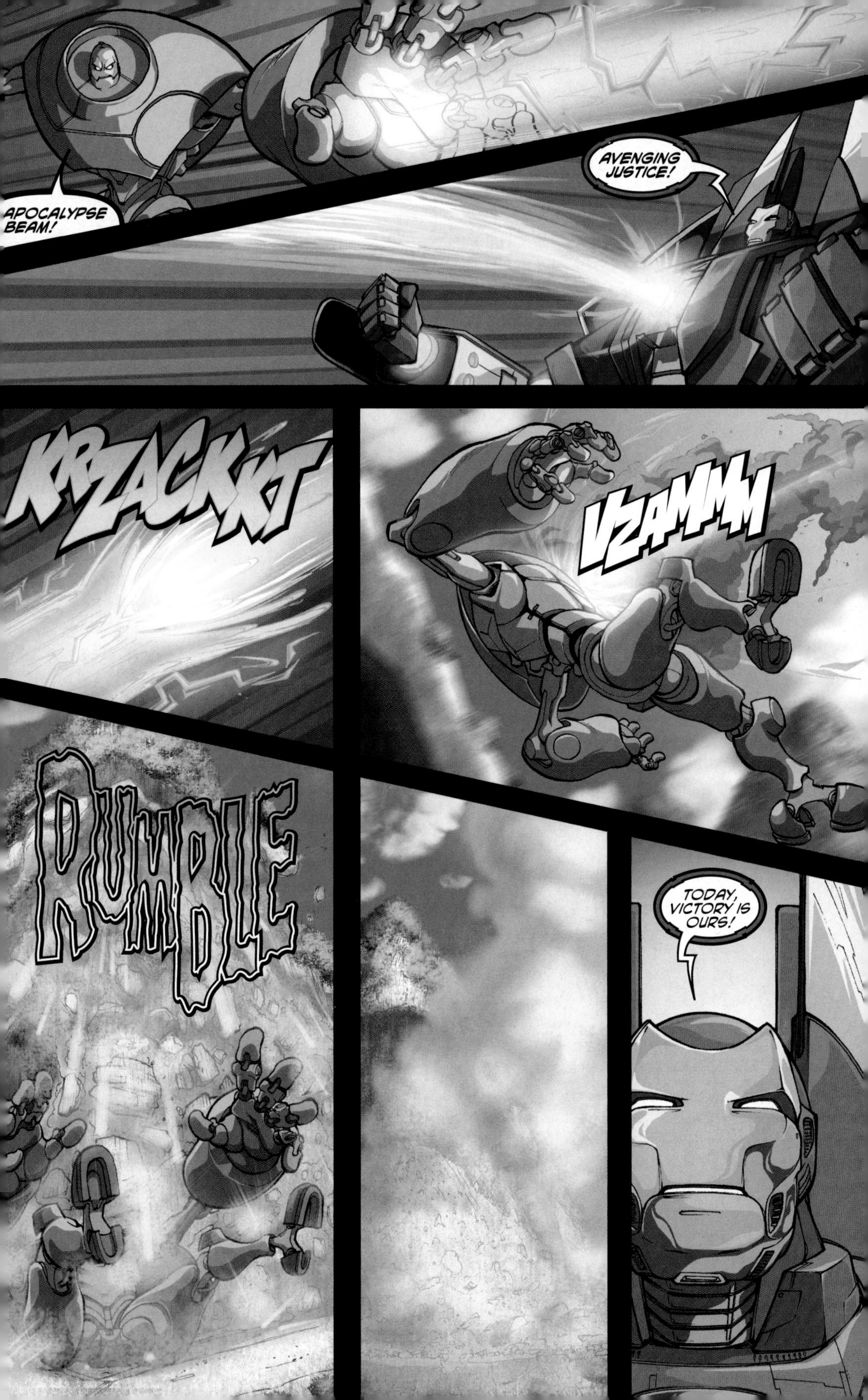
APOCALYPSE BEAM!
AVENGING JUSTICE!
KRZACKKT
VZAMMM
RUMBLE
TODAY, VICTORY IS OURS!

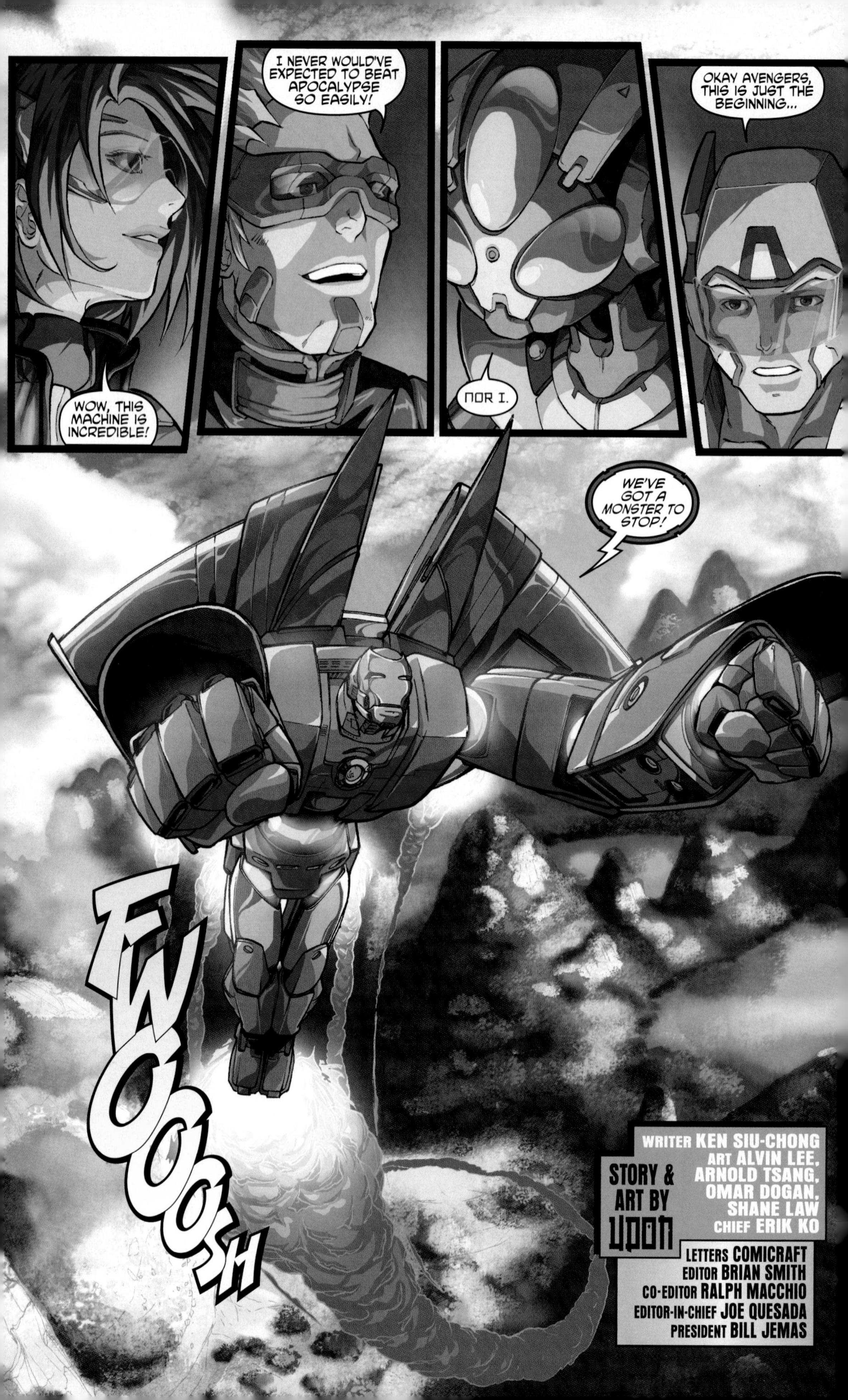
WOW, THIS MACHINE IS INCREDIBLE!
I NEVER WOULD'VE EXPECTED TO BEAT APOCALYPSE SO EASILY!
NOR I.
OKAY AVENGERS, THIS IS JUST THE BEGINNING...
WE'VE GOT A MONSTER TO STOP!
FWOOOOSH
STORY & ART BY UDON
WRITER KEN SIU-CHONG
ART ALVIN LEE, ARNOLD TSANG, OMAR DOGAN, SHANE LAW
CHIEF ERIK KO
LETTERS COMICRAFT
EDITOR BRIAN SMITH
CO-EDITOR RALPH MACCHIO
EDITOR-IN-CHIEF JOE QUESADA
PRESIDENT BILL JEMAS

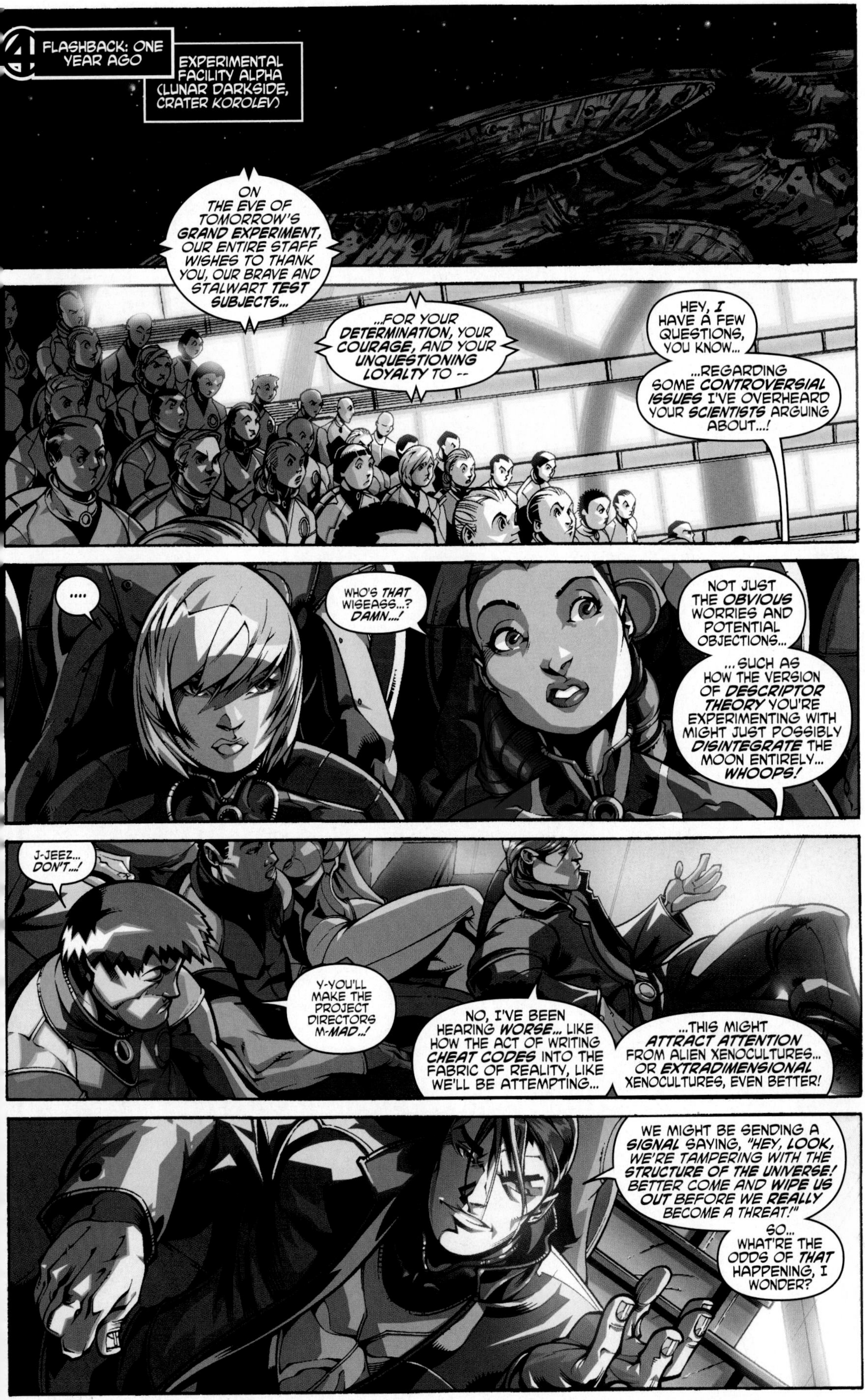

FLASHBACK: ONE YEAR AGO
EXPERIMENTAL FACILITY ALPHA (LUNAR DARKSIDE, CRATER KOROLEV)
ON THE EVE OF TOMORROW'S GRAND EXPERIMENT, OUR ENTIRE STAFF WISHES TO THANK YOU, OUR BRAVE AND STALWART TEST SUBJECTS...
...FOR YOUR DETERMINATION, YOUR COURAGE, AND YOUR UNQUESTIONING LOYALTY TO --
HEY, I HAVE A FEW QUESTIONS, YOU KNOW...
...REGARDING SOME CONTROVERSIAL ISSUES I'VE OVERHEARD YOUR SCIENTISTS ARGUING ABOUT...!
....
WHO'S THAT WISEASS...? DAMN...!
NOT JUST THE OBVIOUS WORRIES AND POTENTIAL OBJECTIONS...
...SUCH AS HOW THE VERSION OF DESCRIPTOR THEORY YOU'RE EXPERIMENTING WITH MIGHT JUST POSSIBLY DISINTEGRATE THE MOON ENTIRELY... WHOOPS!
J-JEEZ... DON'T...!
Y-YOU'LL MAKE THE PROJECT DIRECTORS M-MAD...!
NO, I'VE BEEN HEARING WORSE... LIKE HOW THE ACT OF WRITING CHEAT CODES INTO THE FABRIC OF REALITY, LIKE WE'LL BE ATTEMPTING...
...THIS MIGHT ATTRACT ATTENTION FROM ALIEN XENOCULTURES... OR EXTRADIMENSIONAL XENOCULTURES, EVEN BETTER!
WE MIGHT BE SENDING A SIGNAL SAYING, "HEY, LOOK, WE'RE TAMPERING WITH THE STRUCTURE OF THE UNIVERSE! BETTER COME AND WIPE US OUT BEFORE WE REALLY BECOME A THREAT!"
SO... WHAT'RE THE ODDS OF THAT HAPPENING, I WONDER?

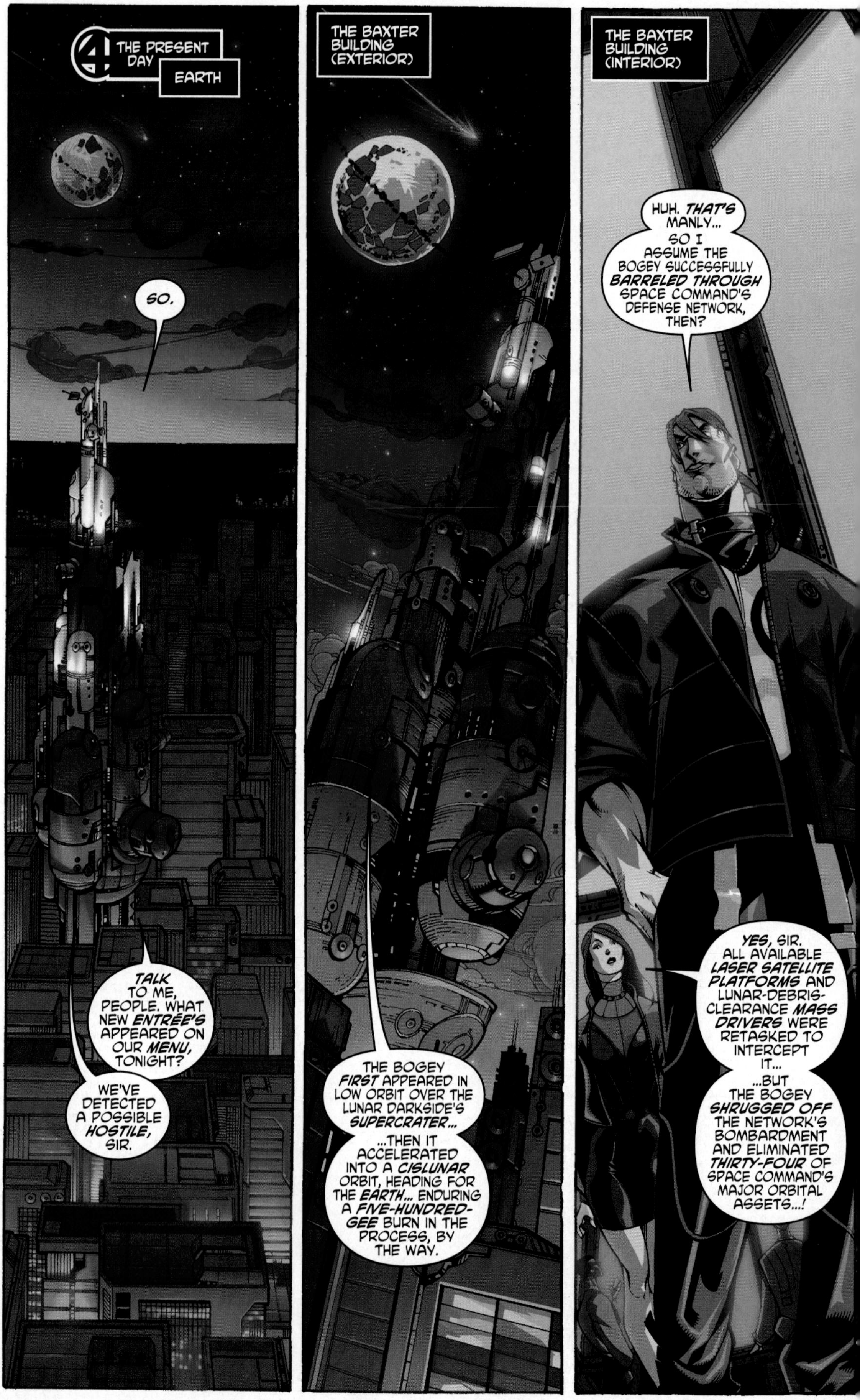
THE PRESENT DAY
EARTH
SO.
TALK TO ME, PEOPLE. WHAT NEW ENTRÉE'S APPEARED ON OUR MENU, TONIGHT?
WE'VE DETECTED A POSSIBLE HOSTILE, SIR.
THE BAXTER BUILDING (EXTERIOR)
THE BOGEY FIRST APPEARED IN LOW ORBIT OVER THE LUNAR DARKSIDE'S SUPERCRATER...
...THEN IT ACCELERATED INTO A CISLUNAR ORBIT, HEADING FOR THE EARTH... ENDURING A FIVE-HUNDRED-GEE BURN IN THE PROCESS, BY THE WAY.
THE BAXTER BUILDING (INTERIOR)
HUH. THAT'S MANLY...
SO I ASSUME THE BOGEY SUCCESSFULLY BARRELED THROUGH SPACE COMMAND'S DEFENSE NETWORK, THEN?
YES, SIR. ALL AVAILABLE LASER SATELLITE PLATFORMS AND LUNAR-DEBRIS-CLEARANCE MASS DRIVERS WERE RETASKED TO INTERCEPT IT...
...BUT THE BOGEY SHRUGGED OFF THE NETWORK'S BOMBARDMENT AND ELIMINATED THIRTY-FOUR OF SPACE COMMAND'S MAJOR ORBITAL ASSETS...!

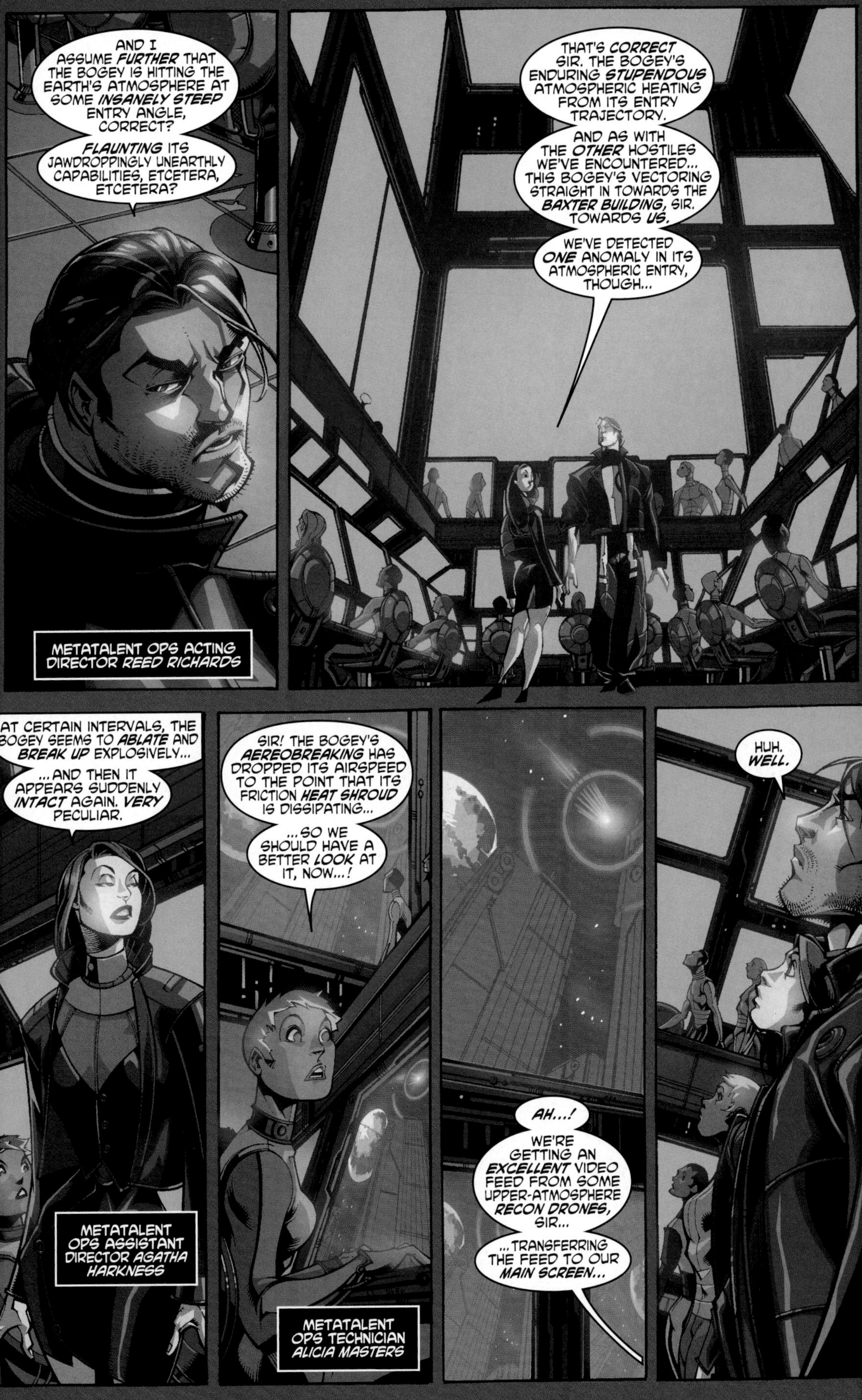
AND I ASSUME FURTHER THAT THE BOGEY IS HITTING THE EARTH'S ATMOSPHERE AT SOME INSANELY STEEP ENTRY ANGLE, CORRECT?
FLAUNTING ITS JAWDROPPINGLY UNEARTHLY CAPABILITIES, ETCETERA, ETCETERA?
METATALENT OPS ACTING DIRECTOR REED RICHARDS
THAT'S CORRECT SIR. THE BOGEY'S ENDURING STUPENDOUS ATMOSPHERIC HEATING FROM ITS ENTRY TRAJECTORY.
AND AS WITH THE OTHER HOSTILES WE'VE ENCOUNTERED... THIS BOGEY'S VECTORING STRAIGHT IN TOWARDS THE BAXTER BUILDING, SIR. TOWARDS US.
WE'VE DETECTED ONE ANOMALY IN ITS ATMOSPHERIC ENTRY, THOUGH...
AT CERTAIN INTERVALS, THE BOGEY SEEMS TO ABLATE AND BREAK UP EXPLOSIVELY...
...AND THEN IT APPEARS SUDDENLY INTACT AGAIN. VERY PECULIAR.
METATALENT OPS ASSISTANT DIRECTOR AGATHA HARKNESS
SIR! THE BOGEY'S AEREOBREAKING HAS DROPPED ITS AIRSPEED TO THE POINT THAT ITS FRICTION HEAT SHROUD IS DISSIPATING...
...SO WE SHOULD HAVE A BETTER LOOK AT IT, NOW...!
METATALENT OPS TECHNICIAN ALICIA MASTERS
AH...!
WE'RE GETTING AN EXCELLENT VIDEO FEED FROM SOME UPPER-ATMOSPHERE RECON DRONES, SIR...
...TRANSFERRING THE FEED TO OUR MAIN SCREEN...
HUH. WELL.

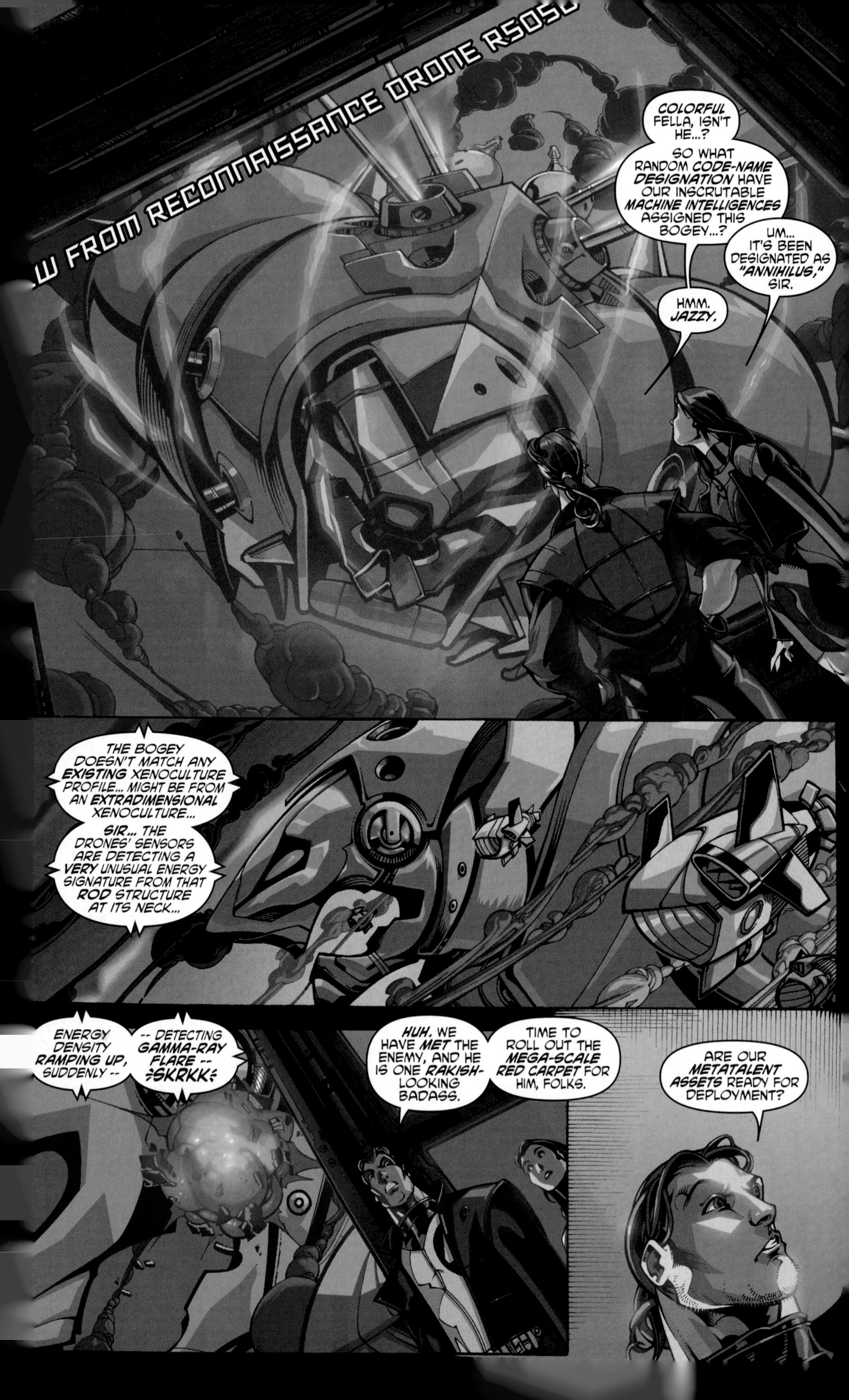
W FROM RECONNAISSANCE DRONE R505
COLORFUL FELLA, ISN'T HE...?
SO WHAT RANDOM CODE-NAME DESIGNATION HAVE OUR INSCRUTABLE MACHINE INTELLIGENCES ASSIGNED THIS BOGEY...?
UM... IT'S BEEN DESIGNATED AS "ANNIHILUS," SIR.
HMM. JAZZY.
THE BOGEY DOESN'T MATCH ANY EXISTING XENOCULTURE PROFILE... MIGHT BE FROM AN EXTRADIMENSIONAL XENOCULTURE...
SIR... THE DRONES' SENSORS ARE DETECTING A VERY UNUSUAL ENERGY SIGNATURE FROM THAT ROD STRUCTURE AT ITS NECK...
ENERGY DENSITY RAMPING UP, SUDDENLY --
-- DETECTING GAMMA-RAY FLARE -- SKRKK
HUH. WE HAVE MET THE ENEMY, AND HE IS ONE RAKISH-LOOKING BADASS.
TIME TO ROLL OUT THE MEGA-SCALE RED CARPET FOR HIM, FOLKS.
ARE OUR METATALENT ASSETS READY FOR DEPLOYMENT?

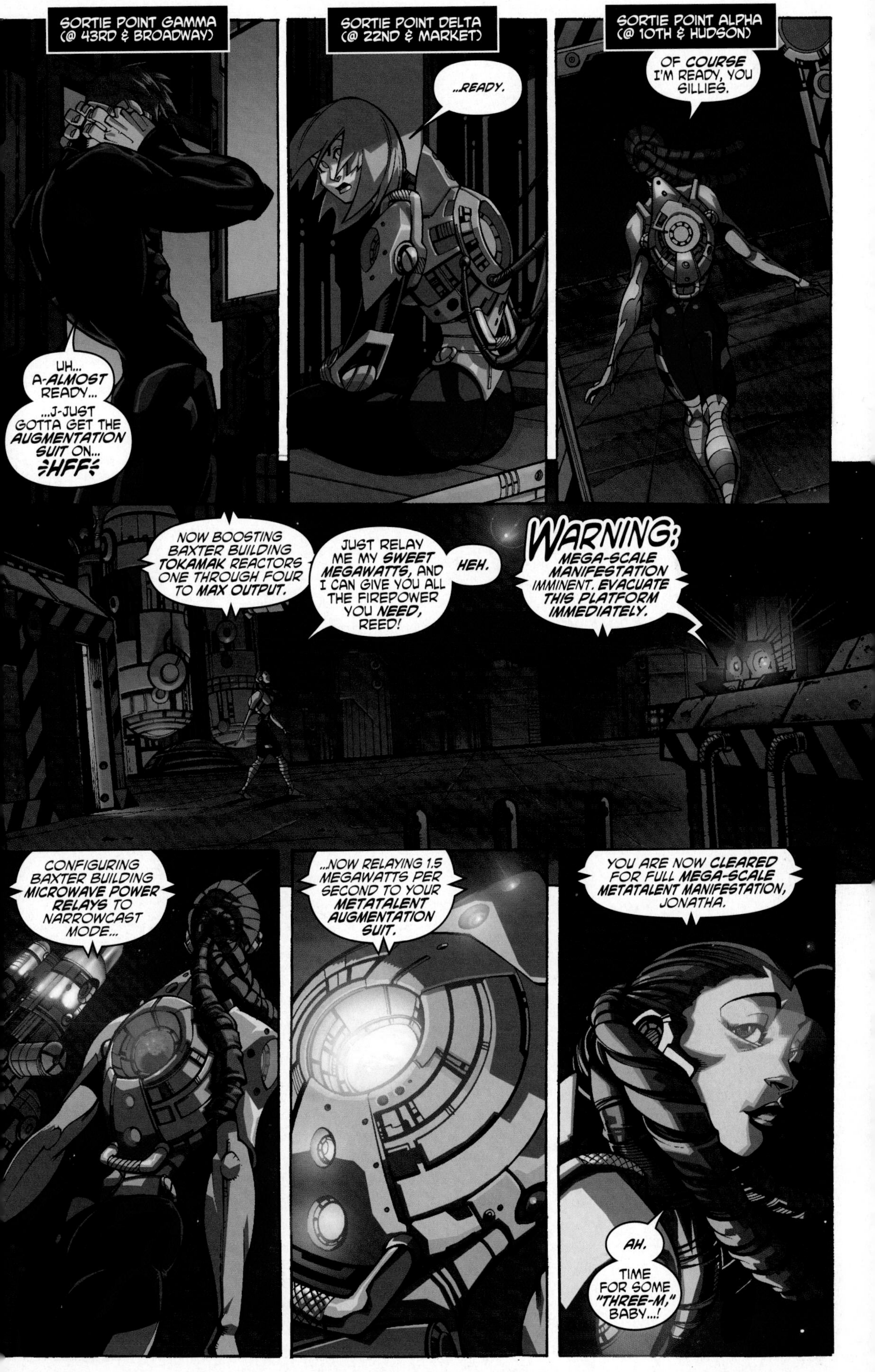
SORTIE POINT GAMMA (@ 43RD & BROADWAY)
UH... A-ALMOST READY... ...J-JUST GOTTA GET THE AUGMENTATION SUIT ON... HFF
SORTIE POINT DELTA (@ 22ND & MARKET)
...READY.
SORTIE POINT ALPHA (@ 10TH & HUDSON)
OF COURSE I'M READY, YOU SILLIES.
NOW BOOSTING BAXTER BUILDING TOKAMAK REACTORS ONE THROUGH FOUR TO MAX OUTPUT.
JUST RELAY ME MY SWEET MEGAWATTS, AND I CAN GIVE YOU ALL THE FIREPOWER YOU NEED, REED!
HEH.
WARNING: MEGA-SCALE MANIFESTATION IMMINENT. EVACUATE THIS PLATFORM IMMEDIATELY.
CONFIGURING BAXTER BUILDING MICROWAVE POWER RELAYS TO NARROWCAST MODE...
...NOW RELAYING 1.5 MEGAWATTS PER SECOND TO YOUR METATALENT AUGMENTATION SUIT.
YOU ARE NOW CLEARED FOR FULL MEGA-SCALE METATALENT MANIFESTATION, JONATHA.
AH.
TIME FOR SOME "THREE-M," BABY...!

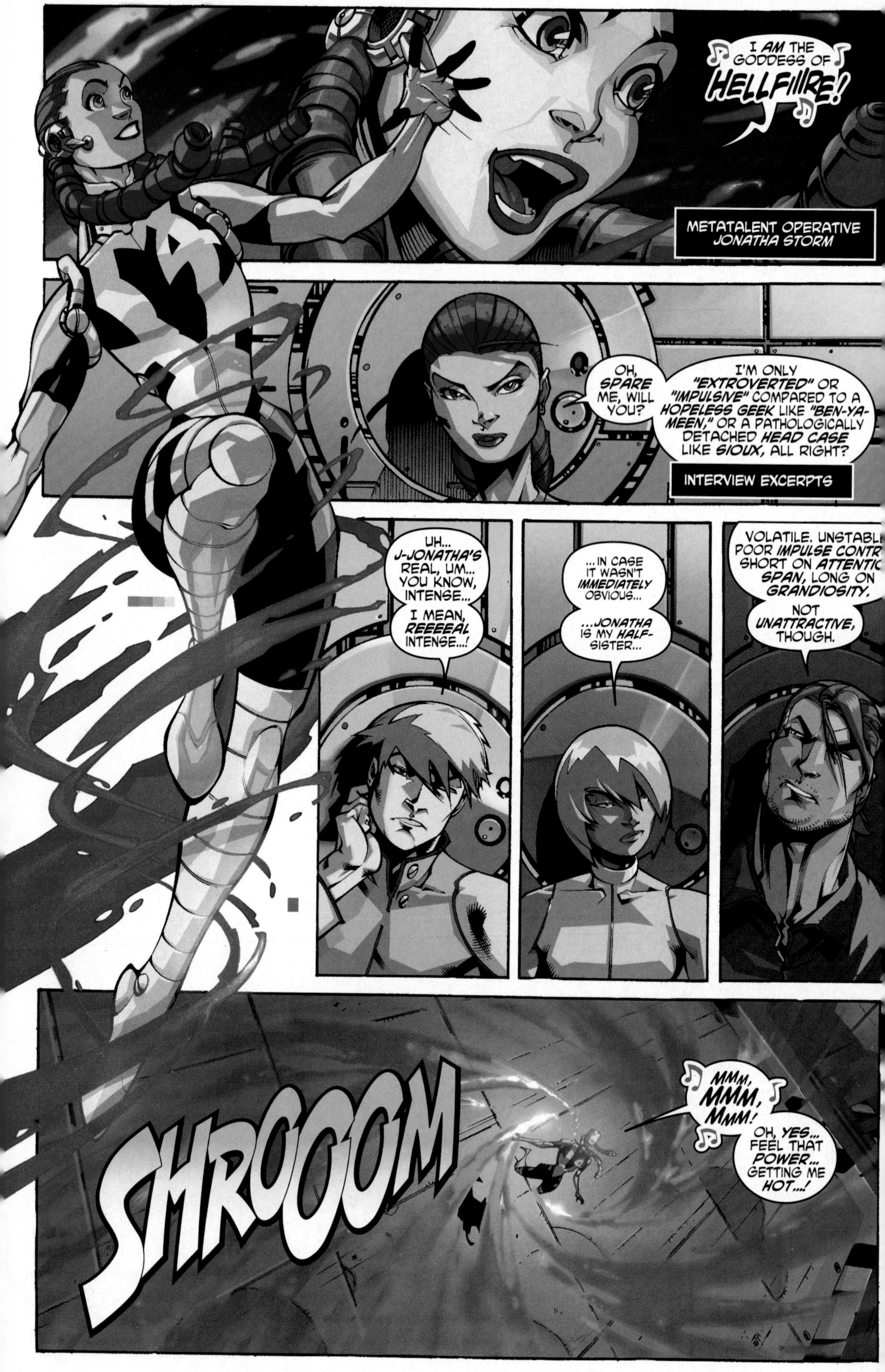
I AM THE GODDESS OF HELLFIIIRE!
METATALENT OPERATIVE JONATHA STORM
OH, SPARE ME, WILL YOU?
I'M ONLY "EXTROVERTED" OR "IMPULSIVE" COMPARED TO A HOPELESS GEEK LIKE "BEN-YAMEEN," OR A PATHOLOGICALLY DETACHED HEAD CASE LIKE SIOUX, ALL RIGHT?
INTERVIEW EXCERPTS
UH... J-JONATHA'S REAL, UM... YOU KNOW, INTENSE...
I MEAN, REEEEAL INTENSE...!
...IN CASE IT WASN'T IMMEDIATELY OBVIOUS...
...JONATHA IS MY HALF-SISTER...
VOLATILE. UNSTABL POOR IMPULSE CONTR SHORT ON ATTENTIC SPAN, LONG ON GRANDIOSITY.
NOT UNATTRACTIVE, THOUGH.
SHROOOM
MMM, MMM, MMM!
OH, YES... FEEL THAT POWER... GETTING ME HOT...!

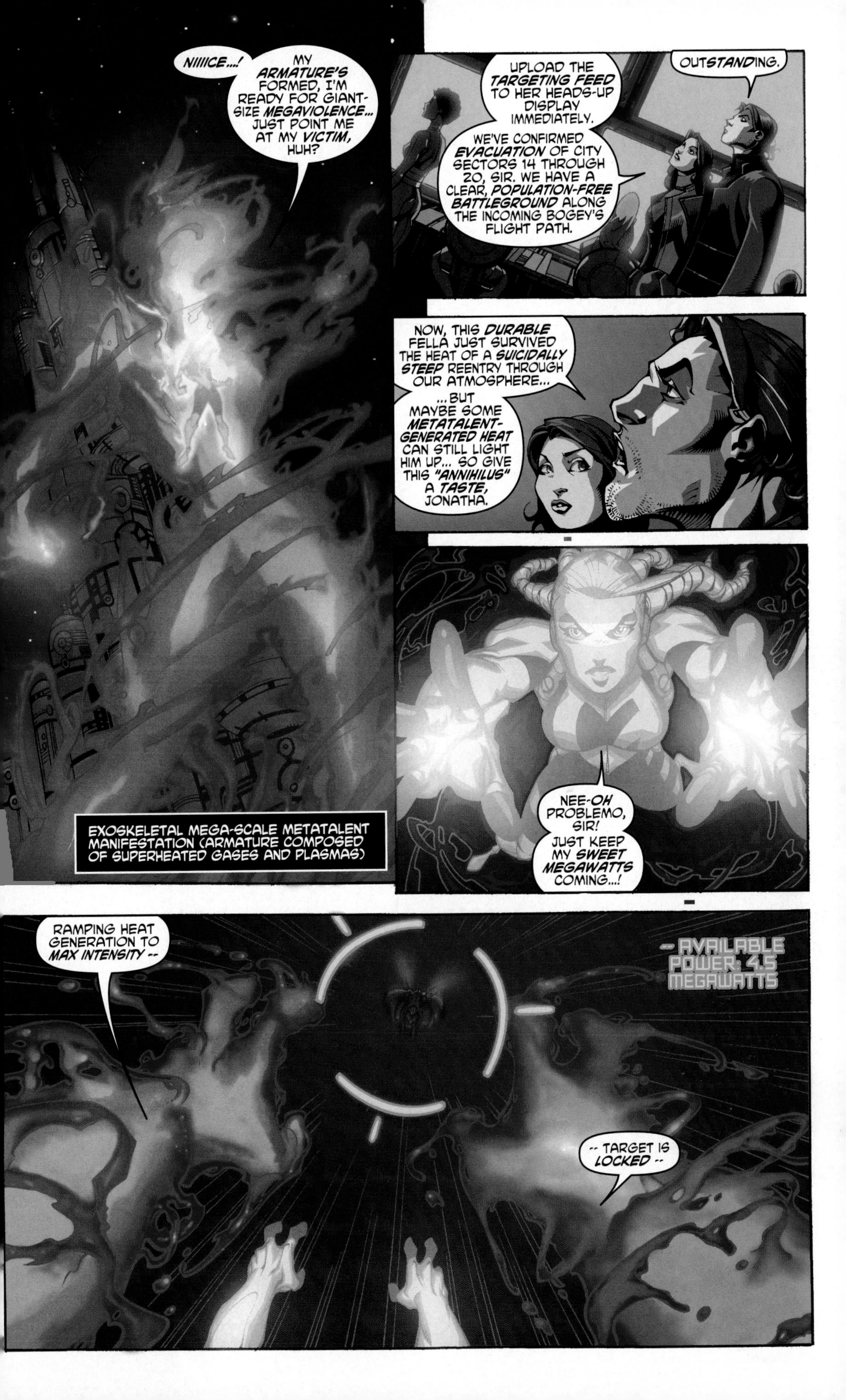
NIIIICE...!
MY ARMATURE'S FORMED, I'M READY FOR GIANT-SIZE MEGAVIOLENCE... JUST POINT ME AT MY VICTIM, HUH?
EXOSKELETAL MEGA-SCALE METATALENT MANIFESTATION (ARMATURE COMPOSED OF SUPERHEATED GASES AND PLASMAS)
UPLOAD THE TARGETING FEED TO HER HEADS-UP DISPLAY IMMEDIATELY.
WE'VE CONFIRMED EVACUATION OF CITY SECTORS 14 THROUGH 20, SIR. WE HAVE A CLEAR, POPULATION-FREE BATTLEGROUND ALONG THE INCOMING BOGEY'S FLIGHT PATH.
OUTSTANDING.
NOW, THIS DURABLE FELLA JUST SURVIVED THE HEAT OF A SUICIDALLY STEEP REENTRY THROUGH OUR ATMOSPHERE...
...BUT MAYBE SOME METATALENT-GENERATED HEAT CAN STILL LIGHT HIM UP... SO GIVE THIS "ANNIHILUS" A TASTE, JONATHA.
NEE-OH PROBLEMO, SIR! JUST KEEP MY SWEET MEGAWATTS COMING...!
RAMPING HEAT GENERATION TO MAX INTENSITY --
-- AVAILABLE POWER: 4.5 MEGAWATTS
-- TARGET IS LOCKED --

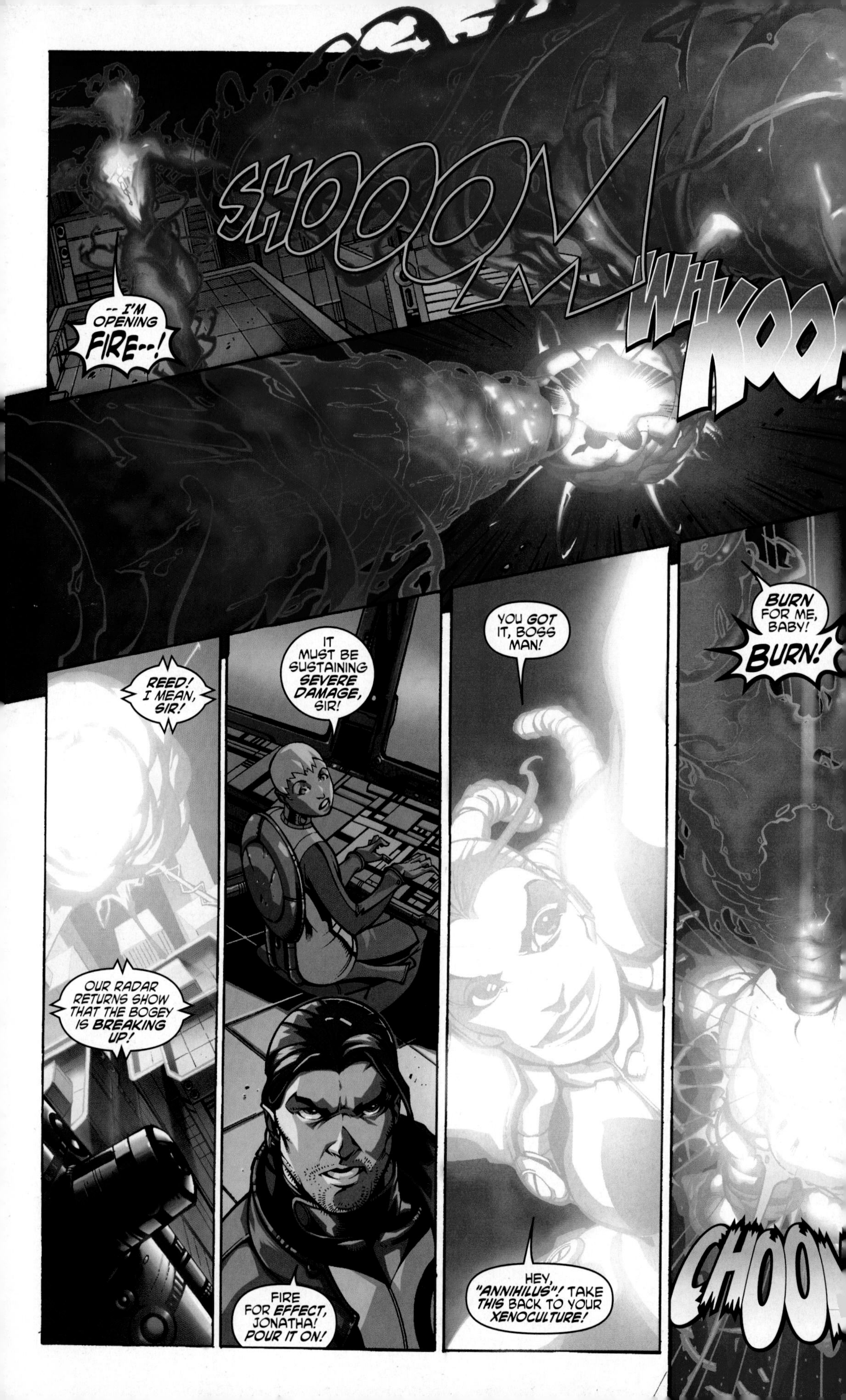
-- I'M OPENING FIRE--!
SHOOOOM
WHKOOM
REED! I MEAN, SIR!
OUR RADAR RETURNS SHOW THAT THE BOGEY IS BREAKING UP!
IT MUST BE SUSTAINING SEVERE DAMAGE, SIR!
FIRE FOR EFFECT, JONATHA! POUR IT ON!
YOU GOT IT, BOSS MAN!
HEY, "ANNIHILUS"! TAKE THIS BACK TO YOUR XENOCULTURE!
BURN FOR ME, BABY! BURN!
CHOOM

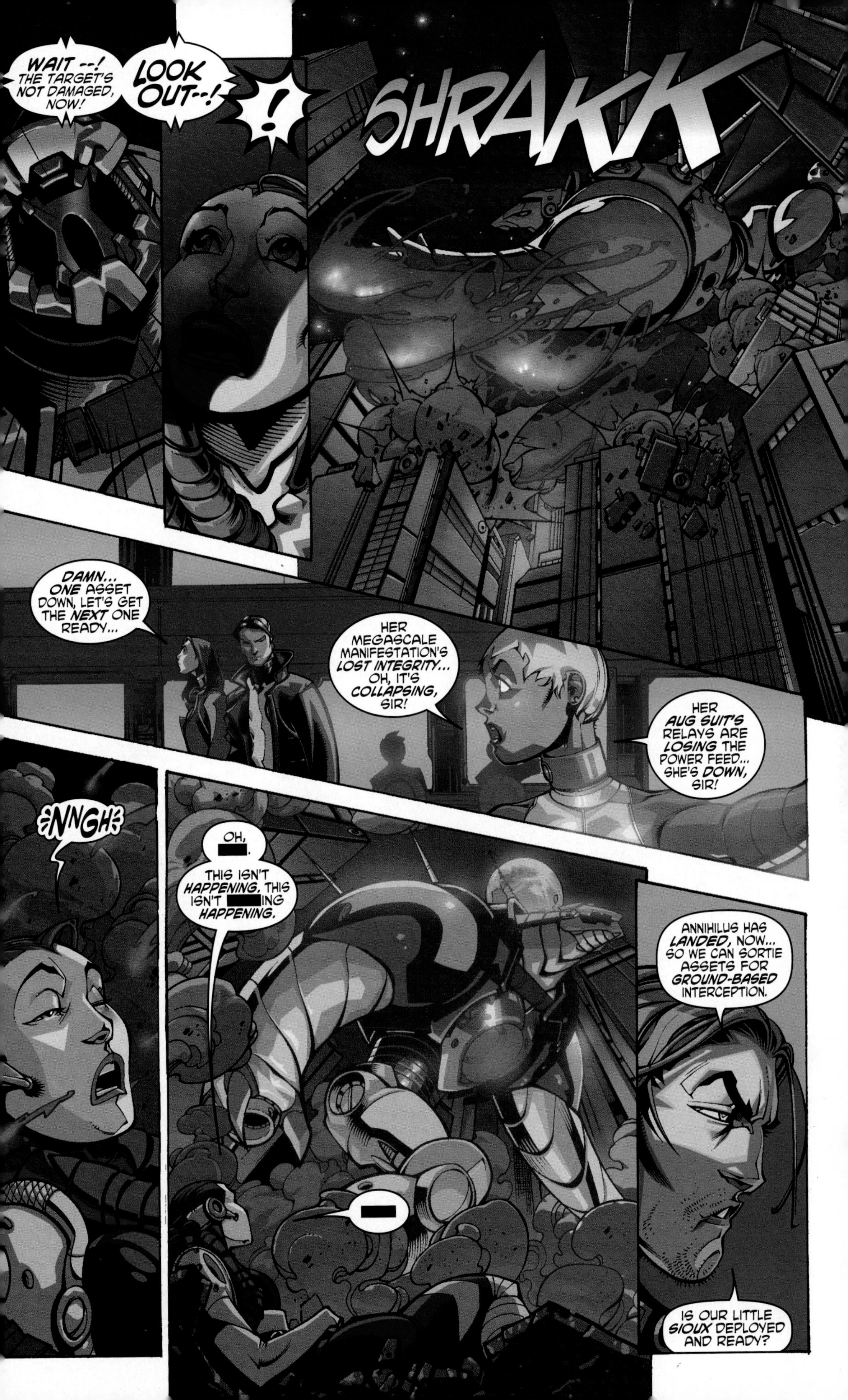
WAIT --! THE TARGET'S NOT DAMAGED, NOW!
LOOK OUT--!
!
SHRAKK
DAMN... ONE ASSET DOWN, LET'S GET THE NEXT ONE READY...
HER MEGASCALE MANIFESTATION'S LOST INTEGRITY... OH, IT'S COLLAPSING, SIR!
HER AUG SUIT'S RELAYS ARE LOSING THE POWER FEED... SHE'S DOWN, SIR!
NNGH
OH, [redacted].
THIS ISN'T HAPPENING, THIS ISN'T [redacted]ING HAPPENING.
[redacted]
ANNIHILUS HAS LANDED, NOW... SO WE CAN SORTIE ASSETS FOR GROUND-BASED INTERCEPTION.
IS OUR LITTLE SIOUX DEPLOYED AND READY?

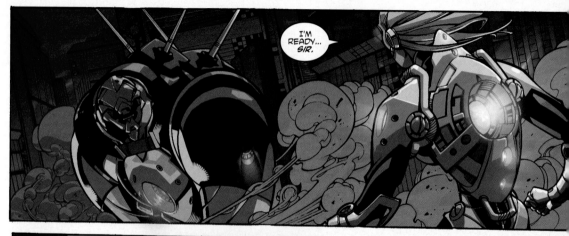

I'M READY... SIR.

MY *INVISIBLE FRIEND* IS FULLY FORMED.

WHAT DO YOU REQUIRE ME TO DO...?

HER *AUG SUIT'S* DUMPING NEAR-OVERDOSES OF *WARDRUGS* AND *AGGRESSOR HORMONES* INTO HER BLOODSTREAM... AND THIS IS AS *PUMPED-UP* AS WE CAN MAKE HER...

GOTTA LOVE THAT NEAR-*PSYCHOSIS*-LEVEL EMOTIONAL DETACHMENT...

ENGAGE THE BOGEY *HAND-TO-INVISIBLE-HAND,* SIOUX. I NEED YOU TO PUT A *SEVERE HURTIN'* ON HIM, UNDERSTAND?

UNDERSTOOD, SIR.

EXOSKELETAL MEGA-SCALE METATALENT MANIFESTATION (ARMATURE COMPOSED OF INVISIBLE FORCE FIELDS)

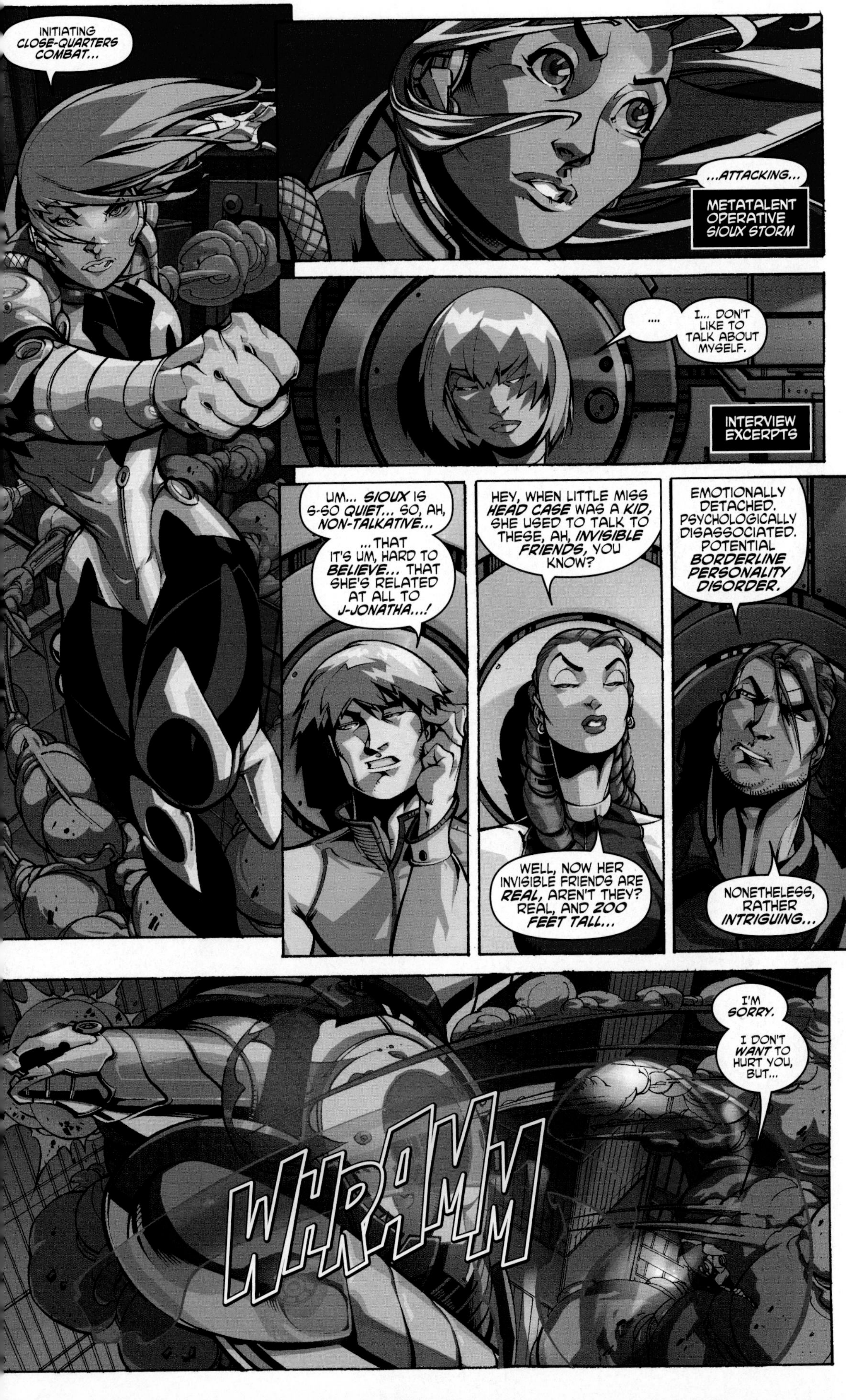
INITIATING CLOSE-QUARTERS COMBAT...
...ATTACKING...
METATALENT OPERATIVE SIOUX STORM
....
I... DON'T LIKE TO TALK ABOUT MYSELF.
INTERVIEW EXCERPTS
UM... SIOUX IS S-SO QUIET... SO, AH, NON-TALKATIVE...
...THAT IT'S UM, HARD TO BELIEVE... THAT SHE'S RELATED AT ALL TO J-JONATHA...!
HEY, WHEN LITTLE MISS HEAD CASE WAS A KID, SHE USED TO TALK TO THESE, AH, INVISIBLE FRIENDS, YOU KNOW?
WELL, NOW HER INVISIBLE FRIENDS ARE REAL, AREN'T THEY? REAL, AND 200 FEET TALL...
EMOTIONALLY DETACHED. PSYCHOLOGICALLY DISASSOCIATED. POTENTIAL BORDERLINE PERSONALITY DISORDER.
NONETHELESS, RATHER INTRIGUING...
I'M SORRY.
I DON'T WANT TO HURT YOU, BUT...
WHRAMM

PRETEND THAT THIS IS HAPPENING TO SOMEONE ELSE...

THAT'S WHAT I ALWAYS USED TO DO...

BOOM

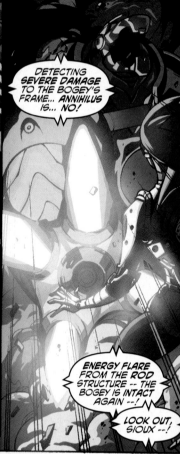

DETECTING SEVERE DAMAGE TO THE BOGEY'S FRAME... ANNIHILUS IS... NO!

ENERGY FLARE FROM THE ROD STRUCTURE -- THE BOGEY IS INTACT AGAIN --!

LOOK OUT, SIOUX --!

:UNNH:

WHRNNCH

GET ME A CRASH ANALYSIS ON THAT ROD'S ENERGY SIGNATURE, AGATHA.

NOW, BENJAMIN...

...IT'S YOUR TURN.

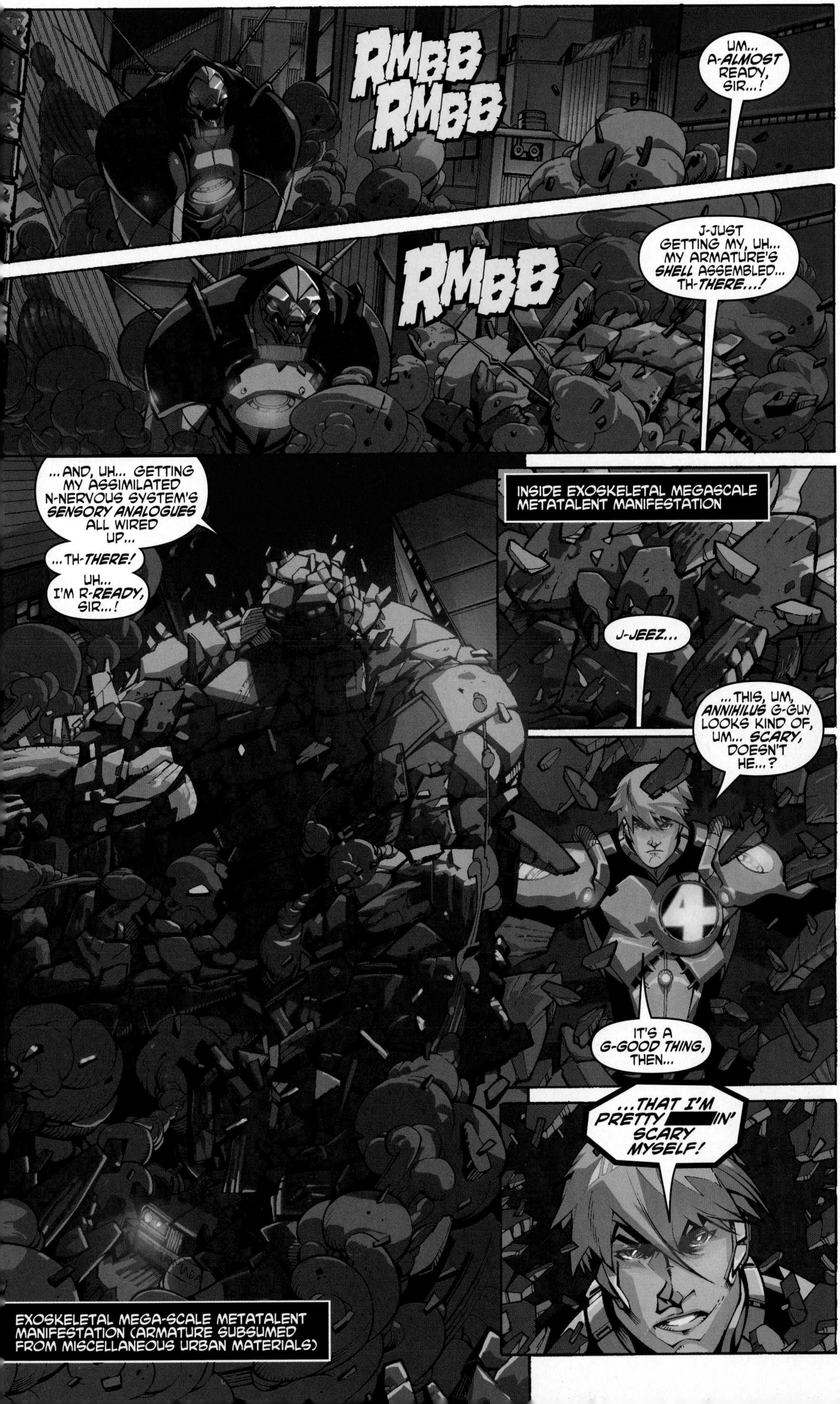
RMBB RMBB
UM... A-ALMOST READY, SIR...!
RMBB
J-JUST GETTING MY, UH... MY ARMATURE'S SHELL ASSEMBLED... TH-THERE...!
...AND, UH... GETTING MY ASSIMILATED N-NERVOUS SYSTEM'S SENSORY ANALOGUES ALL WIRED UP...
...TH-THERE!
UH... I'M R-READY, SIR...!
EXOSKELETAL MEGA-SCALE METATALENT MANIFESTATION (ARMATURE SUBSUMED FROM MISCELLANEOUS URBAN MATERIALS)
INSIDE EXOSKELETAL MEGASCALE METATALENT MANIFESTATION
J-JEEZ...
...THIS, UM, ANNIHILUS G-GUY LOOKS KIND OF, UM... SCARY, DOESN'T HE...?
IT'S A G-GOOD THING, THEN...
...THAT I'M PRETTY [redacted]IN' SCARY MYSELF!

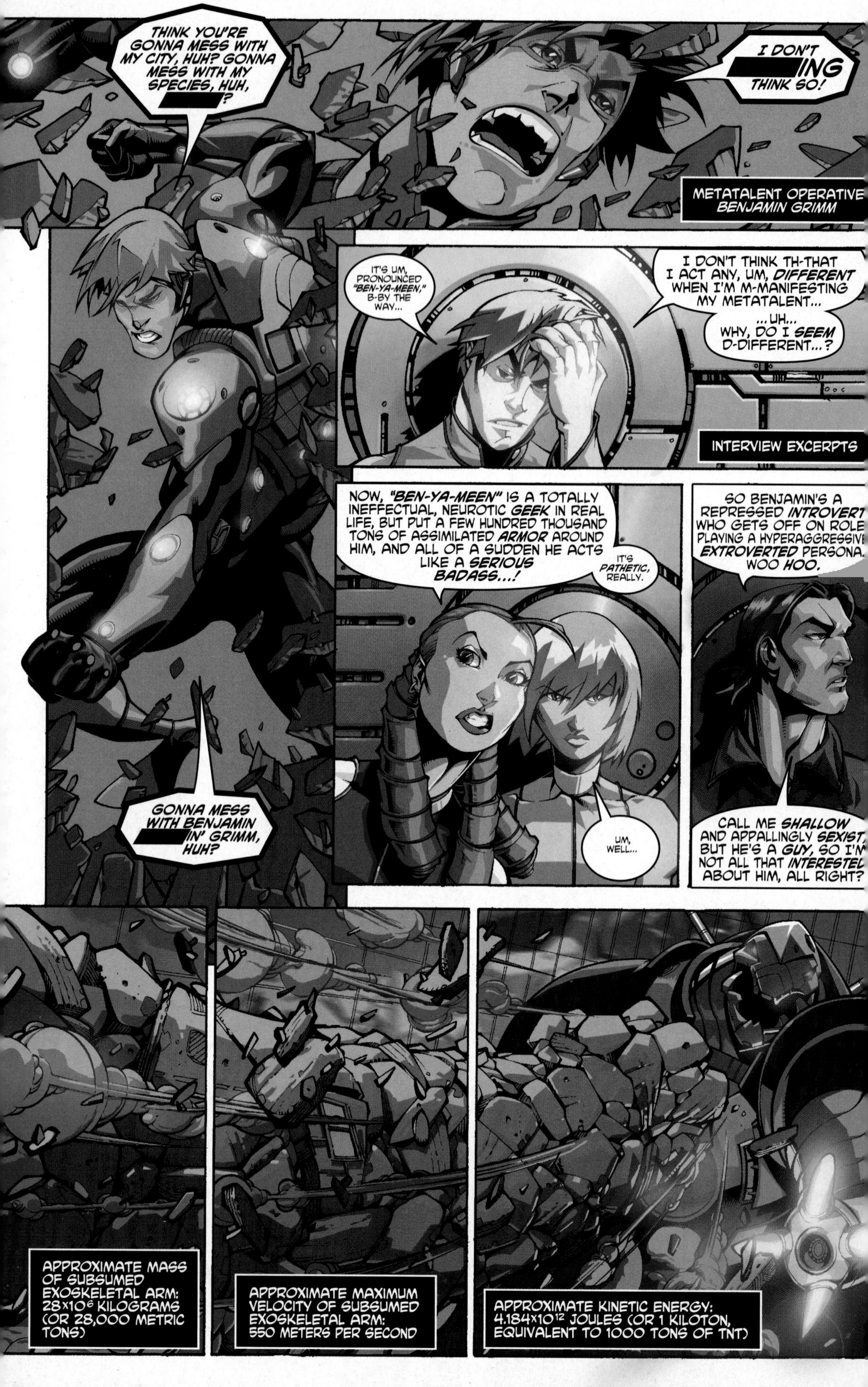
THINK YOU'RE GONNA MESS WITH MY CITY, HUH? GONNA MESS WITH MY SPECIES, HUH, [redacted]?
I DON'T [redacted]ING THINK SO!
METATALENT OPERATIVE BENJAMIN GRIMM
GONNA MESS WITH BENJAMIN [redacted]IN' GRIMM, HUH?
IT'S UM, PRONOUNCED "BEN-YA-MEEN," B-BY THE WAY...
I DON'T THINK TH-THAT I ACT ANY, UM, DIFFERENT WHEN I'M M-MANIFESTING MY METATALENT...
...UH... WHY, DO I SEEM D-DIFFERENT...?
INTERVIEW EXCERPTS
NOW, "BEN-YA-MEEN" IS A TOTALLY INEFFECTUAL, NEUROTIC GEEK IN REAL LIFE, BUT PUT A FEW HUNDRED THOUSAND TONS OF ASSIMILATED ARMOR AROUND HIM, AND ALL OF A SUDDEN HE ACTS LIKE A SERIOUS BADASS...!
IT'S PATHETIC, REALLY.
UM, WELL...
SO BENJAMIN'S A REPRESSED INTROVERT WHO GETS OFF ON ROLE PLAYING A HYPERAGGRESSIVE EXTROVERTED PERSONA. WOO HOO.
CALL ME SHALLOW AND APPALLINGLY SEXIST, BUT HE'S A GUY, SO I'M NOT ALL THAT INTERESTED ABOUT HIM, ALL RIGHT?
APPROXIMATE MASS OF SUBSUMED EXOSKELETAL ARM: 28×10^6 KILOGRAMS (OR 28,000 METRIC TONS)
APPROXIMATE MAXIMUM VELOCITY OF SUBSUMED EXOSKELETAL ARM: 550 METERS PER SECOND
APPROXIMATE KINETIC ENERGY: 4.184×10^{12} JOULES (OR 1 KILOTON, EQUIVALENT TO 1000 TONS OF TNT)

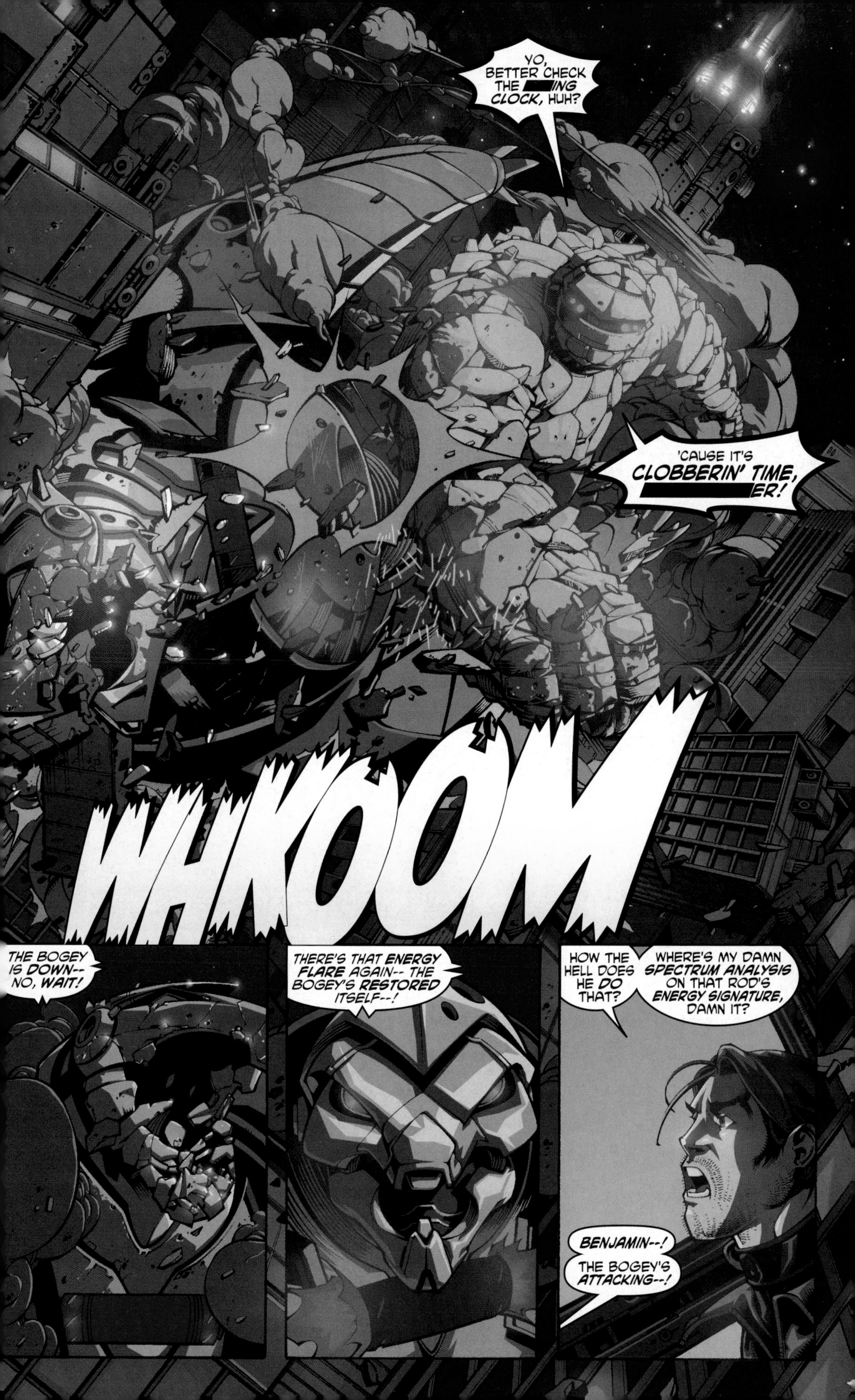
YO, BETTER CHECK THE [redacted]ING CLOCK, HUH?
'CAUSE IT'S CLOBBERIN' TIME, [redacted]ER!
WHKOOM
THE BOGEY IS DOWN-- NO, WAIT!
THERE'S THAT ENERGY FLARE AGAIN-- THE BOGEY'S RESTORED ITSELF--!
HOW THE HELL DOES HE DO THAT?
WHERE'S MY DAMN SPECTRUM ANALYSIS ON THAT ROD'S ENERGY SIGNATURE, DAMN IT?
BENJAMIN--!
THE BOGEY'S ATTACKING--!

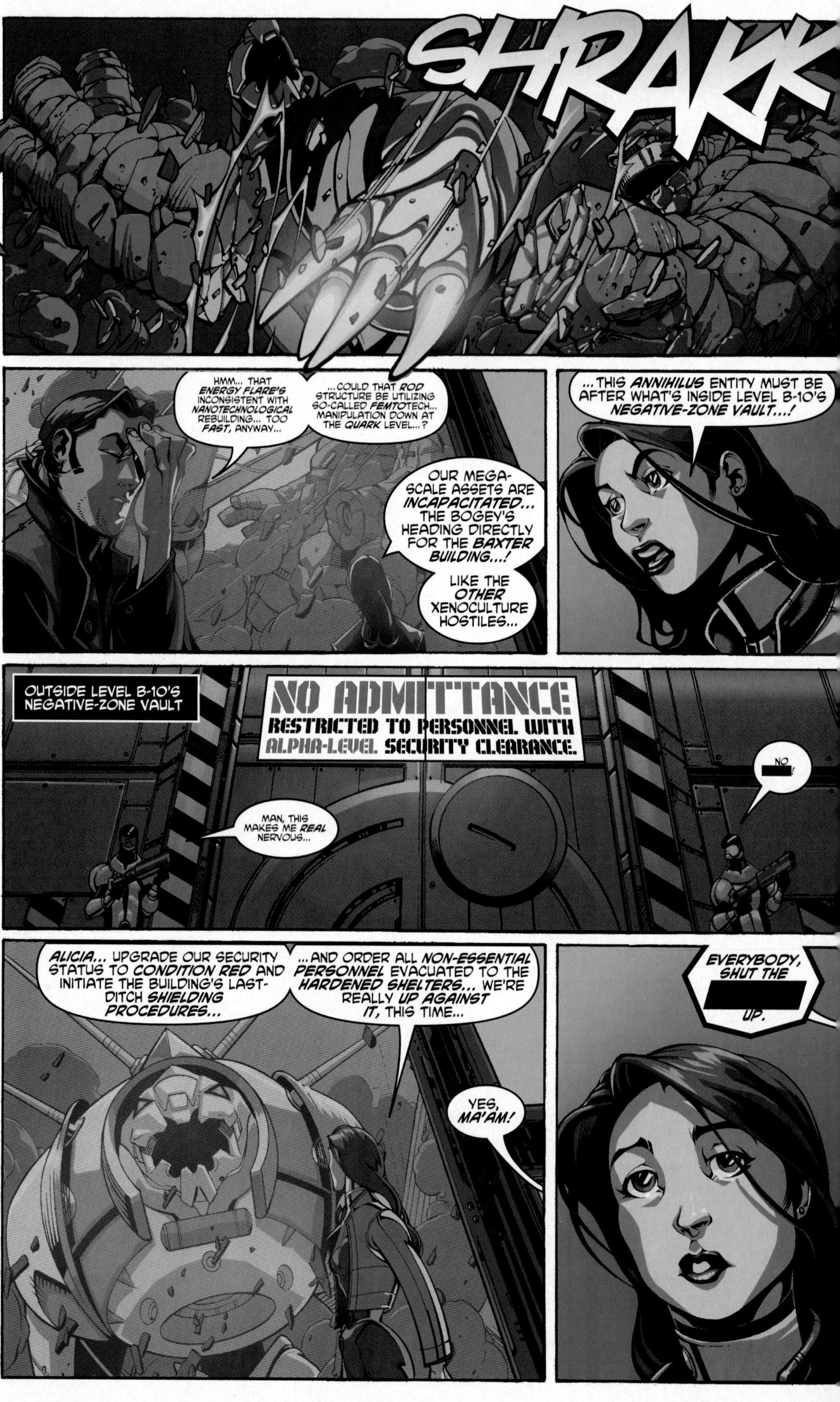
SHRAKK
HMM... THAT ENERGY FLARE'S INCONSISTENT WITH NANOTECHNOLOGICAL REBUILDING... TOO FAST, ANYWAY...
...COULD THAT ROD STRUCTURE BE UTILIZING SO-CALLED FEMTOTECH... MANIPULATION DOWN AT THE QUARK LEVEL...?
OUR MEGA-SCALE ASSETS ARE INCAPACITATED... THE BOGEY'S HEADING DIRECTLY FOR THE BAXTER BUILDING...!
LIKE THE OTHER XENOCULTURE HOSTILES...
...THIS ANNIHILUS ENTITY MUST BE AFTER WHAT'S INSIDE LEVEL B-10'S NEGATIVE-ZONE VAULT...!
OUTSIDE LEVEL B-10'S NEGATIVE-ZONE VAULT
NO ADMITTANCE
RESTRICTED TO PERSONNEL WITH ALPHA-LEVEL SECURITY CLEARANCE.
MAN, THIS MAKES ME REAL NERVOUS...
NO [redacted]!
ALICIA... UPGRADE OUR SECURITY STATUS TO CONDITION RED AND INITIATE THE BUILDING'S LAST-DITCH SHIELDING PROCEDURES...
...AND ORDER ALL NON-ESSENTIAL PERSONNEL EVACUATED TO THE HARDENED SHELTERS... WE'RE REALLY UP AGAINST IT, THIS TIME...
YES, MA'AM!
EVERYBODY, SHUT THE [redacted] UP.

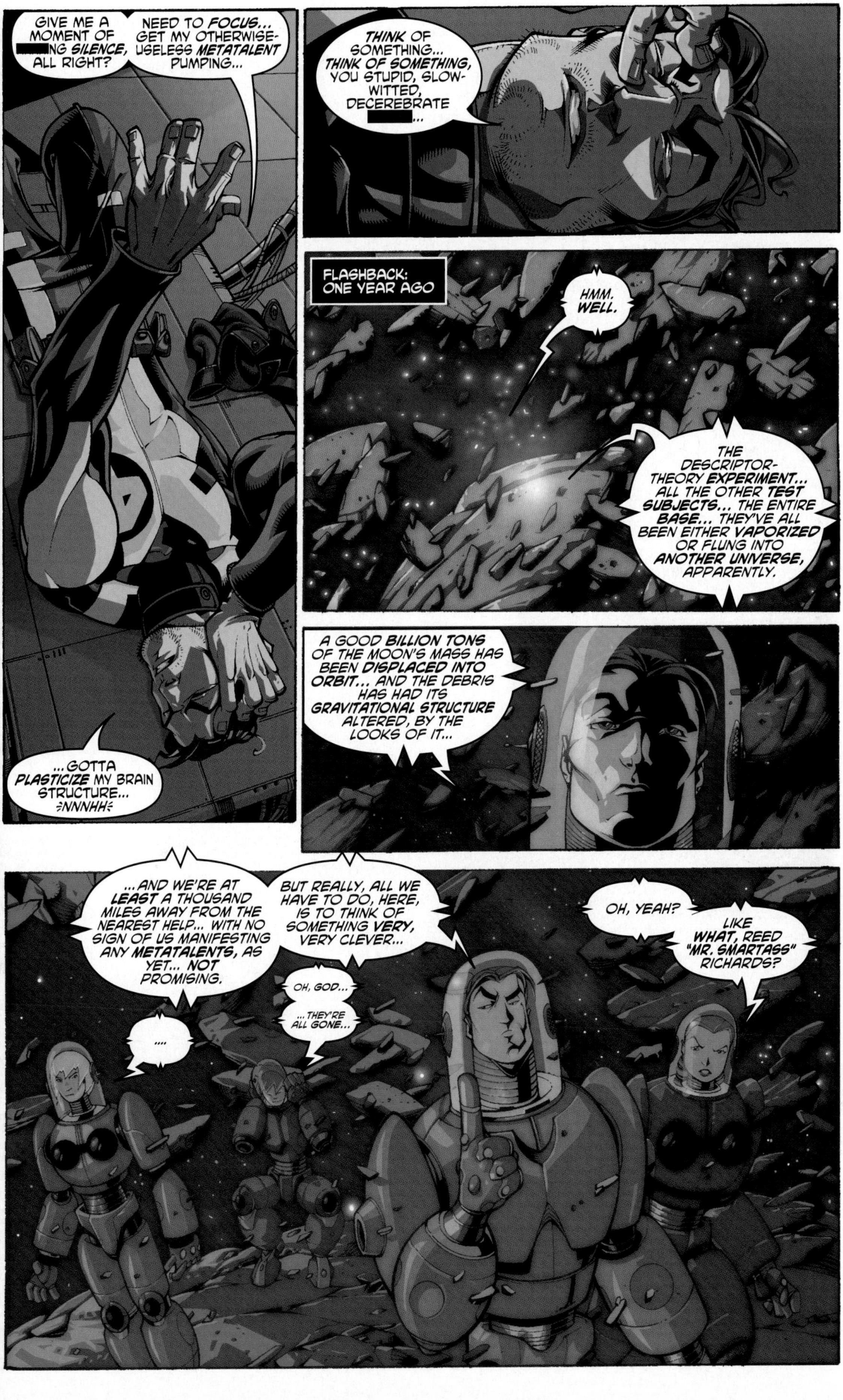

GIVE ME A MOMENT OF [redacted]ING SILENCE, ALL RIGHT?
NEED TO FOCUS... GET MY OTHERWISE-USELESS METATALENT PUMPING...
...GOTTA PLASTICIZE MY BRAIN STRUCTURE... NNNHH
THINK OF SOMETHING... THINK OF SOMETHING, YOU STUPID, SLOW-WITTED, DECEREBRATE [redacted]...
FLASHBACK: ONE YEAR AGO
HMM. WELL.
THE DESCRIPTOR-THEORY EXPERIMENT... ALL THE OTHER TEST SUBJECTS... THE ENTIRE BASE... THEY'VE ALL BEEN EITHER VAPORIZED OR FLUNG INTO ANOTHER UNIVERSE, APPARENTLY.
A GOOD BILLION TONS OF THE MOON'S MASS HAS BEEN DISPLACED INTO ORBIT... AND THE DEBRIS HAS HAD ITS GRAVITATIONAL STRUCTURE ALTERED, BY THE LOOKS OF IT...
...AND WE'RE AT LEAST A THOUSAND MILES AWAY FROM THE NEAREST HELP... WITH NO SIGN OF US MANIFESTING ANY METATALENTS, AS YET... NOT PROMISING.
BUT REALLY, ALL WE HAVE TO DO, HERE, IS TO THINK OF SOMETHING VERY, VERY CLEVER...
OH, YEAH?
LIKE WHAT, REED "MR. SMARTASS" RICHARDS?
....
OH, GOD...
...THEY'RE ALL GONE...

GET THOSE NEURONS STRETCHING... BRANCH OFF THOSE NEW AXONS AND DENDRITES...

THIS ANNIHILUS KEEPS RESTORING HIMSELF EVERY TIME HE'S SERIOUSLY DAMAGED... HOW'S HE DOING IT... AND HOW TO STOP HIM...?

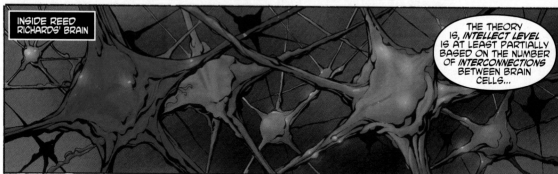

INSIDE REED RICHARDS' BRAIN

THE THEORY IS, INTELLECT LEVEL IS AT LEAST PARTIALLY BASED ON THE NUMBER OF INTERCONNECTIONS BETWEEN BRAIN CELLS...

FLASHBACK: FOUR MONTHS AGO

...SO, CRUDELY PUT, THE MORE CONNECTIONS THERE ARE BETWEEN YOUR BRAIN'S BILLIONFOLD NEURONS, THE SMARTER YOU ARE, RIGHT?

WHICH IS WHERE MY OTHERWISE-UNIMPRESSIVE ELASTICITY METATALENT BECOMES RELEVANT, AGATHA...!

MMM HMM...?

SEE, I CAN USE MY METATALENT TO TEMPORARILY MAKE MY BRAIN CELLS STRETCH EN MASSE, EXTENDING MILLIONS OF NEW CONNECTIONS TO EACH OTHER...

FLASHBACK: TWO MONTHS AGO.

...AND THIS EXPONENTIAL INCREASE IN NEURAL INTERCONNECTIONS GIVES ME A BURST OF AUGMENTED INTELLIGENCE...

...ALLOWING ME SOME OCCASIONALLY CRUIAL COGNITIVE BREAKTHROUGHS AND INTUITIVE LEAPS, RIGHT, ALICIA?

OH, REALLY, REED...?

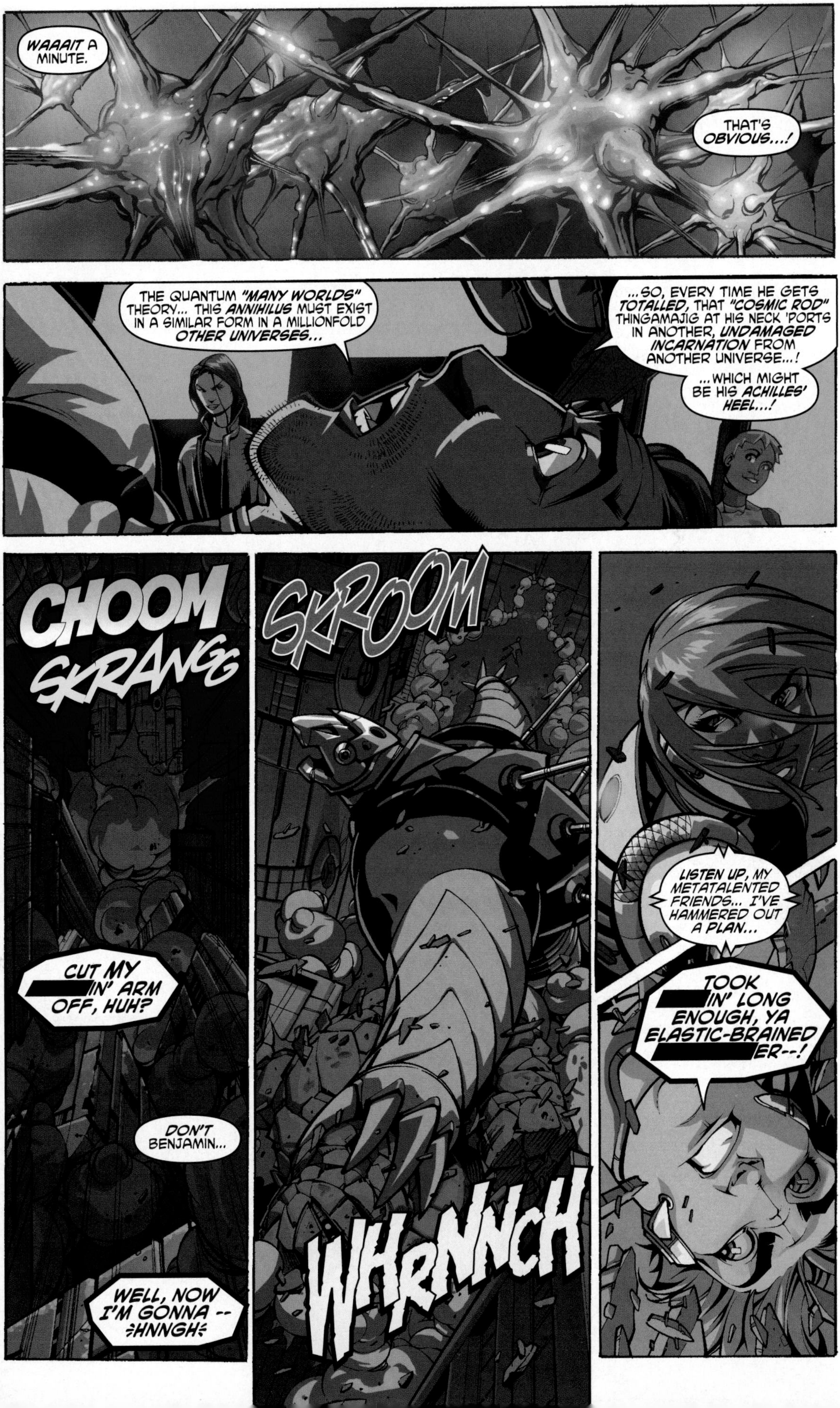
WAAAIT A MINUTE.
THAT'S OBVIOUS...!
THE QUANTUM "MANY WORLDS" THEORY... THIS ANNIHILUS MUST EXIST IN A SIMILAR FORM IN A MILLIONFOLD OTHER UNIVERSES...
...SO, EVERY TIME HE GETS TOTALLED, THAT "COSMIC ROD" THINGAMAJIG AT HIS NECK 'PORTS IN ANOTHER, UNDAMAGED INCARNATION FROM ANOTHER UNIVERSE...!
...WHICH MIGHT BE HIS ACHILLES' HEEL...!
CHOOM
SKRANGG
CUT MY [redacted]IN' ARM OFF, HUH?
DON'T BENJAMIN...
WELL, NOW I'M GONNA -- HNNGH
SKROOM
WHRNNCH
LISTEN UP, MY METATALENTED FRIENDS... I'VE HAMMERED OUT A PLAN...
TOOK [redacted]IN' LONG ENOUGH, YA ELASTIC-BRAINED [redacted]ER--!

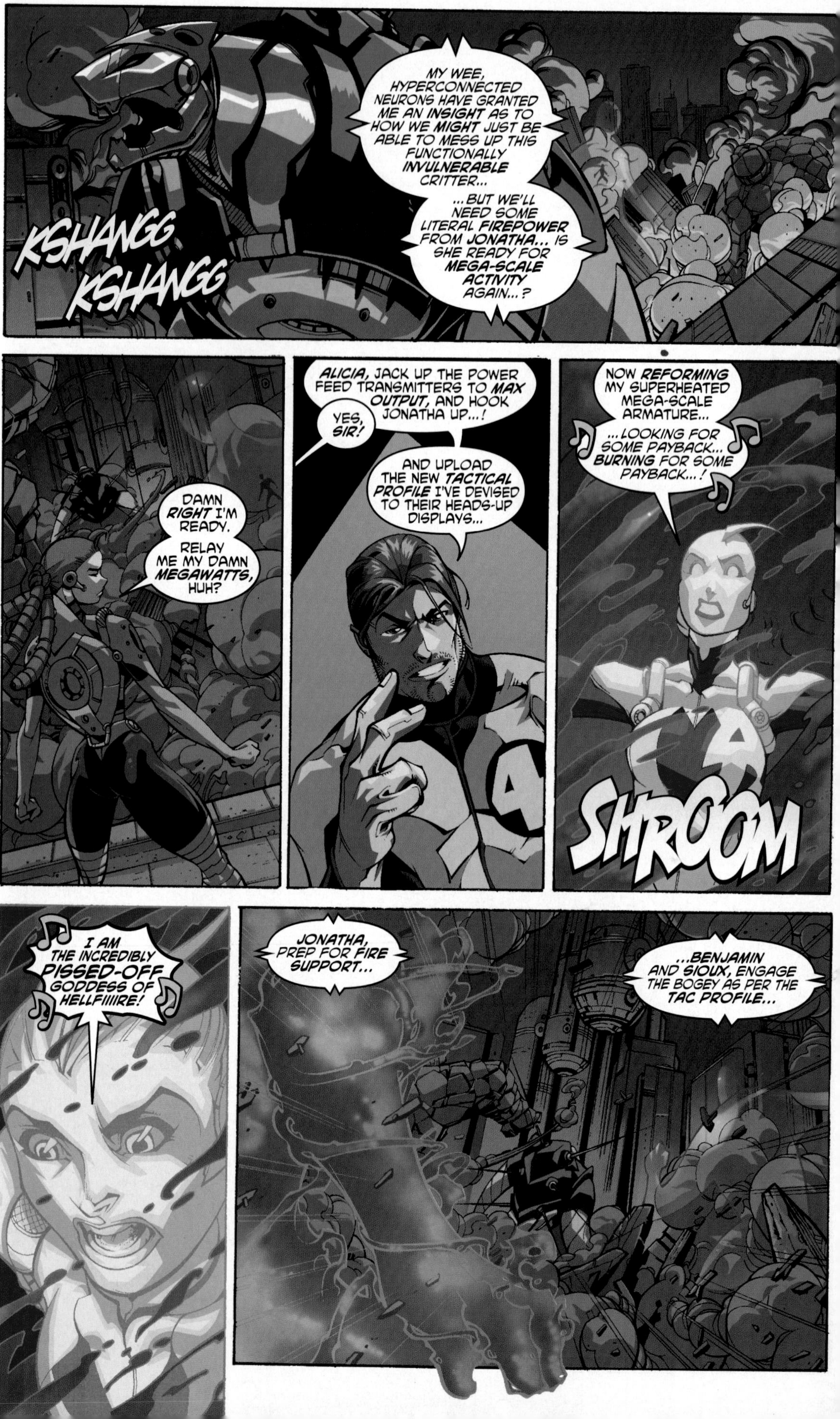
MY WEE, HYPERCONNECTED NEURONS HAVE GRANTED ME AN INSIGHT AS TO HOW WE MIGHT JUST BE ABLE TO MESS UP THIS FUNCTIONALLY INVULNERABLE CRITTER...
...BUT WE'LL NEED SOME LITERAL FIREPOWER FROM JONATHA... IS SHE READY FOR MEGA-SCALE ACTIVITY AGAIN...?
KSHANGG KSHANGG
DAMN RIGHT I'M READY.
RELAY ME MY DAMN MEGAWATTS, HUH?
ALICIA, JACK UP THE POWER FEED TRANSMITTERS TO MAX OUTPUT, AND HOOK JONATHA UP...!
YES, SIR!
AND UPLOAD THE NEW TACTICAL PROFILE I'VE DEVISED TO THEIR HEADS-UP DISPLAYS...
NOW REFORMING MY SUPERHEATED MEGA-SCALE ARMATURE...
...LOOKING FOR SOME PAYBACK... BURNING FOR SOME PAYBACK...!
SHROOM
I AM THE INCREDIBLY PISSED-OFF GODDESS OF HELLFIIIIRE!
JONATHA, PREP FOR FIRE SUPPORT...
...BENJAMIN AND SIOUX, ENGAGE THE BOGEY AS PER THE TAC PROFILE...

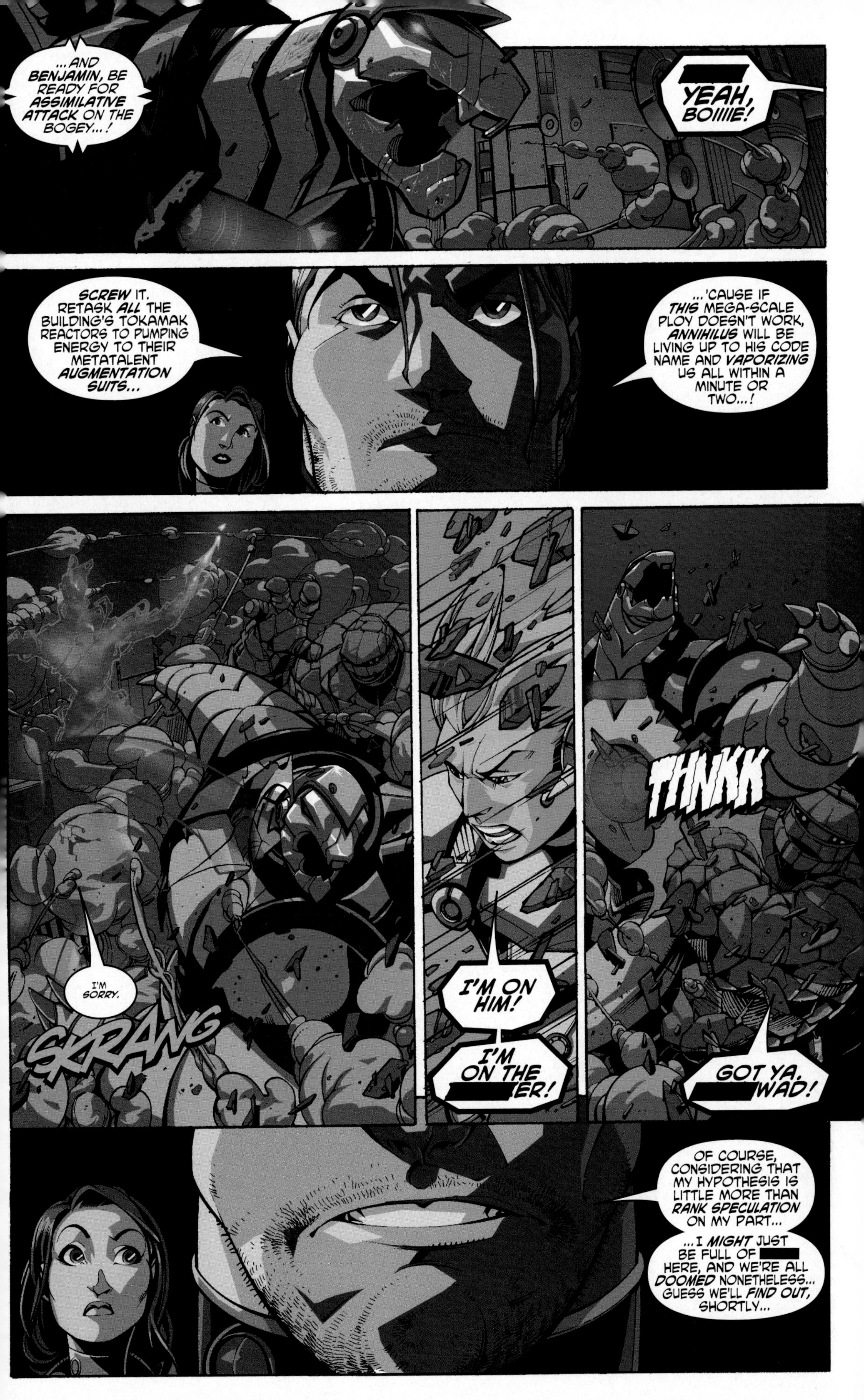
...AND BENJAMIN, BE READY FOR ASSIMILATIVE ATTACK ON THE BOGEY...!
[redacted] YEAH, BOIIIIE!
SCREW IT. RETASK ALL THE BUILDING'S TOKAMAK REACTORS TO PUMPING ENERGY TO THEIR METATALENT AUGMENTATION SUITS...
...'CAUSE IF THIS MEGA-SCALE PLOY DOESN'T WORK, ANNIHILUS WILL BE LIVING UP TO HIS CODE NAME AND VAPORIZING US ALL WITHIN A MINUTE OR TWO...!
I'M SORRY.
SKRANG
I'M ON HIM!
I'M ON THE [redacted]ER!
THNKK
GOT YA, [redacted]WAD!
OF COURSE, CONSIDERING THAT MY HYPOTHESIS IS LITTLE MORE THAN RANK SPECULATION ON MY PART...
...I MIGHT JUST BE FULL OF [redacted] HERE, AND WE'RE ALL DOOMED NONETHELESS... GUESS WE'LL FIND OUT, SHORTLY...

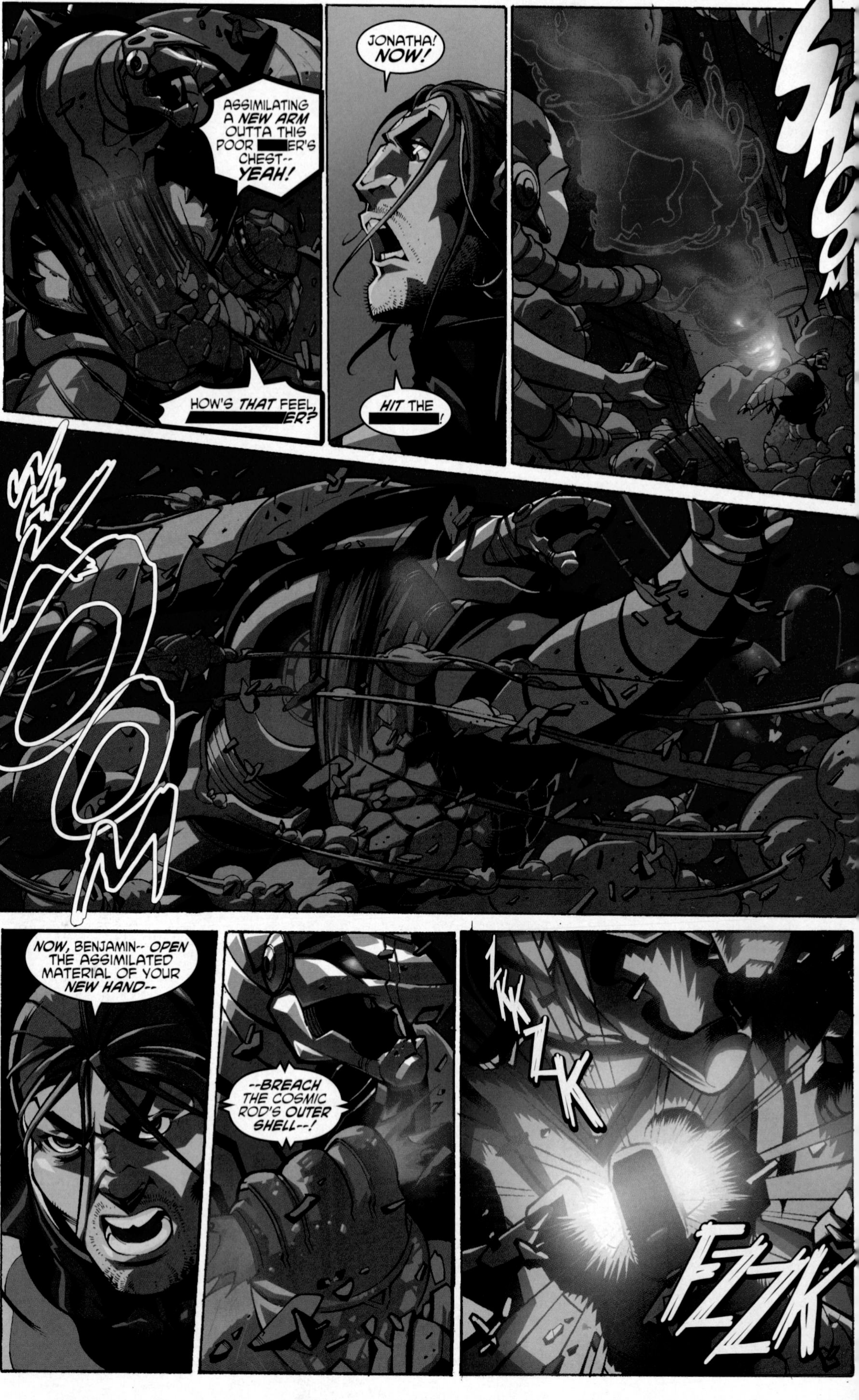

ASSIMILATING A NEW ARM OUTTA THIS POOR [redacted]ER'S CHEST-- YEAH!
HOW'S THAT FEEL, [redacted]ER?
JONATHA! NOW!
HIT THE [redacted]!
SHOOOM
VOOOM
NOW, BENJAMIN-- OPEN THE ASSIMILATED MATERIAL OF YOUR NEW HAND--
--BREACH THE COSMIC ROD'S OUTER SHELL--!
ZKKZK
FZZK

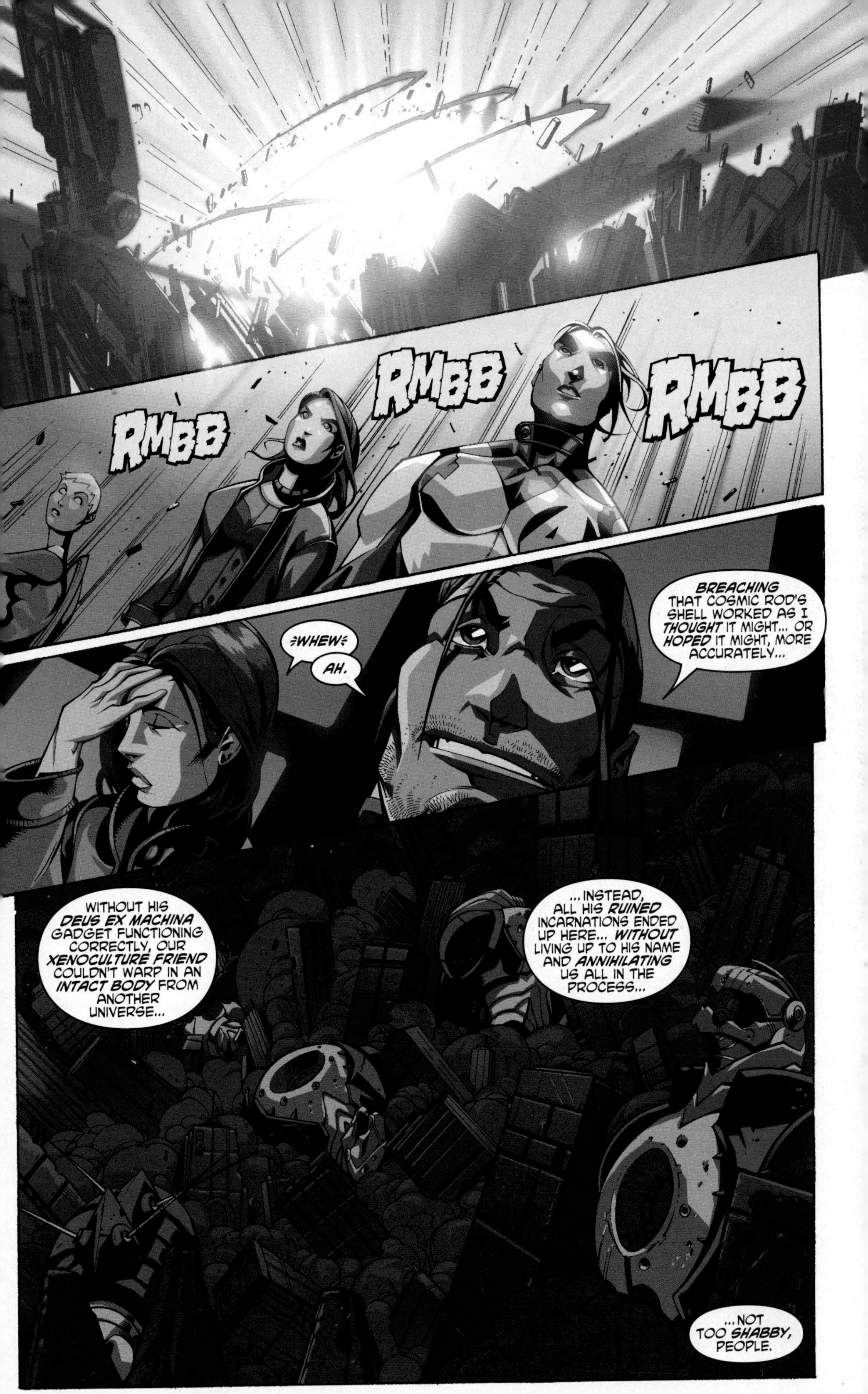
RMBB
RMBB
RMBB
BREACHING THAT COSMIC ROD'S SHELL WORKED AS I THOUGHT IT MIGHT... OR HOPED IT MIGHT, MORE ACCURATELY...
WHEW
AH.
WITHOUT HIS DEUS EX MACHINA GADGET FUNCTIONING CORRECTLY, OUR XENOCULTURE FRIEND COULDN'T WARP IN AN INTACT BODY FROM ANOTHER UNIVERSE...
...INSTEAD, ALL HIS RUINED INCARNATIONS ENDED UP HERE... WITHOUT LIVING UP TO HIS NAME AND ANNIHILATING US ALL IN THE PROCESS...
...NOT TOO SHABBY, PEOPLE.

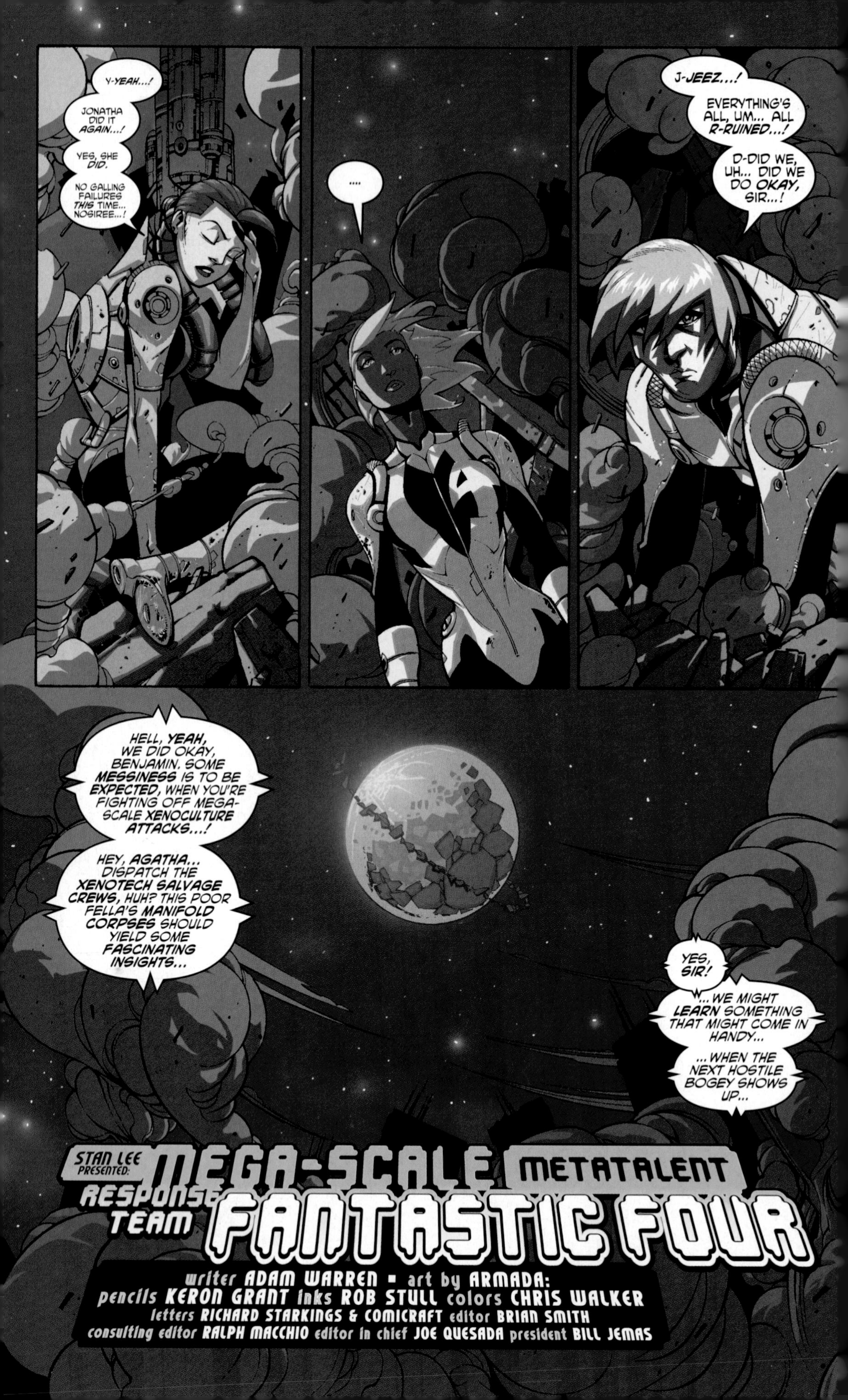

Y-YEAH...!
JONATHA DID IT AGAIN...!
YES, SHE DID.
NO GALLING FAILURES THIS TIME... NOSIREE...!
....
J-JEEZ...!
EVERYTHING'S ALL, UM... ALL R-RUINED...!
D-DID WE, UH... DID WE DO OKAY, SIR...!
HELL, YEAH, WE DID OKAY, BENJAMIN. SOME MESSINESS IS TO BE EXPECTED, WHEN YOU'RE FIGHTING OFF MEGA-SCALE XENOCULTURE ATTACKS...!
HEY, AGATHA... DISPATCH THE XENOTECH SALVAGE CREWS, HUH? THIS POOR FELLA'S MANIFOLD CORPSES SHOULD YIELD SOME FASCINATING INSIGHTS...
YES, SIR!
...WE MIGHT LEARN SOMETHING THAT MIGHT COME IN HANDY...
...WHEN THE NEXT HOSTILE BOGEY SHOWS UP...
STAN LEE PRESENTED: MEGA-SCALE METATALENT RESPONSE TEAM FANTASTIC FOUR
writer ADAM WARREN ▪ art by ARMADA:
pencils KERON GRANT inks ROB STULL colors CHRIS WALKER
letters RICHARD STARKINGS & COMICRAFT editor BRIAN SMITH
consulting editor RALPH MACCHIO editor in chief JOE QUESADA president BILL JEMAS

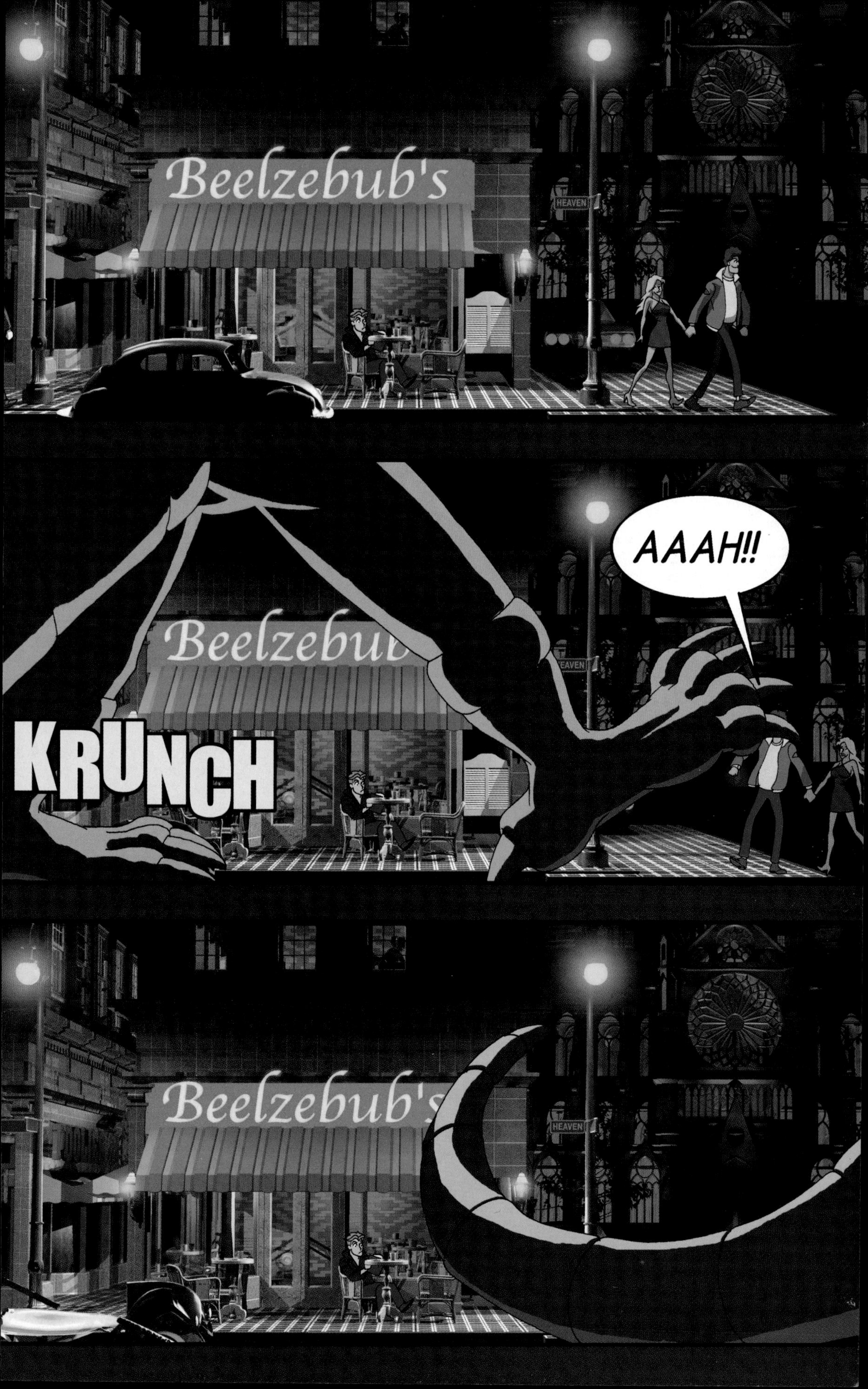
Beelzebub's
HEAVEN
Beelzebub
HEAVEN
AAAH!!
KRUNCH
Beelzebub's
HEAVEN

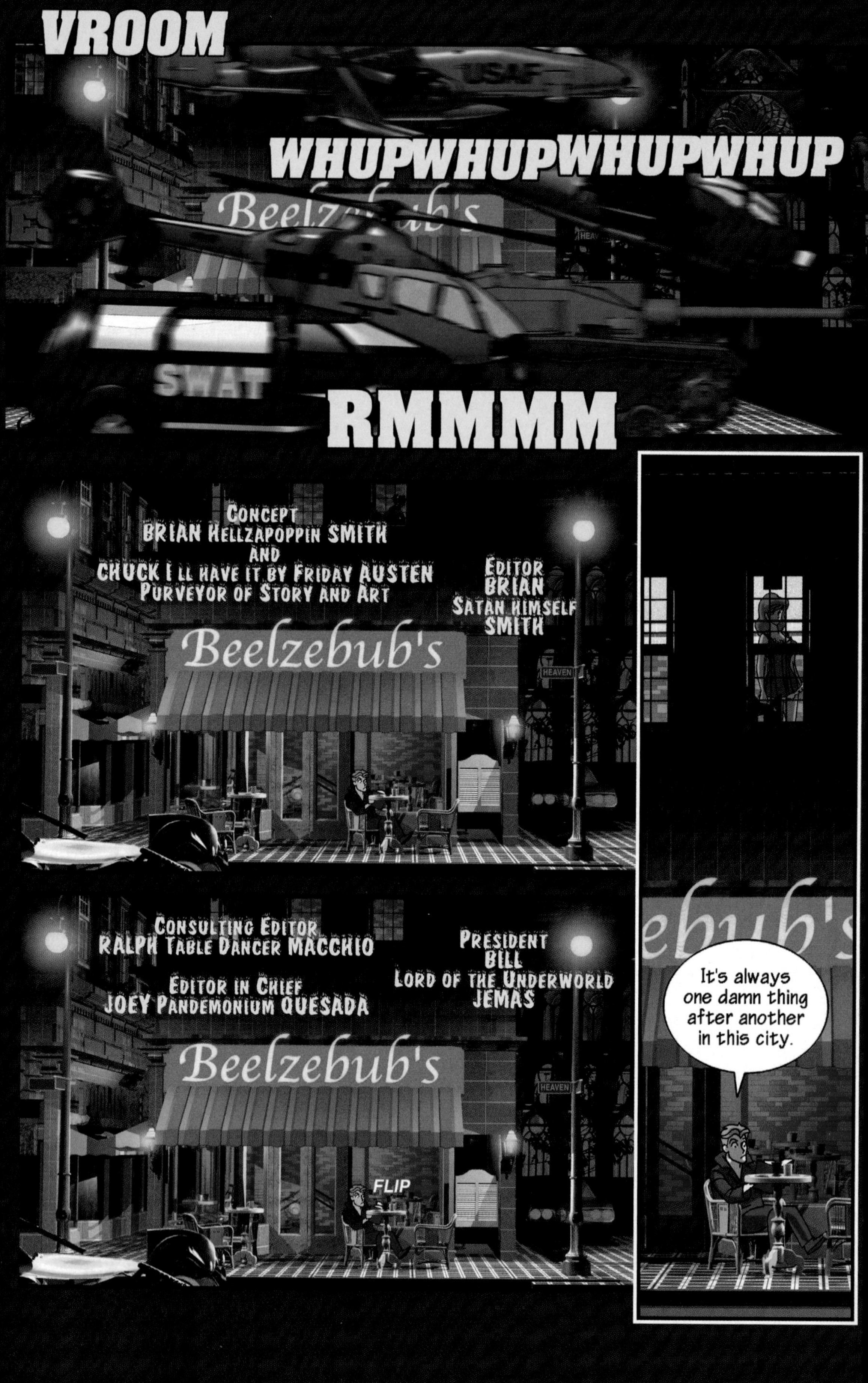
VROOM
WHUPWHUPWHUPWHUP
Beelzebub's
SWAT
RMMMM
CONCEPT
BRIAN HELLZAPOPPIN SMITH
AND
CHUCK I LL HAVE IT BY FRIDAY AUSTEN
PURVEYOR OF STORY AND ART
EDITOR
BRIAN
SATAN HIMSELF
SMITH
Beelzebub's
HEAVEN
CONSULTING EDITOR
RALPH TABLE DANCER MACCHIO
EDITOR IN CHIEF
JOEY PANDEMONIUM QUESADA
PRESIDENT
BILL
LORD OF THE UNDERWORLD
JEMAS
Beelzebub's
HEAVEN
FLIP
ebub's
It's always one damn thing after another in this city.

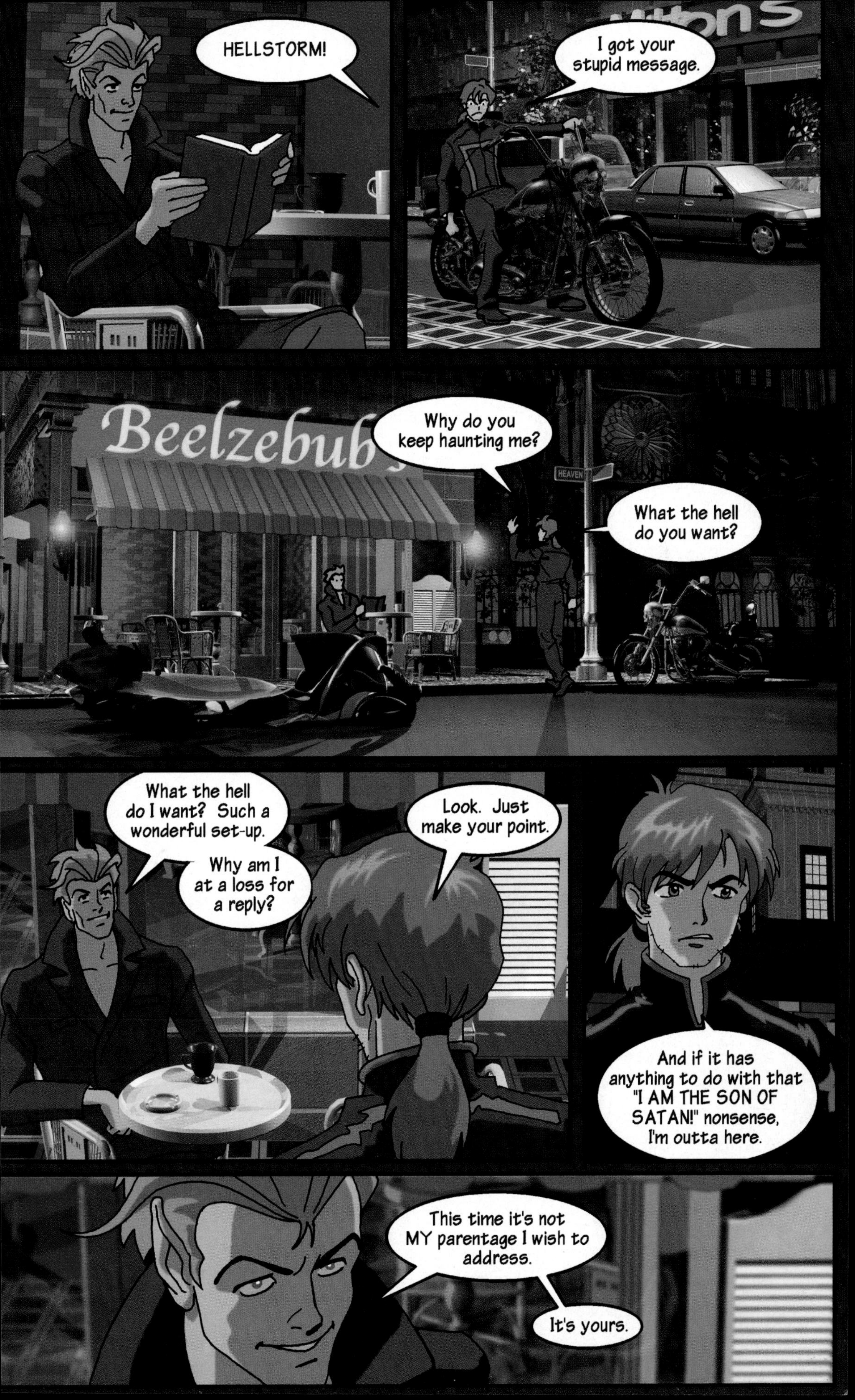
HELLSTORM!
I got your stupid message.
Beelzebub's
HEAVEN
Why do you keep haunting me?
What the hell do you want?
What the hell do I want? Such a wonderful set-up.
Why am I at a loss for a reply?
Look. Just make your point.
And if it has anything to do with that "I AM THE SON OF SATAN!" nonsense, I'm outta here.
This time it's not MY parentage I wish to address.
It's yours.

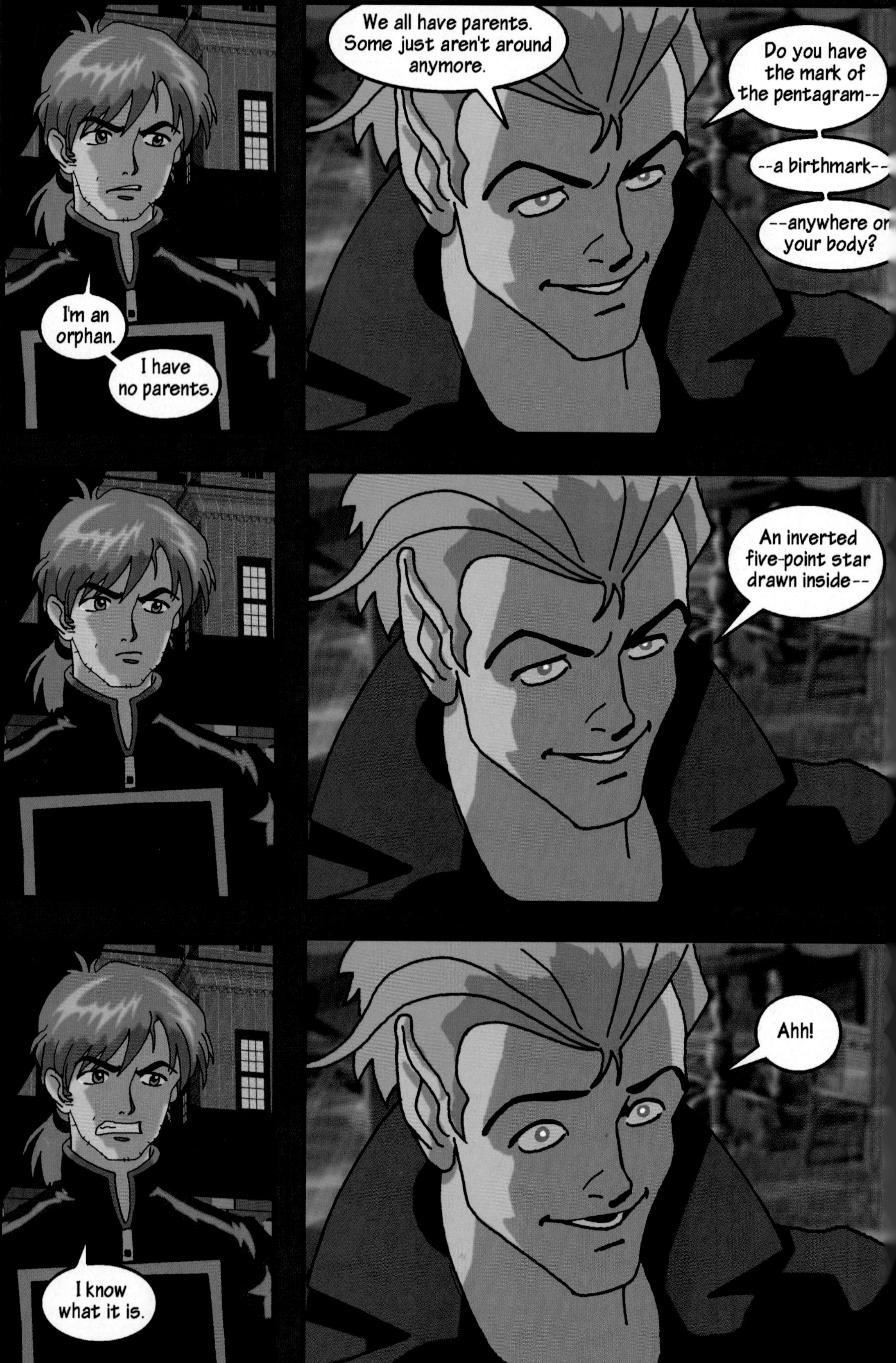
I'm an orphan.
I have no parents.
We all have parents. Some just aren't around anymore.
Do you have the mark of the pentagram--
--a birthmark--
--anywhere on your body?
An inverted five-point star drawn inside--
I know what it is.
Ahh!

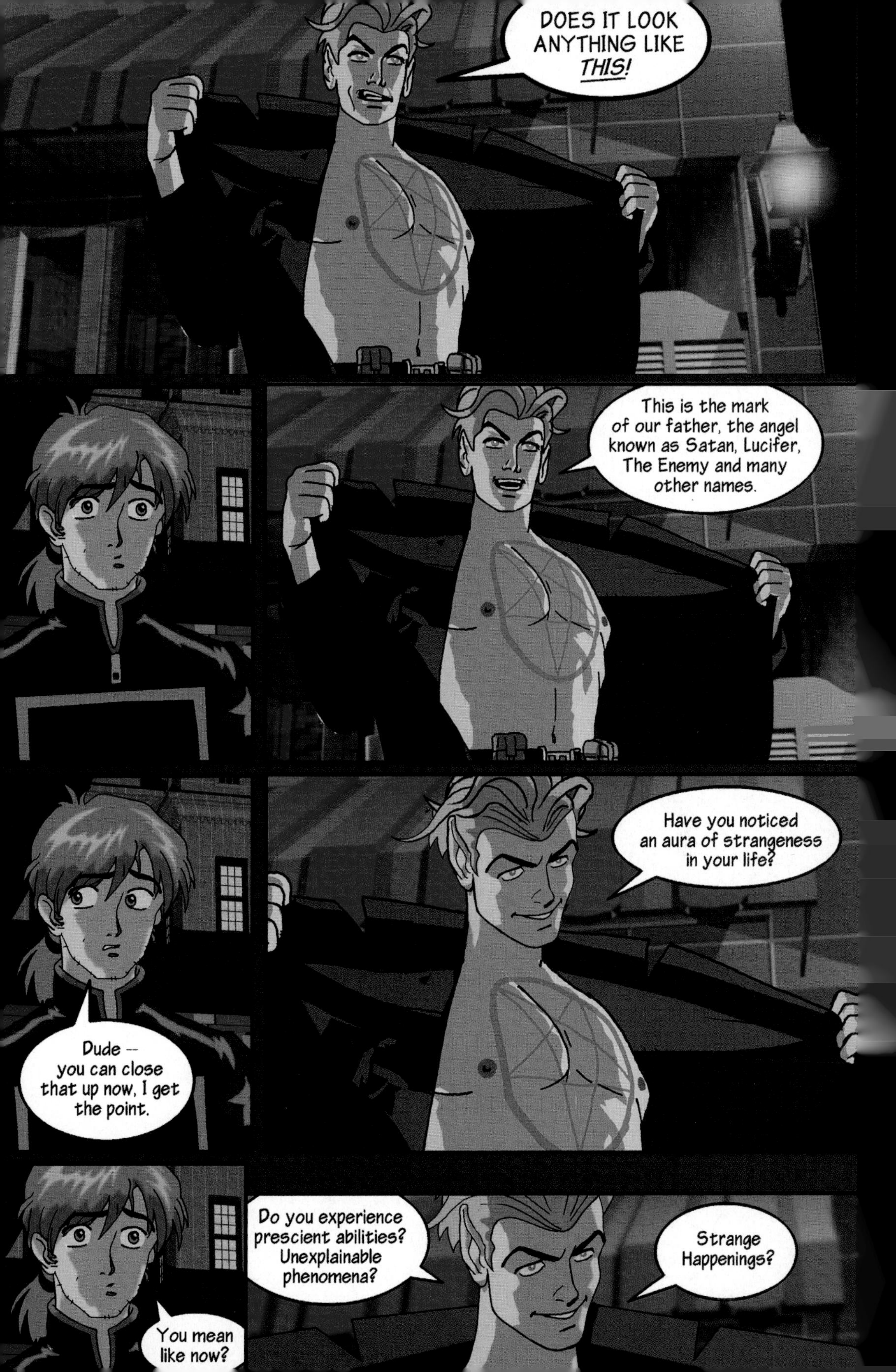
DOES IT LOOK ANYTHING LIKE *THIS!*
This is the mark of our father, the angel known as Satan, Lucifer, The Enemy and many other names.
Have you noticed an aura of strangeness in your life?
Dude -- you can close that up now, I get the point.
Do you experience prescient abilities? Unexplainable phenomena?
Strange Happenings?
You mean like now?

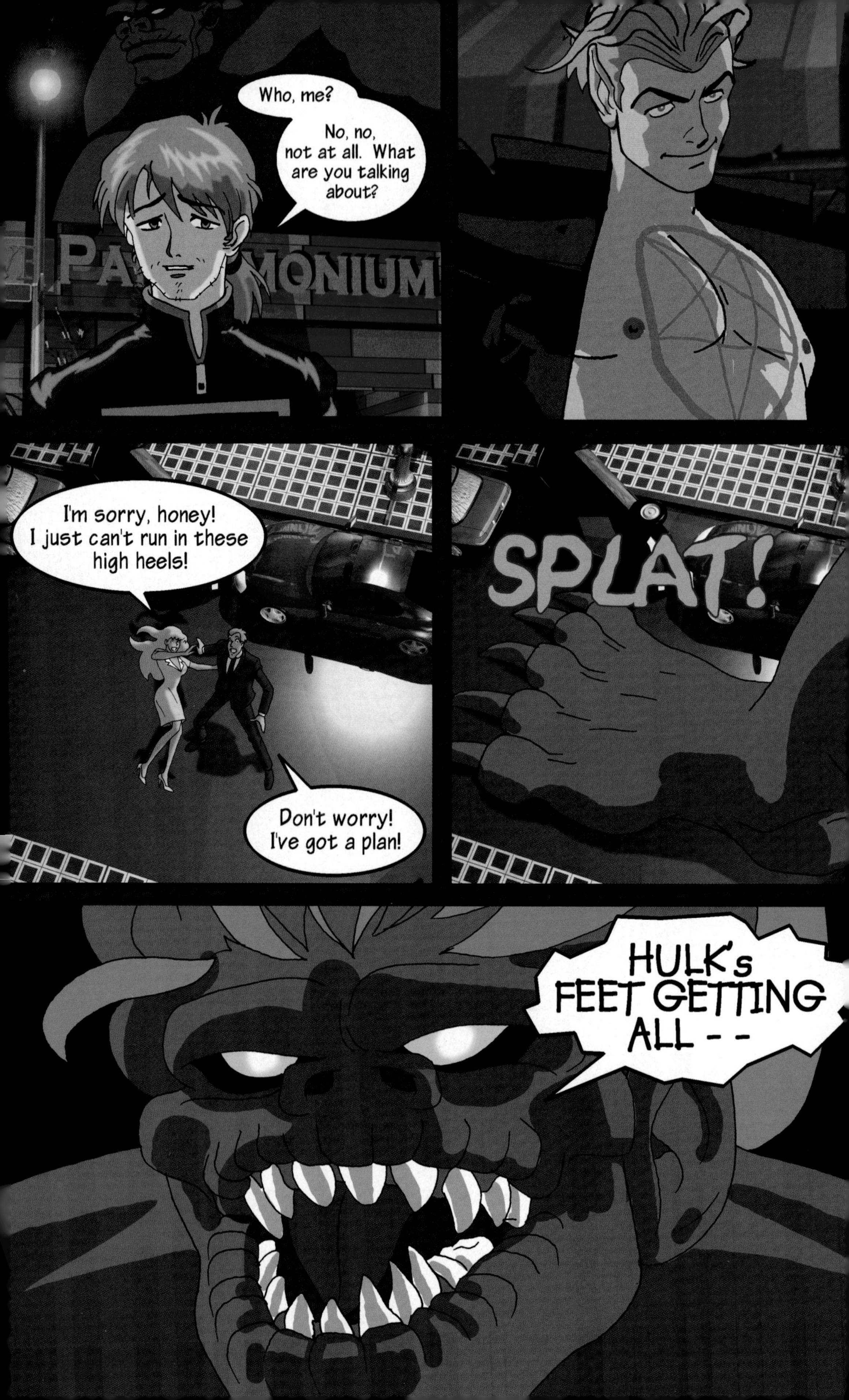

Who, me?
No, no, not at all. What are you talking about?
PANDEMONIUM
I'm sorry, honey! I just can't run in these high heels!
Don't worry! I've got a plan!
SPLAT!
HULK's FEET GETTING ALL - -

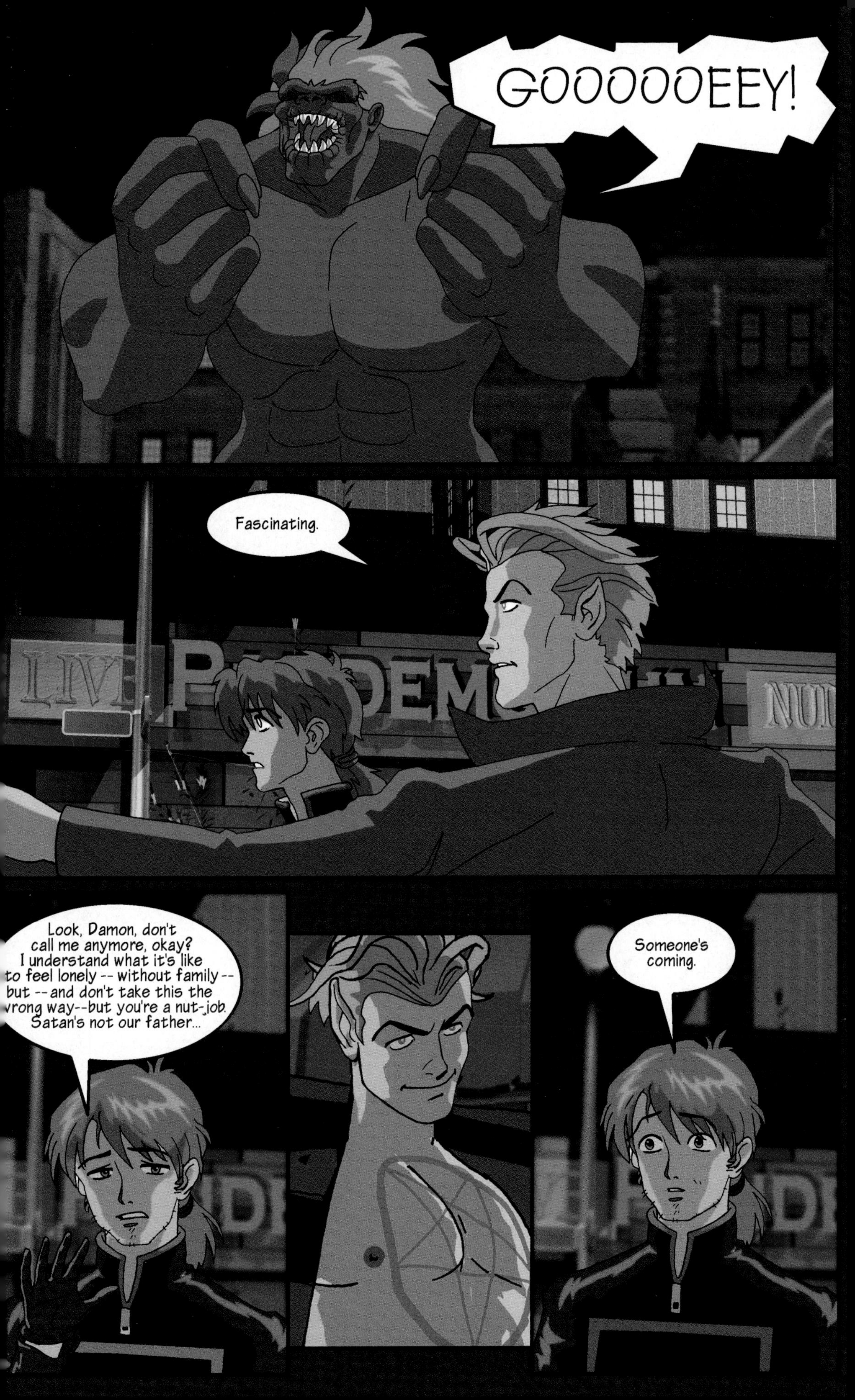
GOOOOOEEY!
Fascinating.
Look, Damon, don't call me anymore, okay? I understand what it's like to feel lonely -- without family -- but -- and don't take this the wrong way--but you're a nut-job. Satan's not our father...
Someone's coming.

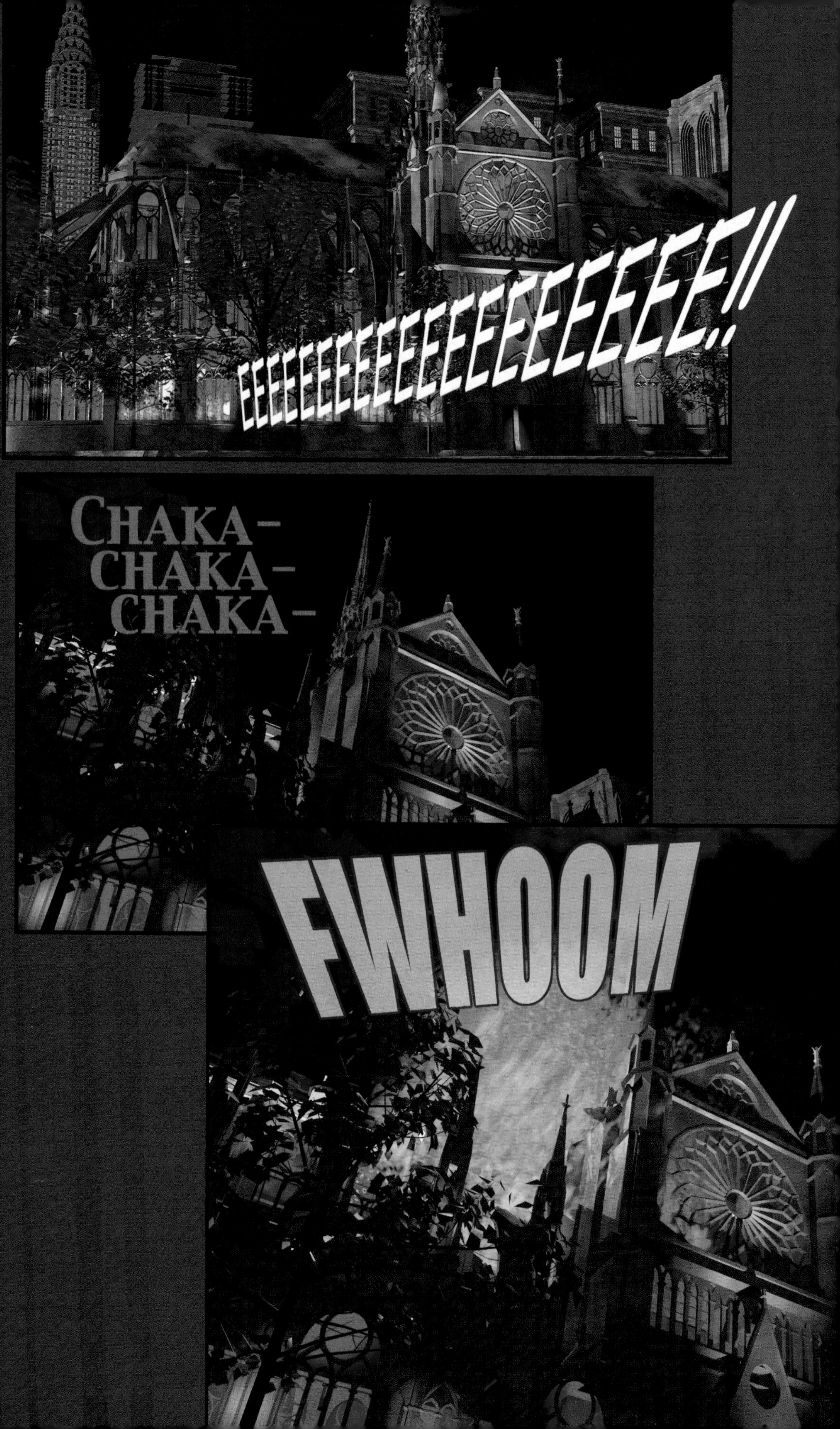
EEEEEEEEEEEEEEEEEE!!
CHAKA-
CHAKA-
CHAKA-
FWHOOM

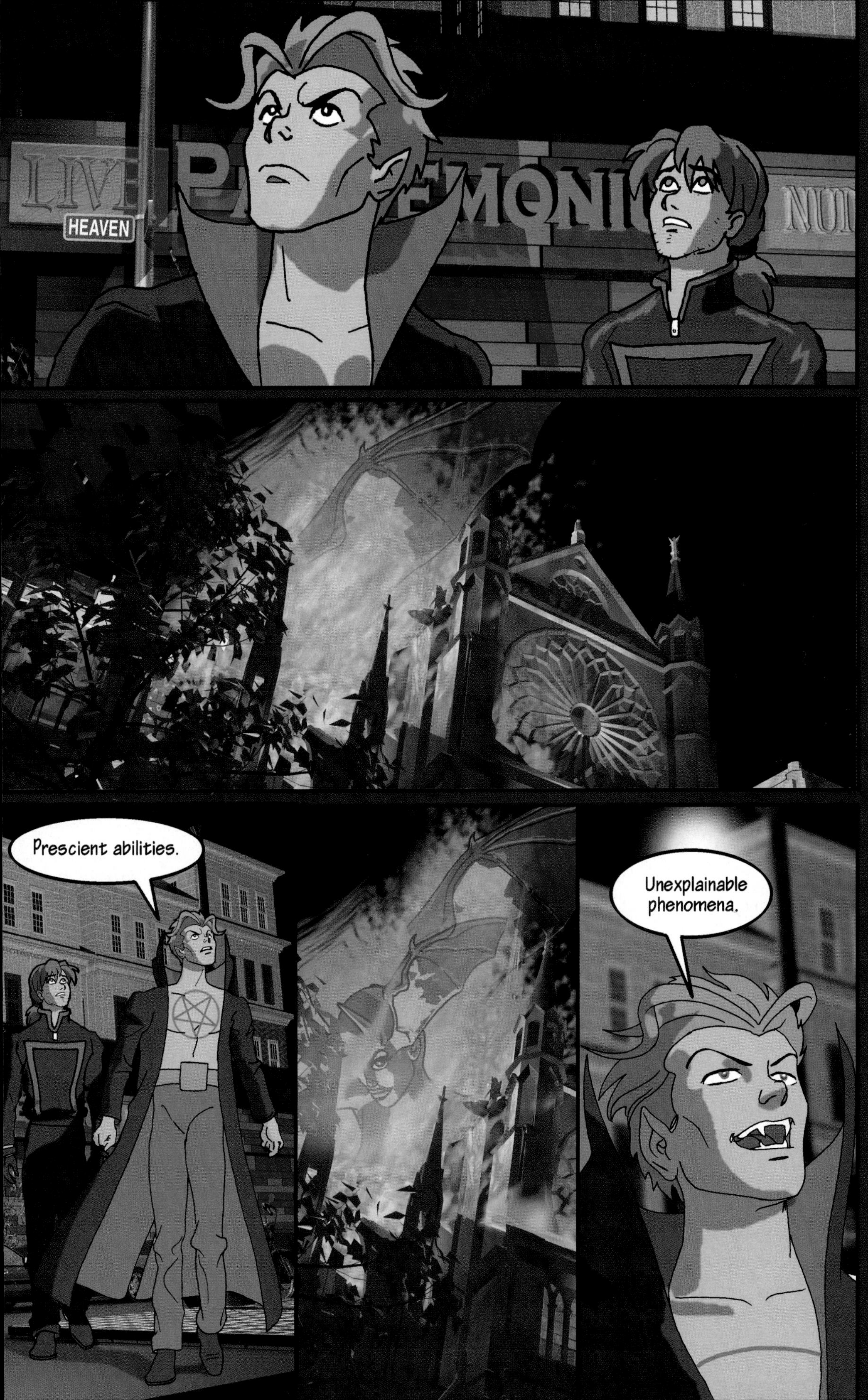
HEAVEN
Prescient abilities.
Unexplainable phenomena.

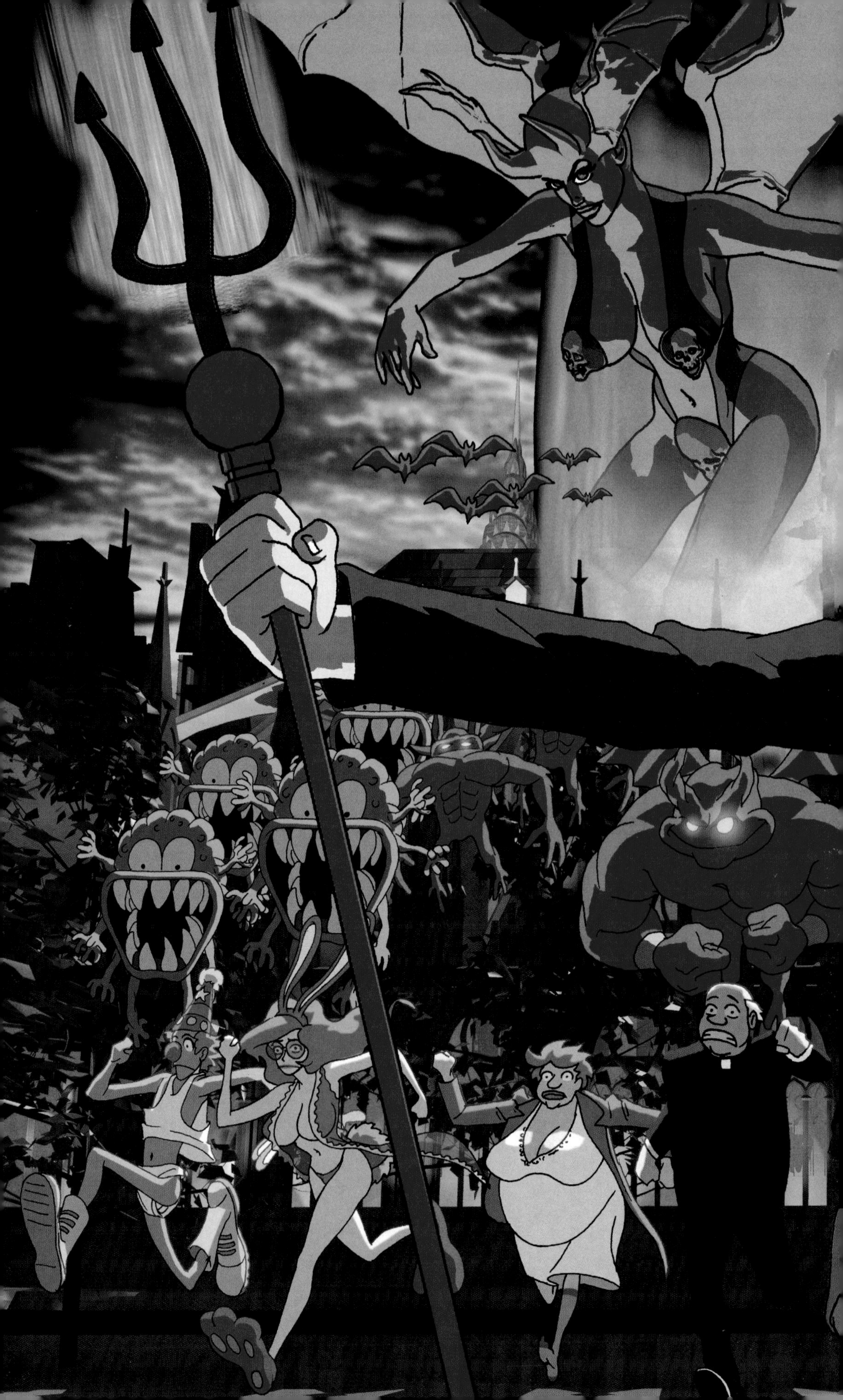

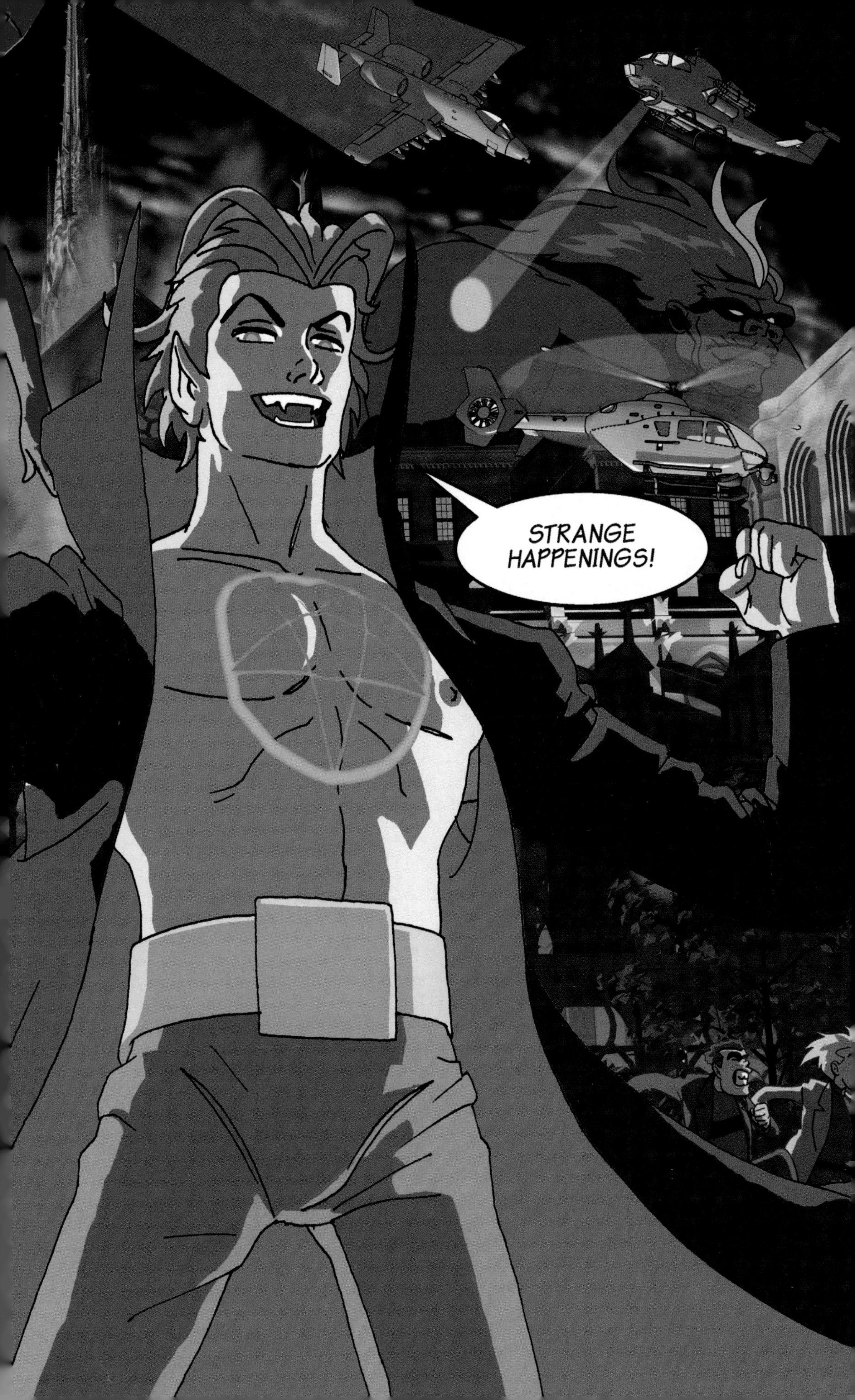
STRANGE HAPPENINGS!

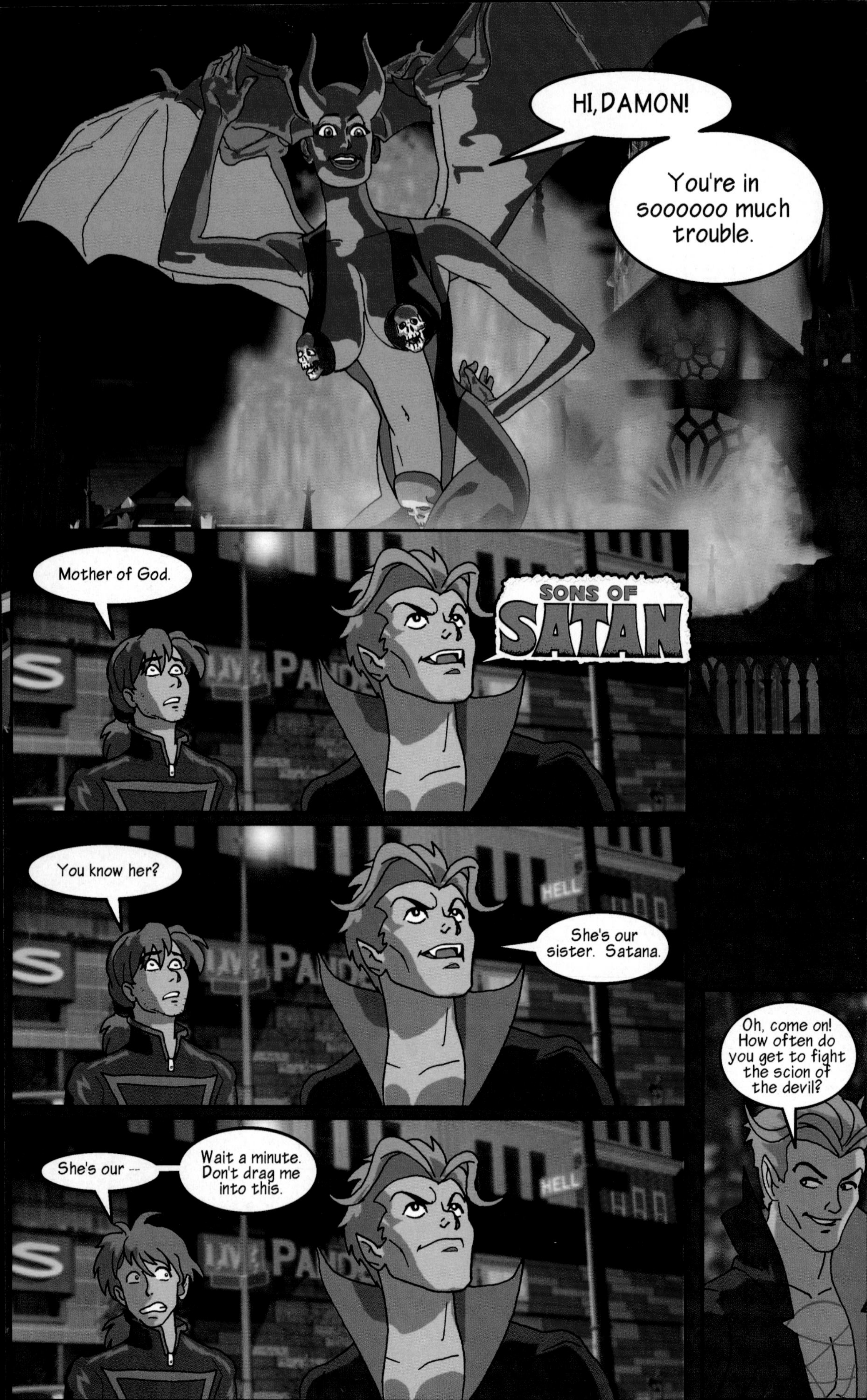
HI, DAMON!
You're in sooooooo much trouble.
Mother of God.
SONS OF SATAN
You know her?
She's our sister. Satana.
She's our --
Wait a minute. Don't drag me into this.
Oh, come on! How often do you get to fight the scion of the devil?

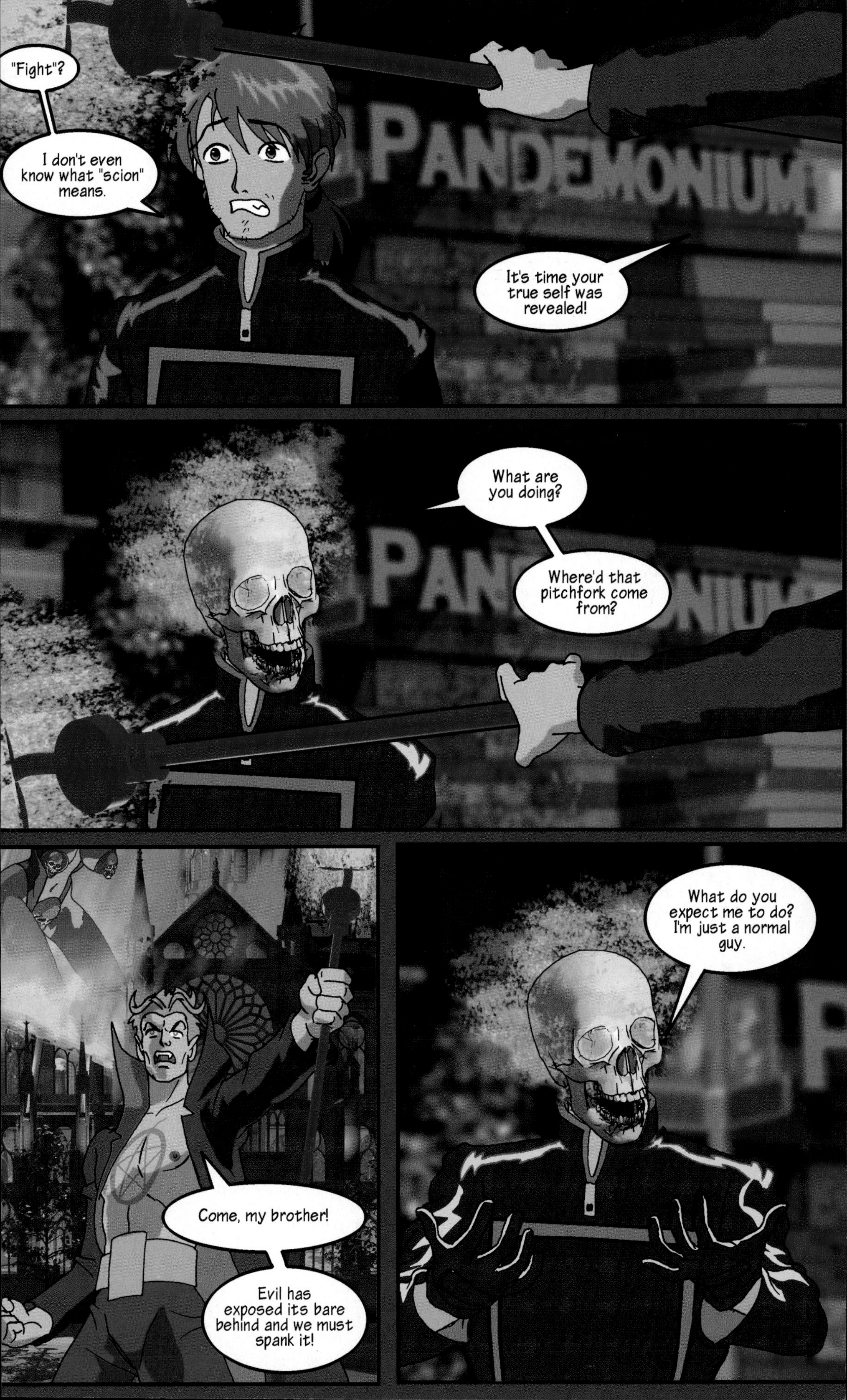
"Fight"?
I don't even know what "scion" means.
PANDEMONIUM
It's time your true self was revealed!
What are you doing?
Where'd that pitchfork come from?
Come, my brother!
Evil has exposed its bare behind and we must spank it!
What do you expect me to do? I'm just a normal guy.

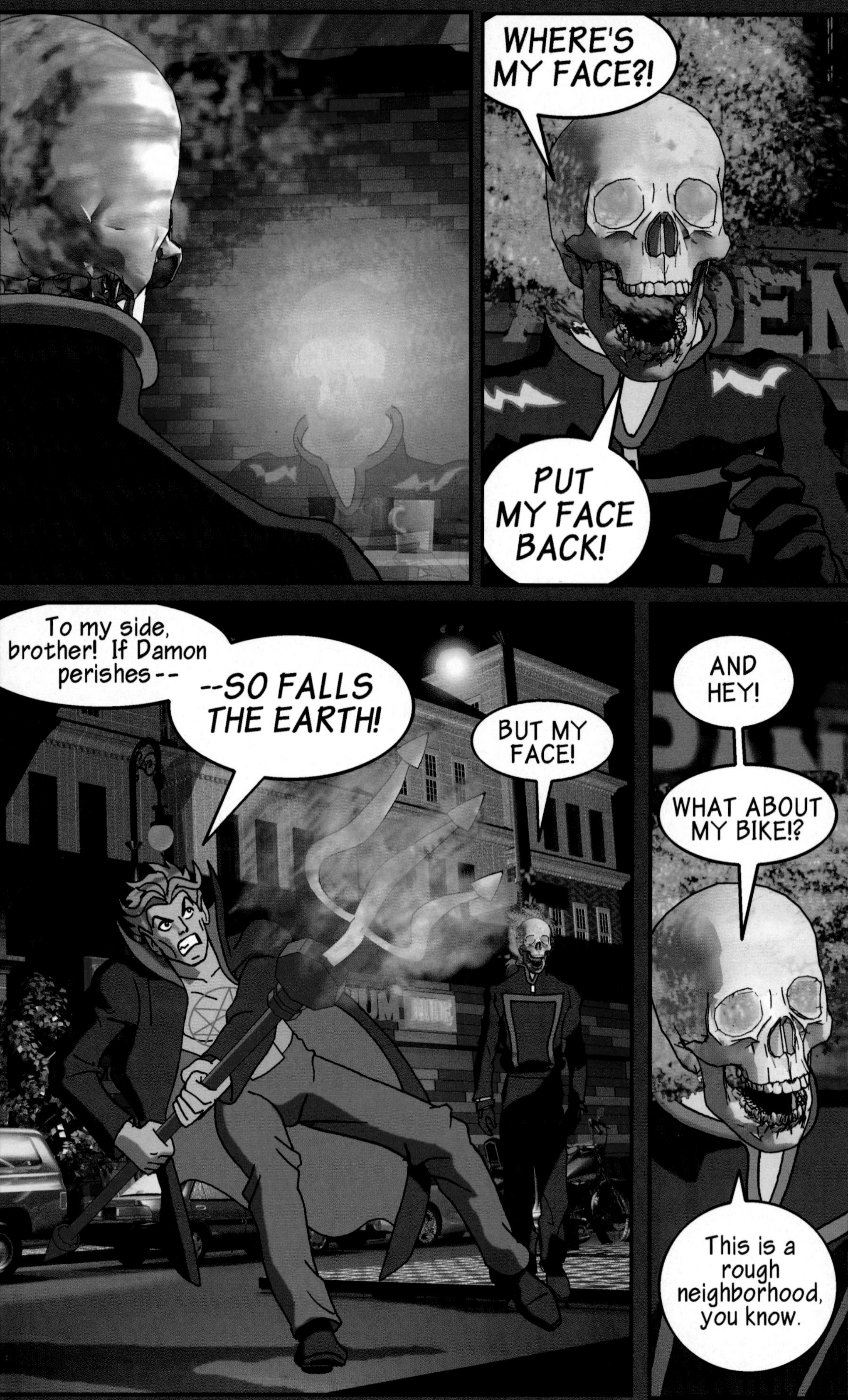
WHERE'S MY FACE?!
PUT MY FACE BACK!
To my side, brother! If Damon perishes--
--SO FALLS THE EARTH!
BUT MY FACE!
AND HEY!
WHAT ABOUT MY BIKE!?
This is a rough neighborhood, you know.

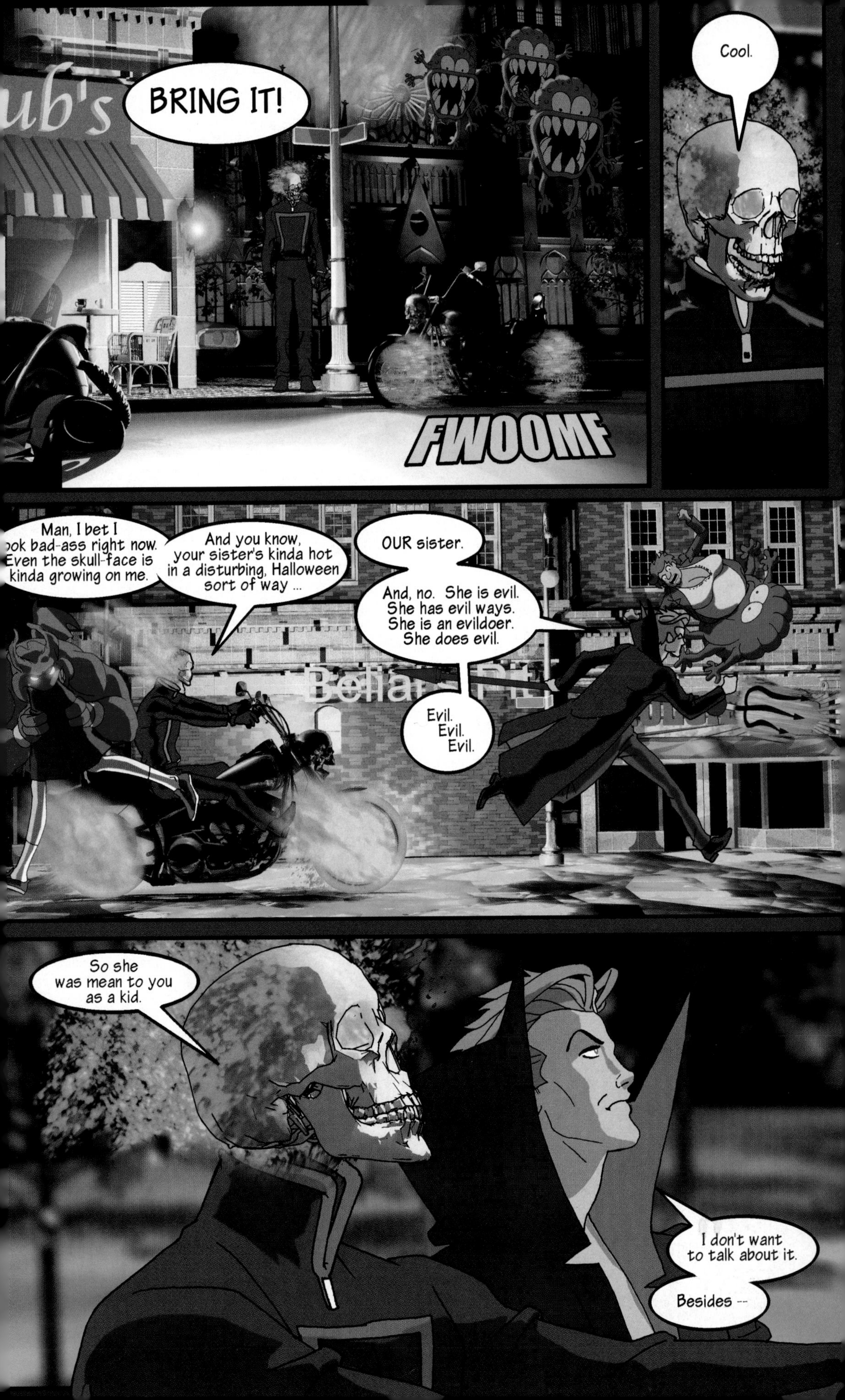
ub's
BRING IT!
FWOOMF
Cool.
Man, I bet I ook bad-ass right now. Even the skull-face is kinda growing on me.
And you know, your sister's kinda hot in a disturbing, Halloween sort of way ...
OUR sister.
And, no. She is evil. She has evil ways. She is an evildoer. She does evil.
Evil. Evil. Evil.
So she was mean to you as a kid.
I don't want to talk about it.
Besides --

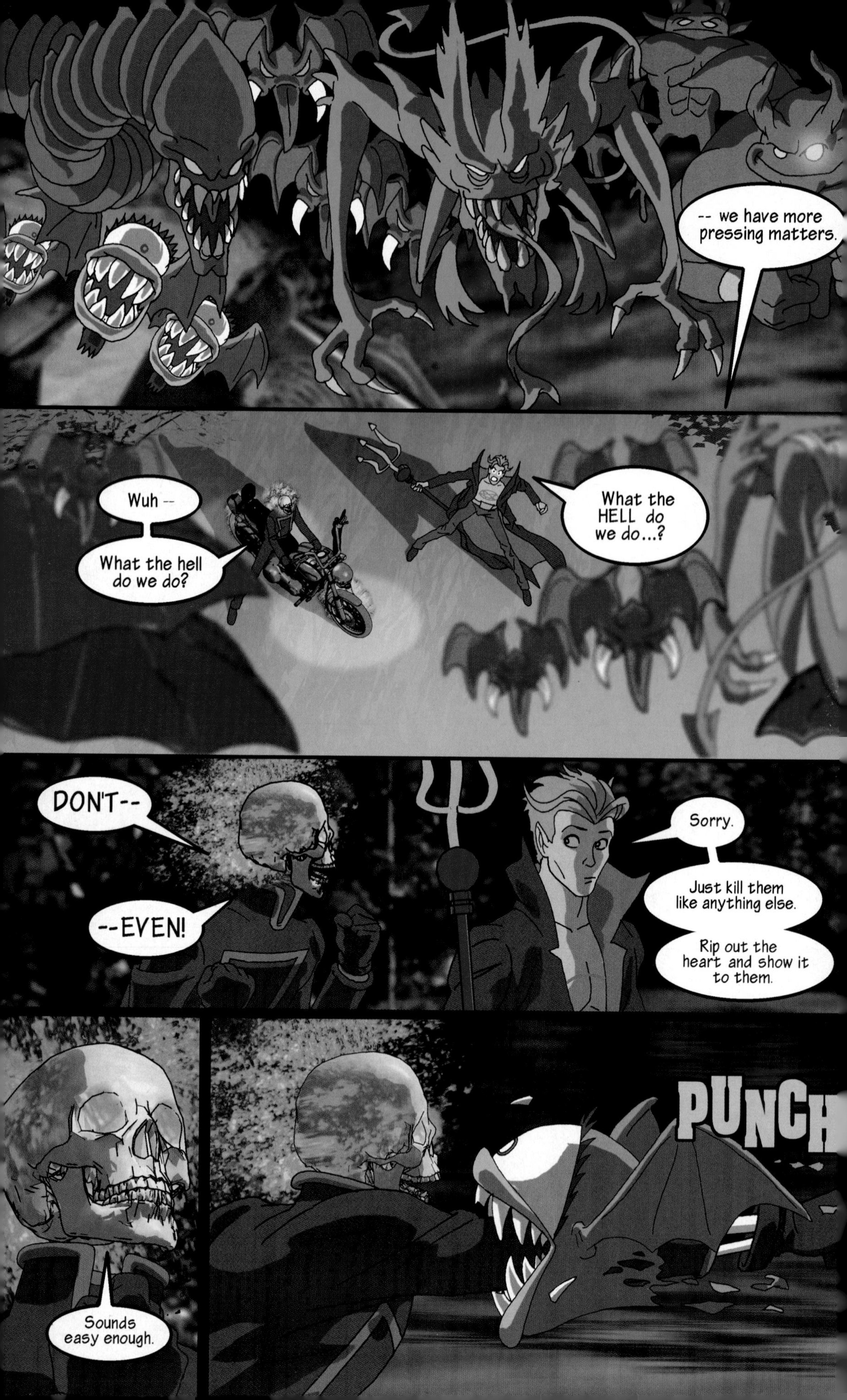
-- we have more pressing matters.
Wuh --
What the hell do we do?
What the HELL do we do...?
DON'T--
--EVEN!
Sorry.
Just kill them like anything else.
Rip out the heart and show it to them.
Sounds easy enough.
PUNCH

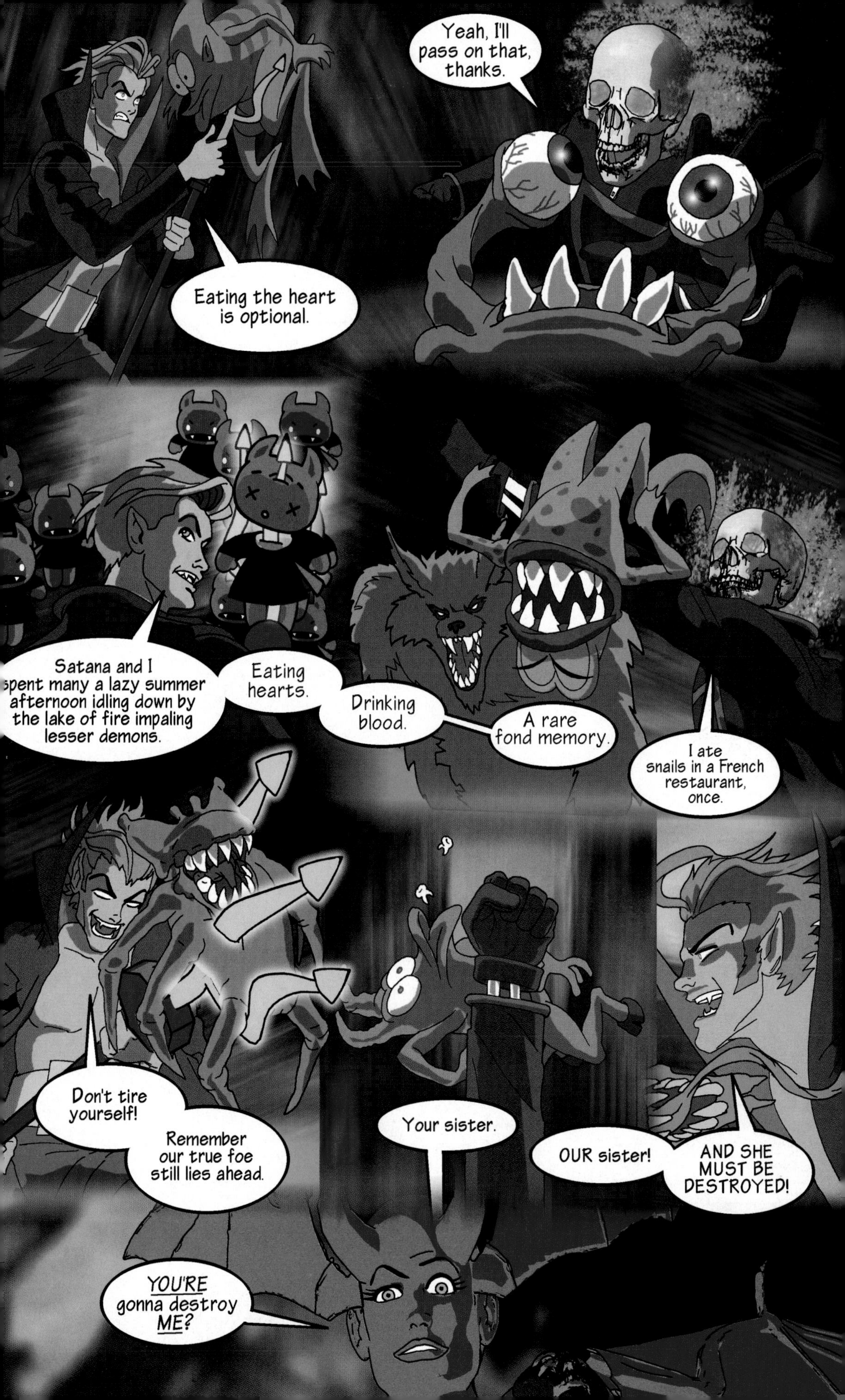
Yeah, I'll pass on that, thanks.
Eating the heart is optional.
Satana and I spent many a lazy summer afternoon idling down by the lake of fire impaling lesser demons.
Eating hearts.
Drinking blood.
A rare fond memory.
I ate snails in a French restaurant, once.
Don't tire yourself!
Remember our true foe still lies ahead.
Your sister.
OUR sister!
AND SHE MUST BE DESTROYED!
YOU'RE gonna destroy ME?

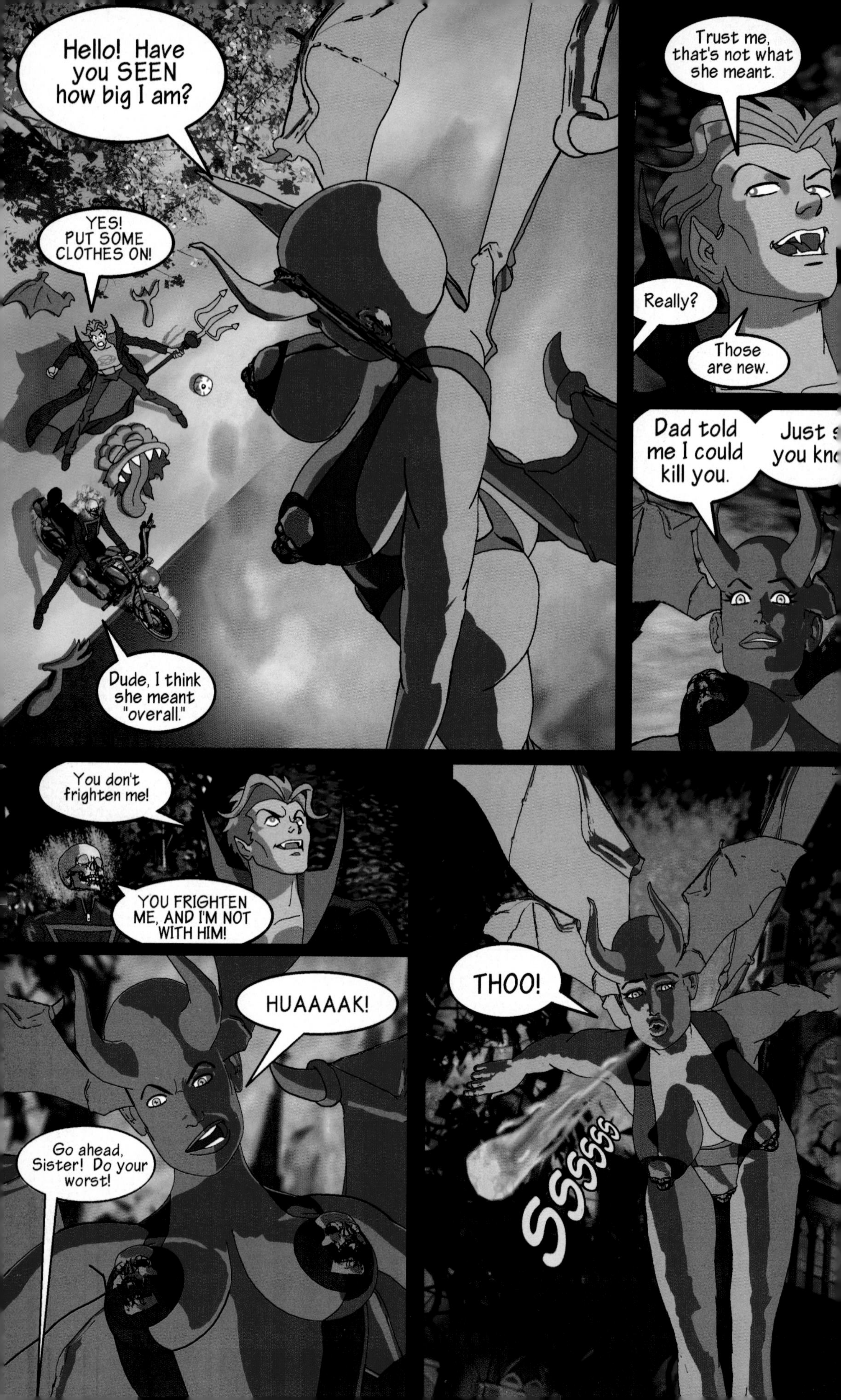

Hello! Have you SEEN how big I am?
YES! PUT SOME CLOTHES ON!
Dude, I think she meant "overall."
Trust me, that's not what she meant.
Really?
Those are new.
Dad told me I could kill you.
You don't frighten me!
YOU FRIGHTEN ME, AND I'M NOT WITH HIM!
HUAAAAK!
Go ahead, Sister! Do your worst!
THOO!
SSSSSS

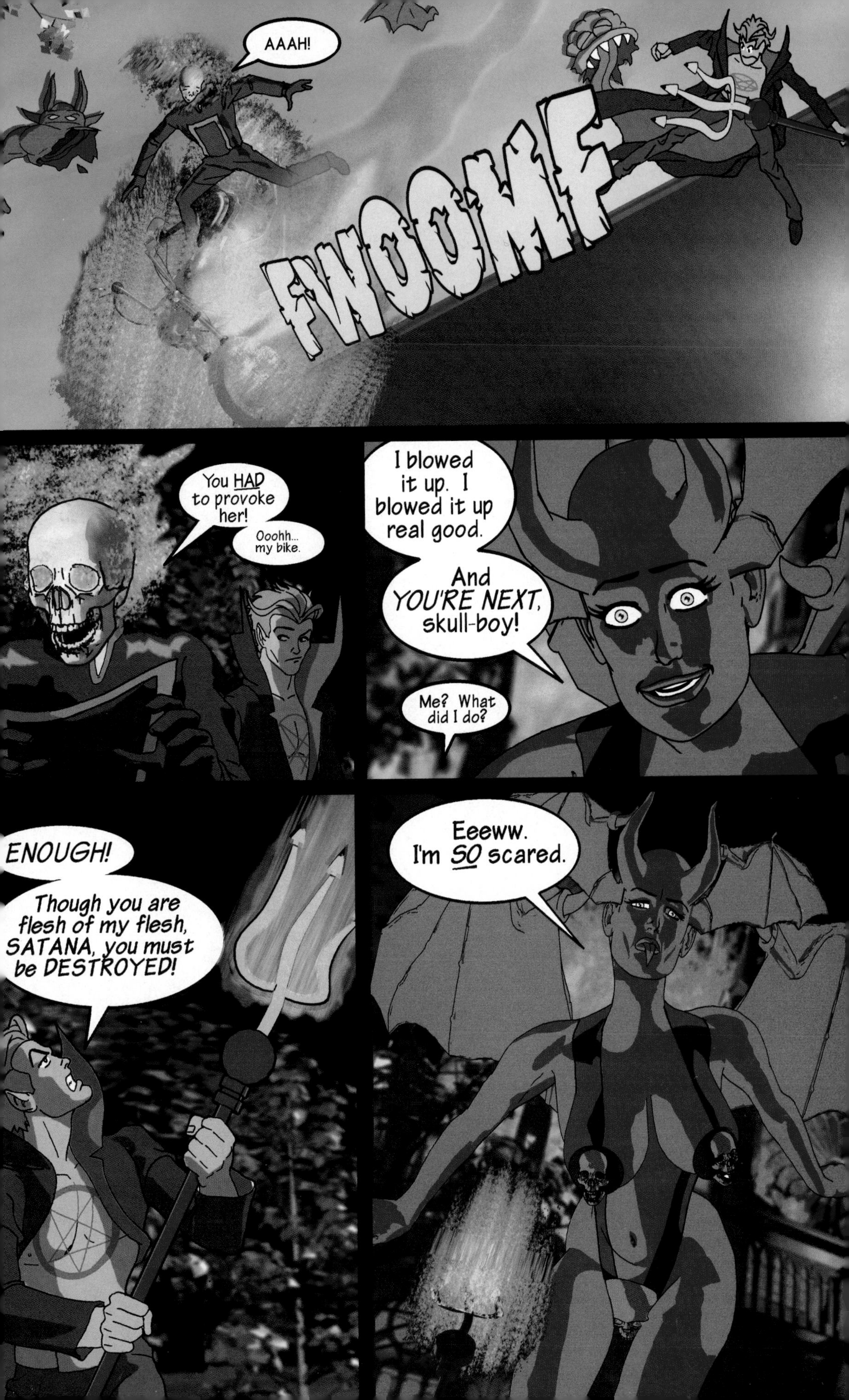
AAAH!
FWOOMF
You HAD to provoke her!
Ooohh... my bike.
I blowed it up. I blowed it up real good.
And YOU'RE NEXT, skull-boy!
Me? What did I do?
ENOUGH!
Though you are flesh of my flesh, SATANA, you must be DESTROYED!
Eeeww. I'm SO scared.

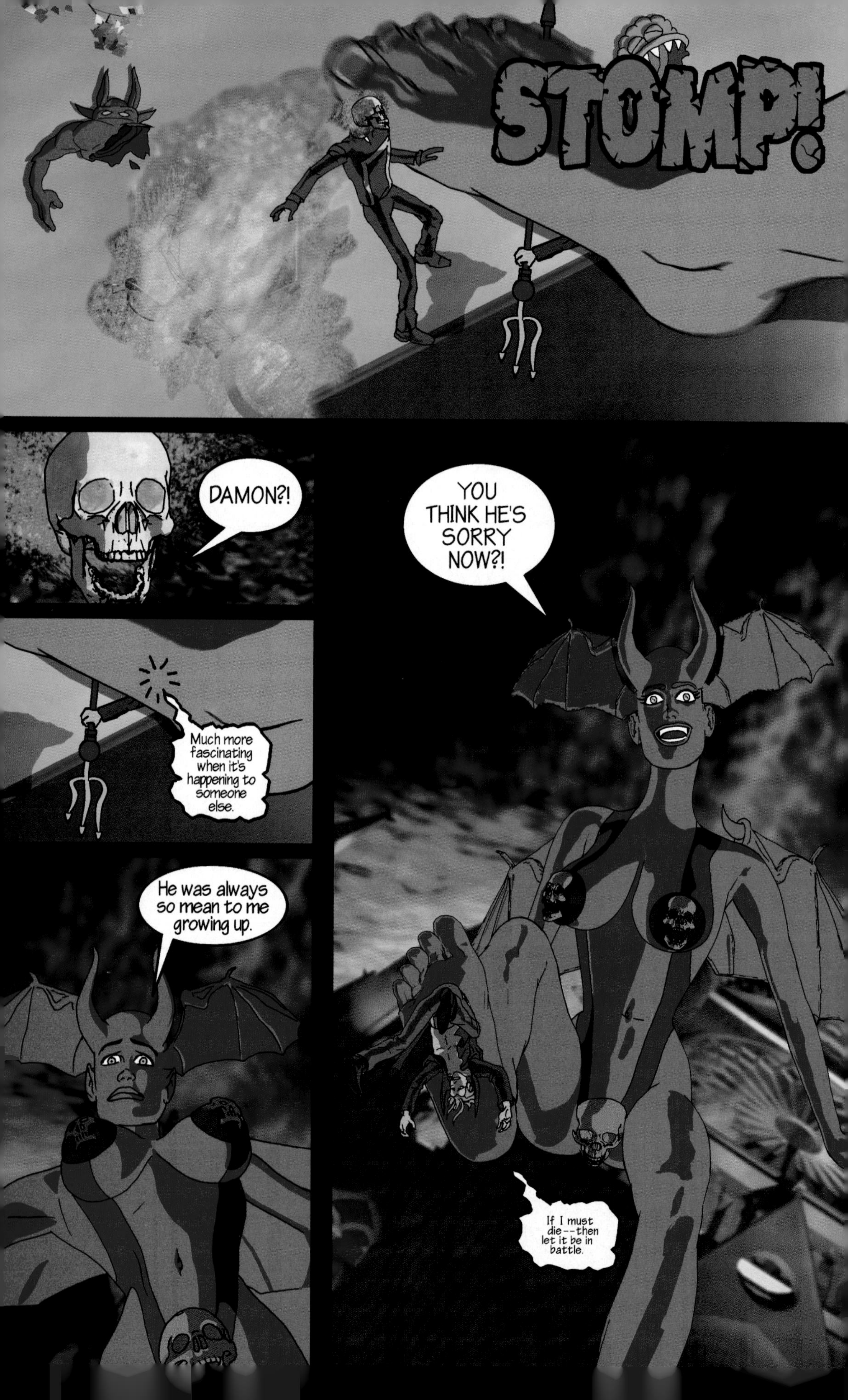
STOMP!
DAMON?!
Much more fascinating when it's happening to someone else.
He was always so mean to me growing up.
YOU THINK HE'S SORRY NOW?!
If I must die--then let it be in battle.

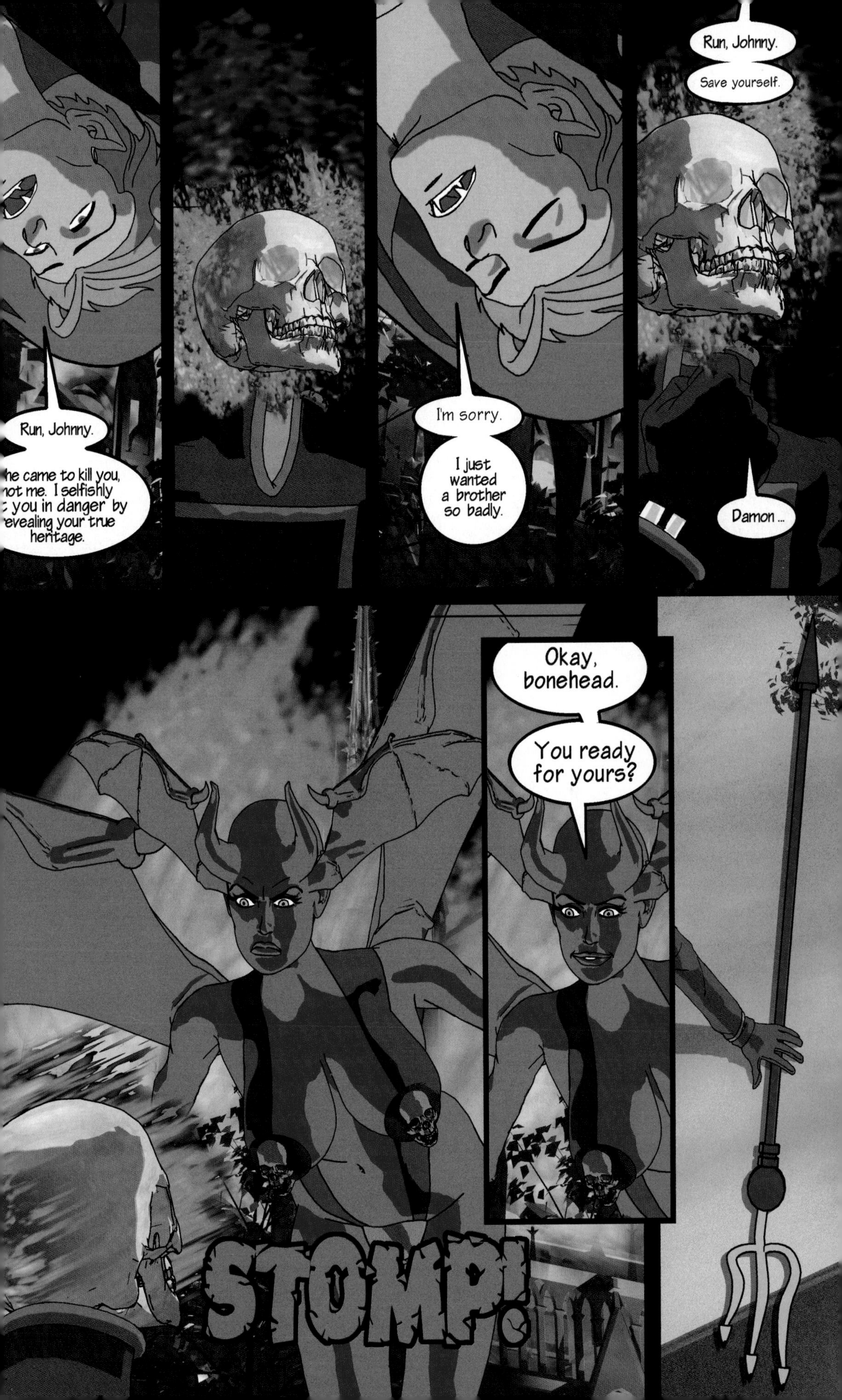

Run, Johnny.
he came to kill you, not me. I selfishly you in danger by evealing your true heritage.
I'm sorry.
I just wanted a brother so badly.
Run, Johnny.
Save yourself.
Damon ...
Okay, bonehead.
You ready for yours?
STOMP!

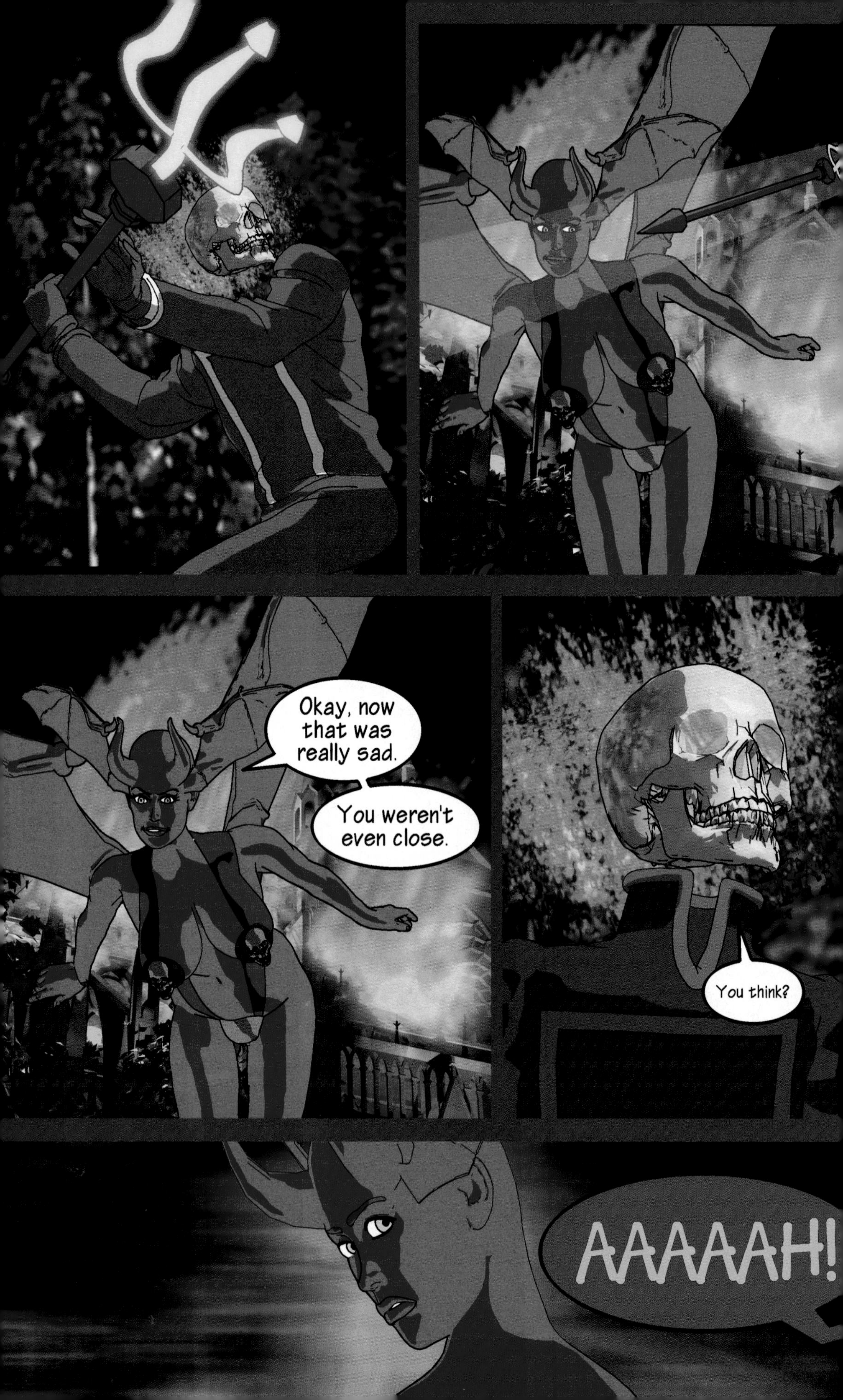
Okay, now that was really sad.
You weren't even close.
You think?
AAAAAH!

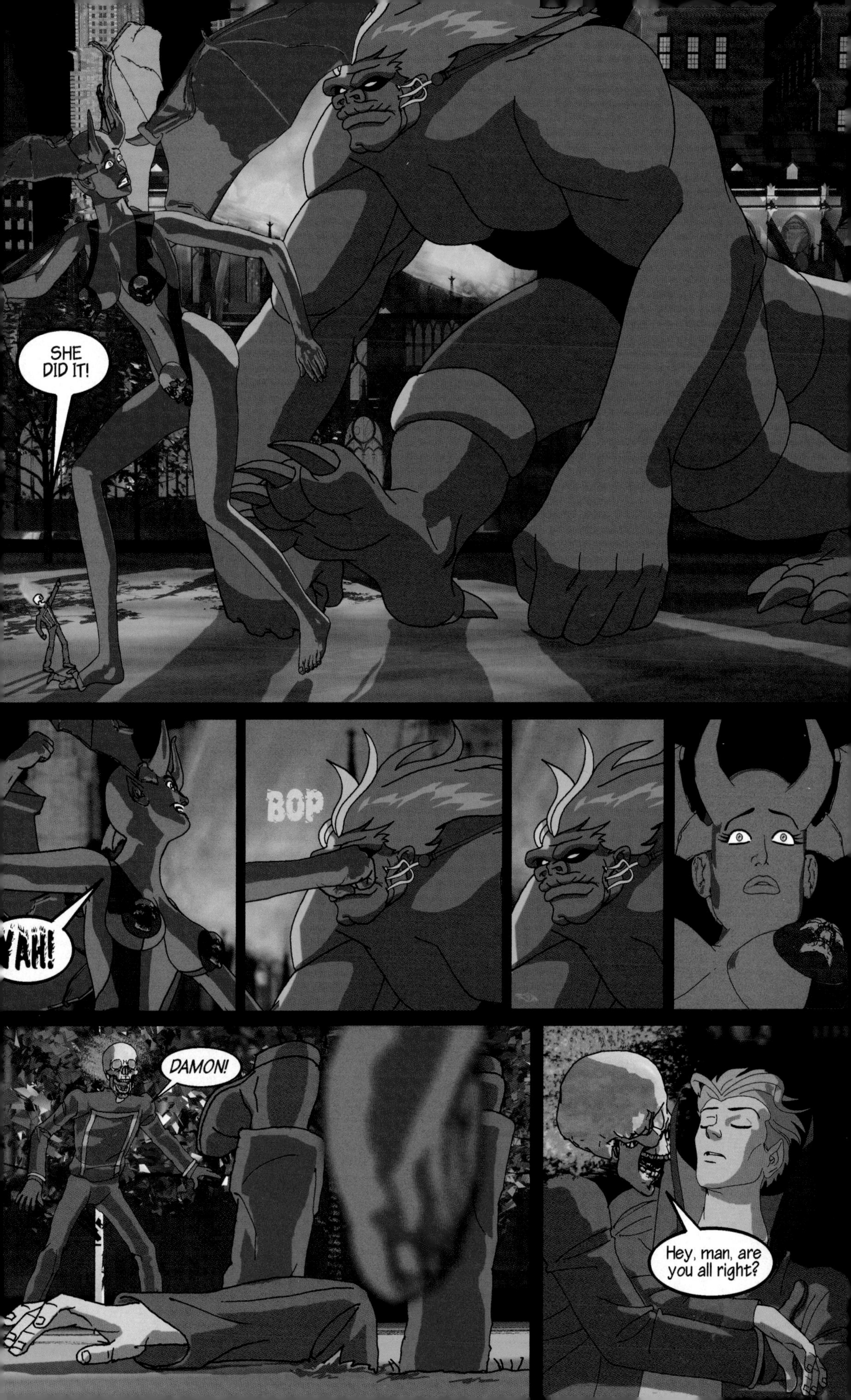
SHE DID IT!
YAH!
BOP
DAMON!
Hey, man, are you all right?

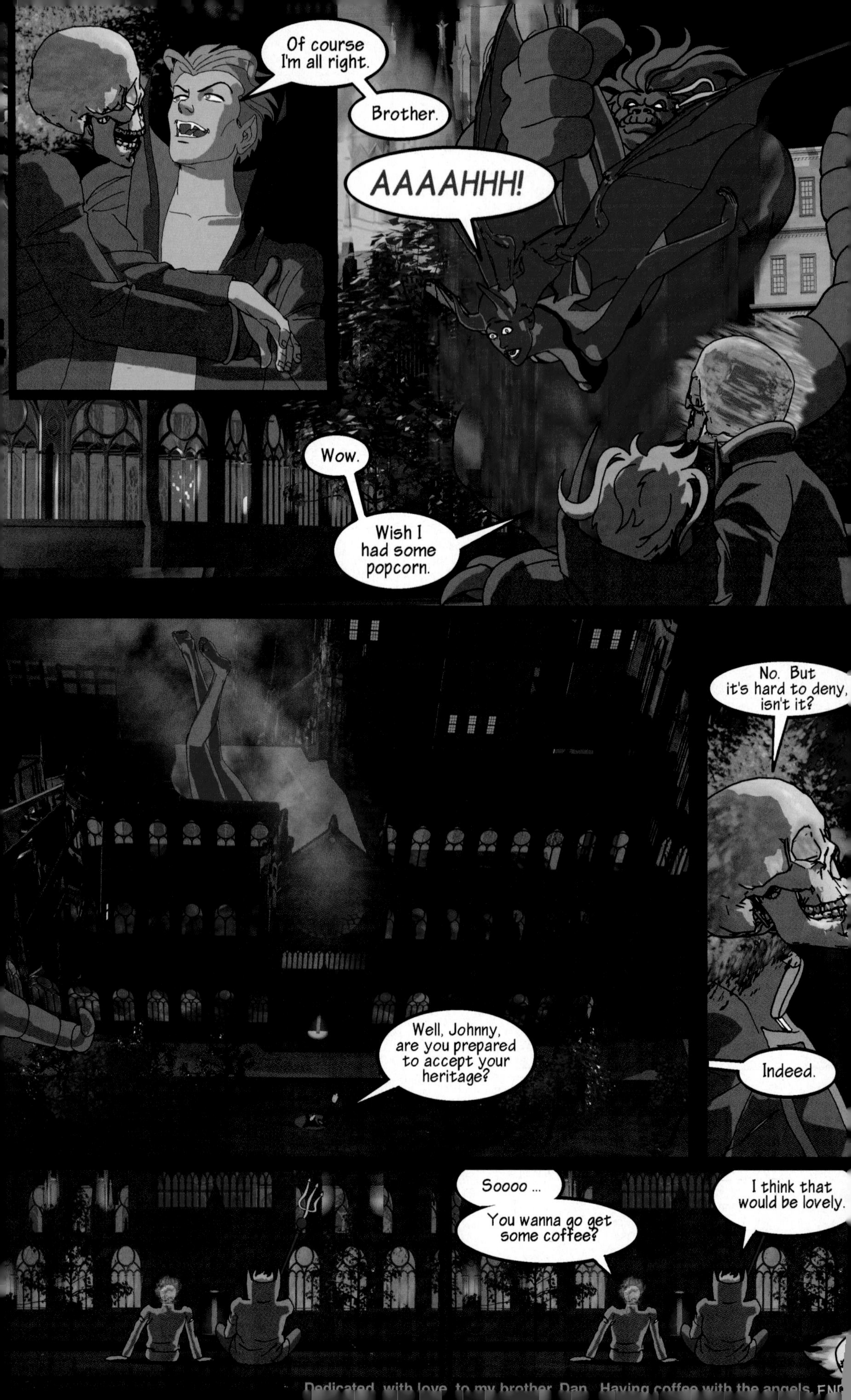
Of course I'm all right.
Brother.
AAAAHHH!
Wow.
Wish I had some popcorn.
No. But it's hard to deny, isn't it?
Well, Johnny, are you prepared to accept your heritage?
Indeed.
Soooo ...
You wanna go get some coffee?
I think that would be lovely.
Dedicated, with love, to my brother, Dan. Having coffee with the angels.

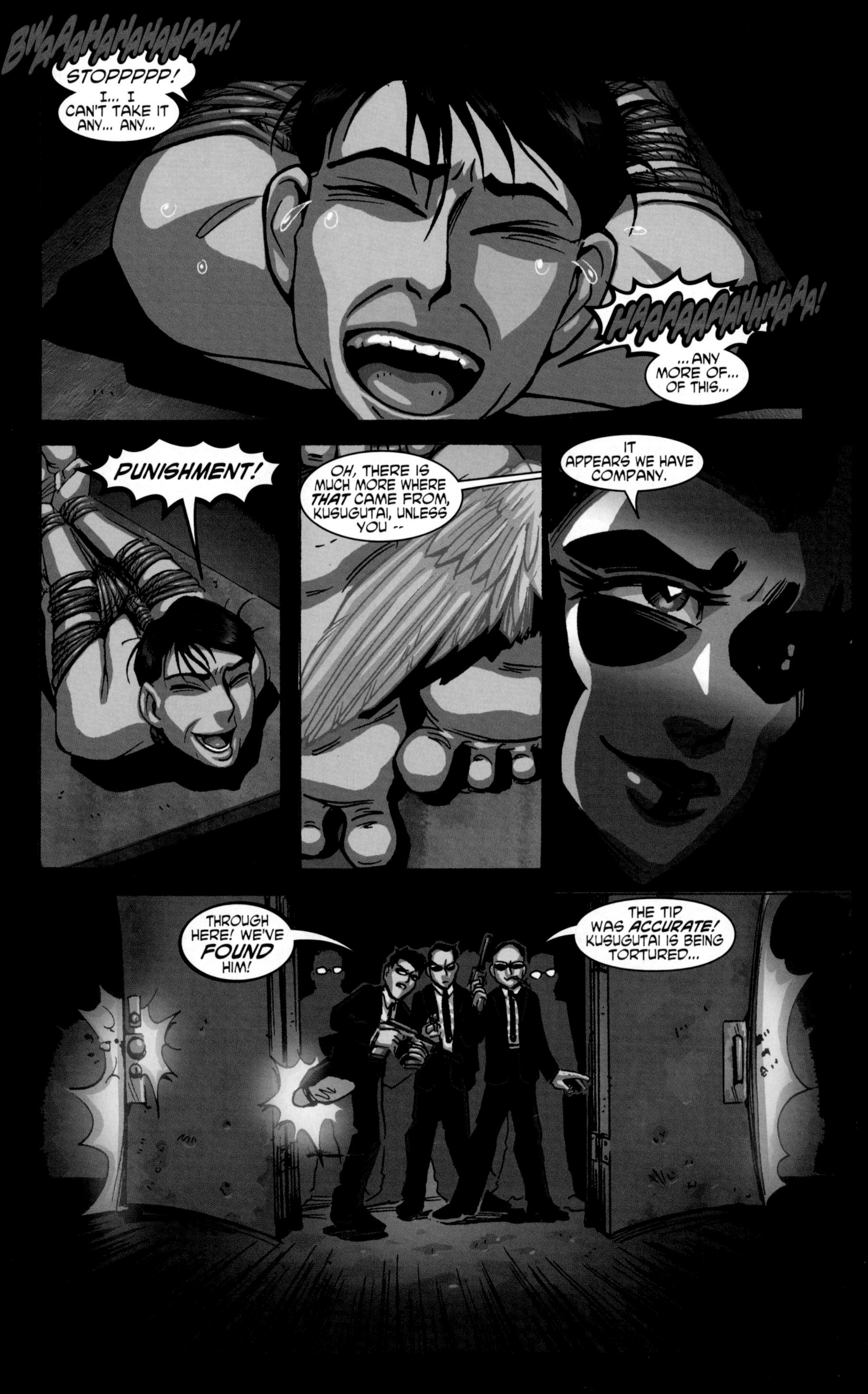
BWAAAHAHAHAHAAA!
STOPPPPPP! I... I CAN'T TAKE IT ANY... ANY...
HAAAAAAAHHAAA!
... ANY MORE OF... OF THIS...
PUNISHMENT!
OH, THERE IS MUCH MORE WHERE THAT CAME FROM, KUSUGUTAI, UNLESS YOU --
IT APPEARS WE HAVE COMPANY.
THROUGH HERE! WE'VE FOUND HIM!
THE TIP WAS ACCURATE! KUSUGUTAI IS BEING TORTURED...

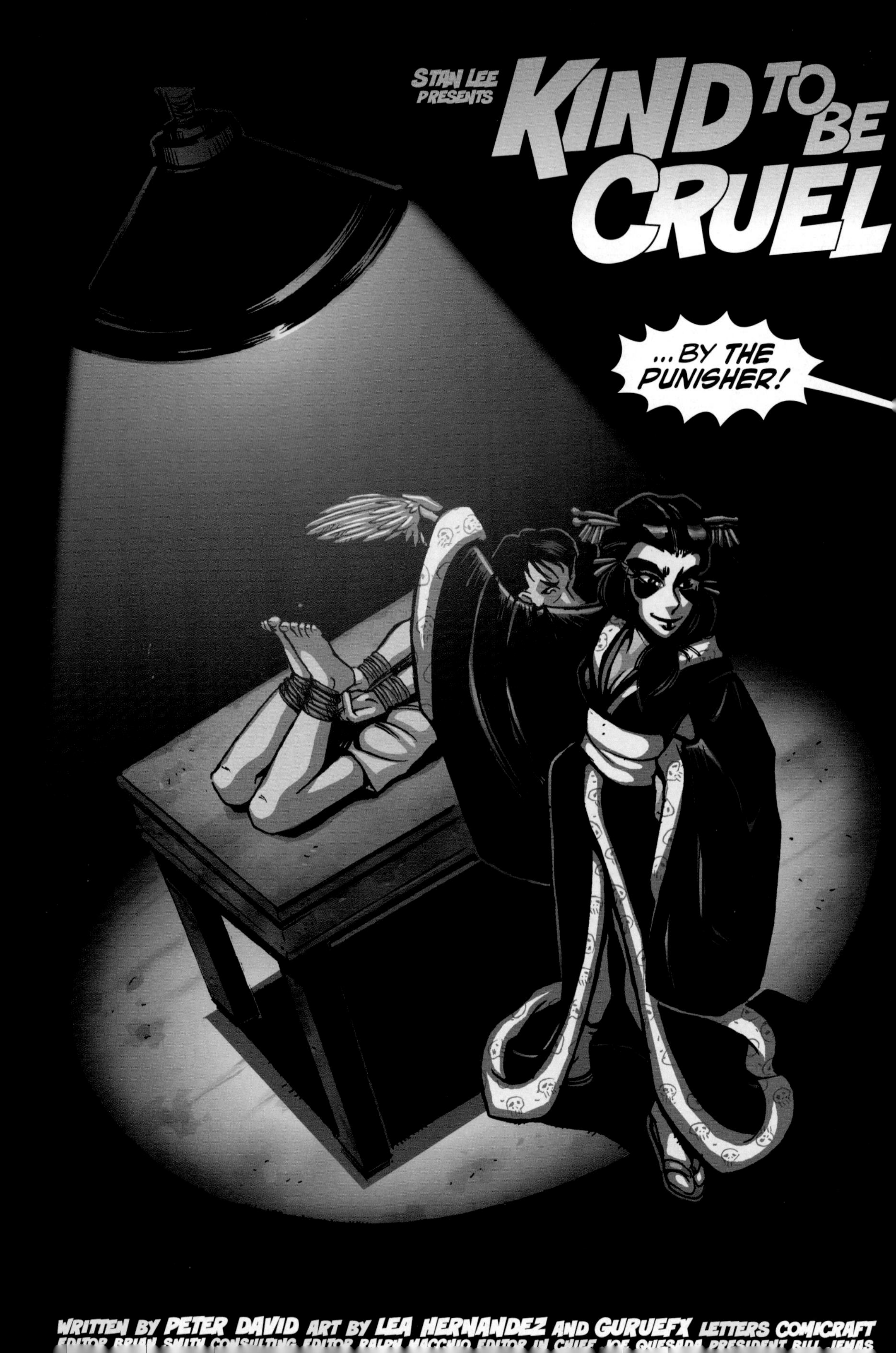
STAN LEE PRESENTS
KIND TO BE CRUEL
...BY THE PUNISHER!
WRITTEN BY PETER DAVID ART BY LEA HERNANDEZ AND GURUEFX LETTERS COMICRAFT
EDITOR BRIAN SMITH CONSULTING EDITOR RALPH MACCHIO EDITOR IN CHIEF JOE QUESADA PRESIDENT BILL JEMAS

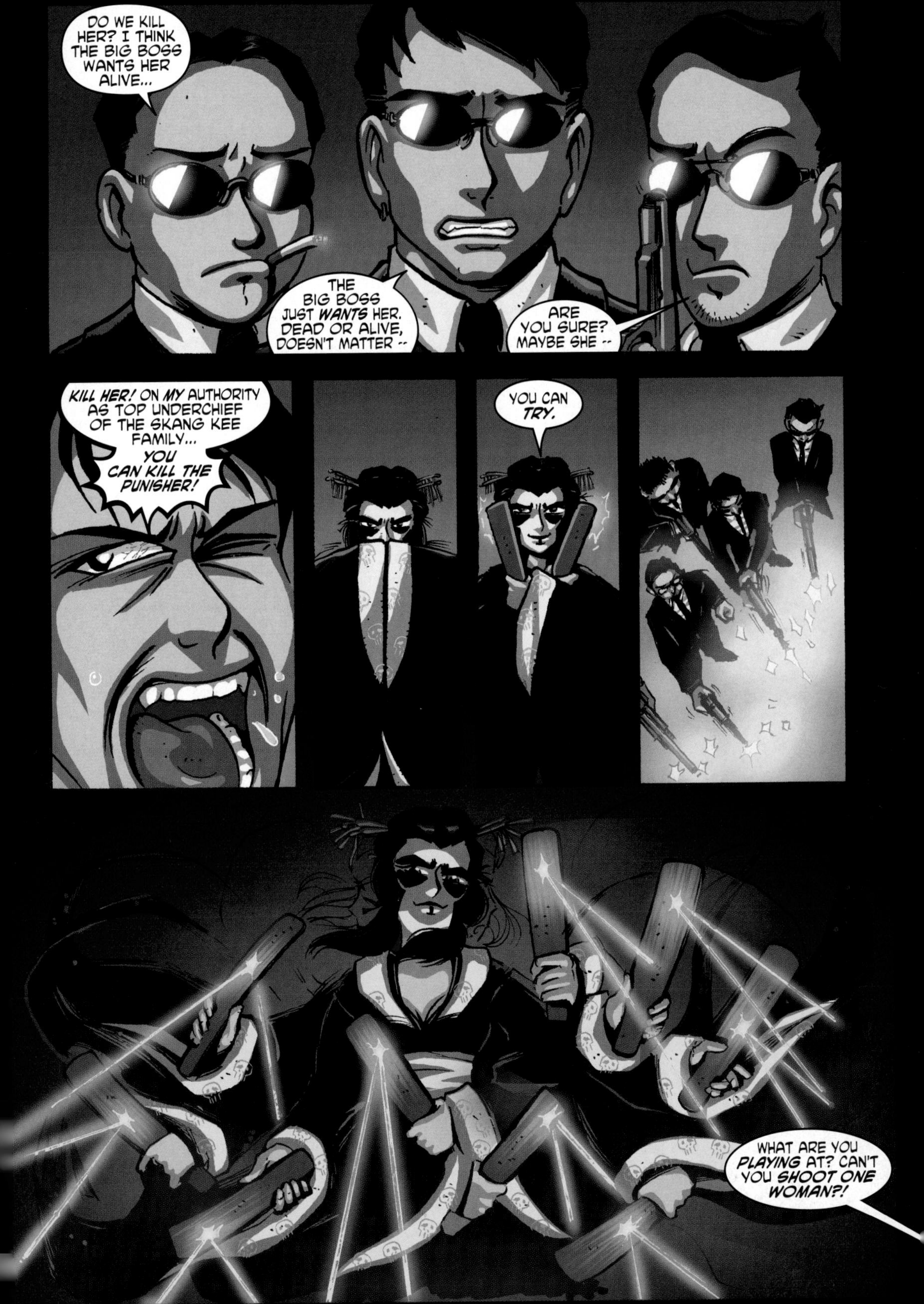
DO WE KILL HER? I THINK THE BIG BOSS WANTS HER ALIVE...
THE BIG BOSS JUST WANTS HER. DEAD OR ALIVE, DOESN'T MATTER --
ARE YOU SURE? MAYBE SHE --
KILL HER! ON MY AUTHORITY AS TOP UNDERCHIEF OF THE SKANG KEE FAMILY... YOU CAN KILL THE PUNISHER!
YOU CAN TRY.
WHAT ARE YOU PLAYING AT? CAN'T YOU SHOOT ONE WOMAN?!

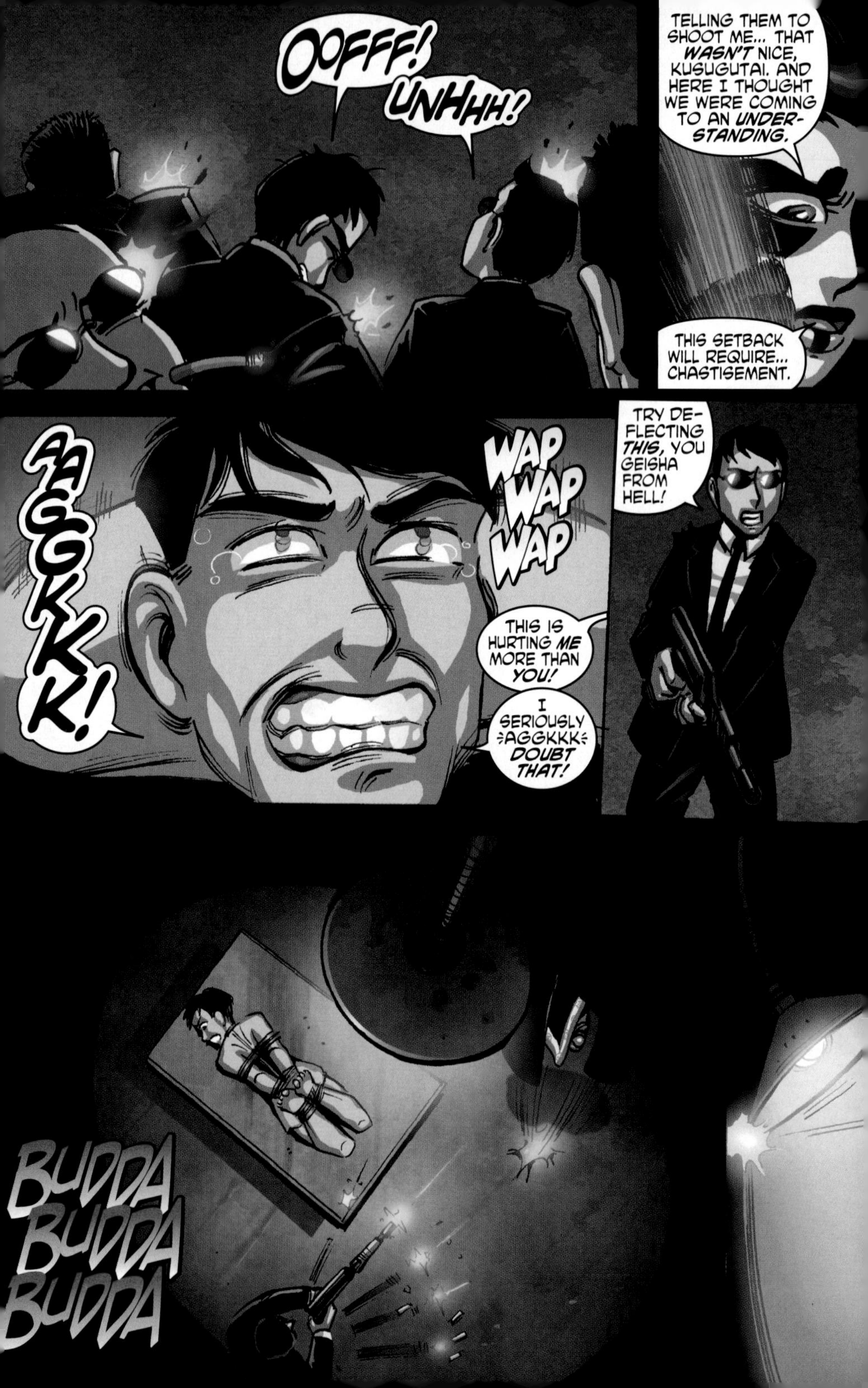
OOFFF!
UNHHH!
TELLING THEM TO SHOOT ME... THAT WASN'T NICE, KUSUGUTAI. AND HERE I THOUGHT WE WERE COMING TO AN UNDER-STANDING.
THIS SETBACK WILL REQUIRE... CHASTISEMENT.
AAGGKKK!
WAP WAP WAP
THIS IS HURTING ME MORE THAN YOU!
I SERIOUSLY AGGKKK DOUBT THAT!
TRY DE-FLECTING THIS, YOU GEISHA FROM HELL!
BUDDA BUDDA BUDDA

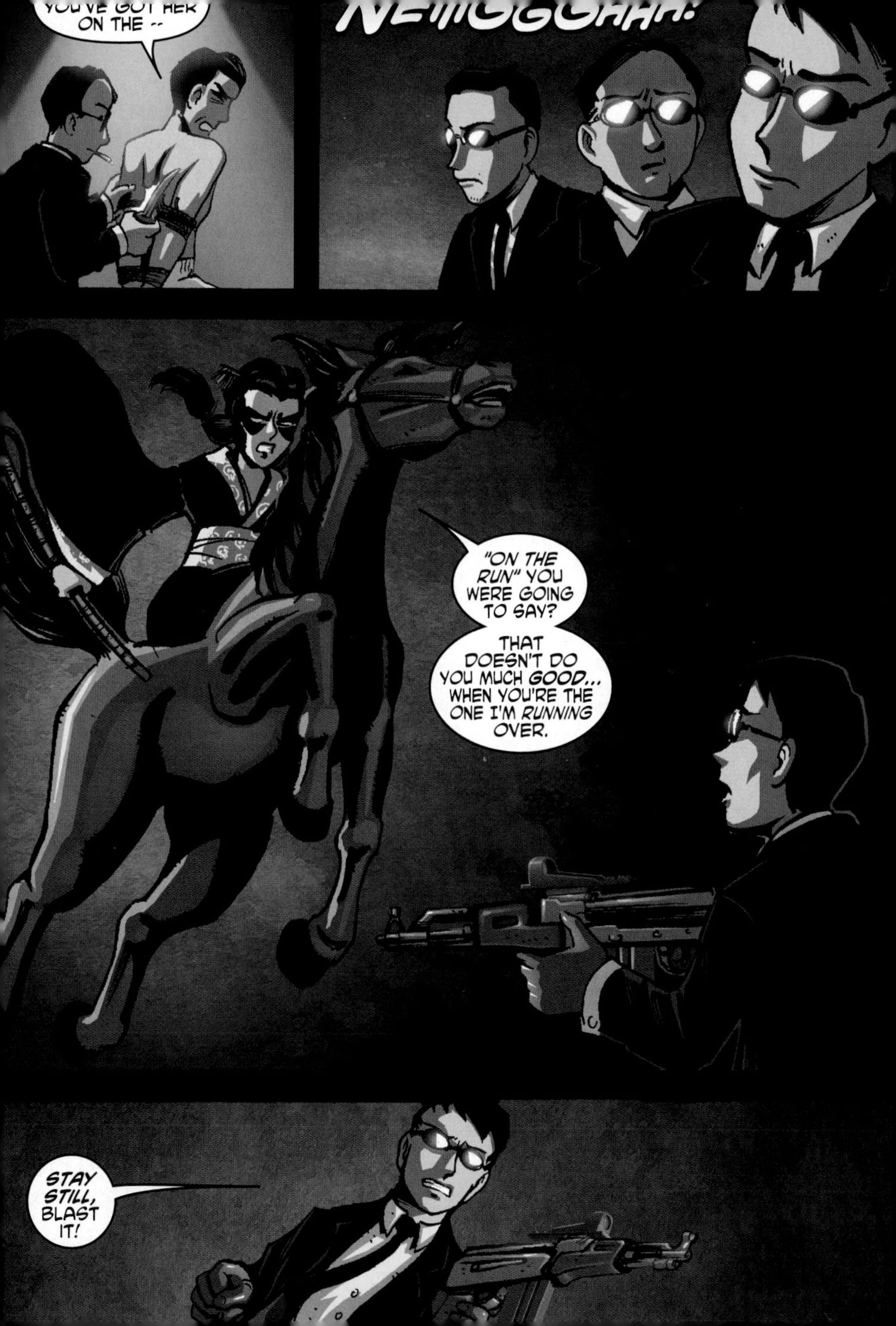
YOU'VE GOT HER ON THE --
"ON THE RUN" YOU WERE GOING TO SAY?
THAT DOESN'T DO YOU MUCH GOOD... WHEN YOU'RE THE ONE I'M RUNNING OVER.
STAY STILL, BLAST IT!

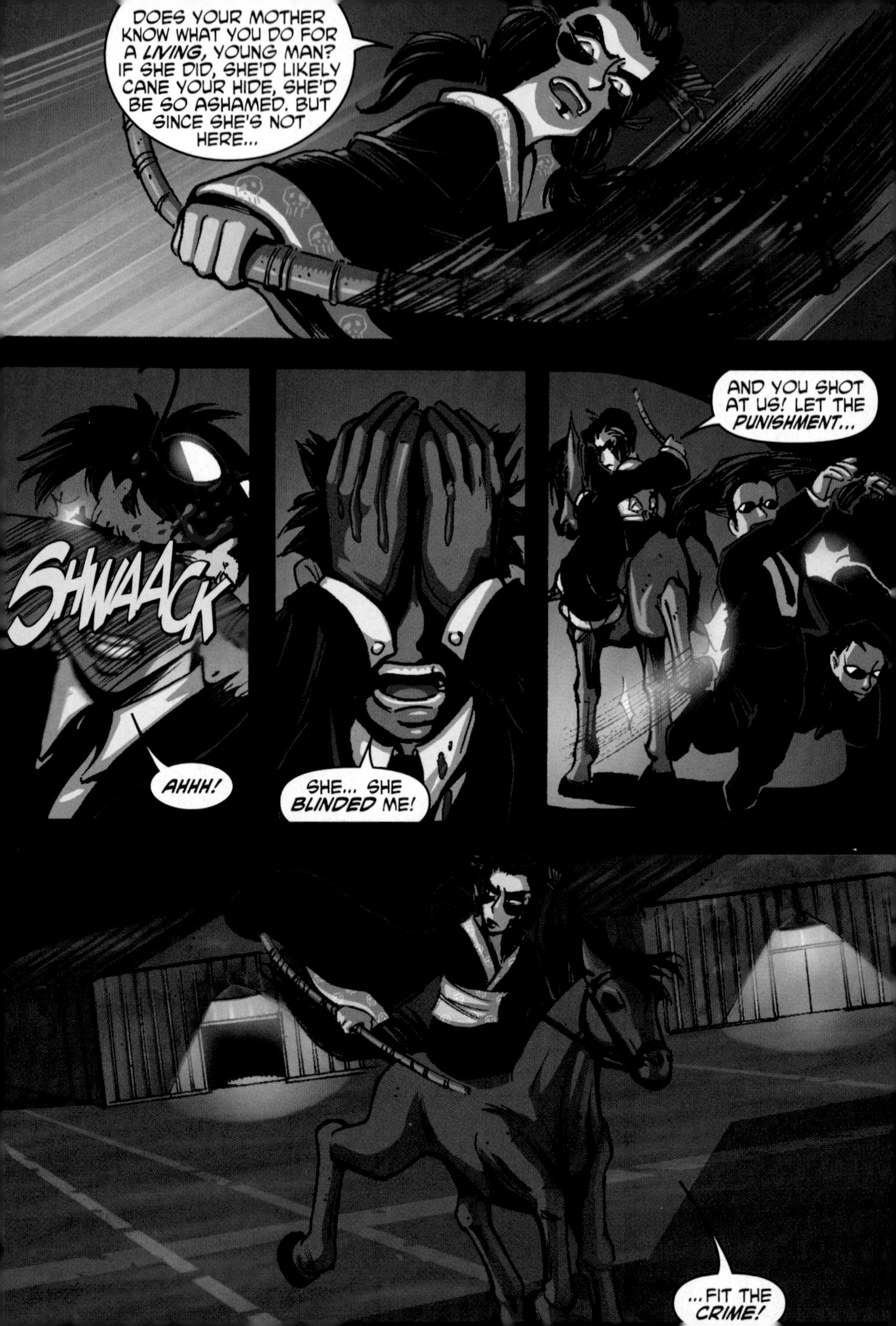
DOES YOUR MOTHER KNOW WHAT YOU DO FOR A LIVING, YOUNG MAN? IF SHE DID, SHE'D LIKELY CANE YOUR HIDE, SHE'D BE SO ASHAMED. BUT SINCE SHE'S NOT HERE...
SHWAACK
AHHH!
SHE... SHE BLINDED ME!
AND YOU SHOT AT US! LET THE PUNISHMENT...
...FIT THE CRIME!

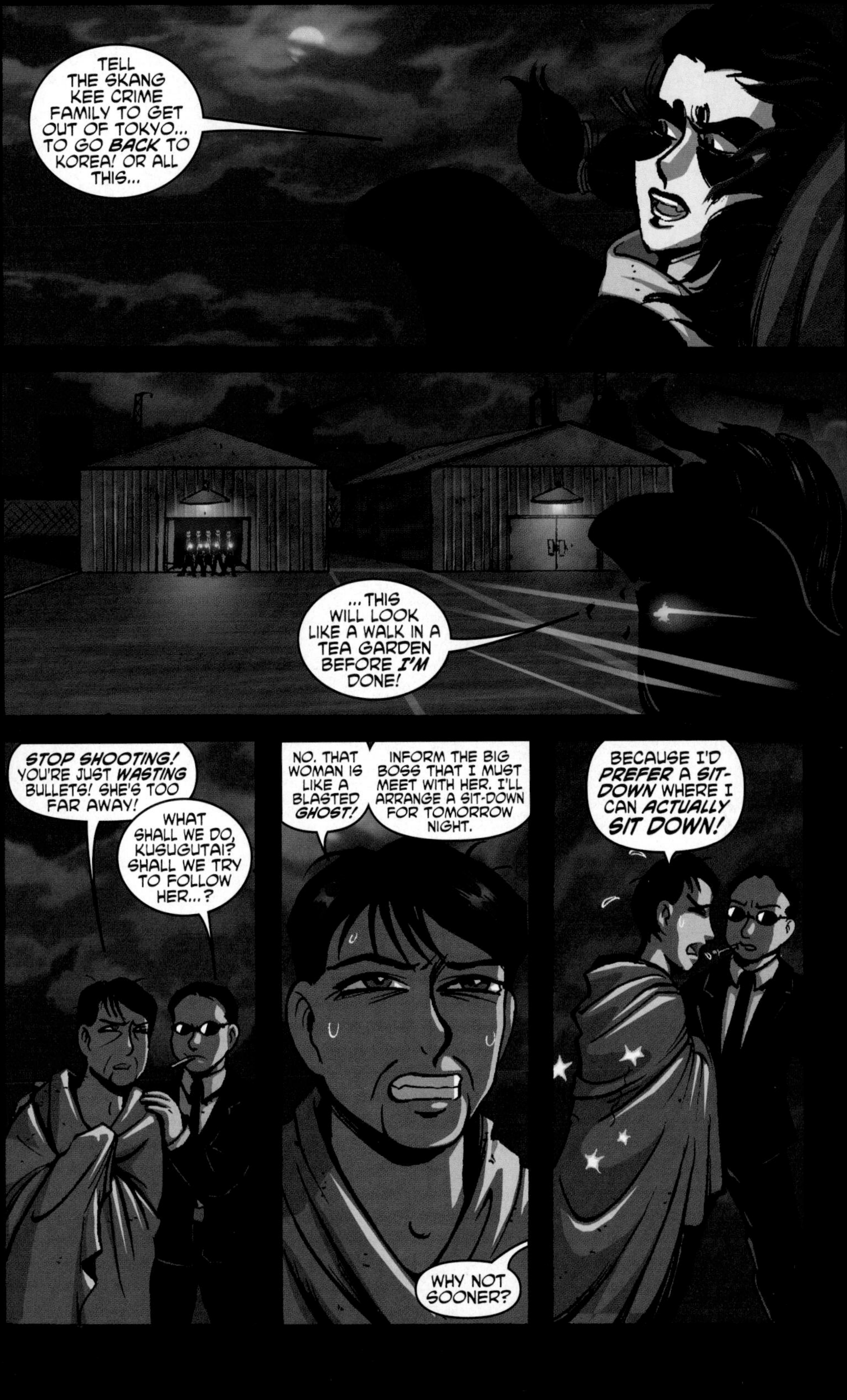
TELL THE SKANG KEE CRIME FAMILY TO GET OUT OF TOKYO... TO GO BACK TO KOREA! OR ALL THIS...
...THIS WILL LOOK LIKE A WALK IN A TEA GARDEN BEFORE I'M DONE!
STOP SHOOTING! YOU'RE JUST WASTING BULLETS! SHE'S TOO FAR AWAY!
WHAT SHALL WE DO, KUSUGUTAI? SHALL WE TRY TO FOLLOW HER...?
NO. THAT WOMAN IS LIKE A BLASTED GHOST!
INFORM THE BIG BOSS THAT I MUST MEET WITH HER. I'LL ARRANGE A SIT-DOWN FOR TOMORROW NIGHT.
WHY NOT SOONER?
BECAUSE I'D PREFER A SIT-DOWN WHERE I CAN ACTUALLY SIT DOWN!

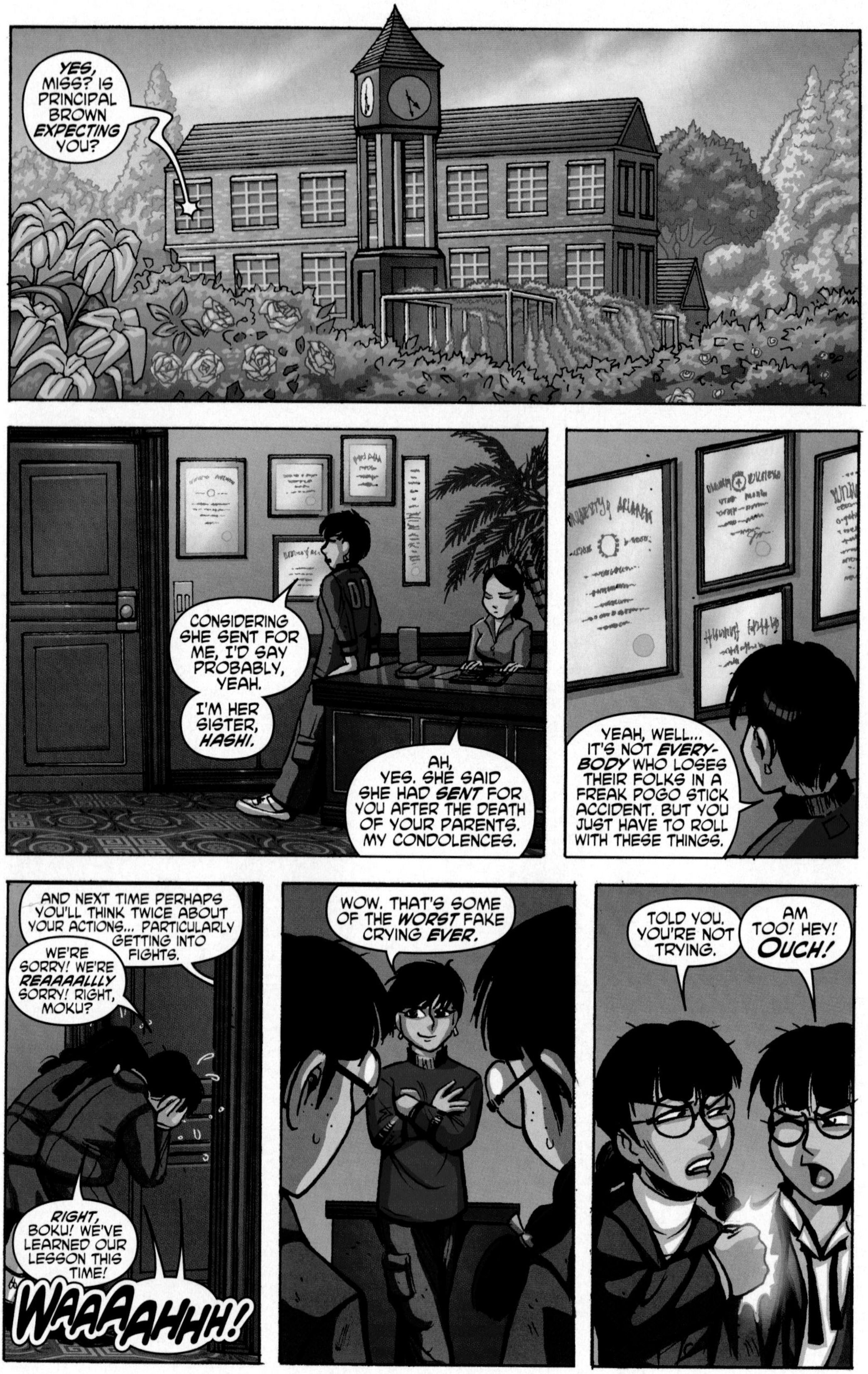
YES, MISS? IS PRINCIPAL BROWN EXPECTING YOU?
CONSIDERING SHE SENT FOR ME, I'D SAY PROBABLY, YEAH.
I'M HER SISTER, HASHI.
AH, YES. SHE SAID SHE HAD SENT FOR YOU AFTER THE DEATH OF YOUR PARENTS. MY CONDOLENCES.
YEAH, WELL... IT'S NOT EVERY-BODY WHO LOSES THEIR FOLKS IN A FREAK POGO STICK ACCIDENT. BUT YOU JUST HAVE TO ROLL WITH THESE THINGS.
AND NEXT TIME PERHAPS YOU'LL THINK TWICE ABOUT YOUR ACTIONS... PARTICULARLY GETTING INTO FIGHTS.
WE'RE SORRY! WE'RE REAAAALLLY SORRY! RIGHT, MOKU?
RIGHT, BOKU! WE'VE LEARNED OUR LESSON THIS TIME!
WAAAAHHH!
WOW. THAT'S SOME OF THE WORST FAKE CRYING EVER.
TOLD YOU. YOU'RE NOT TRYING.
AM TOO! HEY! OUCH!

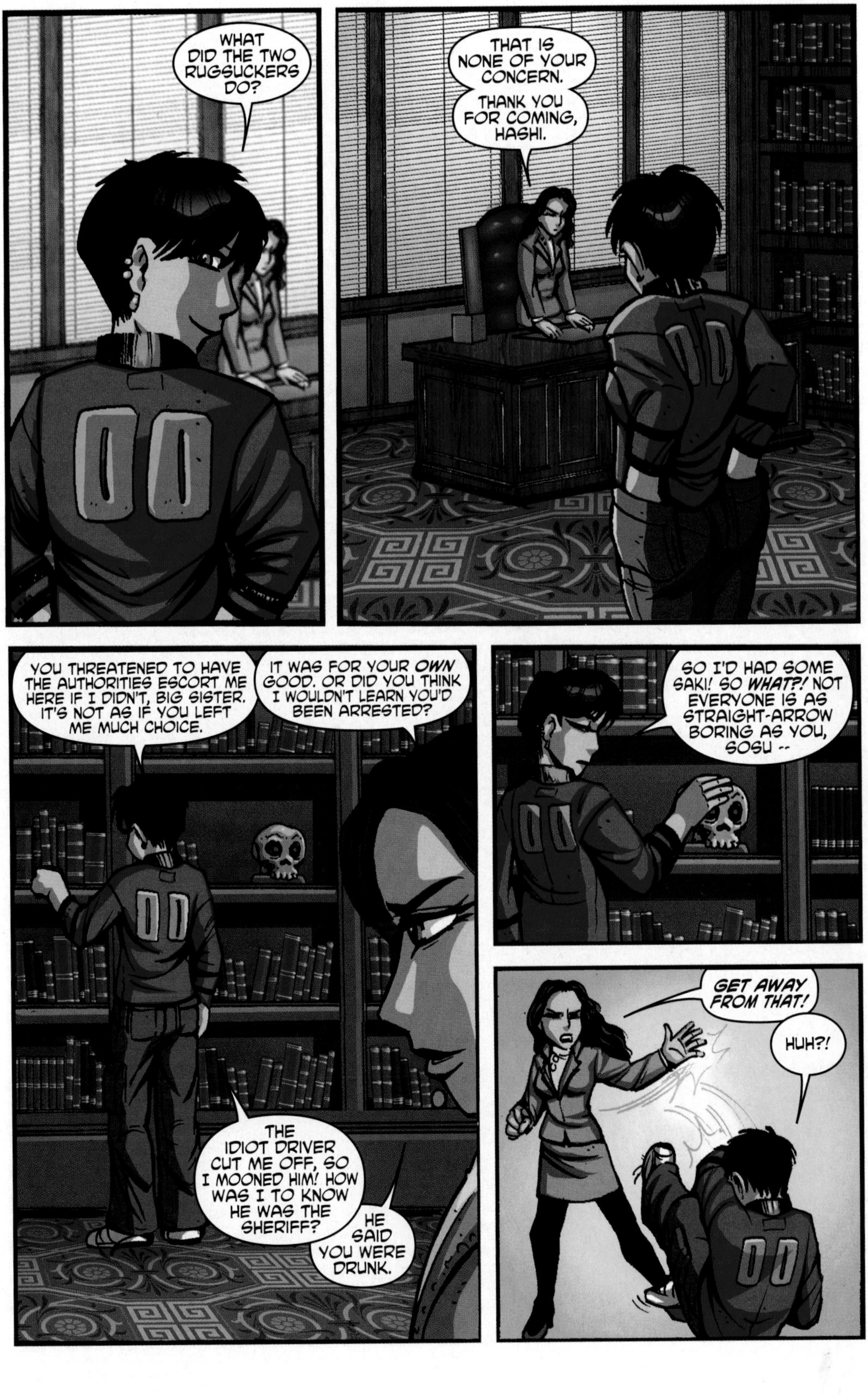
WHAT DID THE TWO RUGSUCKERS DO?
THAT IS NONE OF YOUR CONCERN.
THANK YOU FOR COMING, HASHI.
YOU THREATENED TO HAVE THE AUTHORITIES ESCORT ME HERE IF I DIDN'T, BIG SISTER. IT'S NOT AS IF YOU LEFT ME MUCH CHOICE.
IT WAS FOR YOUR *OWN* GOOD. OR DID YOU THINK I WOULDN'T LEARN YOU'D BEEN ARRESTED?
THE IDIOT DRIVER CUT ME OFF, SO I MOONED HIM! HOW WAS I TO KNOW HE WAS THE SHERIFF?
HE SAID YOU WERE DRUNK.
SO I'D HAD SOME SAKI! SO *WHAT?!* NOT EVERYONE IS AS STRAIGHT-ARROW BORING AS YOU, SOSU --
GET AWAY FROM THAT!
HUH?!

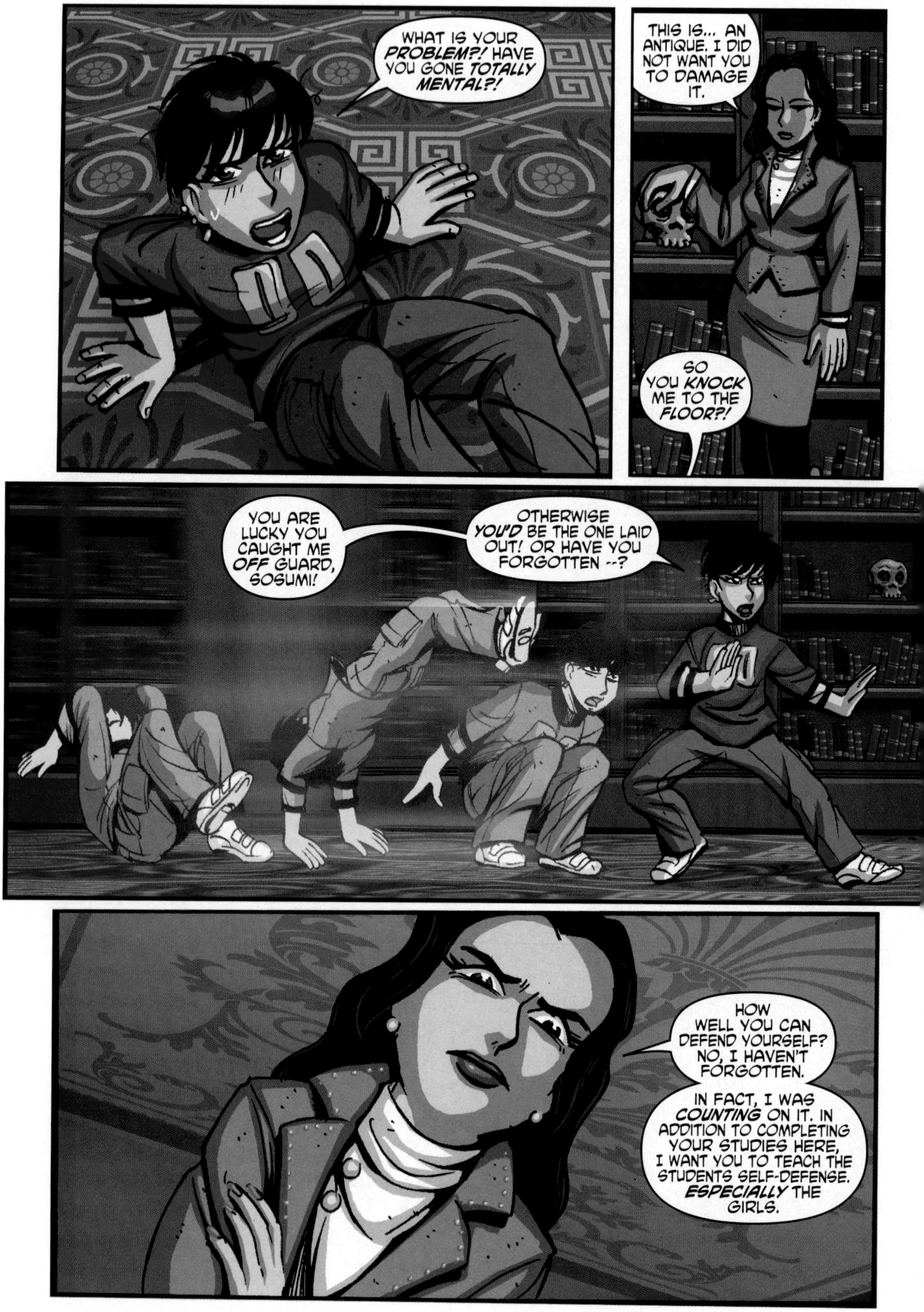
WHAT IS YOUR PROBLEM?! HAVE YOU GONE TOTALLY MENTAL?!
THIS IS... AN ANTIQUE. I DID NOT WANT YOU TO DAMAGE IT.
SO YOU KNOCK ME TO THE FLOOR?!
YOU ARE LUCKY YOU CAUGHT ME OFF GUARD, SOSUMI!
OTHERWISE YOU'D BE THE ONE LAID OUT! OR HAVE YOU FORGOTTEN --?
HOW WELL YOU CAN DEFEND YOURSELF? NO, I HAVEN'T FORGOTTEN.
IN FACT, I WAS COUNTING ON IT. IN ADDITION TO COMPLETING YOUR STUDIES HERE, I WANT YOU TO TEACH THE STUDENTS SELF-DEFENSE. ESPECIALLY THE GIRLS.

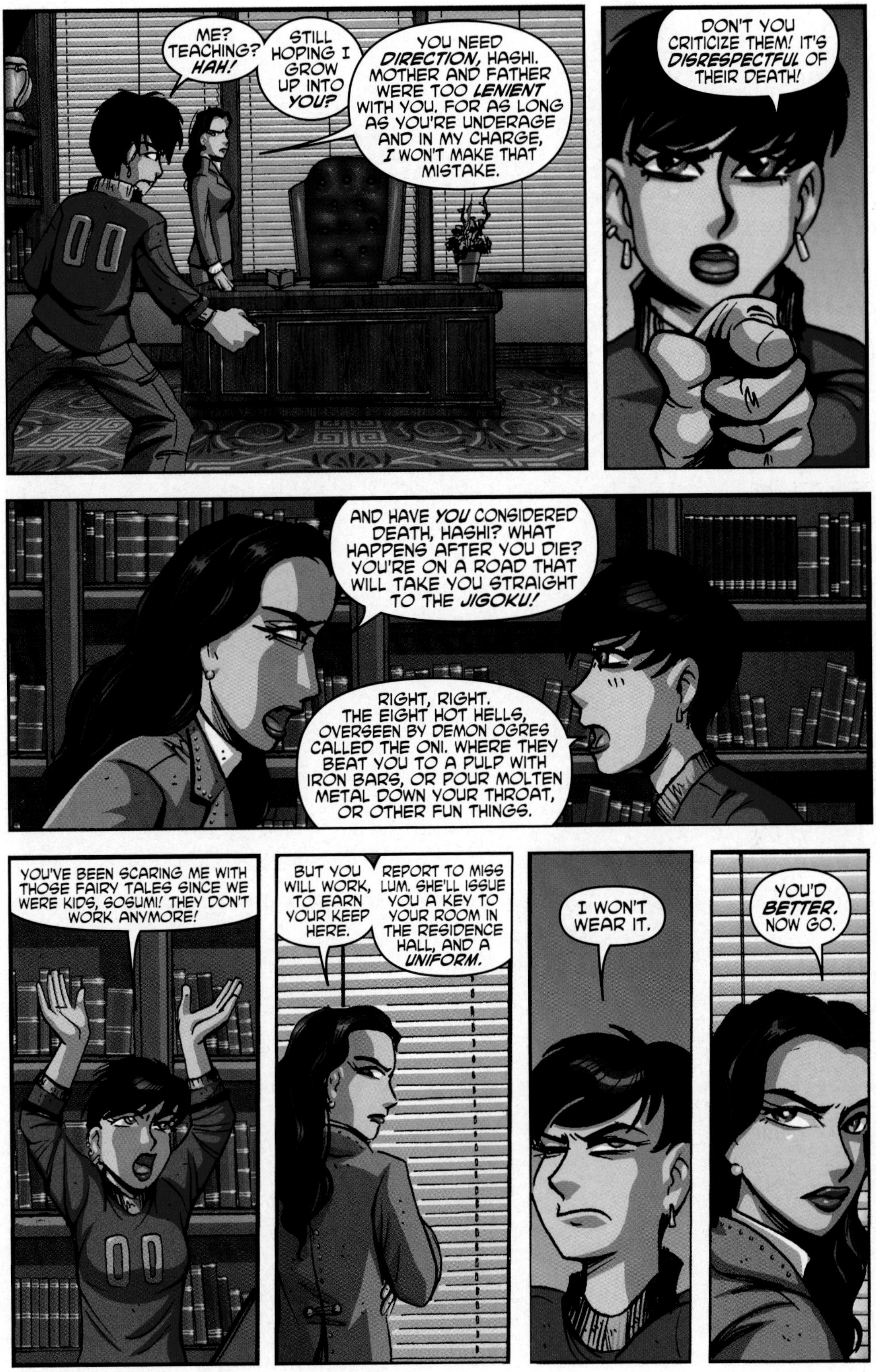
ME? TEACHING? HAH!
STILL HOPING I GROW UP INTO YOU?
YOU NEED DIRECTION, HASHI. MOTHER AND FATHER WERE TOO LENIENT WITH YOU. FOR AS LONG AS YOU'RE UNDERAGE AND IN MY CHARGE, I WON'T MAKE THAT MISTAKE.
DON'T YOU CRITICIZE THEM! IT'S DISRESPECTFUL OF THEIR DEATH!
AND HAVE YOU CONSIDERED DEATH, HASHI? WHAT HAPPENS AFTER YOU DIE? YOU'RE ON A ROAD THAT WILL TAKE YOU STRAIGHT TO THE JIGOKU!
RIGHT, RIGHT. THE EIGHT HOT HELLS, OVERSEEN BY DEMON OGRES CALLED THE ONI. WHERE THEY BEAT YOU TO A PULP WITH IRON BARS, OR POUR MOLTEN METAL DOWN YOUR THROAT, OR OTHER FUN THINGS.
YOU'VE BEEN SCARING ME WITH THOSE FAIRY TALES SINCE WE WERE KIDS, SOSUMI! THEY DON'T WORK ANYMORE!
BUT YOU WILL WORK, TO EARN YOUR KEEP HERE.
REPORT TO MISS LUM. SHE'LL ISSUE YOU A KEY TO YOUR ROOM IN THE RESIDENCE HALL, AND A UNIFORM.
I WON'T WEAR IT.
YOU'D BETTER. NOW GO.

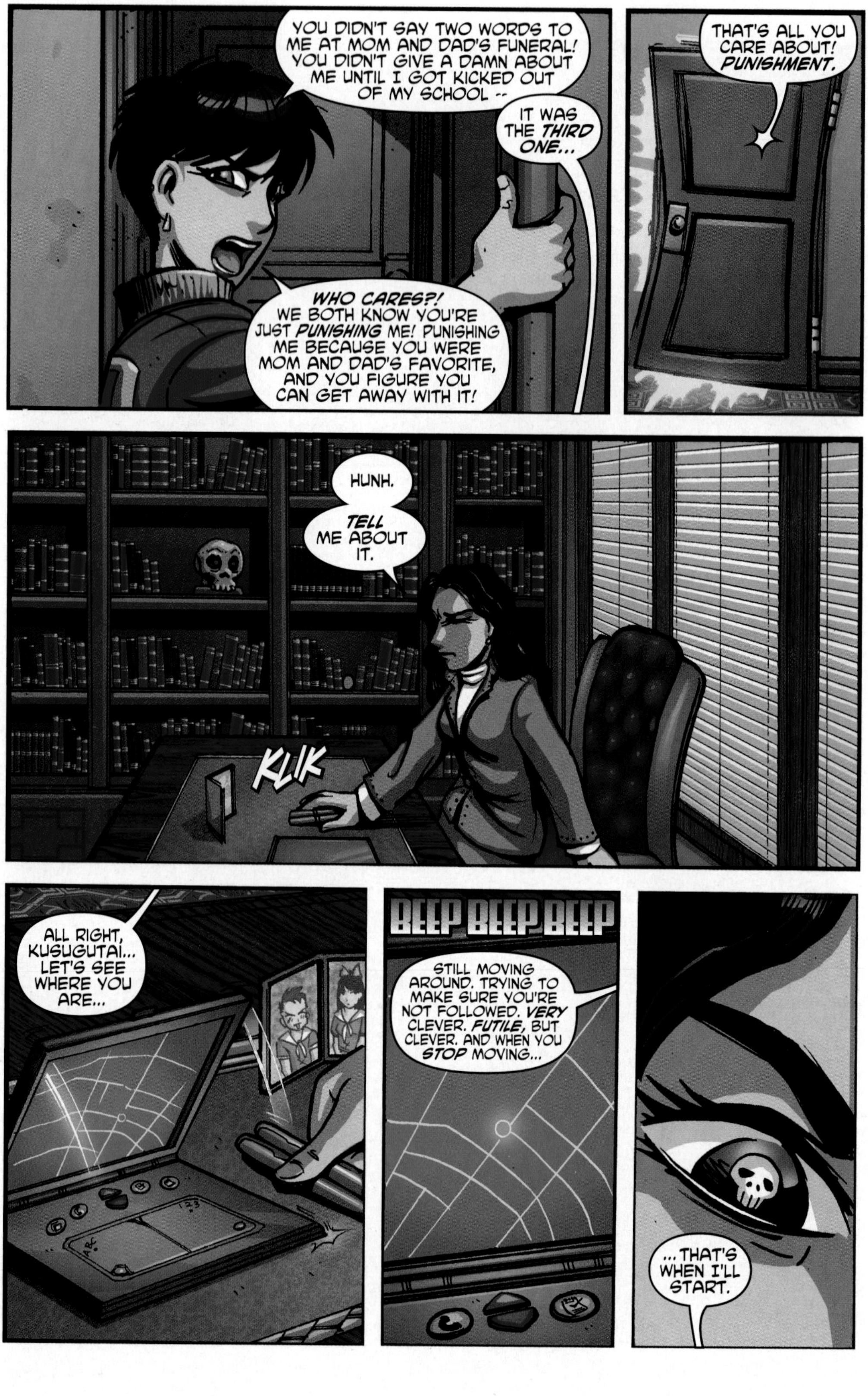
YOU DIDN'T SAY TWO WORDS TO ME AT MOM AND DAD'S FUNERAL! YOU DIDN'T GIVE A DAMN ABOUT ME UNTIL I GOT KICKED OUT OF MY SCHOOL --
IT WAS THE THIRD ONE...
WHO CARES?! WE BOTH KNOW YOU'RE JUST PUNISHING ME! PUNISHING ME BECAUSE YOU WERE MOM AND DAD'S FAVORITE, AND YOU FIGURE YOU CAN GET AWAY WITH IT!
THAT'S ALL YOU CARE ABOUT! PUNISHMENT.
HUNH.
TELL ME ABOUT IT.
KLIK
ALL RIGHT, KUSUGUTAI... LET'S SEE WHERE YOU ARE...
BEEP BEEP BEEP
STILL MOVING AROUND. TRYING TO MAKE SURE YOU'RE NOT FOLLOWED. VERY CLEVER. FUTILE, BUT CLEVER. AND WHEN YOU STOP MOVING...
...THAT'S WHEN I'LL START.

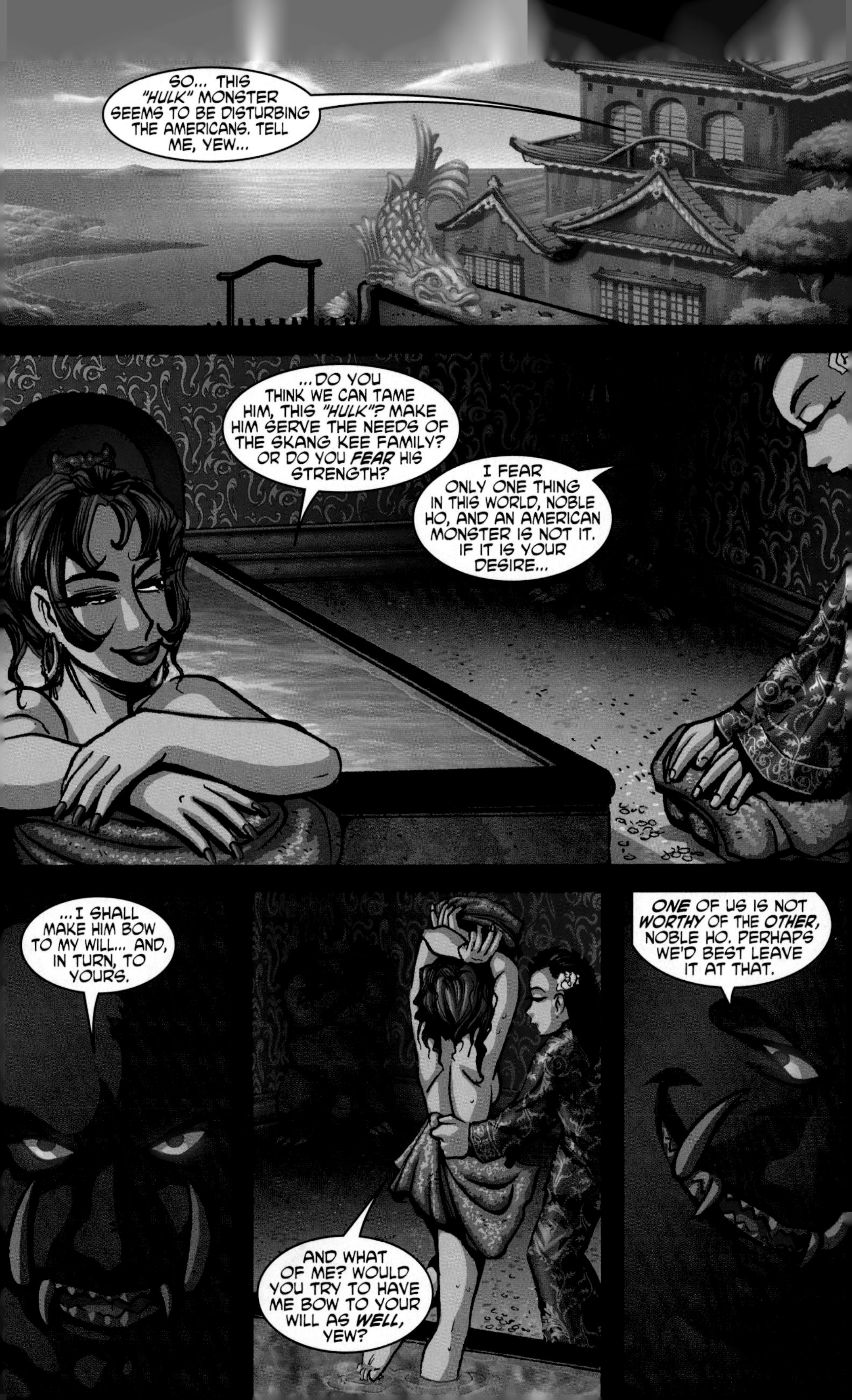
SO... THIS "HULK" MONSTER SEEMS TO BE DISTURBING THE AMERICANS. TELL ME, YEW...
...DO YOU THINK WE CAN TAME HIM, THIS "HULK"? MAKE HIM SERVE THE NEEDS OF THE SKANG KEE FAMILY? OR DO YOU *FEAR* HIS STRENGTH?
I FEAR ONLY ONE THING IN THIS WORLD, NOBLE HO, AND AN AMERICAN MONSTER IS NOT IT. IF IT IS YOUR DESIRE...
...I SHALL MAKE HIM BOW TO MY WILL... AND, IN TURN, TO YOURS.
AND WHAT OF ME? WOULD YOU TRY TO HAVE ME BOW TO YOUR WILL AS *WELL*, YEW?
ONE OF US IS NOT *WORTHY* OF THE *OTHER*, NOBLE HO. PERHAPS WE'D BEST LEAVE IT AT THAT.

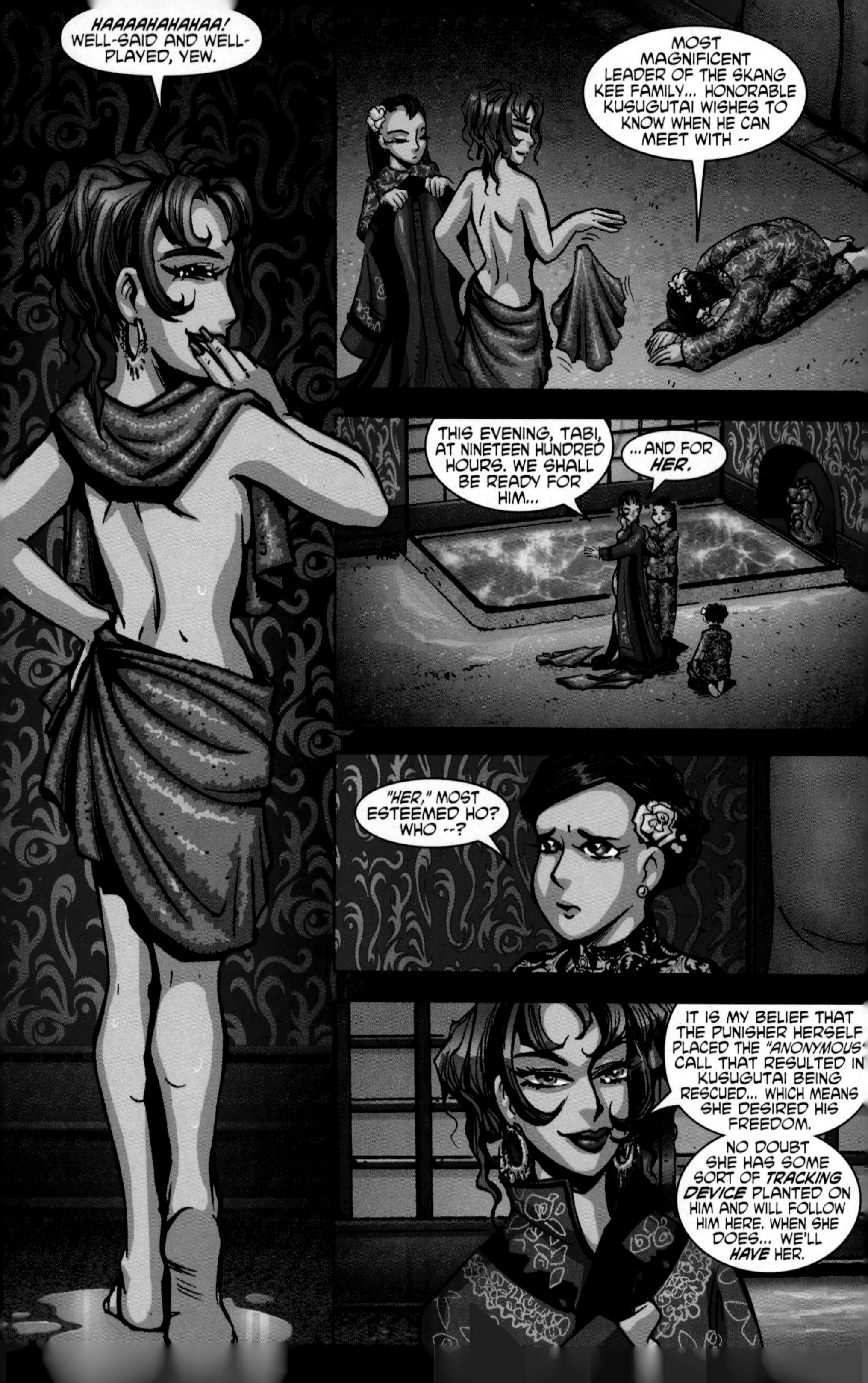
HAAAAHAHAHAA! WELL-SAID AND WELL-PLAYED, YEW.
MOST MAGNIFICENT LEADER OF THE SKANG KEE FAMILY... HONORABLE KUSUGUTAI WISHES TO KNOW WHEN HE CAN MEET WITH --
THIS EVENING, TABI, AT NINETEEN HUNDRED HOURS. WE SHALL BE READY FOR HIM...
...AND FOR HER.
"HER," MOST ESTEEMED HO? WHO --?
IT IS MY BELIEF THAT THE PUNISHER HERSELF PLACED THE "ANONYMOUS" CALL THAT RESULTED IN KUSUGUTAI BEING RESCUED... WHICH MEANS SHE DESIRED HIS FREEDOM.
NO DOUBT SHE HAS SOME SORT OF TRACKING DEVICE PLANTED ON HIM AND WILL FOLLOW HIM HERE. WHEN SHE DOES... WE'LL HAVE HER.

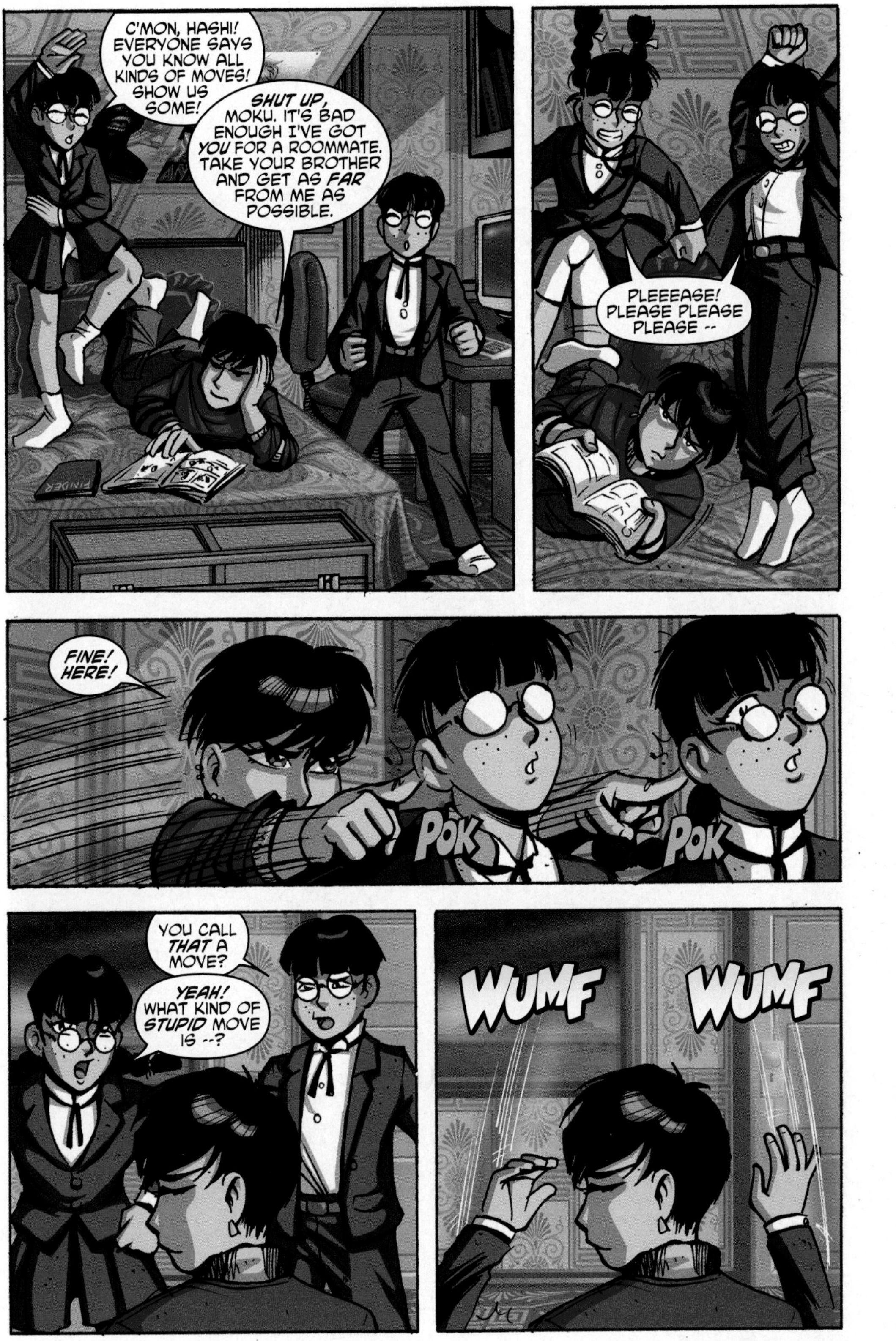
C'MON, HASHI! EVERYONE SAYS YOU KNOW ALL KINDS OF MOVES! SHOW US SOME!
SHUT UP, MOKU. IT'S BAD ENOUGH I'VE GOT YOU FOR A ROOMMATE. TAKE YOUR BROTHER AND GET AS FAR FROM ME AS POSSIBLE.
FINDER
PLEEEASE! PLEASE PLEASE PLEASE --
FINE! HERE!
POK
POK
YOU CALL THAT A MOVE?
YEAH! WHAT KIND OF STUPID MOVE IS --?
WUMF
WUMF

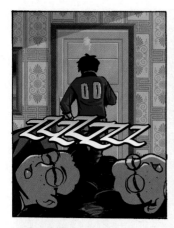

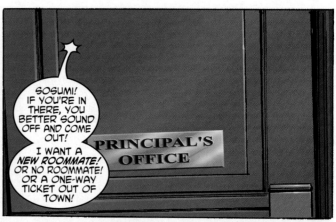

ZZZZZZZ
SOSUMI! IF YOU'RE IN THERE, YOU BETTER SOUND OFF AND COME OUT!
I WANT A *NEW ROOMMATE!* OR NO ROOMMATE! OR A ONE-WAY TICKET OUT OF TOWN!
PRINCIPAL'S OFFICE
SOSUMI!
PRINCIPAL'S OFFICE
HEY, SOSUMI! I'M IN YOUR *OFFICE!* I'M GONNA TOUCH YOUR STUFF! I'M HEADING STRAIGHT TO *JIGOKU* IF I HAVE MY WAY!
SEE? SEE? I'M TOUCHING YOUR FANCY ANTIQUE SKULL! I'M OUTTA CONTROL! SO YOU BETTER...!
KLIK
HUH?!

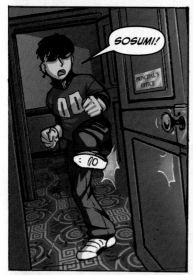

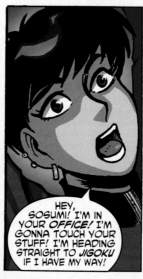

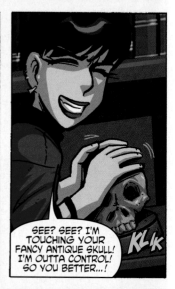

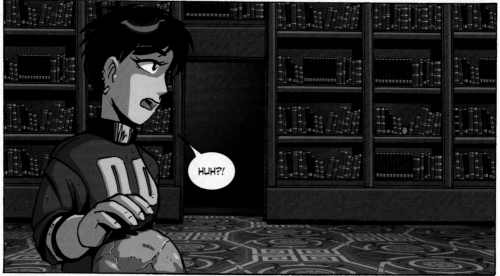

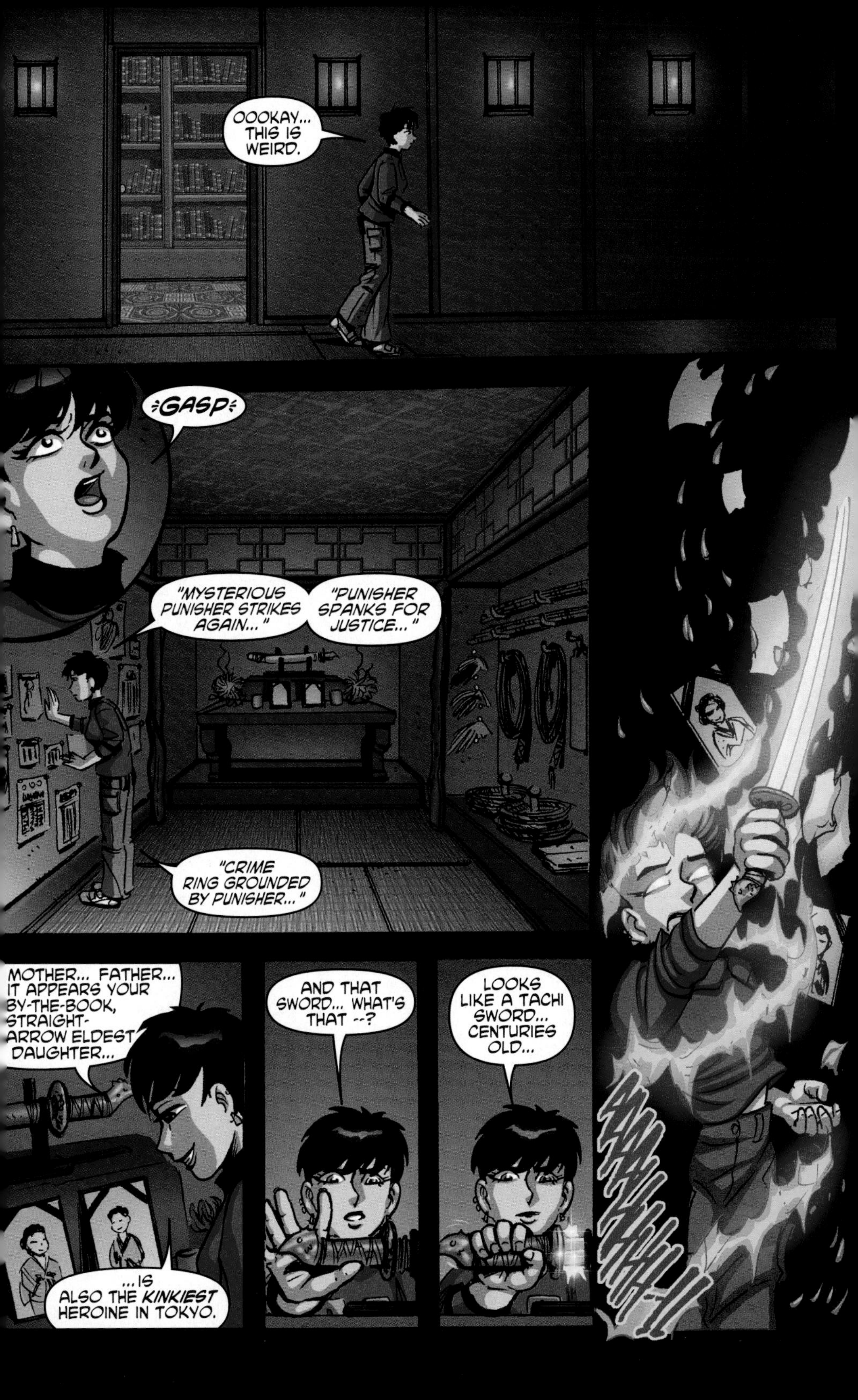
OOOKAY... THIS IS WEIRD.
GASP
"MYSTERIOUS PUNISHER STRIKES AGAIN..."
"PUNISHER SPANKS FOR JUSTICE..."
"CRIME RING GROUNDED BY PUNISHER..."
MOTHER... FATHER... IT APPEARS YOUR BY-THE-BOOK, STRAIGHT-ARROW ELDEST DAUGHTER...
...IS ALSO THE KINKIEST HEROINE IN TOKYO.
AND THAT SWORD... WHAT'S THAT --?
LOOKS LIKE A TACHI SWORD... CENTURIES OLD...

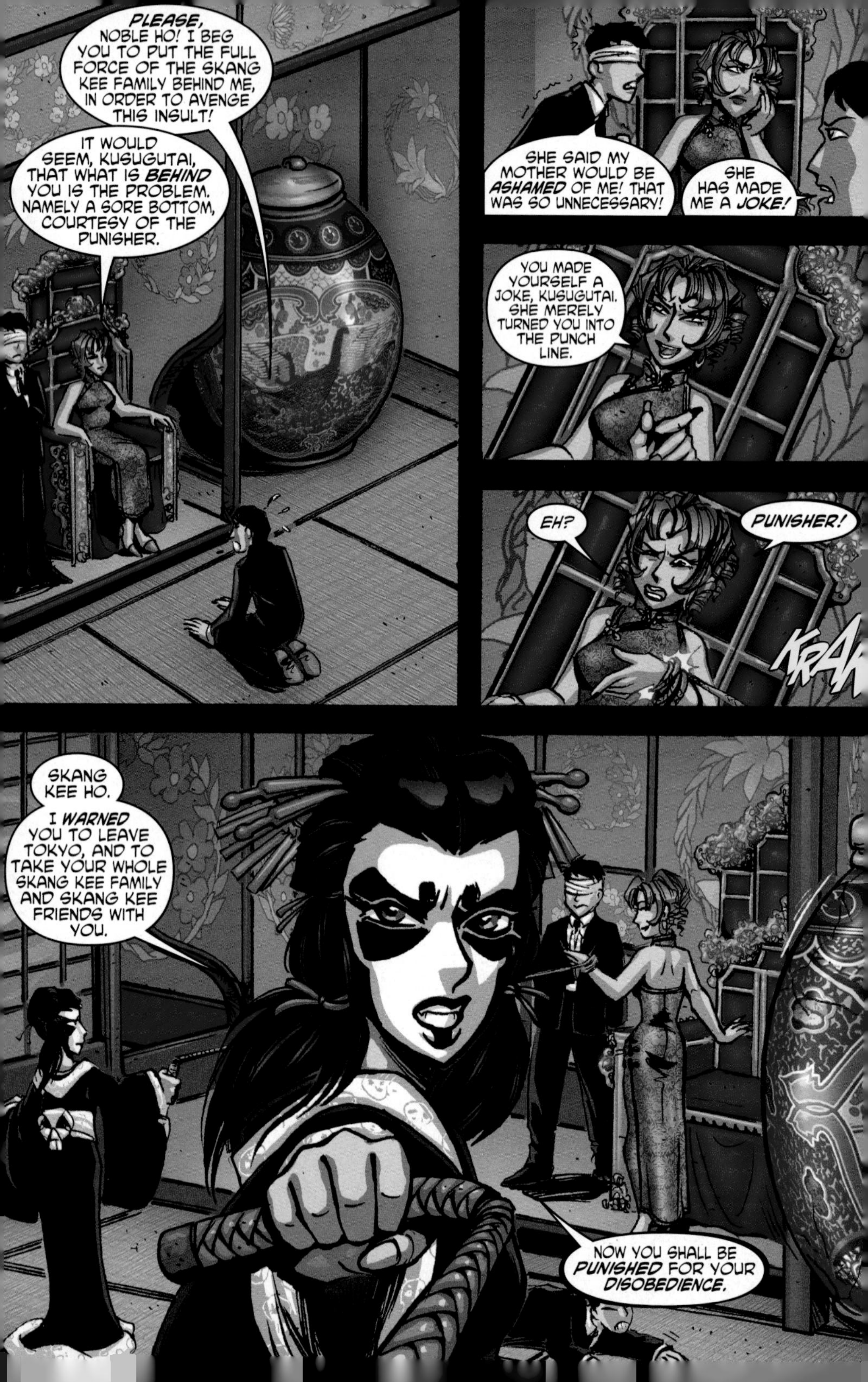

PLEASE, NOBLE HO! I BEG YOU TO PUT THE FULL FORCE OF THE SKANG KEE FAMILY BEHIND ME, IN ORDER TO AVENGE THIS INSULT!
IT WOULD SEEM, KUSUGUTAI, THAT WHAT IS BEHIND YOU IS THE PROBLEM. NAMELY A SORE BOTTOM, COURTESY OF THE PUNISHER.
SHE SAID MY MOTHER WOULD BE ASHAMED OF ME! THAT WAS SO UNNECESSARY!
SHE HAS MADE ME A JOKE!
YOU MADE YOURSELF A JOKE, KUSUGUTAI. SHE MERELY TURNED YOU INTO THE PUNCH LINE.
EH?
PUNISHER!
KRAK
SKANG KEE HO.
I WARNED YOU TO LEAVE TOKYO, AND TO TAKE YOUR WHOLE SKANG KEE FAMILY AND SKANG KEE FRIENDS WITH YOU.
NOW YOU SHALL BE PUNISHED FOR YOUR DISOBEDIENCE.

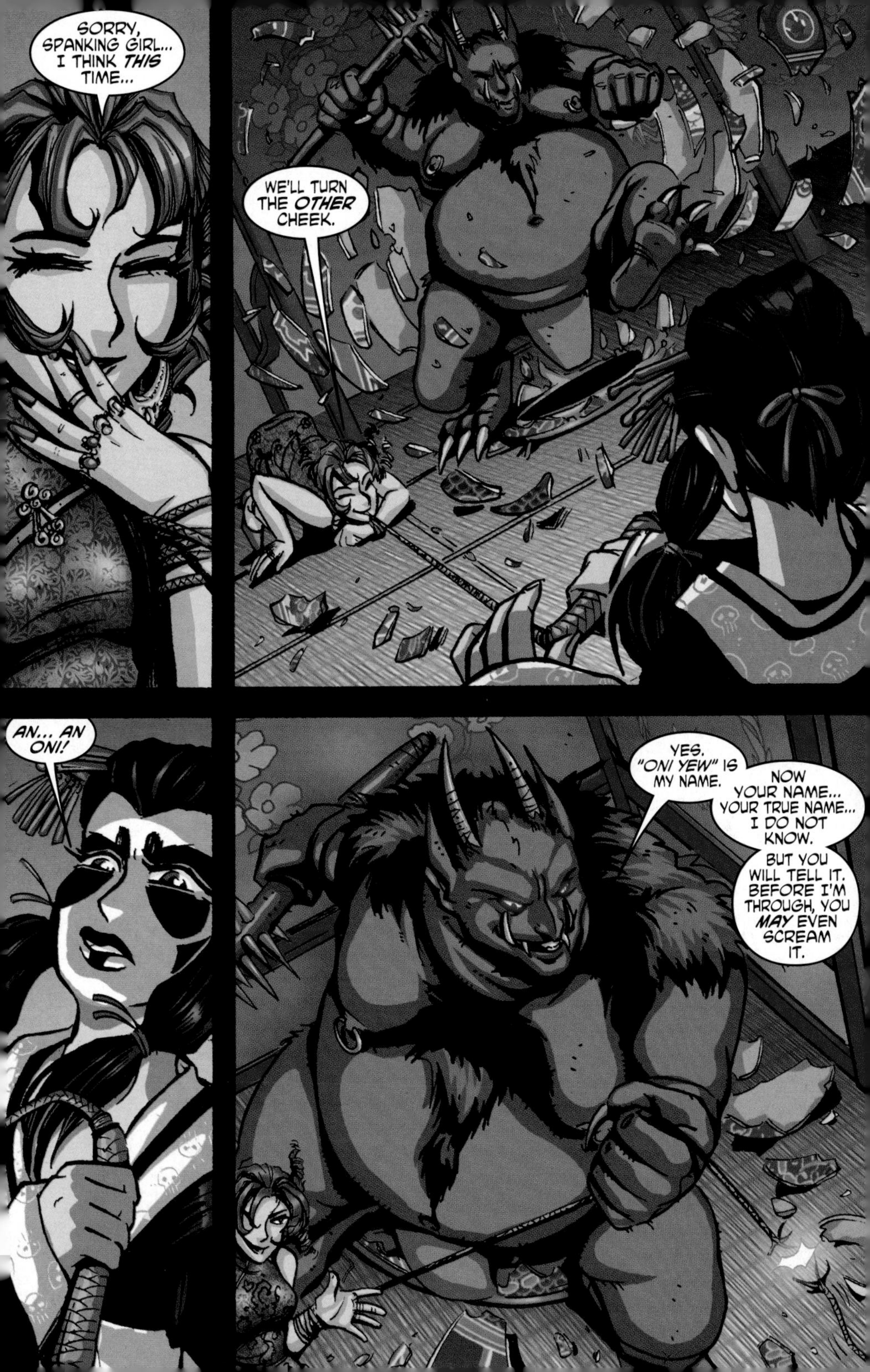
SORRY, SPANKING GIRL... I THINK *THIS* TIME...
WE'LL TURN THE *OTHER* CHEEK.
AN... AN ONI!
YES. "*ONI YEW*" IS MY NAME.
NOW YOUR NAME... YOUR TRUE NAME... I DO NOT KNOW.
BUT YOU WILL TELL IT. BEFORE I'M THROUGH, YOU *MAY* EVEN SCREAM IT.

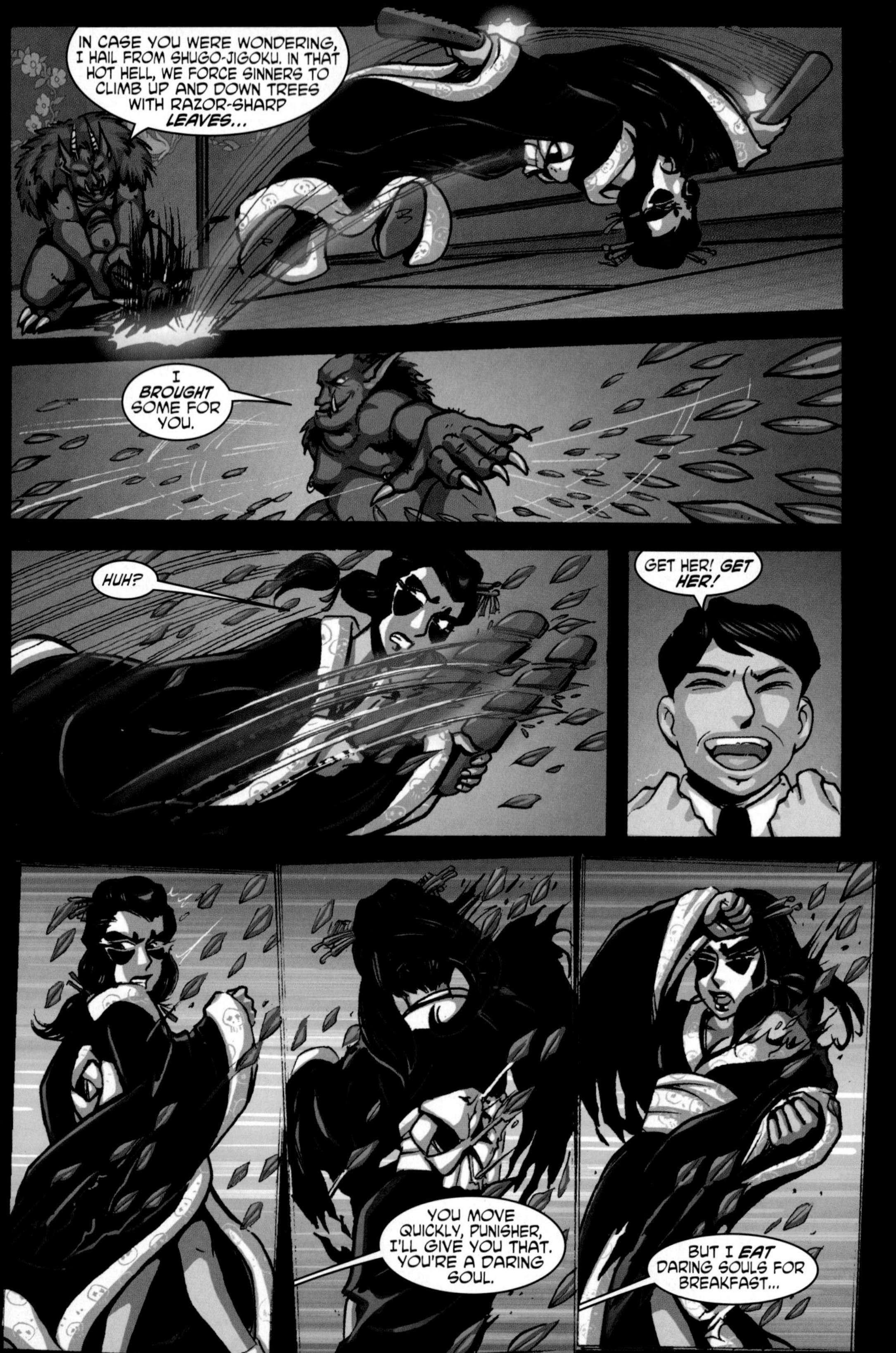
IN CASE YOU WERE WONDERING, I HAIL FROM SHUGO-JIGOKU. IN THAT HOT HELL, WE FORCE SINNERS TO CLIMB UP AND DOWN TREES WITH RAZOR-SHARP *LEAVES...*
I *BROUGHT* SOME FOR YOU.
HUH?
GET HER! *GET HER!*
YOU MOVE QUICKLY, PUNISHER, I'LL GIVE YOU THAT. YOU'RE A DARING SOUL.
BUT I *EAT* DARING SOULS FOR BREAKFAST...

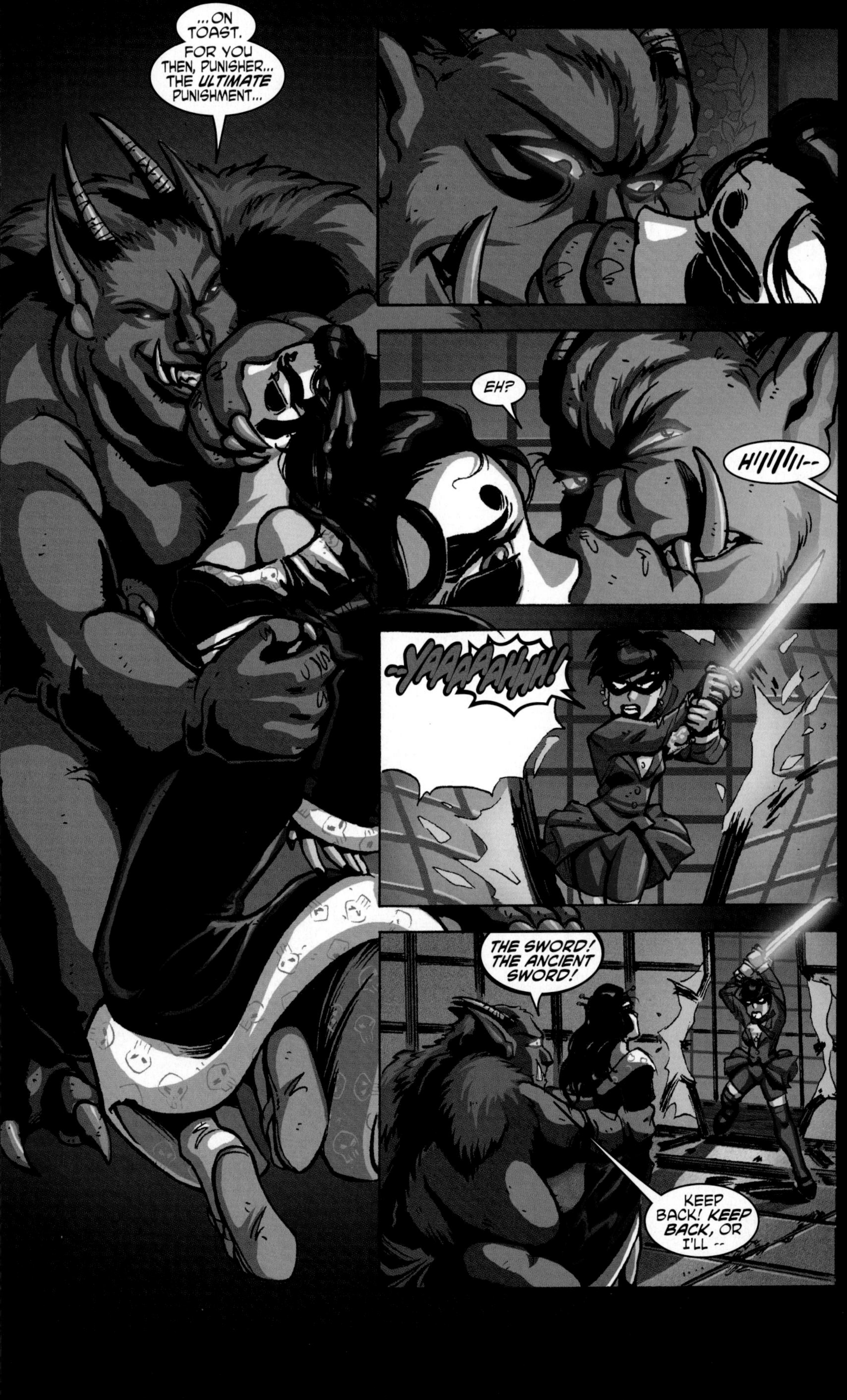
...ON TOAST. FOR YOU THEN, PUNISHER... THE ULTIMATE PUNISHMENT...
EH?
H!!!!!!--
-YAAAAAHHH!
THE SWORD! THE ANCIENT SWORD!
KEEP BACK! KEEP BACK, OR I'LL --

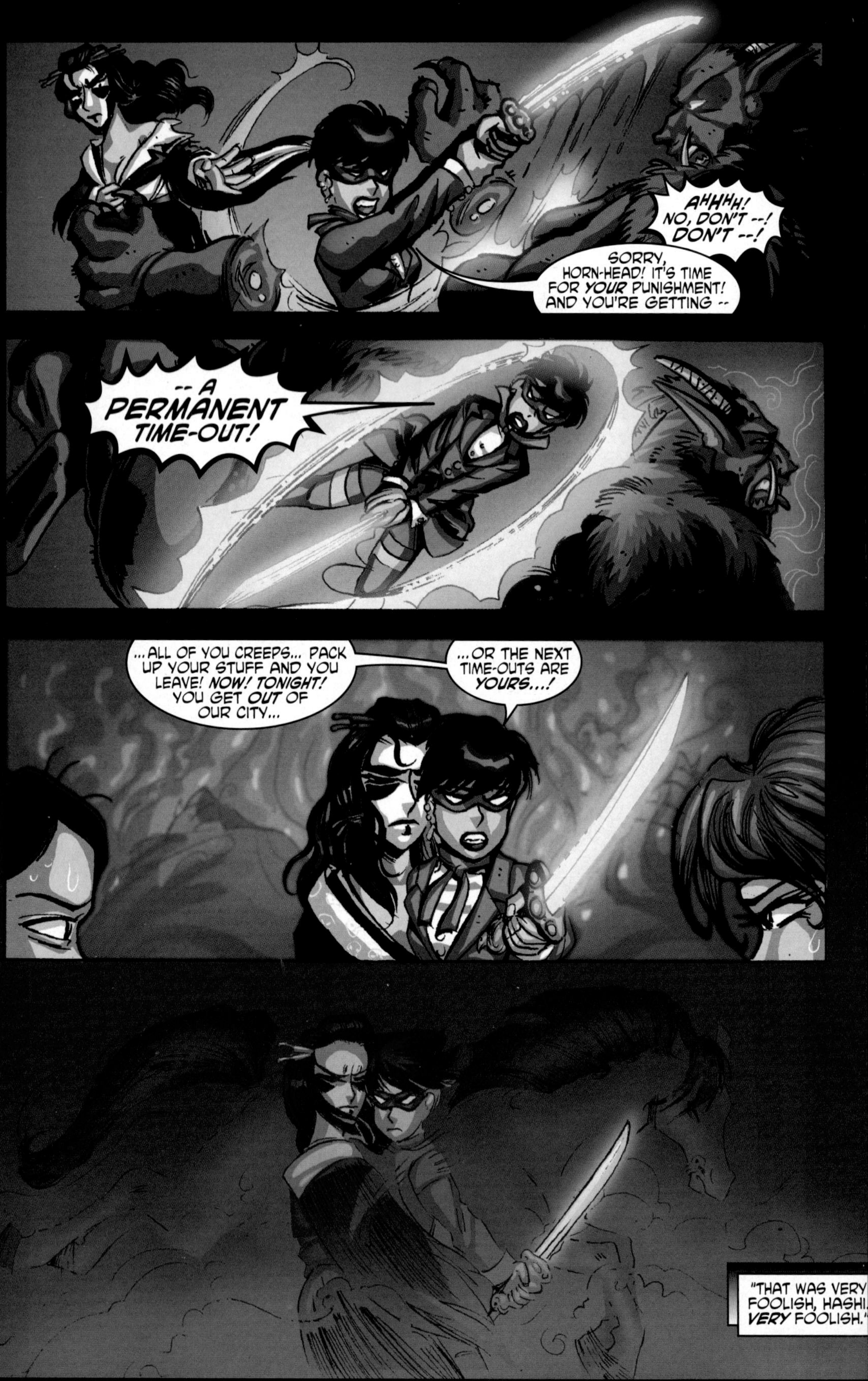
AHHHH! NO, DON'T --! DON'T --!
SORRY, HORN-HEAD! IT'S TIME FOR YOUR PUNISHMENT! AND YOU'RE GETTING --
-- A PERMANENT TIME-OUT!
...ALL OF YOU CREEPS... PACK UP YOUR STUFF AND YOU LEAVE! NOW! TONIGHT! YOU GET OUT OF OUR CITY...
...OR THE NEXT TIME-OUTS ARE YOURS...!
"THAT WAS VERY FOOLISH, HASHI. VERY FOOLISH."

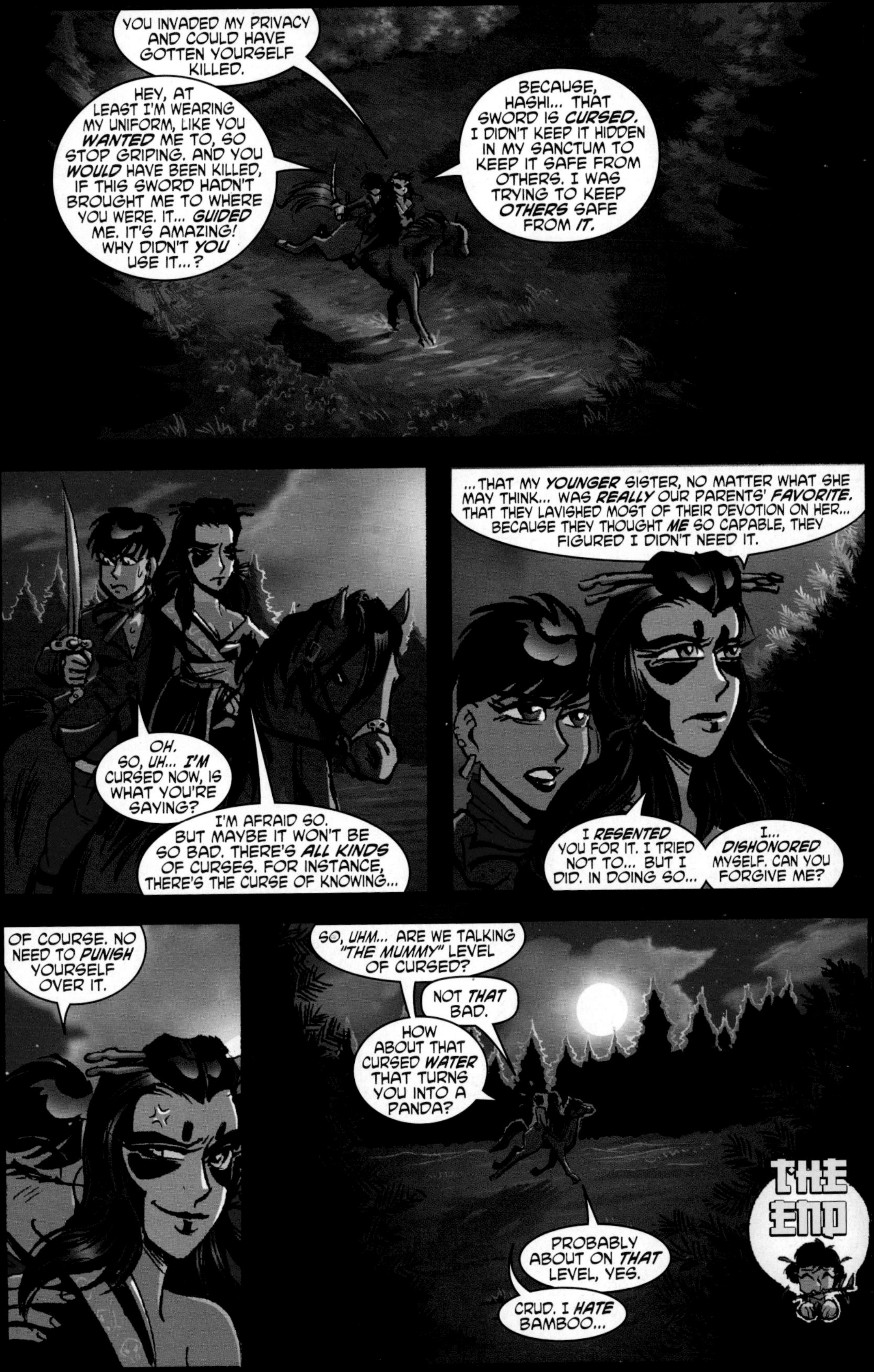
YOU INVADED MY PRIVACY AND COULD HAVE GOTTEN YOURSELF KILLED.
HEY, AT LEAST I'M WEARING MY UNIFORM, LIKE YOU *WANTED* ME TO, SO STOP GRIPING. AND YOU *WOULD* HAVE BEEN KILLED, IF THIS SWORD HADN'T BROUGHT ME TO WHERE YOU WERE. IT... *GUIDED* ME. IT'S AMAZING! WHY DIDN'T *YOU* USE IT...?
BECAUSE, HASHI... THAT SWORD IS *CURSED.* I DIDN'T KEEP IT HIDDEN IN MY SANCTUM TO KEEP IT SAFE FROM OTHERS. I WAS TRYING TO KEEP *OTHERS* SAFE FROM *IT.*
OH. SO, UH... *I'M* CURSED NOW, IS WHAT YOU'RE SAYING?
I'M AFRAID SO. BUT MAYBE IT WON'T BE SO BAD. THERE'S *ALL KINDS* OF CURSES. FOR INSTANCE, THERE'S THE CURSE OF KNOWING...
...THAT MY *YOUNGER* SISTER, NO MATTER WHAT SHE MAY THINK... WAS *REALLY* OUR PARENTS' *FAVORITE.* THAT THEY LAVISHED MOST OF THEIR DEVOTION ON HER... BECAUSE THEY THOUGHT *ME* SO CAPABLE, THEY FIGURED I DIDN'T NEED IT.
I *RESENTED* YOU FOR IT. I TRIED NOT TO... BUT I DID. IN DOING SO...
I... *DISHONORED* MYSELF. CAN YOU FORGIVE ME?
OF COURSE. NO NEED TO *PUNISH* YOURSELF OVER IT.
SO, *UHM*... ARE WE TALKING *"THE MUMMY"* LEVEL OF CURSED?
NOT *THAT* BAD.
HOW ABOUT THAT CURSED *WATER* THAT TURNS YOU INTO A PANDA?
PROBABLY ABOUT ON *THAT* LEVEL, YES.
CRUD. I *HATE* BAMBOO...
THE END

SPIDER-MAN #1

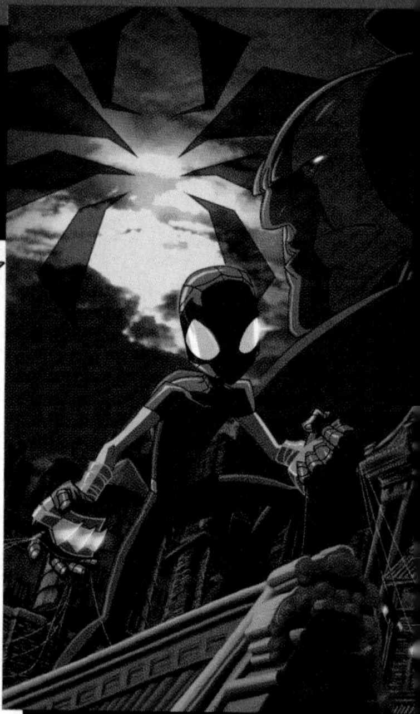

X-MEN #1

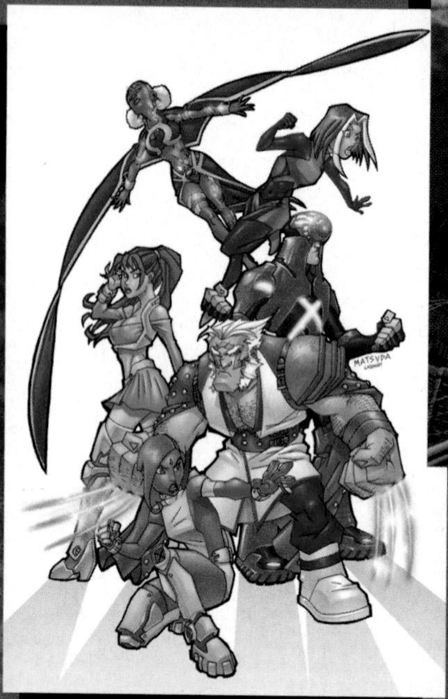
MATSUDA

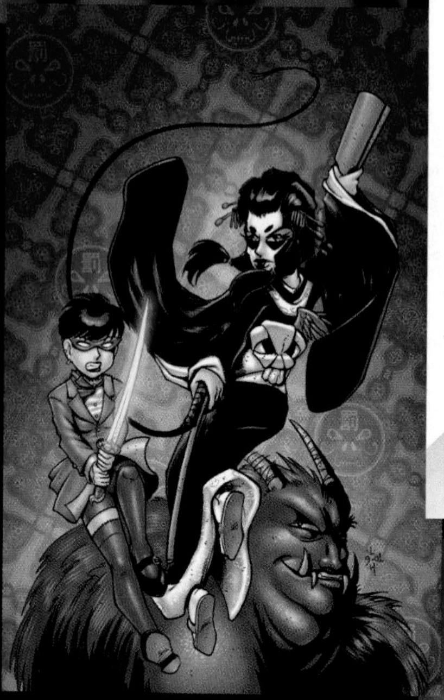

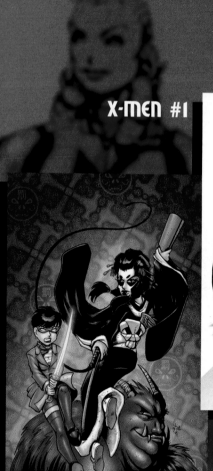

PUNISHER #1

COVER GALLER

ETERNITY TWILIGHT #1

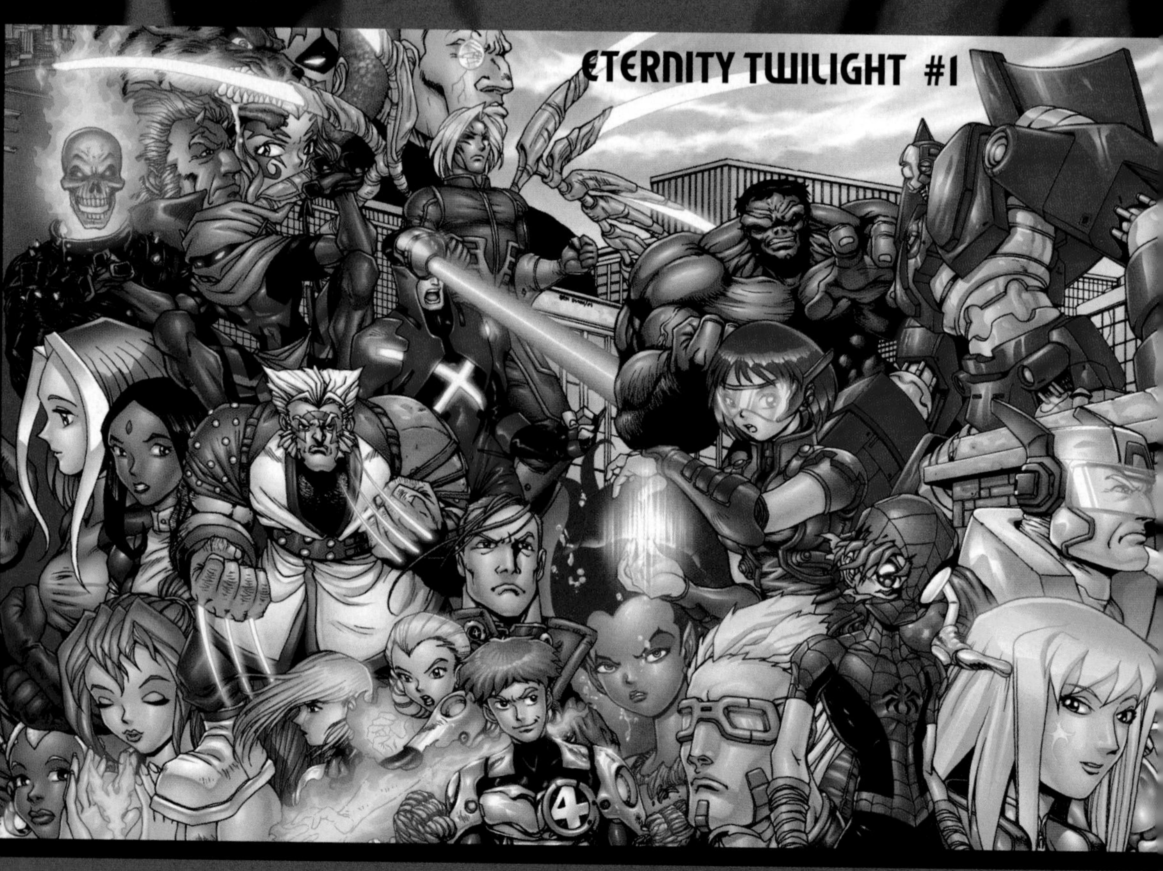

HUF!
HUF!
STUPID...
HUF!
...PRACTICE
HUF!
I AM SO...
HUF!
...LATE...
HUF!
SENSEI, WHY ARE THE DOJO LIGHTS...
...

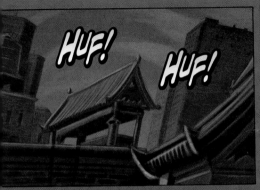

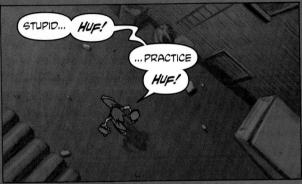

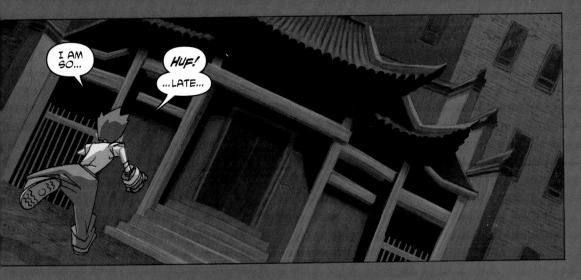

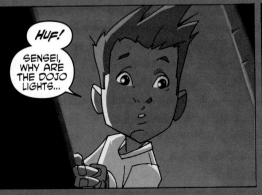

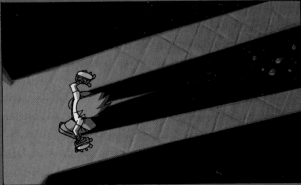

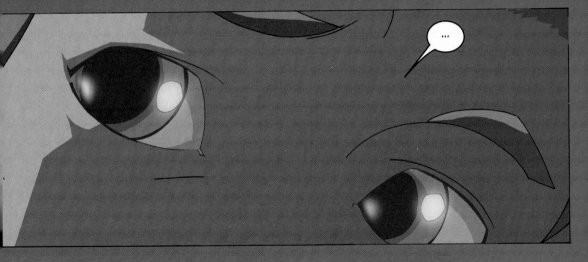

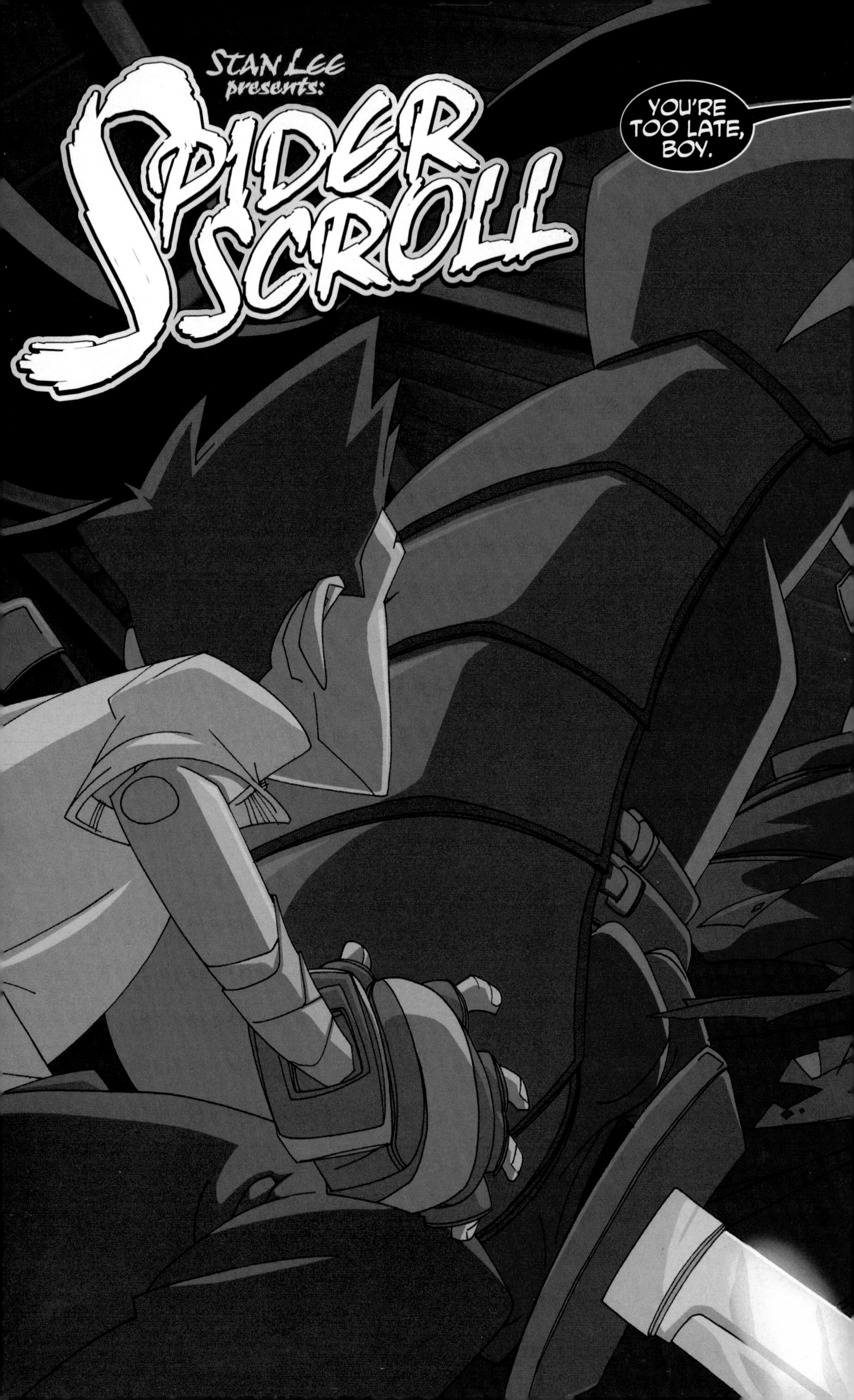
STAN LEE presents:
SPIDER SCROLL
YOU'RE TOO LATE, BOY.

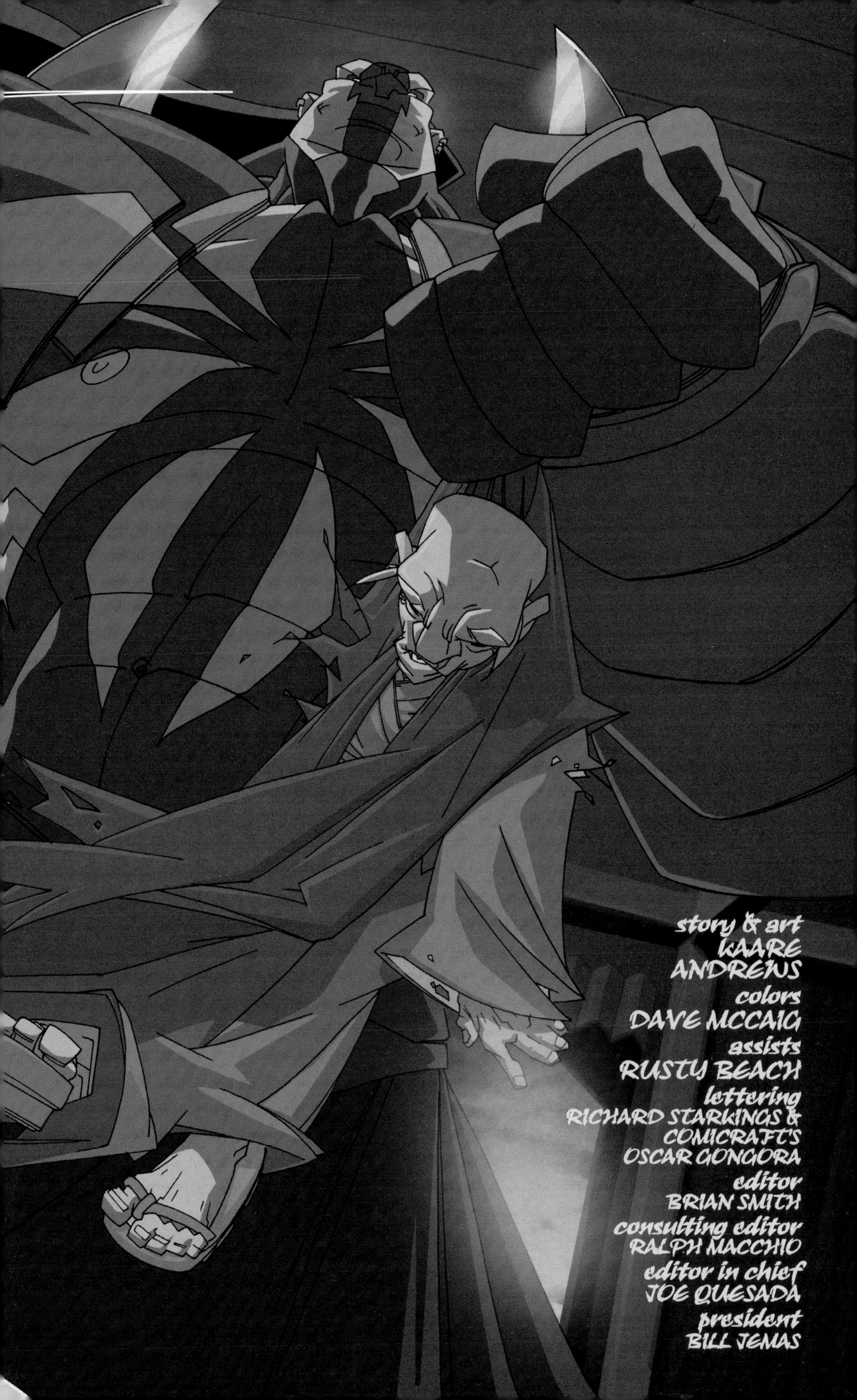
story & art
KAARE ANDREWS
colors
DAVE MCCAIG
assists
RUSTY BEACH
lettering
RICHARD STARKINGS & COMICRAFT'S OSCAR GONGORA
editor
BRIAN SMITH
consulting editor
RALPH MACCHIO
editor in chief
JOE QUESADA
president
BILL JEMAS

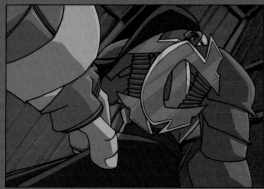

IT IS
DONE.

PETER...

...YOU HAVE
THE POWER,
PETER... HIDDEN
WITHIN.

YOU MUST
TAKE THE
NEXT STEP...
ALONE

SENSEI...
DON'T LEAVE ME.

REMEMBER... WITH
THAT GREAT POWER
MUST COME GREAT
RESPONSIBILITY...

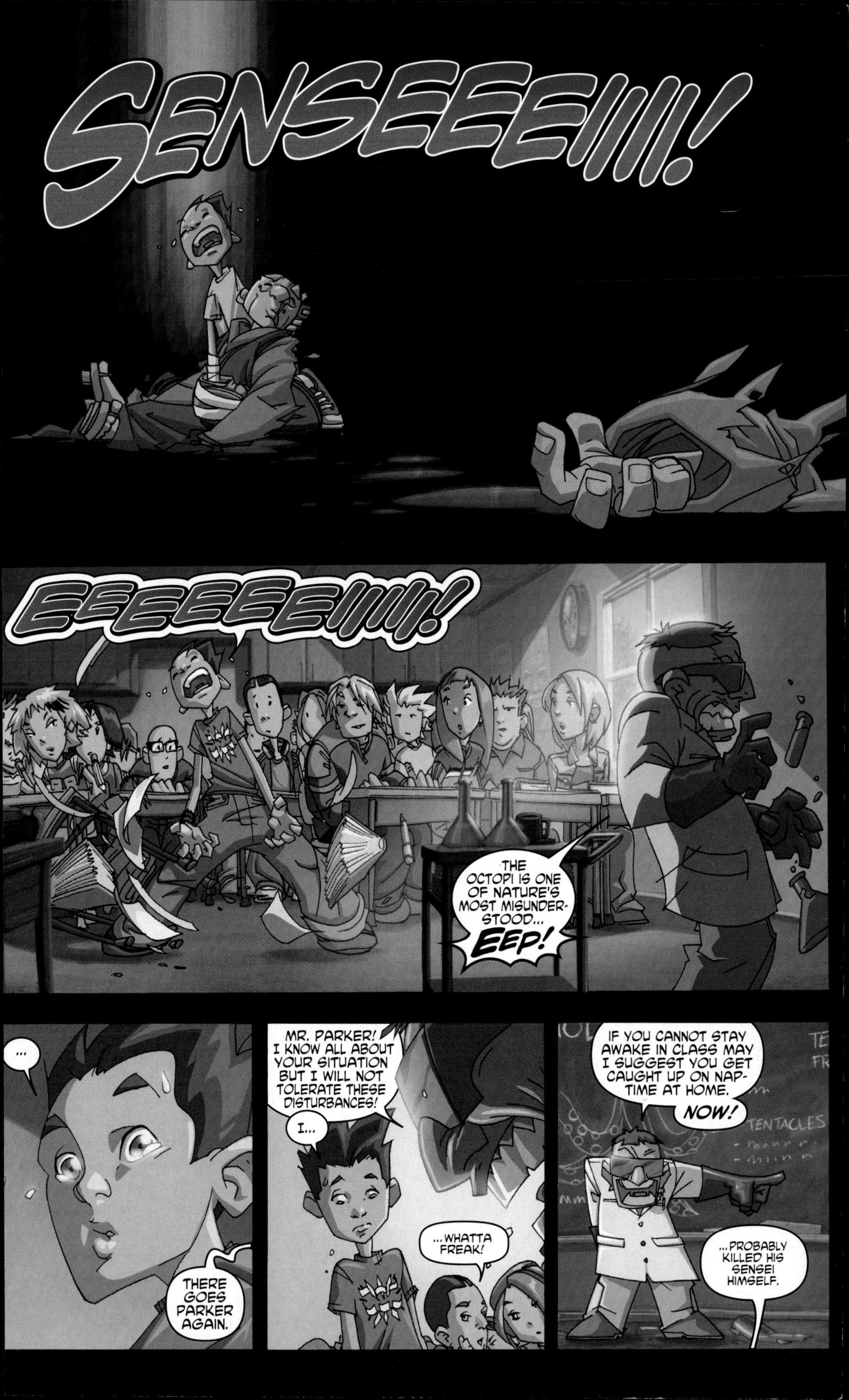
SENSEEEIIII!
EEEEEEEIIIII!
THE OCTOPI IS ONE OF NATURE'S MOST MISUNDER-STOOD... EEP!
...
THERE GOES PARKER AGAIN.
MR. PARKER! I KNOW ALL ABOUT YOUR SITUATION BUT I WILL NOT TOLERATE THESE DISTURBANCES!
I...
...WHATTA FREAK!
IF YOU CANNOT STAY AWAKE IN CLASS MAY I SUGGEST YOU GET CAUGHT UP ON NAP-TIME AT HOME. NOW!
TENTACLES
...PROBABLY KILLED HIS SENSEI HIMSELF.

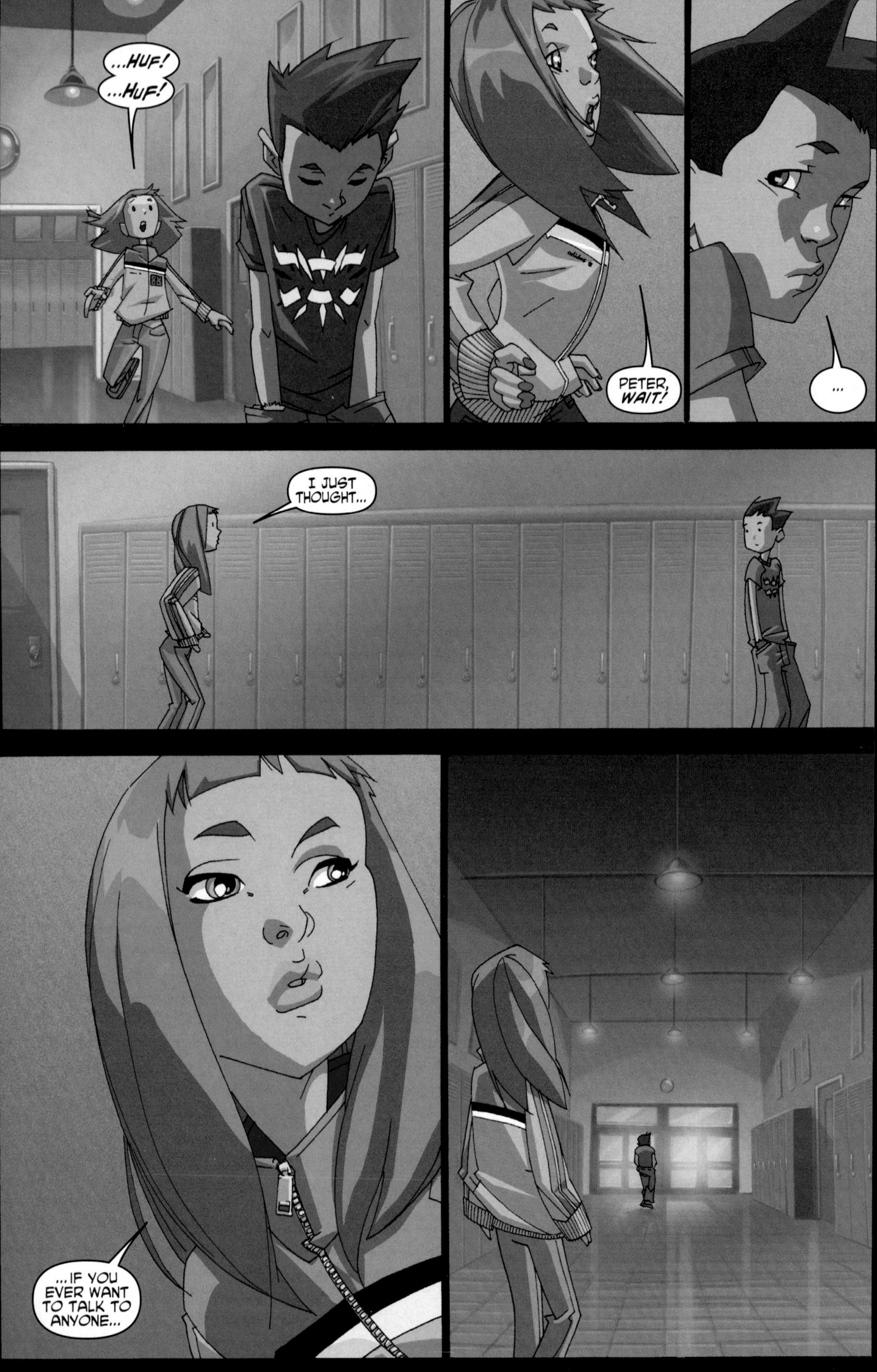
...HUF!
...HUF!
PETER, WAIT!
...
I JUST THOUGHT...
...IF YOU EVER WANT TO TALK TO ANYONE...

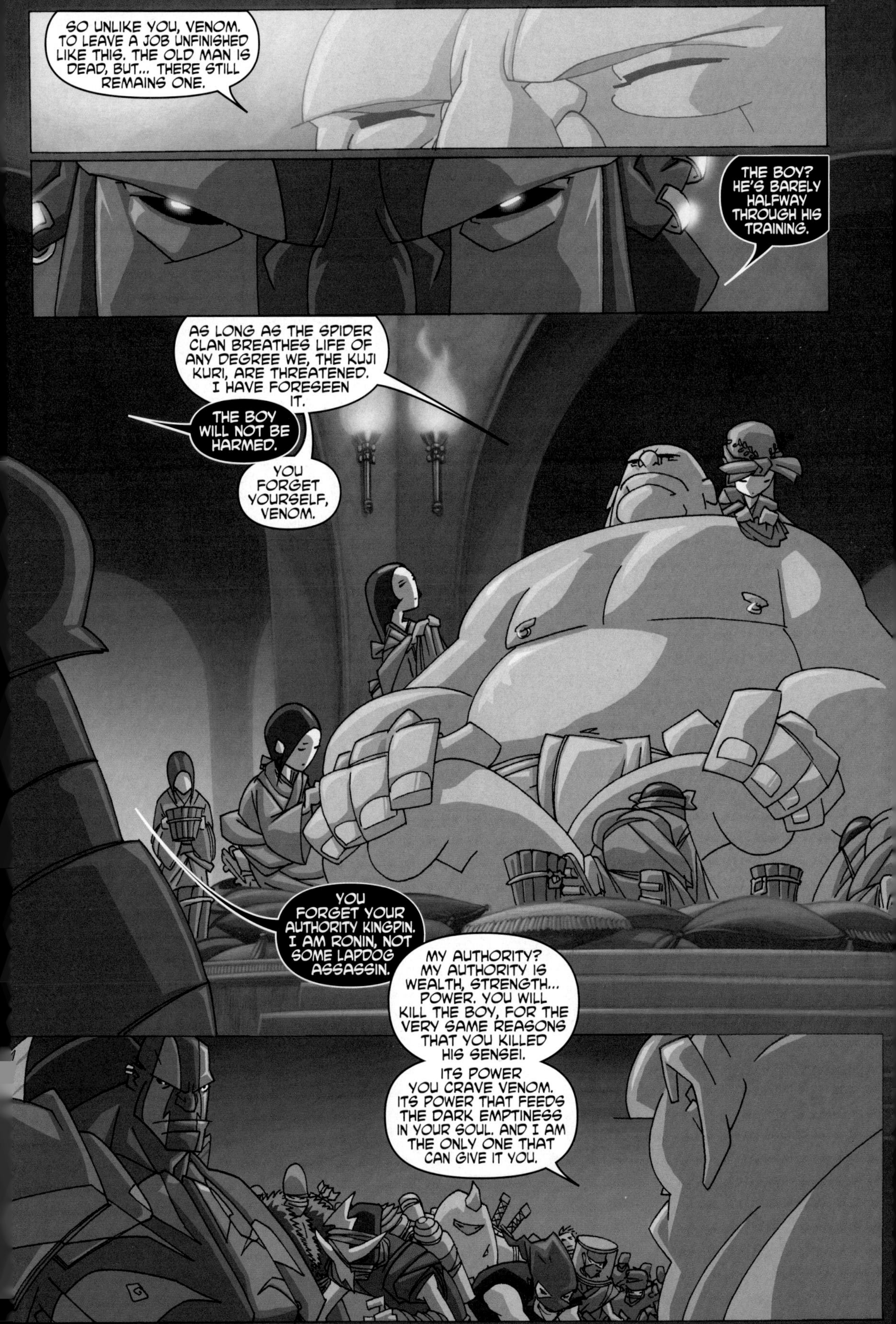
SO UNLIKE YOU, VENOM. TO LEAVE A JOB UNFINISHED LIKE THIS. THE OLD MAN IS DEAD, BUT... THERE STILL REMAINS ONE.
THE BOY? HE'S BARELY HALFWAY THROUGH HIS TRAINING.
AS LONG AS THE SPIDER CLAN BREATHES LIFE OF ANY DEGREE WE, THE KUJI KURI, ARE THREATENED. I HAVE FORESEEN IT.
THE BOY WILL NOT BE HARMED.
YOU FORGET YOURSELF, VENOM.
YOU FORGET YOUR AUTHORITY KINGPIN. I AM RONIN, NOT SOME LAPDOG ASSASSIN.
MY AUTHORITY? MY AUTHORITY IS WEALTH, STRENGTH... POWER. YOU WILL KILL THE BOY, FOR THE VERY SAME REASONS THAT YOU KILLED HIS SENSEI.
ITS POWER YOU CRAVE VENOM. ITS POWER THAT FEEDS THE DARK EMPTINESS IN YOUR SOUL. AND I AM THE ONLY ONE THAT CAN GIVE IT YOU.

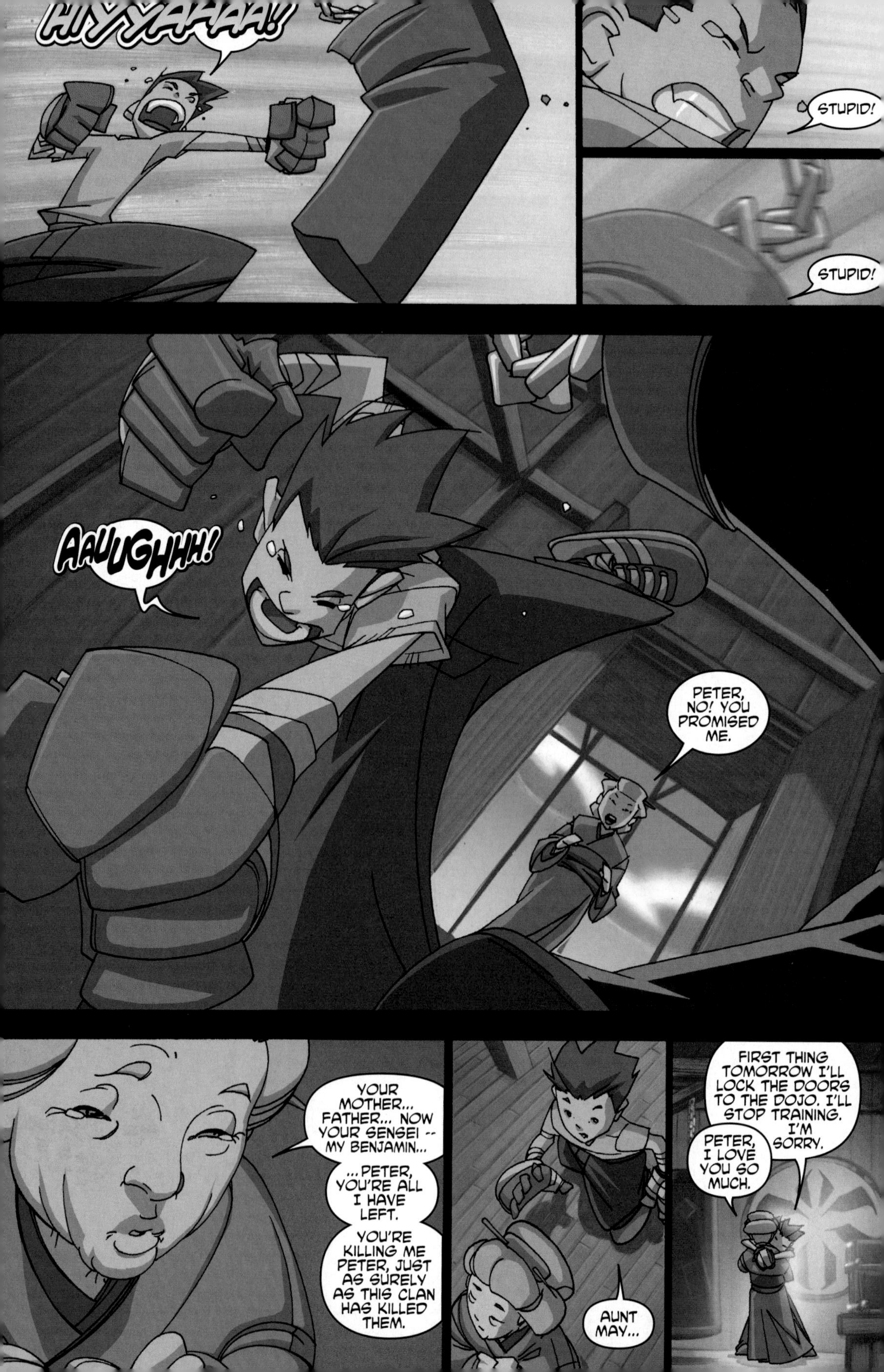
HIYYAHAA!!
STUPID!
STUPID!
AAUUGHHH!
PETER, NO! YOU PROMISED ME.
YOUR MOTHER... FATHER... NOW YOUR SENSEI -- MY BENJAMIN...
...PETER, YOU'RE ALL I HAVE LEFT.
YOU'RE KILLING ME PETER, JUST AS SURELY AS THIS CLAN HAS KILLED THEM.
AUNT MAY...
FIRST THING TOMORROW I'LL LOCK THE DOORS TO THE DOJO. I'LL STOP TRAINING. I'M SORRY.
PETER, I LOVE YOU SO MUCH.

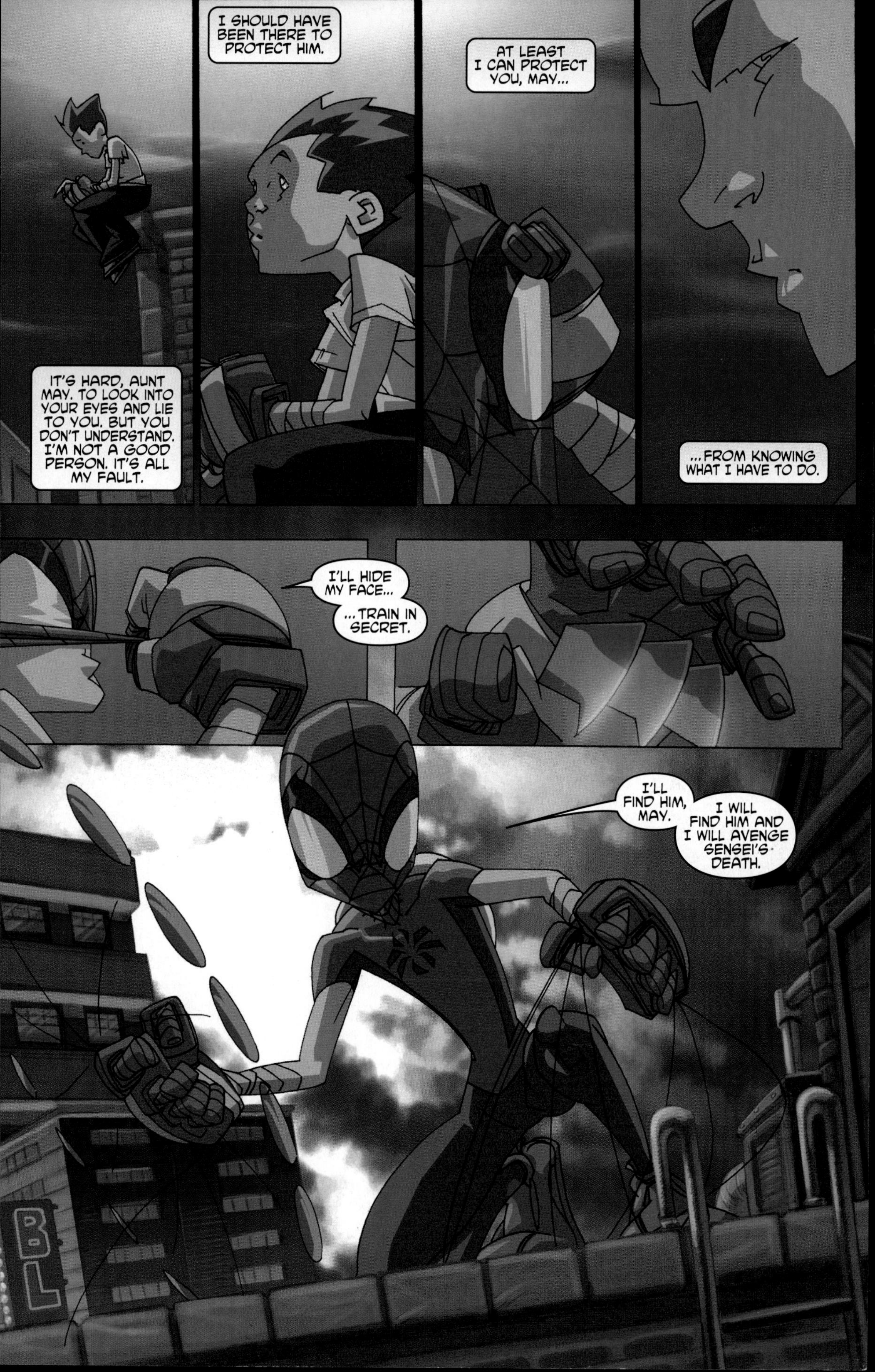
I SHOULD HAVE BEEN THERE TO PROTECT HIM.
IT'S HARD, AUNT MAY. TO LOOK INTO YOUR EYES AND LIE TO YOU. BUT YOU DON'T UNDERSTAND. I'M NOT A GOOD PERSON. IT'S ALL MY FAULT.
AT LEAST I CAN PROTECT YOU, MAY...
...FROM KNOWING WHAT I HAVE TO DO.
I'LL HIDE MY FACE...
...TRAIN IN SECRET.
I'LL FIND HIM, MAY.
I WILL FIND HIM AND I WILL AVENGE SENSEI'S DEATH.
BL

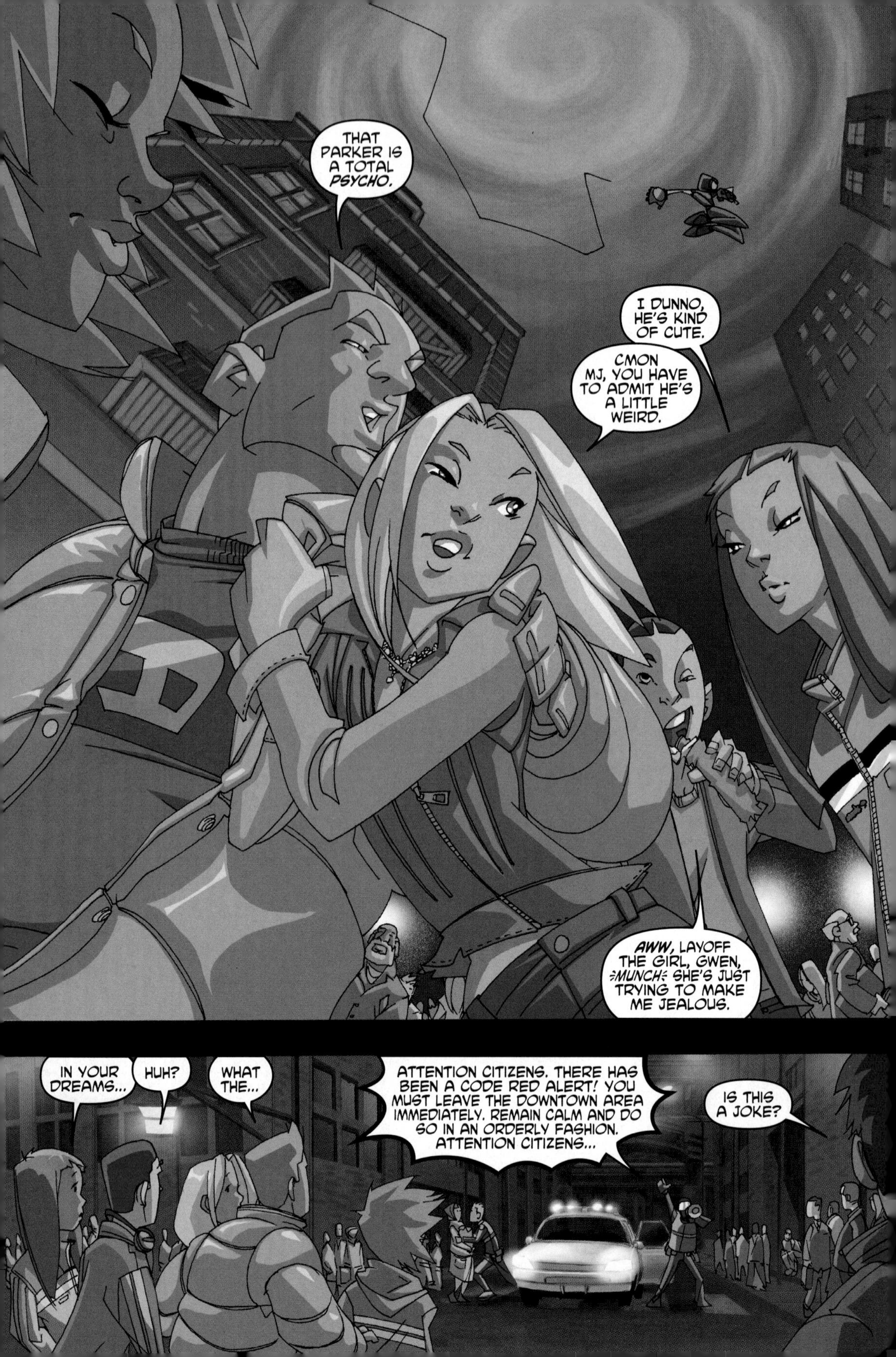
THAT PARKER IS A TOTAL *PSYCHO.*
I DUNNO, HE'S KIND OF CUTE.
CMON MJ, YOU HAVE TO ADMIT HE'S A LITTLE WEIRD.
AWW, LAYOFF THE GIRL, GWEN, *MUNCH* SHE'S JUST TRYING TO MAKE ME JEALOUS.
IN YOUR DREAMS...
HUH?
WHAT THE...
ATTENTION CITIZENS. THERE HAS BEEN A CODE RED ALERT! YOU MUST LEAVE THE DOWNTOWN AREA IMMEDIATELY. REMAIN CALM AND DO SO IN AN ORDERLY FASHION. ATTENTION CITIZENS...
IS THIS A JOKE?

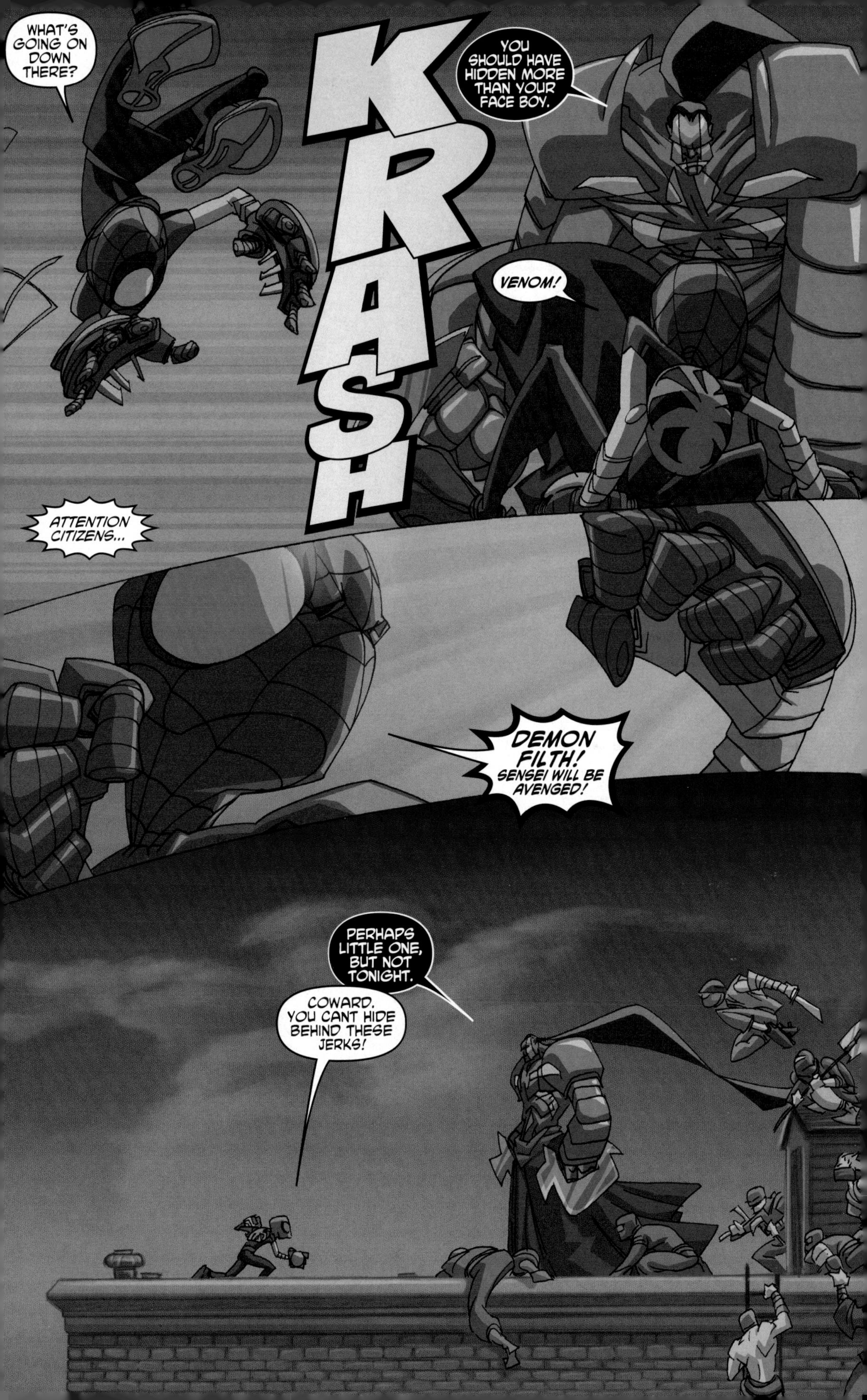
WHAT'S GOING ON DOWN THERE?
KRASH
YOU SHOULD HAVE HIDDEN MORE THAN YOUR FACE BOY.
VENOM!
ATTENTION CITIZENS...
DEMON FILTH! SENSEI WILL BE AVENGED!
PERHAPS LITTLE ONE, BUT NOT TONIGHT.
COWARD. YOU CANT HIDE BEHIND THESE JERKS!

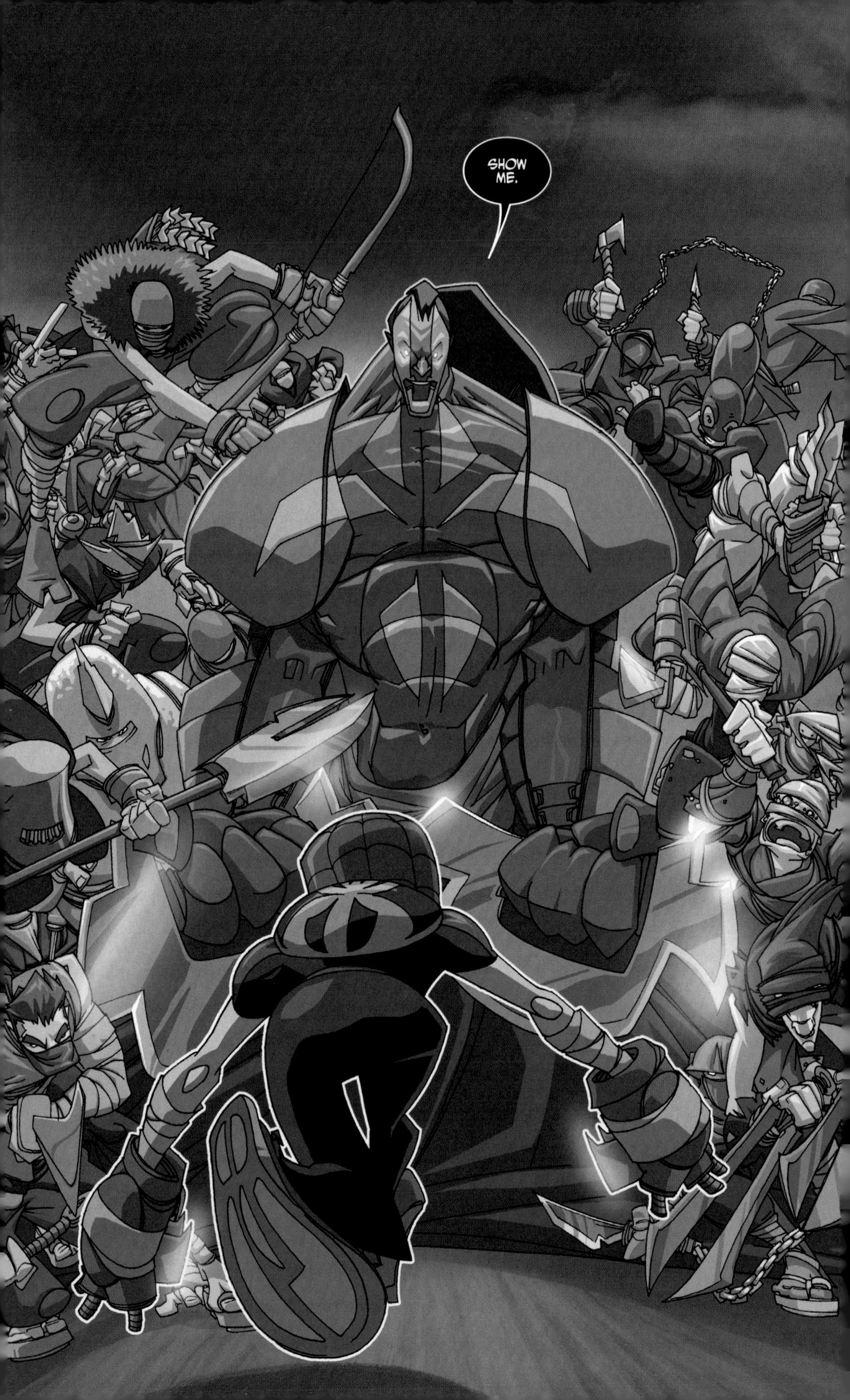
SHOW ME.

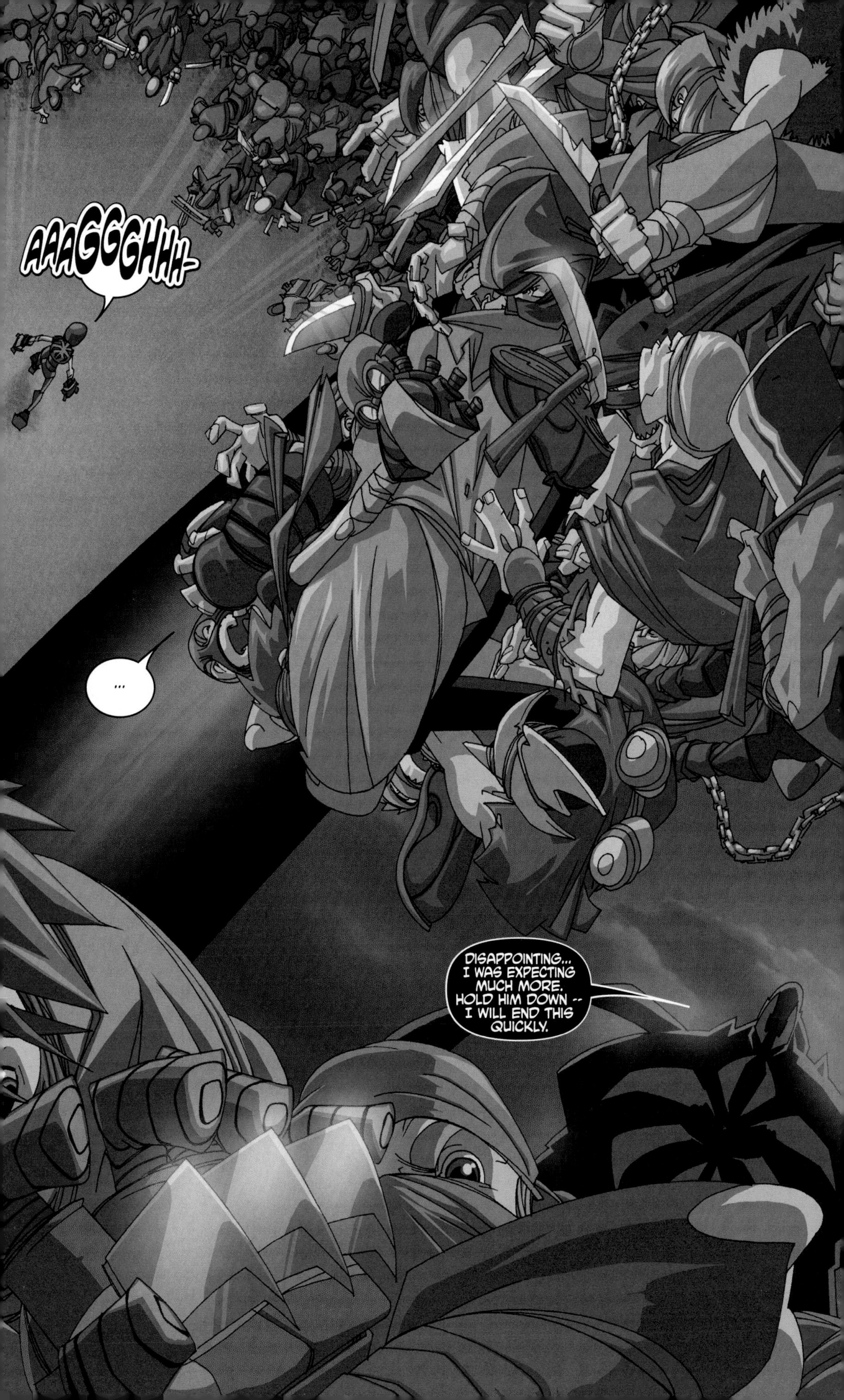
AAAGGGHHH-
...
DISAPPOINTING... I WAS EXPECTING MUCH MORE. HOLD HIM DOWN -- I WILL END THIS QUICKLY.

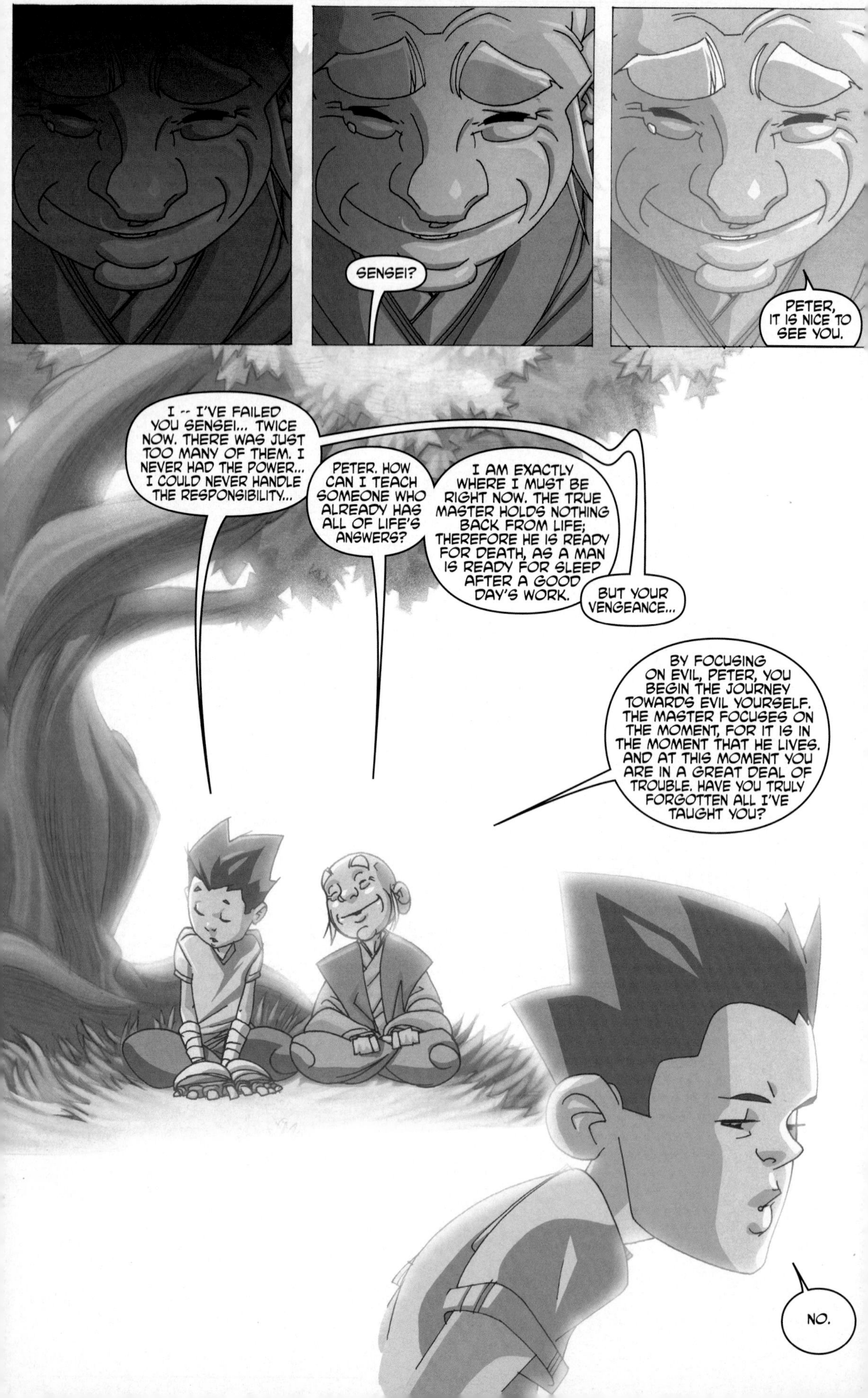
SENSEI?
PETER, IT IS NICE TO SEE YOU.
I -- I'VE FAILED YOU SENSEI... TWICE NOW. THERE WAS JUST TOO MANY OF THEM. I NEVER HAD THE POWER... I COULD NEVER HANDLE THE RESPONSIBILITY...
PETER. HOW CAN I TEACH SOMEONE WHO ALREADY HAS ALL OF LIFE'S ANSWERS?
I AM EXACTLY WHERE I MUST BE RIGHT NOW. THE TRUE MASTER HOLDS NOTHING BACK FROM LIFE; THEREFORE HE IS READY FOR DEATH, AS A MAN IS READY FOR SLEEP AFTER A GOOD DAY'S WORK.
BUT YOUR VENGEANCE...
BY FOCUSING ON EVIL, PETER, YOU BEGIN THE JOURNEY TOWARDS EVIL YOURSELF. THE MASTER FOCUSES ON THE MOMENT, FOR IT IS IN THE MOMENT THAT HE LIVES. AND AT THIS MOMENT YOU ARE IN A GREAT DEAL OF TROUBLE. HAVE YOU TRULY FORGOTTEN ALL I'VE TAUGHT YOU?
NO.

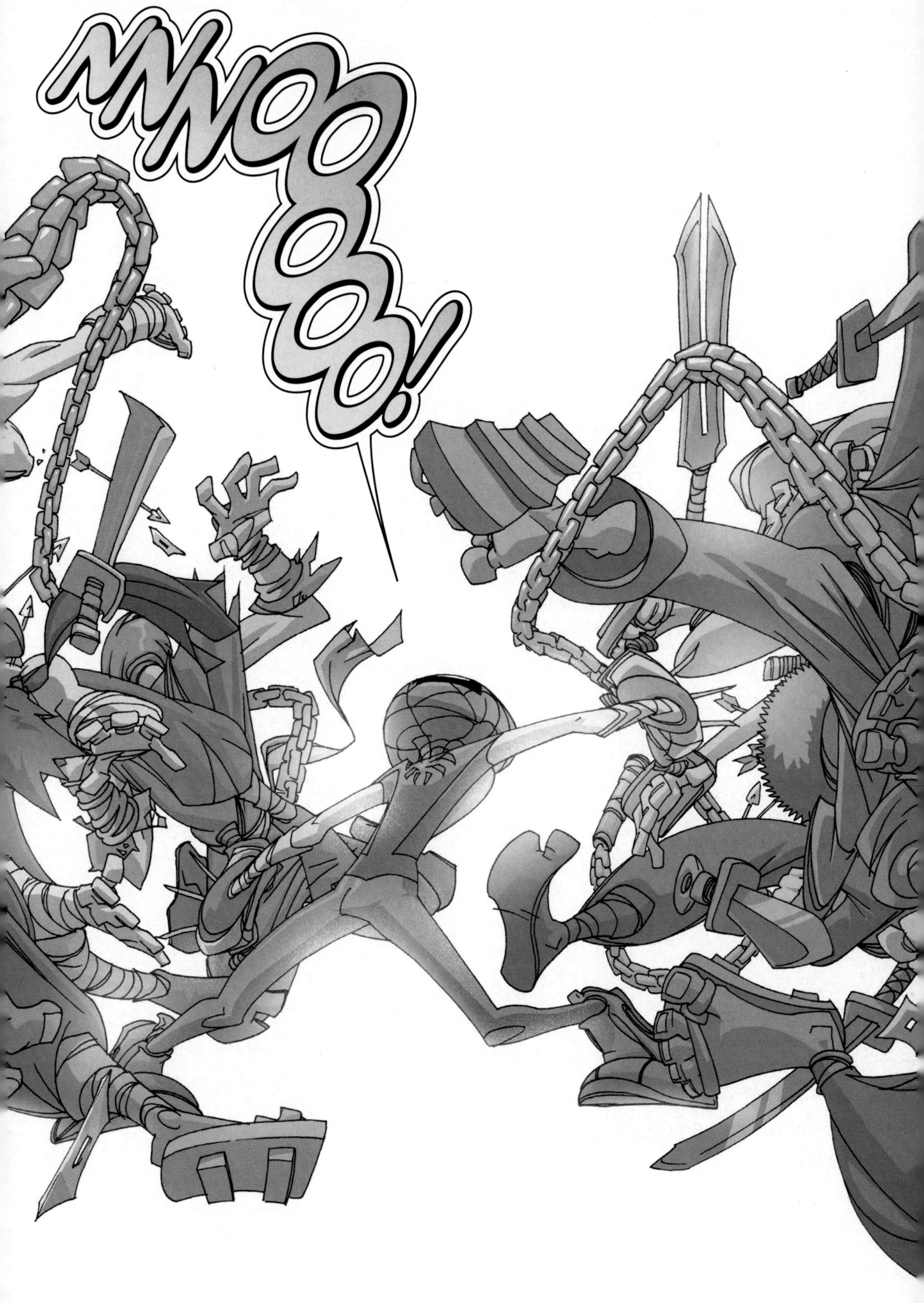
NNNOOOOOOO!

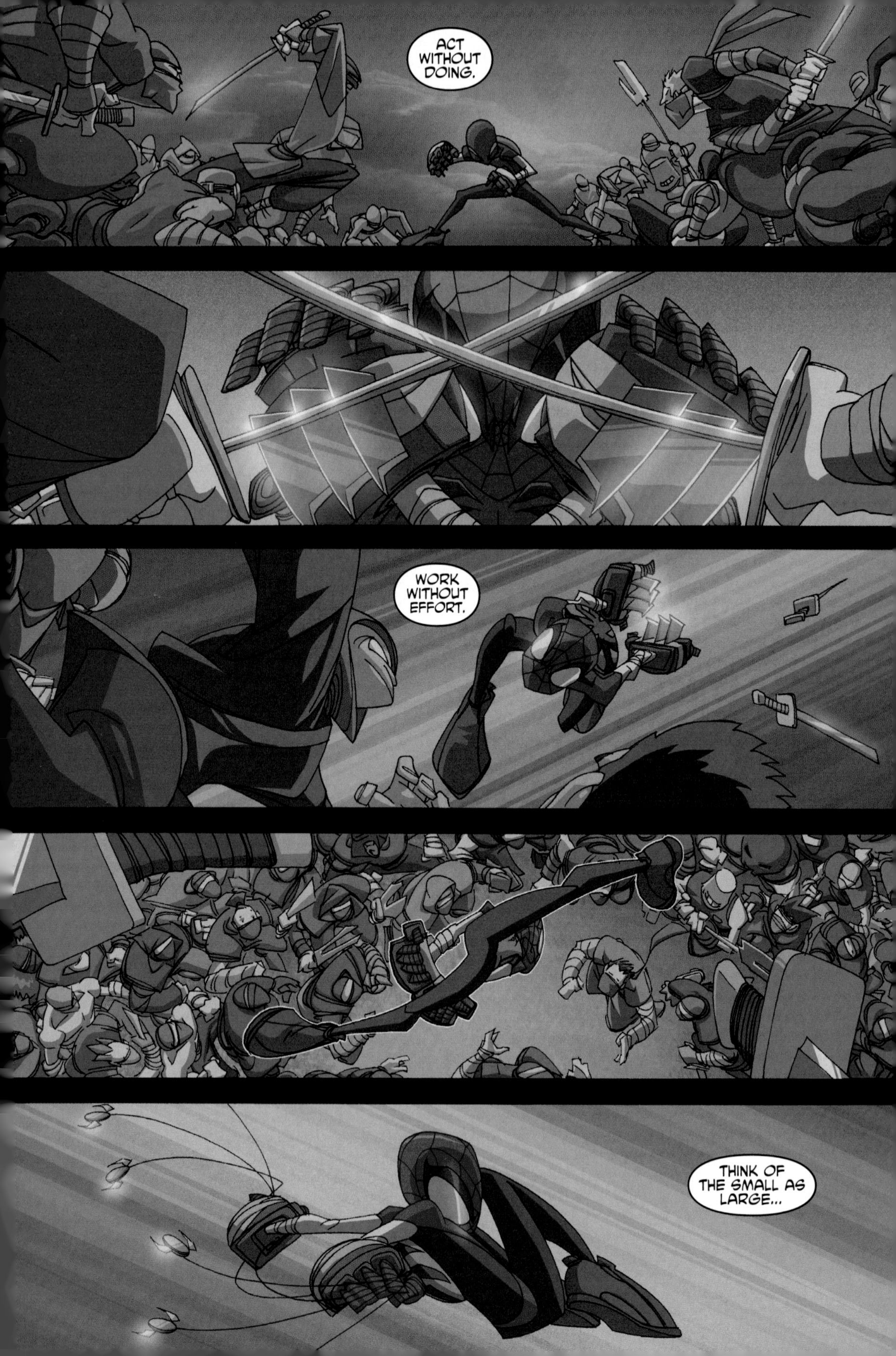
ACT WITHOUT DOING.
WORK WITHOUT EFFORT.
THINK OF THE SMALL AS LARGE...

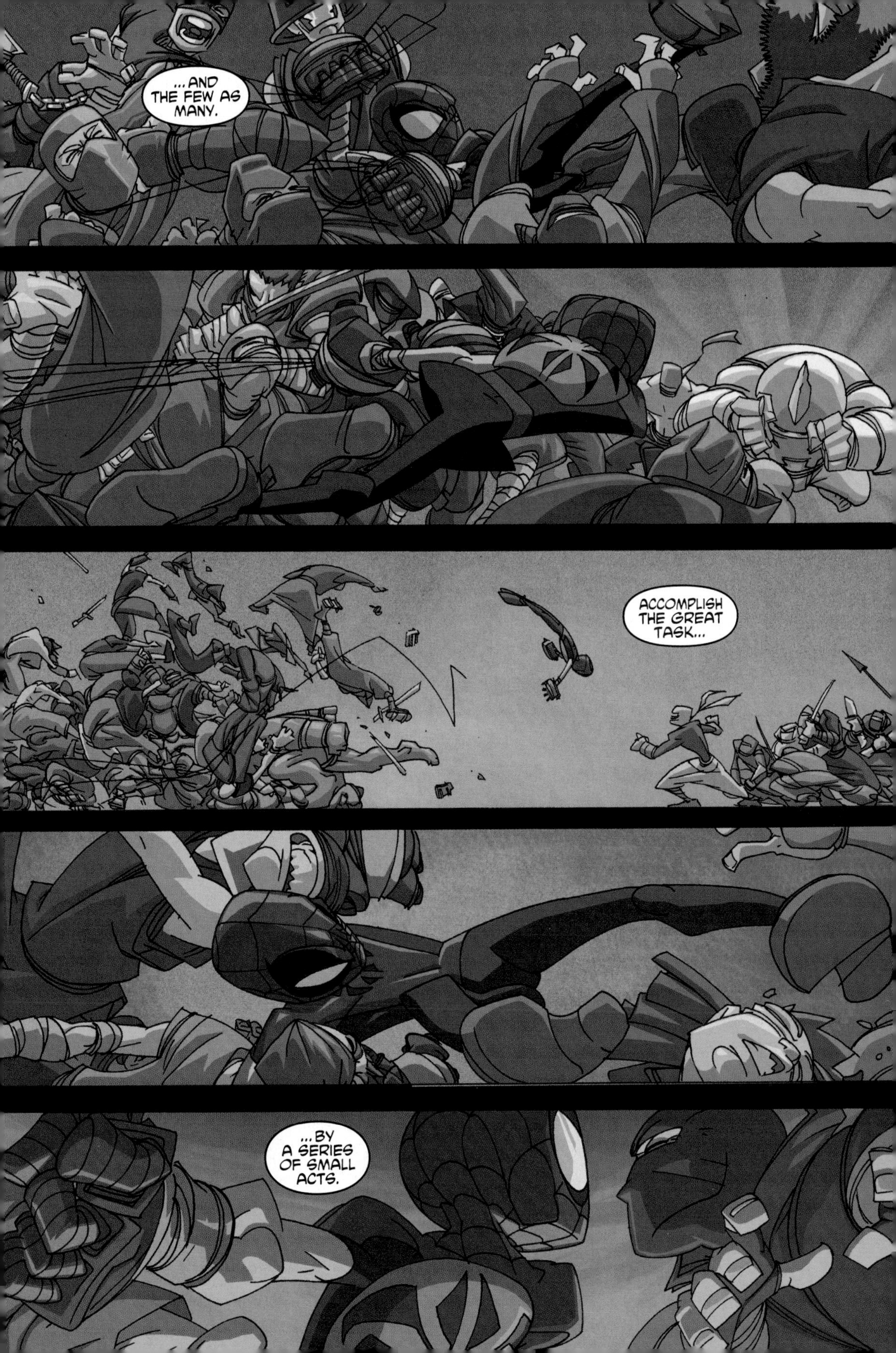
...AND THE FEW AS MANY.
ACCOMPLISH THE GREAT TASK...
...BY A SERIES OF SMALL ACTS.

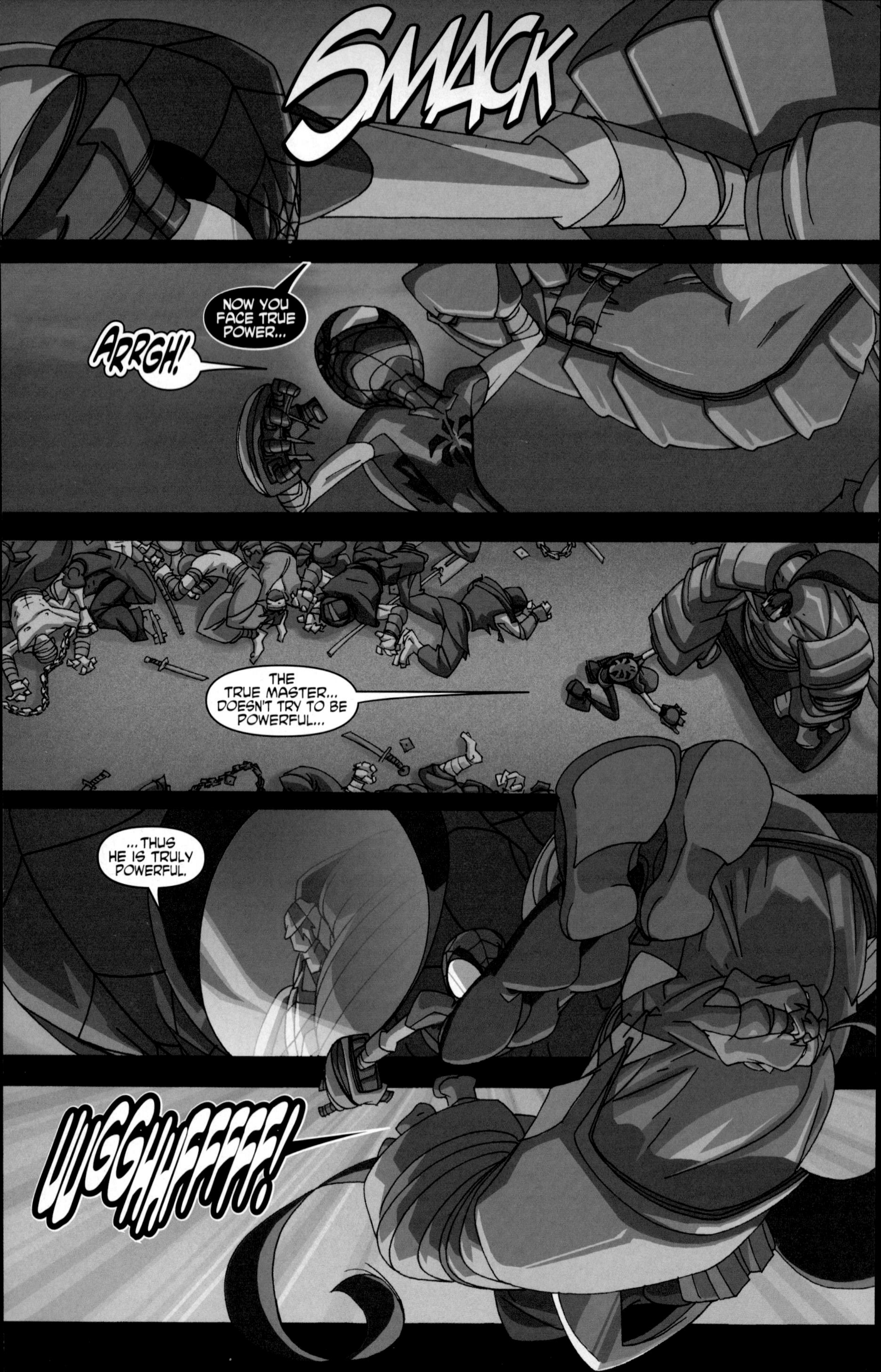
SMACK
NOW YOU FACE TRUE POWER...
ARRGH!
THE TRUE MASTER... DOESN'T TRY TO BE POWERFUL...
...THUS HE IS TRULY POWERFUL.
UUGGHHFFFFF!

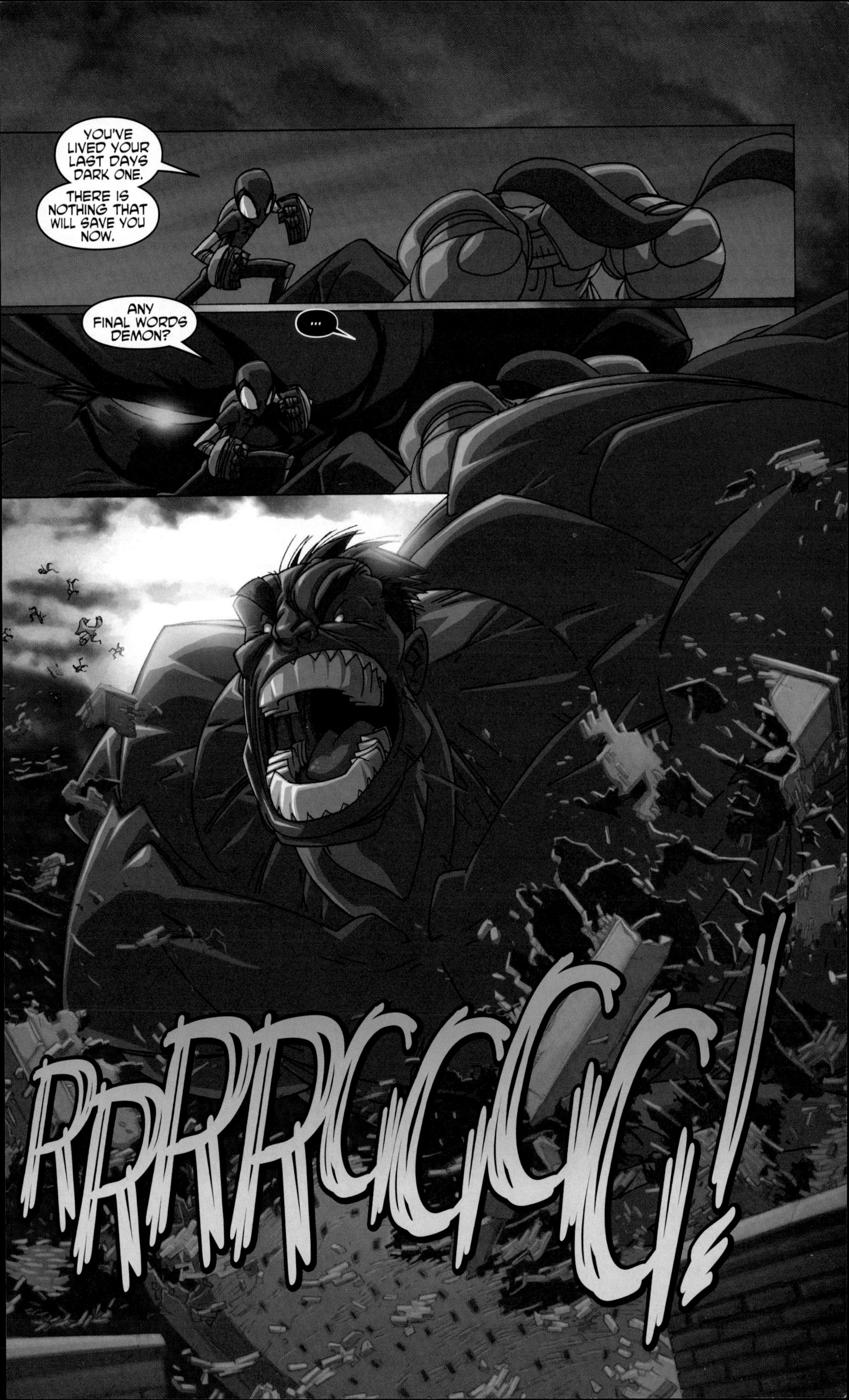
YOU'VE LIVED YOUR LAST DAYS DARK ONE.
THERE IS NOTHING THAT WILL SAVE YOU NOW.
ANY FINAL WORDS DEMON?
...
RRRRGGGG!

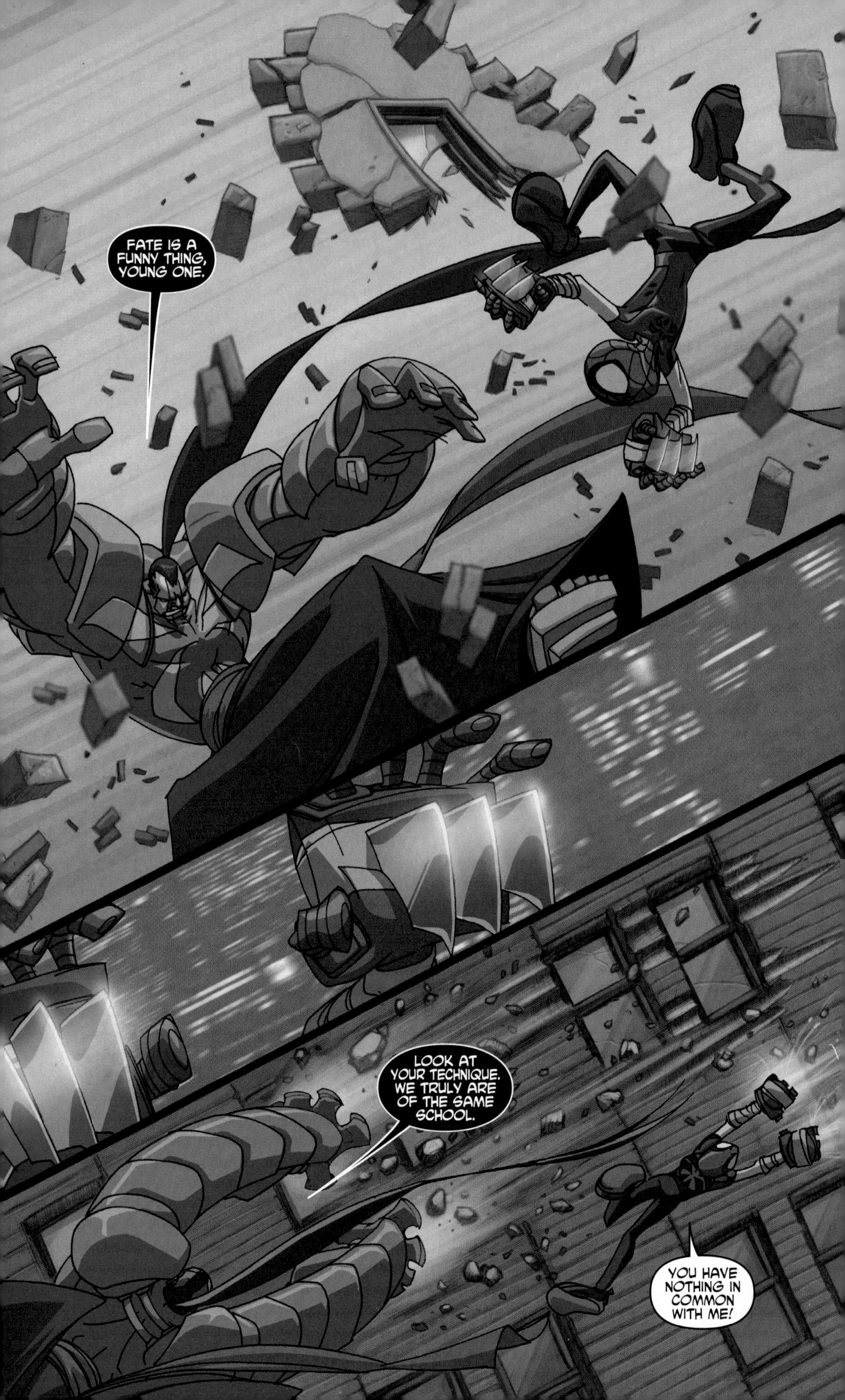
FATE IS A FUNNY THING, YOUNG ONE.
LOOK AT YOUR TECHNIQUE. WE TRULY ARE OF THE SAME SCHOOL.
YOU HAVE NOTHING IN COMMON WITH ME!

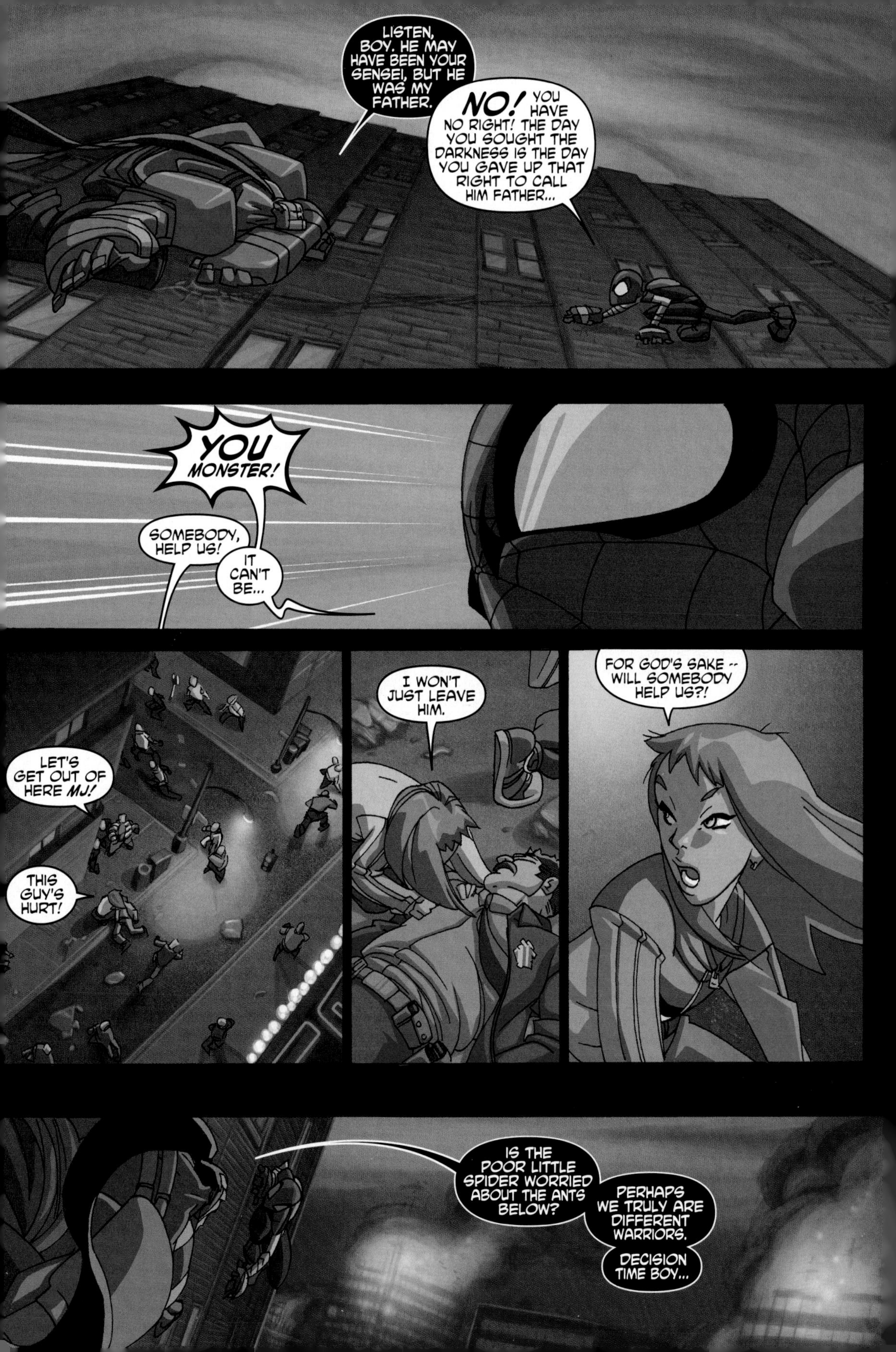
LISTEN, BOY. HE MAY HAVE BEEN YOUR SENSEI, BUT HE WAS MY FATHER.
NO! YOU HAVE NO RIGHT! THE DAY YOU SOUGHT THE DARKNESS IS THE DAY YOU GAVE UP THAT RIGHT TO CALL HIM FATHER...
YOU MONSTER!
SOMEBODY, HELP US!
IT CAN'T BE...
LET'S GET OUT OF HERE MJ!
THIS GUY'S HURT!
I WON'T JUST LEAVE HIM.
FOR GOD'S SAKE -- WILL SOMEBODY HELP US?!
IS THE POOR LITTLE SPIDER WORRIED ABOUT THE ANTS BELOW?
PERHAPS WE TRULY ARE DIFFERENT WARRIORS.
DECISION TIME BOY...

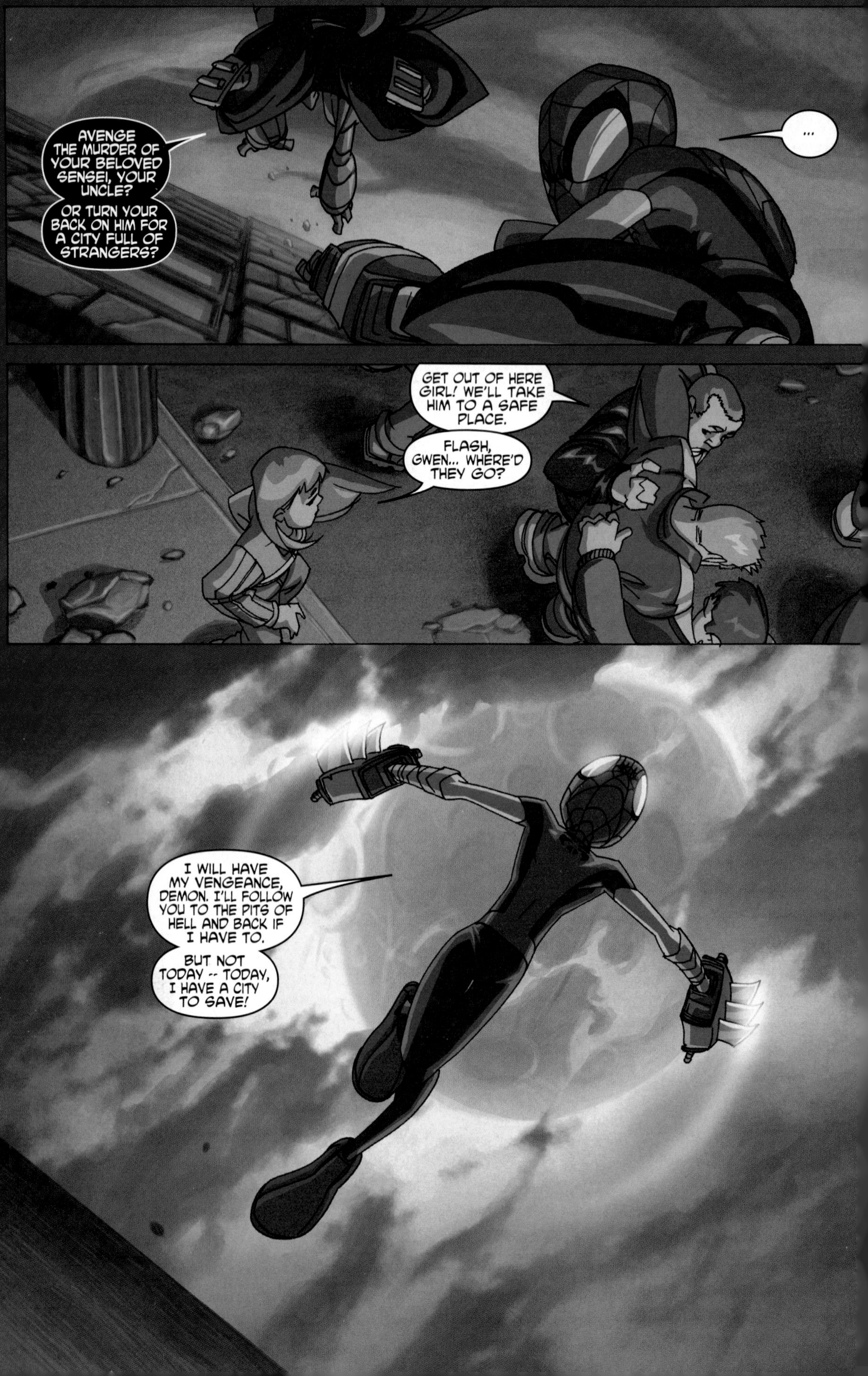
AVENGE THE MURDER OF YOUR BELOVED SENSEI, YOUR UNCLE?
OR TURN YOUR BACK ON HIM FOR A CITY FULL OF STRANGERS?
...
GET OUT OF HERE GIRL! WE'LL TAKE HIM TO A SAFE PLACE.
FLASH, GWEN... WHERE'D THEY GO?
I WILL HAVE MY VENGEANCE, DEMON. I'LL FOLLOW YOU TO THE PITS OF HELL AND BACK IF I HAVE TO.
BUT NOT TODAY -- TODAY, I HAVE A CITY TO SAVE!

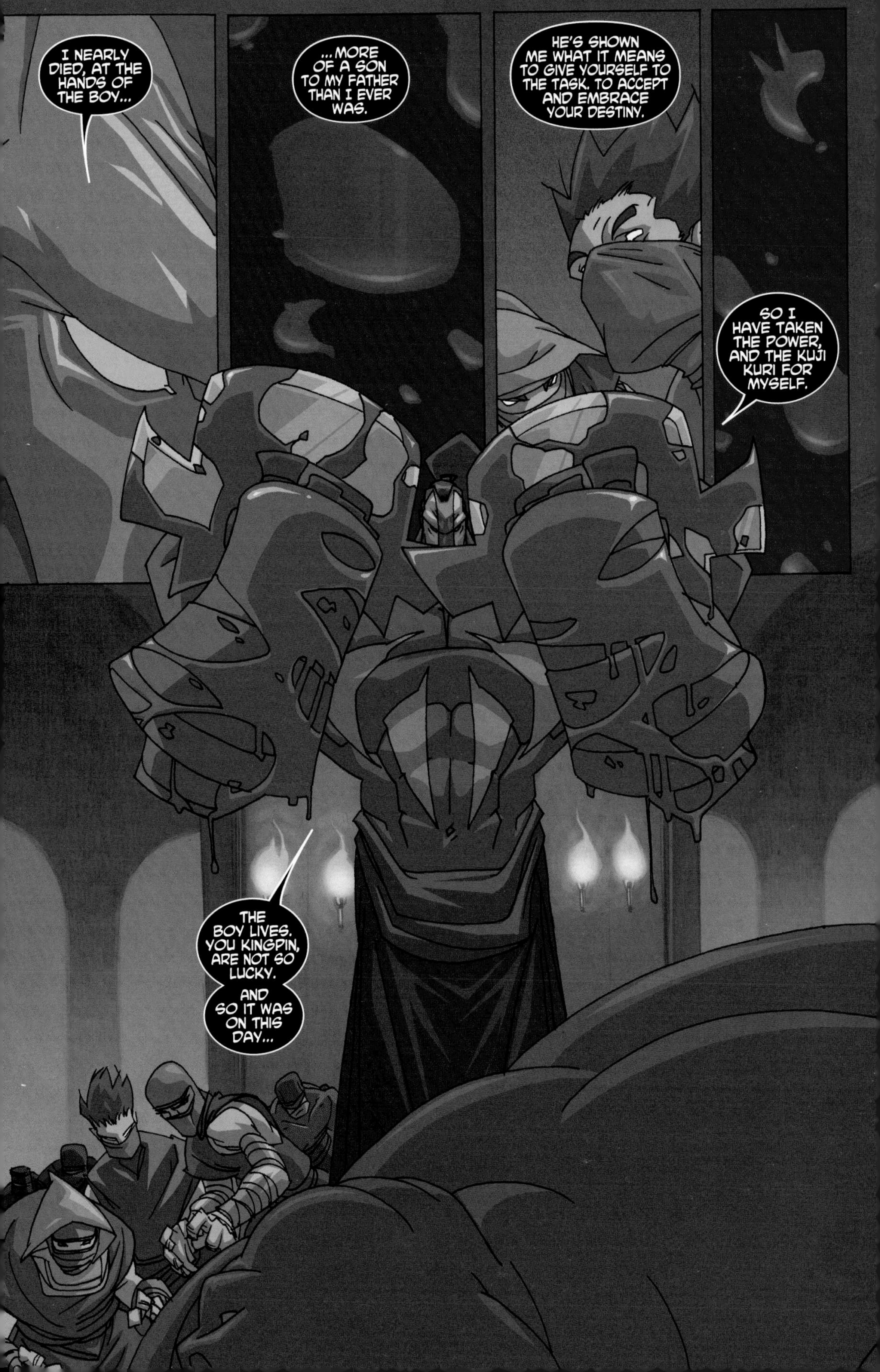
I NEARLY DIED, AT THE HANDS OF THE BOY...
...MORE OF A SON TO MY FATHER THAN I EVER WAS.
HE'S SHOWN ME WHAT IT MEANS TO GIVE YOURSELF TO THE TASK. TO ACCEPT AND EMBRACE YOUR DESTINY.
SO I HAVE TAKEN THE POWER, AND THE KUJI KURI FOR MYSELF.
THE BOY LIVES. YOU KINGPIN, ARE NOT SO LUCKY.
AND SO IT WAS ON THIS DAY...

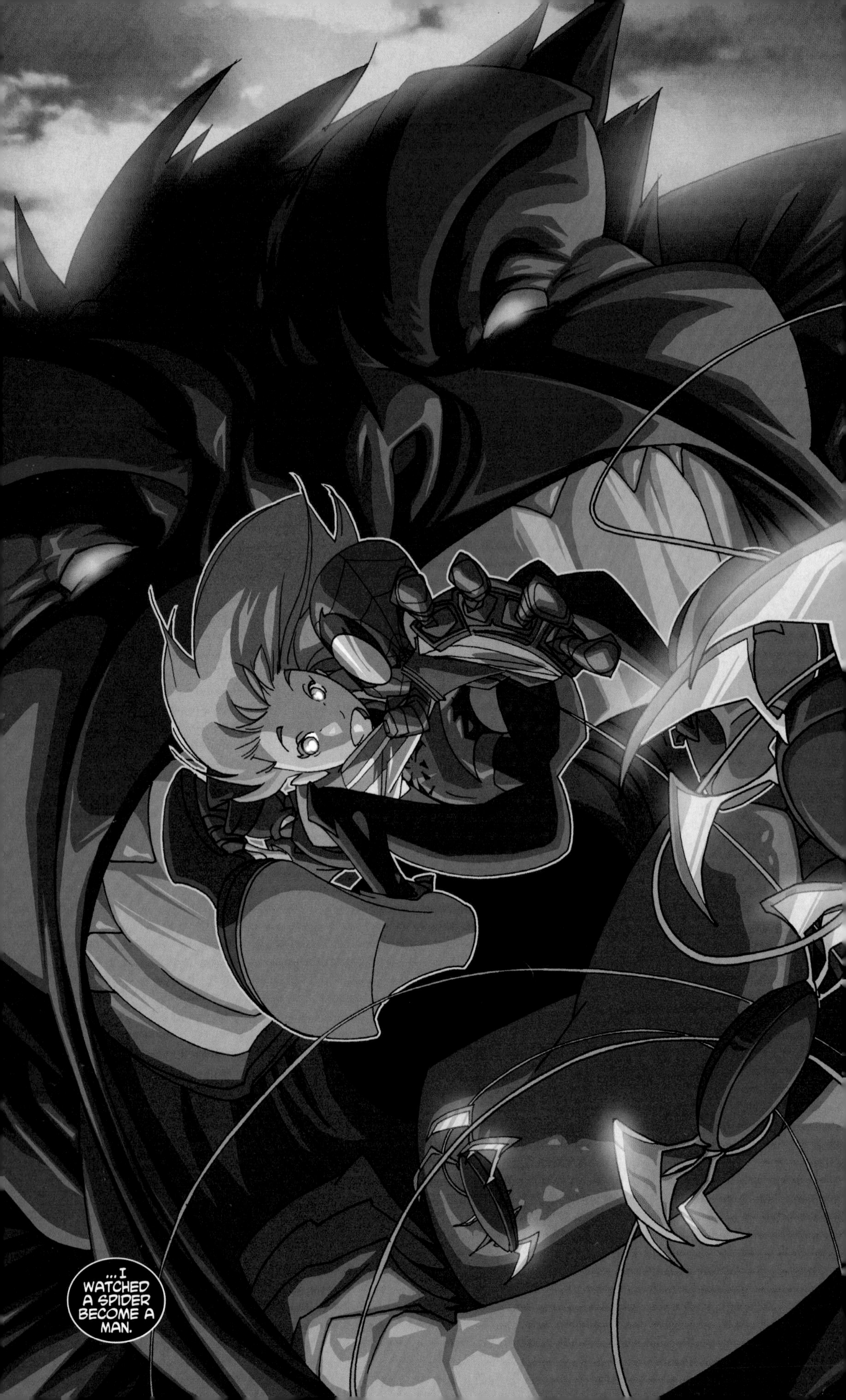
...I WATCHED A SPIDER BECOME A MAN.

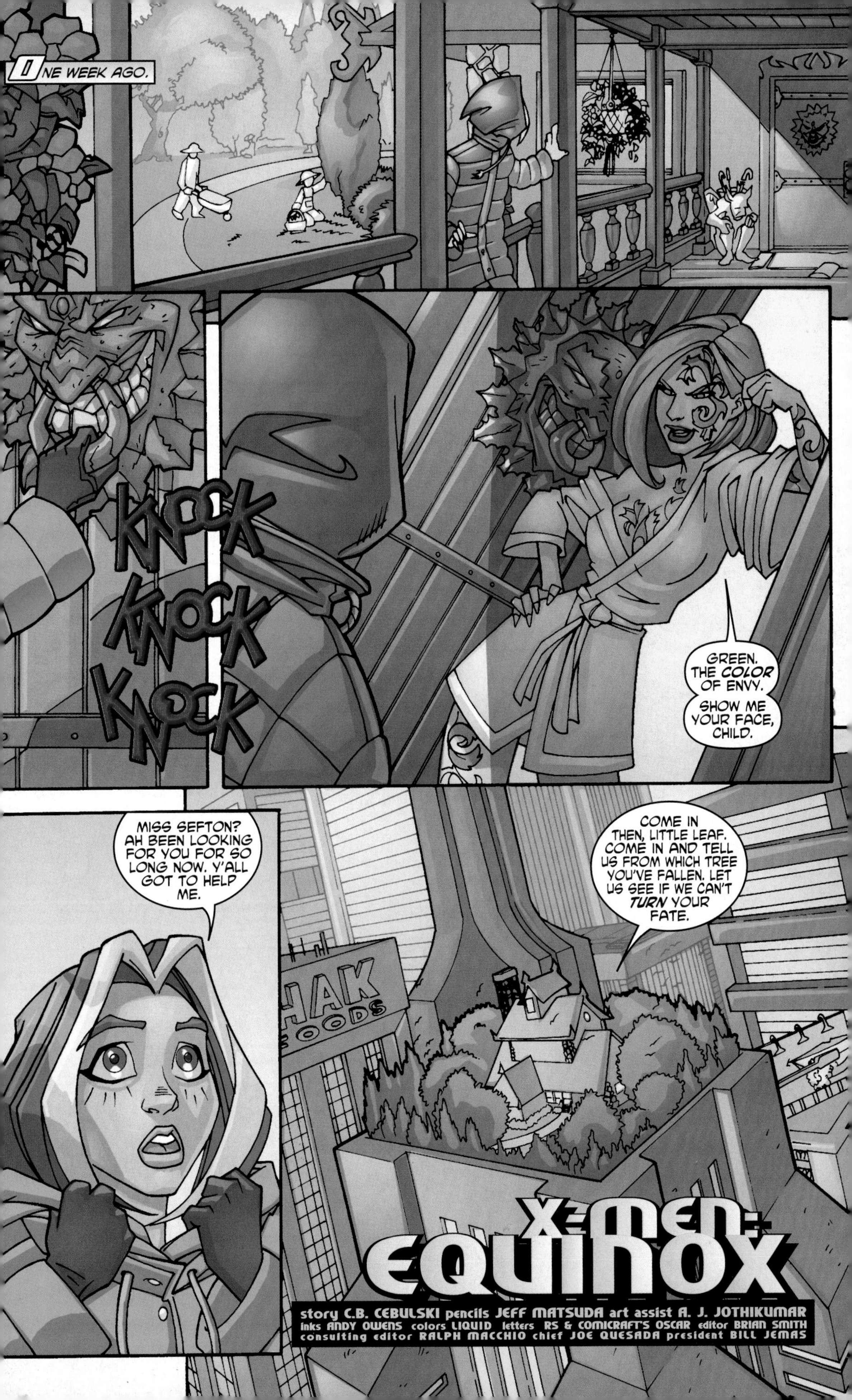
ONE WEEK AGO.
KNOCK KNOCK KNOCK
GREEN. THE COLOR OF ENVY.
SHOW ME YOUR FACE, CHILD.
MISS SEFTON? AH BEEN LOOKING FOR YOU FOR SO LONG NOW. Y'ALL GOT TO HELP ME.
COME IN THEN, LITTLE LEAF. COME IN AND TELL US FROM WHICH TREE YOU'VE FALLEN. LET US SEE IF WE CAN'T TURN YOUR FATE.
X-MEN: EQUINOX
story C.B. CEBULSKI pencils JEFF MATSUDA art assist A. J. JOTHIKUMAR
inks ANDY OWENS colors LIQUID letters RS & COMICRAFT'S OSCAR editor BRIAN SMITH
consulting editor RALPH MACCHIO chief JOE QUESADA president BILL JEMAS

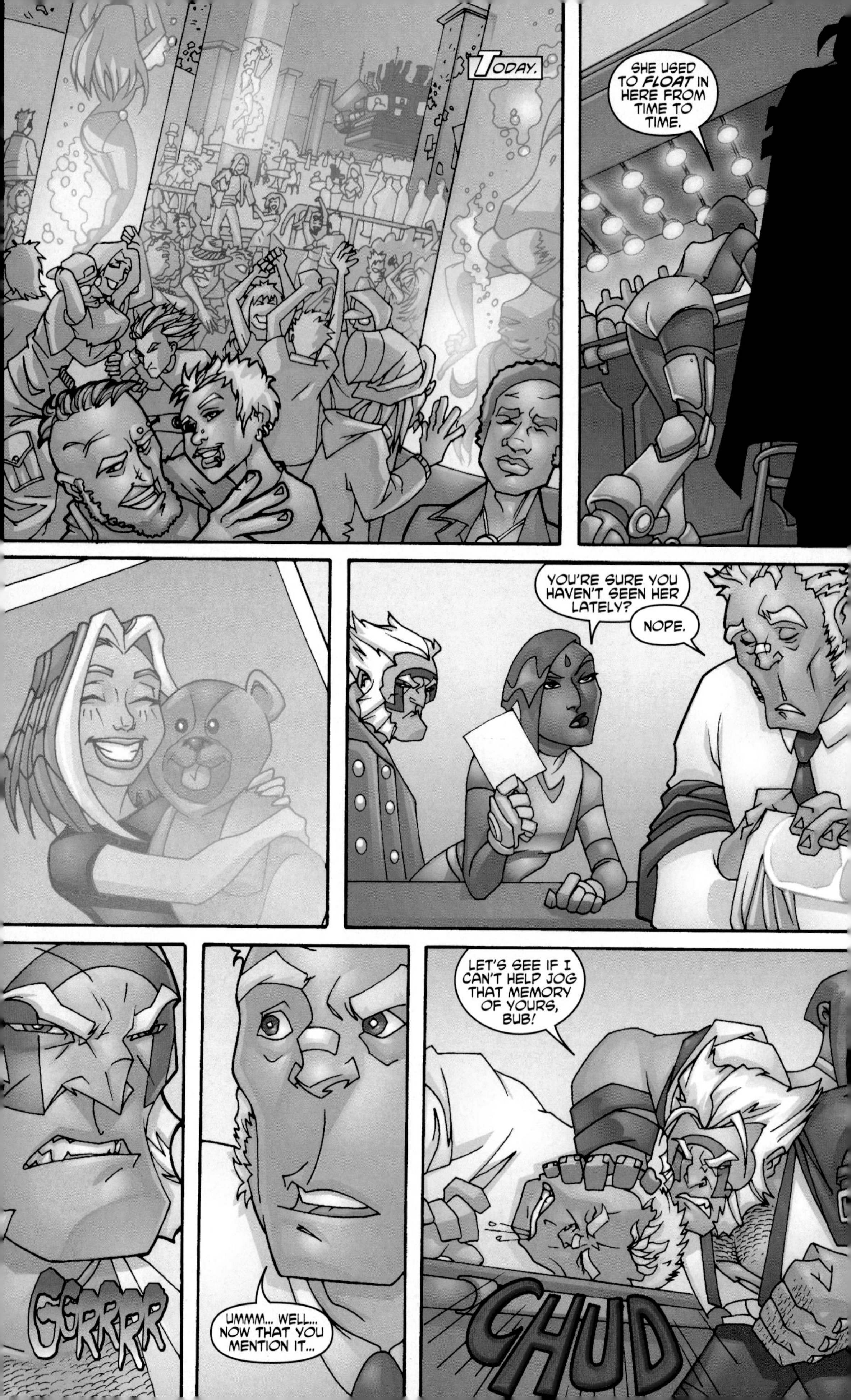
TODAY.
SHE USED TO FLOAT IN HERE FROM TIME TO TIME.
YOU'RE SURE YOU HAVEN'T SEEN HER LATELY?
NOPE.
GGRRRR
UMMM... WELL... NOW THAT YOU MENTION IT...
LET'S SEE IF I CAN'T HELP JOG THAT MEMORY OF YOURS, BUB!
CHUD

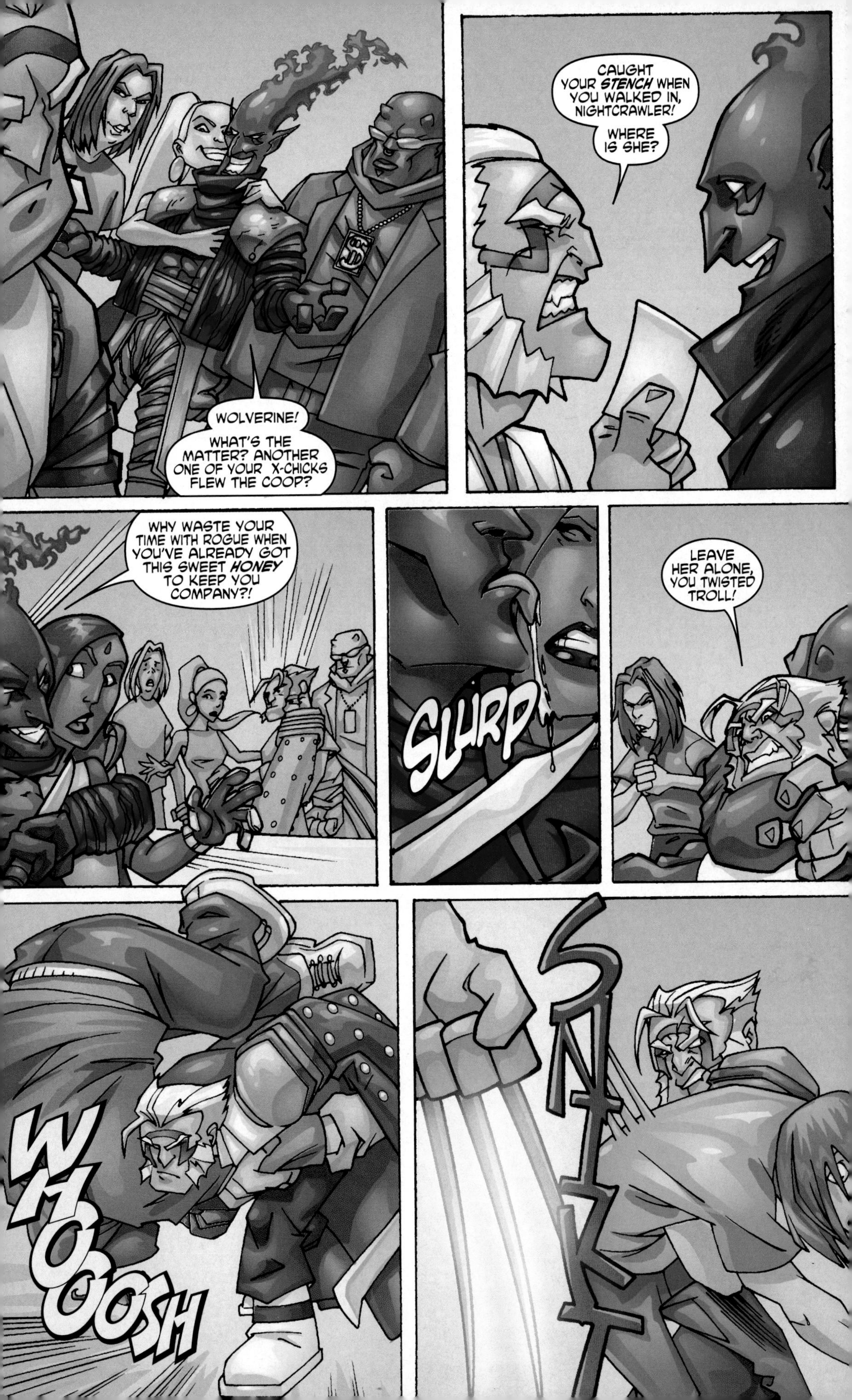
WOLVERINE!
WHAT'S THE MATTER? ANOTHER ONE OF YOUR X-CHICKS FLEW THE COOP?
CAUGHT YOUR STENCH WHEN YOU WALKED IN, NIGHTCRAWLER!
WHERE IS SHE?
WHY WASTE YOUR TIME WITH ROGUE WHEN YOU'VE ALREADY GOT THIS SWEET HONEY TO KEEP YOU COMPANY?!
SLURP
LEAVE HER ALONE, YOU TWISTED TROLL!
WHOOOSH

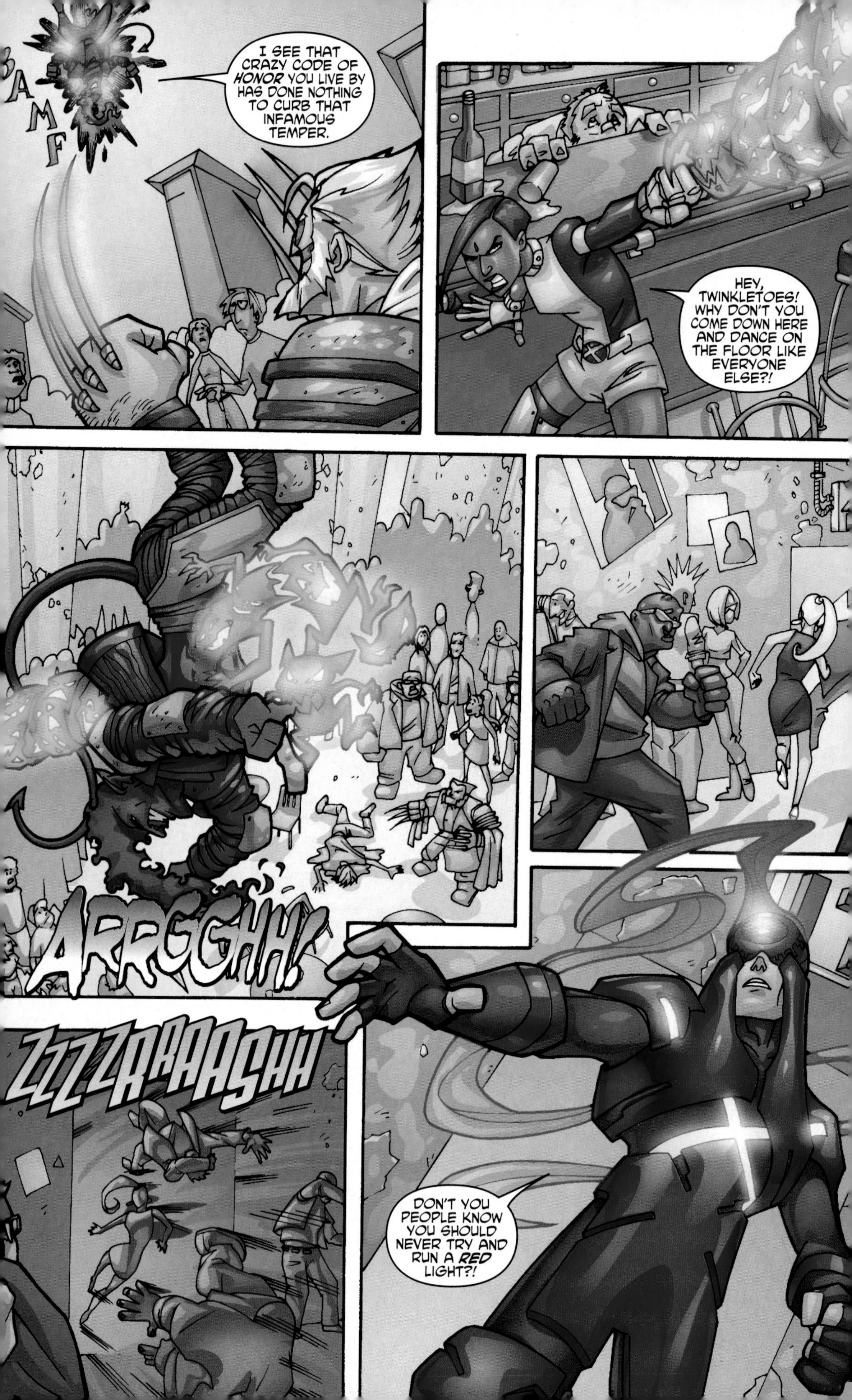
BAMF
I SEE THAT CRAZY CODE OF *HONOR* YOU LIVE BY HAS DONE NOTHING TO CURB THAT INFAMOUS TEMPER.
HEY, TWINKLETOES! WHY DON'T YOU COME DOWN HERE AND DANCE ON THE FLOOR LIKE EVERYONE ELSE?!
ARRGGHH!
ZZZZRRRAASHH
DON'T YOU PEOPLE KNOW YOU SHOULD NEVER TRY AND RUN A *RED* LIGHT?!

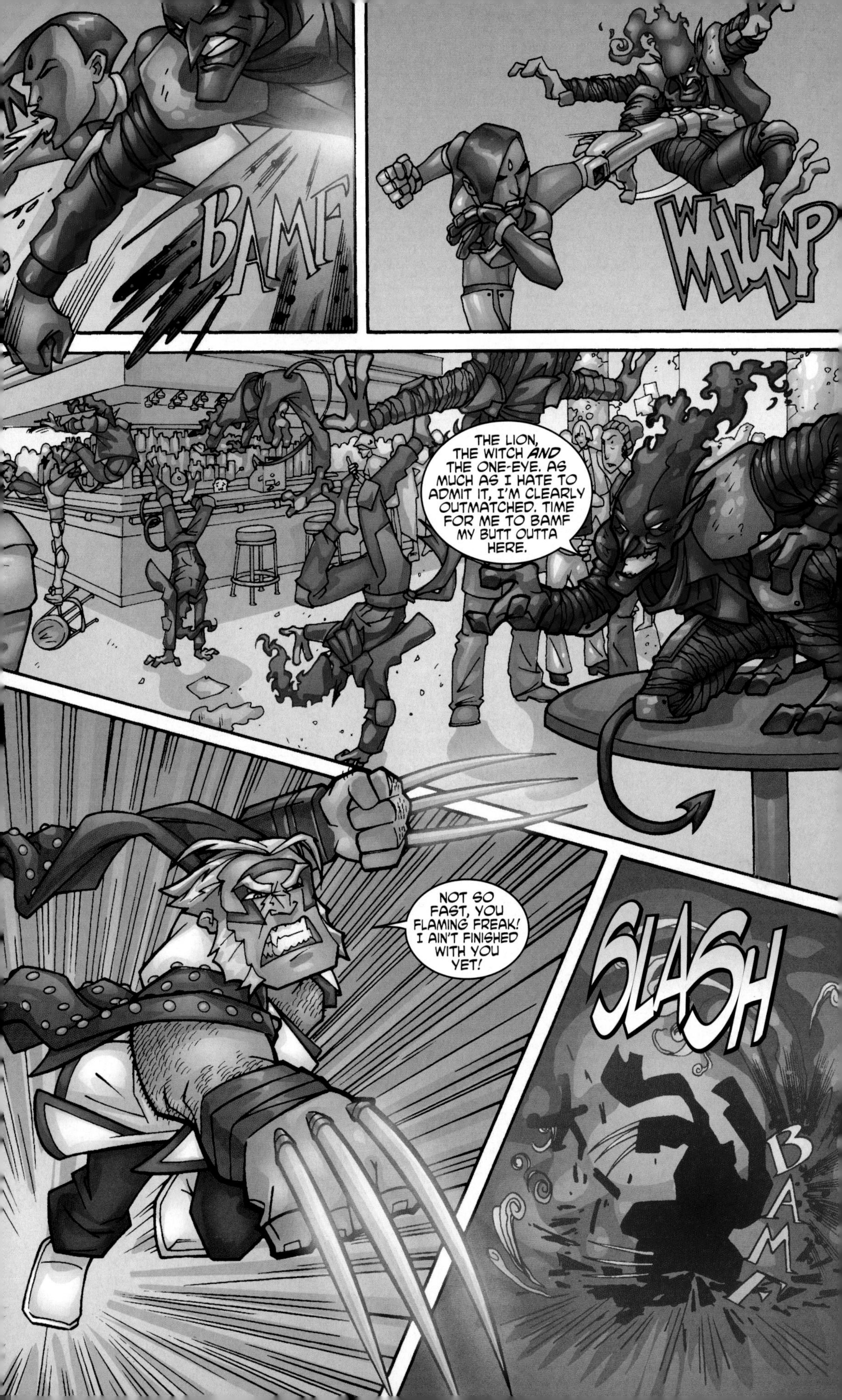
BAMF
WHUMP
THE LION, THE WITCH AND THE ONE-EYE. AS MUCH AS I HATE TO ADMIT IT, I'M CLEARLY OUTMATCHED. TIME FOR ME TO BAMF MY BUTT OUTTA HERE.
NOT SO FAST, YOU FLAMING FREAK! I AIN'T FINISHED WITH YOU YET!
SLASH
BAMF

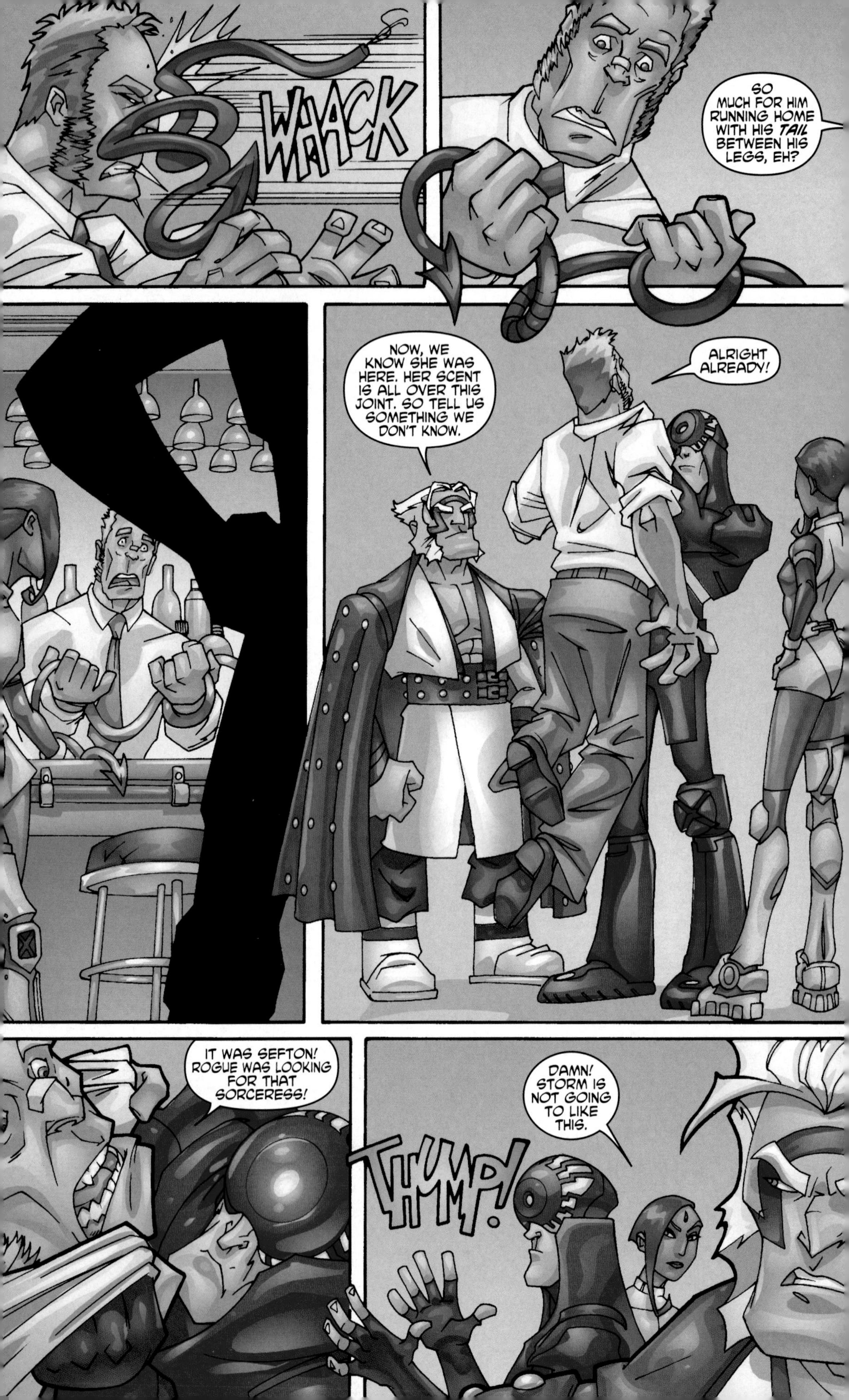
WAACK
SO MUCH FOR HIM RUNNING HOME WITH HIS TAIL BETWEEN HIS LEGS, EH?
NOW, WE KNOW SHE WAS HERE. HER SCENT IS ALL OVER THIS JOINT. SO TELL US SOMETHING WE DON'T KNOW.
ALRIGHT ALREADY!
IT WAS SEFTON! ROGUE WAS LOOKING FOR THAT SORCERESS!
THUMP!
DAMN! STORM IS NOT GOING TO LIKE THIS.

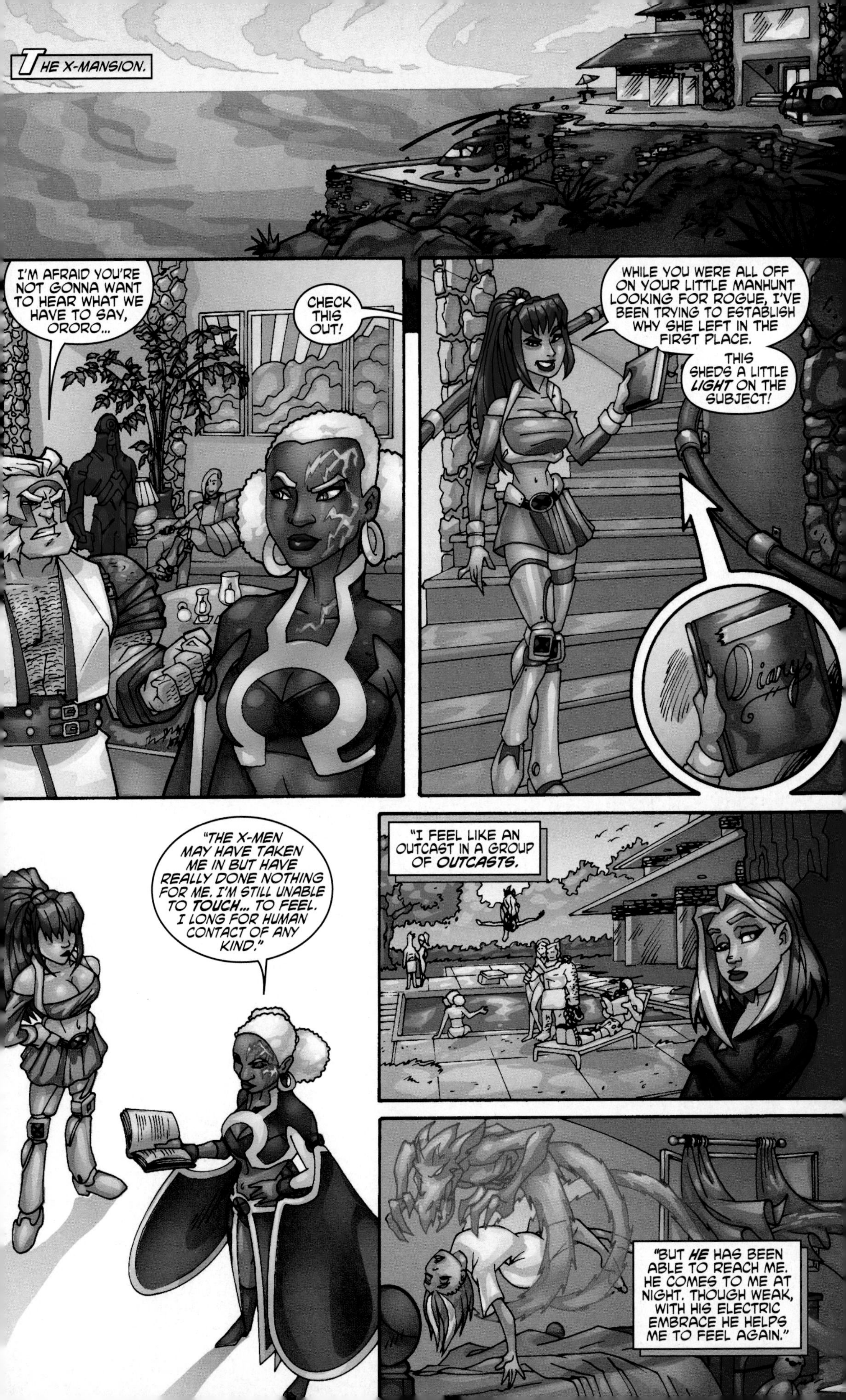
THE X-MANSION.
I'M AFRAID YOU'RE NOT GONNA WANT TO HEAR WHAT WE HAVE TO SAY, ORORO...
CHECK THIS OUT!
WHILE YOU WERE ALL OFF ON YOUR LITTLE MANHUNT LOOKING FOR ROGUE, I'VE BEEN TRYING TO ESTABLISH WHY SHE LEFT IN THE FIRST PLACE.
THIS SHEDS A LITTLE LIGHT ON THE SUBJECT!
Diary
"THE X-MEN MAY HAVE TAKEN ME IN BUT HAVE REALLY DONE NOTHING FOR ME. I'M STILL UNABLE TO TOUCH... TO FEEL. I LONG FOR HUMAN CONTACT OF ANY KIND."
"I FEEL LIKE AN OUTCAST IN A GROUP OF OUTCASTS.
"BUT HE HAS BEEN ABLE TO REACH ME. HE COMES TO ME AT NIGHT. THOUGH WEAK, WITH HIS ELECTRIC EMBRACE HE HELPS ME TO FEEL AGAIN."

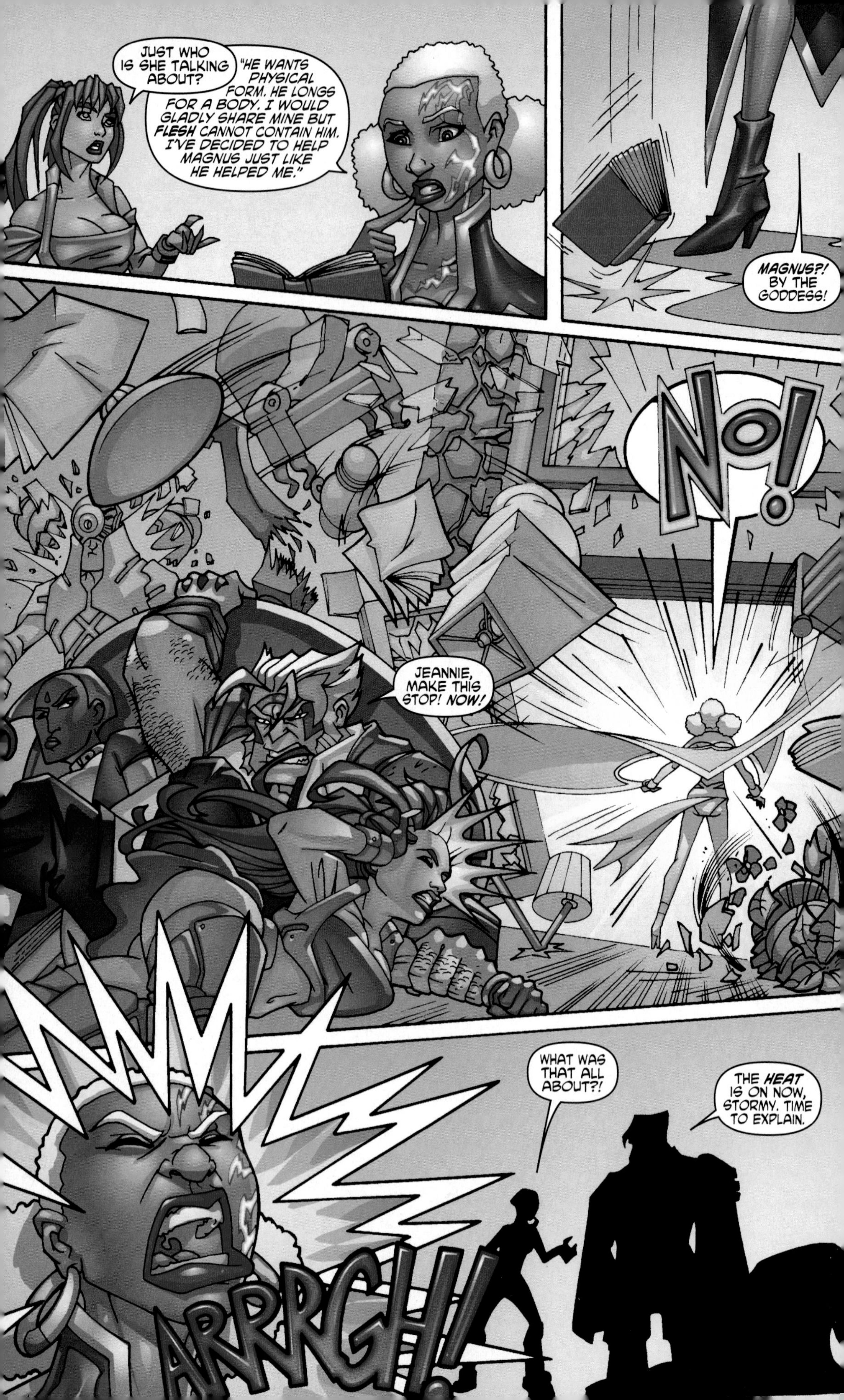

JUST WHO IS SHE TALKING ABOUT?
"HE WANTS PHYSICAL FORM. HE LONGS FOR A BODY. I WOULD GLADLY SHARE MINE BUT FLESH CANNOT CONTAIN HIM. I'VE DECIDED TO HELP MAGNUS JUST LIKE HE HELPED ME."
MAGNUS?! BY THE GODDESS!
NO!
JEANNIE, MAKE THIS STOP! NOW!
ARRRGH!!
WHAT WAS THAT ALL ABOUT?!
THE HEAT IS ON NOW, STORMY. TIME TO EXPLAIN.

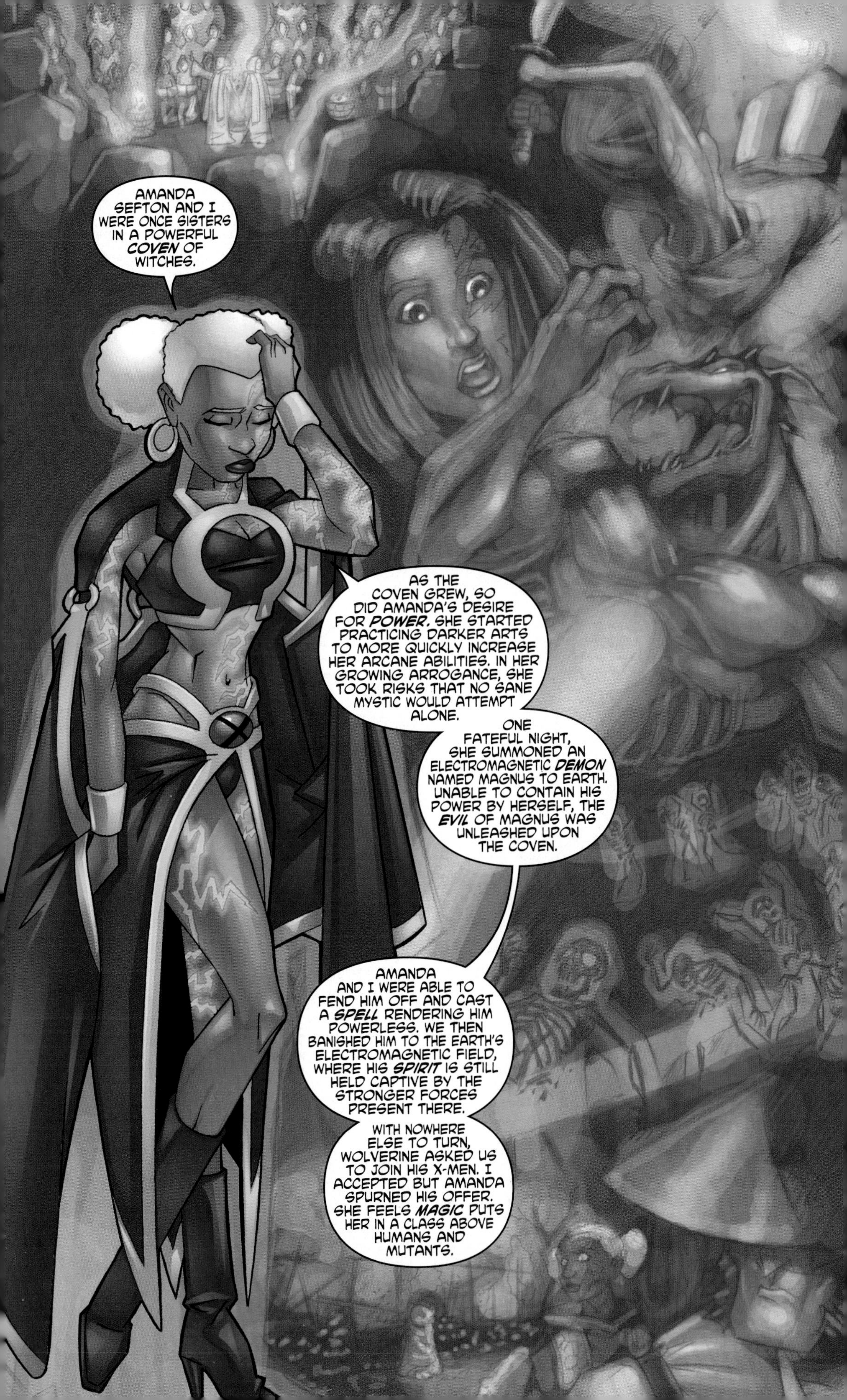
AMANDA SEFTON AND I WERE ONCE SISTERS IN A POWERFUL *COVEN* OF WITCHES.
AS THE COVEN GREW, SO DID AMANDA'S DESIRE FOR *POWER.* SHE STARTED PRACTICING DARKER ARTS TO MORE QUICKLY INCREASE HER ARCANE ABILITIES. IN HER GROWING ARROGANCE, SHE TOOK RISKS THAT NO SANE MYSTIC WOULD ATTEMPT ALONE.
ONE FATEFUL NIGHT, SHE SUMMONED AN ELECTROMAGNETIC *DEMON* NAMED MAGNUS TO EARTH. UNABLE TO CONTAIN HIS POWER BY HERSELF, THE *EVIL* OF MAGNUS WAS UNLEASHED UPON THE COVEN.
AMANDA AND I WERE ABLE TO FEND HIM OFF AND CAST A *SPELL* RENDERING HIM POWERLESS. WE THEN BANISHED HIM TO THE EARTH'S ELECTROMAGNETIC FIELD, WHERE HIS *SPIRIT* IS STILL HELD CAPTIVE BY THE STRONGER FORCES PRESENT THERE.
WITH NOWHERE ELSE TO TURN, WOLVERINE ASKED US TO JOIN HIS X-MEN. I ACCEPTED BUT AMANDA SPURNED HIS OFFER. SHE FEELS *MAGIC* PUTS HER IN A CLASS ABOVE HUMANS AND MUTANTS.

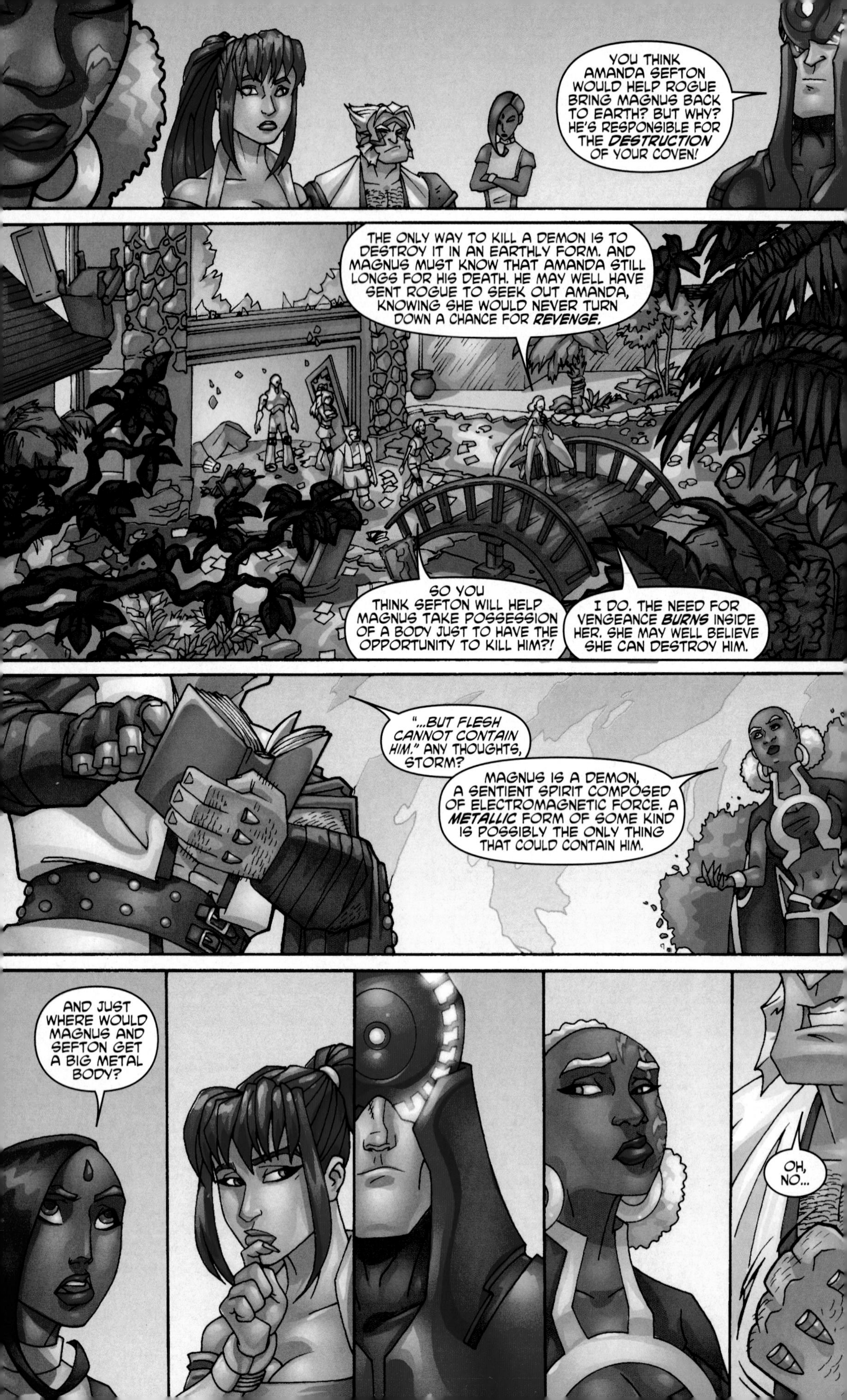
YOU THINK AMANDA SEFTON WOULD HELP ROGUE BRING MAGNUS BACK TO EARTH? BUT WHY? HE'S RESPONSIBLE FOR THE *DESTRUCTION* OF YOUR COVEN!
THE ONLY WAY TO KILL A DEMON IS TO DESTROY IT IN AN EARTHLY FORM. AND MAGNUS MUST KNOW THAT AMANDA STILL LONGS FOR HIS DEATH. HE MAY WELL HAVE SENT ROGUE TO SEEK OUT AMANDA, KNOWING SHE WOULD NEVER TURN DOWN A CHANCE FOR *REVENGE.*
SO YOU THINK SEFTON WILL HELP MAGNUS TAKE POSSESSION OF A BODY JUST TO HAVE THE OPPORTUNITY TO KILL HIM?!
I DO. THE NEED FOR VENGEANCE *BURNS* INSIDE HER. SHE MAY WELL BELIEVE SHE CAN DESTROY HIM.
"...BUT FLESH CANNOT CONTAIN HIM." ANY THOUGHTS, STORM?
MAGNUS IS A DEMON, A SENTIENT SPIRIT COMPOSED OF ELECTROMAGNETIC FORCE. A *METALLIC* FORM OF SOME KIND IS POSSIBLY THE ONLY THING THAT COULD CONTAIN HIM.
AND JUST WHERE WOULD MAGNUS AND SEFTON GET A BIG METAL BODY?
OH, NO...

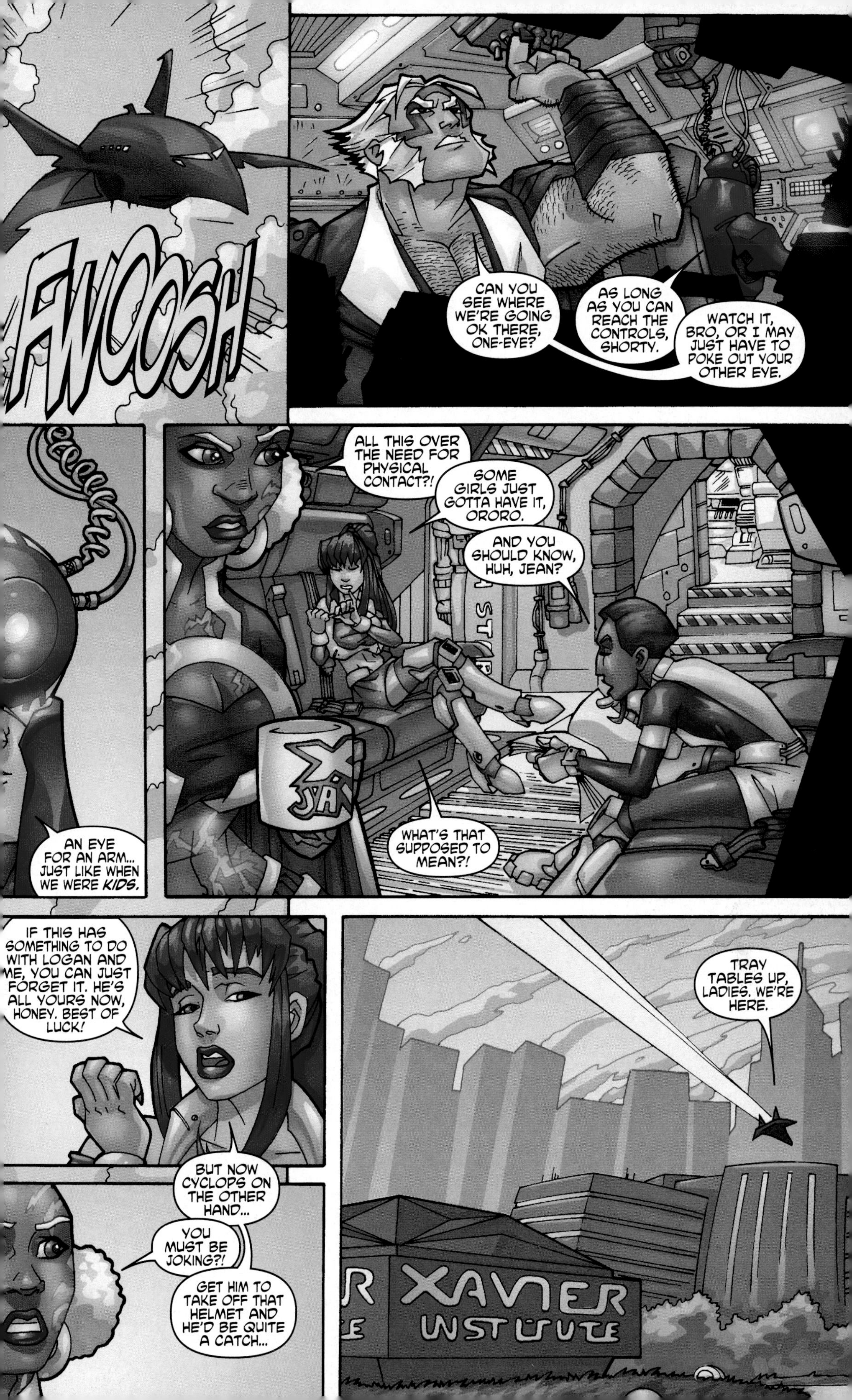
FWOOSH
CAN YOU SEE WHERE WE'RE GOING OK THERE, ONE-EYE?
AS LONG AS YOU CAN REACH THE CONTROLS, SHORTY.
WATCH IT, BRO, OR I MAY JUST HAVE TO POKE OUT YOUR OTHER EYE.
AN EYE FOR AN ARM... JUST LIKE WHEN WE WERE *KIDS*.
ALL THIS OVER THE NEED FOR PHYSICAL CONTACT?!
SOME GIRLS JUST GOTTA HAVE IT, ORORO.
AND YOU SHOULD KNOW, HUH, JEAN?
WHAT'S THAT SUPPOSED TO MEAN?!
IF THIS HAS SOMETHING TO DO WITH LOGAN AND ME, YOU CAN JUST FORGET IT. HE'S ALL YOURS NOW, HONEY. BEST OF LUCK!
BUT NOW CYCLOPS ON THE OTHER HAND...
YOU MUST BE JOKING?!
GET HIM TO TAKE OFF THAT HELMET AND HE'D BE QUITE A CATCH...
TRAY TABLES UP, LADIES. WE'RE HERE.
XAVIER INSTITUTE

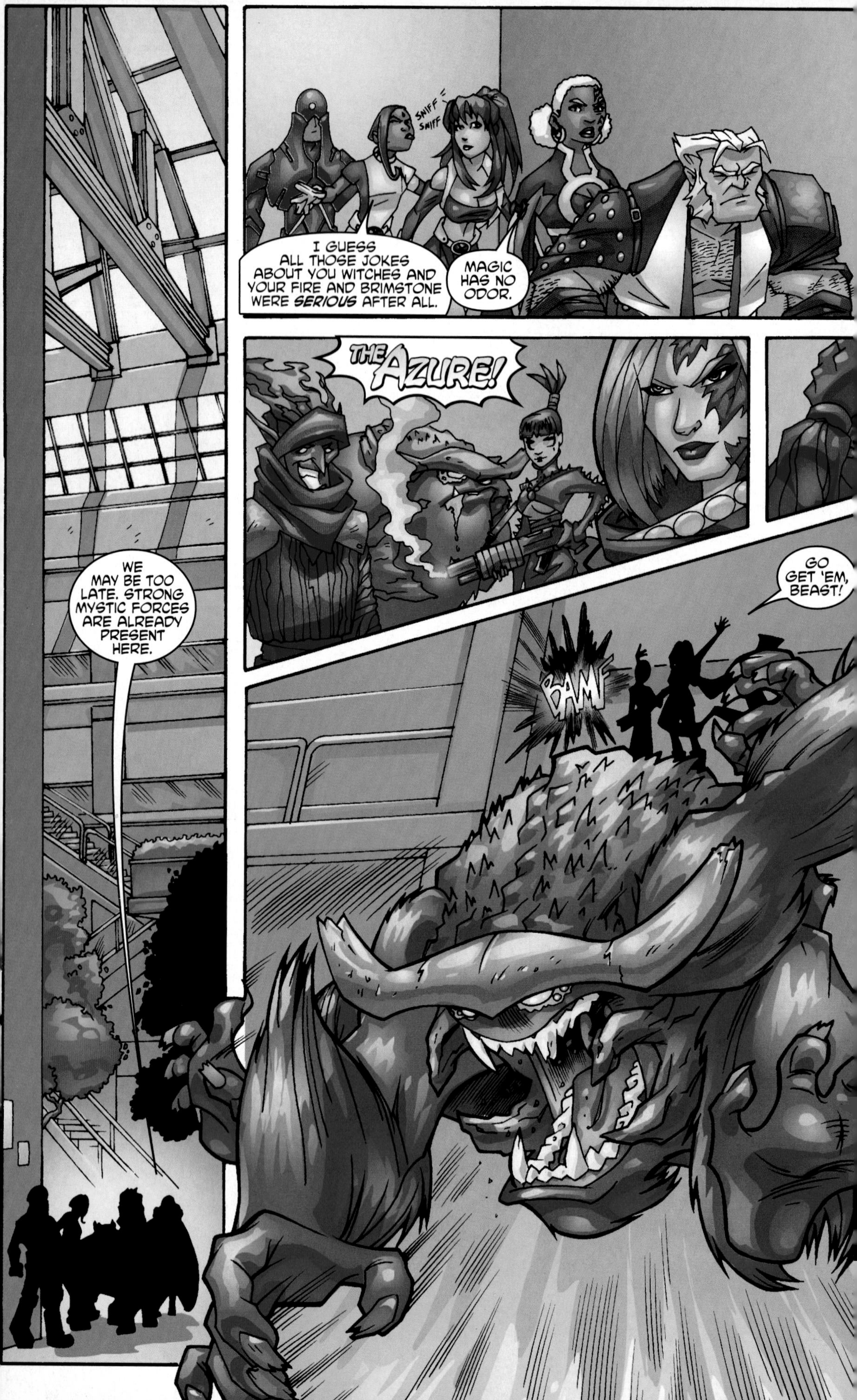
SNIFF SNIFF
I GUESS ALL THOSE JOKES ABOUT YOU WITCHES AND YOUR FIRE AND BRIMSTONE WERE *SERIOUS* AFTER ALL.
MAGIC HAS NO ODOR.
THE AZURE!
WE MAY BE TOO LATE. STRONG MYSTIC FORCES ARE ALREADY PRESENT HERE.
GO GET 'EM, BEAST!
BAMF

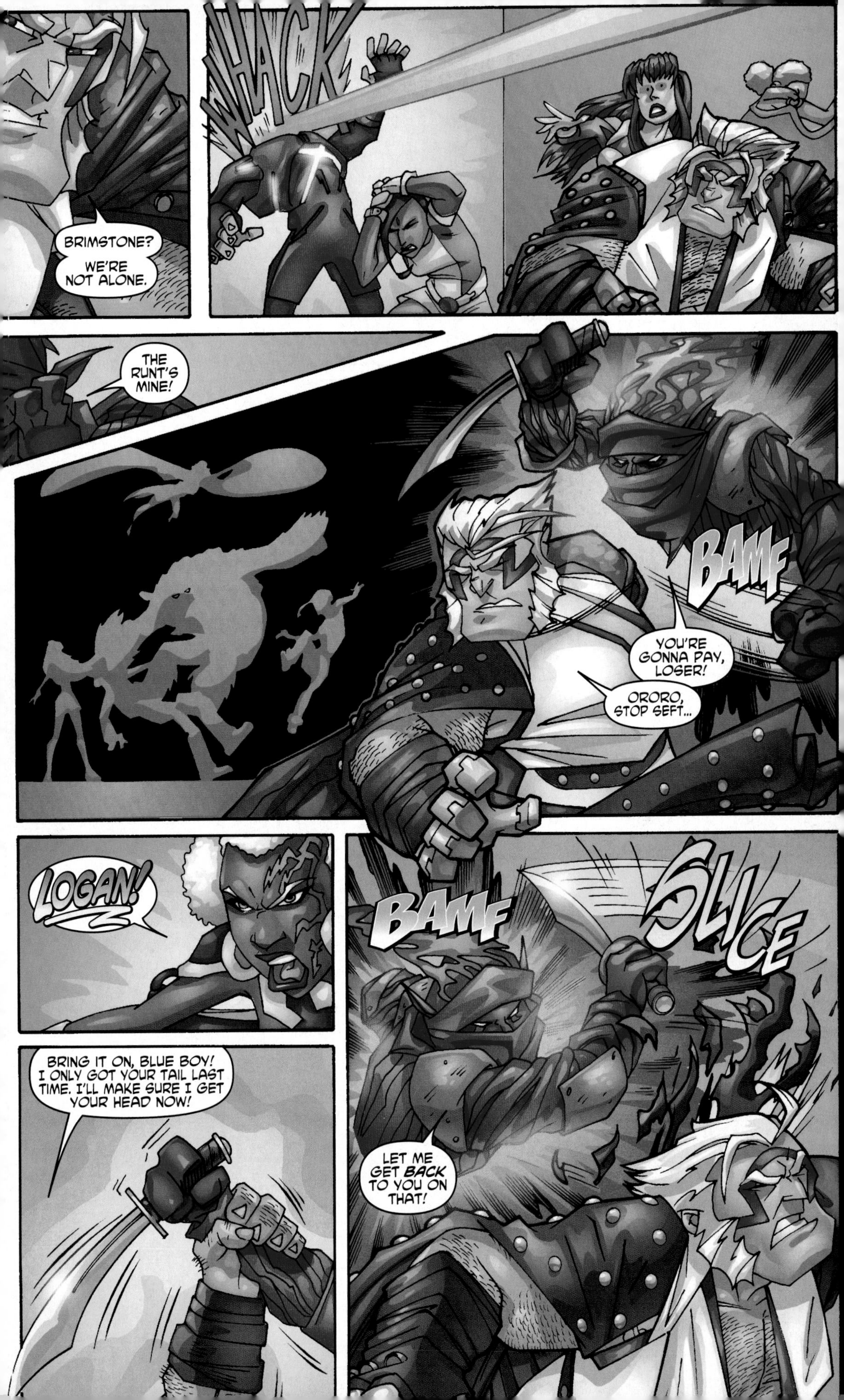
BRIMSTONE? WE'RE NOT ALONE.
WHACK
THE RUNT'S MINE!
BAMF
YOU'RE GONNA PAY, LOSER!
ORORO, STOP SEFT...
LOGAN!
BAMF
SLICE
BRING IT ON, BLUE BOY! I ONLY GOT YOUR TAIL LAST TIME. I'LL MAKE SURE I GET YOUR HEAD NOW!
LET ME GET BACK TO YOU ON THAT!

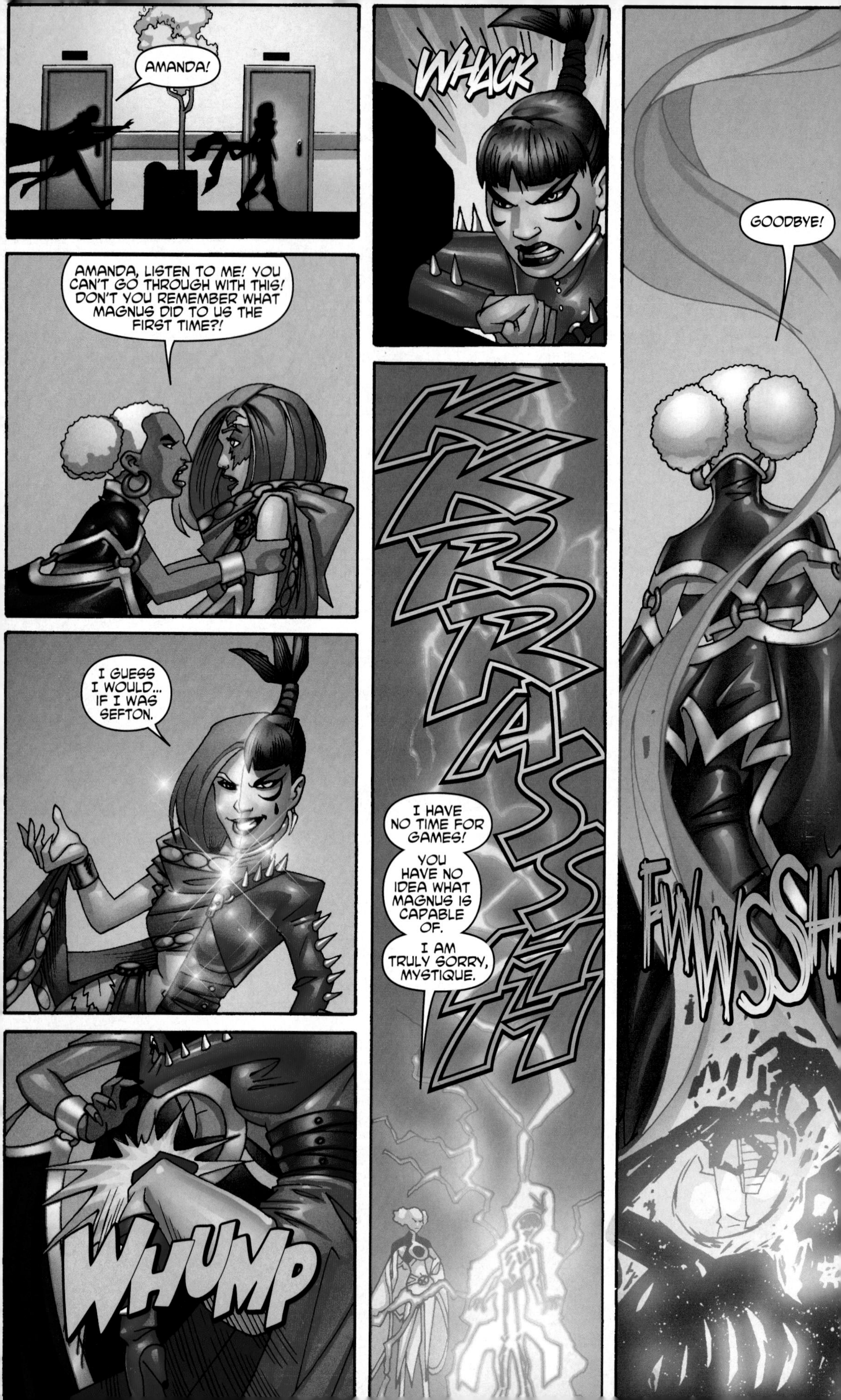
AMANDA!
AMANDA, LISTEN TO ME! YOU CAN'T GO THROUGH WITH THIS! DON'T YOU REMEMBER WHAT MAGNUS DID TO US THE FIRST TIME?!
I GUESS I WOULD... IF I WAS SEFTON.
WHUMP
WHACK
KRRAASSHH
I HAVE NO TIME FOR GAMES!
YOU HAVE NO IDEA WHAT MAGNUS IS CAPABLE OF.
I AM TRULY SORRY, MYSTIQUE.
GOODBYE!
FWWSSH

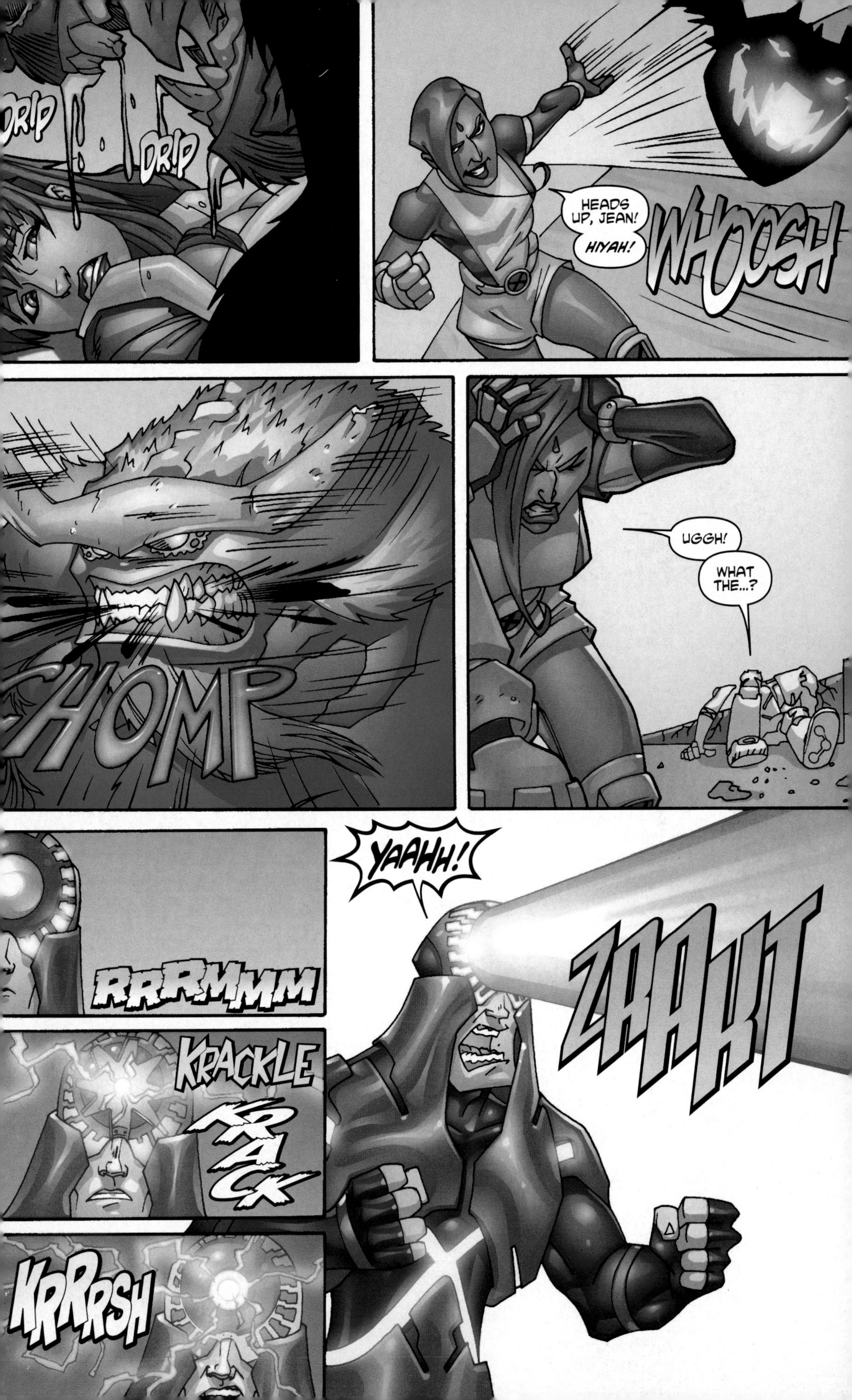

DRIP
DRIP
HEADS UP, JEAN!
HIYAH!
WHOOSH
CHOMP
UGGH!
WHAT THE...?
RRRMMM
YAAHH!
ZAAKT
KRACKLE
KRACK
KRRRSH

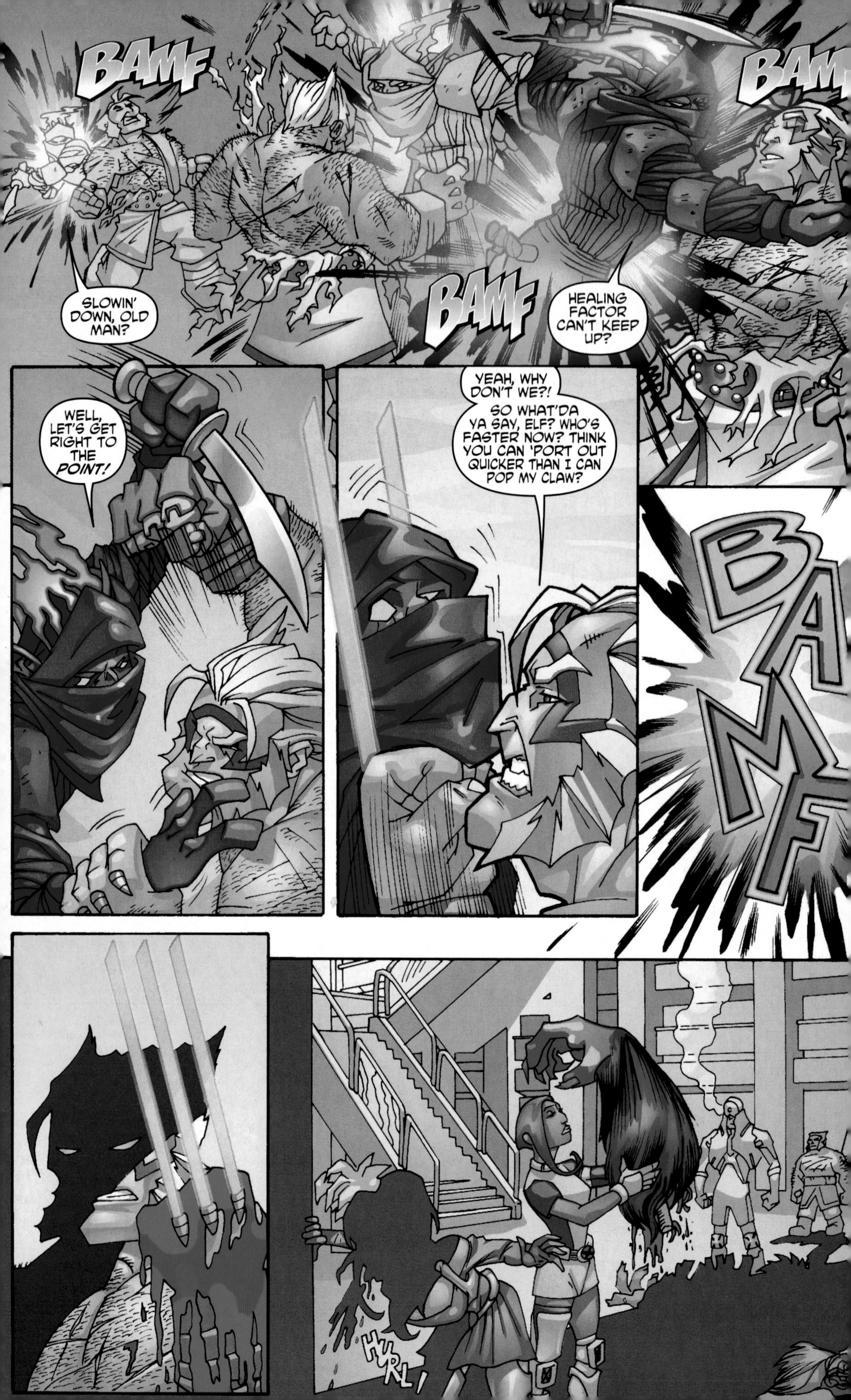
BAMF
BAMF
SLOWIN' DOWN, OLD MAN?
BAMF
HEALING FACTOR CAN'T KEEP UP?
WELL, LET'S GET RIGHT TO THE *POINT!*
YEAH, WHY DON'T WE?!
SO WHAT'DA YA SAY, ELF? WHO'S FASTER NOW? THINK YOU CAN 'PORT OUT QUICKER THAN I CAN POP MY CLAW?
BAMF
HURL!

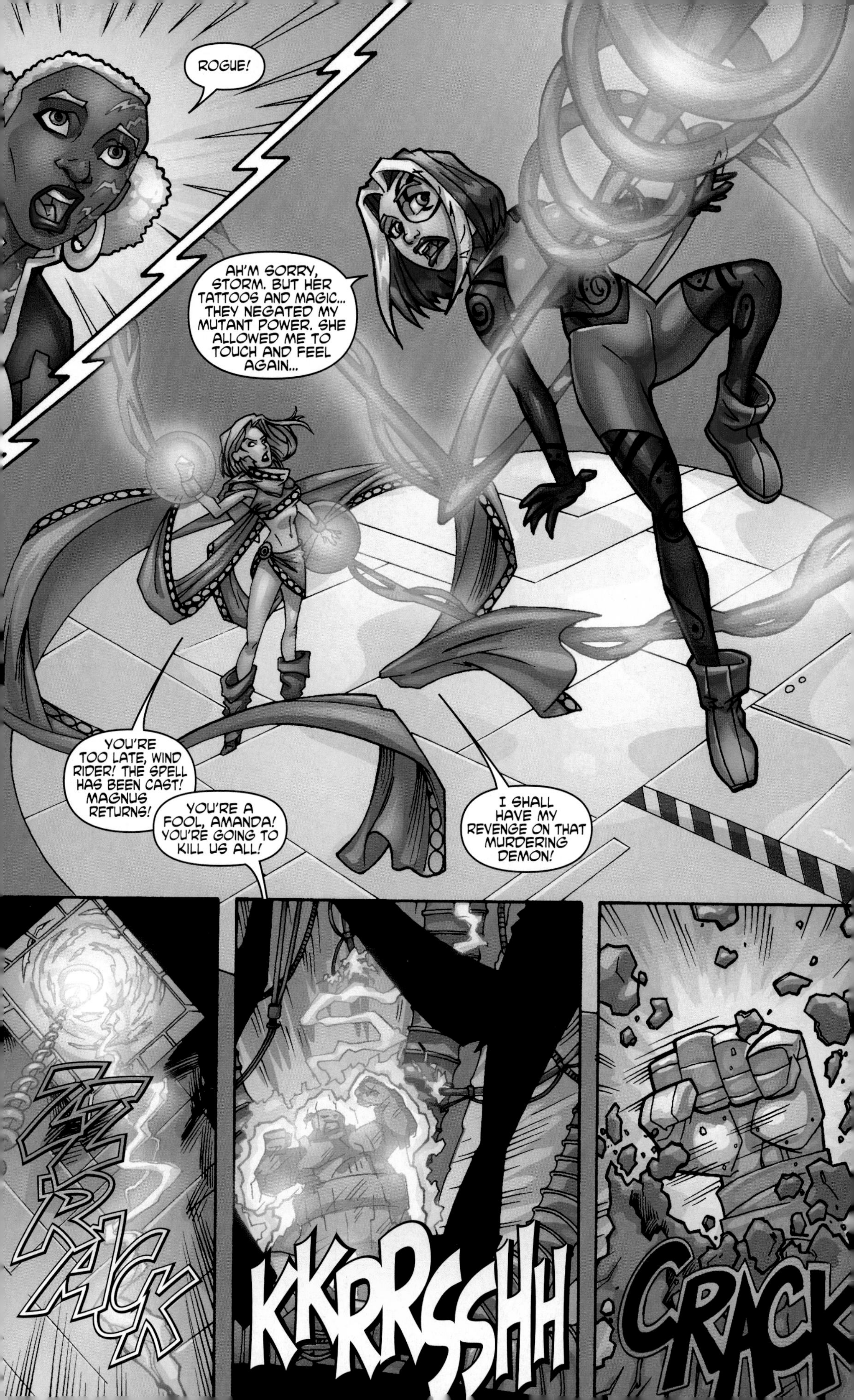
ROGUE!
AH'M SORRY, STORM. BUT HER TATTOOS AND MAGIC... THEY NEGATED MY MUTANT POWER. SHE ALLOWED ME TO TOUCH AND FEEL AGAIN...
YOU'RE TOO LATE, WIND RIDER! THE SPELL HAS BEEN CAST! MAGNUS RETURNS!
YOU'RE A FOOL, AMANDA! YOU'RE GOING TO KILL US ALL!
I SHALL HAVE MY REVENGE ON THAT MURDERING DEMON!
ZZRACK
KKRRSSHH
CRACK

I LIVE!

NOT FOR LONG, YOU SADISTIC SPIRIT!

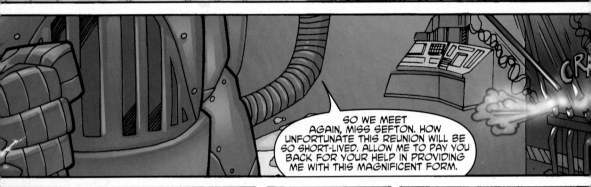

SO WE MEET AGAIN, MISS SEFTON. HOW UNFORTUNATE THIS REUNION WILL BE SO SHORT-LIVED. ALLOW ME TO PAY YOU BACK FOR YOUR HELP IN PROVIDING ME WITH THIS MAGNIFICENT FORM.

CHANG

SPLAT

NO!

THUK

SHE'S DEAD.

WITHOUT HER POWER TO SUSTAIN THE MAGIC, MY MUTANT POWER'S GONNA RETURN.

NOT TO WORRY, CHILD. YOU'LL BE ABLE TO TOUCH ME NOW THAT I CONTROL COLOSSUS' METALLIC BODY. HEH HEH.

WHAT'S THIS?

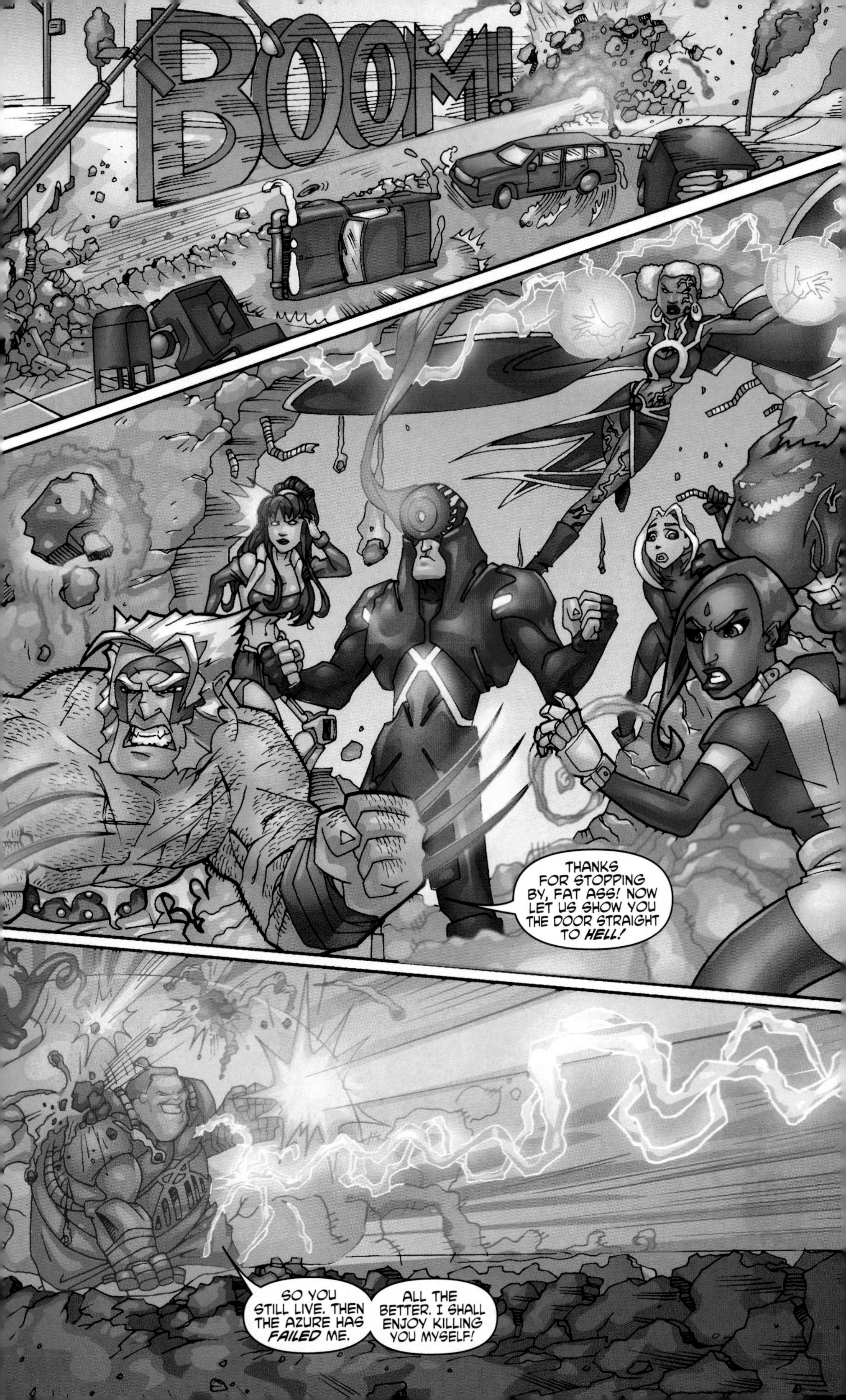
BOOM!
THANKS FOR STOPPING BY, FAT ASS! NOW LET US SHOW YOU THE DOOR STRAIGHT TO *HELL!*
SO YOU STILL LIVE. THEN THE AZURE HAS *FAILED* ME.
ALL THE BETTER. I SHALL ENJOY KILLING YOU MYSELF!

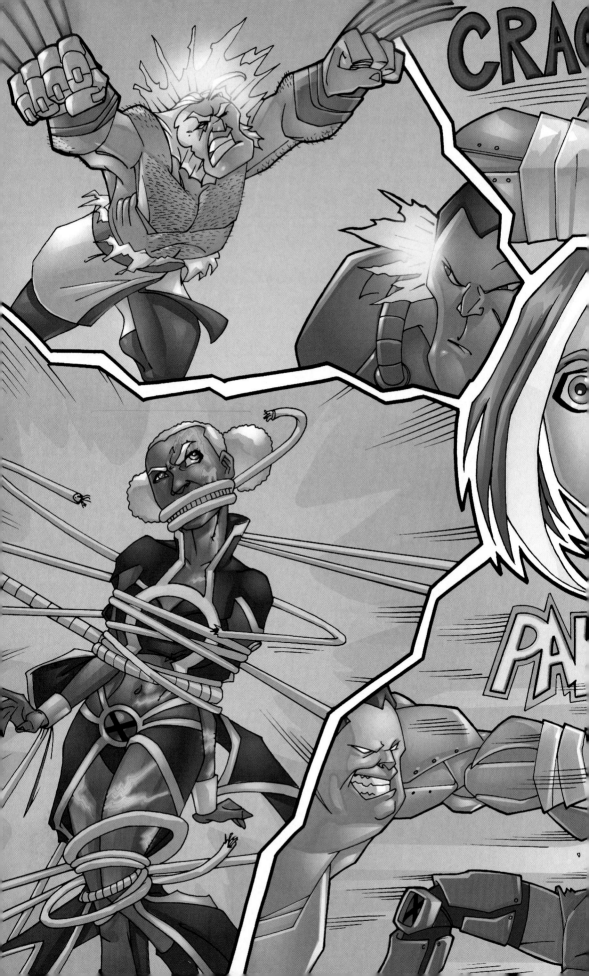

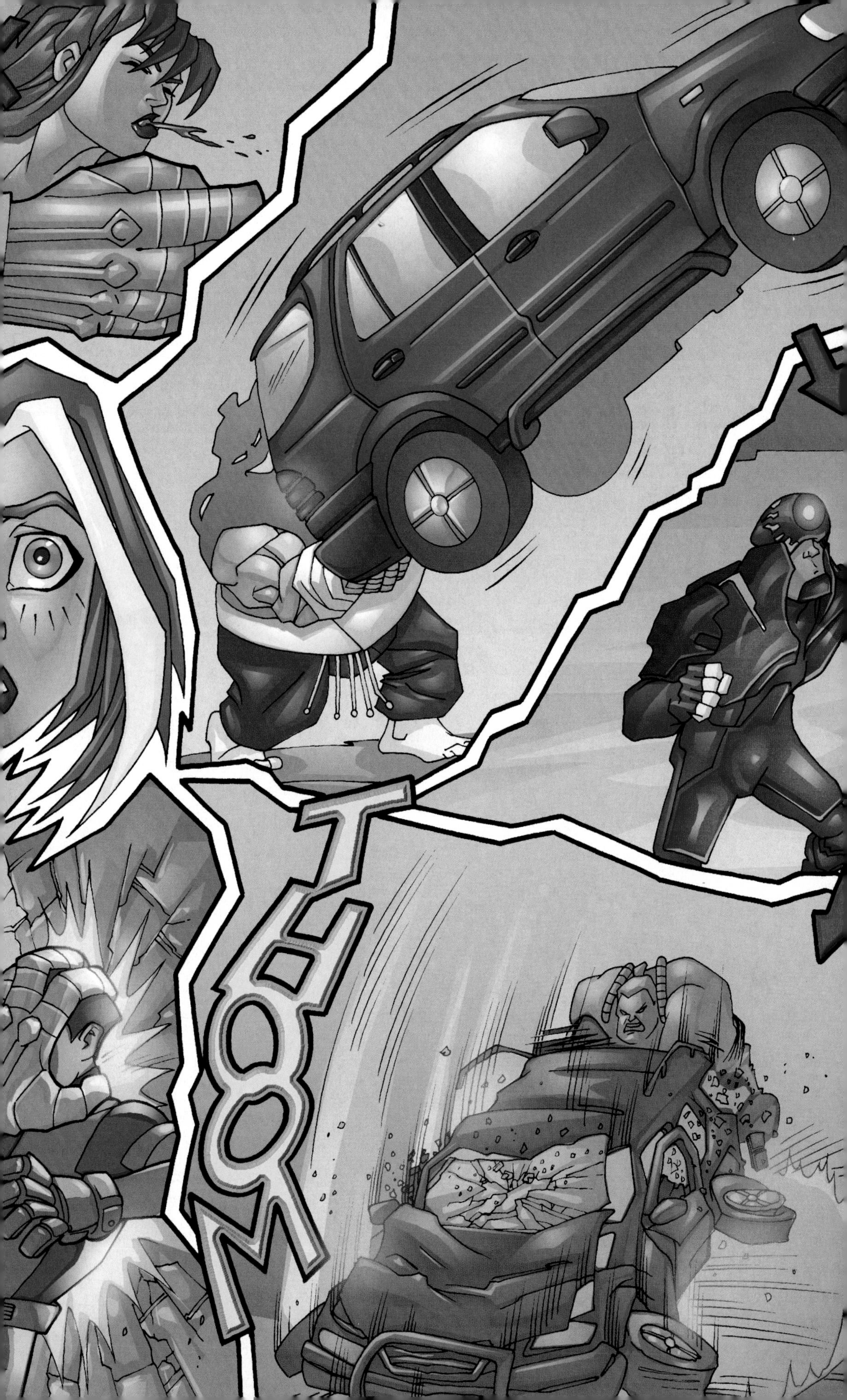
THOOM

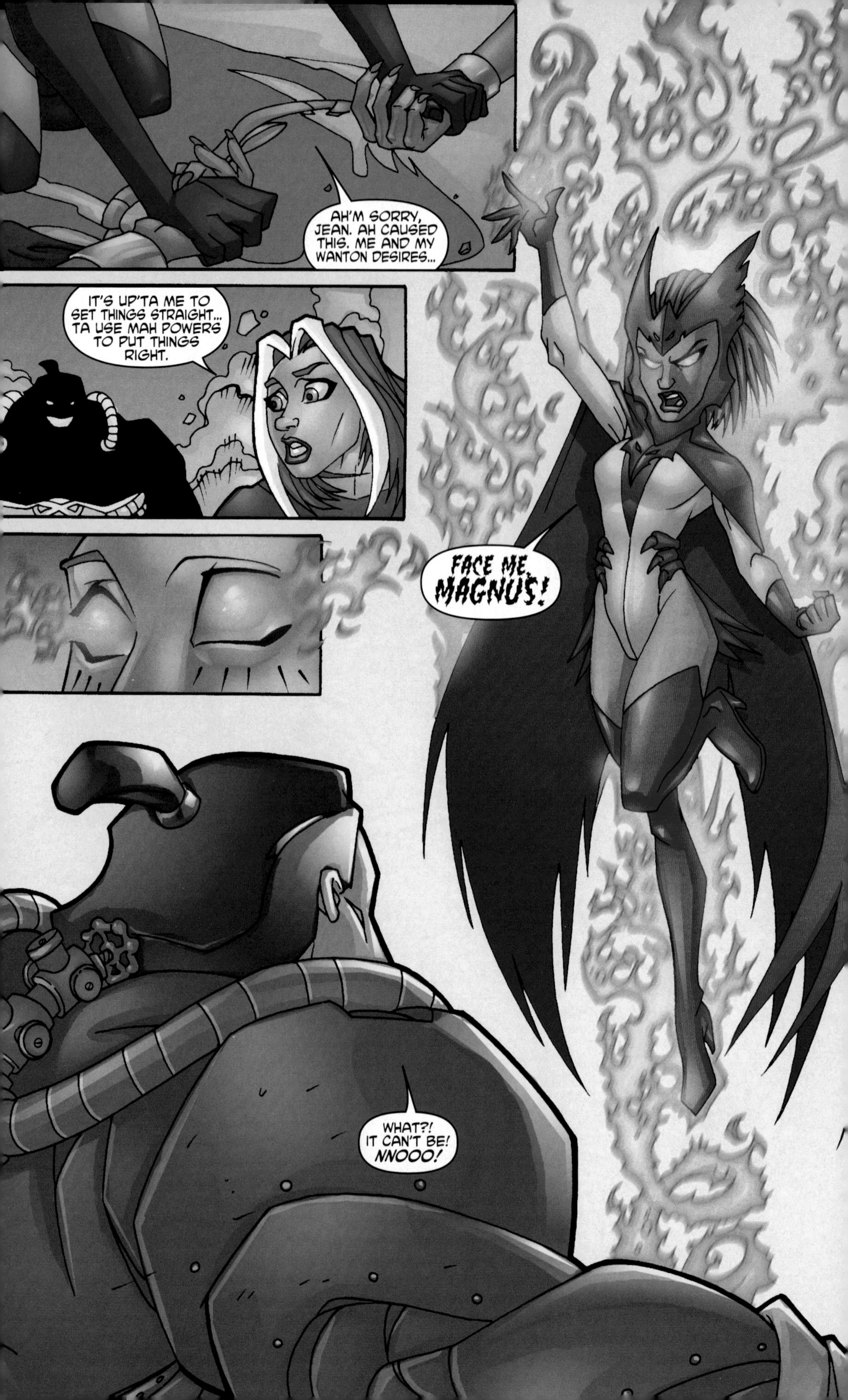
AH'M SORRY, JEAN. AH CAUSED THIS. ME AND MY WANTON DESIRES...
IT'S UP'TA ME TO SET THINGS STRAIGHT... TA USE MAH POWERS TO PUT THINGS RIGHT.
FACE ME, MAGNUS!
WHAT?! IT CAN'T BE! NNOOO!

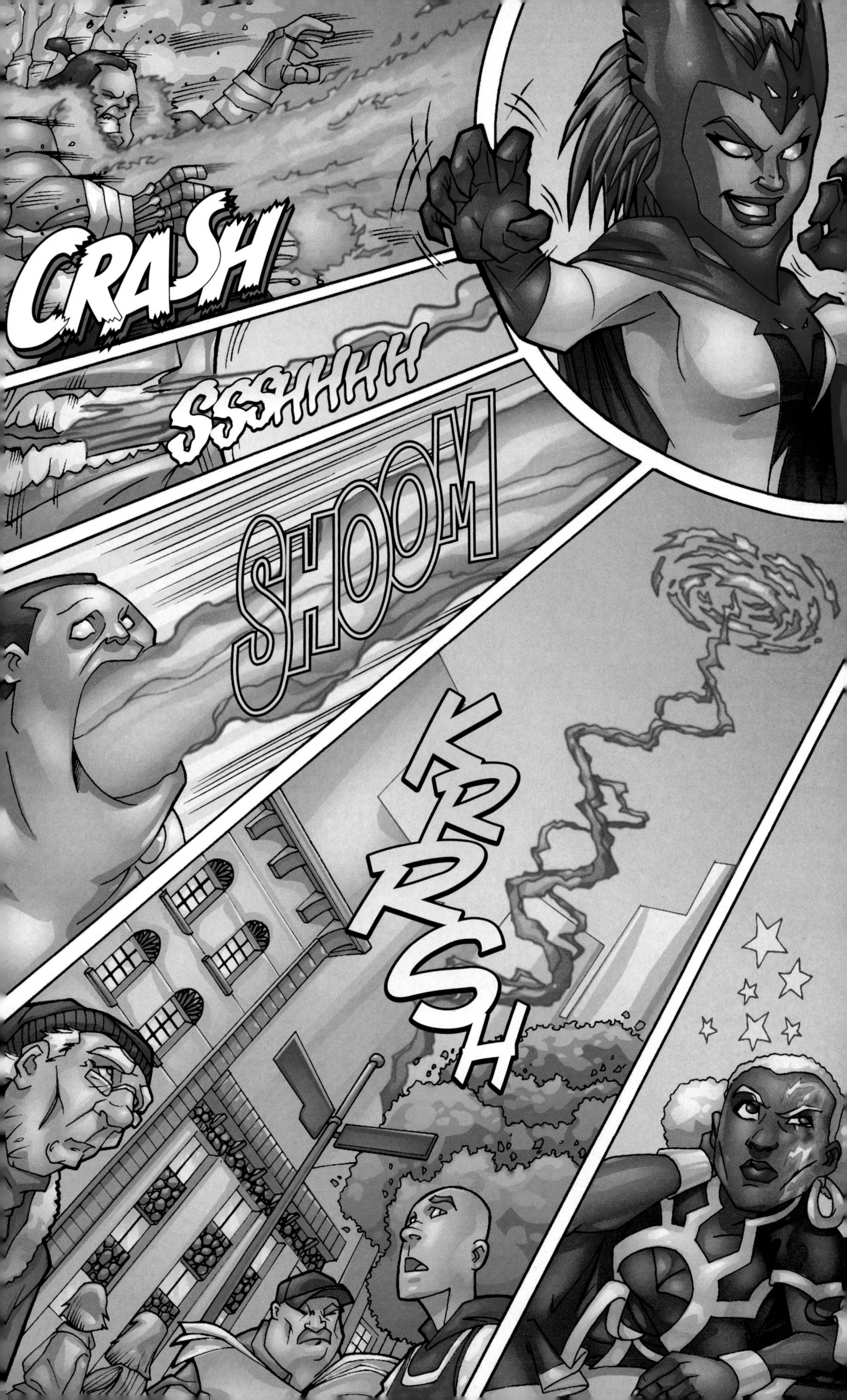
CRASH
SSSHHHH
SHOOM
KRRSH

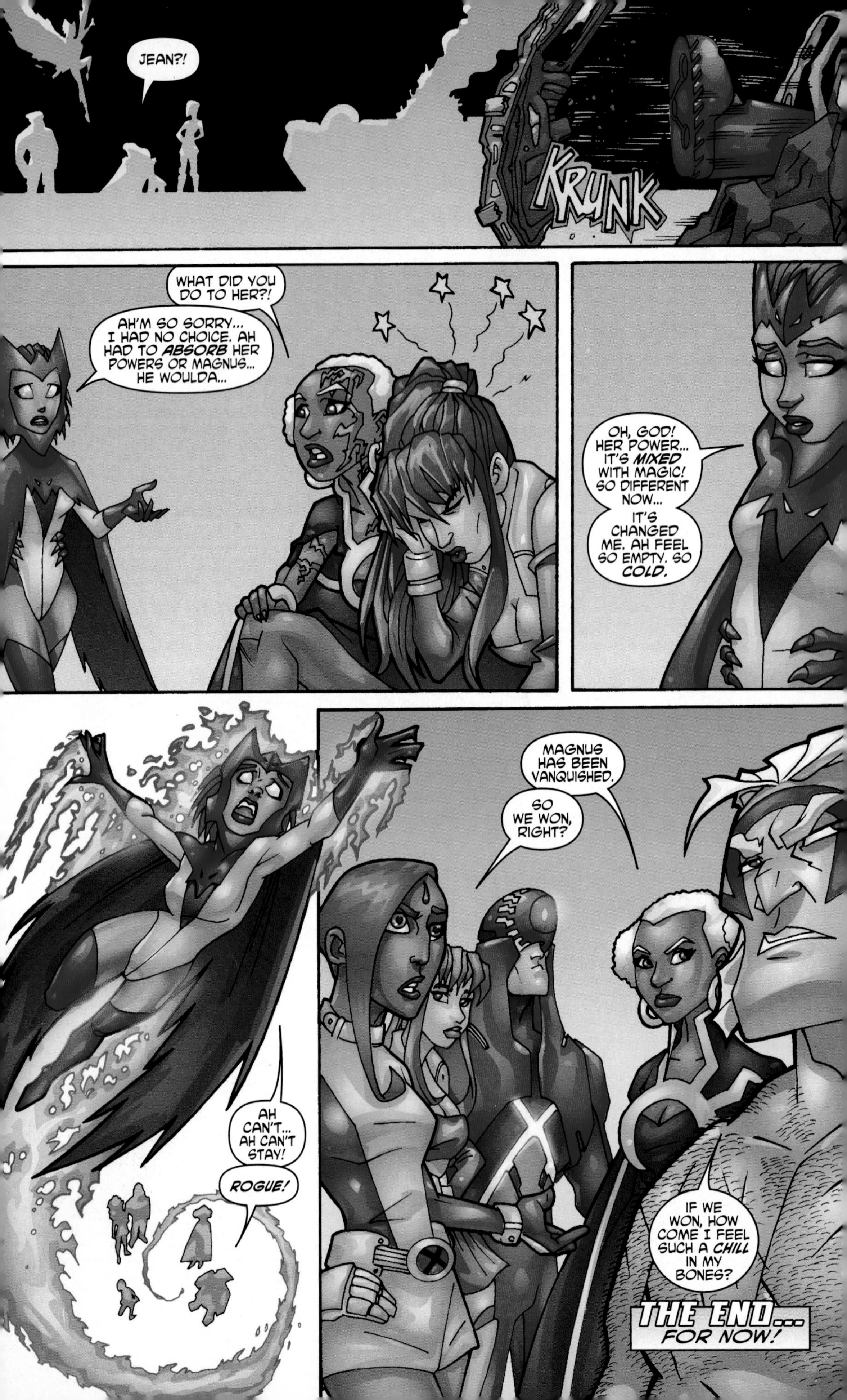
JEAN?!
KRUNK
WHAT DID YOU DO TO HER?!
AH'M SO SORRY... I HAD NO CHOICE. AH HAD TO ABSORB HER POWERS OR MAGNUS... HE WOULDA...
OH, GOD! HER POWER... IT'S MIXED WITH MAGIC! SO DIFFERENT NOW...
IT'S CHANGED ME. AH FEEL SO EMPTY. SO COLD.
AH CAN'T... AH CAN'T STAY!
ROGUE!
MAGNUS HAS BEEN VANQUISHED.
SO WE WON, RIGHT?
IF WE WON, HOW COME I FEEL SUCH A CHILL IN MY BONES?
THE END... FOR NOW!

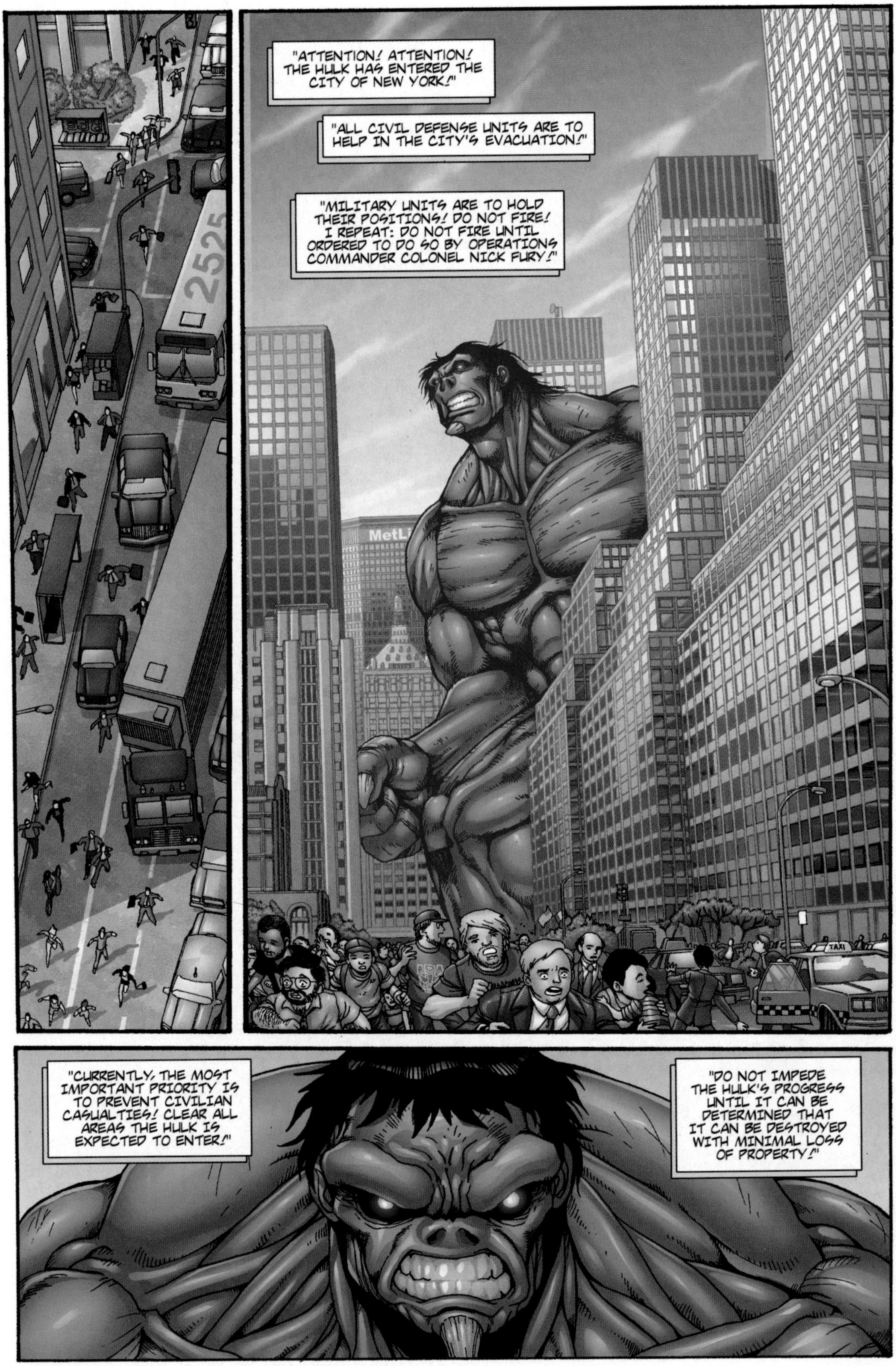
2525
"ATTENTION! ATTENTION! THE HULK HAS ENTERED THE CITY OF NEW YORK!"
"ALL CIVIL DEFENSE UNITS ARE TO HELP IN THE CITY'S EVACUATION!"
"MILITARY UNITS ARE TO HOLD THEIR POSITIONS! DO NOT FIRE! I REPEAT: DO NOT FIRE UNTIL ORDERED TO DO SO BY OPERATIONS COMMANDER COLONEL NICK FURY!"
"CURRENTLY, THE MOST IMPORTANT PRIORITY IS TO PREVENT CIVILIAN CASUALTIES! CLEAR ALL AREAS THE HULK IS EXPECTED TO ENTER!"
"DO NOT IMPEDE THE HULK'S PROGRESS UNTIL IT CAN BE DETERMINED THAT IT CAN BE DESTROYED WITH MINIMAL LOSS OF PROPERTY!"

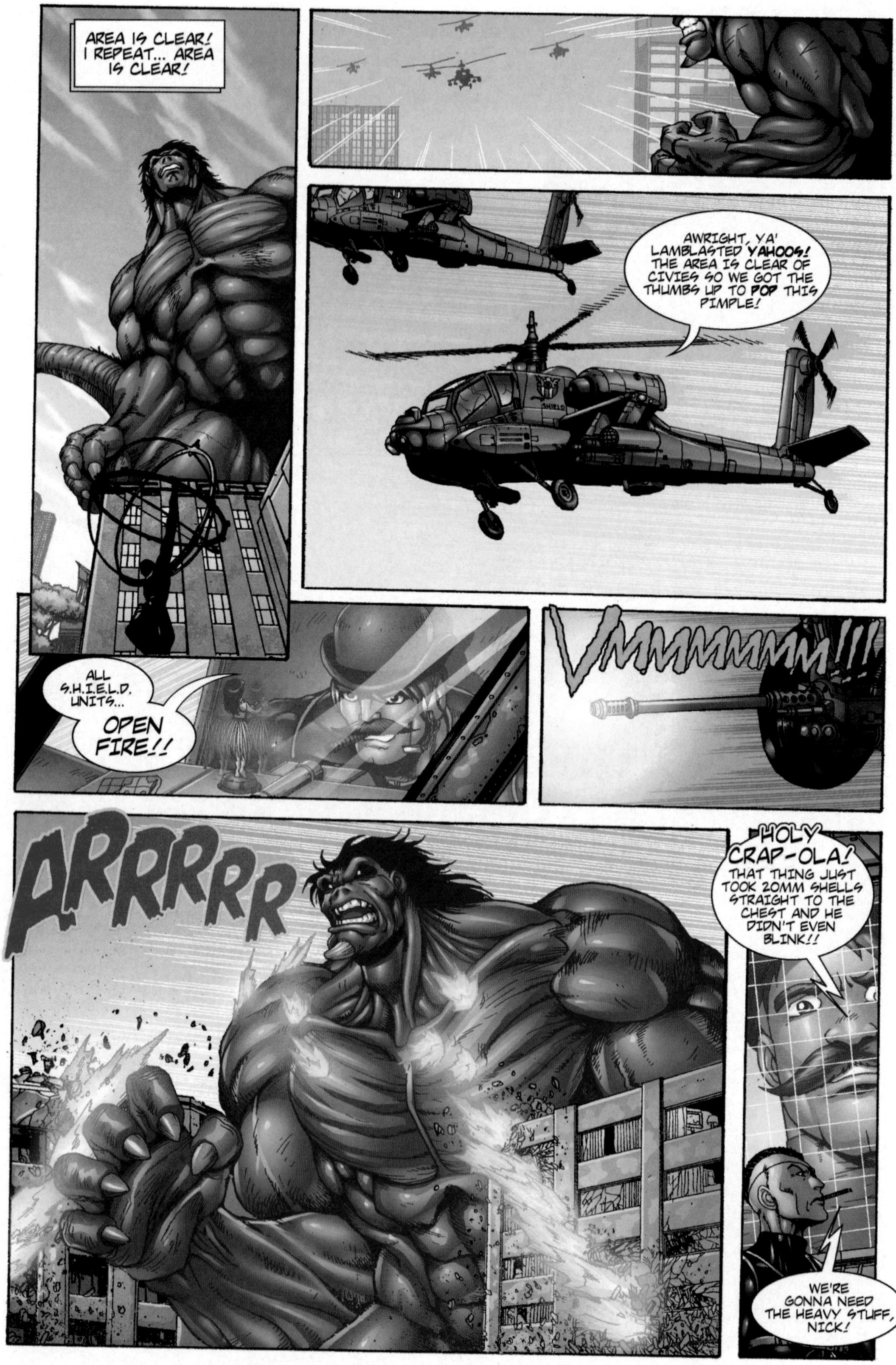
AREA IS CLEAR! I REPEAT... AREA IS CLEAR!
AWRIGHT, YA' LAMBLASTED YAHOOS! THE AREA IS CLEAR OF CIVIES SO WE GOT THE THUMBS UP TO POP THIS PIMPLE!
ALL S.H.I.E.L.D. UNITS... OPEN FIRE!!
VMMMMMMM!!!
ARRRRR
HOLY CRAP-OLA! THAT THING JUST TOOK 20MM SHELLS STRAIGHT TO THE CHEST AND HE DIDN'T EVEN BLINK!!
WE'RE GONNA NEED THE HEAVY STUFF, NICK!

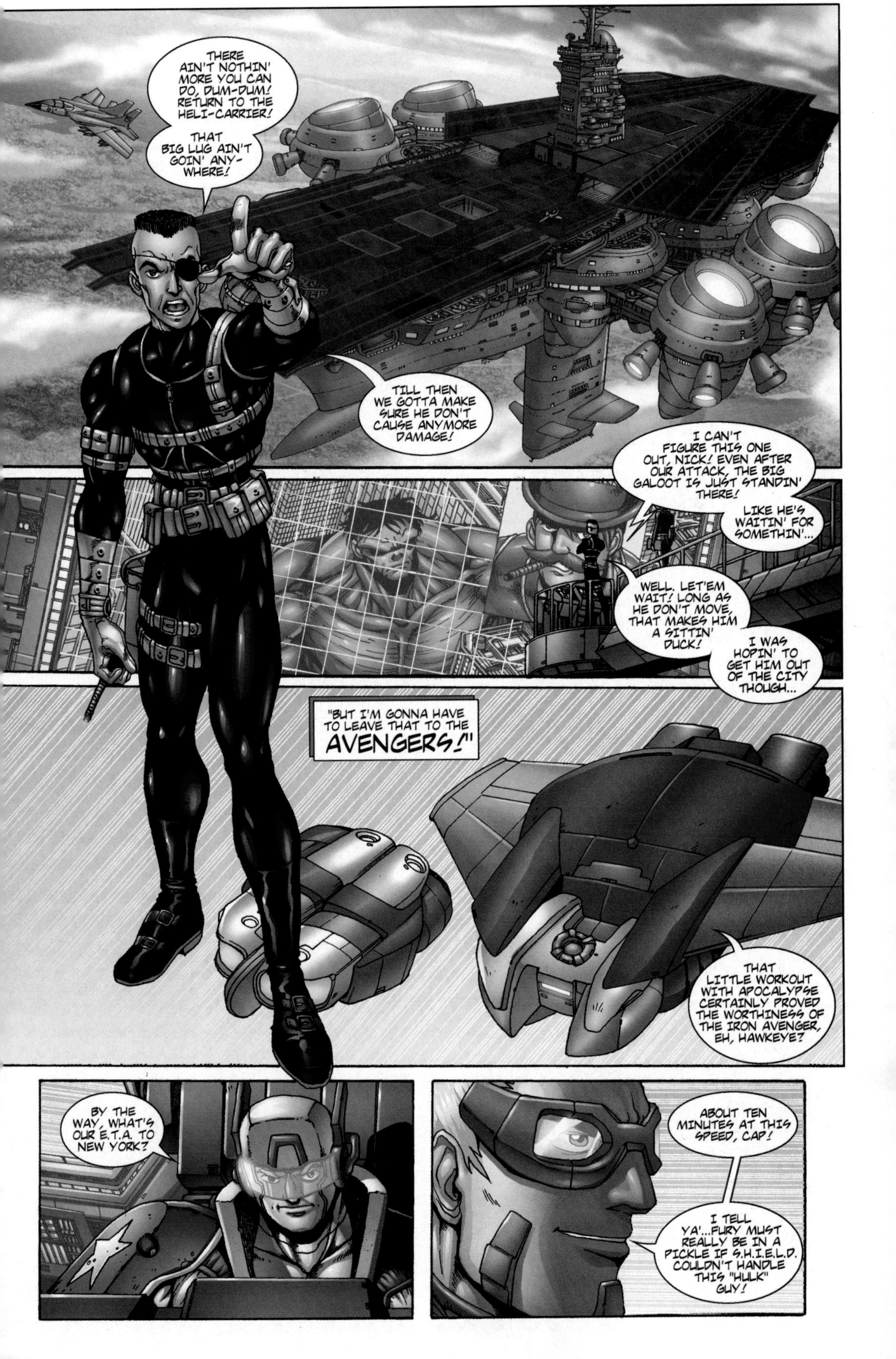
THERE AIN'T NOTHIN' MORE YOU CAN DO, DUM-DUM! RETURN TO THE HELI-CARRIER!
THAT BIG LUG AIN'T GOIN' ANYWHERE!
TILL THEN WE GOTTA MAKE SURE HE DON'T CAUSE ANYMORE DAMAGE!
I CAN'T FIGURE THIS ONE OUT, NICK! EVEN AFTER OUR ATTACK, THE BIG GALOOT IS JUST STANDIN' THERE!
LIKE HE'S WAITIN' FOR SOMETHIN'...
WELL. LET'EM WAIT! LONG AS HE DON'T MOVE, THAT MAKES HIM A SITTIN' DUCK!
I WAS HOPIN' TO GET HIM OUT OF THE CITY THOUGH...
"BUT I'M GONNA HAVE TO LEAVE THAT TO THE AVENGERS!"
THAT LITTLE WORKOUT WITH APOCALYPSE CERTAINLY PROVED THE WORTHINESS OF THE IRON AVENGER, EH, HAWKEYE?
BY THE WAY, WHAT'S OUR E.T.A. TO NEW YORK?
ABOUT TEN MINUTES AT THIS SPEED, CAP!
I TELL YA'...FURY MUST REALLY BE IN A PICKLE IF S.H.I.E.L.D. COULDN'T HANDLE THIS "HULK" GUY!

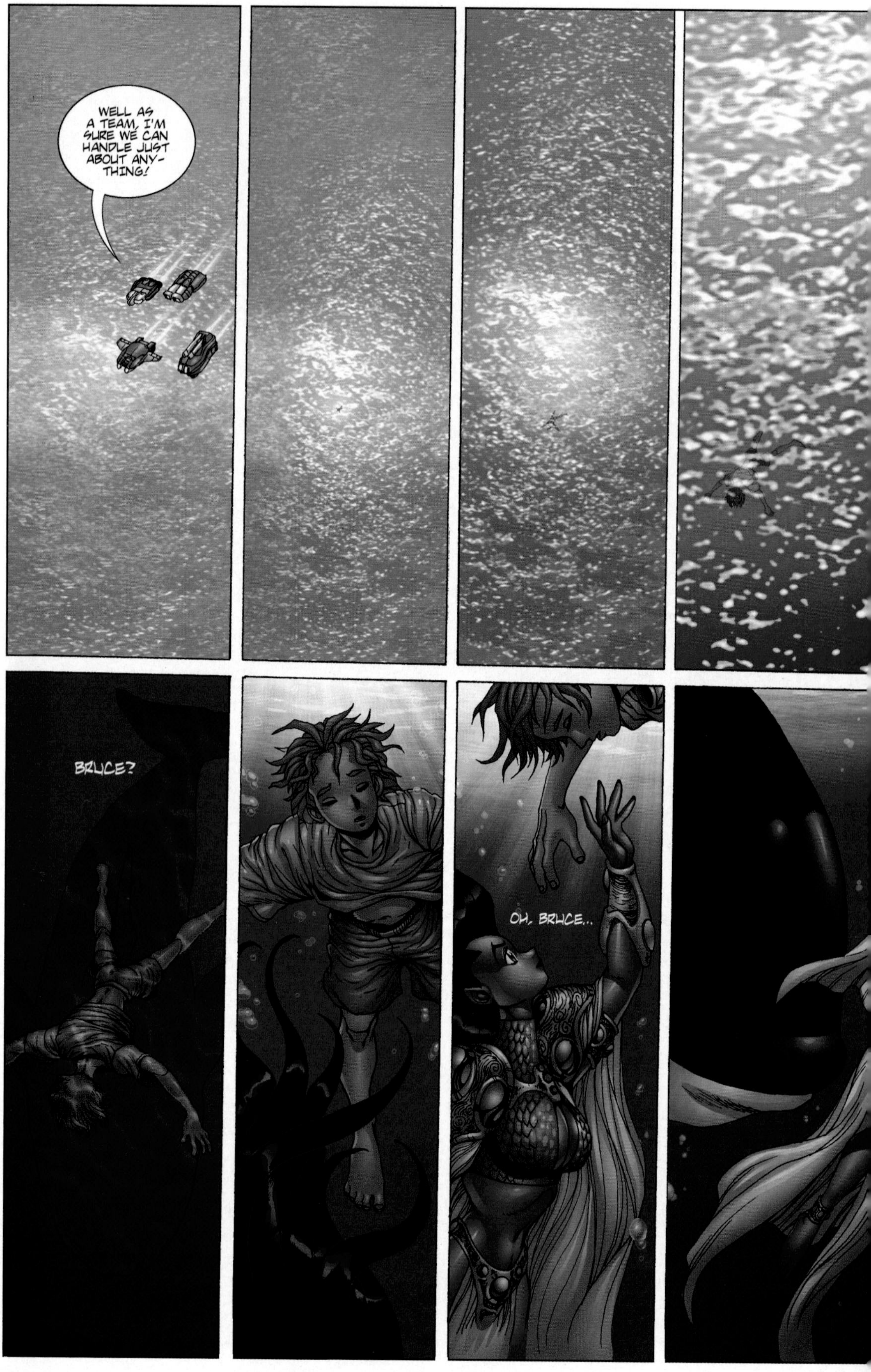
WELL AS A TEAM, I'M SURE WE CAN HANDLE JUST ABOUT ANY-THING!
BRUCE?
OH, BRUCE...

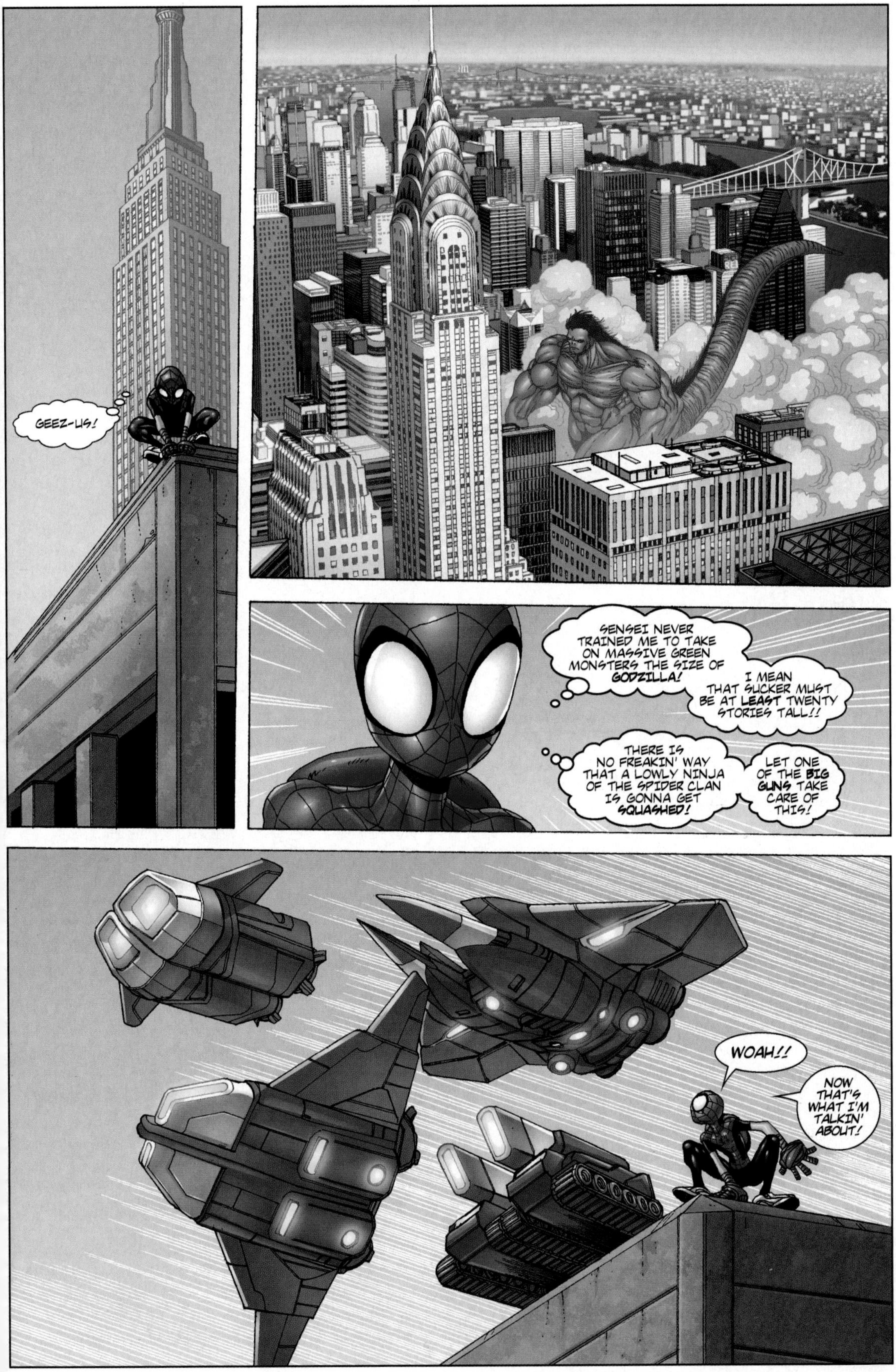
GEEZ-US!
SENSEI NEVER TRAINED ME TO TAKE ON MASSIVE GREEN MONSTERS THE SIZE OF GODZILLA!
I MEAN THAT SUCKER MUST BE AT LEAST TWENTY STORIES TALL!!
THERE IS NO FREAKIN' WAY THAT A LOWLY NINJA OF THE SPIDER CLAN IS GONNA GET SQUASHED!
LET ONE OF THE BIG GUNS TAKE CARE OF THIS!
WOAH!!
NOW THAT'S WHAT I'M TALKIN' ABOUT!

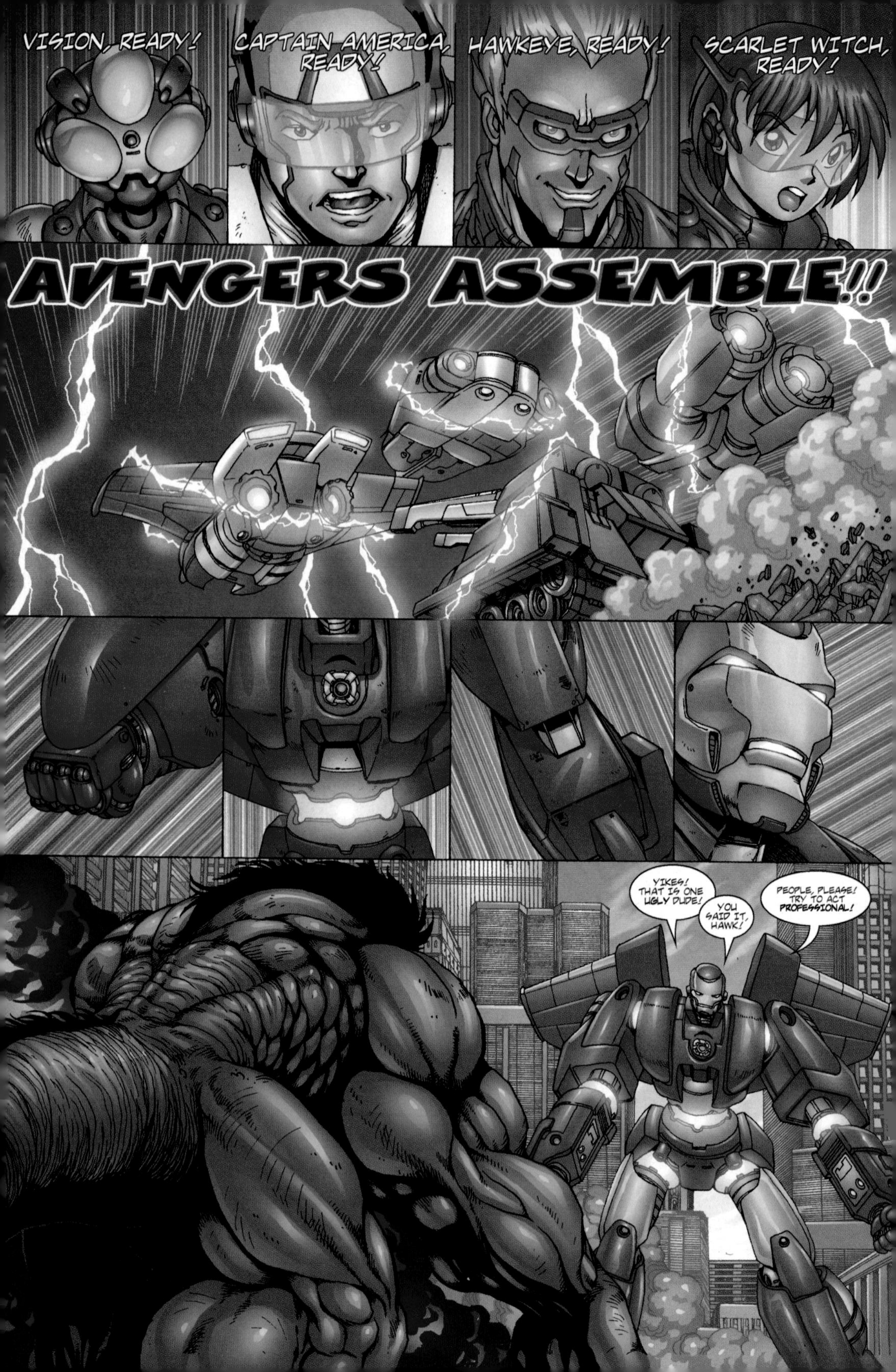

VISION, READY!
CAPTAIN AMERICA, READY!
HAWKEYE, READY!
SCARLET WITCH, READY!
AVENGERS ASSEMBLE!!
YIKES! THAT IS ONE UGLY DUDE!
YOU SAID IT, HAWK!
PEOPLE, PLEASE! TRY TO ACT PROFESSIONAL!

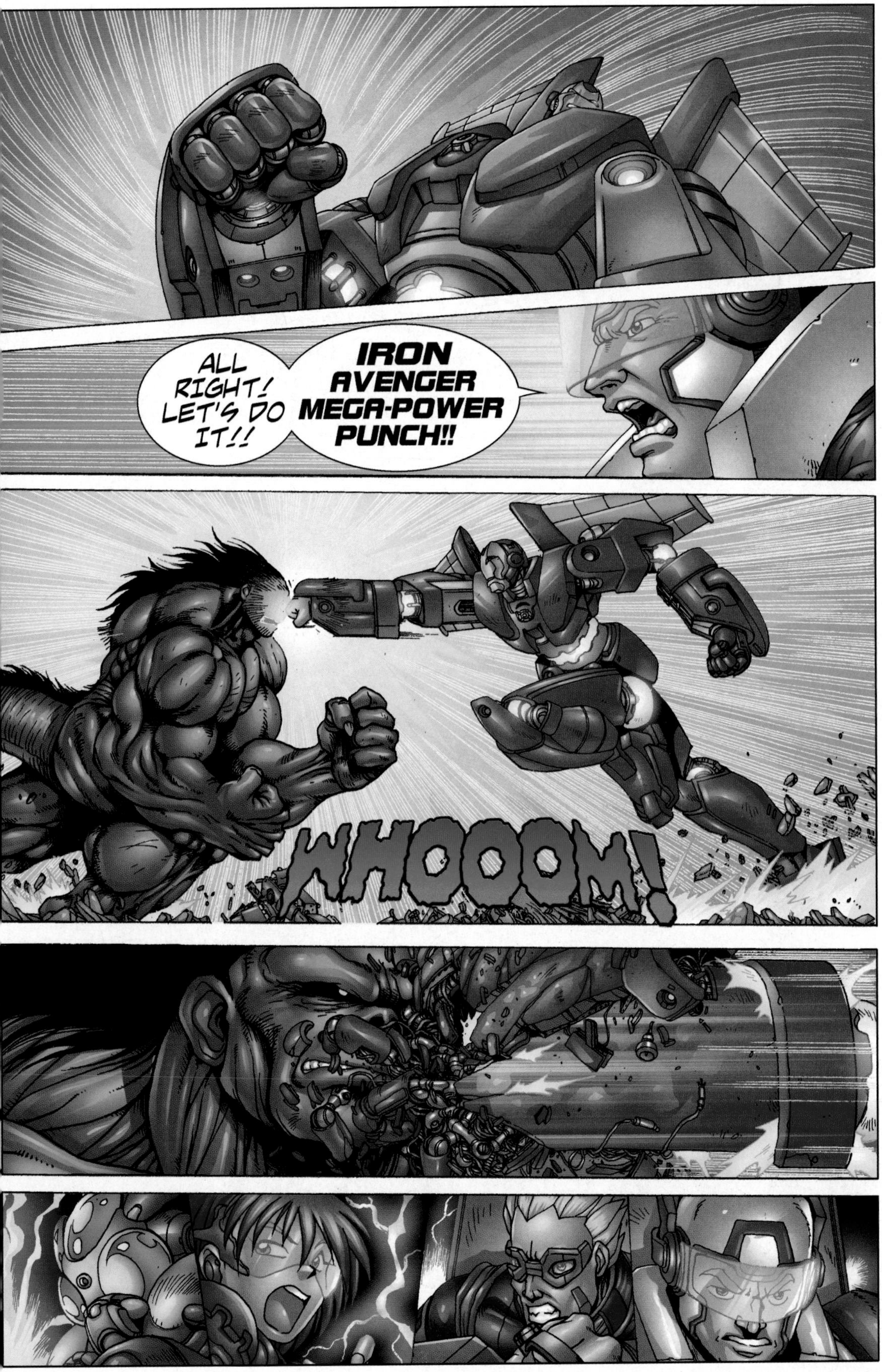
ALL RIGHT! LET'S DO IT!!
IRON AVENGER MEGA-POWER PUNCH!!
WHOOOM!

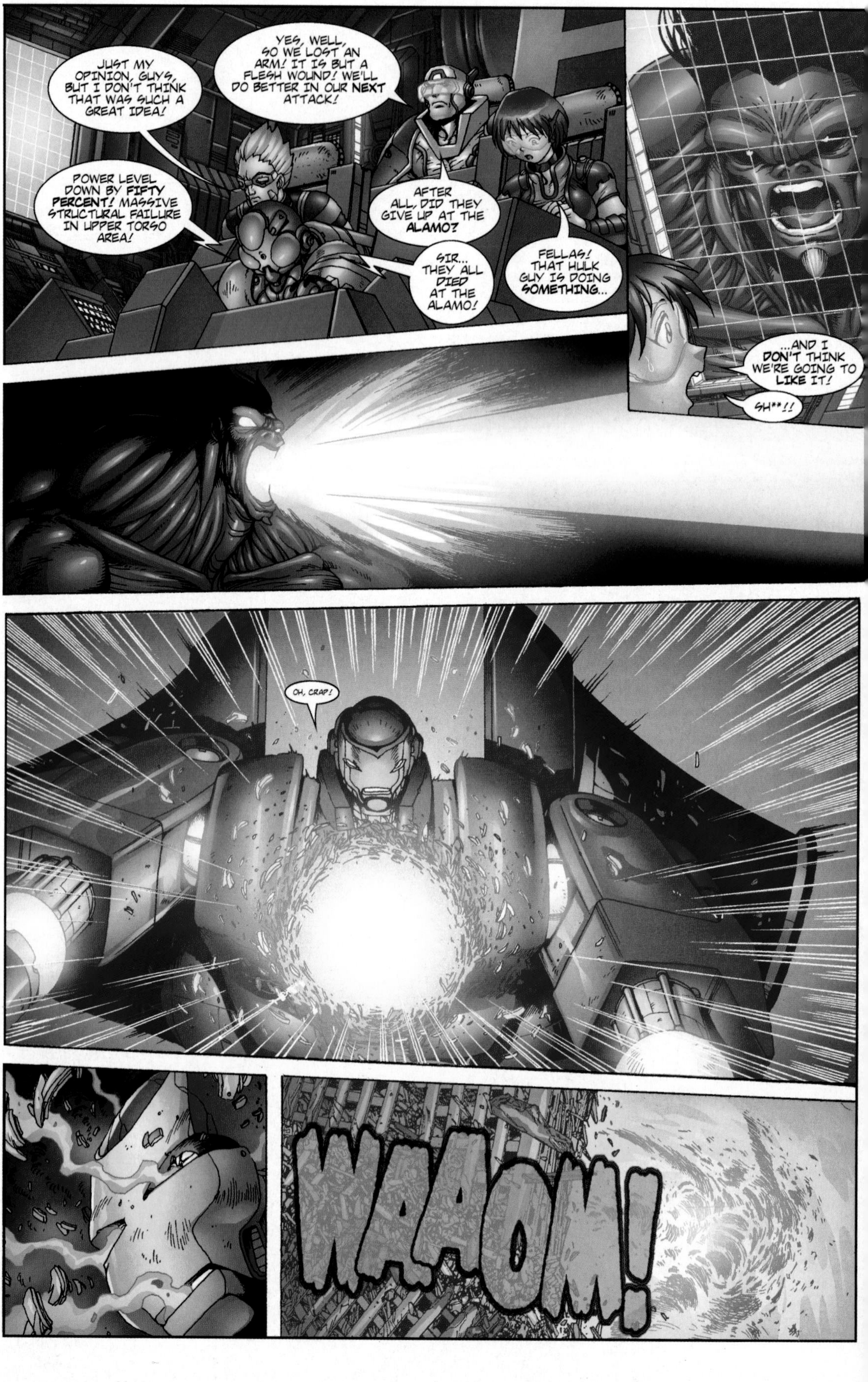
JUST MY OPINION, GUYS, BUT I DON'T THINK THAT WAS SUCH A GREAT IDEA!
YES, WELL, SO WE LOST AN ARM! IT IS BUT A FLESH WOUND! WE'LL DO BETTER IN OUR NEXT ATTACK!
POWER LEVEL DOWN BY FIFTY PERCENT! MASSIVE STRUCTURAL FAILURE IN UPPER TORSO AREA!
AFTER ALL, DID THEY GIVE UP AT THE ALAMO?
SIR... THEY ALL DIED AT THE ALAMO!
FELLAS! THAT HULK GUY IS DOING SOMETHING...
...AND I DON'T THINK WE'RE GOING TO LIKE IT!
SH**!!
OH, CRAP!
WAAOM!

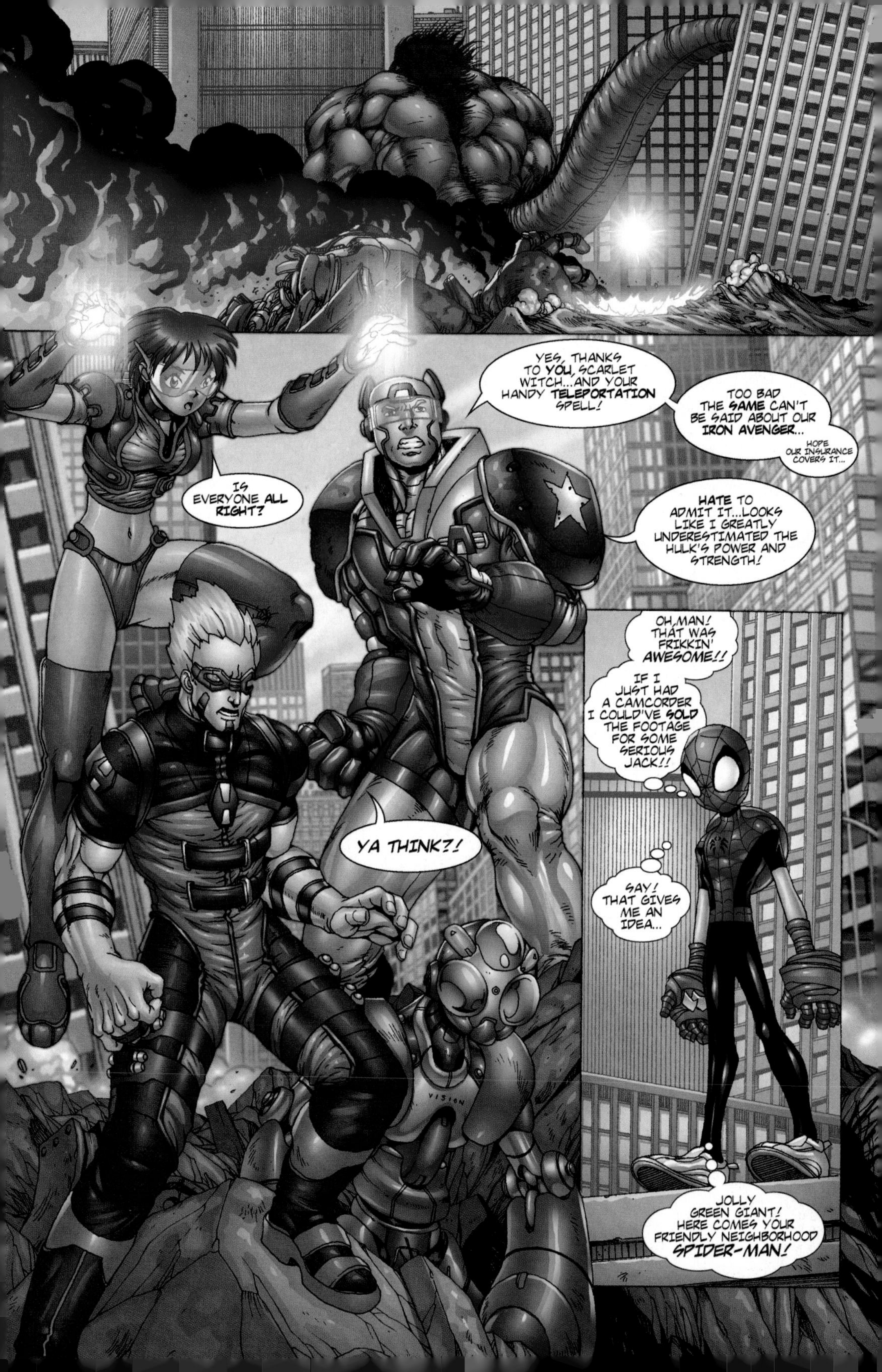
IS EVERYONE ALL RIGHT?
YES, THANKS TO YOU, SCARLET WITCH...AND YOUR HANDY TELEPORTATION SPELL!
TOO BAD THE SAME CAN'T BE SAID ABOUT OUR IRON AVENGER...
HOPE OUR INSURANCE COVERS IT...
HATE TO ADMIT IT...LOOKS LIKE I GREATLY UNDERESTIMATED THE HULK'S POWER AND STRENGTH!
YA THINK?!
OH, MAN! THAT WAS FRIKKIN' AWESOME!!
IF I JUST HAD A CAMCORDER I COULD'VE SOLD THE FOOTAGE FOR SOME SERIOUS JACK!!
SAY! THAT GIVES ME AN IDEA...
JOLLY GREEN GIANT! HERE COMES YOUR FRIENDLY NEIGHBORHOOD SPIDER-MAN!

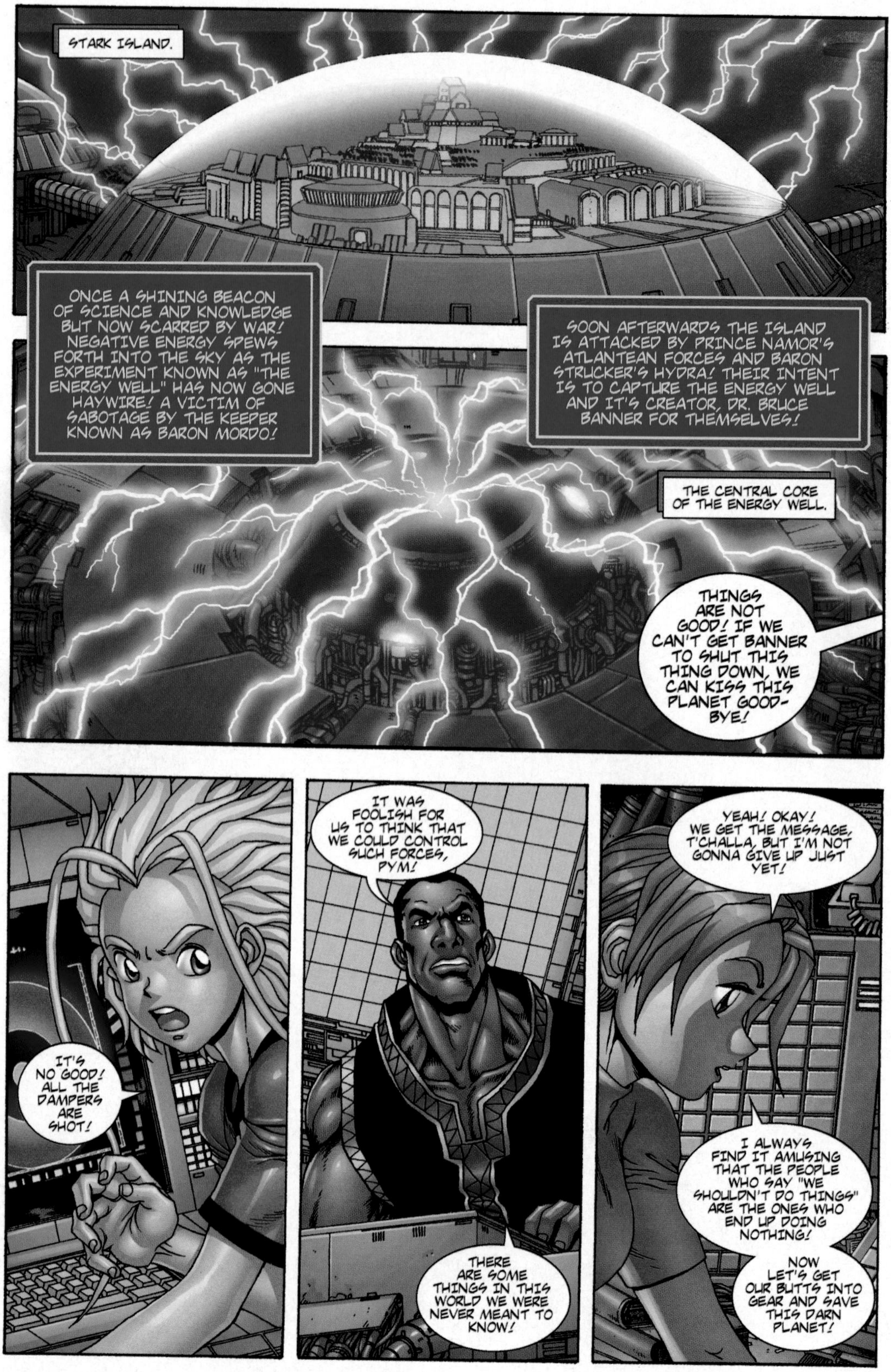
STARK ISLAND.
ONCE A SHINING BEACON OF SCIENCE AND KNOWLEDGE BUT NOW SCARRED BY WAR! NEGATIVE ENERGY SPEWS FORTH INTO THE SKY AS THE EXPERIMENT KNOWN AS "THE ENERGY WELL" HAS NOW GONE HAYWIRE! A VICTIM OF SABOTAGE BY THE KEEPER KNOWN AS BARON MORDO!
SOON AFTERWARDS THE ISLAND IS ATTACKED BY PRINCE NAMOR'S ATLANTEAN FORCES AND BARON STRUCKER'S HYDRA! THEIR INTENT IS TO CAPTURE THE ENERGY WELL AND IT'S CREATOR, DR. BRUCE BANNER FOR THEMSELVES!
THE CENTRAL CORE OF THE ENERGY WELL.
THINGS ARE NOT GOOD! IF WE CAN'T GET BANNER TO SHUT THIS THING DOWN, WE CAN KISS THIS PLANET GOOD-BYE!
IT'S NO GOOD! ALL THE DAMPERS ARE SHOT!
IT WAS FOOLISH FOR US TO THINK THAT WE COULD CONTROL SUCH FORCES, PYM!
THERE ARE SOME THINGS IN THIS WORLD WE WERE NEVER MEANT TO KNOW!
YEAH! OKAY! WE GET THE MESSAGE, T'CHALLA, BUT I'M NOT GONNA GIVE UP JUST YET!
I ALWAYS FIND IT AMUSING THAT THE PEOPLE WHO SAY "WE SHOULDN'T DO THINGS" ARE THE ONES WHO END UP DOING NOTHING!
NOW LET'S GET OUR BUTTS INTO GEAR AND SAVE THIS DARN PLANET!

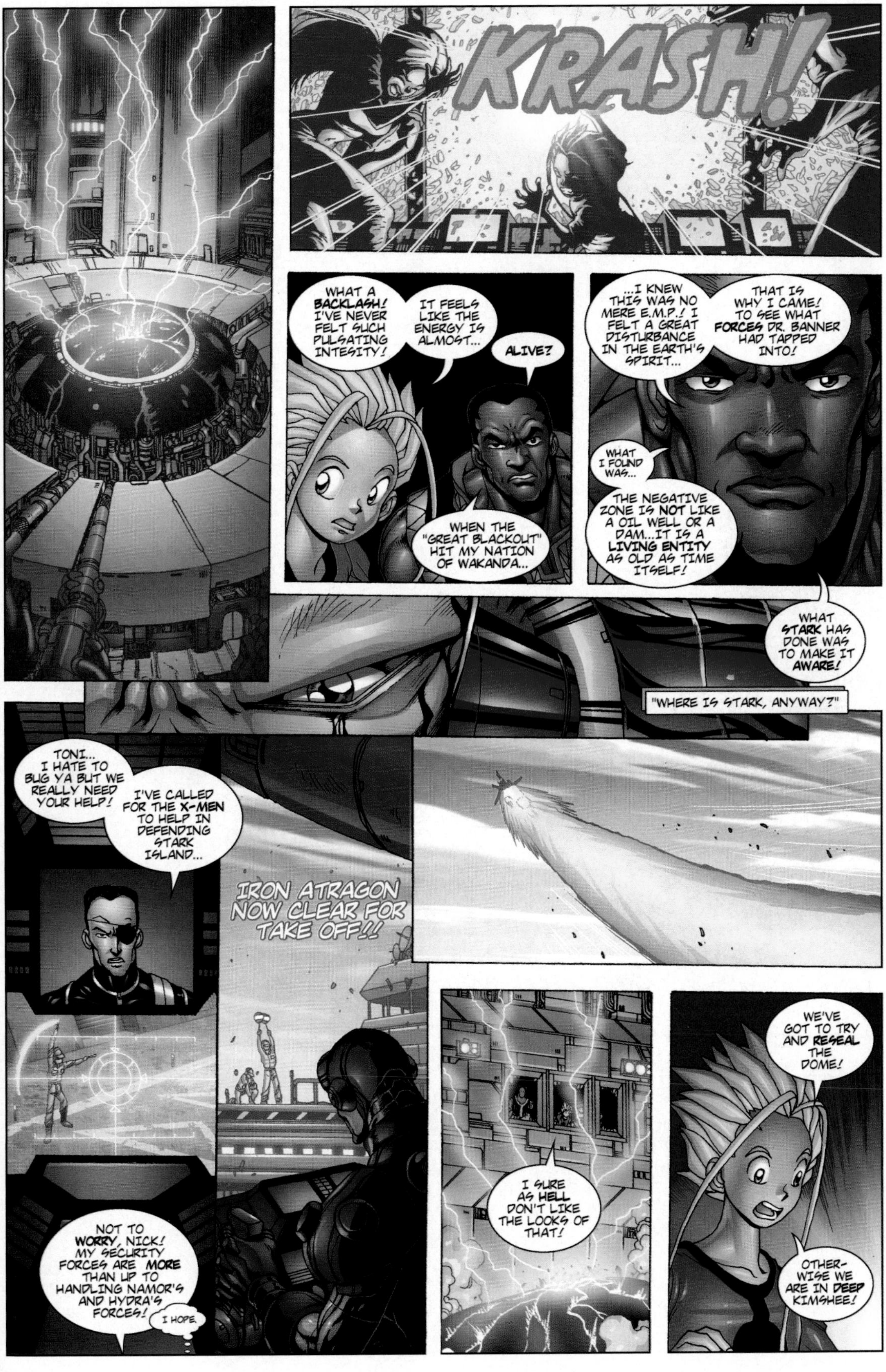
KRASH!
WHAT A BACKLASH! I'VE NEVER FELT SUCH PULSATING INTESITY!
IT FEELS LIKE THE ENERGY IS ALMOST...
ALIVE?
WHEN THE "GREAT BLACKOUT" HIT MY NATION OF WAKANDA...
...I KNEW THIS WAS NO MERE E.M.P.! I FELT A GREAT DISTURBANCE IN THE EARTH'S SPIRIT...
THAT IS WHY I CAME! TO SEE WHAT FORCES DR. BANNER HAD TAPPED INTO!
WHAT I FOUND WAS...
THE NEGATIVE ZONE IS NOT LIKE A OIL WELL OR A DAM...IT IS A LIVING ENTITY AS OLD AS TIME ITSELF!
WHAT STARK HAS DONE WAS TO MAKE IT AWARE!
"WHERE IS STARK, ANYWAY?"
TONI... I HATE TO BUG YA BUT WE REALLY NEED YOUR HELP!
I'VE CALLED FOR THE X-MEN TO HELP IN DEFENDING STARK ISLAND...
IRON ATRAGON NOW CLEAR FOR TAKE OFF!!
NOT TO WORRY, NICK! MY SECURITY FORCES ARE MORE THAN UP TO HANDLING NAMOR'S AND HYDRA'S FORCES!
I HOPE.
I SURE AS HELL DON'T LIKE THE LOOKS OF THAT!
WE'VE GOT TO TRY AND RESEAL THE DOME!
OTHER-WISE WE ARE IN DEEP KIMSHEE!

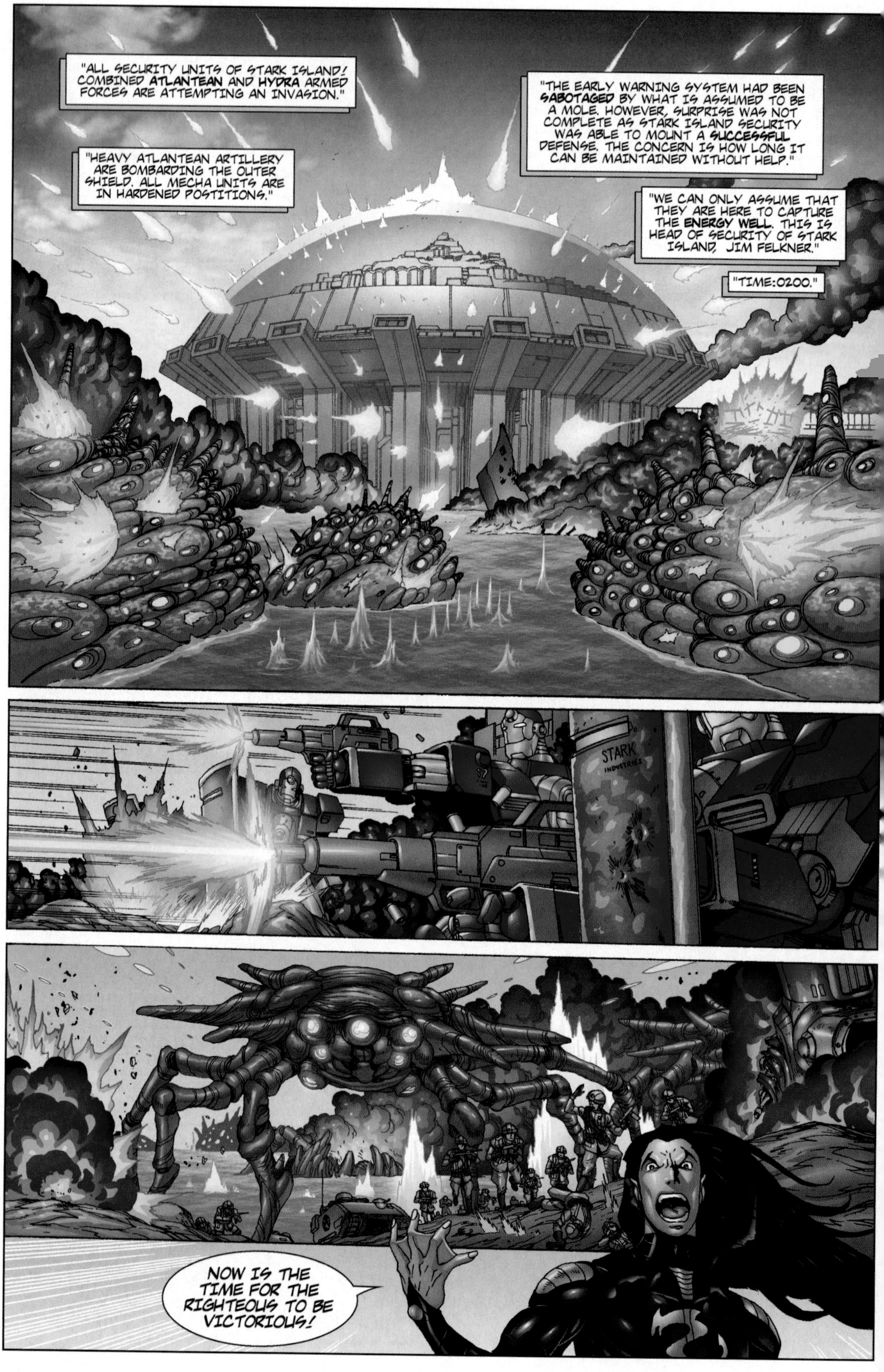
"ALL SECURITY UNITS OF STARK ISLAND! COMBINED ATLANTEAN AND HYDRA ARMED FORCES ARE ATTEMPTING AN INVASION."
"HEAVY ATLANTEAN ARTILLERY ARE BOMBARDING THE OUTER SHIELD. ALL MECHA UNITS ARE IN HARDENED POSTITIONS."
"THE EARLY WARNING SYSTEM HAD BEEN SABOTAGED BY WHAT IS ASSUMED TO BE A MOLE. HOWEVER, SURPRISE WAS NOT COMPLETE AS STARK ISLAND SECURITY WAS ABLE TO MOUNT A SUCCESSFUL DEFENSE. THE CONCERN IS HOW LONG IT CAN BE MAINTAINED WITHOUT HELP."
"WE CAN ONLY ASSUME THAT THEY ARE HERE TO CAPTURE THE ENERGY WELL. THIS IS HEAD OF SECURITY OF STARK ISLAND, JIM FELKNER."
"TIME:0200."
STARK
INDUSTRIES
NOW IS THE TIME FOR THE RIGHTEOUS TO BE VICTORIOUS!

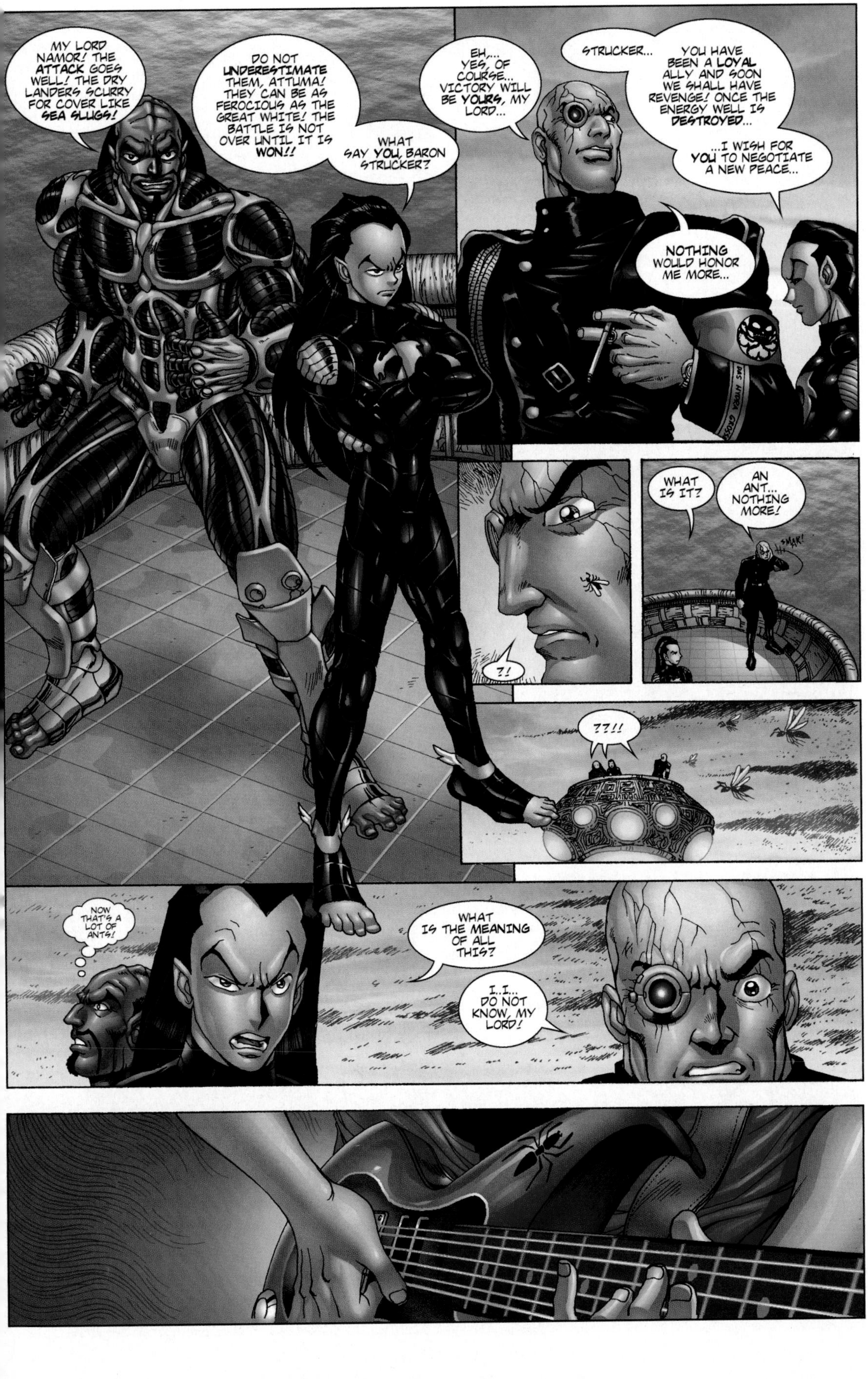
MY LORD NAMOR! THE ATTACK GOES WELL! THE DRY LANDERS SCURRY FOR COVER LIKE SEA SLUGS!
DO NOT UNDERESTIMATE THEM, ATTUMA! THEY CAN BE AS FEROCIOUS AS THE GREAT WHITE! THE BATTLE IS NOT OVER UNTIL IT IS WON!!
WHAT SAY YOU, BARON STRUCKER?
EH,... YES, OF COURSE... VICTORY WILL BE YOURS, MY LORD...
STRUCKER...
YOU HAVE BEEN A LOYAL ALLY AND SOON WE SHALL HAVE REVENGE! ONCE THE ENERGY WELL IS DESTROYED...
...I WISH FOR YOU TO NEGOTIATE A NEW PEACE...
NOTHING WOULD HONOR ME MORE...
?!
WHAT IS IT?
AN ANT... NOTHING MORE!
SMAK!
??!!
NOW THAT'S A LOT OF ANTS!
WHAT IS THE MEANING OF ALL THIS?
I..I... DO NOT KNOW, MY LORD!

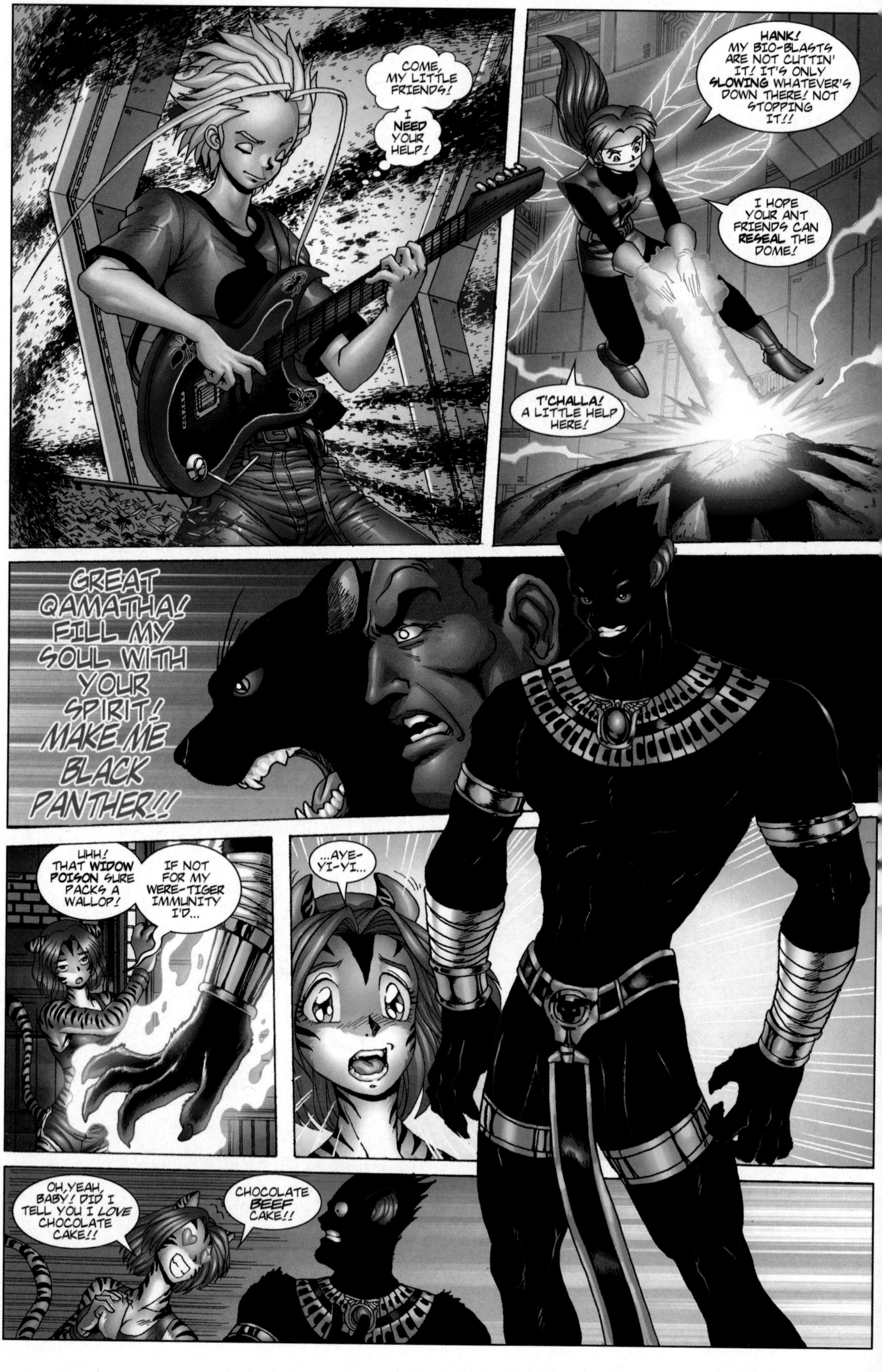
COME, MY LITTLE FRIENDS!
I NEED YOUR HELP!
HANK! MY BIO-BLASTS ARE NOT CUTTIN' IT! IT'S ONLY SLOWING WHATEVER'S DOWN THERE! NOT STOPPING IT!!
I HOPE YOUR ANT FRIENDS CAN RESEAL THE DOME!
T'CHALLA! A LITTLE HELP HERE!
GREAT QAMATHA! FILL MY SOUL WITH YOUR SPIRIT! MAKE ME BLACK PANTHER!!
UHH! THAT WIDOW POISON SURE PACKS A WALLOP!
IF NOT FOR MY WERE-TIGER IMMUNITY I'D...
...AYE-YI-YI...
OH, YEAH, BABY! DID I TELL YOU I LOVE CHOCOLATE CAKE!!
CHOCOLATE BEEF CAKE!!

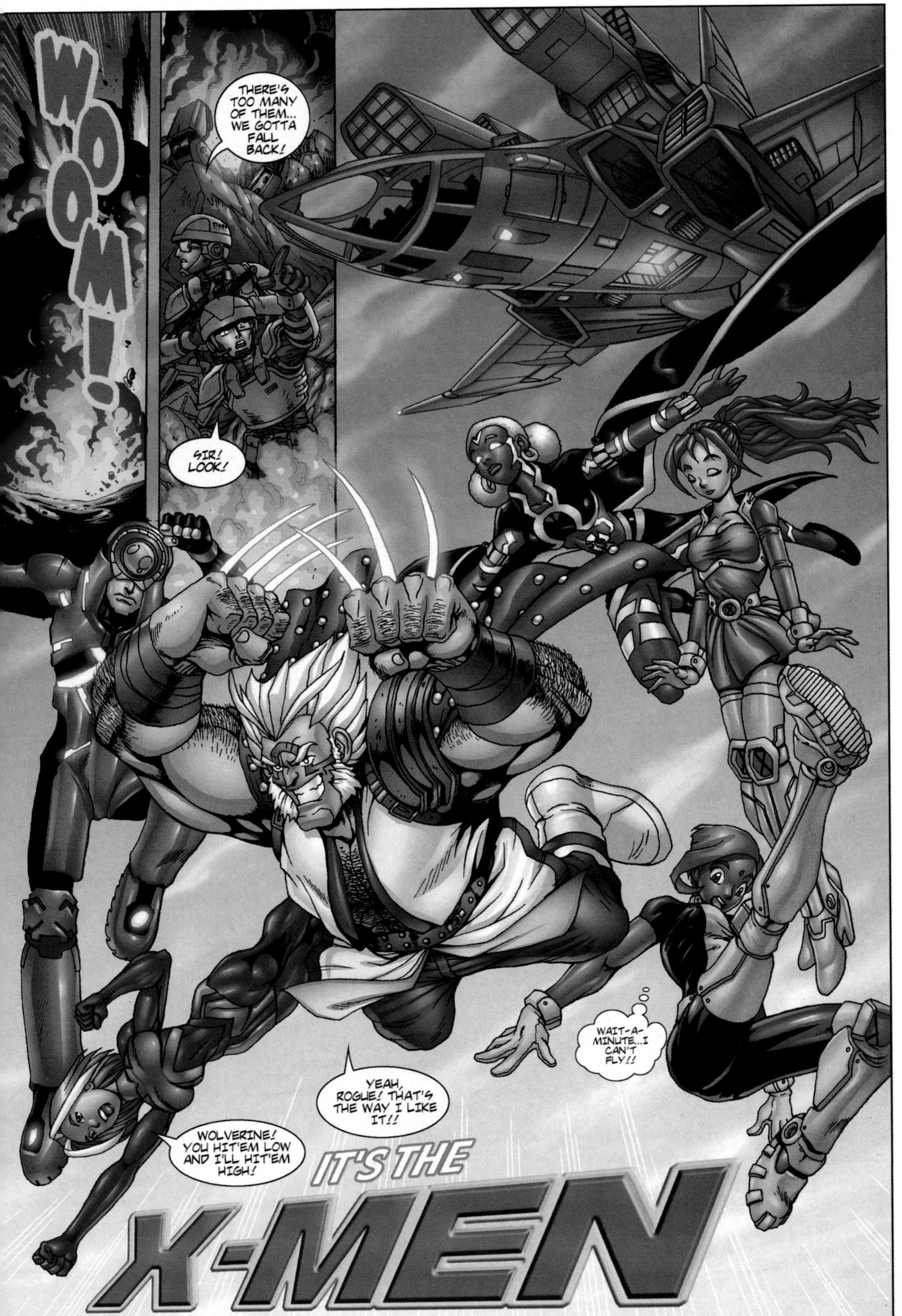
WOOOM!
THERE'S TOO MANY OF THEM... WE GOTTA FALL BACK!
SIR! LOOK!
WAIT-A-MINUTE...I CAN'T FLY!!
YEAH, ROGUE! THAT'S THE WAY I LIKE IT!!
WOLVERINE! YOU HIT'EM LOW AND I'LL HIT'EM HIGH!
IT'S THE X-MEN

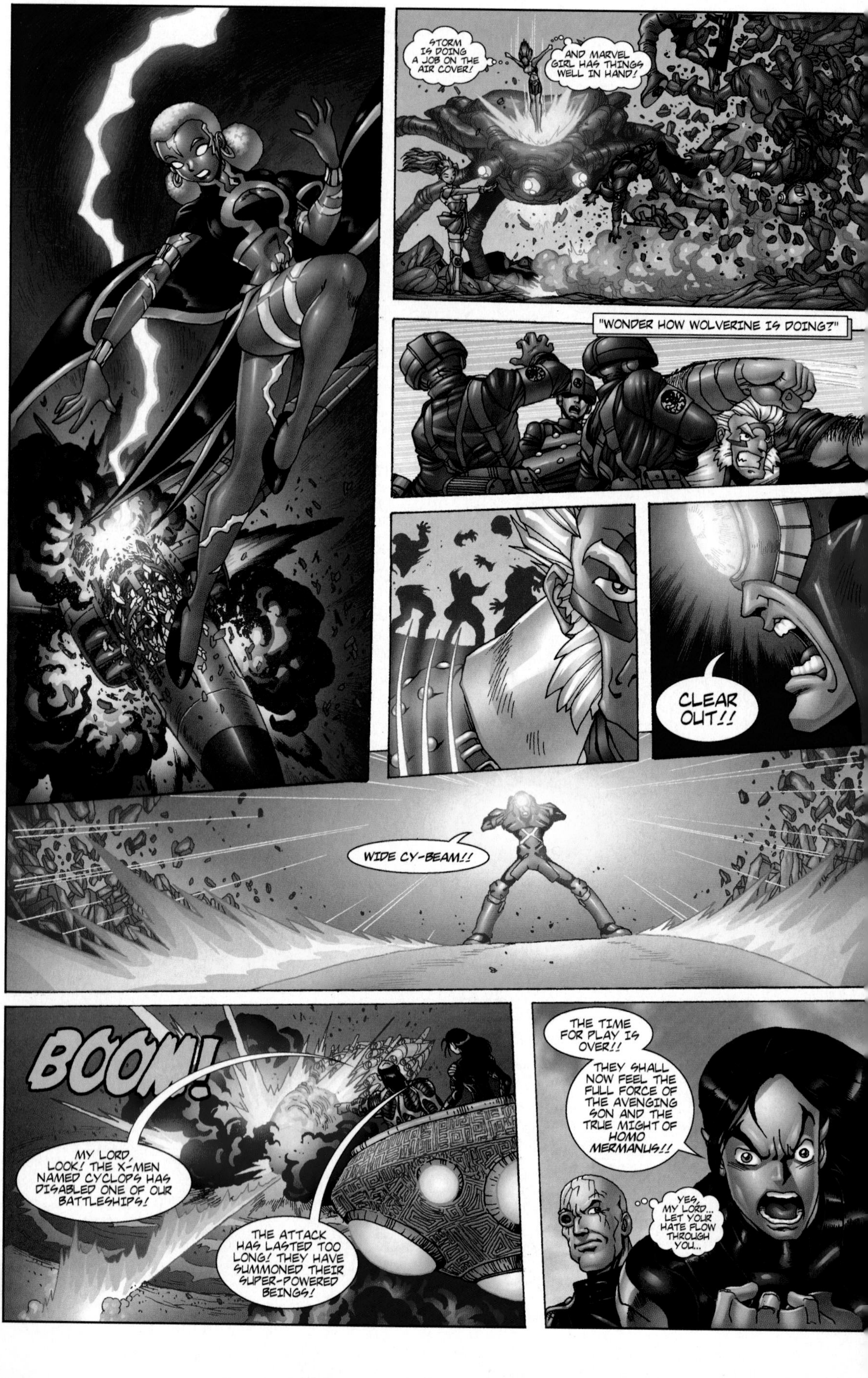
STORM IS DOING A JOB ON THE AIR COVER!
AND MARVEL GIRL HAS THINGS WELL IN HAND!
"WONDER HOW WOLVERINE IS DOING?"
CLEAR OUT!!
WIDE CY-BEAM!!
BOOM!
MY LORD, LOOK! THE X-MEN NAMED CYCLOPS HAS DISABLED ONE OF OUR BATTLESHIPS!
THE ATTACK HAS LASTED TOO LONG! THEY HAVE SUMMONED THEIR SUPER-POWERED BEINGS!
THE TIME FOR PLAY IS OVER!!
THEY SHALL NOW FEEL THE FULL FORCE OF THE AVENGING SON AND THE TRUE MIGHT OF HOMO MERMANUS!!
YES, MY LORD... LET YOUR HATE FLOW THROUGH YOU...

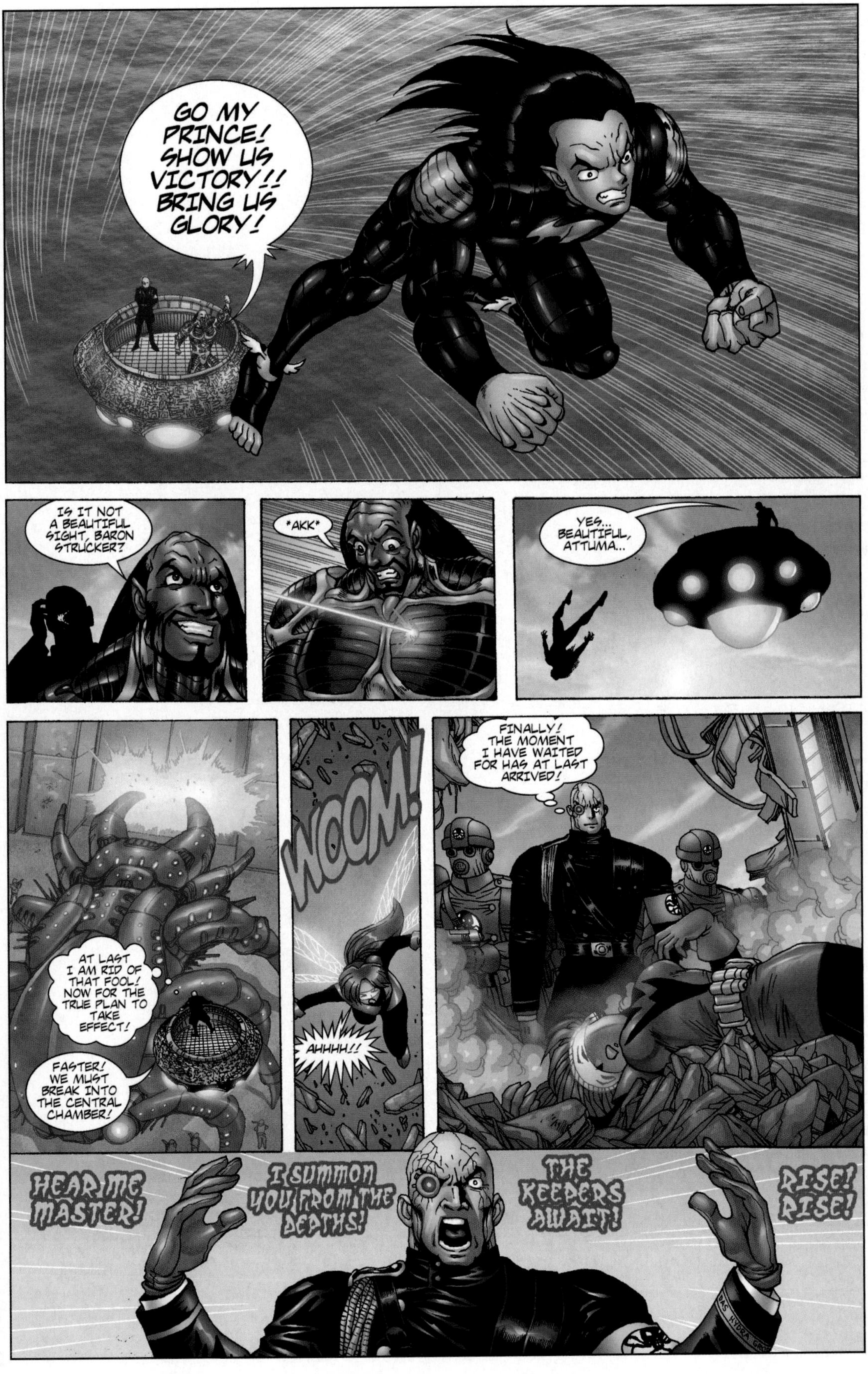
GO MY PRINCE! SHOW US VICTORY!! BRING US GLORY!
IS IT NOT A BEAUTIFUL SIGHT, BARON STRUCKER?
AKK
YES... BEAUTIFUL, ATTUMA...
AT LAST I AM RID OF THAT FOOL! NOW FOR THE TRUE PLAN TO TAKE EFFECT!
FASTER! WE MUST BREAK INTO THE CENTRAL CHAMBER!
WOOM!
AHHHH!!
FINALLY! THE MOMENT I HAVE WAITED FOR HAS AT LAST ARRIVED!
HEAR ME MASTER!
I SUMMON YOU FROM THE DEPTHS!
THE KEEPERS AWAIT!
RISE! RISE!

THE WORLD AWAITS YOUR RETURN!!

AT LAST! AFTER AN ETERNITY!

MY LORD AND GOD DORMAMMU! I, STRUCKER, WELCOME YOU TO YOUR INHERITANCE OF THE PRIMEVAL EARTH!

I AM HONORED TO BE ONE OF YOUR HUMBLE GATE-KEEPERS!

GATEKEEPER! I HUNGER! I DEMAND BLOOD AND SOULS!

THEN PLEASE ACCEPT THESE MEN AS MY HUMBLE GIFT!

MAY THEY PROVIDE THE NOURISHMENT YOU NEED!

!!

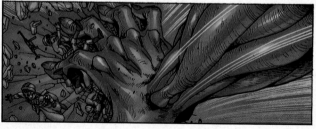

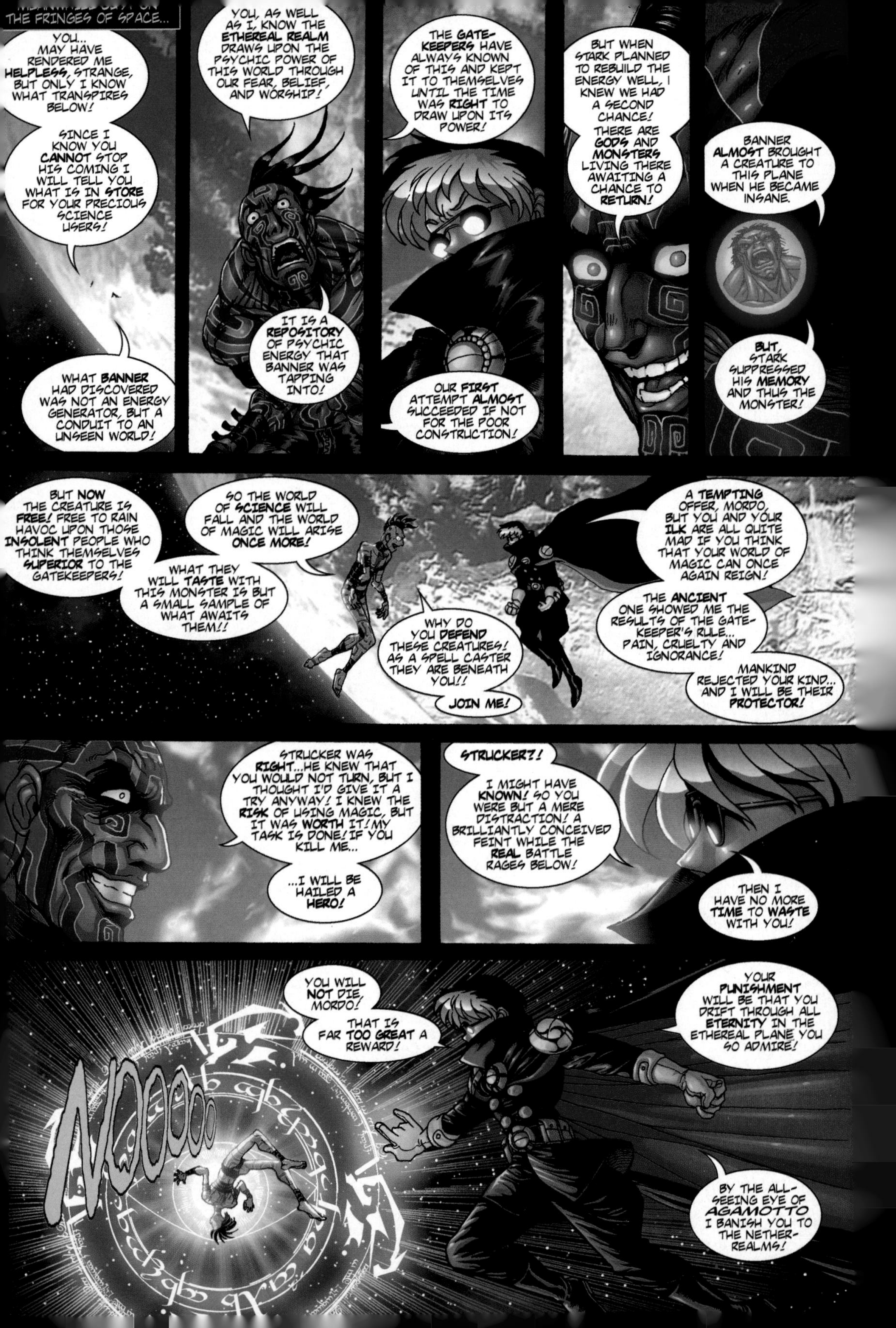
THE FRINGES OF SPACE...
YOU... MAY HAVE RENDERED ME HELPLESS, STRANGE, BUT ONLY I KNOW WHAT TRANSPIRES BELOW!
SINCE I KNOW YOU CANNOT STOP HIS COMING I WILL TELL YOU WHAT IS IN STORE FOR YOUR PRECIOUS SCIENCE USERS!
WHAT BANNER HAD DISCOVERED WAS NOT AN ENERGY GENERATOR, BUT A CONDUIT TO AN UNSEEN WORLD!
YOU, AS WELL AS I, KNOW THE ETHEREAL REALM DRAWS UPON THE PSYCHIC POWER OF THIS WORLD THROUGH OUR FEAR, BELIEF, AND WORSHIP!
IT IS A REPOSITORY OF PSYCHIC ENERGY THAT BANNER WAS TAPPING INTO!
THE GATE-KEEPERS HAVE ALWAYS KNOWN OF THIS AND KEPT IT TO THEMSELVES UNTIL THE TIME WAS RIGHT TO DRAW UPON ITS POWER!
OUR FIRST ATTEMPT ALMOST SUCCEEDED IF NOT FOR THE POOR CONSTRUCTION!
BUT WHEN STARK PLANNED TO REBUILD THE ENERGY WELL, I KNEW WE HAD A SECOND CHANCE!
THERE ARE GODS AND MONSTERS LIVING THERE AWAITING A CHANCE TO RETURN!
BANNER ALMOST BROUGHT A CREATURE TO THIS PLANE WHEN HE BECAME INSANE.
BUT, STARK SUPPRESSED HIS MEMORY AND THUS THE MONSTER!
BUT NOW THE CREATURE IS FREE! FREE TO RAIN HAVOC UPON THOSE INSOLENT PEOPLE WHO THINK THEMSELVES SUPERIOR TO THE GATEKEEPERS!
SO THE WORLD OF SCIENCE WILL FALL AND THE WORLD OF MAGIC WILL ARISE ONCE MORE!
WHAT THEY WILL TASTE WITH THIS MONSTER IS BUT A SMALL SAMPLE OF WHAT AWAITS THEM!!
WHY DO YOU DEFEND THESE CREATURES! AS A SPELL CASTER THEY ARE BENEATH YOU!!
JOIN ME!
A TEMPTING OFFER, MORDO, BUT YOU AND YOUR ILK ARE ALL QUITE MAD IF YOU THINK THAT YOUR WORLD OF MAGIC CAN ONCE AGAIN REIGN!
THE ANCIENT ONE SHOWED ME THE RESULTS OF THE GATE-KEEPER'S RULE... PAIN, CRUELTY AND IGNORANCE!
MANKIND REJECTED YOUR KIND... AND I WILL BE THEIR PROTECTOR!
STRUCKER WAS RIGHT... HE KNEW THAT YOU WOULD NOT TURN, BUT I THOUGHT I'D GIVE IT A TRY ANYWAY! I KNEW THE RISK OF USING MAGIC, BUT IT WAS WORTH IT! MY TASK IS DONE! IF YOU KILL ME...
...I WILL BE HAILED A HERO!
STRUCKER?!
I MIGHT HAVE KNOWN! SO YOU WERE BUT A MERE DISTRACTION! A BRILLIANTLY CONCEIVED FEINT WHILE THE REAL BATTLE RAGES BELOW!
THEN I HAVE NO MORE TIME TO WASTE WITH YOU!
YOU WILL NOT DIE, MORDO!
THAT IS FAR TOO GREAT A REWARD!
YOUR PUNISHMENT WILL BE THAT YOU DRIFT THROUGH ALL ETERNITY IN THE ETHEREAL PLANE YOU SO ADMIRE!
NOOOOO
BY THE ALL-SEEING EYE OF AGAMOTTO I BANISH YOU TO THE NETHER-REALMS!

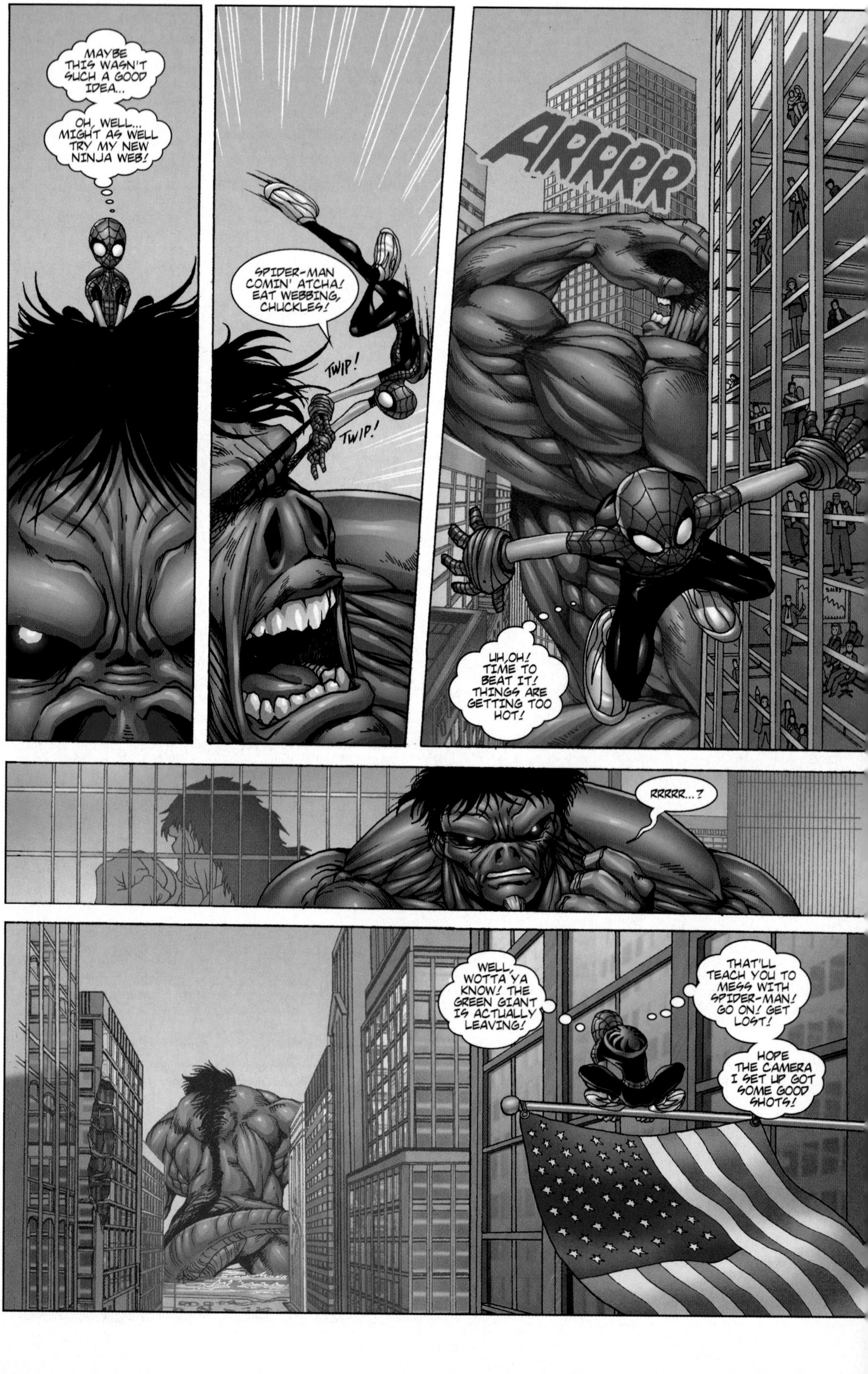
MAYBE THIS WASN'T SUCH A GOOD IDEA...
OH, WELL... MIGHT AS WELL TRY MY NEW NINJA WEB!
SPIDER-MAN COMIN' ATCHA! EAT WEBBING, CHUCKLES!
TWIP!
TWIP!
ARRRR
UH,OH! TIME TO BEAT IT! THINGS ARE GETTING TOO HOT!
RRRRR...?
WELL, WOTTA YA KNOW! THE GREEN GIANT IS ACTUALLY LEAVING!
THAT'LL TEACH YOU TO MESS WITH SPIDER-MAN! GO ON! GET LOST!
HOPE THE CAMERA I SET UP GOT SOME GOOD SHOTS!

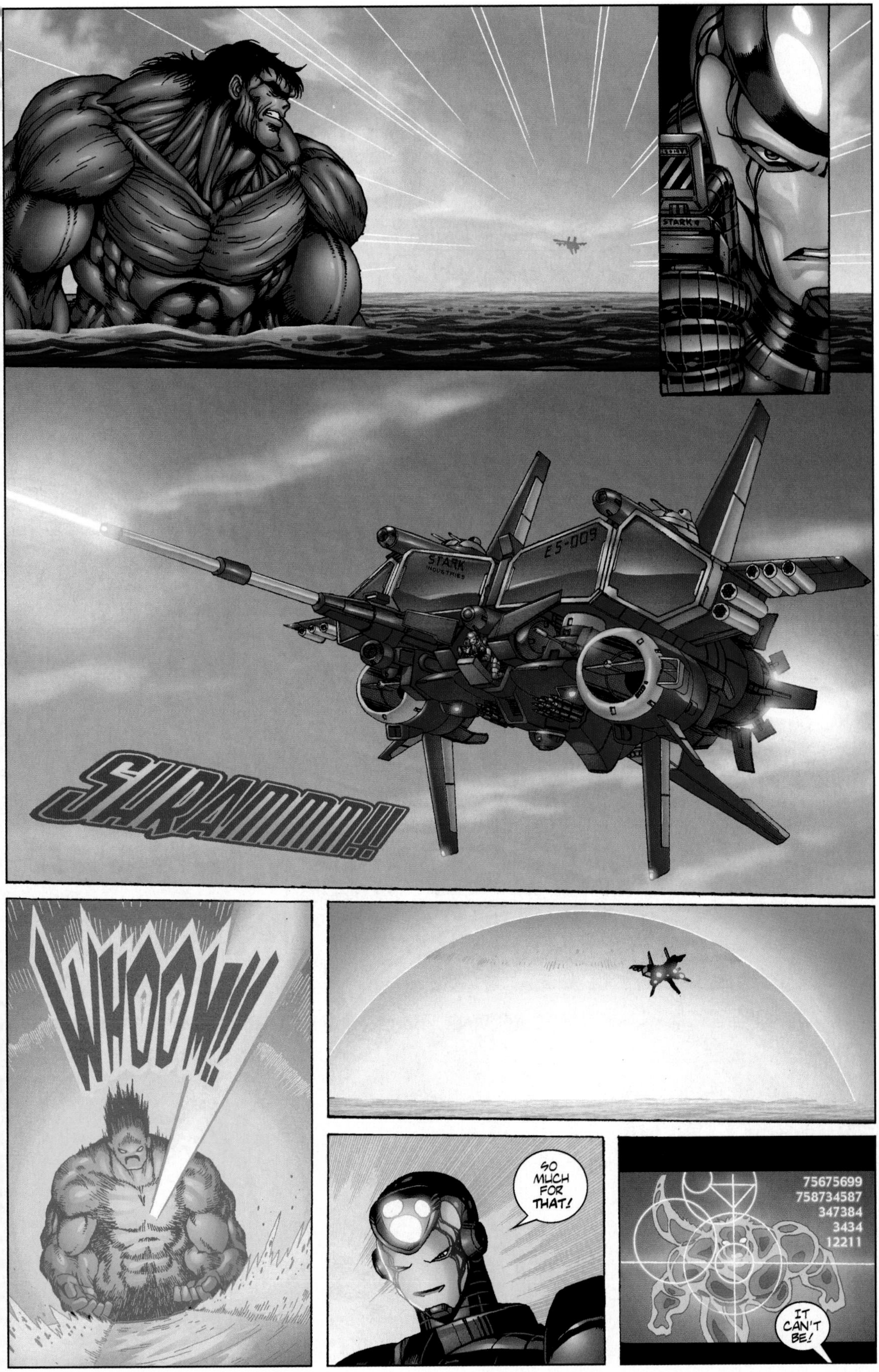
STARK INDUSTRIES
ES-009
SHRAMMM!!
WHOOM!!
SO MUCH FOR THAT!
75675699
758734587
347384
3434
12211
IT CAN'T BE!

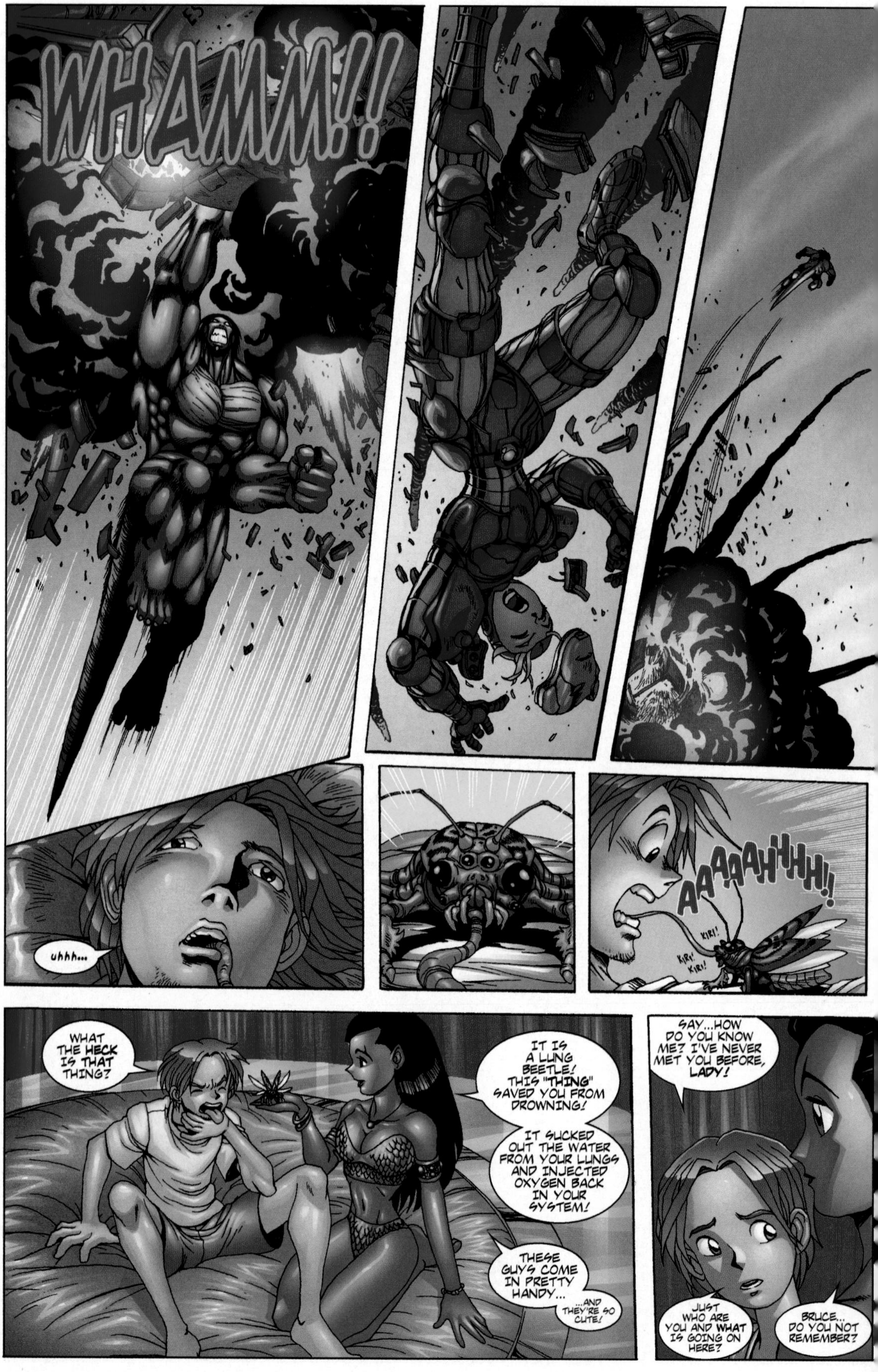

WHAMM!!
uhhh...
AAAAAHHHH!!
KIRI! KIRI! KIRI!
WHAT THE HECK IS THAT THING?
IT IS A LUNG BEETLE! THIS "THING" SAVED YOU FROM DROWNING!
IT SUCKED OUT THE WATER FROM YOUR LUNGS AND INJECTED OXYGEN BACK IN YOUR SYSTEM!
THESE GUYS COME IN PRETTY HANDY...
...AND THEY'RE SO CUTE!
SAY...HOW DO YOU KNOW ME? I'VE NEVER MET YOU BEFORE, LADY!
JUST WHO ARE YOU AND WHAT IS GOING ON HERE?
BRUCE... DO YOU NOT REMEMBER?

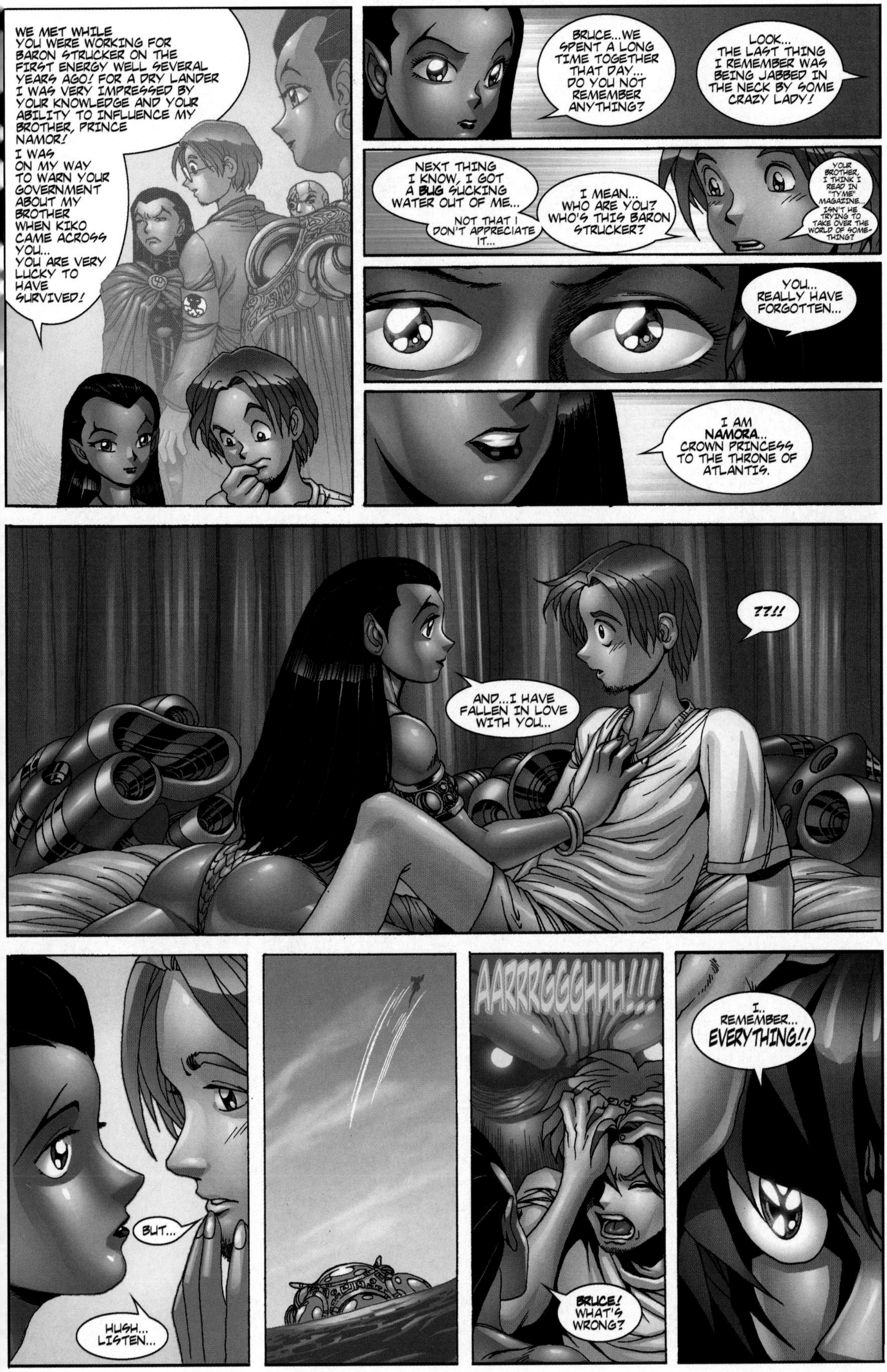
WE MET WHILE YOU WERE WORKING FOR BARON STRUCKER ON THE FIRST ENERGY WELL SEVERAL YEARS AGO! FOR A DRY LANDER I WAS VERY IMPRESSED BY YOUR KNOWLEDGE AND YOUR ABILITY TO INFLUENCE MY BROTHER, PRINCE NAMOR!
I WAS ON MY WAY TO WARN YOUR GOVERNMENT ABOUT MY BROTHER WHEN KIKO CAME ACROSS YOU... YOU ARE VERY LUCKY TO HAVE SURVIVED!
BRUCE...WE SPENT A LONG TIME TOGETHER THAT DAY... DO YOU NOT REMEMBER ANYTHING?
LOOK... THE LAST THING I REMEMBER WAS BEING JABBED IN THE NECK BY SOME CRAZY LADY!
NEXT THING I KNOW, I GOT A BUG SUCKING WATER OUT OF ME...
NOT THAT I DON'T APPRECIATE IT...
I MEAN... WHO ARE YOU? WHO'S THIS BARON STRUCKER?
YOUR BROTHER, I THINK I READ IN "TYME" MAGAZINE...
ISN'T HE TRYING TO TAKE OVER THE WORLD OF SOME-THING?
YOU... REALLY HAVE FORGOTTEN...
I AM NAMORA... CROWN PRINCESS TO THE THRONE OF ATLANTIS.
??!!
AND...I HAVE FALLEN IN LOVE WITH YOU...
BUT...
HUSH... LISTEN...
AARRRGGGHHH!!!
BRUCE! WHAT'S WRONG?
I.. REMEMBER... EVERYTHING!!

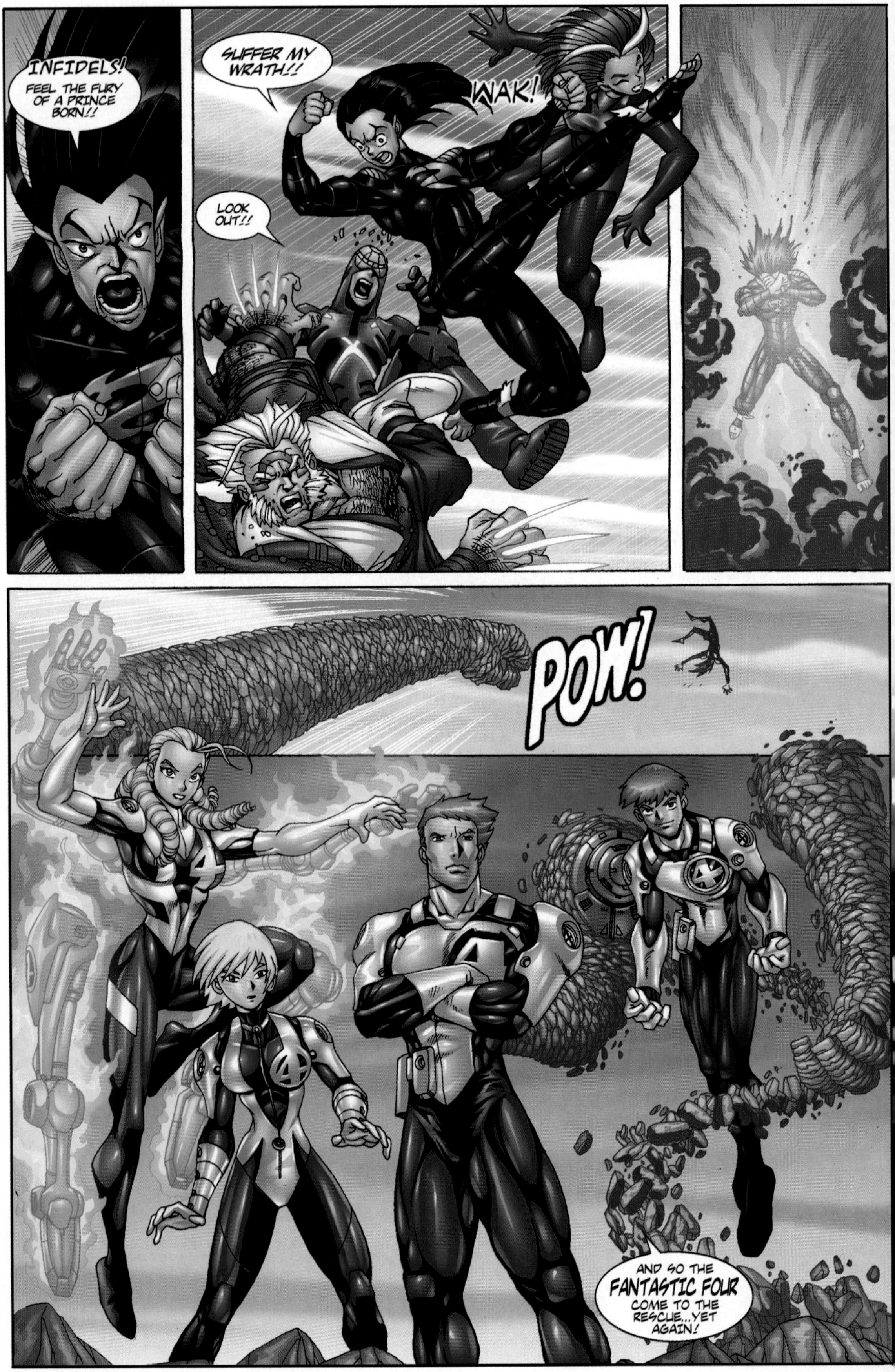
INFIDELS!
FEEL THE FURY OF A PRINCE BORN!!
SUFFER MY WRATH!!
WAK!
LOOK OUT!!
POW!
AND SO THE FANTASTIC FOUR COME TO THE RESCUE...YET AGAIN!

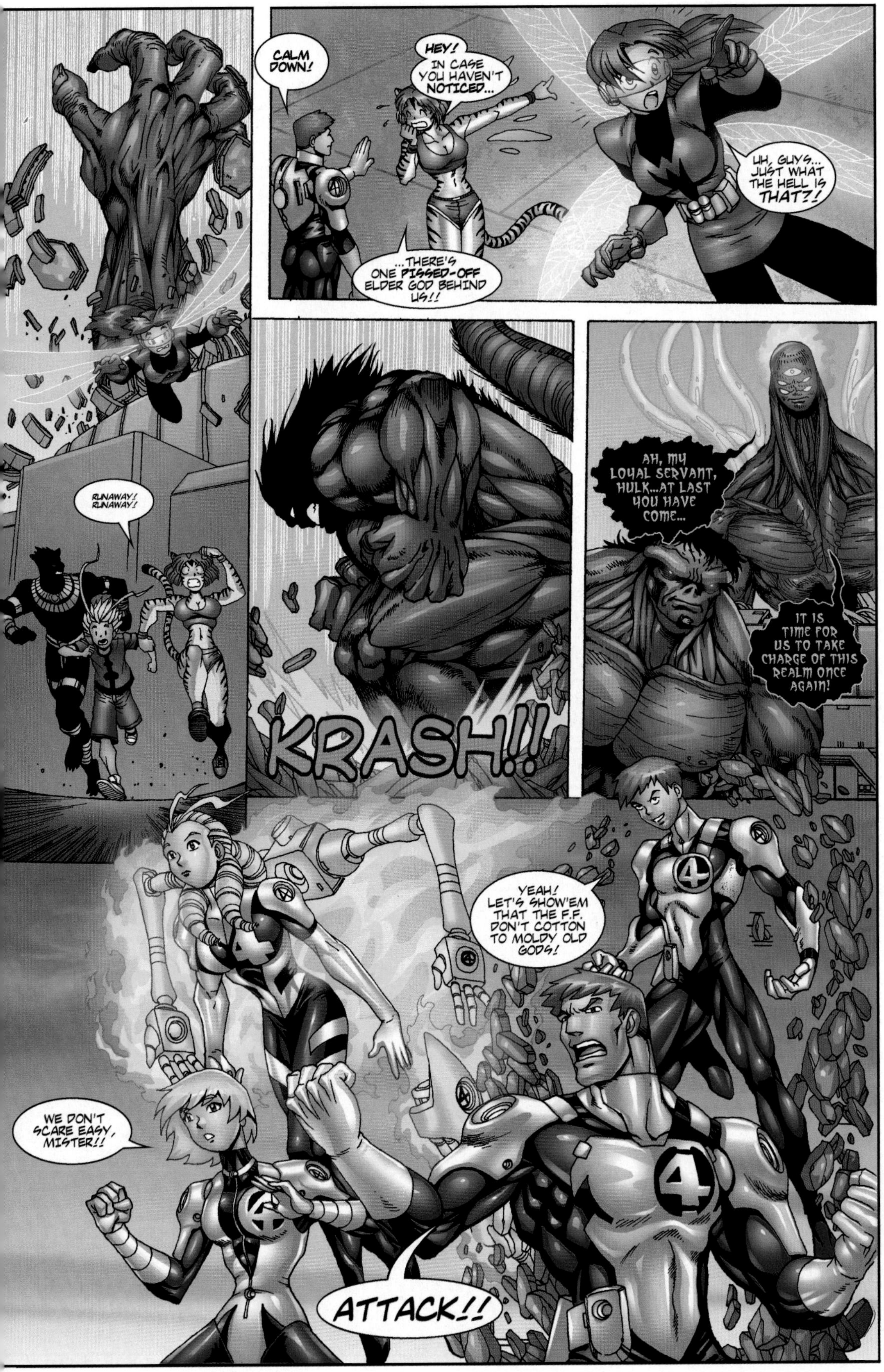

CALM DOWN!
HEY! IN CASE YOU HAVEN'T NOTICED...
...THERE'S ONE PISSED-OFF ELDER GOD BEHIND US!!
UH, GUYS... JUST WHAT THE HELL IS THAT?!
RUNAWAY! RUNAWAY!
KRASH!!
AH, MY LOYAL SERVANT, HULK...AT LAST YOU HAVE COME...
IT IS TIME FOR US TO TAKE CHARGE OF THIS REALM ONCE AGAIN!
YEAH! LET'S SHOW'EM THAT THE F.F. DON'T COTTON TO MOLDY OLD GODS!
WE DON'T SCARE EASY, MISTER!!
ATTACK!!

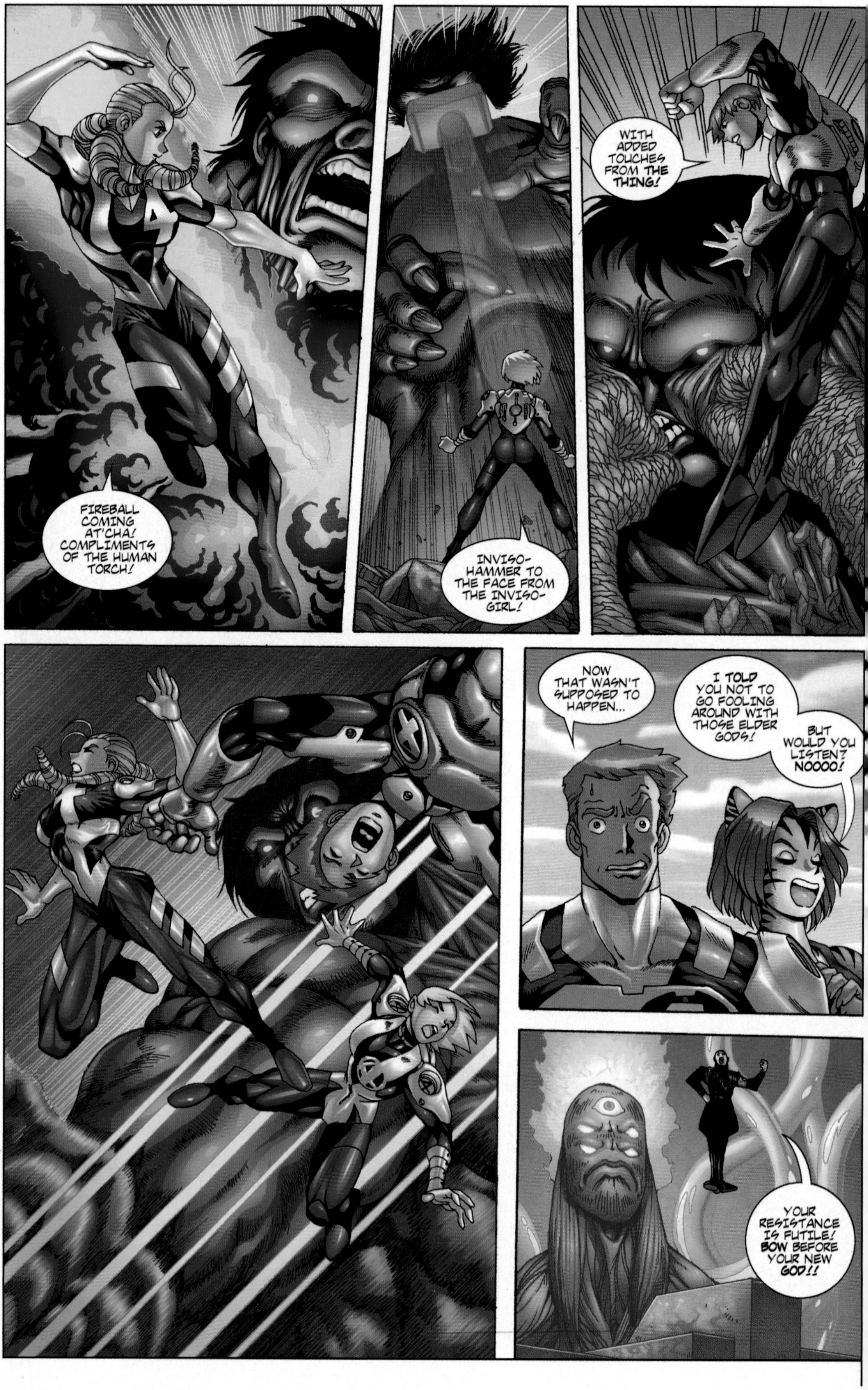
FIREBALL COMING AT'CHA! COMPLIMENTS OF THE HUMAN TORCH!
INVISO-HAMMER TO THE FACE FROM THE INVISO-GIRL!
WITH ADDED TOUCHES FROM THE THING!
NOW THAT WASN'T SUPPOSED TO HAPPEN...
I TOLD YOU NOT TO GO FOOLING AROUND WITH THOSE ELDER GODS!
BUT WOULD YOU LISTEN? NOOOO!
YOUR RESISTANCE IS FUTILE! BOW BEFORE YOUR NEW GOD!!

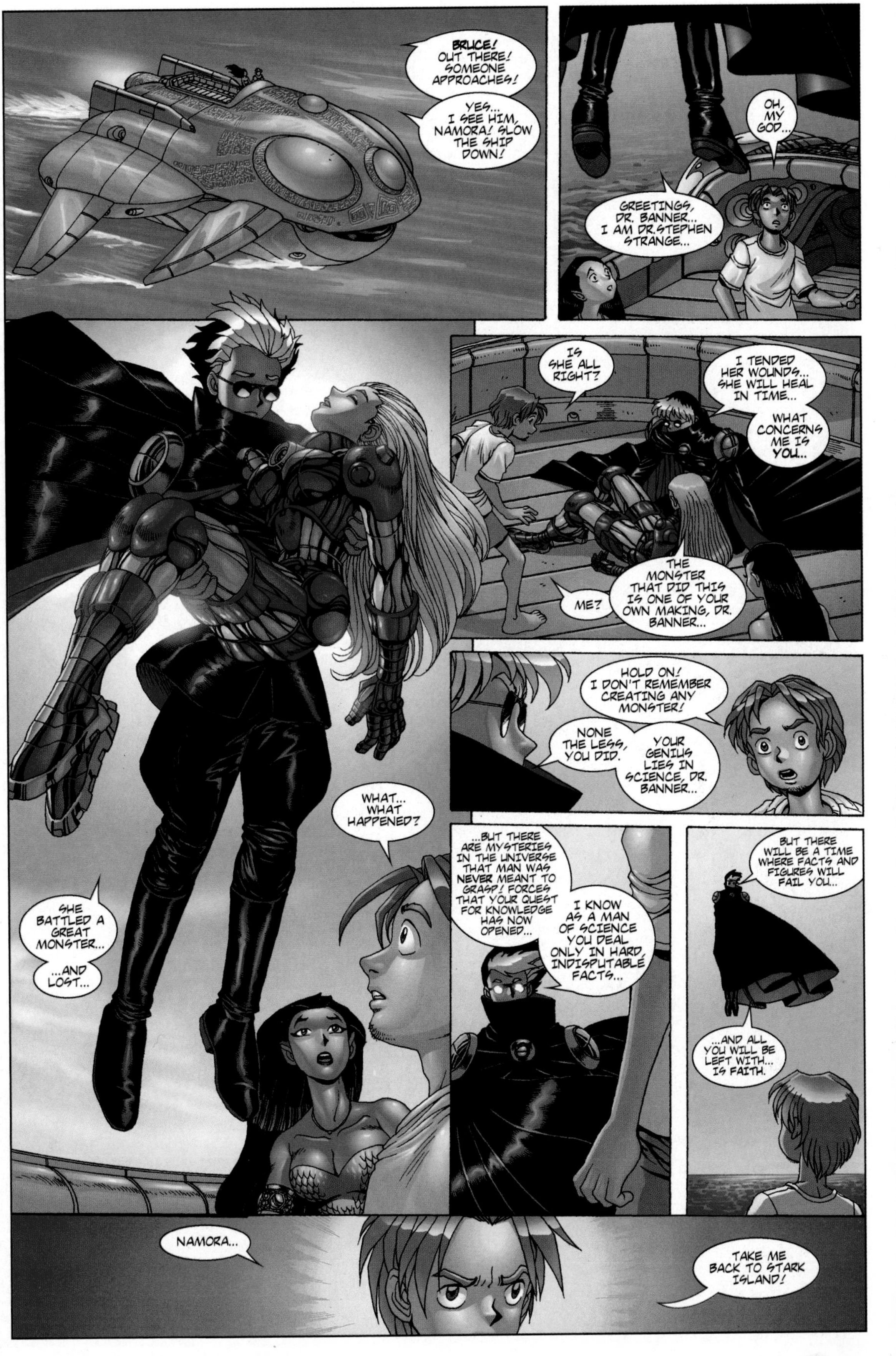
BRUCE! OUT THERE! SOMEONE APPROACHES!
YES... I SEE HIM, NAMORA! SLOW THE SHIP DOWN!
OH, MY GOD...
GREETINGS, DR. BANNER... I AM DR. STEPHEN STRANGE...
WHAT... WHAT HAPPENED?
SHE BATTLED A GREAT MONSTER...
...AND LOST...
IS SHE ALL RIGHT?
I TENDED HER WOUNDS... SHE WILL HEAL IN TIME...
WHAT CONCERNS ME IS YOU...
ME?
THE MONSTER THAT DID THIS IS ONE OF YOUR OWN MAKING, DR. BANNER...
HOLD ON! I DON'T REMEMBER CREATING ANY MONSTER!
NONE THE LESS, YOU DID.
YOUR GENIUS LIES IN SCIENCE, DR. BANNER...
...BUT THERE ARE MYSTERIES IN THE UNIVERSE THAT MAN WAS NEVER MEANT TO GRASP! FORCES THAT YOUR QUEST FOR KNOWLEDGE HAS NOW OPENED...
I KNOW AS A MAN OF SCIENCE YOU DEAL ONLY IN HARD, INDISPUTABLE FACTS...
BUT THERE WILL BE A TIME WHERE FACTS AND FIGURES WILL FAIL YOU...
...AND ALL YOU WILL BE LEFT WITH... IS FAITH.
NAMORA...
TAKE ME BACK TO STARK ISLAND!

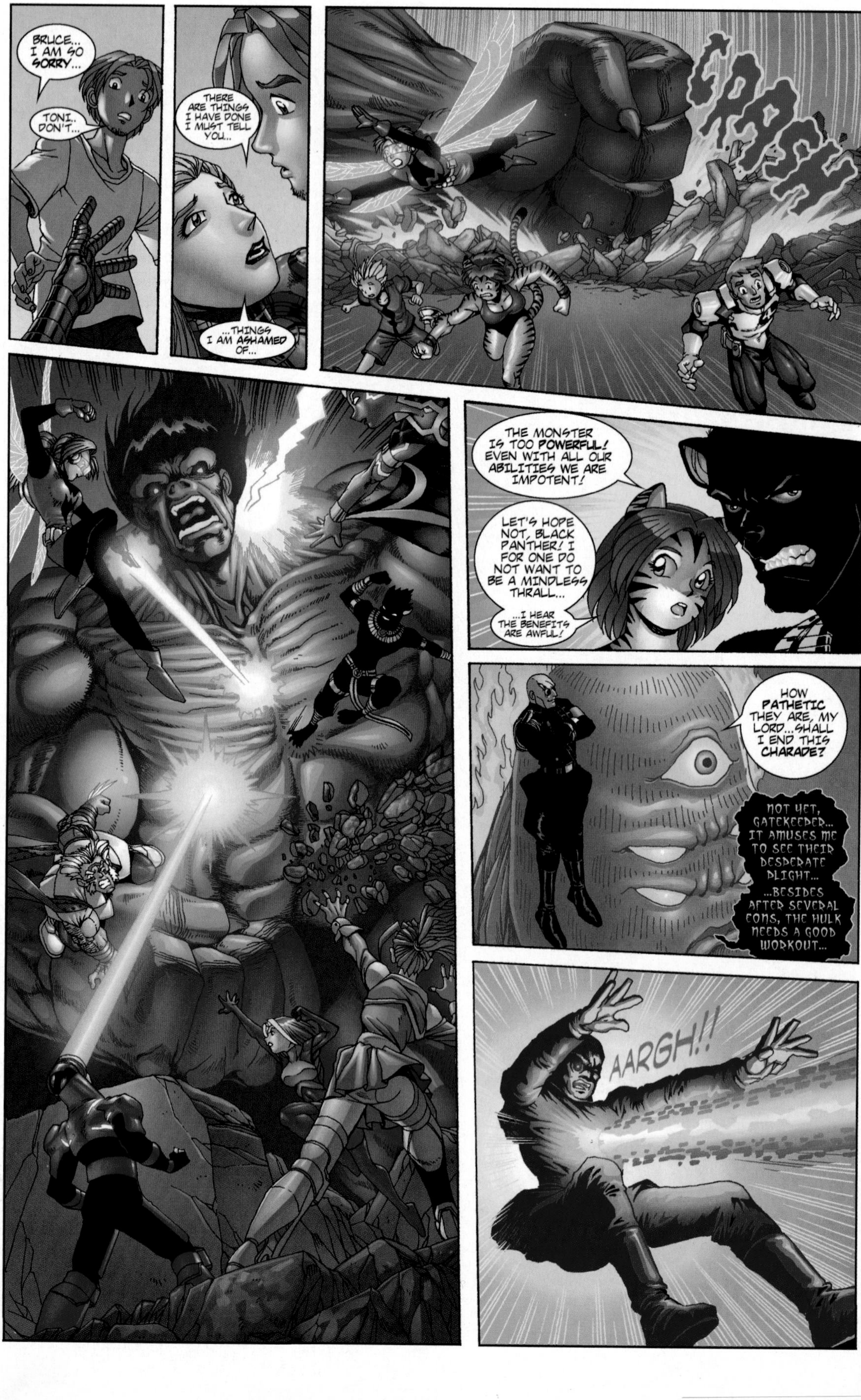
BRUCE... I AM SO SORRY...
TONI.. DON'T...
THERE ARE THINGS I HAVE DONE I MUST TELL YOU...
...THINGS I AM ASHAMED OF...
CRASH
THE MONSTER IS TOO POWERFUL! EVEN WITH ALL OUR ABILITIES WE ARE IMPOTENT!
LET'S HOPE NOT, BLACK PANTHER! I FOR ONE DO NOT WANT TO BE A MINDLESS THRALL...
...I HEAR THE BENEFITS ARE AWFUL!
HOW PATHETIC THEY ARE, MY LORD...SHALL I END THIS CHARADE?
NOT YET, GATEKEEPER... IT AMUSES ME TO SEE THEIR DESPERATE PLIGHT...
...BESIDES AFTER SEVERAL EONS, THE HULK NEEDS A GOOD WORKOUT...
AARGH!!

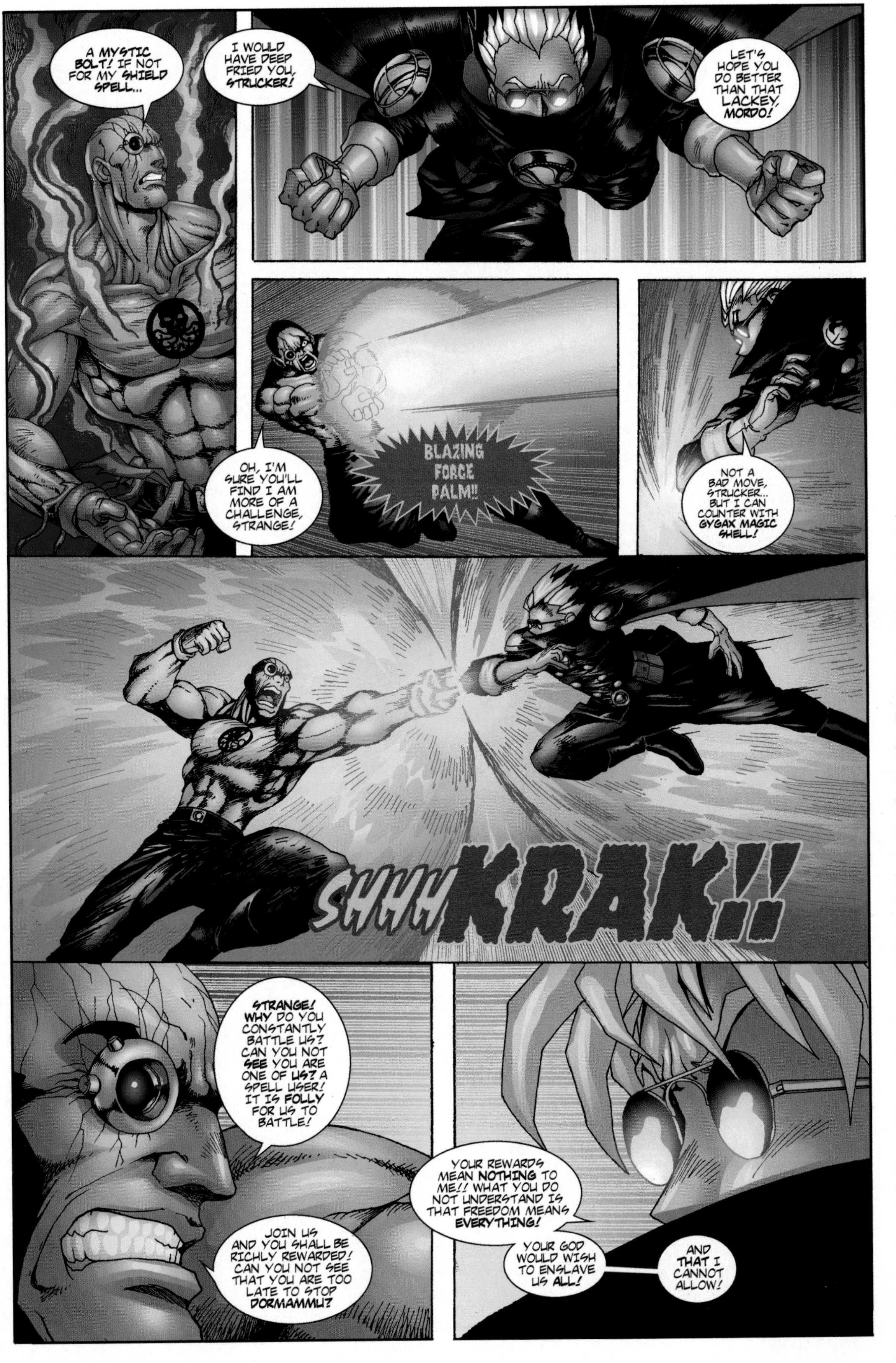
A MYSTIC BOLT! IF NOT FOR MY SHIELD SPELL...
I WOULD HAVE DEEP FRIED YOU, STRUCKER!
LET'S HOPE YOU DO BETTER THAN THAT LACKEY, MORDO!
OH, I'M SURE YOU'LL FIND I AM MORE OF A CHALLENGE, STRANGE!
BLAZING FORCE PALM!!
NOT A BAD MOVE, STRUCKER... BUT I CAN COUNTER WITH GYGAX MAGIC SHELL!
SHHHKRAK!!
STRANGE! WHY DO YOU CONSTANTLY BATTLE US? CAN YOU NOT SEE YOU ARE ONE OF US? A SPELL USER! IT IS FOLLY FOR US TO BATTLE!
JOIN US AND YOU SHALL BE RICHLY REWARDED! CAN YOU NOT SEE THAT YOU ARE TOO LATE TO STOP DORMAMMU?
YOUR REWARDS MEAN NOTHING TO ME!! WHAT YOU DO NOT UNDERSTAND IS THAT FREEDOM MEANS EVERYTHING!
YOUR GOD WOULD WISH TO ENSLAVE US ALL!
AND THAT I CANNOT ALLOW!

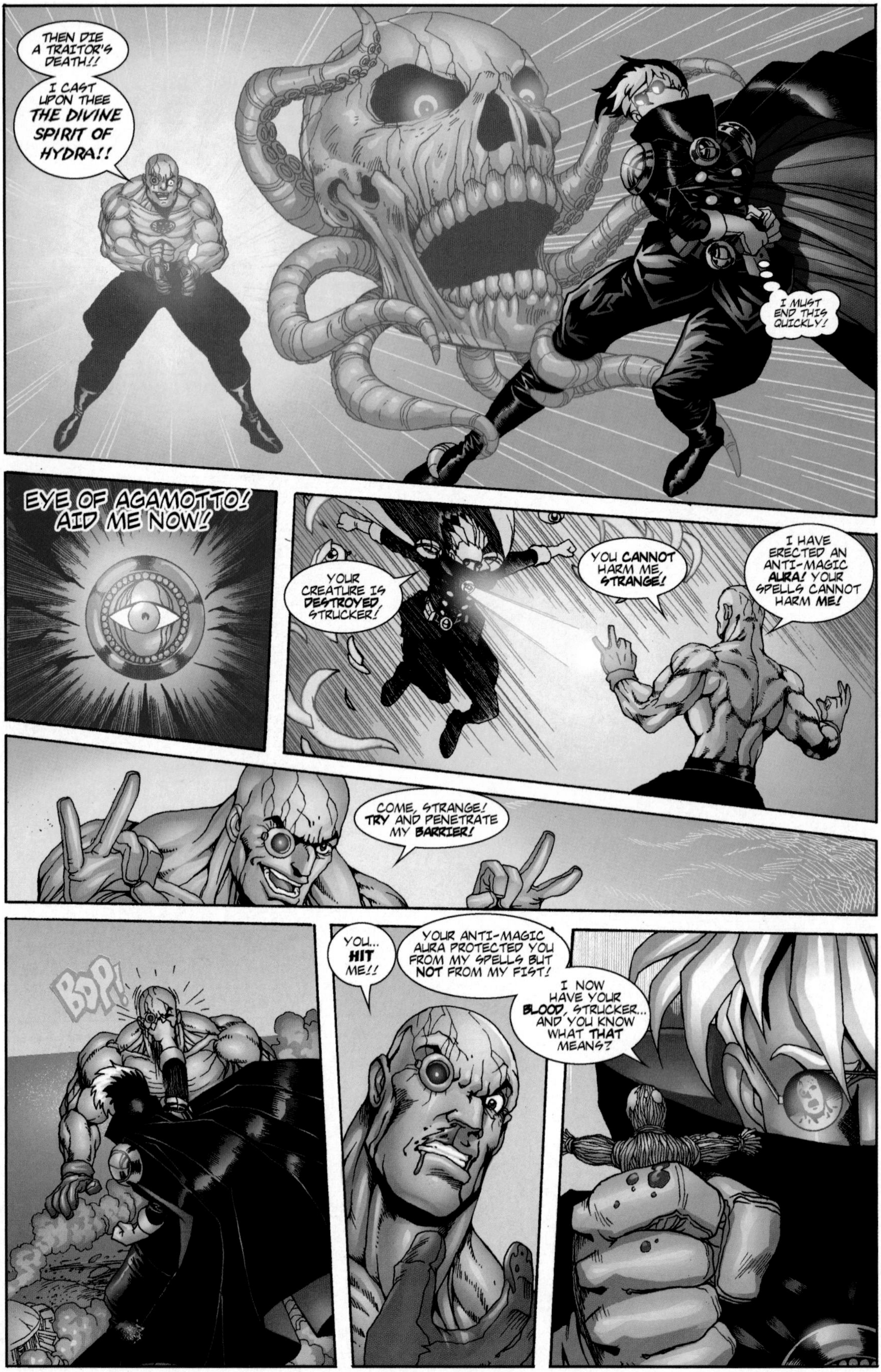
THEN DIE A TRAITOR'S DEATH!!
I CAST UPON THEE THE DIVINE SPIRIT OF HYDRA!!
I MUST END THIS QUICKLY!
EYE OF AGAMOTTO! AID ME NOW!
YOUR CREATURE IS DESTROYED, STRUCKER!
YOU CANNOT HARM ME, STRANGE!
I HAVE ERECTED AN ANTI-MAGIC AURA! YOUR SPELLS CANNOT HARM ME!
COME, STRANGE! TRY AND PENETRATE MY BARRIER!
BOP!
YOU... HIT ME!!
YOUR ANTI-MAGIC AURA PROTECTED YOU FROM MY SPELLS BUT NOT FROM MY FIST!
I NOW HAVE YOUR BLOOD, STRUCKER... AND YOU KNOW WHAT THAT MEANS?

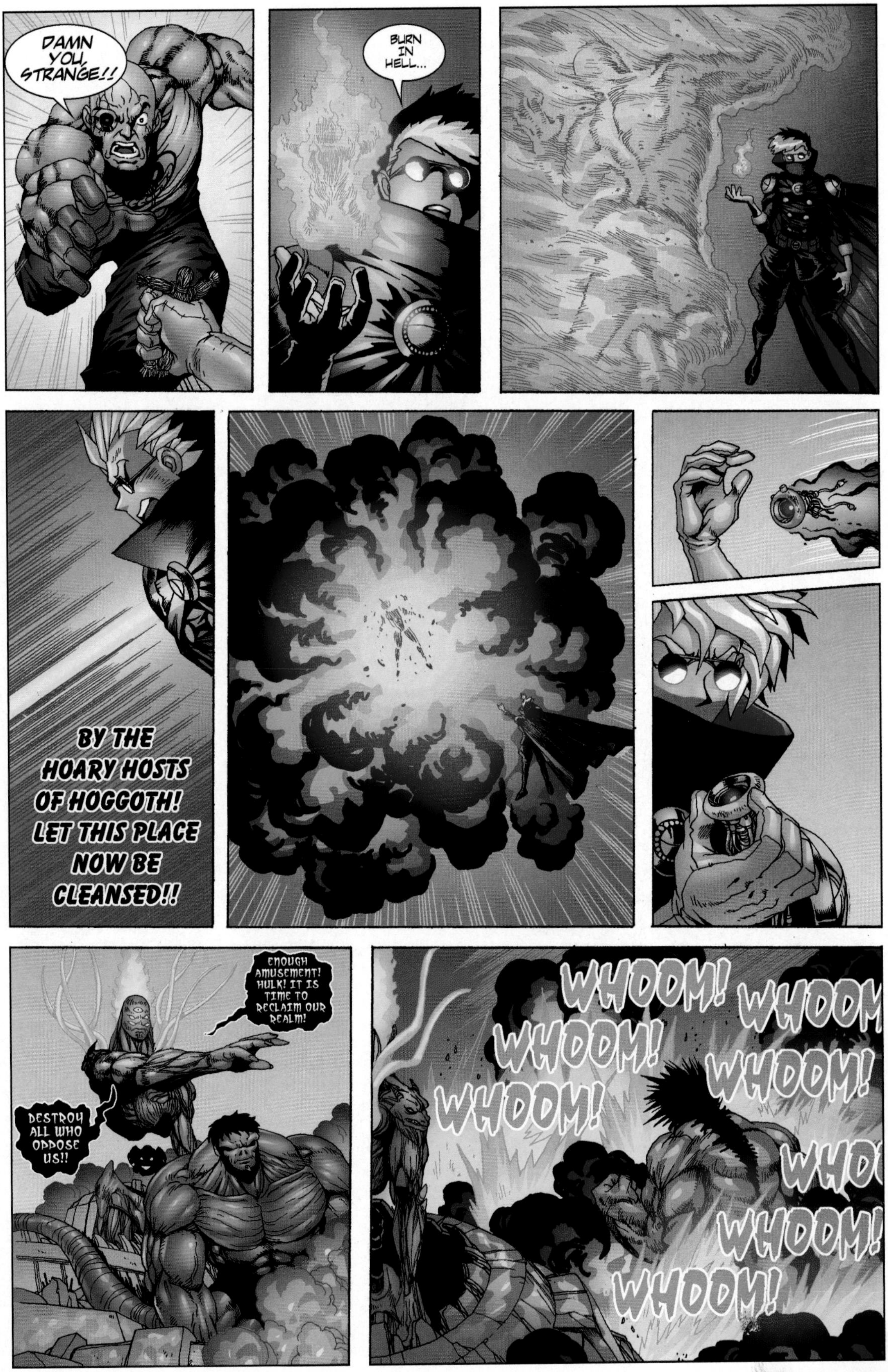
DAMN YOU, STRANGE!!
BURN IN HELL...
BY THE HOARY HOSTS OF HOGGOTH! LET THIS PLACE NOW BE CLEANSED!!
ENOUGH AMUSEMENT! HULK! IT IS TIME TO RECLAIM OUR REALM!
DESTROY ALL WHO OPPOSE US!!
WHOOM!
WHOOM!
WHOOM!
WHOOM!
WHOOM!
WHOOM!
WHOOM!

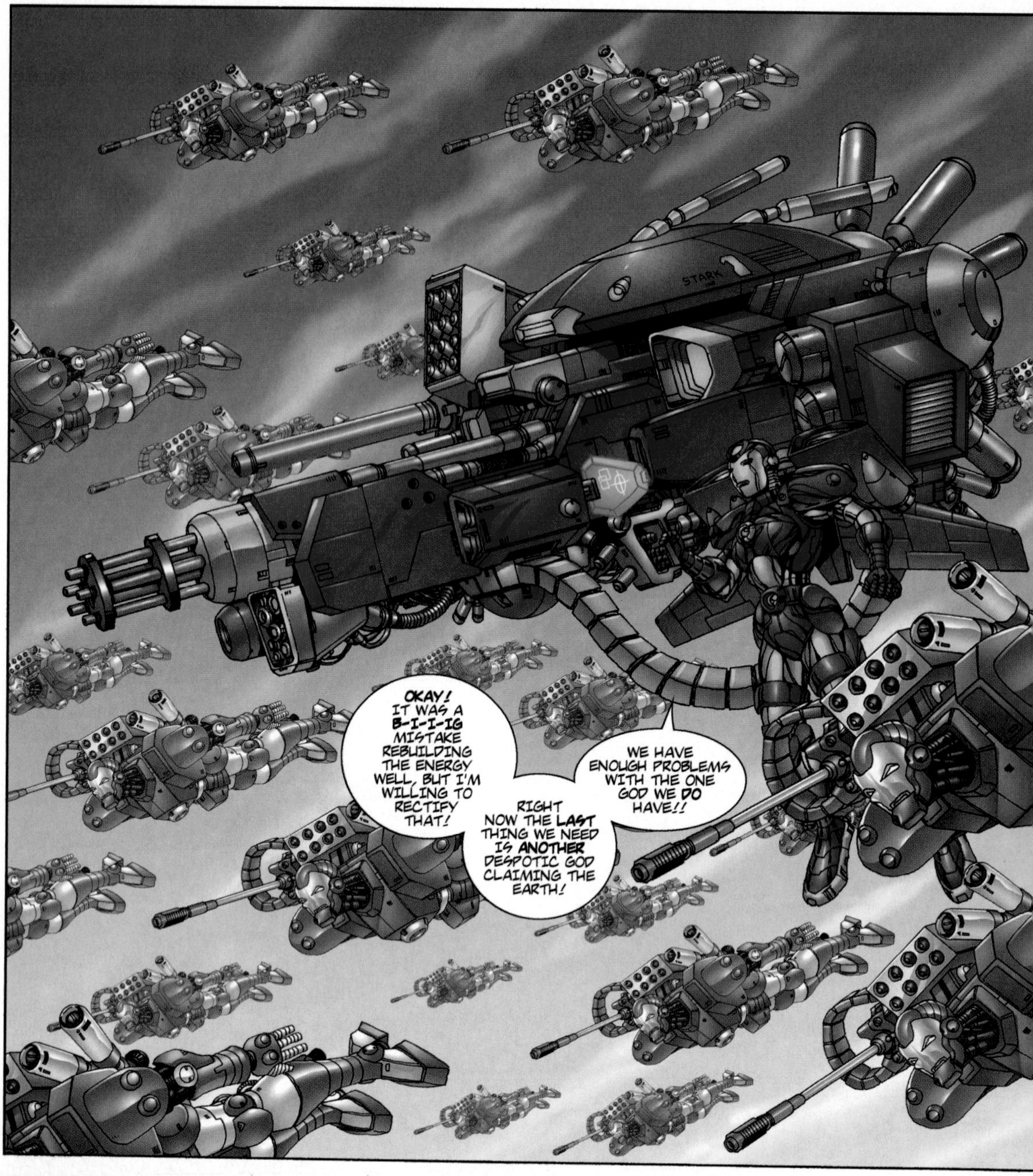
OKAY! IT WAS A B-I-I-IG MISTAKE REBUILDING THE ENERGY WELL, BUT I'M WILLING TO RECTIFY THAT!
RIGHT NOW THE LAST THING WE NEED IS ANOTHER DESPOTIC GOD CLAIMING THE EARTH!
WE HAVE ENOUGH PROBLEMS WITH THE ONE GOD WE DO HAVE!!
STARK

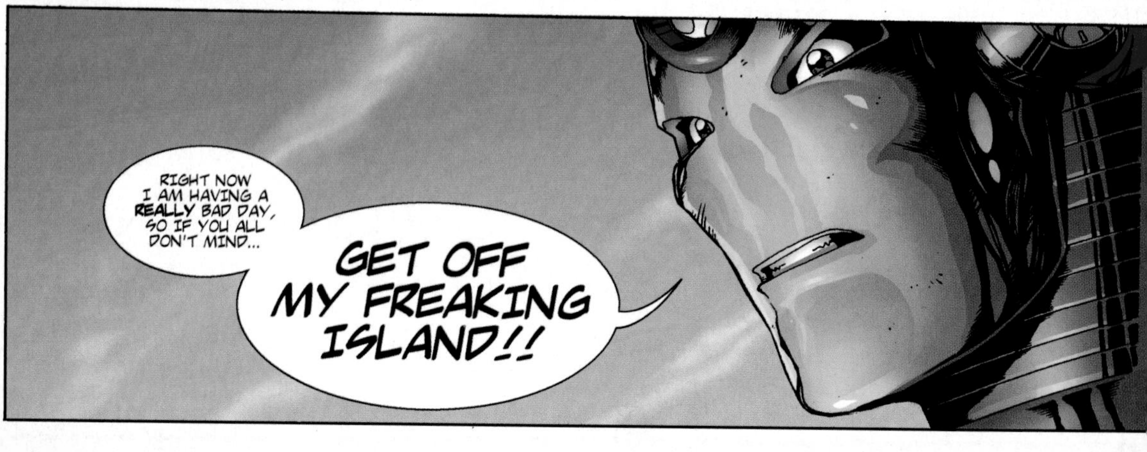
RIGHT NOW I AM HAVING A REALLY BAD DAY, SO IF YOU ALL DON'T MIND...
GET OFF MY FREAKING ISLAND!!

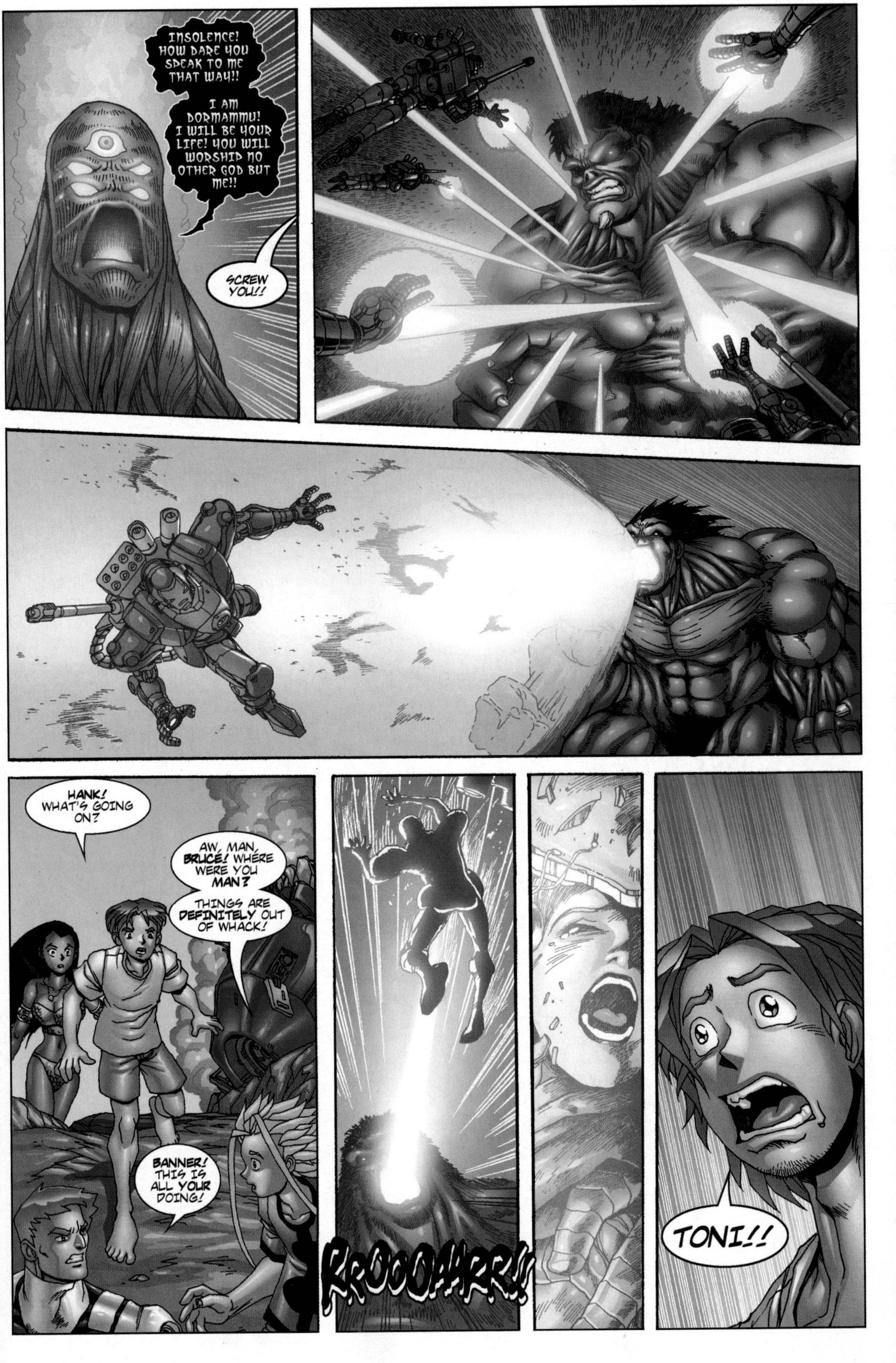
INSOLENCE! HOW DARE YOU SPEAK TO ME THAT WAY!!
I AM DORMAMMU! I WILL BE YOUR LIFE! YOU WILL WORSHIP NO OTHER GOD BUT ME!!
SCREW YOU!!
HANK! WHAT'S GOING ON?
AW, MAN, BRUCE! WHERE WERE YOU MAN?
THINGS ARE DEFINITELY OUT OF WHACK!
BANNER! THIS IS ALL YOUR DOING!
KROOOAARR!!
TONI!!

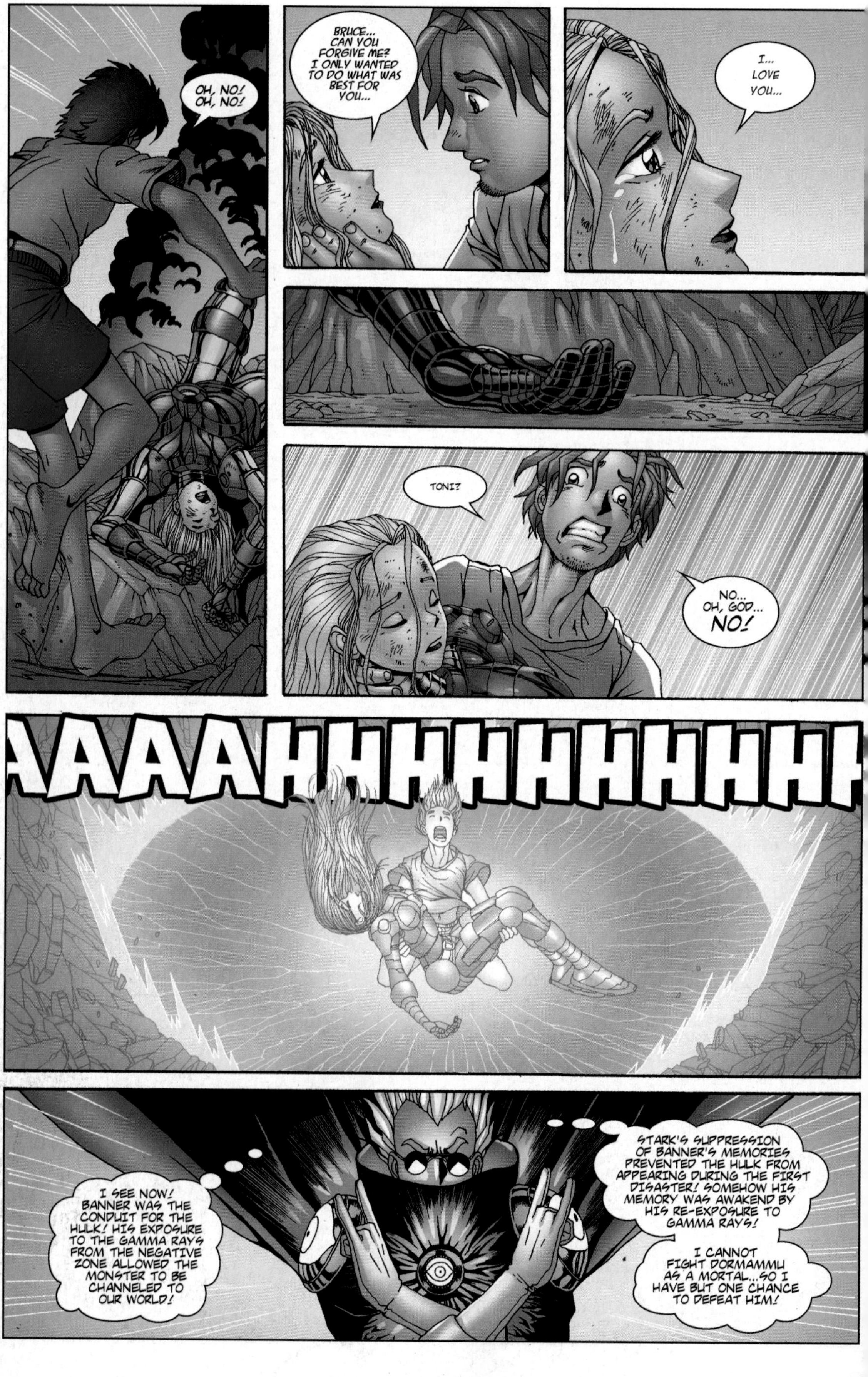
OH, NO! OH, NO!
BRUCE... CAN YOU FORGIVE ME? I ONLY WANTED TO DO WHAT WAS BEST FOR YOU...
I... LOVE YOU...
TONI?
NO... OH, GOD... NO!
AAAAAHHHHHHHHHHHH
I SEE NOW! BANNER WAS THE CONDUIT FOR THE HULK! HIS EXPOSURE TO THE GAMMA RAYS FROM THE NEGATIVE ZONE ALLOWED THE MONSTER TO BE CHANNELED TO OUR WORLD!
STARK'S SUPPRESSION OF BANNER'S MEMORIES PREVENTED THE HULK FROM APPEARING DURING THE FIRST DISASTER! SOMEHOW HIS MEMORY WAS AWAKEND BY HIS RE-EXPOSURE TO GAMMA RAYS!
I CANNOT FIGHT DORMAMMU AS A MORTAL...SO I HAVE BUT ONE CHANCE TO DEFEAT HIM!

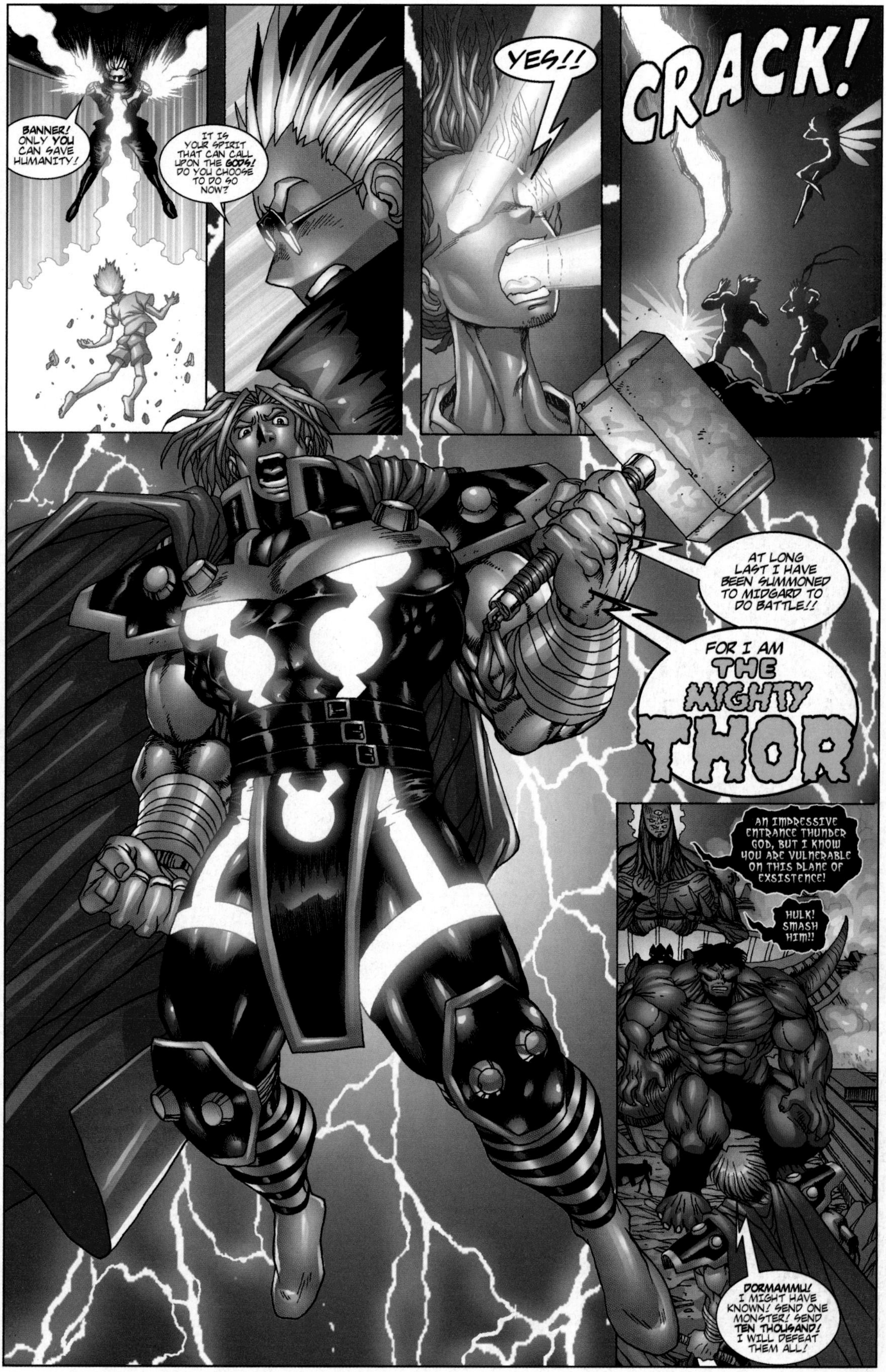
BANNER! ONLY YOU CAN SAVE HUMANITY!
IT IS YOUR SPIRIT THAT CAN CALL UPON THE GODS! DO YOU CHOOSE TO DO SO NOW?
YES!!
CRACK!
AT LONG LAST I HAVE BEEN SUMMONED TO MIDGARD TO DO BATTLE!!
FOR I AM THE MIGHTY THOR
AN IMPRESSIVE ENTRANCE THUNDER GOD, BUT I KNOW YOU ARE VULNERABLE ON THIS PLANE OF EXSISTENCE!
HULK! SMASH HIM!!
DORMAMMU! I MIGHT HAVE KNOWN! SEND ONE MONSTER! SEND TEN THOUSAND! I WILL DEFEAT THEM ALL!

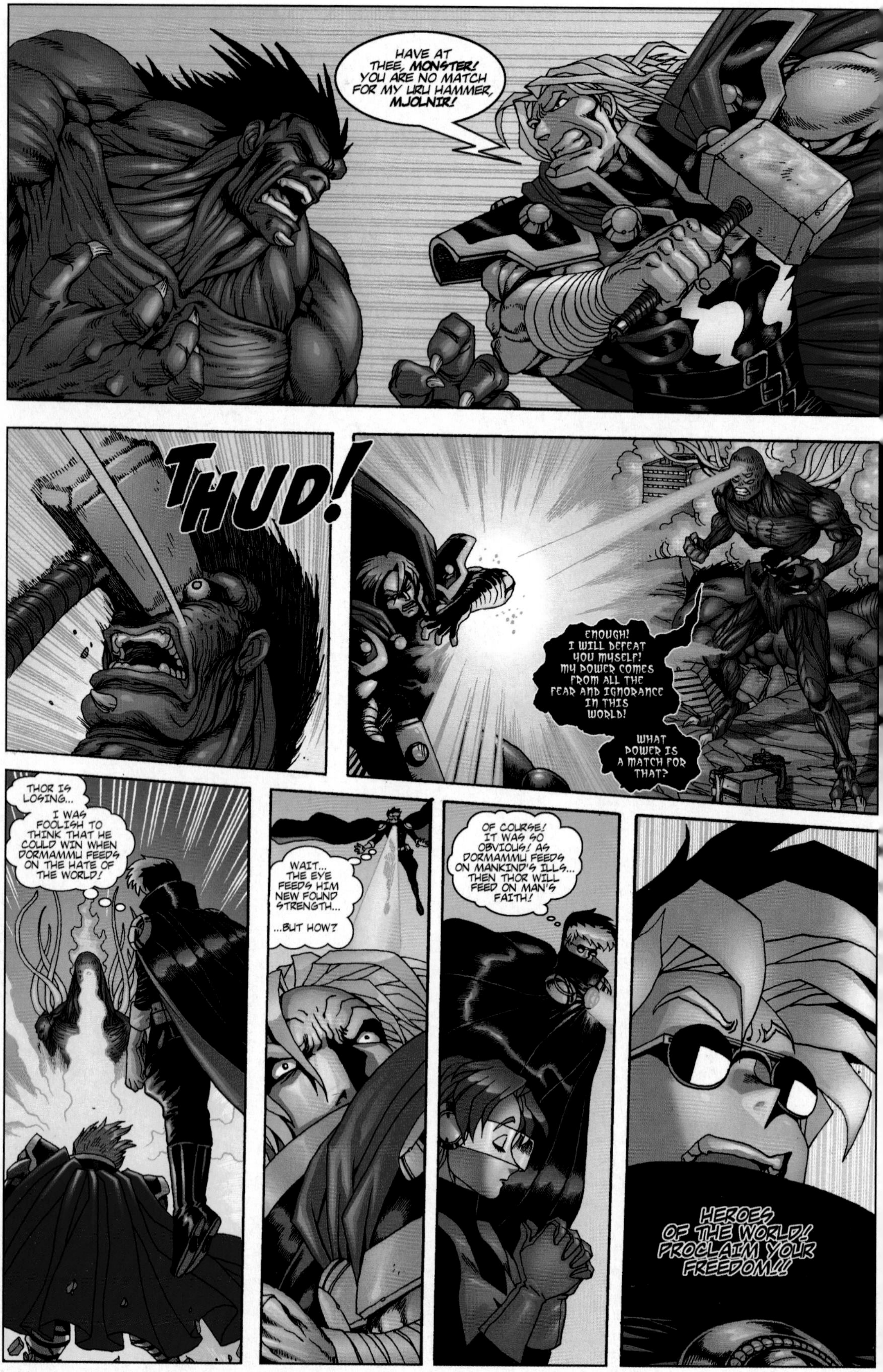
HAVE AT THEE, MONSTER! YOU ARE NO MATCH FOR MY URU HAMMER, MJOLNIR!
THUD!
ENOUGH! I WILL DEFEAT YOU MYSELF! MY POWER COMES FROM ALL THE FEAR AND IGNORANCE IN THIS WORLD!
WHAT POWER IS A MATCH FOR THAT?
THOR IS LOSING...
I WAS FOOLISH TO THINK THAT HE COULD WIN WHEN DORMAMMU FEEDS ON THE HATE OF THE WORLD!
WAIT... THE EYE FEEDS HIM NEW FOUND STRENGTH...
...BUT HOW?
OF COURSE! IT WAS SO OBVIOUS! AS DORMAMMU FEEDS ON MANKIND'S ILLS... THEN THOR WILL FEED ON MAN'S FAITH!
HEROES OF THE WORLD! PROCLAIM YOUR FREEDOM!!

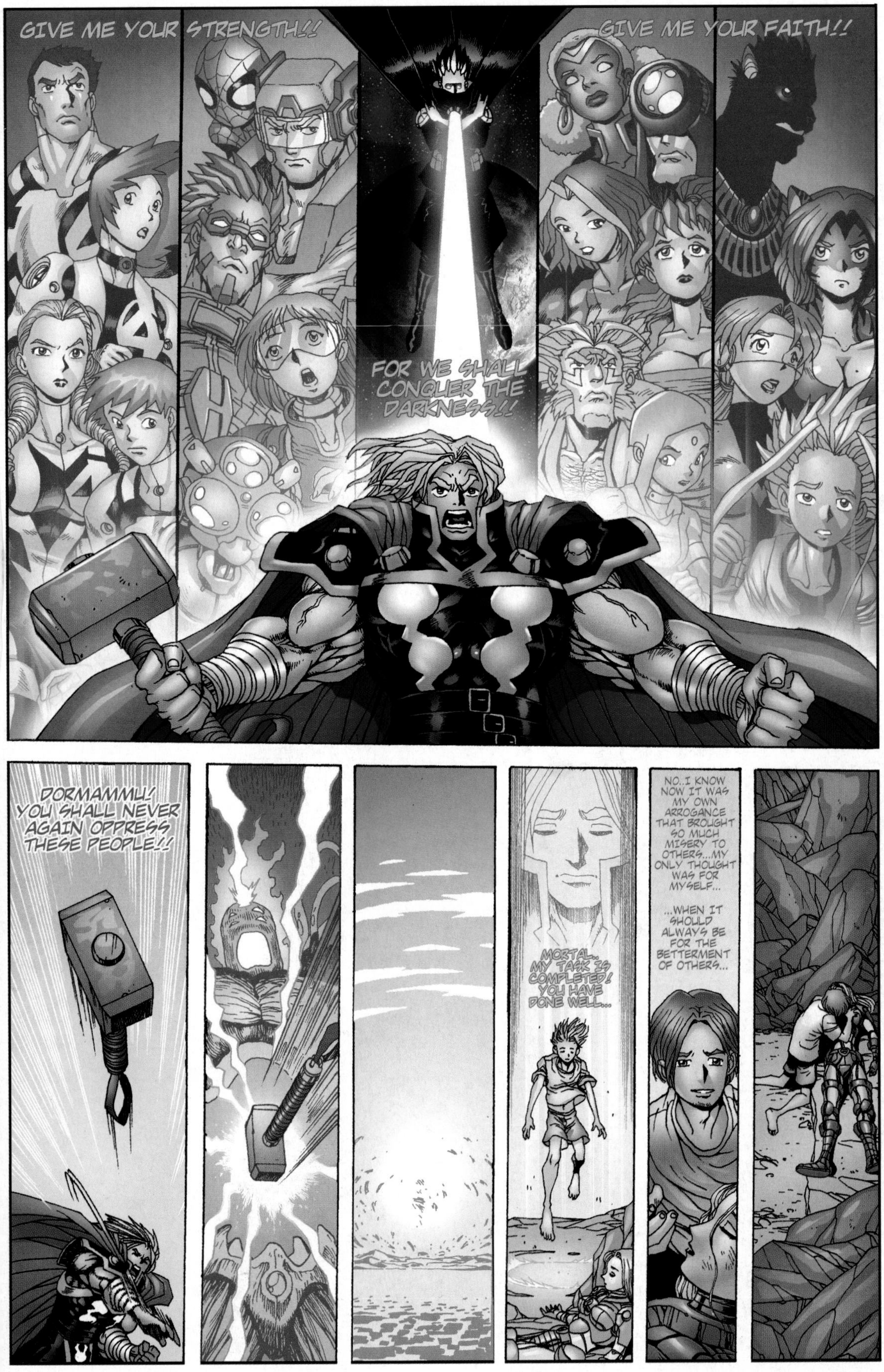
GIVE ME YOUR STRENGTH!!
GIVE ME YOUR FAITH!!
FOR WE SHALL CONQUER THE DARKNESS!!
DORMAMMU! YOU SHALL NEVER AGAIN OPPRESS THESE PEOPLE!!
MORTAL.. MY TASK IS COMPLETED! YOU HAVE DONE WELL...
NO..I KNOW NOW IT WAS MY OWN ARROGANCE THAT BROUGHT SO MUCH MISERY TO OTHERS...MY ONLY THOUGHT WAS FOR MYSELF...
...WHEN IT SHOULD ALWAYS BE FOR THE BETTERMENT OF OTHERS...

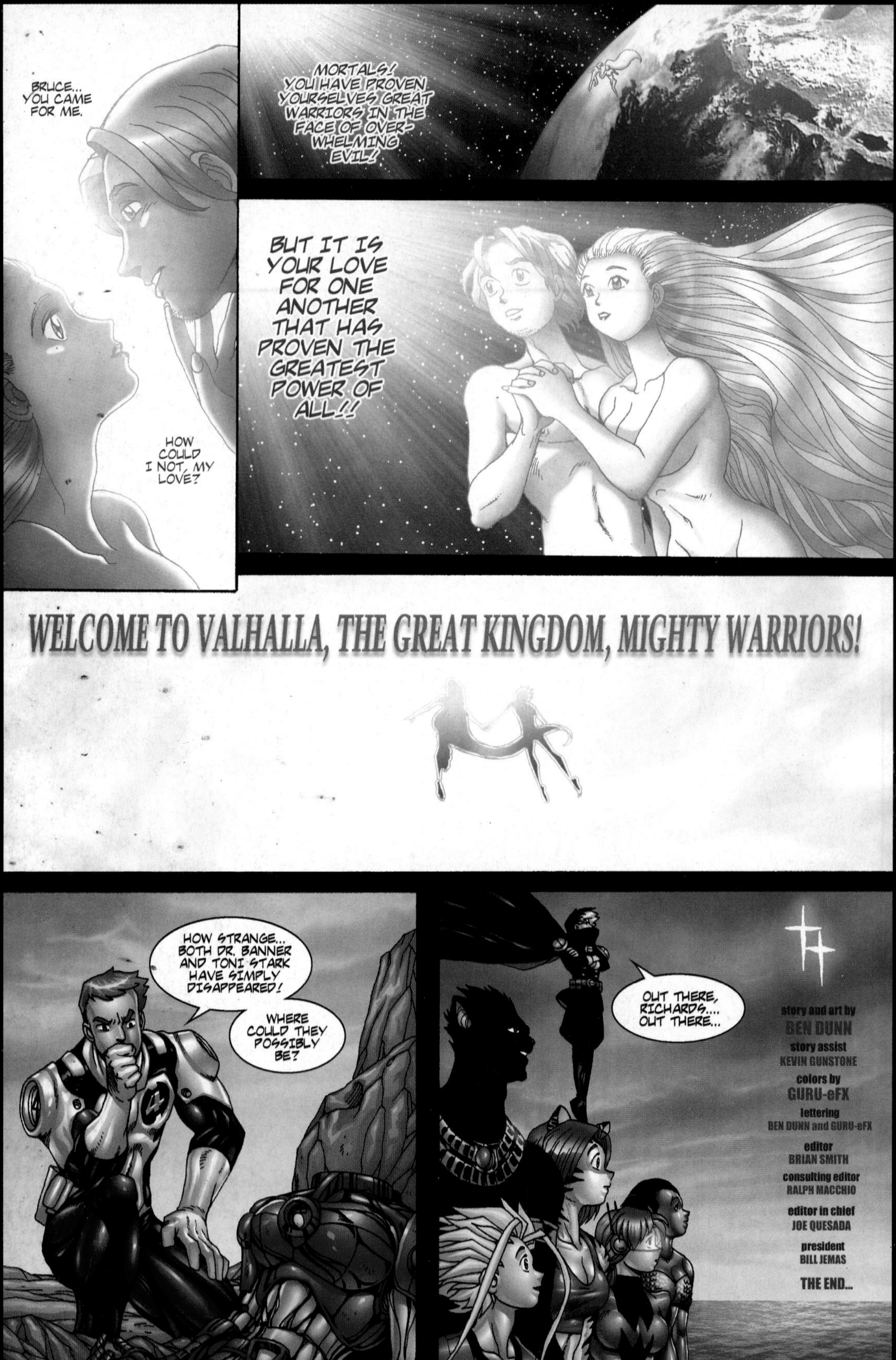
BRUCE... YOU CAME FOR ME.
HOW COULD I NOT, MY LOVE?
MORTALS! YOU HAVE PROVEN YOURSELVES GREAT WARRIORS IN THE FACE OF OVER-WHELMING EVIL!
BUT IT IS YOUR LOVE FOR ONE ANOTHER THAT HAS PROVEN THE GREATEST POWER OF ALL!!
WELCOME TO VALHALLA, THE GREAT KINGDOM, MIGHTY WARRIORS!
HOW STRANGE... BOTH DR. BANNER AND TONI STARK HAVE SIMPLY DISAPPEARED!
WHERE COULD THEY POSSIBLY BE?
OUT THERE, RICHARDS.... OUT THERE...
story and art by
BEN DUNN
story assist
KEVIN GUNSTONE
colors by
GURU-eFX
lettering
BEN DUNN and GURU-eFX
editor
BRIAN SMITH
consulting editor
RALPH MACCHIO
editor in chief
JOE QUESADA
president
BILL JEMAS
THE END...